THE GUERRILLA HUNTERS

CONFLICTING WORLDS

New Dimensions of the American Civil War

T. Michael Parrish, Series Editor

THE GUERRILLA HUNTERS

IRREGULAR CONFLICTS DURING THE CIVIL WAR

EDITED BY

BRIAN D. McKNIGHT & BARTON A. MYERS

FOREWORD BY KENNETH W. NOE

AFTERWORD BY DANIEL E. SUTHERLAND

LOUISIANA STATE UNIVERSITY PRESS BATON ROUGE

Published by Louisiana State University Press

Manufactured in the United States of America
First printing

Designer: Michelle A. Neustrom
Typeface: Sentinel
Printer and binder: McNaughton & Gunn, Inc.

Library of Congress Cataloging-in-Publication Data

Names: McKnight, Brian Dallas, editor, author. | Myers, Barton A., 1980– editor, author.
Title: The guerrilla hunters : irregular conflicts during the Civil War / edited by Brian D. McKnight and Barton A. Myers ; foreword by Kenneth W. Noe ; afterword by Daniel E. Sutherland.
Description: Baton Rouge : Louisiana State University Press, 2017. | Series: Conflicting worlds: new dimensions of the American Civil War | Includes bibliographical references and index.
Identifiers: LCCN 2016041277| ISBN 978-0-8071-6497-6 (cloth : alk. paper) | ISBN 978-0-8071-6498-3 (pdf) | ISBN 978-0-8071-6499-0 (epub) | ISBN 978-0-8071-6500-3 (mobi)
Subjects: LCSH: United States—History—Civil War, 1861–1865—Underground movements. | United States—History—Civil War, 1861–1865—Campaigns. | Guerrilla warfare—United States—History—19th century. | Guerrillas—United States—History—19th century.
Classification: LCC E470 .G867 2017 | DDC 973.7/3—dc23
LC record available at https://lccn.loc.gov/2016041277

The paper in this book meets the guidelines for permanence and durability of the Committee on Production Guidelines for Book Longevity of the Council on Library Resources. ♾

Irregular war is far more intellectual than a bayonet charge.

—T. E. Lawrence, *Seven Pillars of Wisdom*

CONTENTS

ACKNOWLEDGMENTS

Nearly ten years ago, we began talking about the need for a wide-ranging book that could help flesh out the contributions of the growing literature in the "guerrilla studies" subfield. It was our concern that despite the expanding number of works examining irregular forms of violence on the Southern home front during the American Civil War, the scholarly expectations for creative argument and methodological experimentation had largely remained static. In our minds, guerrilla warfare was proving itself to be one of the most complex and elusive areas of Civil War study, and in order to help it grow, the field needed a volume that might push historiographic boundaries and raise new questions for future research. Such a recalibration, as is offered in this collection, would allow the dynamic guerrilla scholarship to move beyond the traditional and outmoded notion of a single compartmentalized irregular war and into a new place where the guerrilla conflicts could stand alongside the conventional battle narrative for serious analysis, rather than being seen as simply an ancillary result of conventional operations. After several years spent clearing our calendars, we finally found the time to invest in this book.

From the beginning of this process, we had the strong support of Rand Dotson of LSU Press and Michael Parrish, editor of the Conflicting Worlds series. Our contributors, aside from being the best in their fields, were patient, timely, and committed to our vision. We thank them individually and collectively for their time and energy expended on this volume. In short, this project seemed to come together with a disarming ease.

We have been fortunate that our past works have been well received and our colleagues remain interested in hearing our thoughts on guerrilla-related issues. It is rare for scholars to toil alongside and sometimes challenge those whom they hold in such high regard, but again, we are fortunate.

* * *

I would like to offer special thanks to Pam and Devin for their constant support and encouragement. Only those who do this kind of work recognize the amount of time a scholar spends either absent or distracted. It takes special people to appreciate the greater meaning and purpose of our work. I would also like to recognize my coeditor, Barton Myers. Working with him on this project over these past years has been a pleasure. Barton and I represent within ourselves the complexity of the guerrilla war: we view this conflict very differently and approach it from dramatically diverse directions, but in the end our individual wars fundamentally look the same.

—**B. McKNIGHT**

* * *

I would like to thank Washington and Lee University for the support provided by the H. F. Lenfest Research Grant, the Filson Historical Society for the C. Ballard Breaux Visiting Research Fellowship, and the Virginia Historical Society for the Andrew W. Mellon Research Grant. These institutions enabled me to complete research for my contributions to this volume and to spend time editing the other pieces included here. I thank my colleagues in the History Department at Washington and Lee, especially Theodore DeLaney, J. Holt Merchant, and Dean of the College Suzanne Keen and Provost Marc Conner for their consistent support of my work. I would like to acknowledge Professor Ricardo Herrera of the School of Advanced Military Studies at the Command and General Staff College at Fort Leavenworth, Kansas, for his reading of the manuscript. I would also like to thank my wife, Molly; son, Warner; and in-laws Barb, Bob, and Richard for their consistent support. Working alongside Brian McKnight on this book has been a true joy. Rarely does one find a collaborator who is equally passionate about the same set of scholarly issues and yet can display excellent editorial judgment and solid gentlemanly criticism without losing sight of the end goal, a groundbreaking scholarly product.

—**B. MYERS**

FOREWORD

KENNETH W. NOE

As most any reader of historical journals knows from the book reviews, edited collections of historical essays often lack much cohesion beyond a broad topic or common dissertation director. It is a common complaint in the back pages. In refreshing contrast, the contributors and editors of this volume explore the guerrilla experience in the American Civil War with remarkable intention and yoked cohesion. In essay after essay, beginning with Brian McKnight and Barton Myers's bold introduction, three intertwined themes appear consistently. That trio of key ideals clearly is coming to define modern Civil War guerrilla studies in the wake of the conflict's sesquicentennial, much as Philip Shaw Paludan's pathbreaking examination of North Carolina's Shelton Laurel Massacre and Michael Fellman's defiantly revisionist *Inside War* first instigated the scholarly reexamination of irregular warfare over thirty years ago.[1]

First among the contributors' aims is confronting the still-dominant counternarrative that guerrilla warfare was in the end an unimportant "sideshow," a trendy distraction then and now that draws attention away from the battlefields and executive offices of traditional scholarship. Echoing the recent work of Daniel Sutherland, the contributors to *The Guerrilla Hunters* reaffirm what Sutherland calls the "decisive" nature of the guerrilla experience. Tracing the "sideshow" approach to postwar Lost Cause narratives that still cast long shadows, Myers and McKnight go on to maintain that it dangerously obscures the war's true history by pushing the dissident voices of people such as Southern Unionists into the background while privileging some participants' war over others. They accordingly call for a much messier but more accurate synthesis of symmetrical and asymmetrical warfare, toward the goal of a more rounded understanding of what the war was really like for the people who lived through it.[2]

The second, related theme running through these pages is the guerrilla war's human diversity. Again and again the contributors stress that there was no one kind of irregular or irregular conflict. These men could be driven by the very same political and social ideologies and motivations that empowered volunteer soldiers, by kin and neighborhood ties, or simply by desire for profit or revenge; others, such as John Gatewood, were likely criminal psychopaths. Some guerrillas had to binge on whiskey before they indulged in killing, but the notorious William Quantrill was a teetotaler. They operated on isolated prairies, in rugged mountains, and along rivers. Irregulars wore uniforms, or wore their opponents' uniforms, or donned beautiful shirts embroidered by sisters and lovers. Some eschewed regularity at all. Bushwhackers committed atrocities against regular troops, and sometimes those supposedly better disciplined soldiers committed atrocities against the assailants and their families. Civilians too responded in a myriad of ways to the chaos irregular warfare brought to their doors. Supporters took guerrillas food and supplies, while survivors occasionally defiled guerrillas' dead bodies and threw their butchered handiwork into ditches to rot. After the war, all of those still living had competing stories to tell.

A third theme, closely tied to the second, involves categorization. Important recent works, grounded in both nineteenth-century law and the nation's most recent counterinsurgencies in the Middle East, increasingly posit clear boundaries for guerrillas and the men who hunted them. Echoing Henry W. Halleck, Lincoln's general in chief for much of the war, as well as Halleck legal advisor Francis Lieber, some scholars suggest that guerrillas seemingly were either real soldiers, civilians in arms, or lawless thugs, depending largely on their relationship with their state and its conventional military. Such characterizations are useful for examining irregular warfare over time, especially when searching for lessons for the modern military.[3] But as many of the contributors here establish, the walls between those strict categories in the 1860s were both remarkably permeable and decidedly murky to contemporaries. Guerrillas often moved in and out of official chains of command. Sometimes they started out in conventional units only to desert. Others joined regiments later in the war. Guerrillas and regular troops could fight side by side, as they did uneasily during Sterling Price's Missouri campaign in 1864. Partisan rangers emerged from a more amorphous irregular war in 1862 and returned to it later on. Nathan Bedford Forrest bristled when people called him a guerrilla, but many Federal authorities did so anyway. Many of John Hunt Morgan's men became guerrillas after the death of their commander, fighting essentially the same kind of war. Likewise, regular troops could fight conventional battles, act like partisans, and then mimic their irregular enemies in counterguerrilla sweeps all within the space of a few days.

To further illustrate these three thematic points, let us consider the instructive case of a stolid, reticent young Ohioan who graduated near the bottom of his class at West Point in 1852. From New York, Brevet 2nd Lieutenant George Crook embarked on a transcontinental journey that not only took him to northern California via Panama but also set him down professionally amid a sporadic, persistent, and often nasty guerrilla war. Looking back nearly forty years later, Crook pronounced himself supremely unprepared for it—but he proved to be a fast learner. For almost a decade, the young officer honed his skills in company-sized expeditions and small-but-escalating local wars against the besieged Indian nations of the Pacific Northwest. Surrounded by a series of incompetent and often-drunken commanders as well as often-unreliable comrades, he gained a largely self-taught yet remarkably effective practical education.[4]

Much of Crook's growing store of knowledge came while off duty. An obsessive hunter in his spare time, he made it a point to learn as much as he could about the topography and geography surrounding the small posts where he was stationed. Understanding the terrain and reading signs became vital when pursuing raiders or small groups attempting to flee reservations. At times Crook hunted with fellow officers, but on other trips he traveled with friendly Indians "and in this way learned something of their habits." Later on, he took subordinates with him in order to teach them what he knew.

By 1857, during an expedition against the Pitt River Indians, Crook realized that he finally had "learned enough about Indian craft to have confidence in my being able to hold my own with them." But there were still more new ideas and experiences to add to his toolbox as regional warfare became more frequent. He worked hard to keep his men healthy and well equipped. Coerced local guides, once including a terrified mother and her hostage infant, facilitated locating enemy parties. Leading small, isolated detachments on "scouts"—miniature search-and-destroy missions—Crook came to understand the value of personal leadership, boldness, and surprise attacks. On one march he captured an outpost by first carefully surrounding it in order to cut off escape routes. This kind of fighting was often brutal, ruthless, and individual. Crook did not just order men to kill, he usually took part himself and—according to a recent biographer—relished it. Up the Columbia River, however, he once turned to a lieutenant who "rather enjoyed that kind of thing" and ordered him to summarily execute a party of suspected "murderers" who had wandered peacefully into camp. Crook continued to hunt, explore, and procure information about potential enemies through gaining the confidence of other Indians. With comrades, he even studied local languages and submitted vocabularies to the Smithsonian Institute.[5]

By 1861, according to historian Paul Magid, Crook had "become as close to an expert on Indian warfare as anyone in the U.S. Army of the time."[6] Yet as war clouds gathered back east, he sought a different, textbook kind of war there. Ordered temporarily to New York, he hurried down to Washington to secure a leave of absence in hopes of securing command of a volunteer regiment. When both President Abraham Lincoln and Adjutant General Lorenzo Thomas resisted releasing yet another regular officer to volunteer service, Crook boldly telegraphed the governor of his home state. Within days he had secured command of the 36th Ohio Infantry, already at the front in the mountains of modern West Virginia. The regiment he found in the garrison town of Summersville during an unseasonably cold and rainy mid-September 1861 must have given him second thoughts about his decision. Eager and willing to learn, the men of the 36th Ohio nonetheless were "as rare as beefsteak," poorly equipped, amateurishly led, sickly, sometimes drunk, and in his opinion completely "demoralized." Much of that poor morale resulted from suffering repeatedly at the almost invisible hand of local Confederate guerrillas, universally derided as "bushwhackers," who had sniped and skirmished with them without consequence throughout their difficult march into Virginia.[7]

Crook worked hard over the next few months to clothe, shod, and properly drill his regiment. What delighted the men most, however, were his reported experiences in the West coupled with his promises to take a similar war to the hated bushwhackers. "Colonel Crook is a regular Old Indian fighter," one of his soldiers wrote proudly. "I reckon he will 'Bushwhack' some of the Bushwhacking cusses in regular Bushwhacking style if they venture across his war path."[8] They read their commander's intentions correctly. Crook first dismissed the locals as "cut-throats" and "cowardly," not to mention barely white, just as he had denigrated the native people of the Pacific Northwest as "filthy, odoriferous, treacherous, ungrateful, pitiless, cruel, and lazy." Othering enabled killing. The regular then turned naturally to the skills and tactics he knew best. "Being fresh from the Indian country," he recalled, "where I had more or less experience with that kind of warfare, I set to work organizing for the task." He chose a group of "the most apt officers," notably a cohort from Marietta, Ohio, "and scattered them through the country to learn it and all the people in it, and particularly the bushwhackers, their haunts, etc." After that came scouting expeditions. "Disgusted" that captured bushwhackers received good treatment and sometimes early release from Federal confinement, the Ohioans began killing all prisoners in the field. "In a short time no more of these prisoners were brought in," Crook later admitted. "When an officer returned from a scout he would report that they had caught so-and-so, but in bringing him in he slipped off a log while crossing a stream and broke his neck, or that he was killed by an accidental discharge of one of the men's guns, and many like reports. But they never brought back any more prisoners."[9]

As the hard western Virginia winter dragged on, Crook's successful scouting tactics inspired other units even as the 36th Ohio mounted bigger and more destructive expeditions. In January 1862, Crook led six companies into Braxton County, a bushwhacker haven, and then left orders that "every thing along the road was to be burned. . . . [W]e simply burned every thing of worth burnable. The destruction was complete."[10] In addition to isolated homes, his men destroyed two small settlements, threatened women in their beds, shot at least one prisoner, and killed upward of twenty other local men who resisted. When parents and siblings back home reacted badly to the news that their boys were not behaving as soldiers should, the troops replied with defiant pride in their tactics and their officers' no-prisoners policy. "If we ant out here to kill Bushwhackers," wrote one, "what are we [here] for?"[11]

Finally, in early April 1862, new Mountain Department commander John C. Frémont, fresh from the guerrilla chaos of Missouri, ordered what twenty-first-century observers might call a "surge." This was a massive, all-out attempt to destroy the region's bushwhacker bands once and for all using their own guerrilla tactics against them. Frémont personally selected Crook to lead elements of three regiments straight into the bushwhacker stronghold of Webster County. But the colonel balked. Instead, he advised a more conventional attack against the regular Confederate troops stationed at the strategic town of Lewisburg, a traditional campaign of the type that he wanted to lead. When Frémont persisted, Crook handed the assignment to an apt subordinate who proceeded to apply the torch to Webster County with enthusiasm.[12]

At first Frémont's surge seemed to work splendidly. Confederate partisans sued for peace, laid down their arms, or fled south. What finally undermined the new campaign was a ramped-up traditional war that overlapped the western Virginia mountains. Thomas J. "Stonewall" Jackson's Valley Campaign distracted Frémont and pulled his men to defeat in the east. Subsequent campaigns in Virginia and Maryland further involved the Mountain Department's forces in set-piece fighting. Crook was in the thick of it, transitioning skillfully from mountain-guerrilla fighter into conventional battlefield commander over the next bloody year. Late in May 1862 he led a newly formed brigade of Ohio and West Virginia troops, including his own regiment, against a Confederate incursion at now-occupied Lewisburg. Crook praised his men, noting that they had performed well "the first time . . . under fire"—scouting apparently did not count as real fighting. In August the army folded his brigade into the new Kanawha Division and sent it into northern Virginia to help block Jackson's march north toward Washington. During the Second Battle of Bull Run, Crook and his detached regiment acted as John Pope's bodyguards. Reunited with the rest of the division, Crook joined George McClellan's force assembling to defend the capital. The Kanawha Division fought well at South Mountain, Maryland, but Crook showed his inexperience and a tendency toward backbiting at Antietam. Promoted nonetheless to the rank of brigadier general of volunteers, Crook took his brigade to Tennessee in January 1863 to reinforce the Army of the Cumberland after the Battle of Stones River.[13]

But the army was not done with Crook's particular talents. After William Rosecrans's Tullahoma Campaign, Crook gave up his brigade to John Turchin, the controversial former Russian officer who had notoriously sacked the Alabama town of Athens in retaliation for Confederate partisan depredations, and took over the army's 2nd Cavalry Division. Commanding horse soldiers for the first time, Crook now metamorphosed into a uniformed partisan along the lines of Nathan Bedford Forrest or Morgan, directing fast-moving raids and reconnaissance missions behind enemy lines. At Chickamauga in September, his cavalrymen briefly reverted to traditional duties and at the bitter end acted as rear guard for the retreating army. During the Chattanooga occupation, Crook initially screened the city from the north, which finally drew his division across the Tennessee River and west into Alabama in a ruthless pursuit of Joseph Wheeler's cavalry.

When George Thomas replaced Rosecrans, however, Crook found himself once again involved in hunting guerrillas.[14] "I received orders to remain in the northern part of Alabama," he remembered, "and break up a band of cut-throats, bushwhackers, and thieves, and besides to break up an illegal traffic that was being carried on between Nashville and the South." Crook's target was Frank

Gurley, an Alabama cavalryman serving under Forrest whose men were notorious in Federal circles for killing Union general Robert McCook inside his ambulance—the same incident that led Turchin to Athens. By Crook's reckoning, he made quick work of them. "He was soon captured," he wrote of Gurley, "and his whole outfit scattered to the four winds, a great many being killed."[15]

In February 1864, after the Kanawha Division's commander was captured, Washington sent Crook back to West Virginia to restore order. Discovering that his "sphere of operations gave me control of country that had never been rid of bushwhackers," the general "organized to suppress them, employing the same principles which were so efficacious when I was in that country before."[16] But there were new principles too; Crook now mounted his scouts, equipped them with better weapons, and authorized them to live off the land. But when Ulysses S. Grant moved against Robert E. Lee in May 1864, the Federal general in chief called upon him to play an important if more traditional role in the Confederate rear. Crook marched his men south through the mountains, defeated a small Confederate force at Cloyd's Mountain in the Virginia interior, and cut the vital Virginia and Tennessee Railroad—the so-called "gut of the Confederacy." Worried by a newspaper report that Grant had been defeated in the Wilderness, Crook then hastily retreated north down the Shenandoah Valley to Lexington. When department commander David Hunter decided to order the destruction of the Virginia Military Institute in that city, Crook led the opposition, though expressing less indignation when Hunter turned away hungry women with threats to burn their houses. After a humiliating retreat back into West Virginia, Crook took practical command of the Army of West Virginia and joined Philip H. Sheridan's growing force in its final struggle against Jubal Early in the Valley, fighting with distinction from Third Winchester to Cedar Creek.[17]

By the end of 1864, Crook had made a name for himself as one of the war's significant commanders. Yet he essentially ended the war the way he began it, fighting irregulars, and not always successfully. In February, partisan rangers captured the general at his hotel in Cumberland, Maryland, where uncharacteristically he had spent much of the winter courting his future wife, the secessionist innkeeper's much-younger daughter. Crook blamed "ignorant Dutchmen" among his pickets; Secretary of War Edwin Stanton blamed Crook. Luckily for the general, the Confederates took him alive instead of later alleging that he had fallen off a log and broken his neck. Soon after his exchange, and with support from Grant, he once again took command of cavalry. By then the war was nearly over. He made it to Appomattox, briefly commanded occupation troops in North Carolina, and then returned to the Pacific Northwest, where his career had begun. For the next quarter of a century in the West, Crook fought various Indian nations and his own high command, gaining a reputation for honesty and humanitarian sympathy toward his foes, but also exhibiting ambition, prickliness, and a steady cultivation of his sometimes eccentric image. Notably, he served on the northern plains with George Custer, attaining mixed results, and in Arizona, more successfully, against the Apaches. There he became known as Nantan Lupan, "Gray Wolf."[18]

Considering his later career in the West, biographer Charles Robinson described Crook as "something of an enigma." He was adored and despised within the army, modest and self-promoting, innovative in the field but often stumbling as well, a sometimes vindictive comrade whose death left both his subordinates and the Apaches in tears. "He, at least, had never lied to us," said the great Oglala Lakota leader Red Cloud.[19] Crucially within the context of *The Guerrilla Hunters,* that same ambiguous if not perplexing character likewise initially seems to apply when dealing more narrowly with Crook's Civil War career. Simply put, historians sometimes behave as if there were several Federal officers named George Crook. One was the fierce enemy of Appalachian bushwhackers who wielded ruthless tactics learned out west against a different "Other" in the East. Another was the brigade commander who led troops on the war's bloodiest day. Then there was the partisan horseman sending mounted raiders behind Confederate lines in Tennessee. The problem is that a single soldier was all of them. His diverse career simply blurred the allegedly hard-and-fast lines of wartime service—and did so consistently. Crook in fact shifted back and forth from conventional to unconventional service with a surprising ease that belies any strict categorization. And while he preferred textbook warfare and the recognition that accompanied it, he never regarded his other activities as part of any "sideshow" or any less part of the Civil War than what he did on South Mountain. And Crook was not unique. Perhaps more importantly, the same assertions can be made about the men he led. The soldiers of the 36th Ohio, for example, followed him through most of his war, from scouting for guerrillas in Braxton County to actions on many a bloody field against Confederate soldiers in line of battle. They fought secessionists of every stripe and tactic, and after a time little differentiated them.

What initially appears to be enigmatic about George Crook's war, then, is really only the effect of viewing the conflict through comfortable lenses that value one kind of service while minimizing others. The enigma is in the eye of the beholder. For readers who want to see a sharper image of the real war that soldiers and civilians experienced across the South, *The Guerrilla Hunters* offers a new prescription that allows us to see both men like Crook and his enemies with renewed clarity.

NOTES

1. Fellman, *Inside War.* For modern approaches, see, for example, Beilein and Hulbert, *Civil War Guerrilla;* and Barton A. Myers, "Guerrillas," chap. 9 of *A Companion to the U.S. Civil War,* 2 vols., ed. Aaron Sheehan-Dean (Malden, Mass.: Wiley-Blackwell, 2014).

2. For the decisive nature of guerrilla fighting, see Sutherland, "Sideshow No Longer"; and Sutherland, *Savage Conflict.* For a more recent and much-discussed demurral, see Gallagher and Meier, "Coming to Terms with Civil War Military History."

3. See, for example, Mackey, *Uncivil War.*

4. George Crook, *General George Crook: His Autobiography,* ed. Martin F. Schmidt, foreword by Joseph C. Porter (1946; Norman: University of Oklahoma Press, paperback ed., 1986), xi–xxiv, 3–13. A useful biography of Crook's early career is Paul Magid, *George Crook: From the Redwoods to Appomattox* (Norman: University of Oklahoma Press, 2011), esp. 11–50. In depicting Crook's 1850s campaigns as guerrilla wars comparable to those he would fight later rather than as a species of warfare that must be considered separately due to the ethnicities of the adversaries, I echo Nelson, "Indians Make the Best Guerrillas."

5. Crook, *General George Crook,* 13–81 (quotations, 21, 63, 64); Magid, *George Crook,* 75–81, 84, 86, 101–2, 110–11.

6. Magid, *George Crook,* 110.

7. Crook, *General George Crook,* 83–86 (quotations 85, 86). I have discussed this stage of Crook's career previously in Noe, "Exterminating Savages," 113–15. See also Magid, *George Crook,* 86.

8. John A. Palmer Diary, Jan. 1, 1862, in *The Salem Light Guard: Company G, 36th Regiment, Ohio Volunteer Infantry, Marietta, Ohio, 1861–1865,* comp. Lester L. Kempfer (Chicago: Adams, 1973), 38. Paul Magid downplays Crook's antiguerrilla activities in West Virginia. See *George Crook,* 116–21.

9. Crook, *General George Crook,* 69, 86–87; Noe, "Exterminating Savages," 115–16.

10. "Diary of Sergeant John Thomas Booth Company 'G' Thirty-Sixth Ohio Volunteer Infantry. In War of the Rebellion. Under the name of 'Foot Prints of the Thirty-Sixth Ohio Volunteer Infantry in the War of the Rebellion,'" Dr. John Booth Papers, Folder 7, Box 1, Collection 180, Ohio Historical Society, Columbus, 102, 104; Noe, "Exterminating Savages," 116–17.

11. J. A. Palmer, Summersville, Va. (future West Virginia), to Margaret, Feb. 12, 1862, and Palmer to Folks at Home, Mar. 31, 1862, in Kempfer, *Salem Light Guard,* 40; Noe, "Exterminating Savages," 116–17.

12. Noe, "Exterminating Savages, 119–21.

13. Crook, *General George Crook,* 89–103 (quotation, 90); Magid, *George Crook,* 144–56.

14. Crook, *General George Crook,* 103–12; Magid, *George Crook,* 157–58.

15. Crook, *General George Crook,* 112–13; Magid, *George Crook,* 164–72.

16. Crook, *General George Crook,* 135; Magid, *George Crook,* 173–76.

17. Crook, *General George Crook,* 113–34; Magid, *George Crook,* 201, 210–11. While Horatio Wright replaced Hunter as departmental commander, Crook took command of the troops in the field.

18. Here I briefly summarize Crook, *General George Crook,* xi–xiii, 135–301. See also Magid, *George Crook,* 288–99; Paul Magid, *The Gray Fox: George Crook and the Indian Wars* (Norman: University of Oklahoma Press, 2015); and Charles M. Robinson III, *General Crook and the Western Frontier* (Norman: University of Oklahoma Press, 2001).

19. Robinson, *General Crook,* 310–11. See also Magid, *Gray Fox,* 396–98.

THE GUERRILLA HUNTERS

INTRODUCTION

Guerrilla Warfare's Place in the History of the American Civil War

BRIAN D. McKNIGHT & BARTON A. MYERS

Writing from Memphis while commanding the District of West Tennessee in July 1862, Major General Ulysses S. Grant expressed the frustration of many senior Union officers facing the problems of guerrilla warfare during the American Civil War. In General Orders No. 60, Grant indicted not just the communities harboring guerrillas but also the Confederate government, which he viewed as wholly responsible for using irregular warfare as part of its military strategy. "Government collections shall be made, of personal property, from persons in the immediate neighborhood, sympathizing with the rebellion, sufficient to remunerate the Government [for] all loss and expense of collection," Grant ordered. "Persons acting as guerrillas without organization, and without uniform to distinguish them from private citizens, are not entitled to the treatment of Prisoners of War, when caught, and will not receive such treatment."[1]

This stern proclamation against irregular warriors further agitated the guerrillas in the Memphis region. Confederate irregular George R. Merritt of Senatobia, Mississippi, responded directly to Grant: "If you intend to make this a war of extermination, you will please inform us of it. . . . We are ready, and more than willing, to raise the 'black flag.' There are two thousand partisans who have sworn to retaliate. If you do not retract your proclamation, you may expect to have scenes of the most bloody character. Henceforth our motto shall be, Blood for Blood, and blood for property. We intend, by the help of God, to hang on the outskirts of your rabble, like lightning around the edge of a cloud." Grant was undeterred.[2]

The difficulties caused by guerrillas during the Civil War reached far beyond the vicious behavior of the many rogues in Tennessee, Missouri, Arkansas, and Mississippi to the very fundamental issues of command and control at the county and neighborhood levels across a substantial section of the South. By 1862, Union generals such as Grant, Henry W. Halleck, and John C. Frémont were struggling to define a counterguerrilla policy to contain this military threat in the West. Back east, the Confederate Congress used the early successes of cavalry raiders like Kentuckian John Hunt Morgan and Virginian Turner Ashby as models to create an authorized partisan service under the April 1862 Partisan Ranger Act. The policy ultimately failed by 1864, but the experiment reveals much about Confederate military culture. It also suggests the societal limits these Southerners were attempting to protect.

Meanwhile, enemies of the Confederacy—Unionists, recusant conscripts, and deserters—were waging local guerrilla wars of survival as they sought the new nation's downfall in hundreds of neighborhoods and communities across the seceding states. The American guerrilla conflicts of the 1860s were messy local affairs that few Confederates wanted to remember in the years after the war. But the internal problems at the county level created widespread instability across the Confederacy by 1864. Ignoring these military issues within the divided South both aids Lost Cause writers such as Virginian Jubal Early and North Carolinian Zebulon Vance, who sought to eliminate the history of political dissent in the Confederacy, and prevents clearer understanding of the origins and course of many people's Civil War experience.[3]

The essays in this volume begin to connect the dots between the conventional, symmetrical battlefield war and the guerrilla conflicts that spread across every state of the Confederacy. Explaining how these two areas of the war relate will at some point in the future enable scholars to offer new synthesis to two areas of military history that seem to talk at, not with, one another. This volume suggests numerous reasons why scholars have either been reluctant to integrate these "other" military stories into larger narratives of the war or faced problems doing so. Taken as a whole, the pieces presented here offer a redefinition of Civil War soldiering and the boundaries of military history in studying the war, which now include a range of irregular fighters, combatants and noncombatants, affected by guerrilla conflict; counterirregulars who saw service fighting guerrillas; policymakers who implemented irregulars and counterirregulars as a strategy; and ultimately an uncovered group of people coping with the subsequent problems this type of warfare caused for West Point–trained officers in both the Union and Confederate regular armies.

While Civil War scholars continue to discuss the importance of classification for irregular warriors during the conflict, most employ a basic definition for guerrilla warfare. In the 1860s, this method of violence deployed the military tactics of hit-and-run attacks, ambush, and surprise. It was fought much of the time with the civilian population at the center of the "guerrilla battlefield." Irregulars could be mounted or dismounted, utilizing shotguns, a brace of pistols, or even their grandfather's squirrel rifle in a personal, independent war. Some wore uniforms, others did not; some even wore the uniforms of their enemy for the purposes of deception. But the central problem for military officials and civilians alike was that these irregulars defied the sacrosanct boundary between combatant and noncombatant, creating a liminal warrior stripped by governments and regular armies of the legal protections of the legitimate combatant. Specific typologies of guerrilla warfare—raiding war, people's war, and partisan war—as well as the term "bushwhacker" help us understand the finer analytical points of these conflicts. But many civilians in the 1860s did not share the subtle interests of scholars such as Columbia College professor Francis Lieber, who first addressed this set of definitional questions in the context of international laws of war. Lieber's pamphlet *Guerrilla Parties: Considered with Reference to the Laws and Usages of War* (August 1862) was distilled into an important section of General Orders No. 100 (April 1863), which guided Union officers on this definitional point about legitimate combatants and the treatment of prisoners of war. This document subsequently became foundational for laws of war in the early twentieth century. Yet discerning the differences and motivations of people that many civilians and military officials considered brigands and criminals, regardless of their loyalty, was not a high priority for many of the Civil War generation.[4]

Scholars of the Civil War's many local guerrilla conflicts have, at times, felt pushed to the periphery of their own field of scholarship—treated as "a sideshow"—as other historians searched for the primary reasons for Confederate surrender in 1865, doing so without engaging the full spectrum of military stories and combatants from beyond the conventional battlefield. The guerrillas who faced Grant's army in West Tennessee in 1862 may not have prevented the ultimate victory of Union men in arms, but the many irregulars fighting both for and against the Confederacy did play a fundamental military role in Southern strategy, policy, and, as a result of massive destabilization, military defeat. That military role, however, has not been fully investigated, from the local, state, or national level. Those guerrillas resisting Confederates at home likewise played a key role in the military history of the war. Yet they are often treated as an afterthought, not a main area for scholarly analysis. Only recently have we seen the first Confederacy-wide study of the issue in Daniel Sutherland's path-breaking book *A Savage Conflict* (2009), in which he concludes that guerrillas played a decisive role in the outcome of the war. Up until this point, local and regional study has dominated the discussion of the origins and course of guerrilla conflict during the Civil War. What military historians need now is better synthesis of the conventional battlefield narrative of the war with the many stories growing out of a less linear and more diffuse use of asymmetric war in its mid-nineteenth-century forms. Several of the essays in this volume ask readers to think about how Civil War scholars will accomplish this.

For decades, historians and biographers of irregular warriors have faced the dual problem of integrating "guerrilla studies" into the broader history of the war and of writing about American guerrillas during the 1860s more generally. There are major obstacles facing those who embark on the journey down one of these guerrilla paths. Some of the problems are source related, while others are historiographical. Regardless, moving beyond them presents the challenge of asking better questions and raising sharper points of analysis about who fought in the Civil War: when, where, and why. This volume collectively makes several penetrating arguments. First, there was not *one* irregular war, easy to compartmentalize and forget. Civil War guerrillas fought in many localized conflicts, motivated by diverse issues, with an influence at the county, regional, state, and national levels. These conflicts emerged in the lower North, the Border South, and across the Confederate States of America. Second, authors within the Lost Cause mythology sought to bury the story of the guerrilla wars to promote the idea of a united white Confederate South after Robert E. Lee's surrender. Lost Cause writers, seeking to minimize the history of dissent and Unionism on the home front, frequently excised local guerrilla histories along with other forms of resistance after the war. The sometimes limited and fragmentary source material of the local irregular conflicts, which involved many illiterate warriors and civilians, compounds this source problem. Confederates also lost or destroyed many of their own records (many Conscription Bureau records, for example) that would have been helpful to later writers. These factors limited the overall amount of material making it into a traditional narrative of the war's events before any historians sat down to write. Third, scholars of the conventional battlefield have been reluctant to examine different forms of combat beyond those that readers expect to see from a war they believe they know. The well-worn story is of Union regiments charging Marye's Heights at Fredericksburg and of the war with a clear beginning, middle, and end. Fourth, even the Confederate leadership did not fully understand the extent of the problem they and the Southern people had created by using this method of violence. Many Confederate military officials saw anti-Confederate guerrillas as a criminal problem, not a military one, as they struggled to roll back the challenges of these self-constituted bands. The war ended just as many began to awake to the many local and regional crises raging at home, which in part brought about the end. Finally, these local irregular wars introduce a certain degree of chaos into a conflict Civil War readers like to think had a neat, clear narrative, which also creates problems for the historian constructing a linear narrative. The resistance by scholars of the conventional battlefield to examine the "guerrilla battlefield" as part of the overall narrative military history of the war is palpable. Embracing that historical problem, not running from it, will help us find a better synthesis of these very different kinds of warfare.[5]

One issue should be clear for Civil War military historians from the recent surge in scholarship on the irregulars: The geographic extent of the Confederate government's guerrilla problem needs to be fully understood and better disseminated to other military historians. Even scholars who have little interest in studying the local wars within the Confederacy concede that those conflicts were "disruptive," but they do not seem interested in investigating how disruptive guerrilla warfare was, preferring to keep attention laser-focused on the "real" fighting that mattered as opposed to what those scholars perceive as "atypical" or "ancillary" engagements. But in much of the Confederacy—places like greater Appalachia, as historian Brian McKnight has suggested—these irregular conflicts were "the war" that mattered a great deal in scores upon scores of counties. In part, this resistance to studying guerrillas and military occupation demonstrates the need to push for a well-staffed National Park Service site to commemorate the irregular conflicts of the American Civil War—a park or monument that would serve as a place of national conversation on these issues, a dedicated place of reflection apart from such battlefields as Vicksburg and Gettysburg. Far more people were affected directly by guerrilla conflict between 1861 and 1865 than fought for three days in July 1863 on those Pennsylvania fields or over the besieged Mississippi town. Excellent possibilities for a federal park of this kind exist in the Mosby Heritage Area in northern Virginia and at Centralia Battlefield in Missouri. Both are sites of important and decisive events of Civil War guerrilla conflict and offer a perfect eastern and western pole for public conversation. They also have been well preserved by local historical organizations from modern development. Another promising public history "guerrilla option" resides in the local movement in eastern Ohio to secure a National Park Service site for the events of Confederate general John Hunt Morgan's infamous 1863 raid. Morgan's role as a principal model for the Confederacy's authorized partisan ranger force and the military strategy of raiding warfare would be further integrated into the narrative of the Civil War by the addition of such a National Park site in the Buckeye State.[6]

With the passing of the Civil War's sesquicentennial, specialists in the field are taking an inventory of progress and deficiency. The centennial saw its own challenges to Civil War orthodoxy as scholars of social history were growing in influence at precisely that same time. In the years that immediately followed, social history exploded, bringing into public consciousness heretofore marginalized groups and propelling them to the forefront of new interpretations. The subsequent decades were a heyday for scholars looking at the war "from the bottom up" and finding a different kind of conflict missed by previous generations. Amid this movement there emerged a new kind of military history, that of the guerrilla and his influence upon his surrounding society. The irregular soldier seemed to capture some element of all that was going on in the historical profession at the time: He was a citizen first and soldier second, a member of his community before a member of an army. At the same time, he was brutally effective either fighting an enemy or instilling a terrific fear by representing the unknown. One thing is certain: the subfield of guerrilla studies has developed into one of the most vibrant and creative in Civil War historiography and has contributed significantly to future reinterpretations of the conflict.

This volume speaks to the innovative nature of Civil War guerrilla studies and does so in the spirit of other developing fields. This area of study is barely five years from the publication of the first attempt at a comprehensive examination of these shadowy figures, Sutherland's *A Savage Conflict*. The past two decades have witnessed the appearance of numerous biographies and regional studies that speak to the irregular war, with new and innovative works appearing frequently. It seems that guerrilla studies is providing a new intellectual direction for Civil War scholars. That is not to say that the process of developing a new field is an easy one. The past few years have seen growing criticism of this direction, with one article seemingly arguing that guerrilla studies has become a distraction to the examination of the real Civil War.[7] This reaction is to be expected as historiographical trends evolve.

Guerrilla studies achieved its initial influence because of its ability to bridge military and social history. There is little question that military history has dominated Civil War studies, with political history running a strong second. In the past fifty years, though, there has been a groundswell of social history that has offered new opportunities to understand heretofore misunderstood or neglected populations. African American history and women's history have been the greatest beneficiaries of this movement, and countless scholars have constructed an impressive corpus of information. Despite the mass and intellectual level of this work, it did little to treat regions and people unknown to historians. Residents of regions like the mid-nineteenth-century Appalachians and Ozarks did not have a strong tradition of literacy, making internal record keeping difficult, but did have a well-developed oral tradition that helped future generations write histories. Their stories were further complicated by a Civil War experience markedly different from the traditional kind of warfare employing conventional armies. The result was a dearth of good scholarship owing to attempts to fit an unconventional experience into an outdated, linear narrative. The modern scholar of the Civil War guerrilla conflict can add to the literature by combining newer techniques and methods for a much more comprehensive picture of a region's experience than that traditionally achieved by using military or political history where very little conventional warfare took place.

The essays in this volume convey the number, variety, and complexity of issues motivating guerrillas and their style of warfare. Most of the contributors have spent their careers studying, and therefore defining, the nature of the irregular conflict in the mid-nineteenth century with an eye toward appreciating the multiple understandings of it held by the perpetrators, their enemies, and those innocents who felt their effect. The volume begins with a piece on the intersection of Confederate military policy and the official debate over guerrilla warfare within the South, also drawing on records of irregulars across the Confederacy. It then moves to a regional overview of the Appalachian interior. Essays addressing issues in the Border and Middle South follow before the volume moves to the western and Trans-Mississippi theaters of the war, returning to the Deep South and to the issues of counterirregular warfare for the Union army. The final piece offers international context to the American Civil War guerrilla experience. Collectively, the essays demonstrate the nationwide problem that Confederate use of irregular warfare wrought for soldiers and civilians, Union and Confederate. In addition to each essay offering an avenue for better integration of irregular warriors and their unique form of conflict into the narrative of the Civil War, they collectively argue for a more comprehensive and inclusive definition of military history that includes all combatants from the 1860s, not just those who fought on the fields of northern Virginia.

The volume's editors open the collection with geographically broad and theoretically challenging contributions. In "Partisan Ranger Petitions and the Confederacy's Authorized *Petite Guerre* Service," Barton A. Myers examines many of the men who desired independent military service and the government's creation of a national policy on authorized *petite guerre* service that would eventually touch every state in the Confederacy and most of the Border South. Myers delves into the Confederate high command, which initially viewed partisan service in a positive light but, under the strain of diminishing manpower and public outcry over outrages visited upon civilians, began to see the guerrillas as an unrelenting, if dimly understood, problem. Brian D. McKnight's "Finding the Guerrillas: The Power of Shadow and Perception in the Appalachian Theater" seeks to view the guerrilla from the ground up, examining the appeal of irregular service to the individual and how guerrillas' activities complicate traditional military lines of thought. McKnight argues that simple self-interest cannot be ignored as the defining element of the average guerrilla's decision-making process.

McKnight's Appalachian-focused essay is followed by Brian Steel Wills's exploration of Tennessee and the gray area connecting the regular and irregular wars. "Nathan Bedford Forrest and Guerrilla War" is a study of the duality of this most controversial Confederate. Wills finds that while Forrest appeared to embody the guerrilla ideal in his approach to warfare, he held the formalities of armed conflict in high regard.[8] For the "Wizard of the Saddle," war was serious business to be practiced by serious-minded men. Stephen Rockenbach's "Home Rebels, Amnesty, and Antiguerrilla Operations in Kentucky in 1864" chronicles that state's difficult progress resisting insurgent threats and reaffirming the safety of its citizens from marauders. By the end of the year, much progress had been made, although most Kentuckians continued to face a very real threat of violence if they voiced their opinions too loudly.[9] Primarily shared between Kentucky and Tennessee, the Cumberland Plateau was home to Aaron Astor's subject. "'Who is "Tinker Dave" Beaty?': Hunting Guerrilla Social Networks" reaches deep into the communities and social networks of the Upper Cumberland region of Tennessee and Kentucky and finds that the men who made up Beaty's irregular band joined for the protection it provided. Astor explains how pragmatism and self-interest motivated denizens of this region to respond to the crisis that came to surround them. His approach opens new avenues of interpreting people and communities that did not leave traditional records of their experiences.[10]

Moving east, Scott Thompson's "The Irregular War in Loudoun County, Virginia" looks at John Mobberly's band of irregulars and the Loudoun Rangers, who sought to eliminate their threat. Ultimately, Mobberly was killed and his band put down by the rangers, but only after a years-long struggle that affected most everyone in the county and surrounding region. In "American Warlord? Reconsidering 'Guerrilla' Leader John Gatewood," Adam H. Domby reconfirms the bandit thesis that frequently applies to the basest of irregular warriors. Using Gatewood as his foil, Domby illustrates how guerrillas often sought to couch their criminal behavior in patriotic mythology. For Gatewood, the war was about opportunism. Sharing the southeastern area of operations with Domby's piece is Lisa Tendrich Frank's "The Union War on Women," which refutes the traditional interpretation that women were innocent bystanders caught up in a war that did not seek to harm them, replacing it with a fascinating argument that they were intended targets. Frank is attuned to the fact that Unionist guerrillas have received preferential treatment by continuing to be viewed as regular soldiers engaged in regular warfare, while their activities differ very little from those of their Confederate counterparts.

The Trans-Mississippi theater of guerrilla operations has enjoyed significant attention thanks to the infamous figures who operated in that region. In "Guerrilla Warfare and the Environment in the Trans-Mississippi Theater," Matthew M. Stith makes the argument that the conflict in the Trans-Mississippi, which at that time was still a developing region in comparison to the more established and active states in the other theaters of war, suffered from the conflict in such a way that its progress and development were severely stifled in most cases and sometimes completely halted. This occurred because of the danger individual isolation presented during wartime. By 1865, the same isolation that had felt so liberating for residents before the war was considered a mortal danger, with the result that forests were allowed to return to wilderness and settlement in townships for mutual protection was encouraged. Laura June Davis also challenges existing geographic conventions in her contribution, "Irregular Naval Warfare along the Lower Mississippi." In it she argues convincingly that these riverine guerrillas were very effective at destroying boats, killing civilians, and causing substantial economic loss through their unconventional tactics. By the middle of the war, these men had grown so notorious that actions dismissed in previous years as accidents were now instinctively laid at their feet.

One important epicenter of guerrilla conflict in the West was the Missouri-Kansas border region. Joseph M. Beilein Jr. contributes "Whiskey, Wild Men, and Missouri's Guerrilla War," which confirms the influence of alcohol on the dirty underbelly of the conflict. The guerrillas of Missouri were drinking men who used "liquid courage" to help them carry out some of the most heinous atrocities of the war. It also assisted them in moving beyond some of the terrible things they had done. Matthew C. Hulbert's "Larkin M. Skaggs and the Massacre(s) at Lawrence" follows Beilein's piece. In it he makes a strong case that the Lawrence Massacre was a series of individual fights occurring in numerous pockets of isolated violence. This is a powerful argument that should influence the way people study larger violent activities. If this is the way such actions took place, then the household war—that from within, fought by women at home acting as the storekeeper and information carrier to husbands operating as guerrillas in the hills and valleys—was also a viable arena for guerrillas. Andrew Fialka is a pioneer in the spatiotemporal study of Civil War guerrilla activity. In "A Spatial Approach to Civil War Missouri's Domestic Supply Line," he finds heretofore-unrecognized patterns that help connect irregular warfare to the society in which it operates.

The volume closes as it opened, by returning to a much wider stage. Andrew F. Lang makes a compelling argument in "Challenging the Union Citizen-Soldier Ideal" that those soldiers who engaged in guerrilla operations were intellectually changed as a result. They began to see the true complexity of war as a conflict in which civilians were targeted and violence was unfettered and disconnected from the traditional monopoly of conventional armies. It was a war of people trying to destroy men, property, and institutions that otherwise and at other times would be supported and encouraged. Earl Hess closes the volume with his first work to explore the guerrilla wars, "Civil War Guerrillas in a Global, Comparative Context," arguing that irregular warfare is a much better established and more frequently employed tactic than modern scholars often care to admit. He finds that much of the international community, while aware of the role of the guerrilla in other conflicts, knew nothing of such combatants in the American Civil War and primarily view the fight as a battle between large, formal, and conventional armies.

This anthology presents Civil War guerrilla studies in their full complexity, not as a field unto itself. The editors and contributors view the "guerrilla school" as a way to supplement existing knowledge by showing the interconnections between the conventional and unconventional. Guerrilla warfare thus becomes an integral part of the larger whole in the same way that race, class, gender, and cultural approaches came to expand and illuminate Civil War history during the latter half of the twentieth century.

Future developments in Civil War scholarship are dependent upon researchers who not only write within their fields but also seek out other, intellectually foreign spheres in which they can learn new techniques not yet applied to this time and place. Topically, the same is also true. Civil War history has traditionally been the dominion of military and political scholars. In the past several decades, however, social, cultural, and economic historians have made landmark contributions to a broader understanding of the conflict and helped the field more fully mature. Guerrilla studies will likewise enhance and advance traditional historical approaches and interpretations.

NOTES

1. Ulysses S. Grant, *The Papers of Ulysses S. Grant,* vol. 5, *April 1–August 31, 1862,* ed. John Y. Simon (Carbondale: Southern Illinois University Press, 1973), 190.

2. Ibid.

3. Gallagher and Meier, "Coming to Terms with Civil War Military History." It may be noted that one of Gary Gallagher's most important contributions to Civil War historiography was his Confederate nationalism thesis, developed in *Confederate War.* Gallagher alleges that the Confederacy enjoyed the unflagging support of its populace but was failed by an army that lost too many battles to ultimately win the war. In *The South vs. the South,* William Freehling takes direct issue with Gallagher's thesis by arguing that the Confederacy's greatest weakness was its failure to unite white Southerners from all of the slaveholding states behind the cause of Confederate nationalism. For a more recent critique of the Gallagher-Meier approach, see Sutherland, "Memories of a Rooted Sorrow."

4. For an overview of the historical development and scholarly debates within the field of American Civil War "guerrilla studies," see Barton A. Myers, "Guerrillas," chap. 9 of *A Companion to the U.S. Civil War,* 2 vols., ed. Aaron Sheehan-Dean (Malden, Mass.: Wiley-Blackwell, 2014).

5. See Myers, *Rebels against the Confederacy* and "Future of Civil War Era Studies." Myers

offers a more extensive discussion at http://journalofthecivilwarera.org/forum-the-future-of-civil-war-era-studies.

6. Gallagher and Meier, "Coming to Terms with Civil War Military History"; Beilein and Hulbert, *Civil War Guerrilla;* "Mosby Heritage Area Association Gets American Battlefield Protection Program Grant," *Clarke Daily News,* Aug. 23, 2012; Friends of Centralia Battlefield, "Centralia Battlefield," n.d., http://www.centraliabattlefield.com (accessed, Apr. 13, 2016); "Park Proposed for Ohio Civil War Battle Site from Morgan's Raid," *Columbus Dispatch,* Feb. 11, 2016.

7. Gallagher and Meier, "Coming to Terms with Civil War Military History." Other recent scholarly overviews of the Civil War historiography do not examine the growing scholarship on guerrilla warfare and its effect. See John H. Matsui, "Seven Score and Ten: American Civil War Historiography at the Close of the Sesquicentennial," *Journal of Military History* 80 (Apr. 2016): 487–509.

8. See also Wills, *Battle from the Start.* This book was republished as *The Confederacy's Greatest Cavalryman* (Lawrence: University Press of Kansas, 1998).

9. Rockenbach's forthcoming book *"War upon Our Border": Two Ohio Communities Navigate the Civil War* promises to expand our current knowledge of the borderland's wartime experience.

10. See also Astor, *Civil War along Tennessee's Cumberland Plateau;* Astor, *Rebels on the Border.*

PARTISAN RANGER PETITIONS AND THE CONFEDERACY'S AUTHORIZED *PETITE GUERRE* SERVICE

BARTON A. MYERS

"I have lately noticed that our Government is directing its attention to the organization of independent partisan Companies of Mounted Rangers or Garillus," wrote Captain F. M. Marks of the Fourth Louisiana Infantry Battalion on May 4, 1862, in a letter to Confederate secretary of war George Wythe Randolph (Thomas Jefferson's youngest grandson). "In my humble estimation, this a wise step, and must ultimately prove fruitful, and be of incalculable benefit to our cause—*the great cause of Southern Liberty and Southern Independence.*" As he penned his elegant six-page petition, Captain Marks requested authority to take his company out of line-infantry service and into one of the American Civil War's guerrilla conflicts. Although his main concern was to gain permission to operate against Union soldiers in the area of Louisiana along the Mississippi River, his letter illustrates many of the other motives and goals found in the formal requests of would-be partisan chieftains. He appealed boldly and pragmatically to the Confederate War Department about a fundamental strategic concern, manpower. "In the new position we seek to occupy; with the indomitable determination that pervades the company, aye, the entire Battalion, we must prove equal to a regular field army of at least 2,500 men." If guerrilla warfare maximized manpower as opposed to drawing it away from the key strategic aims of the Confederate war effort, then it might prove a valuable military solution to the beleaguered Confederacy's problems of controlling more than 750,000 square miles of territory.[1]

Captain Marks exhibited Southern patriotism and commitment to the cause of Confederate nationalism in his petition for a partisan ranger unit, but at the same time, he offered insight into why some men wanted out of the regular army. His discussion of the harsh winter weather in western Virginia, poor command decisions of Brigadier General John B. Floyd in that theater, and idleness and boredom associated with regular-army service exemplified the aspects of military duty that many Confederate soldiers found intolerable.

These same features of infantry soldiering would drive many men out of line service and into localized guerrilla wars across every state of the Confederacy between 1861 and 1865.[2]

Although the application of Captain Marks could be read as just a disgruntled soldier seeking an easy way out of infantry service, under the surface his petition shows a deep concern with maintaining Southern social order. Through his citation of and identification with established political and military officials, Marks sought to uphold the prewar hierarchical structure of Louisiana society as he related his motives for seeking independent military service. Concurrently, he sought to preserve that social order by using a form of political violence that would erode the protections for legal military conduct in the interior of the Confederacy, encourage criminality, and ultimately bring about the collapse of order in hundreds of communities and neighborhoods in the South. These partisan ranger petitions, and the internal governmental debate over an authorized irregular warfare policy, provide an important window into both the initial motives of Confederate guerrillas and the subsequent problems created by the official partisan ranger service.[3]

Between the spring and fall of 1862, Captain Marks was one of scores of Southern men responding through official channels to a new, and they believed exciting, military policy adopted by the Confederate government. That April, the Confederate Congress had passed the Conscription Act, the first national draft in American history, to address the declining number of volunteers and consequent manpower shortages of its field armies. This law was not the only policy that many in the government hoped would address the challenges of defending the remote border regions of the nascent nation. During the same month, Confederates also passed into law the Partisan Ranger Act, an authorized partisan service of sanctioned *petite guerre* units placing trusted officers and their commands on detached service from the regular field armies to harass, gather intelligence, and secure supplies from the Union army. What supportive congressmen from South Carolina, Kentucky, Louisiana, and Missouri all had in mind was a new military force that capitalized on the intense Southern desire for individual military service, deeds of daring, local defense in areas the armies could not or would not have time to protect, as well as a strong desire for mounted home-front service to protect families and loved ones. For the men who petitioned the Confederate War Department, an authorized policy promised local service and might offer the opportunity to garner martial accolades and honor in front of one's community, not on some distant conventional battlefield. The added benefits of being able to sell captured materiel of war to the Confederate Quartermaster's Department, see loved ones, and perhaps even live at home were alluring.[4]

The Partisan Ranger Act had been designed, largely in closed secret session, with a two-fold purpose. Its first aim was to regulate and control who could use guerrilla warfare as part of a Confederate military strategy of raids into the Border South, lower North, and remote, contested areas of the Confederate interior. This was part of the Jefferson Davis administration's offensive military strategy, which required Confederate armies to protect the geographic boundaries of all seceding slave states and project military forces into border-slave areas as well. The act gave Davis and his secretary of war power to regulate partisan ranger units, including the total number of such units, their number of commissioned officers, their size and organization as either infantry or cavalry, and their authority to confiscate materiel of war for resale to the Confederate government. Yet it also placed them under the same regulations as regular soldiers, including the Confederate Articles of War, which held men liable for their good behavior on line of march, prohibited wanton plundering of civilian property, and harshly punished capital crimes committed by soldiers.[5]

Initially, congressmen did not view these sanctioned partisan units as incompatible with the control needed to administer the institution of slavery, either. After all, slaveholding families during the War for Independence had used *petite guerre* successfully to resist the British in many regions of the South. General Robert E. Lee's own father, Henry Lee III, known by his hard-earned *nom de guerre* "Light-Horse Harry," had been a prime example of a successful partisan commander in the conflict. Some Confederate legislators versed in the long history of eighteenth- and nineteenth-century European and American wars knew that partisans and free corps often were used as detached soldiers from a main army. These troops proved valuable in gathering intelligence, disrupting the supply and communications of the enemy, and attacking the enemy army's foraging parties. If not always viewed as legitimate by regular infantry officers, such units were recognized as technically legal, with prisoner-of-war protections awarded in a time of conflict as long as such combatants abided by certain rules: wearing a regulation uniform, responding to the chain of command and the commander of their main army, and limiting attacks to regular soldiers of opposing armies. If any of these lines were crossed, the protections evaporated, and the controversy over the irregulars' status commenced.[6]

The second purpose of the Partisan Ranger Act was to promote the use of guerrilla warfare to maximize Confederate manpower in areas that supportive congressmen knew were not really going to be protected by the limited strength of the major armies or that were under Federal military occupation or control. Already behind Union lines, some Southern men were beyond the reach of Confederate recruiting and conscription officers, but they might be of service if given sanction and recruited by a chieftain into a local unit. In 1862 lawmakers had not fully considered either the potential popularity of the policy leading to a drain on manpower for the major armies or the difficulty in controlling the irregulars' activities once in service. The new law led many Southerners to believe that guerrilla warfare in *any* form was now sanctioned by the Confederate government, making the regulatory purpose of the act difficult, if not impossible, for the War Department to enforce. Essentially, trying to control all forms of guerrilla warfare in areas only contested but not formally controlled by the Confederacy became impossible during the twenty-two months the law was in force. Yet the policy began with optimism attached to it. From the viewpoint of supportive congressmen and War Department officials in the spring of 1862, officially sanctioned partisan ranger units were both legal and legitimate. For many Union soldiers and officers, however, the use of guerrilla warfare brought to the fore difficult areas of legal decision making. In addition, the irregulars operated on a different type of battlefield from which most Union citizen-soldiers had been trained to fight—one centered on civilians.[7]

Eventually, the Union army would employ one of the greatest academic minds of the nineteenth century, Dr. Francis Lieber, to address the thorny legal and definitional issues raised by the use of irregular warfare. In an erudite pamphlet published in late 1862, Lieber outlined the long history of "partisans" used for detached service and detailed how they were recognized and appropriate for certain pursuits in a time of war. In 1863 he was the lead author in drafting "Lieber's Code," General Orders No. 100. In several key articles as issued by President Abraham Lincoln to the U.S. Army, Lieber outlined the different categories—legal and extralegal—for how the tactics of guerrilla warfare might be used in a conflict. In the end, the code provided prisoner-of-war and lawful protection for officially sanctioned partisans: "Art. 81. Partisans are soldiers armed and wearing the uniform of their army, but belonging to a corps which acts detached from the main body for the purpose of making inroads into the territory occupied by the enemy. If captured, they are entitled to all the privileges of the prisoner of war." The lines remained very thin, however, between an official "partisan" and the other Lieberian categories, including "armed prowlers," "war-rebels," scouts," and self-constituted groups of men using the deception and tactics of guerrillas, all of whom were subject to death if captured. The pillars of Lieber's definitions rested largely on the foundation of a military commission, wearing a regulation uniform, and the importance of being part of a recognized, responsive unit on detached service from the main body of the army. Confederates in the highest levels of government envisioned a service of sanctioned *petite guerre* forces that would use the range of tactics associated with irregular warfare but be responsive to military commanders and to government officials. By their use of guerrilla tactics, such men would be authorized partisans, but they were not to be bushwhackers, brigands, or freebooters. In practice, this distinction would be difficult to police. Actual authorized service would frequently test the boundaries of each of these areas and place the Confederate partisan rangers in jeopardy throughout the war. By the end of the war, the partisan rangers would show how easy it was to march or ride across the metaphorical line between the conventional and unconventional battlefields.[8]

On the guerrilla battlefields of the American Civil War, there were essentially four manifestations of irregular warfare (four broad analytical categories). Self-constituted groups or bands (sometimes called bushwhackers, outliers, or for some, simply criminals) formed one group. Their loyalty could be Unionist or Confederate, or they could be waging a personal war of vendetta or simply be out for gain. A second group were the partisan rangers, authorized *petite guerre* forces under the 1862 Partisan Ranger Act passed by the Confederate Congress. Additionally, regular cavalry on both sides sometimes appropriated the hit-and-run tactics of irregular war as raiders and counterguerrillas in small or large groups. Finally, individuals using assassination or sabotage can be categorized as a fourth group, even though their war frequently was even more personally directed and outside the chain of command or cooperation with regular, or even other irregular, forces. These analytical categories are useful for discerning the basic nature, motives, recruitment, and origins of a local guerrilla conflict; they were even used by soldiers and scholars of the mid-nineteenth century, like Lieber, though sometimes debated. But people did move back and forth across the definitional lines of irregular warriors and between the conventional and unconventional conflicts. This movement made discernment and enforcement of the laws of war difficult, frustrating, sometimes deadly, and occasionally impossible to apply with consistency in those areas of the eastern and western theaters where irregular warfare was common.[9]

While scholars have looked at many successful partisans, cavaliers, and guerrillas in book-length biographical studies, would-be chieftains and less distinguished irregulars have been largely overlooked. The experience of these men highlights the experimental nature of the Confederate military project, the difficulty of controlling the activities of warriors seeking independent action, the problems of deploying such an aggressive strategy early in the war, and the critical issue of manpower deficiency, with the South outnumbered four to one in white manpower. In the spring, summer, and fall of 1862, petitions arrived at the Confederate War Department desiring local, independent military service outside the ranks of the large armies, while many others sent such requests directly to commanders in the field. Many of these men wanted permission to raise new companies for irregular service. Others simply wanted transfers for themselves or their units directly from infantry to partisan service. Still other soldiers petitioned to keep their cavalry or infantry units in their home state for local defense. Yet another group of petitions came from concerned citizens asking for additional local defense troops or partisan ranger units to better protect their interests. While the response from the secretary of war was frequently a polite declination in favor of bringing more troops into the line infantry, some soldiers did receive permission to organize partisan units both from the War Department and a commanding officer in the field. In general, these petitions raise red flags about the entity that Confederates had authorized and offer an early warning of many of the emerging military problems of the Southern interior.[10]

In September 1862 the Confederate adjutant and inspector general, Samuel Cooper, reported nearly one hundred company-sized units of partisan rangers in service or actively forming. While it is not a definitive accounting of partisan rangers, Cooper's official report made to Secretary of War Randolph lists seventy-three companies accepted and another twenty-four that had forwarded muster rolls to Richmond. This list includes companies from eight Confederate states; only Tennessee, Arkansas, and Texas, where self-constituted bands were regularly active in attacking both local Unionists and Union soldiers, had not forwarded paperwork for approval by this date. The border states of Kentucky, Maryland, and Missouri also had partisan ranger units accepted into Confederate service, and despite further restriction on the age of new recruits adopted after September, the program continued to grow in the remote areas behind Union lines into the summer of 1863. The policy spread its tentacles far and wide; eventually, partisan ranger units would be recruited in every state of the Confederacy, Indian Territory (present-day Oklahoma), and each state of the Border South save Delaware. The Confederate military governor of the Arizona Territory, John R. Baylor, was even given authority by the Southern secretary of war to raise partisan ranger units in Texas for deployment in the far Southwest.[11]

Given the scarcity and disorganization of Confederate records related to the partisan rangers, it is difficult to assess exactly how many men were officially part of this program during the period from April 1862 through February 1864, when it was repealed by Congress. The duration of *petite guerre* service for each unit is also difficult to calibrate for many of the sanctioned companies and regiments. Nevertheless, even if only sixty-four men mustered in a partisan company (this was the standard for new units accepted into service), and there were full battalions and regiments of partisans recruited, this meant that more than six thousand men were officially part of the program by the time of Cooper's September 1862 report—and given the continued proliferation of units in 1863, the number was likely much higher. Roughly, by late 1862, the *authorized* partisan rangers spread across the South were at least the size of a division in the Army of Tennessee or the Army of Northern Virginia. And this did not include the numerous self-constituted bands of both Unionist and Confederate irregulars already in the field. Many partisan ranger units did not form until mid-1863. For example, not listed on the Cooper report was the most famous partisan ranger unit of the war: the famed Forty-Third Battalion of Virginia Cavalry commanded by the "Gray Ghost," Lieutenant Colonel John Singleton Mosby. Mosby practiced full-spectrum, nineteenth-century *petite guerre* in his personal war for national survival. Known for his daring raids behind enemy lines, intelligence-gathering prowess, and ability to evade Union cavalry, Mosby became a favorite of General Lee. But Mosby and his well-ordered battalion, which usually operated in only small company-sized groups and at its height had roughly two thousand soldiers listed on muster rolls, were the exception in terms of conduct, not the rule for Confederate irregulars.[12]

What becomes clear from the internal Confederate government and officer-corps debate about guerrilla warfare is that what was once heralded as a potential strategic solution ultimately became a major military problem. The Partisan Ranger Act's consequences stretched beyond those who were authorized to raise units, having a disproportionate effect on the Confederacy beyond those officially sanctioned by the secretary of war. The promotion of the act, which was issued nationally to Confederate soldiers as General Orders No. 30 by General Cooper alongside the text of the earlier Conscription Act, inspired many men to organize their own local defense without government or military approval. The Partisan Ranger Act and those officers who were models for the policy (namely Brigadier Generals John Hunt Morgan and Turner Ashby) became an inspiration to independent-minded individuals in many areas of the Southern interior. The ultimate repercussions of the local guerrilla wars were devastating for communities from the coast of North Carolina to the Ozarks of Arkansas and from farms in northern Virginia to the coast of Florida. Confederates' use of irregular warfare, hit-and-run tactics, and raiding behind enemy lines was not solely due to the Partisan Ranger Act, but the overall negative experience with authorizing and attempting to control/regulate irregular units in the field did little to persuade skeptical West Point–trained commanders that this type of service was helpful in the cause of Southern independence. Popular understanding of the Lieberian analytical categories was highly limited. One man's partisan ranger was another's bushwhacking criminal. Indeed, most Southern soldiers and civilians did not spend an enormous amount of time distinguishing between the various types of irregular units used by the Confederacy.[13]

The positive conduct that Captain F. M. Marks and many other aspiring partisans proposed was to protect Southern civilians in the interior and border regions. Social conduct in this sense was directly linked to social ascension, for appropriate conduct could guarantee a position of honor, or at least respectable status, in the white South. The communities and government of the Confederacy were concerned about whom they gave this right of protection to, since violence in the wrong hands could mean severe retribution from Yankees or even empower unethical Confederate irregulars to betray the very people they swore to protect. The ultimate fear about guerrilla conduct was that partisan ranger units, if left under no governing control, might subvert, not reinforce, prewar social norms.[14]

Despite these fears expressed by some congressmen and military officials, immediately following the proclamation of the policy, letters flooded the Confederate War Department with requests for units. Individuals and communities from all across the South, frightened by the threat of Federal invasion and the destruction of their property, began to negotiate with the War Department for rangers. These petitions also express the motivations of men who wanted to become partisan chieftains. Most importantly, these requests signal the formal entrance of civilians and common soldiers into the larger debate over the role of irregular warfare. The negotiation between Southerners and their government sheds light on the new world Confederates tried to create.

This spirited correspondence reveals a complex relationship connecting the individual, community, and government in the white South and demonstrates a negotiation among these three groups over military control in the Confederacy. Correspondence came from all over the South, from the most remote regions of the periphery to the cities of Charleston, Richmond, and Savannah. The petitions came from ministers, farmers, state senators, the wealthy, the poor, the well educated, and some who did not even write their own requests. By discussing the proposed behavior of would-be partisans, Confederates of different social classes related what they perceived as an acceptable level of political violence within their society. The adoption of a formal partisan service by the Confederate government exhibited a desire to maintain control over rampant guerrilla activity. The approval of this policy by white elites exemplified an attempt to reconcile the individualism of irregular service with the pressing concerns of forming a cohesive nation-state that brought together all Southerners under one government. In their letters, smaller communities requested specific members of their societies to operate as guerrilla protectors. They did this not only to maintain control over the military conduct of these partisans but also to retain power over local defense—some communities simply pled desperation in the face of encroaching Union forces. By negotiating with the government, Southern towns and villages sought a degree of local autonomy while assuring the government in Richmond of their stalwart loyalty.[15]

Many government officials supported the partisan service out of concern for their constituency on the home front. Confederate senators and representatives from threatened areas sought an innovative mechanism to control and perhaps repel Union invasion. Among the most powerful supporters of the partisan ranger policy was the former mayor of Charleston and chairman of the Confederate House of Representatives Military Affairs Committee, William Porcher Miles. While the South Carolinian acknowledged a certain level of nationalism by joining the Confederate Congress, his views on guerrillas illustrate that he still believed the Confederacy had a responsibility to defend the sovereignty of his state as well as every local community.[16]

In late May, Miles endorsed the application of H. Smith Bass, who had been the captain of police in Charleston when Miles was mayor. This endorsement by a high-ranking figure demonstrates the importance of having trustworthy men at the head of irregular units. The congressman even offered that while Bass was police chief, he "enjoyed my entire confidence during my whole term of office."[17] Miles elsewhere stated, "There should be as little delay as possible in organizing this Partisan service for which we all anticipate such useful results."[18]

Eager men from across the South, with far less power and influence than military officers and congressmen, found endorsements a powerful way to request units for home-front protection.[19] M. McDaniel of Columbia County, Georgia, cited Confederate vice president Alexander H. Stephens as a reference when he submitted his application. The petitions frequently reinforced the old social order established in the prewar years, and those who sought service in guerrilla units often did so for some form of social ascension in the communities in which they lived or to secure an elevation in military rank.[20]

The partisan petition of Adjutant John B. McLenahan was accompanied by a note from the officers of the Fifteenth North Carolina Volunteer Infantry, who assured the government that the adjutant was an excellent candidate "for that species of warfare which the Confederate Government had indicated would be acceptable." The letter was also endorsed by John S. Pender, who had already received authority from Major General Theophilus H. Holmes to raise an entire battalion of rangers, of which McLenahan's company would become a part.[21]

Writing from Savannah to Brigadier General A. R. Lawton, John M. Millen, a prewar judge and later a first lieutenant in the Tenth Georgia Infantry until resigning his commission in March 1862, sought the endorsement of his regional commander *before* writing directly to the War Department to request service along the coast of Georgia with an independent "squadron of mounted scouts." In his letter, Millen deferred to General Lawton when he offered "to report to any officer designated" as long as his unit was "detailed as a guerilla command along our rivers and marshes." Like the letters of McLenahan and McDaniel, Millen included a political endorsement in his application. The honorable R. B.

Hilton of Florida, a member of the House Military Affairs Committee who strongly advocated coastal defense, cited Millen's "intelligence, bravery, and energy" as well as his "noble and reckless ambition to distinguish himself in the service of his count[r]y." Millen would eventually command the Twentieth Battalion, Georgia Partisan Rangers, which served along the coast of that state until the spring of 1864, when it was sucked into the northern Virginia meat grinder of the Overland Campaign. The unit, recruited in part from Liberty County, Georgia, in the summer of 1862, fought as a battalion in Brigadier General Pierce M. B. Young's brigade of Wade Hampton's cavalry division on conventional battlefields at Wilderness, Spotsylvania Court House, Cold Harbor, and along the James River before being ordered to disband and its men dispersed into various regular cavalry regiments. Although partisan units often sought independence, unattached from the military command structure, Millen's initial request clearly demonstrates a dependence on connected officials. His personal experience and that of his battalion make clear that the subsequent movement of combatants back and forth across the regular-irregular line was common for many partisan rangers.[22]

Lieutenant Colonel John Tyler Morgan (a distant relative of President John Tyler) of the Fifth Alabama Infantry also sent a request to Richmond. His petition contained the endorsement of Alabama's William P. Chilton, a member of the Confederate House of Representatives and Morgan's brother-in-law, and alludes to another way in which would-be partisans sought government authorization. Clearly understanding the existing social hierarchy, Morgan and others cited their military experience and expertise to help them stand out.[23] By appealing to the practical aspects of military training and experience, such men hoped the government would see the benefit in sanctioning their proposed units. These exhibitions of preparedness were created to show commitment to the Confederate cause as well as a perceived understanding of what the government wanted in a partisan. Morgan eventually resigned his infantry commission and raised the Fifty-First Alabama Partisan Rangers, which operated in conjunction with Major General Nathan Bedford Forrest's cavalry command later in the war.[24]

A petition written by R. S. McKeen of Galveston, Texas, and signed "Captain of Guerilla Guards" sought service in Arkansas, Tennessee, or Virginia.[25] McKeen's request inquired as to whether the War Department would "accept a well drilled Company of Texans" who were "well Mounted and armed with

Double Barrell Shot Guns as a Guerilla company." H. C. Cook assured Richmond authorities that he was "well acquainted" with the "topography and people" of Middle Tennessee and Missouri, where he desired to operate. He believed that the "Southern cause might be enhansed by [the] efficiency of the [guerrilla] service."[26] Like McKeen and Cook, Lieutenant Millen also claimed that his men would be "excellent woodsmen, armed with rifles or double barralled shotguns" and prove "a scourge to the enemy wherever they could meet him."[27]

Archie McCrane, an orderly sergeant from Savannah, Georgia, also highlighted his military prowess and experience. He promised that his men "was [*sic*] raised on the frontier of Georgia and is [*sic*] Sharp Shooter and good horsemen [and would] make a company up that would do good execution." Although he could not write an argument as polished as a well-educated Louisianan or Virginian, he attempted to demonstrate military bearing and skill.[28]

The War Department received a transfer request for an entire company of cavalry under J. R. McCain, a captain in the Eleventh Tennessee Cavalry Regiment. On May 6, 1862, Captain McCain pled that the new conscription law interfered with a previous War Department order for him to raise a corps for independent service. McCain had previously promised his men "detached" service from the regiment before they reenlisted on the assurance of the secretary of war that they would be mounted. He desired to return to Middle or West Tennessee and fight in the areas where most of his men originated. The captain also discussed his correspondence with R. S. Smith, a Secret Service agent working for Major General Edmund Kirby Smith, who at that time commanded the Confederate District of East Tennessee. From this information, the captain believed, "The citizens of Middle Tenn of all ages are anxious for an opportunity to engage in the partisan service." The accompanying letter from the secret agent noted the motivations behind the interest of many in partisan service. The agent was "convinced that any quantity of men[,] men who have property at stake, and do not wish to leave home, but to the contrary, want to fight for their firesides in Middle Tenn.," would serve as partisans, and if allowed to remain in the region, prominent citizens would do "anything in their power" for "'the Partisan Rangers' in their midst." An additional letter from the Executive Headquarters in Memphis, Tennessee, referred the request to General Albert Sidney Johnston, commander of the entire theater in which Captain McCain sought to operate.[29]

McCain's request highlights the emerging problem of how the conscription law, which required the service of all white men from eighteen to thirty-five who were not exempted to enlist in the regular army, related to the Partisan Ranger Act and the overall control of guerrilla warfare. Officially, Section 5, Article XII of the Conscription Act blocked the formation of any new corps for guerrilla service unless they were expressly authorized "partisan rangers." In reality, self-constituted units would be impossible to regulate, and Confederate governors were actively complaining about the Partisan Ranger Act's interference with the enforcement of conscription. Furthermore, War Department–sanctioned partisan rangers jealously guarded both their autonomy and freedom to sell captured goods, and regular Confederate soldiers grew to resent their special status. McCain's men desired to serve in their own communities, which also raises questions of local manpower control. Since guerrillas are in essence warriors distinctly associated with the communities they serve, a certain level of public consent was necessary for irregulars to survive without being forced to steal from the very people they purported to protect. Local autonomy and control over who commanded new authorized partisan units were aspects of protection that some communities expected from the government. This also contradicted the conscription law's intent of tight control over manpower. Guerrillas not only lived in the same communities they sought to protect but also were often related to many townspeople. This local relationship with partisan rangers, therefore, becomes vital to understanding the story of Confederate irregulars.[30]

Walter P. MacFarland and L. D. Lusk of Guntersville, Alabama, offer an example of this community involvement in promoting partisan ranger service. Their request, penned by a probate judge from the area in which the men resided, states, "it is the wish of our people that Walter P. MacFarland and L. D. Lusk be commissioned to raise a company or companies of Partisan Rangers." By using a local dignitary to affirm community consent, the would-be partisans showed the desire of this particular town to remain within Confederate law while at the same time retaining local authority over their own defense.[31] The letter also questions whom the men would have to take orders from over the rank of captain, further supporting the belief that many communities in the South desired to retain control over their own defense through these units.[32]

Because of the direct relationship between Confederate civilians and partisans, one of the most important considerations for the government became the requestors' understanding of the appropriate use of violence in war since each man's conduct in practice shaped Northern and Southern opinions of partisan soldiers. It is evident in many of the petitions for sanctioned *petite guerre* units that, although these prospective chieftains understood the Southern social order, control over their units' specific actions in battle was *not* first on their minds. The Confederate government's desire to protect its civilians from Union soldiers necessitated partisan rangers who could be trusted to operate judiciously within the boundaries of the Confederate Articles of War. Therefore, the applicants illustrating less restraint in their plans offer considerable insight into why authorized partisan service ultimately failed to prove its worth with much of the Confederate regular-officer corps or as a military mechanism for helping Confederates win their independence.

Typical of the absence of restraint expressed in a petitioner's military plans is H. A. Melson of Potomac Mills, Virginia, who posited, "There are many here whose peculiar private affairs prevent them from regularly enlisting in the military service." Yet Melson added vehemently, "If supplied with arms we will pledge ourselves to take the field the greater part of every year during the war and kill or capture some of the enemy every two or three days." This letter is one example of the great degree of naïveté among potential partisans about the laws of war. By suggesting that he and his men would operate wherever and whenever they wanted, Melson was giving up his status as a legitimate combatant in the eyes of the enemy and was probably positioning himself outside the boundaries of the Partisan Ranger Act itself, which aimed to keep such men in close contact with a commander in the regular army while they were on detached service.[33] In fact, few would-be chieftains seemed to realize the precarious position in which irregular service would place them or the people and economic interests they sought to protect. At this point in the war, early 1862, it remained ambiguous as to whether the Union army would recognize captured partisan rangers as prisoners of war, even if Confederates argued for their legitimacy. Even under the 1863 Lieber Code, if irregulars were captured out of uniform, operating without a commission, or functioning outside the Confederate command hierarchy, Union soldiers would have authority under the laws of war to execute them as murderers, thieves, and brigands.[34]

Presbyterian minister W. W. Morrison from New Harmony, Alabama, also forwarded his own guerrilla plan "to take 'special care' of the gunboats" along the Mississippi River by raising a group of men to "kill the pilots." This lack of restraint seems odd coming from a member of society entrusted with public well-being. Morrison cited military training at Washington College in Lexington, Virginia, as evidence of his military experience and his acquaintance with Governor John Letcher of Virginia for legitimacy. Although he was exempted from the draft by occupation, the prospective guerrilla minister exhibited a malleable, if illuminating, understanding of wartime conduct in the white South. Men from all walks of life could become partisans, and many were quite willing to put aside peacetime beliefs and use deceptive tactics that might later endanger Confederate civilians.[35]

The partisan petitions of 1862 establish that a net positive opinion about irregular warfare prevailed in the minds of many Confederate citizens and soldiers early in the war. These documents, coupled with the approval of official legislation endorsing a form of guerrilla warfare, also show that there were many proponents of experimenting with irregular conflict at the highest levels of the Confederate government during the first two years of the war. These petitions and the discussion of partisan ranger service also demonstrate an enormous amount of inexperience with the problems this service could entail for Confederate soldiers, citizens, and their government. Although partisan ranger units continued to muster during the spring and summer of 1863, the consequences of all types of irregular warfare began to turn some of those initially supportive officers and civilians against the service. This change, in turn, made the chances of securing authorization for a unit more difficult, and the War Department and Confederate armies began to consolidate and reorganize many of the original partisan companies, battalions, and regiments into regular infantry and cavalry units throughout 1863 and 1864. The understanding of guerrilla warfare would continue to evolve throughout the war. During the period from late 1862 to early 1864, when the Partisan Ranger Act was law, a major shift would occur in how many in the Confederate government and population viewed the use of irregular warfare in a civil war.[36]

Many of the partisan rangers who became active during the spring and summer of 1863 enjoyed a period of detached service as scouts and guides to large bodies of regular cavalry. Others remained "more detached" from the main Confederate armies while employing raiding warfare against blockhouses, train tracks, and telegraph lines as well as gathering intelligence and supplies. Many of the consolidated and reorganized companies and battalions, now back in the regular service, were sent to the Army of Northern Virginia and the Army of Tennessee in the spring and summer of 1864 as each prepared for spring campaigning. Yet there were other units that remained active in the irregular conflicts or proved impossible to corral.[37]

While the repercussions of the Partisan Ranger Act and the Confederacy's use of a raiding strategy in the border areas of the South can be seen in many communities, one region's story highlights the problems for military officials and civilians of novice irregulars playing at home defense. Following the adoption of the act in April 1862, Confederates in northeastern North Carolina's Albemarle region began to recruit men to form a regiment of partisan rangers. The unit was never officially sanctioned by the War Department, but the former Confederate soldiers who would have been part of this command divided into independent companies and preyed on local Unionists and Union soldiers in the six-county region for the remainder of the war. Eventually, the Union army sent a large force of U.S. Colored Troops to the region on a counterirregular raid in December 1863 that hunted down many guerrillas and brought freedom to hundreds of North Carolina slaves. But the operation did not permanently defeat the irregular companies, which would remain hazards for locals and Union forces for the remainder of the war. Citizens of Union and Confederate loyalty in the region, however, were so disgusted with this conflict that they actually tried to negotiate with both governments for the removal of the guerrillas and black soldiers from the region, leading to an attempt at negotiated neutrality, essentially opting out of the war. Far from being a successful strategy, the irregular war in this region of North Carolina backfired on Richmond. Eventually many, though not all, of the guerrillas were organized through strenuous effort into a regular Confederate regiment, the Sixty-Eighth North Carolina Infantry, in the spring of 1864. In the Tar Heel State, a careful analysis at the neighborhood level demonstrates that one-third of the counties were embroiled in one form of guerrilla war or another by early 1864. The greatest disruption and violence occurred in the old Whig congressional strongholds of the state like the northeastern region, which was extremely politically divided.[38]

While several historians have pointed to the extent to which John Mosby forced Union troops to devote outsize numbers to capture him—and have even offered that guerrilla warfare may have prolonged the Confederacy's existence by several months—this is far too narrow a view geographically and credits the positive dimensions of a very negative phenomenon for most white Southerners. By 1863, guerrilla warfare was a national problem for Confederates, and the Richmond government helped make it so by adopting an act that promoted it.

The law had some minor successes in the form of Virginia partisan rangers and intelligence gatherers like Mosby and John Hanson McNeill, who commanded McNeill's Rangers, originally Company E, Eighteenth Virginia Cavalry, but the policy largely backfired. Even Mosby's Rangers would eventually suffer for their status. Mosby's relatively disciplined command experienced heavy losses. In late September 1864, in response to what Union soldiers believed was the murder of a lieutenant by one of Mosby's men after the officer had surrendered, Union brigadier generals Wesley Merritt and George Custer executed six partisan rangers near Front Royal, Virginia; another of Mosby's men was executed in a separate incident. A sign left on the body of one partisan read simply, "Such is the fate of all of Mosby's men." In response, the "Gray Ghost" had twenty-three captured Union soldiers draw for seven lots; three of the unfortunate men were eventually hanged in retaliation, two were shot, and two escaped. Even the relatively tidy partisan war of Mosby was beginning to unravel into retaliatory killing. The Virginian struggled to rationalize and control the chaos that irregular warfare brought: "It was not an act of revenge," Mosby wrote, "but a judicial sentence to save not only the lives of my own men, but the lives of the enemy. It had that effect. I regret that fate thrust such a duty upon me; I do not regret that I faced and performed it."[39]

While Mosby himself survived the war and went on to become a Republican, a friend of Ulysses S. Grant, and eventually U.S. consul to Hong Kong, many of his men were not so fortunate. A brief walk around the cemetery in Warrenton, Virginia, shows the costs. The attrition rate in the famed Company A, Forty-Third Battalion of Virginia Cavalry, was telling: only one officer, commissioned or noncommissioned (a sergeant), was available for service by April 1865. The rest were all killed, wounded, or captured.[40]

Most of the men inspired by and who eventually operated as partisan rangers or in self-constituted guerrilla bands fell into the trap of living off of the local white Southern population while operating against Union forces, which either remained confused about how to treat guerrillas in the field or did not deploy the nuance of the Lieber Code on the question of irregulars. In some regions of the slaveholding South, guerrilla warfare used to defend a slave society actually led to less slave control.[41]

By early 1864, the entire partisan ranger program was a massive miscalculation from the perspective not only of Confederate generals like Robert E. Lee and Joseph E. Johnston but also of the Confederate secretary of war, James

Seddon. Partisan rangers were liminal, dangerously straddling the line between the regular and irregular wars in the American South. The Confederate Congress had designed them loosely to bridge a gap between a war on the front lines and one behind the lines. This attempt was largely a failure. Congress, desperate for manpower, had not considered that those who served in the regular armies would want to leave for more independent and hometown service or that this exodus from the ranks would happen in such large numbers to be a problem. The repercussions of violence perpetrated by or in reprisal for Confederate guerrilla activity was also not something they had anticipated. In February 1864, after prodding from numerous generals, including Lee, Congress repealed the Partisan Ranger Act, after only twenty-two months in effect. This did not end the use of guerrilla warfare, but it did end the Confederate government's experiment in trying to control it as a national policy and as part of its intended military strategy.[42]

The Confederate partisan ranger service was ultimately a failed experiment in authorizing and directing guerrilla warfare for national defense. Attempts to control the subsequent chaos caused within the South were largely unsuccessful. Confederate authorities lacked the manpower to rein in both self-constituted bands and other units inspired by the misguided law. And there just were not enough officers like John Mosby capable of *petite guerre* miracles. Like Frankenstein's monster, the Partisan Ranger Act and the authorized guerrilla service it spawned became a creature that was uncontrollable even by its creators and had unforeseen repercussions for all involved. And like Dr. Frankenstein, the fathers of the Partisan Ranger Act had positive intentions for their creation. Many dedicated Confederate nationalists believed that the policy could be "of incalculable benefit" to the cause of independence, but ultimately it was poorly calculated. Guerrilla warfare's repercussions led to unforeseen and dangerous consequences: less security in some locales in the South, the proliferation of military atrocity by both sides, hostage taking, executions, plundering, murders of civilians, and a war of punitive measures by the Union army against unruly guerrillas in the vast areas of the Confederacy and Border South where irregular warfare spread. In sum, the partisan rangers constituted a self-inflicted wound on the Confederate body politic.

NOTES

1. Request of F. M. Marks, May 10, 1862, Letters Received, Confederate Secretary of War, RG 109, M-437, roll 60, National Archives and Records Administration (NARA), Washington, D.C. (hereafter cited by the name of the petitioner, date received, and roll number). This collection contains thousands of letters submitted to the Confederate secretary of war and War Department during the four years of the Civil War. Although the topics and the concerns of these letters vary widely, the items received include applications for partisan ranger service, requests for conscription exemption, and civilian complaints about military conduct on the Confederate home front. The research for this essay examined more than three dozen petitions from this collection for partisan ranger service and local defense troops submitted by citizens to the Confederate War Department.

2. Ibid.

3.Ibid.; Gerald Linderman, *Embattled Courage: The Experience of Combat in the American Civil War* (New York: Free Press, 1989), 2, 197–200. Linderman discusses a dearth in the analysis of Civil War guerrilla motivations.

4. The Confederate congressional debate over the Partisan Ranger Act and conscription law is found in the minutes of the Confederate Congress published in Jones et al., *Southern Historical Society Papers* (hereafter cited as *SHSP*), and Confederate States of America, Congress, *Journal of the Congress of the Confederate States of America, 1861–1865* (Washington, D.C.: Government Printing Office, 1904), vol. 2. For the full text of the Partisan Ranger Act, see General Orders No. 30, Apr. 28, 1862, U.S. War Department, *War of the Rebellion,* ser. 4, 1:1094–1100 (hereafter cited as *O.R.*).

5. General Orders No. 30, Apr. 28, 1862, *O.R.*, ser. 4, 1:1094–98; Confederate States of America, War Department, *Articles of War, for the Government of the Army of the Confederate States* (Montgomery, Ala.: Barrett, Wimbish, 1861).

6. Ricardo A. Herrera, "'[T]he Zealous Activity of Capt. Lee': Light-Horse Harry Lee and *Petite Guerre,*" *Journal of Military History* 79, no. 1 (Jan. 2015): 9–36; Lieber, *Guerrilla Parties Considered,* 11; Minutes of the First Confederate Congress, 1st and 2nd sess., Apr.–Sept. 1862, *SHSP,* 45:153, 160–61, 221, 253. Another excellent source on *petite guerre* and its use in early American history is John Grenier, *The First Way of War: American War Making on the Frontier* (New York: Cambridge University Press, 2005).

7. Minutes of the First Confederate Congress, 1st sess., Apr. 1862, *SHSP,* vol. 45; *Journal of the Congress of the Confederate States,* 2:199–201, 220.

8. Lieber, *Guerrilla Parties Considered,* 5–22; "Instructions for the Government of Armies of the United States in the Field," General Order No. 100, U.S. War Department, Apr. 24, 1863, *O.R.*, ser. 3, 3:148. For examinations of the emerging laws-of-war debate during the Civil War, see Witt, *Lincoln's Code;* and Burrus M. Carnahan, *Lincoln on Trial: Southern Civilians and the Law of War* (Lexington: University Press of Kentucky, 2010).

9. For an extensive overview of the historiography of the Civil War's guerrilla conflicts and leaders, see Barton A. Myers, "Guerrillas," in *A Companion to the U.S. Civil War,* ed. Aaron Sheehan-Dean (Hoboken, N.J.: Wiley-Blackwell, 2014). Scholars who have examined and debated the definitional issues related to guerrilla warfare in the Civil War include Sutherland, *Savage Conflict;* Grimsley, *Hard Hand of War;* and Myers, *Rebels against the Confederacy.*

10. Theodore Ropp, *War in the Modern World* (Baltimore: Johns Hopkins University Press, 2000), 185.

11. Samuel Cooper to G. W. Randolph, Sept. 12, 1862, *O.R.*, ser. 4, 2:82–83; *Journal of the Congress of the Confederate States*, 377; George W. Randolph to John R. Baylor, 29 May 1862, in John C. Stafford Service Record, U.S. War Department, Compiled Service Records of Confederate General and Staff Officers and Nonregimental Enlisted Men, M331, Record Group 108, roll 235, NARA. Brief thumbnail histories of many partisan ranger units can be found in Joseph H. Crute Jr., *Units of the Confederate States Army* (Gaithersburg, Md.: Olde Soldier Books, 1987); and Stewart Sifakis, *Compendium of the Confederate Armies*, vols. 1–10 (New York: Facts on File, 1991). On the confusing organizational structure of Missouri's Confederate units during the war, see U.S. War Department, *Missouri Troops in Service during the Civil War* (Washington, D.C.: Government Printing Office, 1902), 320–23. In Arkansas, major generals Earl Van Dorn and Thomas Hindman used the authority of the Partisan Ranger Act to recruit independent companies, but many never mustered formally with the War Department. See *O.R.*, ser. 1, 13:827–28, 835. Another source on the geographic distribution of partisan ranger units across the Confederacy is Register of Partisan Rangers, War Department Archives of Confederate Records, RG 109, NARA.

12. Samuel Cooper to G. W. Randolph, Sept. 12, 1862, *O.R.*, ser. 4, 2:82–83. The Cooper report accounts for the status of the partisan ranger program by September 1862, but groups like John Mosby's, which formed in early 1863, and John McNeill's continued to recruit throughout the war, bringing the numbers far higher than what the secretary of war had originally reviewed in this 1862 report. Furthermore, the number of total authorized and unauthorized guerrilla units from Missouri became virtually impossible to sort out even after the war. See U.S. War Department, *Missouri Troops in Service during the Civil War*, 320–23. On the standard number of privates in a company, see A. Johnson, *Partisan Rangers of the Confederate States Army*, 129–30. Johnson was commissioned a colonel of partisan rangers in 1862; his 10th Kentucky Partisan Rangers formed in 1863.

13. General Orders No. 30, Apr. 28, 1862, *O.R.*, ser. 4, 1:1094–95. On John Hunt Morgan, see Ramage, *Rebel Raider*. On Turner Ashby, see Anderson, *Blood Image*.

14. Request of F. M. Marks, May 10, 1862, roll 60.

15. Wilbur J. Cash, *The Mind of the South* (New York: Alfred A. Knopf, 1941), 38. Cash offers a penetrating look at the continuity of the southern "mind" throughout American history and the importance of community in promoting and regulating violence in the American South. The wartime deployment of partisan warfare continues a white southern tradition of individual violent conduct promoted by notions of masculinity, honor, and social rank. For a closer analysis of southern martial identity as it relates to personal warfare, see John Hope Franklin, *The Militant South, 1800–1861* (Boston: Beacon, 1956). Franklin's chapter "Personal Warfare" offers an illuminating study of individual southern militancy, especially the practice of dueling. For a thorough review of southern attitudes toward social conduct and the system of honor's functionality, see Bertram Wyatt-Brown, *Southern Honor: Ethics and Behavior in the Old South* (New York: Oxford University Press, 1982).

16. Minutes of the First Confederate Congress, 1st and 2nd sess., Apr.–Sept. 1862, *SHSP*, 45:153, 160–61, 221, 253. The discussion in the Confederate Congress of adding a section to the original partisan ranger bill that would have included a reimbursement to members for dead Union soldiers

at "five dollars per head" is indicative of how obtuse some members were being about the Federal reaction to Confederate military excesses caused by irregular soldiers.

17. Request of H. Smith Bass, May 20, 1862, roll 60.

18. Request of William M. Hale, May 21, 1862, ibid.

19. For additional examples of endorsements for partisan ranger units, see Request of H. C. Cook, Apr. 29, 1862, ibid.; Request of B. D. McKie, June 2, 1862, ibid.; Request of A. S. Maxwell on behalf of A. C. Blount, May 12, 1862, ibid.; Request of J. W. Moore on behalf of a Captain Allans, May 21, 1862, ibid.; Request of C. McLaurin, May 28, 1862, ibid.; and Request of Jas. W. Brown, May 6, 1862, ibid.

20. Request of M. McDaniel, Apr. 29, 1862, ibid.

21. Request of John B. McLenahan, May 22, 1862, ibid.

22. Request of John M. Millen, Apr. 18, 1862, ibid. Millen was eventually killed in action at the Battle of Haw's Shop on May 28, 1864, and is buried in Hollywood Cemetery in Richmond, Virginia. Brief biographical information on Millen and many other partisan chieftains can be found in U.S. Bureau of the Census, *Eighth Census of the United States, 1860,* M653, RG 29, NARA; Compiled Service Records of Confederate Soldiers Who Served in Organizations from the State of Georgia, http://www.Fold3.com; and "LTC John M. Millen," Find a Grave, http://www.finda grave.com/cgi-bin/fg.cgi?page=gr&GSln=Millen&GSfn=John&GSbyrel=all&GSdy=1864&GS dyrel=in&GSst=48&GScntry=4&GSob=n&GRid=30144973&df=all&. For biographical information on R. B. Hilton and other members of the Confederate Congress involved in the Partisan Ranger Act debates, see Ezra J. Warner and W. Buck Yearns, *Biographical Register of the Confederate Congress* (Baton Rouge: Louisiana State University Press, 1975), 119–20; and Crute, *Units of the Confederate States Armies,* 98.

23. For additional examples that cite military experience and expertise, see Request of Samuel McCutcheon, May 17, 1862, roll 60; Request of J. M. Magee, May 20, 1862, ibid.; and Request of Jas. W. Brown, May 6, 1862, ibid.

24. Request of John T. Morgan, May 10, 1862, ibid.; Joseph A. Fry, *John Tyler Morgan and the Search for Southern Autonomy* (Knoxville: University of Tennessee Press, 1992), 18–23. The best work on Nathan Bedford Forrest remains Wills, *Battle from the Start.*

25. Request of R. S. McKeen, Apr. 22, 1862, roll 60. Each of these states would later have extensive guerrilla conflicts at the local level, partially because of the large numbers of Southern Unionists within the Confederate home front. For an excellent discussion of Southern unionism as it relates to Civil War guerrilla conflicts, see William W. Freehling, *South vs. the South.* For analysis of Border South unionism during the early war period, see Daniel Crofts, *Reluctant Confederates: Upper South Unionists in the Secession Crisis* (Chapel Hill: University of North Carolina Press, 1989).

26. Request of H. C. Cook, Apr. 29, 1862, roll 60.

27. Request of John M. Millen, Apr. 18, 1862, ibid.

28. Request of Archie McCrane, Apr. 24, 1862, ibid.

29. Request of J. R. McCain, May 12, 1862, ibid.

30. Henry T. Clark to G. W. Randolph, July 13, 1862, *O.R.,* ser. 4, 2:4–5; G. W. Randolph to Jefferson Davis, Aug. 12, 1862, ibid., 48. The Confederate War Department eventually mandated that only units receiving the formal approval of the general commanding in their military district

would be sanctioned as authorized partisan rangers. Nevertheless, it is difficult to ascertain if the petitioners knew of this order prior to submitting their applications. The department requirement explains some of the endorsements from general officers, but it does not explain why a large number of applicants turned to lower-ranking military officials and civilian elites for sanction in their letters. For an example of a community concerned with conscription and conduct as it relates to militia, see Complaint of J. M. McCran on Behalf of the Town of Barksdale, Halifax County, Va., May 8, 1862, roll 60. Added pressure on the conscription and partisan ranger laws came from local militias associated with these Southern communities. In some areas of the Confederacy during the spring of 1862, the government was already experiencing problems with men in militia units refusing to respond to the calls of compulsory military service. In Halifax County the Hailey brothers, Carville and Robert, stayed home when the conscription act drafted the rest of the 84th Virginia Militia. People of the town of Barksdale wrote to the War Department complaining about this behavior. The case of the Hailey brothers offers an important insight into the community and local defense relationship of which partisans were a part. The town complained that these men were "of no service to their neighborhood nor to themselves." Although complaints for exemptions were common during this period of the war, few were granted. According to one study, only 7 percent of all exemption requests in the Confederacy were actually granted.

31. On the thorny problem of supporting Confederate nationalism and guerrilla warfare, see Sutherland, "Guerrilla Warfare, Democracy, and the Fate of the Confederacy."

32. Request of W. T. May and James Lamar on behalf of Walter P. McFarland and L. D. Lusk, May 14, 1862, roll 60.

33. Request of H. A. Melson, Apr. 19, 1862, ibid.

34. For a short excerpt of Francis Lieber's most important writings on guerrilla warfare, see Walter Laqueur, ed., *The Guerrilla Reader: A Historical Anthology* (New York: Meridian Books, 1977), 101–106. Confederates never produced a scholar on the laws of war equivalent to Lieber.

35. Request of W. W. Morrison, May 10, 1862, roll 60.

36. A categorical response to many of the partisan ranger requests was to send the petitioner a copy of General Orders No. 30, which included the text of the Partisan Ranger Act and the conscription law. For two examples of this, see Request of A. S. Maxwell on Behalf of A. C. Blount, May 12, 1862, ibid.; and Request of J. R. McCain, May 12, 1862, ibid. This response can be interpreted as the War Department requiring the prospective partisan to gain the approval of the commander of the military department in which the unit would operate before it would consider the application.

37. On organizations of partisan rangers that were reorganized in 1863 and 1864, see Crute, *Units of the Confederate States Army,* 13, 33, 115–16.

38. Myers, *Executing Daniel Bright;* Myers, *Rebels against the Confederacy,* chap. 4.

39. Roger U. Delauter Jr., *McNeill's Rangers* (Lynchburg, Va.: H. E. Howard, 1986); John S. Mosby, "The Execution of Seven Prisoners," *SHSP,* 27:314–22; V. Jones, *Ranger Mosby,* 208–11, 223–28.

40. Williamson, *Mosby's Rangers,* 359.

41. Myers, *Executing Daniel Bright,* chaps. 3–4.

42. Robert E. Lee to Samuel Cooper, Apr. 1, 1864, in Lee, *Wartime Papers,* 688–89; Ramage, *Gray Ghost,* 135–36. In his now-classic work on Civil War guerrillas in the eastern theater, *Gray Ghosts and Rebel Raiders,* Virgil Carrington Jones argues that Confederate guerrillas were a primary reason that the Southern cause in the East did not fail in the summer or fall of 1864 (pp. xi–xiv).

While Virginia did produce the most important, successful partisan rangers, Jones's early work was limited geographically. Broader analysis demonstrates that most of the partisan ranger units and self-constituted guerrilla bands were a drain on Confederate support, manpower, and the overall cause of establishing a Southern nation. Mosby and McNeill certainly aided the cause in Virginia, but Virginia was not the entire Confederacy.

FINDING THE GUERRILLAS

The Power of Shadow and Perception in the Appalachian Theater

BRIAN D. McKNIGHT

In late 1862, a supremely frustrated Colonel Frank Wolford made a request of the newly appointed commander of the Army of the Cumberland, Major General William Rosecrans, for permission to take the war to the enemy. For more than a year, Wolford had shared the area of south-central Kentucky with a formidable collection of enemy guerrillas. First it was Champ Ferguson, then Oliver Hamilton and John P. Gatewood, and most recently John Hunt Morgan. By December, Wolford could stand by no longer. Rosecrans, who had opened the war in the region that would later become West Virginia, proved to be an able commander, even under poor circumstances and surrounded by unsteady loyalty. Understanding that President Abraham Lincoln expected him to be an active commander, he gave Wolford permission to move on the Cumberland guerrillas with the advice, "Let him be careful not to get caught himself."[1] Six days after receiving Rosecrans's sanction, Wolford's troopers spotted some of Ferguson's and Hamilton's men near Lebanon, Kentucky.

Unknown to Wolford, these notorious figures were en route to join a Confederate raiding force. Hailing from Lexington, Kentucky, John Hunt Morgan had begun the war opposed to secession but joined the Confederacy, via the Kentucky State Guard, in July 1861. One year later he and his men were seasoned veterans, raiding their home state in an attempt to pave the way for an invading Confederate army. Five months later Morgan's command, at the time more than three thousand strong, embarked on what would become known as the Christmas Raid.[2] Like the soldiers before them, historians often find more than they expect when they go seeking the guerrilla: Colonel Wolford certainly did when he anticipated facing a small, irregular group but instead discovered himself pursuing a large Confederate raiding force. For Wolford, these units were small, independent, unaffiliated, and generally undisciplined, so there was little chance that they could make a stand against something so formidable as a conventional military unit. The reality, however, was often very different.

One of the most pervasive elements in the study of American Civil War guerrillas is the necessary but frustrating need of classifying them within the context of their peers and their roles in the larger conflict. Contrary to the traditional popular perception, Civil War irregulars were complex figures in multifaceted groups. Although often assumed to be undisciplined and untrained, they sometimes fought alongside regular soldiers, and many of them had conventional military backgrounds that would naturally fit better in the regular service. Irregulars often understood why the war was being fought and frequently were members of the class most likely to benefit from a Southern victory. They also moved fluidly between various roles. In reality, these men enjoyed a truly democratic existence insofar as one might be found in wartime through their ability to choose the nature of their service. They could remain at home with family, tending crops and caring for business concerns, choosing to fight only for personally beneficial reasons. They frequently enjoyed significantly more martial independence as guerrillas than any regular military service, with its command structure, would permit. And they often had the advantage of fighting selectively insomuch as they could choose to participate in activities or sit them out at will. Researchers, however, have consistently failed to fully appreciate the complexity of these warriors. Instead of seeing the irregulars' true nature, they have often simplified them to the point of caricature and myth, while reality paints a much different picture.

The challenge of positioning guerrillas within the larger narrative of the war is not new for the tradition-bound discipline of military history. In 2004 Robert R. Mackey, an officer in the U.S. Army, clearly delineated the different classifications of the Civil War's irregular warriors. He divides the irregular actors into three groups: guerrillas, who created their own units and missions and acted independently of the organized forces; partisans, who were recognized and sanctioned conventional bodies operating independently; and bushwhackers, whom he placed "on the bottom rung of the ladder" astride "criminality and guerrilla warfare."[3] As one might expect, Mackey's work was highly dependent on the nineteenth-century definition of "guerrilla" as explained by Francis Lieber, the respected jurist who helped the Union high command develop policies toward captured irregulars and their status as prisoners of war.

A few years later, Daniel Sutherland defined guerrillas by distinguishing between independent and official figures. He notes that in the earliest days of the war, guerrillas preferred to use the name "partisan," and even the Confederacy adopted that term for those who operated in the military margins with government sanction. Whereas the common guerrilla operated when, where, and how he saw fit, the partisan was considered a loosely connected member of the army and expected to behave as a soldier in exchange for his operational independence and the protection of military law. The common guerrilla was a complex figure, however, as indicated by the failure of Union officials to clearly classify such warriors. Sutherland acknowledges that they took on many forms, though usually as bushwhackers (Sutherland's preferred term) who often operated alone taking potshots at unsuspecting targets.[4] It appears that the current state of scholarship would agree with the Latin American Marxist approach: "Scholars play the state's (and the dominant classes') game when they define banditry solely along traditional legal lines."[5]

T. R. C. Hutton's study of Breathitt County, Kentucky, agrees. Consciously attempting to avoid the growing trend of classifying violence into categories of feuds and wars, Hutton strives to sever the clear lines of categorization. By doing so, he enables readers to free themselves from the neat classifications that frequently limit how they might think about such complex problems.[6] Hutton further states that misinterpretation of the region's history and culture "has deep roots, namely, an abiding refusal among educated people to acknowledge complexity within what they hold to be 'simple societies.'"[7] If the categories are removed, historians and their subjects will find it necessary to consider guerrillas in the full flower of their existence rather than as simple, myopic figures whose only tools were violence and deception.[8]

Men like John Hunt Morgan and John Singleton Mosby have been embraced as part of the military storyline of the Civil War primarily because they associated very closely with conventional forces. Even the most respected scholars faintly sanction this approach when they discuss Mosby, whose reputation as a guerrilla and raider was preeminent, exclusively as a part of the conventional military narrative.[9] This is not to say that this position is wrong; Mosby did play a significant conventional role. For historians writing in the context of the postwar period, that element of regular service was of primary interest. Yet Mosby, like any number of other guerrillas, understood that he derived his legitimacy from being officially associated with the conventional army, attacked only conventional forces, and knew that he exposed himself to risk if he chose to eschew organized service for a life of operational independence. That link clearly places the cooperating guerrilla in the military realm.

That official sanction was extended down into the ranks. Captain Jerome Marcellus Clarke was with Morgan in Greeneville, Tennessee, on March 4, 1864, the day the famed Confederate raider was killed. Clarke was only nineteen years old at the time but a sage veteran, having fought at Stones River, Vicksburg, and Chickamauga. That day, he was commanding the Confederate artillery overlooking the town. When he saw that Union cavalry had made it into the center of Greeneville, where Morgan's headquarters was located, he directed his guns to rain shot down into the streets, hoping to create enough chaos to permit the general's escape. It did not work: Morgan ran headlong into a young Federal soldier who shot him dead in a vegetable garden. Shortly after Morgan's death, Clarke left the Confederate army and returned home to Kentucky, where he led a small band across the state robbing homes, stagecoaches, and trains. In response to this sort of guerrilla activity, *Louisville Courier* editor George Prentice had created "Sue Mundy," a long-haired, small-framed man engaged in criminal activity throughout the state. As a result of Prentice's stories, Clarke became the embodiment of Sue Mundy. Arrested on March 12, 1865, the former captain was quickly tried, convicted, and hanged in Louisville only three days later.[10] Clarke, an established and veteran figure, not only understood how Morgan's connection protected him but also worked on both sides of the line of acceptability.

Most who preferred to operate independently saw the advantages of official sanction. Be they guerrillas or brigands, men like Champ Ferguson—whose notorious reputation was known throughout the borderland region of Kentucky, Tennessee, and Virginia—joined Morgan's command for periodic raids into Kentucky. By acting as a guide to the general, Ferguson was able to move deeper into the state than was otherwise comfortable for him and remain free enough to prosecute the war in his own vicious way. When Colonel Basil Duke, Morgan's brother-in-law and second-in-command, first met Ferguson, he wished "to impress upon him the necessity of observing—while with us—the rules of civilized warfare, and that he must not attempt to kill prisoners." Offended by Duke's suggestion that he did not understand the subtleties of war, Ferguson responded: "Why Colonel Duke, I've got sense. . . . I know it ain't looked on as right to treat reg'lar soldiers tuk [took] in battle that way."[11] While Duke never speculated on Ferguson's reasons to come into camp and pledge his cooperation, the guerrilla voluntarily joined several such regular units throughout the war for the protection their legitimacy provided. Similarly, Vincent Witcher stood astride the line of legitimacy at various points during the war. Witcher was a southside Virginian who spent the bulk of the Civil War in western Virginia patrolling alternately with conventional and irregular forces. A skilled guerrilla fighter in Appalachia, in June 1863 he was on Fleetwood Hill at Brandy Station with Major General J. E. B. Stuart and a few weeks later at East Cavalry Field at Gettysburg.[12] After tasting the "real" war, Witcher returned to Appalachia and within four months had invaded East Tennessee with a small band, killing nine Carter County Unionists.[13] It appears that Witcher, like so many others, wore many hats during the war, even an occasional kepi.

In eastern Kentucky, the hills seemed alive with criminals and outlaws, many of whom used the war for their own purposes. One of the most notorious was Bill Strong, a dedicated Unionist who had joined the Sixth Kentucky Cavalry (U.S.) in the fall of 1862, serving in that unit until Major General Rosecrans, then commanding the Army of the Cumberland, ordered his transfer to the Fourteenth Kentucky Cavalry (U.S.). While Strong was commissioned a captain and originally served in a traditional capacity, once he returned home as part of the Fourteenth Kentucky, he became the region's most ferocious Unionist enforcer. With military and political support for his wartime activities, Strong seemed to understand that providing political security for Unionists in his home county would result in the official sanction necessary for him to engage in more-criminal activities. Running Democrats out of town was good politics in largely loyal eastern Kentucky, so who cared if they were robbed beforehand?[14]

Strong's counterparts in Breathitt County were the men of the South family. Although the Souths often roved in the counties outside of Breathitt for fear they would be targeted by Strong, when Brigadier General Humphrey Marshall invaded Kentucky in the spring of 1863, Andrew Jackson South volunteered to serve as a local scout for the Confederates and wreaked havoc along the way. Reportedly, he and his gang attacked more than forty Unionist homesteads, and despite the fact they failed to arrest any of the local Union guerrillas, they stole a tremendous number of horses and cattle, burned numerous houses, and destroyed the county's court records.[15]

General Marshall knew and worked with many irregular warriors during the Civil War. In command of Confederate forces in southwestern Virginia, he operated in guerrilla territory, frequently employing such men as guides and scouts. Although he had spent the majority of his adult life as a lawyer and politician, Marshall was an 1832 graduate of West Point and had reentered the army during the war with Mexico. In keeping with his traditional military background, the general was concerned about the message irregular operations sent to regional residents who were loyal or potentially loyal to the Confederacy. With comparatively few soldiers guarding more than a hundred miles of the border between Kentucky and Virginia, Marshall's job was tough enough without having to explain criminal activity. At the same time, he understood that many of the region's men could not leave their homes and families amid such danger. Marshall needed local knowledge and agreed to involve irregular elements in his campaigns, but he never felt comfortable depending on them for anything beyond local intelligence.[16]

The Twenty-Fifth Tennessee Infantry presents a window into the close relationship between conventional and unconventional warfare. Organized like so many other regiments in the summer of 1861, the Twenty-Fifth was the destination for many of the men who lived along the contentious Cumberland Plateau, which served as a border between Middle and East Tennessee and extended northward into Kentucky. By the time it had incorporated the Twenty-Eighth Tennessee Infantry and later the Forty-Fourth Tennessee, the Twenty-Fifth had become home to some of the war's great villains. With leaders like John Hughs, John P. Murray, George Dibrell, and Willis Scott Bledsoe, the regiment included men destined for regional notoriety. It is no wonder that one scholar has identified the Twenty-Fifth Tennessee as "a kind of an organizational superstructure for many guerrilla outfits on the Cumberland Plateau."[17] An examination of unit rosters quickly makes it apparent that the men who commanded the regiment and its subunits saw advantages in bringing untutored mountaineers into the fold and permitting them to operate as guerrillas under Confederate sanction.

Men like Champ Ferguson, Raine Philpott, and John P. Gatewood stood in their first formations as members of the Twenty-Fifth Tennessee, and although none of them remained very long in camp, they maintained contact with their former officers and often joined them on the battlefield. Ferguson and Philpott fought alongside Dibrell at the Battle of Wild Cat Creek in July 1863. Taking place near Sparta, Tennessee, this engagement was partially fought on Dibrell's family farm. Mobilized to meet the invading Fourth Michigan

Cavalry, led by Colonel Robert Minty, Dibrell called upon the assistance of all Southern-leaning men in the neighborhood, and Ferguson and Philpott were among those who appeared. For them, the battle was very much a home-guard activity alongside regular soldiers commanded by a duly commissioned officer. More than a year later, they again joined regular forces at Saltville, Virginia, in a similar manner. Modern scholars are hard pressed to find more brutal and violent men than Ferguson, Philpott, and Gatewood, but that proclivity did not keep them from recognizing a duty to their community, a common cause with their neighbors, and the benefit of having a man like Brigadier General George Dibrell able to speak on their behalf.[18]

It would be easy to see these figures exclusively as guerrillas, but as other scholars have shown about Mosby and Morgan, such simple answers are seldom comprehensively correct. Ferguson, Philpott, and Gatewood were wise enough to understand that while they could operate as guerrillas with relative impunity, a day of accountability would come requiring a legitimate military figure to speak for them in order perhaps to save their lives.

Some of these men were capable of transitioning from legitimate, officially sanctioned warriors to cold-blooded murderers in a matter of hours, thereby tying themselves to both the traditional approach to military history and the dirty underbelly of criminal behavior. On the morning of the Saltville Massacre in October 1864, Champ Ferguson was under the command of Brigadier General Felix Robertson, who at best lost control of his men and at worst gave them permission to wantonly murder wounded and captured Federal horsemen.[19] Brian Steel Wills makes a similar argument in his work on Nathan Bedford Forrest, a Confederate commander who many conventionalists have been comfortable thinking of as a guerrilla despite the facts of his service.[20]

Furthermore, many duly appointed officers behaved in shocking ways while doing their duty. Ezekiel Counts was a native of Wise County, Virginia, when he organized Company E, Twenty-First Virginia Cavalry Regiment. The captain needed to fill his ranks and was unconcerned by the finer points of recruitment. Earning the nickname "Devil Zeke," he adopted a variety of unorthodox practices. When brothers Jim and Isaac Hale were caught by Counts returning from West Virginia, he pushed them to join his unit. When they refused, he ordered them arrested and confined to an open-air pigpen where he fed them dry corn. After three days of living in filth and eating food intended for livestock, the brothers relented and joined Counts's company, but "they did not stay with it long."[21]

On a much larger scale, the Civil War guerrilla played a transformational role in the development of American warfare. Kenneth Noe has challenged the traditional interpretation of a slowly evolving conflict that began with limited goals and evolved into the more American concept of total war. In his study of the West Virginia Campaign of 1861–62, Noe finds that the historic precedent of civilians taking up arms and skulking was well established, and the military transitioned relatively quickly in places under constant threat of guerrilla activity as a result of its previous experiences with such warfare. As the army moved into communities, it met the bushwhackers whose irregular, unprofessional, yet terrifyingly effective tactics awakened the traditional military forces to the stark realities of fighting a war seemingly surrounded by one's enemy. This informal and spontaneous form of warfare resulted in a much broader response to specific activities and incidents, which often reached into the lives of innocents.[22]

Two examples provide evidence to support this claim. In his essay, Noe concludes that the first day of the western Virginia mountaineer's Civil War was May 26, 1861, when Major General George McClellan's troops began crossing the Ohio River. Only two days later, secessionists burned railroad bridges near Farmington in the hopes of slowing the Union advance. From there they quickly expanded their destructive activities "in both tenor and ferocity," resulting in the arrest and imprisonment of dozens of suspected guerrillas. As the arrests increased, so did the bushwhacking, thus beginning a cycle of ever-escalating conflict between the military presence and local civilians.[23] Four months later in East Tennessee, local Unionists followed the lead of the Virginians by making bridge burning a central part of their much larger goal. Hoping for a coordinated Federal invasion of East Tennessee, William Blount Carter met with Union political and military figures and informed them of his plan to burn nine railroad bridges on a single night. Expecting this coordinated attack would slow the Confederate response to the planned invasion, Carter issued the order to attack the bridges on the night of November 8. By the next morning, five of the nine structures had been destroyed, while coincidence and fortune had saved the remaining four. With this guerrilla operation only partially successful, the Union army remained in Kentucky.[24] As in western

Virginia only months before, the result for Unionist East Tennesseans was widespread exposure to what can only be described as a nineteenth-century witch hunt amid a true civil war; in short, there seemed to be no real difference between combatants and noncombatants.

One of the biggest misconceptions about the guerrilla was that he came from the poorest and most ignorant elements of his society. Kenneth Noe explored this issue in an article on the socioeconomic backgrounds of West Virginia guerrillas. Surprising to many historians, the irregulars tracked by Noe tended to be older men, sometimes well into their sixth decade, who chose to fight because they felt that they had something worth protecting. He identified forty-seven guerrillas, and only twelve—around 25 percent—were landless. The remaining thirty-five were all landowners or the sons of landowners, and thirteen of those owned more than $2,000 in property. Noe further notes that the twelve who were not landowners still averaged about $800 in real property.

Farther west, Champ Ferguson inhabited a similar socioeconomic position. The oldest son in a large and relatively poor family, Ferguson inherited his father's farm in 1850. In the ten years that followed, he steadily built his fortune to include 194 acres, one resident hired man, and 3 slaves in a county having barely more than 250 bondsmen. While 3 slaves may not sound like real prosperity, in a small Appalachian community like Clinton County, Kentucky, it allowed Ferguson to stand among the top 5 percent of slaveholders.[25] Vincent Witcher was another descendant of regional royalty. He came from one of southside Virginia's most influential political families. From Pittsylvania County, the Witchers had fought with merit during the American Revolution and had occupied numerous state-level offices.[26] The same was true of William Hildreth. His brother, Reese T. Hildreth, served as state senator from Overton, Fentress, Morgan, and Scott Counties and had cast an affirmative vote on the question of Tennessee's secession.[27]

In the mountains of western North Carolina, James Keith, a native of Marshall and a member of that community's small but influential elite, served as an officer in the Sixty-Fourth North Carolina Infantry Regiment. Organized in the summer of 1862, the unit had spent its first few months in service in East Tennessee. By early 1863, Lieutenant Colonel Keith was detached with two hundred men to return to western North Carolina to guard against Unionist depredations. In January he heard that Captain John Peek, while home on leave in Marshall, was attacked in the middle of the night by a group of Unionist rabble led by locally notorious John Kirk. From there the perpetrators had visited the home of Colonel Lawrence Allen, the regiment's commander, where they harassed his wife and children, who at the time were suffering from scarlet fever. When this news reached the regiment, then only eighty miles away at Bristol, Tennessee, Keith met with Brigadier General Henry Heth and received instructions to take two hundred men into his home county to hunt down guerrillas and restore order.[28]

As Keith's command moved out of Bristol, the Unionists who had descended on Marshall receded into the hills around the Laurel Valley. As the Confederates moved through the region, they met scattered resistance but finally found a considerable force at Shelton Laurel. In the meantime, Colonel Allen had rushed home shortly after the death of one young child just in time to visit with a second before she died. He returned to the camp in Shelton Laurel. The recent transgressions of the local Unionists and subsequent deaths of two of Allen's already sick children apparently whipped the poorly trained and ill-disciplined men into a frenzy. The Confederates fanned out through Shelton Laurel and began arresting suspects. Finally ending up with thirteen, Keith's small command left camp, marching the prisoners to Knoxville. A few miles down the road, Keith suddenly stopped the column and ordered his men to prepare to execute the prisoners. As the Unionists pled for their lives, their would-be assassins hesitated in their duty. Finally, after being threatened with execution themselves, the infantrymen began shooting their prisoners. There, all the prisoners—aged between thirteen and sixty years—were killed in cold blood and buried in shallow graves.[29]

James Keith is an excellent example of a regular soldier who never really evolved from his basic guerrilla inclinations. Although he held a duly proffered commission, he was fundamentally untrained, which would place him in a position of authority without the tools necessary to manage those responsibilities. Despite his socioeconomic position in his hometown, he was still a "wild" character in comparison with his more conventional colleagues. Phillip Shaw Paludan analyzed the conversation between Keith and Heth that precipitated the North Carolinian's return to his native state in search of the Unionist offenders. While it is possible that Heth knew of Keith's guerrilla background, if he did, he would have probably considered it an advantage for the kind of work he ordered done. Keith likely only knew one way to operate, and any orders to the contrary would have required clear explanation. Nevertheless, he also understood that the ununiformed rogues who had attacked the community did not require the same treatment as regular soldiers until the point at which they became prisoners, a status that offered protection. After the killings took place, Heth sought to separate himself from the crimes, while Keith claimed that the general had ordered him to not send any more prisoners to Knoxville and even explicitly ordered him to kill all who were taken.[30] North Carolina governor Zebulon Vance, angry over the massacre, encouraged Confederate secretary of war James Seddon to bring Keith and the other participants to justice. Uninterested in prosecuting the men, Seddon allowed the officer to resign his commission and return home in May 1863, effectively unpunished for his crimes.[31]

The primary motivation of the guerrilla was pragmatic opportunism. His position outside the mainstream of military service gave him ample opportunity to watch for moments that gave him an advantage beyond those normally available. One of the central contexts within which this can be seen is the treatment guerrillas gave to prisoners of war. The Shelton Laurel example is powerful, and other similar events tell familiar stories. In April 1864 at Fort Pillow, Major General Forrest lost control of his troops, resulting in the killing of more than one hundred black soldiers and civilians.[32] The orgy of destruction visited upon the victims grew out of racial frustration at seeing black soldiers, which was very similar to the anger felt by the Confederates at Shelton Laurel who were avenging attacks on their homes and families.

Not far from Shelton Laurel, Saltville goes further to confirm the frustrations that drove such irregular behavior and how they manifested themselves in soldiers' behavior on the battlefield. In October 1864, Brigadier General Stephen Burbridge entered Virginia intending to raid the saline works at Saltville. Among the men with him on the expedition were the Fifth U.S. Colored Cavalry and part of the Sixth U.S. Colored Cavalry, made up mostly of former slaves with only weeks of military experience. After a spirited fight that found the black troops amid the carnage, the two armies settled in for the evening. That night, Burbridge secretly withdrew his men, leaving dozens of wounded troops on the field, including many blacks. The next morning Confederates roamed the field, randomly shooting many of the wounded and imprisoning others. The most notorious transgressor was Ferguson, the Tennessee guerrilla who had joined conventional forces for the defense of this important natural resource. In command of that section of the line that morning was the Texan Robertson, a twenty-one-year-old brigadier general.[33] In these cases, frustrations boiled over when opportunity presented itself with a reasonable possibility of escaping responsibility.

Although many historians tend to dismiss guerrilla violence as an anomaly within a much more structured history of American warfare, a powerful argument can be made that the Civil War irregular and his atrocities became mainstream as a result of the Mexican War. Using the history of the Texas Rangers as a starting point, the nexus of race and retribution can be clearly seen. As defenders of the Texas frontier, the rangers earned fierce reputations in their dealings with Indians. During the Mexican War, their character more fully developed, with enhanced components of recklessness, insubordination, and racially based violence—central elements in the breakdown at Saltville. None other than Brigadier General Zachary Taylor cast doubt on the effectiveness of the Texas Rangers and spoke to their habits early on when he wrote of the men, "I expect if they could be made subordinate they would be the best, at any rate as good as any volunteer corps in service; but I fear they are & will continue too licentious to do much good." In a similar assessment, he noted, "The Mexicans dread the Texians more than they do the devil, and they have good reason for it, if all the reports that we hear are true." A troubled Taylor again wrote, "The mounted men from Texas have scarcely made one expedition without unwarrantably killing a Mexican." During the Battle of Monterey in 1846, the extracurricular activities of the rangers affirmed the general's feelings about them and forced him to send them home, explaining, "With their departure we may look for a restoration of quiet and order in Monterey for I regret to report that some shameful atrocities have been perpetrated by them since the capitulation of the town."[34] Clearly, the ultraviolent behavior of the Texans was driven by their attitudes toward those whom they considered their racial and cultural inferiors. As for the massacre at Saltville, Robertson's leadership on the field and his ability to permit his men to operate without discipline was likely rooted in his experiences as the son of Texas revolutionary Jerome Bonaparte Robertson.[35] In the case of the Confederate general, and likely many others with a connection to the Mexican War, what would become irregular, guerrilla-styled activity had been learned in this earlier conflict.

The massacre at Saltville represents a racial element of guerrilla activity that has often been missed in the context of the Appalachian experience. If guerrilla warfare is unsystematic, indiscriminate, and devoid of the discipline of legitimate command, the incidents at Fort Pillow and Saltville qualify. It is obvious that Forrest lacked control over his men at Fort Pillow and questionable if Robertson considered himself to have any legitimate authority over Ferguson and others at Saltville. At Simpsonville, Kentucky, on January 25, 1865, another racial incident exploded, coincidentally on the Fifth U.S. Colored Cavalry, which had borne the brunt of the massacre at Saltville less than four months earlier. This time about eighty men of the regiment, primarily from Company E, were acting as drovers pushing government cattle to Louisville. As it was a very cold day with no apparent threat in the air, half of the men were guarding the front of the column while the other half pushed from the rear. Along the way, some of the men straggled out of the loose formation to warm and feed themselves in private and public houses.[36]

The perpetrators that day were Dick Taylor, Isaac Colter, Jerome Clarke (by now known as Sue Mundy), and Samuel "One-Armed" Berry, all notorious figures with deep guerrilla roots. Taylor was a native of Anderson County, just south of Simpsonville, while sources suggest that Colter first came to the Confederacy as a member of a Missouri Home Guard unit. While Mundy was Prentice's creation, Berry was a college graduate and ordained minister who had served under Morgan, at which time he first befriended Clarke. The *Louisville Journal* reported that the small group of about fifteen guerrillas robbed the town before riding out in pursuit of the slow-moving herd. About a half-mile out, they apparently took the drovers by surprise and quickly killed several. It was speculated that the black soldiers surrendered and were gunned down in cold blood since only two on rear guard survived, both by running and hiding. A later update placed the number of dead at fourteen, with eight others "so severely wounded that many of them will die." As searches progressed throughout farms and fields surrounding the site, it was expected that several other bodies would be found.[37] Although guerrillas are not normally associated with the racial aspect of the Civil War, they certainly participated in the major racially motivated atrocities and did so using their usual tactics.

The nature of guerrilla warfare often defies clear explanation. Despite the best efforts of scholars to clarify the roles of these irregular actors, the simple truth is that most participants did not have a clear understanding themselves. Men like Champ Ferguson may have fallen into a comfortable guerrilla existence, but if asked, he would not have been able to offer much in the way of clarifying his role in the war. Perhaps this inability to fully explain the guerrilla's purpose takes the mystery so far that it actually becomes a form of strength. When outsiders look at a region in the throes of an irregular conflict, they often diagnose the antisocial activity as paranoia. Yet when a populace is under constant threat, this analysis is dismissive of the real danger of violence that often forced civilians to behave irrationally.

Patsy Keel Boggs was just a child when the Civil War came to her home in southwestern Virginia. At the time, she and her family were living with her grandparents in a small community in one of many mountain hollows. Also living in the neighborhood was a deserter from the Union army simply known to Boggs as "Benny." Every day Benny would emerge from the hills and wander through the community begging for food. One day Patsy's grandfather became convinced that Benny was planning to kill the family and sent them away. When Benny appeared, the grandfather yelled for him and invited him into the house, where he shot the deserter dead.[38]

The old man's fear of Benny was rooted in paranoia, but the fear that drove his actions was real. Although the deserter depended on the community for his existence and would have paid a dear price for any transgressions, the grandfather could only see danger emanating from the stranger. In locations like the western Virginia mountains, the same prime locations that brought travel and prosperity before the war brought danger during it. Strangers in the form of soldiers both friendly and hostile arrived in even the most isolated communities and often took whatever they wanted from residents. As a result, strangers were increasingly viewed as inherently dangerous, and in isolation they often disappeared.

The same basic fear that skewed this grandfather's thinking also affected senior military minds. Most famously, Brigadier General William T. Sherman was in command of the Department of the Cumberland at Louisville, Kentucky, in the fall of 1861. At that early point in the war, the mountains of eastern Kentucky were of great importance to the Union, which hoped to move south through western Virginia into loyal East Tennessee. The most important element of this plan was securing the region and accurately reading its loyalty. Meeting with Brigadier General Lorenzo Thomas on October 16, Sherman painted an uncharacteristically pessimistic picture, saying, "The young men [of the eastern Kentucky mountains] were generally secessionists and had joined the Confederates, while the Union men, the aged and conservatives, would not enroll themselves to engage in conflict with their relations on the other side."

Within weeks, the ever-changing nature of loyalty in the Cumberlands forced Sherman to take a leave to regain his confidence and mental health.[39]

In the title of his now-standard treatment of guerrilla warfare in the Civil War, Daniel Sutherland uses the word "decisive" to describe the effect of guerrillas on the larger war. Some scholars worry that his use of the term overreaches; however, guerrilla warfare did affect most military facets of the conflict, particularly in contested regions, and influenced the outlooks of conventional leaders—most notably Grant and Sherman. As Sutherland suggests and many others agree, the real influence of irregular warfare comes through subtlety—small and isolated moments that shape how great numbers of men view the world around them and are then motivated to alter the landscape. Its chameleonlike and fluid qualities aid in its asymmetrical development, its ability to obscure its true self, and ultimately its capability to disappear into the background of nature and environment.

NOTES

1. Chas. R. Thompson to Major General Thomas, Dec. 15, 1862, U.S. War Department, *War of the Rebellion,* ser. 1, 20(2):185 (hereafter cited as *O.R.*).

2. McKnight, *Confederate Outlaw,* 107.

3. Mackey, *Uncivil War,* 6–8.

4. Sutherland, *Savage Conflict,* xi–xii.

5. Gilbert M. Joseph, "On the Trail of Latin American Bandits: A Reexamination of Peasant Resistance," *Latin American Research Review* 25, no. 3 (1990): 22.

6. Hutton, *Bloody Breathitt,* 5–7.

7. Ibid., 234. Hutton is discussing Malcolm Gladwell's controversial conclusion in *Outliers: The Story of Success* (New York: Back Bay Books, 2008), 161–70.

8. Sensing, *Champ Ferguson;* O'Brien, *Mountain Partisans,* 155–57.

9. Gary W. Gallagher, *Lee and His Generals in War and Memory* (Baton Rouge: Louisiana State University Press, 1998), 161.

10. Ramage, *Rebel Raider,* 238–39; Sutherland, *Savage Conflict,* 225–26.

11. Duke, *Civil War Reminiscences,* 123–24; Matthews, *Basil Wilson Duke,* 62.

12. J. E. B. Stuart to General [Samuel Cooper], Nov. 26, 1863, RG 109, Microfilm 324, Roll 189, Compiled Service Records of Confederate Soldiers Who Served in Organizations from the State of Virginia, National Archives and Records Administration, Washington, D.C.; Jeffrey C. Hall, *The Stand of the U.S. Army at Gettysburg* (Bloomington: Indiana University Press, 2009), 387.

13. Paludan, *Victims,* 78.

14. Hutton, *Bloody Breathitt,* 52, 65.

15. Ibid., 63.

16. Ibid., 59.

17. Astor, *Civil War along Tennessee's Cumberland Plateau,* 126.

18. "Spirited Engagement in White County during Civil War," *Cookeville (Tenn.) Herald-Citizen,* Oct. 12, 2014; McKnight, *Confederate Outlaw,* 115–17.

19. William C. Davis, "The Massacre at Saltville," *Civil War Times Illustrated* (Feb. 1971): 4, 5.

20. Wills, *Battle from the Start,* 189–96; John Cimprich, *Fort Pillow, a Civil War Massacre, and Public Memory* (Baton Rouge: Louisiana State University Press, 2005), 122–23.

21. Margaret [Peggy Yates] Hale Reminiscence, June 16, 1925, in *Pioneer Recollections of Southwest Virginia,* ed. Elihu Jasper Sutherland (Clintwood, Va.: H. S. Sutherland, 1984), 38.

22. Noe, "Exterminating Savages," 105–106.

23. Ibid., 106.

24. Fisher, *War at Every Door,* 54–56.

25. McKnight, *Confederate Outlaw,* 17–19.

26. Scott C. Cole, *34th Battalion Virginia Cavalry* (Lynchburg, Va.: H. E. Howard, 1993), 176; Jeffrey C. Weaver, *The Civil War in Buchanan and Wise Counties* (Lynchburg, Va.: H. E. Howard, 1994), 83–84.

27. Census records bear out the relationship between William and Reese Hildreth. Regional census data is compiled at "York's Fentress County Tennessee," updated Dec. 8, 2014, Rootsweb, http://wc.rootsweb.ancestry.com/cgi-bin/igm.cgi?op=GET&db=bruceyork&id=I9299.

28. Paludan, *Victims,* 85–88; Inscoe and McKinney, *Heart of Confederate Appalachia,* 118–19.

29. Paludan, *Victims,* 86–98; Inscoe and McKinney, *Heart of Confederate Appalachia,* 119.

30. Paludan, *Victims,* 86–88.

31. Gordon B. McKinney, *Zeb Vance: North Carolina's Civil War Governor and Gilded Age Political Leader* (Chapel Hill: University of North Carolina Press, 2004), 145–47.

32. Cimprich, *Fort Pillow,* 84–85.

33. Davis and Swentor, *Bluegrass Confederate,* 546–47; McKnight, *Confederate Outlaw,* 142–55; McKnight, *Contested Borderland,* 206–13.

34. Z. Taylor to My dear Doctor [R. C. Wood], July 7, 1846, in Zachary Taylor, *Letters of Zachary Taylor from the Battle-Fields of the Mexican War* (Rochester, N.Y., 1903; reprint, New York, 1970), 24; Lawrence R. Clayton and Joseph E. Chance, eds., *The March to Monterrey: The Diary of Lieutenant Rankin Dilworth, U.S. Army* (El Paso: Texas Western, 1996), 24; Stephen B. Oates, "Los Diablos Tejanos!," in *Visions of Glory: Texans on the Southwestern Frontier* (Norman: University of Oklahoma Press, 1970), 33 (final Taylor quote). For a more expansive discussion of the various racial and ethnic atrocities perpetrated by the Texas Rangers during the Mexican War, see Robert M. Utley, *Lone Star Justice: The First Century of the Texas Rangers* (New York: Berkley, 2002); Foos, *Short, Offhand, Killing Affair,* 114, 119, 121, 131; and Oates, "Los Diablos Tejanos!," 25–52.

35. Biographical information taken from Ezra J. Warner, *Generals in Gray: Lives of the Confederate Commanders* (Baton Rouge: Louisiana State University Press, 1987), 260–61.

36. Report of Brig. Gen. Hugh Ewing, Jan. 26, 1865, *O.R.,* 49(1):9.

37. *Louisville Journal,* Jan. 26, 1865.

38. Patsy [Keel] Boggs, Sept. 28, 1941, in Sutherland, *Pioneer Recollections of Southwest Virginia,* 38.

39. John F. Marszalek, *Sherman: A Soldier's Passion for Order* (New York: Free Press, 1993), 162–65; McKnight, *Contested Borderland,* 36–37.

NATHAN BEDFORD FORREST AND GUERRILLA WAR

BRIAN STEEL WILLS

Confederate general Nathan Bedford Forrest achieved widespread renown for his ability to conduct deep-penetrating mounted raids against Union supply centers and support infrastructure during the American Civil War. As the "Wizard of the Saddle," he seemed particularly capable of striking targets behind the main lines and raising the anxiety of Federal field leadership and political authority at the highest levels. Quick of mind, despite a lack of any significant formal education, and possessing a keen understanding of human nature and the importance of identifying elements that would enhance his advantage on any battlefield, Forrest applied his life's lessons to his combat experiences. Likewise, his ferocity in engagements with his opponents matched his mental capacities. By war's end, he could claim thirty opponents killed in close-hand fighting to offset twenty-nine of his horses shot from beneath him in battle.[1] Of his fiery subordinate, Lieutenant General Richard Taylor observed simply, "He was a host in himself, and a dangerous adversary at any reasonable odds."[2]

Forrest's ability to lead effective cavalry operations also created a context for the soldier and his style of warfare. Contemporaries who witnessed his actions or their results offered descriptions that fit their notions of such combat. The family of a Union soldier serving in West Tennessee in the summer of 1864 worried that Forrest's far-ranging and fast-moving troopers might appear suddenly to threaten him. "The regiment is doing picket duty three miles from Memphis," Lyman Allen's daughter observed, "and expecting an attack daily from Gen. Forrest's guerrilla cavalry."[3]

Numerous postwar Union reminiscences and other accounts utilized some variation of "guerrilla" to describe Forrest and his men. An 1867 report by Brigadier General Nathaniel B. Baker to the governor of Iowa referred to the transfer of troops to Memphis to "operate against General Forrest's guerrilla bands, who were committing depredations in the vicinity."[4] An Iowa cavalryman referred to the Confederate's forces similarly, as did a former infantryman from Indiana. "Forrest's guerrillas" seemed the term in vogue as retired Union warriors reflected on their service against the celebrated Southern horseman.[5]

In describing the action that had occurred in the aftermath of Shiloh at Fallen Timbers in April 1862, William T. Sherman employed another term for the intrepid Confederate cavalryman and his men, telling his brother John, "In this charge they wounded Col. Forrest, and killed 5 Dragoons, we lost in all 18 killed whom we buried and some 30 wounded." In just over a year of warfare, Sherman explained to his wife, Ellen, concerning Forrest, "It is exceedingly difficult to deal with these Mounted Devils and I am sure all we can do is to make the Country feel that the People must pay for these wandering Arabs." Although he had not applied the epithet "guerrilla" to Forrest, Sherman was prepared to employ a common remedy for dealing with the support system that allowed such irregular activities to take place by holding "the people" of an affected area accountable.[6]

At the time of Forrest's death, newspapers across the land sought to present the fallen leader in a manner designed to appeal to their readerships. For the *New York Times,* this meant tying the cavalry commander to the type of fighting that contrasted him with other, conventional, and therefore more acceptable warriors of the day. To the writer, the former Confederate had demonstrated himself to be "the most regularly successful of all the Southern cavalry leaders," and although he could not match Major Generals Joseph Wheeler or James Ewell Brown "Jeb" Stuart "as a scientific commander . . . , he had all the qualities of a guerrilla chieftain, and the history of his exploits abundantly proves that he displayed them." In recalling the raid on Memphis in August 1864 that compelled the return of a Union invading column under Major General Andrew Jackson Smith, the writer was less generous, terming the operation a "sudden dash through Memphis, with no more result than the killing of a few men on either side, [and] was the recklessness of the mere guerrilla chief—which Forrest essentially was."[7] Such terminology represented the means by which individuals sought to come to grips with Forrest, his men, and their actions in a context that was familiar and recognizable.

Likewise, modern scholars have struggled occasionally with descriptions regarding Forrest and his compatriots. Historian Robert B. Asprey examined guerrilla warfare primarily in terms of the Vietnam conflict, discussing the antecedents that included the Civil War, which "featured definite guerrilla overtones." Asprey was careful not to place "such capable if flamboyant leaders as Forrest, [John H.] Morgan and [John S.] Mosby" in the category of guerrilla fighters, but he saw in them the capability to strike "on the flanks and in the rear of enemy armies—operations invariably aided by local sympathizers."[8] Frederick J. Chiaventone posited, "During the Civil War, the outnumbered Confederate forces featured several guerrilla leaders, including Col. John Singleton Mosby and Gen. Nathan Bedford Forrest." Thus, a combination of a force associated with partisan warfare and another raised through and operating under conventional methods occurred in one all-encompassing description meant to guide prospective military scholars in their assessments.[9] John Tierney Jr. offered the characterization of Forrest as "another great guerrilla leader of the Kentucky-Tennessee area" alongside John Hunt Morgan, argued that the Tennessean's "band of guerrilla horsemen" and his "mobility as a guerrilla raider was helping the South to hold out in the last year of the war."[10]

In his examination of "anti-Confederate Southerners," historian William Freehling describes the events of Fort Pillow in 1864 colorfully as a slaughter carried out by "Nathan Bedford Forrest's Confederate guerrillas" and considers such actions effective in shaping Union strategy. "This and other Forrest sprees, together with raids by dozens of other rebel irregular warriors, made an army of occupation mandatory," he maintains. "The Rebels *did* use irregular warfare, very successfully," Freehling insists, citing Forrest as a prominent example of a practitioner of this style of fighting. "Kentucky's John Hunt Morgan and Tennessee's Nathan Bedford Forrest, 'that devil Forrest,' as Union soldiers called the Confederates' prize guerrilla warrior, perfected the mounted assault on railroads."[11]

Jay Winik's discussion of April 1865 as "the month that saved America" includes the possibility that the Confederacy might have extended the struggle by turning to a full-fledged guerrilla war. He suggests that the "battle-hardened and well-trained veterans" who would undertake the matter would provide a "Confederate guerrilla army [that] could be among the most effective partisan groups in all of history." For this writer, Forrest was among the individuals whose roles as Civil War "guerrillas" offered potential leadership as contemporary Francis Marions.[12]

Forrest scholar Michael R. Bradley has noted the "trend" among such authors and scholars to label Morgan and Forrest "guerrillas." "This designation," he argues, "reflects either ignorance of the two men or of guerrillas or of both." According to Bradley, these officers "operated within the structure of the Confederate Army" and carried out "routine duties" expected of mounted troops during the war. The "innovative tactics" they employed called for them to operate deeply "behind enemy lines" before "returning to the main army." As such, Bradley asserts, these cavalry raiders could in "no sense" be considered "guerrillas."[13] Anthony James Joes, author of a volume on guerrilla warfare in America, has viewed the matter similarly, at least by virtue of excluding Forrest and Morgan from a chapter devoted to analyzing Confederate guerrillas.[14]

As the Francis Marion reference illustrates, just as problematic for scholars attempting to assess Forrest's place in the Civil War has been the difficulty of identifying and applying appropriate historical comparisons for understanding it. In his study of guerrilla warfare, Walter Laqueur insists that while Forrest's "operations resembled those of Denis Davydov in the War of 1812" against Napoleon's invading French army in Russia, the connection lay in regard to their employment of "deep-penetration raids into the enemy's rear rather than guerrilla warfare."[15] John Arquilla places the Confederate cavalryman in the company of the Russian Davydov, Americans Nathanael Greene and George Crook, Boer Christiaan de Wet, Briton T. E. Lawrence, and Vietnamese Vo Nguyen Giap, among others. Labeling Forrest "a quintessential master of irregular warfare" who "built substantially on the methods pioneered by Denis Davydov," Arquilla praises the Southern horseman for his ability to understand that the dependence of large armies on communication and transportation infrastructures increased their vulnerability to swift-moving cavalry raids such as those the Confederate conducted.[16]

Whatever difficulties others might have in defining his actions during the Civil War, Forrest did not waver concerning his status as a regular in the service of his country. His sense of his military role and his understanding of it for others, including his opponents, found its expression early in the war. In late 1861, as Colonel Forrest sought to apprehend a Kentucky Unionist he intended to hold in exchange for a pro-Southern captive, the wanted individual fired at the Confederate party from the cover of his cabin. Under the assumption that the leader must be the most ornately attired member of the entourage, Jonathan Bells chose as his target Forrest's aide, the unit's surgeon, riding alongside his commander. The shot emptied the saddle, killing Dr. Van Wyck. In the confusion Bells made good his escape, but Forrest determined to exact retribution. Although he failed to apprehend the fugitive, the Confederate cavalryman reported subsequently to his superior that he had achieved some success against the rogue elements in the region. "I remained in the vicinity of Marion another day, and my scouts arrested one Federal soldier and brought him as prisoner, and killed one Scott, the leader of the band, who had sworn to shoot Southern men from their houses and behind trees." Scott had managed to wound several horses with a shotgun, and a search of his effects produced "three guns and a pistol," which the colonel duly directed to be "returned to the Ordnance Department."[17] In operating as he had, Forrest was demonstrating the degree to which he would enforce the rules of warfare with regard to others while continuing to adhere to accepted practices concerning the disposition of prisoners and captured enemy materiel.

Forrest could surprise those who knew him only by a reputation for ruthlessness or battlefield ferocity with his displays of a rustic code of honor. When a Northern clergyman came into his camp, the Confederate offered a level of refinement the cleric had not expected. The guest noted that he might wish to remain longer, to which Forrest responded that he would accommodate the preacher "if you were not needed so much more by the sinners on the other side."[18] Forrest's sense of honor, and humor, could be quaint in expression but existed nonetheless.

As a cavalry raider, Forrest excelled in disturbing the equilibrium of his opponents on the field as well. He embodied the doctrine expressed by Thomas J. "Stonewall" Jackson: "Always mystify, mislead, and surprise the enemy if possible, and when you strike and overcome him, never let up in the pursuit as long as your men have strength to follow; for an army routed, if hotly pursued, becomes panic-stricken, and can then be destroyed by half their number."[19] Forrest's phraseology for the same philosophy of battle appeared as "Get 'em skeered and then keep the skeer on 'em." Even when numbers were not to one's advantage, mitigating elements that one controlled could be applied: "Whenever you meet the enemy, show fight," the Tennessean maintained, "[n]o matter how few there are of you or how many of them show fight. If you show fight, they will think there are more of you, and will not push you half so hard." Forrest understood that seizing the initiative and forcing an opponent to react benefited the aggressor. His combination of these effects could be summed up thus: "Whenever you see anything blue, shoot at it, and do all you can to keep up the scare."[20]

Forrest's ability to keep his adversaries off balance also worked when he had to conduct defensive operations. Through the disposition or fabrication of forces, he worked to create the impression either that he had more troops on the field than he actually had or that significant numbers of them were in place to threaten key points of Union positions. Even then, his choice was to initiate an attack rather than stand to receive one. By sending troops to "hit 'em on the e-e-end," as he described flank attacks, or materialize unexpectedly in the rear of an enemy formation, Forrest exacerbated the uncertainty of his foes.[21] But he understood the same principle would serve him when conducting raids, too. Before moving through Brentwood and Nashville on one expedition, Forrest dispatched scouts, including a young soldier, to reconnoiter. The youth provided such thorough information that the commander chided the others for failing to be as effective. He looked at the wide dispersal of scouts as essential to success in such cases in order "[t]o know where they aint—as to know where they are."[22]

If Forrest appeared in his general associations as homespun and unrefined, he nevertheless constructed a public persona that could be useful on the battlefield. He had learned early in life that presenting an intimidating presence could often obtain the results he desired. If an opponent feared Forrest on the basis of what might happen, the Confederate already enjoyed a significant advantage. Close aide and associate David C. Kelley recognized that his superior possessed a valuable "insight" that appeared to allow him "to know, what the other fellow knew."[23] Forrest was aware of the manner in which others perceived him, and while this might reflect a latent sense of insecurity, he masked it with bluff and bluster, turning even the most challenging circumstances into potential gains. These skills he had perfected at the gaming table, where he learned to observe his opponents. In warfare he rapidly understood that although the stakes were greater, the essence of human nature remained the same. Confederate general Dabney Maury recalled Forrest saying, "I will give 'em a dare, anyhow," when he wanted to probe an unknown situation. Maury explained, "He was a great poker-player and illustrated some of its principles and technicalities upon the battle-field."[24] Of course, unconventional tactics did not mean that Forrest was waging unconventional warfare, but rather that he would use every device or tactic in his arsenal to improve his chances of defeating his opponents.

As he achieved his successes in the war, Forrest seemed to recognize that there ought to be a formula that had allowed him to do so. In one form or another, the man whose philosophy appeared most apt in phrases such as "War means fighting and fighting means killing" or "Forward men and mix with 'em" felt that he could display his martial prowess best by insisting that "he got there first with the most men."[25] Even in colloquial forms that would have tortured the tongue by employing "fustest" and "mostest," the mantra was less an indication of reality for the mounted warrior than a reflection of his beliefs as to the best method to use to explain the frequency of his victories.

An articulation of this famous aphorism, provided in his unique style of wording, came in a session with fellow Confederate commanders who had gathered after the Battle of Chickamauga as each sought to learn the secrets of the others for their accomplishments: "Wall, General," Forrest was supposed to have asserted to his interested comrades, "if I git youah idee, you want to know, sah, what I considah the main pint." The description went further than to note simply that he preferred to "git the most men thar furst" by adding that if matters went awry, he considered it equally important "ef you can't whup 'em, [you] outrun 'em."[26]

The last portion of Forrest's assessment reveals his true measure for success. One could not always arrive at an engagement first or with the greatest numbers, but to continue one had to win or at least be able to survive a loss. Forrest knew that he might have to "outrun" an opponent and considered such a course as counting in his favor. At the Battle of Parker's Cross Roads on December 31, 1862, when the Confederate found himself threatened between two Union forces and was supposed to have responded in the crisis that his men should "Charge 'em both ways!," Forrest slipped away with the bulk of his command.[27]

One of the Confederate cavalryman's best assets was his ability to absorb and process information. A limited educational foundation did not prevent him from learning as much as he could from as many sources as were made available to him. Likewise, his communications reflected his design if not his style of speech. Staff officers and clerks who worked for Forrest remained busy with his dictations, and when one of them used terms of which the Tennessean did not approve, he corrected the error instantly. "I give it a new tune," Forrest observed.[28] Consequently, one staffer explained that the general "has made me write the same letter or order three times over," admitting that he thought that each new incarnation was better than the one that preceded it. Another aide noted that the cavalry chieftain was "a hard worker" who kept those around him amply occupied. "I think he calls for 'them clerks' a dozen times a day." He recalled that his commander "attends to everything himself" and seemed "as clear as crystal" in relating his points, although he sometimes struggled to find "good language" to convey them. Still, Forrest could be adamant when he had made his choices. "Leave the message as I dictated it," he declared testily when one of his writers tried to improve on his description. To another he offered a compliment before scolding: "You write very well, but you don't seem to see what I'm driving at. I want you to recollect that it ain't your letter, but my letter. All I ask of you is to see that the spelling an' grammar are right. I'll furnish the words and ideas."[29] Such attention to detail might not enamor the commander with every one of his scribes, but it was bound to ensure that the words being used to convey his points were exactly what he intended.

For all of those around him who understood that the rudiments of language and cultural refinement in Forrest were hardly indicative of his mental prowess, there were others who failed to appreciate them. After Chickamauga, the Tennessean's superior, General Braxton Bragg, became incensed at the perceived failure of his cavalry. "I have not a single general officer of cavalry fit for command—look at Forrest.... The man is ignorant, and does not know anything of cooperation. He is nothing more than a good raider."[30] Forrest would have his chance to confront Bragg, but as his cantankerous commander had indicated, he excelled as a raider.[31] Indeed, the cavalryman's ability to achieve results out of proportion to the forces he used often paid substantial dividends for the South.

Forrest's relations with superiors were occasionally stormy, and as Bragg found out to his own chagrin, the fiery officer could be outspoken and insubordinate. But the appearance of lack of discipline in Forrest did not translate to his men. These troopers were no hodgepodge of warriors left to their own devices. Forrest expected discipline and exacted stern measures to assert it. The result was a force that frequently exceeded expectations for conduct in the field. Lieutenant General Daniel Harvey Hill commented that the behavior of Forrest's horse soldiers at Chickamauga invited favorable comparison to other branches of the service as he watched them "moving across that field like veteran infantry."[32] In his official report, Hill underscored the cooperation and "valuable service" Forrest's men had rendered: "I would ask no better fortune if again placed on a flank, than to have such a vigilant, gallant, and accomplished officer guarding its approaches." Major General Maury recognized his subordinate's capabilities, remarking to Forrest: "It is with no small satisfaction I reflect that of all the commanders of the Confederacy you are accustomed to accomplish the very greatest results with small means when left to your untrammeled judgment. Upon that judgment I now rely."[33] Even Ulysses S. Grant appreciated this feature of his talented adversary, writing that Forrest led a force "composed of thoroughly well-disciplined men, who under so able a leader were very effective." He remained impressed throughout the war, noting, "for the particular kind of warfare which Forrest had carried out neither army could present a more effective officer than he was."[34]

Grant may have been thinking of guerrilla fighting in his remarks. But the closest that Forrest came to implementing that style of warfare, in the sense of employing a small mobile command that would have to operate in isolated Union-occupied areas and seek sanctuary among sympathetic citizens, appeared in his proposal to Adjutant General Samuel Cooper for transfer to the Mississippi River valley, where he could raise an irregular force to interdict Federal waterborne traffic. Calling on his knowledge of the region from his prewar slave-trading days and the intimate familiarity of local residents now serving in his command, the cavalryman explained his plan to "harass and destroy boats on the river, [and thus] seriously, if not entirely obstruct . . . navigation." He noted the advantages of having "resided on the Mississippi River for over twenty years. Was for many years engaged in buying and selling negroes, and know the country perfectly from Memphis to Vicksburg on both sides of the river; and am well acquainted with all prominent planters in that region, as well as above Memphis." In addition, he noted, "I . . . have officers in my command and on my staff who have rafted timber out of the bottom and know every foot of ground . . . to Vicksburg."[35] Forrest did not refer to this type of activity with the Federals as "guerrilla" in nature, but he must have known that with a relatively small force, any effect he might have made would garner a response that would keep his command on the move and force them to look for the next target of opportunity in hit-and-run fashion.

Bragg forwarded Forrest's scheme, purporting that he knew "no officer to whom I would sooner assign the duty proposed, than which none is more important, but it would deprive this army of one of its greatest elements of strength to remove General Forrest." Forrest had anticipated that his superior might be reluctant to endorse the notion and broke protocol to communicate directly with Jefferson Davis. But the ambitious plan was not to be. President Davis indicated that the general "would no doubt be valuable in that portion of the country to which he refers, and in the character of service described," but deferred the matter for further consideration.[36]

As a standard method to increase the effectiveness of his operations, Forrest also engaged in a longstanding practice of dispatching troops into regions behind Union lines, or at least beyond easy Confederate reach, to collect absentees and deserters, gather intelligence on Federal dispositions, and obtain horses and supplies. These details were not meant to remain where they had gone but to return to their regular commands when their missions were complete.[37] In December 1863, General Sherman purported to be "rather indifferent" to Forrest's activities in this regard, observing to Major General Stephen Hurlbut in Memphis: "He may cavort about the country as much as he pleases. Every conscript they now catch will cost a good man to watch."[38] Sherman might appear to be dismissive of the effectiveness of these tactics, but the Confederate activity garnered recruits and kept Union forces scrambling. Unfortunately for some of the men tasked with performing these duties, the activity also exposed them to capture or death.

An example of this occurred when Forrest dispatched Lieutenant Willis Dodds into West Tennessee on such a mission. The officer became a prisoner while stopping at his family residence and, according to one report, subsequently suffered brutal treatment at the hands of his captors. The individual who disclosed the incident claimed to have seen the remains of the soldier "very soon after his murder" and observed the effects of severe mutilation, including evidence of "the face having been skinned, the nose cut off, the under jaw disjointed, the privates cut off, and the body otherwise barbarously lacerated and most wantonly injured." This person was convinced that Dodds's demise "was brought about by the most inhumane process of torture."[39]

For Forrest, the treatment of Lieutenant Dodds was as beyond the bounds of acceptable behavior for military personnel as it was a despicable act of inhumanity. A product of the Middle Tennessee backcountry, with only six months of formal classroom study, the general nevertheless had crafted a sense of soldierly honor and honed an understanding of accepted military practices. The "death by torture" of one of his men on a legitimate assignment enraged his sensibilities. Others had also lost their lives at the hands of Union troops who had executed them on one premise or another.[40] Already well known for a fiery temper and ferociousness on the battlefield, Forrest no doubt would seek an accounting from the men he held responsible for these heinous acts.[41]

Another of the Confederate chieftain's former subordinates endured capture at the hands of the Federals, although he suffered more from the psychological uncertainty of his fate than from any actual practice against him. Captain Frank Gurley, who had served effectively in Forrest's West Tennessee campaign at the end of 1862, was operating independently when he became involved in a confrontation that led to the death of Union brigadier general Robert McCook. Disabled by an illness, McCook was traveling in an ambulance when Confederate horsemen appeared suddenly. During an attempted dash for safety, the Union general received a mortal wound and died the next day. Northern accounts referred to Gurley and his men as "guerrillas," reflecting the sentiment that those who had been involved in this incident should be hunted down for the murder of a defenseless victim. In December 1863, the captain was among a number of Confederates captured by the Federals. His pending fate of hanging for the alleged crime brought reactions from numerous figures in the Confederacy, including General Forrest.

On December 12, the Confederate commander forwarded a message to General Hurlbut under flag of truce in which he maintained Gurley's legitimacy as a regular soldier, insisting, "these General are facts and when known I confidently rely upon his being treated as a Prisoner of War and not as a Guerrilla or robber." Forrest hoped to spare the life of his subordinate but took the opportunity to expand the scope of his discussion to include his views on irregular warfare. "While communicating with you General on the subject," he explained, "allow me to say that it is my purpose to drive Guerrillas from the Country, they must join the service regularly on the one side or the other, otherwise be disbanded or driven off, and while I deplore the existence of such men and their lawless conduct, I desire respectfully to call your attention to facts self evident and undenied[.]" Forrest found the effects of the mayhem they created especially disturbing, noting, "the charred walls of many dwellings have met my eye, the naked chimneys and devastated premises of now homeless [families]." He closed by observing his attitude regarding legitimate warfare: "It has eve[r] been my desire to see this War conducted according to the rules of Civilized Warfare, and as far as I am concerned will so conduct it, at the same time I a[m] determined to execute, on the spot, every house burner and robber that may fall into my hands, whether he claims to be a Federal or Confederate."[42] Even under these assurances of conducting warfare according to accepted practices, sectional tensions remained heightened as Forrest prepared to engage various Tennessee Unionist units in another raid into western Tennessee and Kentucky.

When his column set out on March 22, 1864, into territory that had earlier proven to be lucrative in both supplies and recruits, Forrest also hoped to interject a sense of stability in the troubled region. The general instructed a subordinate, "Impress upon the officers commanding the regiments sent out to scour and breast the country to do the work thoroughly and catch, if possible, the men who are going through the country and impressing and stealing horses without authority." Yet in ways that even he did not anticipate, this movement into western Tennessee uncovered the degree to which residents were experiencing the hardships of war. Forrest's report illustrated the conditions of people who had suffered at the hands of Union columns "and by roving bands of deserters and tories." Many were now destitute and forced to measures of desperation for survival. He hoped that stationing a body of troops in the area "would be the means of driving out of the country or placing in our army the deserters and tories infesting that region, whose lawless appropriation of provisions, horses, and other property is starving out defenseless and unprotected citizens of a large scope of country." The general concluded, "The whole of West Tennessee is overrun by bands and squads of robbers, horse thieves and deserters, whose depredations and unlawful appropriations of private property are rapidly and effectually depleting the country."[43]

Forrest hoped to quell the freelance activity he saw plaguing the region, but he found the actions of certain Federal units particularly offensive. He considered Colonel Fielding Hurst's activities reprehensible and thought that exposing them to the general public was not only warranted but also bound to have a positive effect on the course of the war as it related to noncombatants. In an overview that accompanied the detailed report of a subordinate tasked with investigating these irregularities, Forrest explained the desire to list the grievances to be laid against the Tennessee Unionists, and "with the approval of the lieutenant-general commanding, that this report may be sent to some newspaper for publication." He concluded simply, "Such conduct should be known to the world."[44]

In addition to the Dodds mutilation and the deaths of other personnel while on detached duty, another action had helped Forrest reach this state of mind regarding Hurst—the collection of funds, under threat of arson, from the residents of at least one town. "On the 12th of February, 1864, the entire amount, $5,139.25," he explained, "was paid into the hands of Col. Fielding Hurst by the citizens of Jackson, Tenn." Yet the general was not content with moral suasion to resolve the matter. Forrest closed the same communication on the state of affairs in West Tennessee by drawing special attention to "Hurst and his regiment of renegade Tennesseans." The Federal commander had spurred his adversary's wrath to such an extent as to induce Forrest to issue a special order condemning "the aforesaid Fielding Hurst, and the officers and men of his command, [as] outlaws, and not entitled to be treated as prisoners of war falling into the hands of the forces of the Confederate States." The best chance Forrest had to fulfill his threat came on March 29, 1864, when Colonel James J. Neely's troops confronted "the traitor Hurst" and "drove" him "hatless into Memphis." Such a punishment was not as rigorous as the one the Confederate commander had preferred, but produced the satisfaction of defeating him.[45]

During the course of his expedition, Forrest announced his intentions to his superiors when he identified a target he believed to be vulnerable to an assault; tellingly, these did not include exacting retribution for supposed Union transgressions. "There is a Federal force of 500 or 600 at Fort Pillow, which I shall attend to in a day or two, as they have horses and supplies which we need."[46] Situated on a high bluff on the eastern bank of the Mississippi River, part of the original Confederate defense network for Memphis, Fort Pillow now protected a river landing and outpost that allowed a Union presence in the region. Garrisoned by some six hundred men, evenly divided between Tennessee Unionists and African American soldiers, the isolated post seemed ideal for a swift operation.[47] In a brief engagement on April 12, Forrest's men overwhelmed the defenders and in the excessive aftermath inflicted casualties among men who were no longer capable of resisting effectively, attempting to surrender, or simply trying to escape. Labeled widely in the North as a "massacre," the affair produced a congressional investigation and motivated retaliatory acts by Union forces that often matched the vehemence of those Confederates who had reacted so violently to the appearance of black troops in blue uniforms. Forrest thereafter became, for many, the "Butcher of Fort Pillow."[48]

Among the men who perished under questionable circumstances was the post's commander when the fort fell, Major William Bradford. Succeeding Major Lionel Booth when that officer died from a sharpshooter's bullet early in the fighting, Bradford rejected calls for surrender. The Tennessee Unionist survived the combat and became a prisoner of war, only to be singled out later and killed.[49] And as his forces approached Purdy, Tennessee, General Forrest had an opportunity for vengeance against the family of the man he had labeled a criminal. Confederate sympathizers in the town, which contained Hurst's home, had felt the wrath of the Union colonel's Sixth Tennessee when the regiment had moved out. Forrest recognized that the situation could spiral out of control quickly into a flurry of retaliation and retribution if he did not act to forestall it. To that end, he detailed a trusted officer, Charles Anderson, and a handpicked group from his own escort to secure the Hurst property before the main body arrived. The colonel's wife, occupant of the home, expressed her gratitude "for this unexpected kindness," and Forrest enforced the order with "my personal request that it be obeyed to the letter; and I am sure no soldier of my command will disobey the one or disregard the other." But lest it appear that he had softened his stance toward his adversaries, the Confederate added hastily of "Hurst and his cowardly regiment [that] if we are so fortunate as to find them in our front, I will wipe them off the face of the earth."[50]

Fort Pillow once again raised questions of Forrest's legitimacy as a soldier. If the general and his men purported to engage in warfare using conventional methods, the treatment of prisoners following this action would have to be addressed where such obvious abuses had occurred. In subsequent correspondence with Union major general Cadwallader C. Washburn, Forrest addressed matters related to Fort Pillow and the treatment of black prisoners in particular: "I regard captured negroes as I do other captured property, and not as captured soldiers." He explained that his practice toward prisoners had not altered. "Since the war began I have captured many thousand Federal prisoners, and they, including the survivors of the Fort Pillow massacre (black and white) are living witnesses of the fact that with my knowledge or consent, or by my order, not one of them has ever been insulted or in any way maltreated."[51]

Similarly, Forrest responded to another inquiry: "You ask me to state whether 'I contemplate either their [African American soldiers'] slaughter or their return to slavery.' I answer that I slaughter no man except in open warfare, and that my prisoners, both white and black, are turned over to my Government to be dealt with as it may direct."[52] This interpretation of Confederate policy toward captured African American troops was self-serving, but aide David Kelley noted that the general "was opposed to the killing of negro troops; that it was his policy to capture all he could and return them to their owners."[53] Forrest had ordered such a disposition for those black prisoners from the fort for whom identification could be made and substantiated.[54]

The Bradford killing raised additional questions for the general to address.

In his exchange with Washburn, Forrest insisted that he had not heard of the death of the Union major "until eight or ten days after it is said to have occurred." Bradford had been "arrested" right after the battle by men Forrest had sent out "hunting deserters," and "he [Bradford] claimed to be a Confederate soldier belonging to Bragg's army." Lacking appropriate "papers," the officer remained in custody, then once identified accurately, was scheduled to be removed as a prisoner. "I understand that he attempted to escape, and was shot," Forrest explained. "If he was improperly killed nothing would afford me more pleasure than to punish the perpetrators to the full extent of the law, and to show you how I regard such transactions[,] I can refer you to my demand . . . for the delivery to Confederate authorities of one Col. Fielding Hurst and others of his regiment, who deliberately took out and killed 7 Confederate soldiers, one of whom they left to die after [torturing him.]" Forrest wanted to hear no more of such matters and promised his continued "determination" to suppress "the adoption of the policy [for brutality] which you seem determined to press."[55]

The general remained sensitive to charges that he had breached any code of military ethics at Fort Pillow or elsewhere. He proved vehement in denials that he perpetrated actions against anyone that did not conform to the strictures of legitimate warfare. "I took particular pains when I entered the army to make myself fully acquainted with all rules and usages pertaining to civilized warfare," Forrest explained to a friend after the war. In wording similar to that which he had once used regarding Colonel Hurst, he then denounced anyone "who says I ever overstepped the bounds of civilized warfare."[56]

Hurst's culpability for the actions Forrest attributed to him would have to await either formal Union inquiry or resolution in the field. But for the Confederate general, in addition to the negative reaction it had generated in the North and the reputation it secured for him of brutality, Fort Pillow represented a setback in his pursuit of justice. The individual he had tasked with investigating and reporting on Hurst's involvement in excesses against Confederates and sympathetic civilians, Wiley Reed, was among the fatalities from the attack on the post.[57] Other battlefield imperatives would intrude as well, but Reed's loss silenced a voice that would otherwise have been available to press for a response to the charges Forrest had laid before his opponents.

Forrest's greatest battlefield victory came in the summer of 1864 at Brice's Cross Roads as he confronted and defeated a formidable Union advance from Memphis, Tennessee, under Brigadier Generals Samuel Sturgis and Benjamin

Grierson. The ability to concentrate his troops after scattering them deliberately to cover as many approaches as possible and his use of terrain and the soaring June temperatures of Mississippi against his adversaries worked to Forrest's credit. But these Union expeditions kept the cavalry leader occupied and away from the more significant movement of Sherman toward Atlanta. When Forrest finally turned against the Ohioan's supply lines in Middle Tennessee, capturing vessels and destroying the depot and facilities at Johnsonville in late October and early November, the strike came well after the loss of Atlanta and too late to be more than a nuisance to the Federals. For all of the dramatic elements of sinking gunboats and transports and burning warehouses of supplies, "that devil Forrest," as Sherman termed the general for the havoc he had created, could not affect the momentum of the conflict or alter the fortunes of the Confederacy.[58]

After Johnsonville, Forrest joined General John Bell Hood for the Tennessee Campaign and played a pivotal role in covering the retreat of the Army of Tennessee from the environs of Nashville in December after its defeat by Major General George H. Thomas. The effect on the cavalry of the near decimation of the principal Confederate army in the West and the exertions required in protecting its withdrawal left morale low and rest and refitting imperative. Forrest knew that he would have to inject a renewed sense of purpose in his men for the fighting to come. To that end, he issued General Orders No. 99 on March 3, 1865. Although not intended for this express purpose, the document illustrates the distance at which he sought to hold himself and his men from the taint of guerrilla warfare. Every aspect of the "rules and regulations" laid down deal with the degree to which order and discipline would be expected to be maintained in camp or in the field. The men would participate in regular drills and abide by standard "calls" for camp activities, avoid wasteful practices ("Galloping and other unnecessary use of horses about camp, or on the march, is positively forbidden"), undertake routine duties, and exercise discipline in all circumstances, including by avoiding straggling or "depredation [regarding] private property and citizens" and by exhibiting the strict movement of units under fire. "Finally," the orders underscored, "there must be system, order, and discipline in every department of the command; promptness and precision on the part of all in the performance of every duty, and in the execution of all orders."[59]

Circumstances had reduced the number of recruits from which any conventional forces could draw replacements. Forrest was among the field commanders who recognized that some individuals remained who still might be brought into the ranks. From his headquarters at West Point, Mississippi, the general reported to Secretary of War John Breckinridge his desire to bring to official attention the "existing evils" rampant in the District of Southern Kentucky. "No other motive than the 'good of the service' prompts me to address you," he explained as justification for raising the matter directly, although his department commander, Lieutenant General Taylor, forwarded the message with his own approval for "the views and recommendations of Major-General Forrest."[60]

The Tennessean speculated that if the district had come into being either to enhance the raising of troops or to establish some Confederate presence in territory occupied by Union forces, "the experiment was a complete failure." Few men were currently under arms, and most of these were "scattered to the four winds." Subsequent attempts to restore control had not improved conditions significantly. "Nothing has been added to our army," Forrest concluded, and such remnants as reasserted themselves "scattered" again with the appearance of any sizable Union force. "[M]y opinion is that they can never be brought out or organized until we send troops there in sufficient numbers to bring them out by force." Once more, Forrest advocated having men of military age and capabilities "brought out" to serve in the regular Confederate forces rather than being left to harass the Federals in guerrilla-style campaigning. The general needed men for his conventional cavalry command, and his Kentucky brigade, now reduced to approximately 300 men, required a boost in numbers to become effective again.

Forrest's assessment of affairs in areas under Union control also reflected his attitude toward unconventional warfare. "They have deserted," he observed of the men who remained in Kentucky, "and attached themselves to the roving bands of guerrillas, jayhawkers, and plunderers who are the natural offspring of authorities given to parties to raise troops within the enemy's lines." Disdainful of those who acted in such a fashion as well as those who aided and abetted them, Forrest condemned the "would-be colonels" who "delegated to would-be captains and lieutenants" authority that had "created squads of men who are dodging from pillar to post, preying upon the people, robbing them of their horses and other property, to the manifest injury of the country and our cause."

The people of West Tennessee and the Mississippi River region had already fared poorly and were now subjected to even worse abuse. The men there "never organize [formally], report to nobody, are responsible to no one, and exist by plunder and robbery." Compounding matters, Forrest thought that the ramifications were detrimental to regular forces, with "twenty men out of the army to one placed in it." He argued that those responsible for these deplorable conditions should "be ordered to report with what men they have to the nearest department commander within a limited period for consolidation and organization, and those failing so to report to have their authorities revoked and themselves subjected to conscription whenever caught." Forrest recognized the larger consequences involved if conventional forces could not be "occasionally sent in under good and reliable officers to arrest and bring out deserters and break up the bands of lawless men who not only rob the citizens themselves, but whose presence in the country gives a pretext to Federal authority for oppressing the people."[61]

Even as he sought to establish greater control over his men and differentiate his command from the type of forces he condemned, it became increasingly clear that Forrest would face many difficult challenges during the campaigning season of 1865. The general would try every tack, from persuasion to intimidation, to inspire the soldiers and citizenry and cobble together a force to resist penetrations into Confederate territory. He reminded his men of their past accomplishments and encouraged them to remember the fallen as they continued the struggle for Southern independence.[62]

Forrest faced an impressive Union force, assembled under the command of Brigadier General James Harrison Wilson, that threatened the Confederate industrial center of Selma, Alabama, in March. The aggressive advance and overpowering firepower forced the Southern horsemen to give ground grudgingly from point to point. Yet stressed as it was, Forrest's command did not dissolve into individuals or small groups that would enable the men to engage Wilson's troops independently. Scattering his forces so that they could strike and run would only expose Selma without providing any real chance of success in defending the city. Instead, Forrest attempted to utilize the traditional tactics that had worked before in the hopes of delaying the advance sufficiently to concentrate his forces and improve his odds. That these methods would not be successful now did not prevent him from waging war conventionally.

When General Forrest reached the Selma defenses, he impressed citizens to augment his ranks, promising to pitch anyone into the Alabama River that refused to go into the defensive works.[63] He assured the anxious residents, "I am for fighting as long as there is a man left to fight with."[64] General Taylor had watched as Forrest arrived, "horse and rider covered in blood, and announced the enemy [was] at his heels" before the department commander left on the last train. "Forrest fought as if the world depended on his arm," Taylor recalled.[65] But these efforts, and the cavalryman's personal example in conducting the defense, could not prevent Selma's fall on April 2.

Exhausted and bloodied from his earlier bouts with Union opponents, Forrest and a remnant of cavalry escaped from the city but encountered members from the Fourth U.S. Cavalry, which the Confederates still held responsible for the shooting of their popular comrade Samuel Freeman in 1862 after his capture. The Southerners sought permission to assault the unsuspecting cavalry while Forrest remained behind. When the affair ended, thirty-five Federals lay dead or wounded, with five captured, while the attackers had lost only one of their number wounded.[66] The officer who led the strike insisted "not a single man was killed after he surrendered," but comparisons to the aftermath of Fort Pillow would be impossible to avoid.[67]

A Union account of the matter concluded that Forrest and his men "came across a party of Federals asleep in a neighboring field, and charged on them, and, refusing to listen to their cries for surrender, killed or wounded the entire party, numbering twenty-five men."[68] Sergeant James Larson of the Fourth Cavalry labeled the incident a "repitition of Ft. Pillow."[69] In memoirs that appeared years later, Wilson observed that the Confederates had "killed the last one of them" and concluded, "Such incidents as this were far too frequent with Forrest." The young general explained that his opponent's "ruthless temper . . . impelled him upon every occasion where he had a clear advantage to push his success to a bloody end, and yet he always seemed not only to resent but to have a plausible excuse for the cruel excesses that were charged against him."[70]

Forrest could do nothing to prevent Wilson from capturing Selma, then Montgomery, and found the exercise of trailing the Union forces toward Georgia pointless from a military perspective. He moved westward to regroup and consider his options, but the possibilities for continued operations became increasingly limited as other Confederate forces surrendered and General Taylor opened negotiations with his Federal counterpart as well. Union adversaries from Sherman to Thomas thought Forrest's choice would be to continue the war in guerrilla fashion. Sherman, who had earlier expressed his desire "to have Forrest hunted down & Killed," felt that the Confederate was now among a desperate class of soldiers who would resort to continued resistance by any means. Grant predicted that Forrest would be among the "numberless bands of desperadoes" that would resort to guerrilla warfare rather than face capitulation.[71] Along the same line he confided his concerns to his wife, Ellen: "There is great danger of the Confederate armies breaking up into Guerillas and that is what I most fear. Such men as Wade Hampton, Forrest, Wirt Adams, etc., never will work, and their negros are all gone their plantations destroyed, etc."[72]

Thomas promised the most extreme retribution to those areas that supported such guerrilla forces. "Send under a flag of truce a summons to Forrest to surrender upon the terms given by General Grant to Lee and Johnston," he directed a subordinate. "Inform him of the rumors which have reached you, and that you are prepared for him." Should the Confederate turn guerrilla, Thomas insisted, "if he attempts such a reckless and bloodthirsty adventure he will be treated thereafter as an outlaw, and the States of Miss and Alabama will be so distroyed that they will not recover for fifty years."[73]

As it turned out, Forrest had no intention of embracing the guerrilla option. He had operated throughout the war in a conventional fashion and would end his military career in the same manner. When called upon to continue resistance by Mississippi governor Charles Clark and former Tennessee governor and friend Isham Harris, the general answered definitively, "Any man who is in favor of a further prosecution of this war is a fit subject for a lunatic asylum, and ought to be sent there immediately."[74] As Forrest would do at Gainesville, Alabama, Robert E. Lee had already distanced himself from calls for a guerrilla or partisan phase of the conflict as the conventional one wound down, telling President Davis, "A partisan war may be continued, and hostilities protracted, causing individual suffering and the devastation of the country; but I see no prospect by that means of achieving a separate independence."[75] Historian Charles Roland accepts Lee's importance in this context: "Lee no doubt could have inspired a formidable guerrilla movement, though both his reason and his sense of honor prohibited him from resorting to it." Although Roland adds that Forrest would have been one of the Confederates whose "talent[s] were ideally suited to such a program," the cavalryman rejected that course along the same lines as his illustrious superior.[76]

Forrest could be unconventional in his approach to combat operations, which he insisted gave him advantages over those constrained by West Point tactics, but he maintained his position of spurning guerrilla-style warfare as a viable option. In his request for a pardon, forwarded to President Andrew Johnson in July 1865, the former soldier explained that he had joined the service of his state and "had fought the ones who were opposed to it—in arms—when ever and whereever I could find them," but he accepted the outcome of the war and encouraged "all soldiers under my command to pursue the same course—to lay aside all ideas of 'guerrilla' warfare—and to return at once to the peaceful avocations of citizens." Despite being "whipped" in the recent conflict, the ex-Confederate offered the use of his sword against any new enemies that might arise to challenge the flag of the United States.[77]

During the course of the American Civil War, "that devil Forrest" seemed to embody much more than a regularly commissioned officer fulfilling his duty. He appeared to represent the worst elements of the Confederate character, including embracing a style of irregular warfare that set him at odds with conventional methods and measures. Yet Forrest operated under a code of honor that informed his life and military career. Guerrilla activity did not fit in any positive sense under that code. For all of his zeal in combat and willingness to engage personally in the killing that defined combat as he understood it, Forrest professed not to tolerate actions that did not conform to legitimate conduct under arms. Threatening extermination became part of the method by which he sought to achieve bloodless victories over wavering opponents, just as he had done with bluff and bluster at the poker table. Forrest was at his best in free-ranging raids and independent operations, but he always carried these out under the flag and the authority of his government and military superiors. Those who worked outside these parameters received his disdain and risked raising his ire. For the individual, such as Fielding Hurst, who failed to conform to Forrest's sense of strict adherence to the rules of warfare, any price was a legitimate one to pay.[78] Far from accepting a description of himself as a "guerrilla," Nathan Bedford Forrest would have agreed with the assessment passed down by a person who had experienced such warfare firsthand: "The Yankees were bad, but them old guerrillas were worse!"[79]

NOTES

1. For an account of Forrest's life, wartime career, and personal characteristics, see Wills, *Battle from the Start.* For accounts left by two of Forrest's commanders, see Richard Taylor, *Destruction and Reconstruction: Personal Experiences of the Late War* (New York: Longmans, Green, 1955),

242–43; and Dabney Herndon Maury, *Recollections of a Virginian in the Mexican, Indian, and Civil Wars* (New York: Charles Scribner's Sons, 1894), 204–21.

2. Taylor, *Destruction and Reconstruction,* 268.

3. Lyman Allen, *The Family of Major Lyman Allen during the American Civil War, Compiled from Letters and Diaries,* ed. Harriet Stevens (Iowa City: Press of the Camp Pope Bookshop, 1998), 49 (Monday, June 20, 1864).

4. Nathaniel B. Baker, *Report of Brig.-Gen. Nathaniel B. Baker, Adjutant General and Act'g Q.M.G. and Act'g as P.M.G., to Hon. William M. Stone, Governor of the State of Iowa,* vol. 2 (Des Moines: F. W. Palmer, 1867), 513.

5. Charles H. Lothrop, *A History of the First Regiment Iowa Cavalry, Veteran Volunteers, from Its Organization in 1861 to Its Muster Out of the United States Service in 1866* (Lyons, Iowa: Beers & Eaton, 1890), 209; William R. Hartpence, *History of the Fifty-First Indiana Veteran Volunteer Infantry: A Narrative of Its Organization, Marches, Battles, and Other Experiences in Camp and Prison; from 1860 to 1866* (Cincinnati: Robert Clarke, 1894), 128, 154.

6. William T. Sherman (hereafter WTS) to John Sherman, Hd. Qrs. 5th Divn., camp before Corinth, May 12, 1862, in William T. Sherman, *Sherman's Civil War: Selected Correspondence of William T. Sherman, 1860–1865,* ed. Brooks D. Simpson and Jean V. Berlin (Chapel Hill: University of North Carolina Press, 1999), 218; WTS to Ellen Ewing Sherman, Memphis, Jan. 11, 1864, ibid., 584. With regard to one town and guerrillas, see, for example, WTS to John A. Rawlins, Memphis, Sept. 26, 1862, ibid., 306–307; and WTS to Edwin M. Stanton, Memphis, Dec. 16, 1862, ibid., 347. See also Grimsley, *Hard Hand of War,* 114–17.

7. *New York Times,* Oct. 30, 1870.

8. Asprey, *War in the Shadows,* 1:176.

9. Frederick J. Chiaventone, "Guerrilla Warfare," in *The Oxford Companion to American Military History,* ed. John Whiteclay Chambers II (New York: Oxford University Press, 1999), 306.

10. John J. Tierney Jr., *Chasing Ghosts: Unconventional Warfare in American History* (Washington, D.C.: Potomac Books, 2006), 72–73.

11. Freehling, *South vs. the South,* 4, 11, 153.

12. Jay Winik, *April 1865: The Month that Saved America* (New York: Harper Collins, 2001), 147–66 151.

13. Michael R. Bradley, *The Raiding Winter* (Gretna, La.: Pelican, 2013), 13–14.

14. Joes, *America and Guerrilla Warfare,* 51–101. Joes includes Mosby alongside William Clarke Quantrill, though noting their role in opposite poles morally as well as the possibility of continuing a guerrilla-style war after the surrender of the armies of Robert E. Lee and Joseph E. Johnston.

15. Laqueur, *Guerrilla Warfare,* 81–82.

16. John Arquilla, *Insurgents, Raiders, and Bandits: How Masters of Irregular Warfare Have Shaped Our World* (Chicago: Ivan R. Dee, 2011), 111.

17. Forrest report, Hopkinsville, Ky., Dec. 5, 1861, U.S. War Department, *War of the Rebellion,* ser. 1, 7:5 (hereafter cited as *O.R.*).

18. John Allan Wyeth, *Life of General Nathan Bedford Forrest* (New York: Harper & Bros., 1899), 631.

19. John D. Imboden, "Stonewall Jackson in the Shenandoah," in *Battles and Leaders of the Civil War,* ed. Robert U. Johnson and Clarence C. Buel, 4 vols. (reprint, New York: Thomas Yoseloff, 1956), 2:297.

20. Wyeth, *Life of General Nathan Bedford Forrest,* 198, 569.

21. Robert Selph Henry, *"First with the Most" Forrest* (Indianapolis: Bobbs-Merrill, 1944), 293.

22. Newton Cannon memoir, Newton Cannon Papers, Tennessee State Library and Archives, Nashville, 9; J. L. Weaver to Mr. and Mrs. J. A. Clark, Apr. 5, 1917, Joseph Dent Clark Papers, ibid.

23. Bradley, *Forrest's Escort,* 178.

24. Dabney Herndon Maury, *Recollections of a Virginian in the Mexican, Indian, and Civil Wars* (New York: Charles Scribner's Sons, 1894), 206.

25. Ibid.; James R. Chalmers, "Forrest and His Campaigns," in "Meeting at the White Sulphur Springs," *Southern Historical Society Papers* 7 (Oct. 1879): 454; Taylor, *Destruction and Reconstruction,* 244; Basil W. Duke, *Reminiscences of General Basil W. Duke, C.S.A.* (Garden City, N.Y.: Doubleday, Page, 1911), 345–46; James Harrison Wilson, *Under the Old Flag: Recollections of Military Operations in the War for the Union, the Spanish War, the Boxer Rebellion, etc.,* 2 vols. (New York: D. Appleton, 1912), 2:184.

26. James Compton, "Atlanta Paper, No. 8, the Second Division of the 16th Army Corps, in the Atlanta Campaign," in *The Atlanta Papers,* comp. Stanley C. Kerksis (Dayton, Ohio: Press of Morningside Bookshop, 1980), 239.

27. Henry, *"First with the Most" Forrest,* 118; Dan Kennerly, *The Dawn of Lightning War—General Forrest and Parker's Crossroads* (Houston: Dan Kennerly, 1982), 15.

28. Wyeth, *Life of General Nathan Bedford Forrest,* 374.

29. "General Forrest," Filson Historical Society, Louisville, Ky.; G. W. Cable to My Dear Mother, Gainesville, Ala., Apr. 16, 1865, in Lucy Leffingwell Bikle Cable, *George W. Cable: His Life and Letters* (New York: Russell and Russell, 1967), 23; George W. Cable, "George W. Cable's Recollections of General Forrest," ed. Arlin Turner, *Journal of Southern History* 21 (May 1955): 224–25.

30. James Lee McDonough, *Chattanooga—A Death Grip on the Confederacy* (Knoxville: University of Tennessee Press, 1984), 32.

31. Wyeth, *Life of General Nathan Bedford Forrest,* 264–66.

32. Quoted in ibid., 252–53.

33. D. H. Hill report, n.d., *O.R.,* ser. 1, 30(2):146;
Maury to Forrest, Meridian, Aug. 2, 1864, ibid., 39(2):748.

34. Ulysses S. Grant, *Personal Memoirs of U. S. Grant,* 2 vols. (New York: Charles L. Webster, 1886), 2:108–109.

35. Forrest to S. Cooper, Jackson, Tenn., Aug. 9, 1863, *O.R.,* ser. 1, 30(4):508–509.

36. Bragg endorsement, Chattanooga, Aug. 14, 1863, ibid., 509; Forrest to Davis, Kingston, Tenn., Aug. 19, 1863, ibid, 507; Davis endorsement, n.d., ibid, 510.

37. See, for example, Forrest to Joseph E. Johnston, Jackson, Tenn., Dec. 6, 1863, ibid., 31(3):789; Forrest to S. Cooper, Jackson, Tenn., Dec. 8, 1863, ibid., 797; Forrest to Braxton Bragg, Jackson, Tenn., Dec. 8, 1863, ibid., 798; Forrest to B. S. Ewell, Jackson, Tenn., Dec. 13, 1863, ibid., 817; and Forrest to Joseph E. Johnston, Jackson, Tenn., Dec. 18, 1863, ibid., 844–45.

38. WTS to Hurlbut, Bridgeport, Nov. 18, 1863, ibid., 32(3):187.

39. W. M. Reed to J. P. Strange, Jackson, Tenn., Mar. 21, 1864, ibid., 118–19.

40. Gary Blankinship notes the execution-style killings of thirteen captured Confederates, along with Confederate misdeeds that included the killing of Colonel Hurst's nephew, William, in "Colonel Fielding Hurst and the Hurst Nation," *West Tennessee Historical Society Papers* 34 (Oct. 1980): 83.

41. N. B. Forrest, in the field, Mar. 22, 1864, ibid., 119.

42. Quoted in Donald H. Steenburn, *The Man Called Gurley* (Meridian, Ala.: Elk River, 1999), 173–74.

43. J. P. Strange to R. McCulloch, Columbus, Miss., Mar. 12, 1864, *O.R.*, ser. 1, 32(3):617; Forrest to T. M. Jack, Jackson, Tenn., Mar. 21, 1864, ibid., 664.

44. Forrest to T. M. Jack, Jackson, Tenn., Mar. 21, 1864, ibid., 663.

45. W. M. Reed to J. P. Strange, Jackson, Tenn., Mar. 21, 1864, ibid., 118–19; N. B. Forrest, in the field, Mar. 22, 1864, ibid., 119; Chalmers address, Apr. 20, 1864, ibid., 32(1):623.

46. Forrest report, Apr. 4, 1864, ibid., 608–609.

47. Wyeth, *Life of General Nathan Bedford Forrest,* 335–37; Albert Castel, "The Fort Pillow Massacre: A Fresh Examination of the Evidence," *Civil War History* 4 (1958): 38–39.

48. Two studies of the engagement are Brian Steel Wills, *The River Was Dyed with Blood: Nathan Bedford Forrest and Fort Pillow* (Norman: University of Oklahoma Press, 2014); and John Cimprich, *Fort Pillow, a Civil War Massacre, and Public Memory* (Baton Rouge: Louisiana State University Press, 2005).

49. Washburn to Forrest, Memphis, June 19, 1864, *O.R.*, ser. 1, 32(1):589; McLaglan statement, Memphis, Apr. 25, 1864, ibid., 557–58; McLaglan testimony, *"Fort Pillow Massacre,"* H. Rpt. 65, 38th Cong., 1st sess. (Washington, D.C.: U.S. Government Printing Office, 1864), 101–103.

50. *Confederate Veteran* 23 (1915): 451.

51. Forrest to Washburn, Tupelo, June 23, 1864, *O.R.*, ser. 1, 32(1):590.

52. Ibid., 591; Forrest to Washburn, in the field, June 23, 1864, ibid., 593.

53. Quoted in Wyeth, *Life of General Nathan Bedford Forrest,* 390.

54. Goodwin report, Apr. 21, 1864, *O.R.*, ser. 1, 32(1):619.

55. Forrest to Washburn, in the field, June 23, 1864, ibid., 592.

56. Forrest to C. A. White, Nov. 16, 1868, Nathan Bedford Forrest Papers, Pearce Civil War Collection, Navarro College Archives, Corsicana, Tex.

57. G.W.A., "From Gen. Forrest's Command," Jackson, Tenn., Apr. 27, 1864, in *Memphis Daily Appeal,* May 13, 1864. See also Charles W. Anderson, "Col. Wiley M. Reed," *Confederate Veteran* 5 (Mar. 1897): 101–102.

58. WTS to Grant, Nov. 6, 1864, *O.R.*, ser. 1, 39(3):659.

59. General Orders No. 99, West Point, Miss., Mar. 3, 1865, ibid., 49(1):1024–26.

60. Taylor endorsement, Forrest to John C. Breckinridge, Mar. 18, 1865, ibid., 49(2):1125.

61. Forrest to John C. Breckinridge, Mar. 18, 1865, ibid., 1124–25.

62. Forrest address, n.d., ibid., 45(2):759–60.

63. Wyeth, *Life of General Nathan Bedford Forrest,* 603.

64. Quoted in James Pickett Jones, *Yankee Blitzkrieg: Wilson's Raid through Alabama and Georgia* (Athens: University of Georgia Press, 1976), 81.

65. Taylor, *Destruction and Reconstruction,* 268–69.

66. Thomas Jordan and J. P. Pryor, *The Campaigns of Lieut.-Gen. N. B. Forrest and of Forrest's Cavalry* (New Orleans: Blelock, 1868), 676–77.

67. Lt. George Cowan quoted in Henry, *"First with the Most" Forrest,* 432–33. Jordan and Pryor argue that the Union troops had been engaged in plundering local civilians. See Jordan and Pryor, *Campaigns of Lieut.-Gen. N. B. Forrest,* 676–77.

68. Salter report, n.d., *O.R.*, ser. 1, 49(1):406.

69. Quoted in Jones, *Yankee Blitzkrieg*, 97.

70. Wilson, *Under the Old Flag*, 2:240.

71. WTS to George H. Thomas, Savannah, Jan. 21, 1865, *O.R.*, ser. 1, 45(2):622; WTS to Grant, Raleigh, Apr. 25, 1865, ibid., 47(3):303.

72. WTS to Dearest Ellen, Raleigh, Apr. 22, 1865, in *Sherman's Civil War*, 871–72.

73. Thomas to Hatch, Nashville, May 2, 1865, George H. Thomas Papers, William R. Perkins Library, Duke University, Durham, N.C., 2–3.

74. Jason Niles Diary, May 6, 1865, Southern Historical Collection, University of North Carolina, Chapel Hill; Dan T. Carter, *When the War Was Over: The Failure of Self-Reconstruction in the South, 1865–1867* (Baton Rouge: Louisiana State University Press, 1985), 9.

75. Lee to Davis, Apr. 20, 1865, in Lee, *Wartime Papers*, 939. See also Lee's views to Edward Porter Alexander in Alexander, *Fighting for the Confederacy: The Personal Recollections of General Edward Porter Alexander* ed. Gary W. Gallagher (Chapel Hill: University of North Carolina Press, 1989), 530–33.

76. Charles P. Roland, *An American Iliad: The Story of the Civil War* (Lexington: University Press of Kentucky, 1991), 261.

77. Forrest to Andrew Johnson, ca. July 1, 1865, in Andrew Johnson, *The Papers of Andrew Johnson*, vol. 8, ed. Paul H. Bergeron (Knoxville: University of Tennessee Press, 1989), 331.

78. Hurst survived the war, dying on April 3, 1882. Blankinship, "Colonel Fielding Hurst and the Hurst Nation," 71–87.

79. Quoted in McKenney, *Jack Hinson's One-Man War*, 118.

HOME REBELS, AMNESTY, AND ANTIGUERRILLA OPERATIONS IN KENTUCKY IN 1864

STEPHEN ROCKENBACH

Brigadier General Joseph Holt's first trip back to his native Kentucky after three years serving as judge advocate general for the Union army was one of business, not pleasure. As part of his job, Holt advised President Abraham Lincoln on a number of sensitive issues concerning the prosecution and punishment of unruly soldiers, disloyal citizens, and captured Confederate soldiers. Now Secretary of War Edwin Stanton had dispatched him to investigate reports of disloyalty and antigovernment conspiracies in the region and to meet with state and military authorities. Among other observations, Holt described the serious threat posed by pro-Confederate guerrillas in Kentucky by concluding that "these outlaws are banded together in the same interest, are animated by the same spirit, and seek the accomplishment of the same guilty ends." He advocated immediate and severe measures to respond to the threat, including repeal of President Lincoln's Proclamation of Amnesty, which had allowed former Confederates to return to Kentucky and resume their citizenship. Holt was speaking of fellow Kentuckians who took up arms against their Unionist neighbors when he declared, "they are a brotherhood of traitors and felons, and the public safety demands that they should be held responsible *in solido* for the crimes of each and all of their members."[1] By the summer of 1864, irregular warfare had reached unprecedented levels in the state due to evolving Federal policy, resistance to emancipation and black enlistment, and heightened political competition between those Kentuckians who continued to support the Union government and former Confederates who now turned to settling old scores. The state's guerrilla war had become a fight for home rule that pitted unconditional Unionists against small yet effective bands of homegrown insurrectionists, many of whom had abandoned the Confederate cause in favor of using terror and intimidation to challenge government authority.

The political divide between unconditional and conditional Unionists widened, while pro-Confederate guerrillas used extralegal methods to remove Unionist opposition on the local level. Historian Christopher Phillips has identified the intensification of postemancipation guerrilla violence, noting that black enlistment had "irreversibly racialized the hard war in the western Border States."[2] Although guerrilla violence had occurred previously in Kentucky, most notably during the 1862 Confederate invasion of the state, the postemancipation irregular conflict was different. J. Michael Rhyne points out that "many guerrillas evinced intense hatred of both black recruits and unconditional Unionists who remained loyal to the United States despite its military policies regarding slavery."[3] Late-war violence was therefore not simply a sideshow to the military conflict between Union and Confederate forces, but instead was a localized effort to maintain the racial status quo and undermine Federal authority in the state. The competing sides that clashed along the border after 1863 have been described by Aaron Astor as "two full-on rebellions" facing conservative Unionists, "one from secessionists bent on an increasingly destructive guerrilla insurgency across the border states, and the other from slaves, abolitionists, opportunistic Union military commanders, and an increasingly radical administration."[4] The common thread of white supremacy had made it difficult to distinguish between conservative Unionists and secessionists early in the war, but as emancipation and black enlistment divided the state politically, pro-Confederate guerrillas exploited this weakness and sought to blend into embattled communities and dismantle Union influence from the inside.[5]

By January 1864, resistance to Federal authority was strengthened by an odd mélange of disloyal citizens, former Confederate soldiers, lawless bandits, self-proclaimed partisan rangers, disgruntled Democrats, "Copperheads," and Confederate sympathizers. If one adds Lincoln's Proclamation of Amnesty and Reconstruction, the Emancipation Proclamation, and the enlistment of African American soldiers to the mix, the result is a boiling concoction overflowing Kentucky's borders and destabilizing Unionist support in the region. The Proclamation of Amnesty has remained an underappreciated link in this increase in partisan violence against unconditional Unionists and state and Federal troops. Although military commanders could previously administer the oath of allegiance on an individual basis, this proclamation guaranteed that eligible parties would have their citizenship restored. A resident of Georgetown informed Brigadier General Stephen G. Burbridge, then commander of Union forces in Kentucky, that "home rebels" were applying for pardons and using threats and intimidation to force others to sign petitions supporting their requests. This loyal citizen used the term "home rebels" to convey that these men were indeed still disloyal and in rebellion against the government, returning home to continue the fight from within their communities. Loyal Kentuckians knew they were supporting the amnesty petitions of lawless men but felt they had no other way to protect themselves and their property.[6] The efforts of these home rebels to strike at Union authority and support in the region was not a desperate bid to change the course of the war or to draw military attention away from the battlefront—they sought to eliminate unconditional Unionist support in Kentucky.

Lincoln's Proclamation of Amnesty and Reconstruction is better known for its postwar effects than any wartime repercussions. Announced on December 8, 1863, the policy offered amnesty to anyone who had committed treason by participating in the rebellion against the U.S. government. The president announced that some of the individuals who had participated in the rebellion now wished "to resume their allegiance to the United States, and to reinaugurate loyal state governments within and for their respective states:"[7] In this initial decree, Lincoln expressly excluded loyal states from his effort because the purpose was to gain the support of former Confederates in reestablishing state governments in seceded states. Yet the proclamation allowed any disloyal individual to take the oath of allegiance and thereby regain his rights as a citizen, including claims to property. This did not, however, include regaining slaves confiscated by the Federal government or declared free by the Emancipation Proclamation. Only the rank and file of the Confederate military (those at the rank of colonel and below) were eligible to take the oath. Anyone involved in the so-called Confederate government, or those who left prior positions in the U.S. military or government to serve the Confederacy, were excluded. Further, anyone who did not treat white and black Union military personnel as prisoners of war would also be excluded from receiving a pardon. Lincoln's goal was to quickly allow for the creation of loyal governments in seceded states occupied by Union troops and to fashion a blueprint of restoration to use as the war continued.

The Proclamation of Amnesty garnered an immediate response in loyal states but also raised questions about the actual effect and purpose of Lincoln's action. In the border region, there was profound support from Republicans for the spirit of the proclamation. Former Ohio governor William Dennison wrote Lincoln two days after the announcement and praised him, remarking,

"I shall be surprised if a very large majority of the loyal people of the country don't heartily approve your programme for the reconstruction of the insurgent States." From Dennison's point of view, offering amnesty and encouraging the induction of loyal state governments would promise a speedy resolution to the war; in his opinion and those of Republican colleagues, Lincoln had "said the right word at the right time."[8] In the months following the president's announcement, however, several Unionists who wrote in support of the plan voiced concerns about the clarity of the message. The policy did not indicate whether the oath would apply to current prisoners or to those who previously violated an oath of loyalty or other bond, nor did it indicate if the rights of Confederate soldiers would be restored as opposed to simply placing them in prison or the Union army.[9] On March 26, 1864, Lincoln released a clarification of the proclamation that specifically excluded those men already in custody or under arrest. In short, the move was not meant to empty military prisons, but instead to shrink Confederate formations and repopulate seceded states with now-loyal men.[10]

It did not take long for the proclamation's consequences to become apparent in the border region, where guerrillas intensified their resistance to the Union government. Several Kentuckians expressed their concerns over the amnesty's potential for allowing rebels to return to the state under the guise of taking the oath of allegiance and then aid disloyal forces. Border State radical Republicans gathered at the Louisville Freedom Convention on February 22 and discussed forming an independent radical party and the abolishment of slavery. Before departing the following day, the majority of these unconditional Unionists supported a resolution advising the revocation of the Proclamation of Amnesty.[11] According to these Unionists, anyone who fought against the Federal government should not retain the right to vote. Beyond opposition to the lenient nature of the proclamation, others saw it as having immediate and more damaging effects. Bland Ballard wrote directly to Lincoln from Louisville in early June, declaring that he did "not believe there is a Union man in this state who does not believe the Amnesty Proclamation ought to be revoked." He went on to point out that although amnesty had the potential of doing good, the recent campaign by Confederate brigadier general John Hunt Morgan into Kentucky had complicated the situation. Ballard admitted that he did not know how many men took the oath but confidently concluded that "every one of them whose health is sufficiently restored will, if he has opportunity, join

Morgan in his present raid and carry off as many recruits as he has been able to influence."[12] In Ballard's opinion, the measure was premature in Kentucky because disloyal elements continued to operate in the state and there was no way to prevent those who swore the oath from aiding guerrillas.

Unionists in Kentucky faced a significant challenge in dealing with disloyal citizens already in the state, which made repeal of the Proclamation of Amnesty and Reconstruction seemingly the only way to keep order. A Dr. Henderson, writing from Louisville, begged Mr. Blakely (likely Ebenezer Blakely of New York) to convince Lincoln to repeal the proclamation, stating emphatically that "every loyal, truly loyal man, who loves his country, says that it ought to be promptly revoked." Henderson echoed Ballard's assertion that the president was well intentioned but pointed out that traitors were taking advantage of the amnesty offer and using it against loyal men in the state. Certainly, Henderson saw this as dangerous to the interest of Unionist Kentuckians, noting, "we want Kentucky all loyal, we cannot and we will not be among traitors." The solution, he declared, was not to bring traitors into loyal states, but instead to ship them off to Confederate lines.[13] This proposition was very similar to a suggestion Major General William T. Sherman made to Burbridge only a few days later, when he outlined a plan to banish disloyal Kentuckians aiding guerrillas. He informed Burbridge that "the recent raid of Morgan and the concurrent acts of men styling themselves Confederate partisans or guerrillas call for determined action on your part." First, he advised directing officers to treat guerrillas not as soldiers but as "wild beasts unknown to the usages of war." Additionally, he suggested arresting any citizens, male or female, who encouraged or aided guerrillas and shipping them down the Mississippi River to places unknown. Sherman concluded of these disloyal residents, "if they won't live in peace in such a garden as Kentucky, why we will kindly send them to another, if not a better land, and surely this would be a kindness and a God's blessing to Kentucky." The general made sure to specify that simply having "southern feelings" did not merit exile as long as the individuals were peaceful and law abiding.[14]

The deportation of any citizen aiding guerrillas would have been a difficult task indeed, but these extreme measures were actually a response to the problem posed by continued partisan violence within the state, which was in turn complicated by the amnesty proclamation. General Holt made the strongest indictment of the policy's effect and joined the calls for repeal of the measure. Although his description of Kentucky's "deplorable condition" and conclusion that "these guerrilla bands are the fruit of the Presidents amnesty policy" are well known, the letter itself was a plea for harsher measures and an observation of the shifting nature of partisan violence in the state. The judge advocate general carefully explained to the secretary of war that "a very large portion of the state is completely overrun with guerrillas, who plunder farm-houses, and fields and villages at will, and often murder the helpless victims of their robberies." Holt went on to describe small groups of twenty or so fighters moving swiftly from town to town on fast horses with weapons concealed in their clothing.[15] This vivid description was followed by a characterization of loyal citizens as preferring to give up horses and other supplies to guerrillas to avoid the violent results of refusal or resistance. Holt was describing bands of home rebels who, although seemingly set upon meaningless destruction, were targeting unconditional Unionists in communities across the state.

Holt's portrayal of the guerrilla problem in Kentucky was not confined to concerns over the effect of partisan warfare on loyal citizens. It was part of a response to a perceived conspiracy that threatened not only Kentucky but also the free states of Indiana, Illinois, and Ohio. According to the general, rebels had used the oath of allegiance "as a means for returning to the state, visiting their friends, making observations upon our military affairs, and then arming, mounting, and equipping themselves either for Confederate service or for the career of robbers and cut-throats." Holt concurred with Burbridge's desire to suspend the Proclamation of Amnesty in Kentucky and suggested that a conspiracy existed in that and adjoining states for cooperation with rebel forces. With Kentucky's government not strong enough to resist such widespread treason, he justified Burbridge's policy of punishing sympathizers and executing guerrilla prisoners. He also claimed that the recent execution of three guerrillas had prevented further violence and "inspired a most wholesome terror." Additionally, Holt advocated the enlistment of black soldiers in the state, noting that while some white Kentuckians had attacked enslaved men escaping to enlist, public support and effective government policy had made recruitment a success. The letter concluded with his confident assertion that Kentucky's governor, given sufficient help, could root out the conspiracy against the government in his state, although efforts to clear out Ohio, Indiana, and Illinois would require a greater military presence in each.[16]

The inability of authorities to properly quell guerrilla violence at the local level was directly related to conflicts between military and civil authorities at the state and national levels. In 1863, when Thomas E. Bramlette assumed his position as governor of Kentucky on the Union ticket, there was every indication that he would fully support the war effort and firmly crush rebel sympathy in the state. Yet the new governor made clear his objection to any direct interference with slavery in his state, including the recruitment of black soldiers. At first Lincoln and Bramlette seemed to have an understanding about delaying black enlistment, but this broke down by December 1863, about the same time the president issued his amnesty proclamation. Federal recruiters began enlisting free black Unionists in Kentucky, but the Conscription Act of February 24, 1864, allowed for the recruitment of enslaved men and conferred upon their owners $300 in compensation. An incensed Bramlette traveled to Washington to meet personally with the president, who was able to assuage some of the governor's concerns. But in April 1864 General Burbridge, a Kentucky slave owner who Bramlette had recommended for military command in the state, actively pursued the enrollment and training of black Kentuckians, a violation of the governor's agreement with Lincoln, to make up for low enlistment in some counties. All of this conflict unfolded during a time of political turmoil and social upheaval.[17] When a lenient policy for the pardoning of former Confederates was added to this tense situation, the result was tantamount to declaring open season on unconditional Unionists.

The complexity of Bramlette's relationship with national authority was exacerbated by the need to depend on government troops to protect Unionist civilians. In 1863 Kentucky was allowed by congressional act to raise up to 20,000 Federal troops that could be used to defend the state unless a greater need arose. These troops, which included regiments of mounted infantry, patrolled Kentucky counties for guerrillas while still subject to the authority of Federal commanders. By May 1864, the state was still desperately in need of soldiers dedicated to defending communities against roving bands of guerrillas and outlaws, prompting Inspector General Daniel Lindsey to order that the enrolled militia would be responsible for responding to the threat. Shortly afterward, Bramlette called for 10,000 state troops to serve six months to defend the citizens, urging potential volunteers that "if you would escape desolations of war—lift your hand and strike the despoiler."[18] As the governor scrambled to raise sufficient forces to keep order in Kentucky communities, Burbridge intensified antiguerrilla operations by adopting a policy of retaliation, issuing General Orders No. 59. This measure allowed for the deportation of any citizens living within five miles of irregular activity and for the execution of four guerrilla prisoners in retaliation for the murder of each Unionist.[19] Troops immediately acted on this order, and in the bluegrass region two guerrillas were executed in July near Georgetown, while another four were killed in Frankfort in November. One of the prisoners executed in the capital was Thornton Lafferty, who Union troops had previously arrested and sent to Camp Chase, Ohio. Lafferty had taken the oath of allegiance in November 1862 and gained his freedom, but he later violated that pledge and joined a guerrilla band known for the murder of a discharged Union soldier. Although Lafferty had not taken the oath under Lincoln's Proclamation of Amnesty and Reconstruction, the incident shows that guerrillas had no qualms about violating promises to a government they were fighting to undermine.[20]

The exact effect of the Proclamation of Amnesty and Reconstruction is difficult to ascertain because most of the documentation regarding irregulars mentions only guerrilla leaders or those unfortunate enough to be killed or captured. Beyond this, the shadowy majority of partisan fighters are hard to identify. In his letter to Stanton, Holt referred to a letter from Burbridge estimating that nine out of ten guerrillas had taken the oath of amnesty. This was probably an exaggeration and, much like the conspiracy claims, meant to urge immediate action. Yet there is evidence of Confederate soldiers returning to Kentucky in large numbers during the last two years of the war. A large ledger of oaths given in 1864 and 1865 serves as evidence of this influx of men, most of whom are listed as "civilians," indicating that they came to take the oath on their own as opposed to being captured. A significant number of these men were allowed to take the oath but were required to move north of the Ohio River. This notation occurs especially during the final months of the war, although the ledger does not include the reason behind this measure.[21]

Often these prodigal sons were former members of cavalry units that operated in irregular fashion and who quickly made the transition to small-scale partisan warfare. Nineteen Confederate soldiers took amnesty oaths in Louisville in April 1864 after Major General Nathan Bedford Forrest reportedly disbanded several regiments. In August more of Forrest's men, including four of his officers, had accepted amnesty in Cairo, Illinois. The ability of Confederate soldiers to take the oath and then travel to loyal states had even inspired a rumor that some of these men had crossed into Indiana and Illinois in order to lead an uprising among Copperheads in the free states along the border. Union authorities in Cairo also arrested a man alleged to be a soldier in Forrest's command who had entered Illinois as a spy.[22] In an extreme example of the problematic nature of Lincoln's policy, H. H. Parker, a former Confederate soldier, wrote to Bramlette in February asking for authority to raise a company of cavalry to operate against guerrillas in Kentucky. It was not uncommon for Unionists to ask the governor for permission to raise such companies, but the idea of a former Confederate soldier raising a company to fight pro-Confederate guerrillas bordered on the absurd. Parker was writing from Ohio, where he took the oath of allegiance, and explained that he was "a Kentuckian by birth and education and after having tried the merits of the Rebel government and know it to be a failure I feel it my duty to do something now for my state." He added that during his service to the Confederacy, he participated in raiding parties and therefore would know how to counter their movements. Kentucky authorities did not allow him to lead his own company of guerrilla scouts, although it is unclear if he found some other way to protect the state from his former compatriots.[23]

Much of the anxiety and paranoia that border Unionists experienced was due to the fact that the bulk of Federal troops had moved farther south to engage regular forces, leaving mostly militia and state troops behind. Several prominent Kentucky Unionists criticized the ability of these units to adequately deal with the threat. W. H. Faris, formerly of the Third Kentucky Cavalry, wrote the governor explaining what he believed the problem to be. The state troops were able to guard the frontier against larger groups of 500–1,000 men, but in Faris's mind they could do little to stop around thirty fighters from "slipping in between the posts" in order to "effect every species of robbery and commit every depredation they wish, and pass out again with perfect impunity." Faris described a "scouting system" used by "flying bands of guerrillas" who passed through counties so quickly that once the militia was called up in response, the riders were plundering the next county over. Indeed, even if the militia was called up, the former quartermaster had little faith in the "parcel of illy mounted men on horses and mules, with shotguns and rifles, who feeling so little confidence in themselves, they would prefer not meeting a well-armed and disciplined force though far inferior in number." Faris then outlined a plan to raise a company of men in every border county to be kept in permanent state service for the purpose of preventing invasion.[24]

The problem of guerrilla violence was complex, involving both local factions and the threat of semiorganized bands entering the state and systematically moving from county to county. Faris, who was writing from Muhlenberg County, used the example of Jacob "Jake" Bennett, a man he identified as one of Morgan's captains, who had robbed a bank in Hartford County, then searched a steamboat on the Green River and "wantonly fired into her as she passed on away from them." Bennett went on to raid through surrounding counties, committing what Faris referred to as "smaller depredations."[25] Bennett was indeed a former officer in the Confederate cavalry and had escaped from the Ohio Penitentiary with General Morgan after the unsuccessful Indiana and Ohio Raid in 1863. He then joined Adam Johnson's Tenth Kentucky Cavalry, a unit operating under the Confederacy's Partisan Ranger Act. Some historians have classified partisan rangers as being separate from guerrillas, suggesting that their objectives and operations made them legitimate military units, even if they did use irregular tactics.[26] While Bennett did belong to an organized partisan regiment and occasionally attacked railroads and other targets of military value, his willingness to seek retribution from Unionists reveals a baser impulse for violence.

In August 1864, Bennett demonstrated the complex motivations of some irregulars by staging a raid on Owensboro that seemed to have less to do with achieving victory for the Confederacy and more to do with punishing residents for hosting Union troops. His gang of about twenty men shot up the town, robbed a jewelry store, burned a boat loaded with goods, and killed three black Union soldiers and one white Unionist, who had recently been discharged from the army. This raid occurred immediately after Union authorities had garrisoned Owensboro and recruited soldiers for the 118th U.S. Colored Infantry. Even though these guerrillas seemingly were intent on simple robbery and senseless killing, their attack was actually a well-timed and intentional reaction to Union military policy.[27] Smaller bands of guerrillas like Bennett's often targeted private citizens or important public institutions like banks and businesses. Their intent was to terrorize those who in any way supported Union recruitment and military activities and encourage both political and physical opposition to local Unionists.

These "flying" guerrilla bands were often led by men who were described as "captains" in Morgan's cavalry, indicating that they had some former association with regular Confederate forces, even though they were now operating independently. Richard Massey of Monroe County, which bordered Tennessee, voiced a concern to Bramlette similar to Faris's, noting that when militia returned home after being called up, they were susceptible to visits by groups of five to ten guerrillas who would "punish these men, rob and destroy their property."[28] These were the same type of irregular bands Holt described, and they presented a unique problem for Kentucky Unionists. Citizens alone were neither prepared nor willing to oppose these brazen gangs, who often had the firepower, training, and ruthlessness, if not the numbers, to defeat any who resisted. These men singled out people they knew to be loyal and towns that were not garrisoned, indicating that their main goals were to threaten the security of loyalists and discourage anyone who would restrict their movement.

In 1864 Kentucky's southern border was not secure from small groups or individuals seeking to organize as guerrillas, and Unionists quickly realized that local action was needed to prevent further incursions by former Confederates returning to the state seeking amnesty or simply looking to cause trouble. John Reynolds of Pulaski County wrote Governor Bramlette, requesting authority to question or arrest people passing through his county who he suspected to be spies. He also observed men he described as "disloyalists" and noted "prowling bands of guerrillas who when cut off from their commands scatter through the county and become citizens."[29] Colonel S. M. Starling, commander of the enrolled militia, wrote to Colonel John Mason Brown in June from Hopkinsville explaining that due to the "devilish disloyalty" of citizens in part of Christian County, it was "necessary frequently to send an escort with the sheriff when in discharge of his ordinary duties." Speaking of the militia in this area, Starling admitted that he had "never been able to force them to drill or have company musters."[30] Although Federal troops had some success in hunting guerrillas along the Kentucky-Tennessee border, they often found citizens unwilling or too fearful to help track down the perpetrators. The infamous outlaw Champ Ferguson was able to slip in and out of Kentucky on several occasions, which demonstrates that the border was by no means protected against those who sought to return to counties farther north.[31] Militia were able to do very little to stop the movement of former Confederates back into the state, and guerrillas were free to terrorize loyal citizens and add to their own numbers.

Just as Kentucky's southern border seemed impossible to secure from small bands of guerrillas, its northern border experienced widespread partisan violence as well. There, the problem was not groups passing through, but irregulars operating in specific neighborhoods and undermining the efforts of local Unionists. Although these guerrilla infestations were common throughout the state, Meade County, located along the Ohio River about forty miles west of Louisville, serves as an example of one of the more extreme northern incursions of partisan fighters. Guerrillas and Confederate sympathizers made life extremely hard for Unionists, and although the area was the scene of several skirmishes after the failed Confederate invasion of 1862, the county had become a lawless frontier town by 1864.[32] Lizzie Schrieber, a young girl living near Brandenburg, kept a diary in an old atlas in which she recorded the movements and actions of both Union troops and Confederate guerrillas. The most intriguing thing about her account is her lack of interest in trying to differentiate between uniformed Confederate cavalry raiders and small bands of lawless guerrillas. In July 1863, Morgan's command passed through Meade County and crossed the Ohio River into Harrison County, Indiana, beginning the dash along the southern border of Indiana and Ohio that ended in the general's capture. Schreiber simply commented that "there was a band of thieves crossed the Ohio River" and noted that "it was Morgan's band." She later wrote that Union troops captured the "Morganites" in Ohio, stating, "good for them." Her detailed diary reveals a pattern of guerrilla depredation and Unionist reprisal that intensified in 1864. During that year, Schreiber recorded sixteen separate accounts of guerrilla activity, ranging from the killing of Union soldiers and citizens to a few unusual occasions where guerrillas passed through and "did not touch a thing."[33]

While Schreiber and other valley residents had no trouble identifying irregular forces, historians have struggled with classifying guerrillas and attempting to differentiate between regular cavalry troops using irregular tactics and bands of reckless partisan killers. Some maintain that the term "bushwhacker" represented a separate type of villain, one who sniped from cover and killed for sport, while "guerrilla" applied to anyone who adopted the irregular tactics of taking property, operating behind enemy lines, and otherwise targeting civilians as well as military forces. Kentucky Unionists were less concerned about commissions and uniforms than the actions and intent of these aggressors.[34] They referred to Morgan and his men as guerrillas so often that the general felt the need to answer the accusations in an 1863 handbill during one of his forays. Morgan declared that his "brave army is stigmatized as a band of guerrillas and marauders" but claimed that his men "come to not molest peaceful individuals or destroy private property, but guarantee absolute protection to all who are not in arms against us."[35] The good citizens of Indiana and Ohio would most certainly beg to differ, however, when Morgan's troops engaged in the destruction of private property and the terrorizing of citizens during their July 1863 raid. Additionally, during Morgan's 1864 Kentucky raid, his men enhanced their reputation for lawlessness and wanton destruction.[36] The mere association of Confederate troops with guerrilla tactics was enough to classify them as such. Yet there were often very real connections between bands of home rebels and the larger, more organized cavalry raiders. Guerrillas often broke away from the cavalry columns to operate on their own or joined raids at their convenience.[37]

The large-scale raid perpetrated by Morgan's force in July 1863 was a precursor to a number of smaller incursions and skirmishes the following year. Just as Unionist authorities had little ability to prevent irregulars from moving through southern border counties, violence and depredation spread across the Ohio River despite efforts to contain it. After Morgan's notorious seizure of the steamboat *Alice Dean* and his crossing of the Ohio, any sizable guerrilla force led Unionists on both banks to conclude that another invasion was underway. In the wake of the raid, the *New Albany Daily Ledger* reported with much concern the gathering of these "myrmidons of Jeff Davis" in western Kentucky between the Ohio and Tennessee Rivers. The editor explained that "the recent successful raid of Morgan through our state is an invitation and encouragement to other adventurers" who were "made desperate by the dark clouds now overhanging their sinking cause."[38] In late September 1864, a large group of guerrillas entered Brandenburg in Meade County, which caused forces in Indiana to scramble to defend the river border.[39] Diarist Schreiber noted on October 14, 1864, that "more rebels came in under Major Harris and Capt. Brown," which caused the trigger-happy home guard on the Indiana shore to fire toward the southern bank of the river "all day Wednesday after they were all gone away."[40] This was the same group that the *Daily Ledger* claimed to be under the command of C. L. Hinds and numbering more than one thousand men. The Indiana Legion, a state-guard organization, was mobilized in the counties bordering Meade County, and the editor warned the citizens of nearby New Albany to also prepare to defend themselves against "desparados [*sic*]." Additionally, he noted that "the whole lower Kentucky border is swarming with armed guerrillas."[41] Even though southern Indianans' reactions might seem extreme, the frequency of smaller raids and acts of violence in the northernmost Kentucky counties explains this paranoia. There was real concern for smaller attacks along the river border, and the frequency of these bold strikes increased in 1864.

The Ohio River was by no means a barrier for travelers but was instead a busy commercial conduit that thrived with traffic during the war. Hoosiers immediately noticed the increase of refugees arriving in southern Indiana. Sherman had sent Southern refugees and deserters to the Indiana counties bordering the Ohio, where they congregated and sought jobs and shelter. Eventually, military authorities sent these individuals farther north, which was a cause of relief for loyal citizens who viewed these visitors with suspicion. The exodus of Southern refugees, formerly enslaved persons, and deserters across the river added to the confusion and made it impossible to secure the region. Indeed, many of these refugees were actually well-off Kentucky farmers who took their livestock and belongings north of the river. Under threat from Union forces, foragers, gangs of robbers, and the retaliation of guerrilla raiders, Kentuckians who could pick up and move to safety did so. Others fled areas where industrious guerrillas were conscripting men to aid them in their desperate efforts to oppose Federal authority. This caused the editor of the *Ledger* to conclude that "no loyal people ever suffered more than the people of Kentucky."[42] Indeed, in late January 1865 a guerrilla identified only as "Captain Bradley" took two young men, James J. Mitchell and John McMahon, from their homes in Hancock County at gunpoint while their helpless parents watched. Although this area bordered the Ohio River, Unionists there could not ensure the safety of their family members. Such brazen acts created a ripple effect in neighboring states and destabilized the upper border.[43]

This prolonged guerrilla presence had a lasting effect in Meade County and other communities where armed bands sought to secure the racial status quo. In Brandenburg, black soldiers returned to reunite with their families and were met with the threats of "regulators," who vowed to kill black veterans. A former member of the 118th U.S. Colored Infantry tried to liberate his wife and children after the Thirteenth Amendment took effect on December 18, 1865, but the former master refused. Regulators also targeted white citizens who had either allowed their former slaves to cross the Ohio River and pursue freedom in Indiana or planned on recognizing the status of freedpeople by paying them wages. White and black Unionists fled Meade County in the face of continued violence, although with the Confederacy defeated, one could no longer refer to these regulators as guerrillas. Instead, they had become the de facto law in these border communities, reinforcing the white supremacy they fought so hard to maintain during the war.[44]

Unionist control of the Ohio River had proven essential to military success in the Midwest, but that important transportation link was also a tempting target to guerrillas. In 1864, guerrilla attacks on steamboats on the river intensified and signaled an important shift in partisan violence. Along with targeted attacks on Union soldiers or Unionist civilians, which were still common, guerrillas frequently stalked the banks of the Ohio, looking for floating prey. During the summer of 1864, irregulars seized three steamboats carrying cattle, which both frustrated military officials and demonstrated to civilians that the river border was not secure.[45] While lawless individuals would occasionally fire at passing boats with no intention other than to terrorize the passengers, many Hoosiers feared that guerrillas had a "bitter hate toward the citizens residing on the Indiana shore" and intended to capture these boats and raid into that state.[46] Guerrillas occupying the town of West Point, Kentucky, a short distance downriver from Louisville, fired on the steamboat *Echo* with no effect, while in a separate incident the *Lewellen* steamed past a gang of guerrillas pursued by Unionists in Meade County. In another shockingly bold action, five guerrillas boarded the *Taracon* at Lewisport, Kentucky, and searched the boat, finding only one soldier from an Indiana regiment. They paroled the Hoosier infantryman and left without discovering the black recruits hidden below deck. These irregulars were part of a larger force of thirty or more under the command of Captain Tom Henry, a former member of Morgan's cavalry, who had occupied the town, but surprisingly they did not take anything from the boat or its passengers besides a few shots of whiskey.[47] Near Brandenburg, guerrilla leader Sim Horsely and his men attempted to capture a steamboat on New Year's Day, 1865, but an onboard detachment of fifteen Union soldiers held off the rebels with musket fire.[48] Some of these attacks were merely harassment, while others were attempts to seize and search the vessels. Yet they all had the same result—to throw the upper Kentucky border into chaos at a time when the fighting and suffering had supposedly moved farther south.

The mere presence of pro-Confederate forces was enough to destabilize Unionist efforts and disrupt life along the border, even when these men were not committing murder and theft. Major Walker Taylor and other Confederate officers who attempted to fight an irregular conflict without resorting to retribution against civilians found their efforts undermined by the home rebels in their vicinity. The editor of the *Ledger* noted that Taylor's men were operating in Kentucky along the Ohio River but declared that they were "a remarkably well-behaved set of desperadoes as they do not plunder and murder on the wholesale principle like a majority of the gangs do that infest that state." But Unionists still did not consider Taylor a Confederate soldier and only half-heartedly referred to him as "major." The editors of the *New Albany Daily Ledger* and the *Louisville Journal* opined that Taylor and his "marauders" should go south and fight for the Confederate government on the battlefield.[49]

Even irregular cavalry like Taylor's command could not disassociate themselves from the terror and intimidation caused by smaller groups of home rebels. In December 1864, a gang led by Captain William Davidson of Hawesville boarded the *Morning Star* as the steamboat stopped at Lewisport on the Ohio River, robbing civilians and killing five Union soldiers. Captain Lewis Buckner of the Fifty-Second Kentucky Infantry was on board the steamer and concluded that the gang was part of Taylor's force. John Allen, another passenger, disagreed with Buckner and defended Taylor by describing him as a "gentleman who would condemn such conduct." Buckner then arrested Allen on suspicion of communicating with guerrillas. This confusion over who was responsible for the depredations caused by home rebels resulted in Taylor agreeing to a truce with the home guard in Hardinsburg to protect the town from Davidson's gang.[50] Despite Taylor's desire to prove his official status as a regular combatant, his critics had made a salient point. Whether he intended to or not, Taylor's presence so far behind Union lines disrupted the security of border communities and encouraged retribution by home rebels and lawless bands of outlaws, which could operate freely while Union troops pursued Taylor's force.

In the bluegrass region, one of the centers of Unionist support and Federal activity in Kentucky, guerrillas operated with little resistance and concentrated on eliminating opposition and generally terrorizing citizens. Former Kentucky governor James Robinson had returned to Georgetown after leaving office in 1863, but there was no peace for the conservative Unionist in Scott County. He wrote to Bramlette in August 1864 requesting that a company be raised because the town was being threatened by guerrillas.[51] These irregulars were most likely part of the group that captured and hanged Gabriel Innis the previous month. Innis was a former soldier in the Third Kentucky Cavalry and a lieutenant in the Thirty-Sixth Regiment Kentucky Enrolled Militia, targeted probably because he was a "good and true Union man" and had just been discharged from Federal service. Colonel Edgar Keenon, in command of twenty mounted militia from the

Thirty-Sixth Regiment, went in pursuit and tracked the killers to the northern edge of Franklin County, where the hilly terrain prevented the capture of the culprits.[52] Lieutenant Valentine Grebenstein, in command of a detachment of the Sixteenth Illinois Cavalry, also pursued this group of guerrillas, estimated at about fifty men, prowling the countryside around Georgetown and reportedly having killed a local Unionist. A later attempt to track down these outlaws resulted in disaster in neighboring Owen County as the group broke into smaller gangs of five to ten men, then waited in ambush for the cavalry, killing five of the troopers in the chaotic fray.[53] The prevalence of guerrilla activity so close to Kentucky's capital indicates that these were home rebels, men who knew their Unionist neighbors and the area they operated in. Their goal was not to support Confederate military efforts but to topple already wavering support for the Lincoln administration and Federal policy.

Attacks on outspoken Unionists and discharged soldiers intensified both before and after the presidential election, demonstrating that these were political acts of retribution and focused violence. At the end of November, a band of about twenty-five guerrillas under Sam Berry and Isaiah Coulter rampaged through Springfield, plundering businesses and robbing everyone they encountered. These home rebels killed two discharged cavalrymen, Sam Green and John Foster, who had previously served under outspoken conservative Unionist colonel Frank Wolford. The brigands pulled Green out from under his bed, where he was hiding, and shot him in the head. Similar brutal treatment was served on Isaac Bateman, a Union infantryman home on furlough, who was robbed and killed. The bloodthirsty group then descended on the home of Ken Hall, an officer in the militia. Hall fought back, wounding several of his assailants, until he ran out of ammunition and was forced to surrender. The guerrillas shot Hall seven times as his wife and child clung to him, pleading for mercy. The brigands then declared that they would kill anyone who had served in the Union army. This group was like many other small bands of home rebels who operated throughout several adjacent counties and were known to stay near Bloomfield. Their intent was the same as the group operating near Georgetown. Killing discharged Union soldiers or men active in the enrolled militia would eliminate opposition and send a sobering message to those who intended to challenge the irregulars' influence in that area.[54]

Guerrilla violence during the last winter of the war devolved into a small-scale civil war centered on political divisions and local power as opposed to military campaigns and Confederate objectives. Union men clearly understood what was at stake and reacted quickly to the threat of partisan fighters. Several Unionists in Harrodsburg wrote to Daniel Lindsey in December, warning, "Coulter's gang have sworn they will burn our town, we are in danger of life and limb." These citizens requested weapons and ammunition to arm seventy-one men who were in state service and would protect Harrodsburg. They desperately proclaimed that "*these gangs* are the enemies of all mankind—have no principles, fight for no cause and they ought to be exterminated."[55] Along Kentucky's southern border, Unionists under Edward Young squared off against the Crabtree Gang, killing three members. Young had banded together fifteen citizens acting on their own, though Unionists hoped to raise a company of fifty men if the state could pay and supply the recruits. These citizens looked to the state government to give them the tools and authority to defend themselves, with Young noting, "if we do not get some relief in this way I do not see how we are to get along and keep any property in the South East portion of Wayne."[56] While the excited tone of these petitioners was surely meant to quickly procure the desired state financial support, in other cases Unionists were more concerned about the authority to act against these gangs and volunteered to form companies and supply their own weapons. Their concern was not so much pay or equipment but simply the ability to fight off the small bands of irregulars targeting Unionists.[57] The widespread acts of terrorism that guerrillas perpetrated against Union men during the last year of the war destabilized local politics and undermined state and Federal authority. The result was a lawless environment of retribution and punishment, which caused even Unionists to embrace acts of terror and intimidation.

Requests for help from the state military establishment peaked after the presidential election, demonstrating both the political nature of the contest and the violent effort of home rebels to punish any "Lincolnites" left in Kentucky. Unconditional Unionists also stepped up their retaliation against real and perceived enemies in the state. The most notorious of guerrilla hunters was Captain James H. Bridgewater of Lincoln County, who had mastered nineteenth-century counterguerrilla warfare by operating in small groups throughout the countryside. Bridgewater, however, had obtained a reputation for taking property from suspected rebel sympathizers and operating outside the authority of the state government. This prompted a Mercer County citizen to write the governor in early November, concerned about two men who were attempting a raise a company based on Bridgewater's example. Joseph Buford declared that J. S. Hail and Captain Henry Burns (formerly of the Ninth Kentucky Cavalry) were "men of very bad feeling and they have many enemies in the country." Buford described them as "both strong for Lincoln" and noted that if they received commissions they would use their authority to "intimidate many from voting for McClelland [*sic*]." Buford admitted that he got along well with both men but feared that "they would only prey upon certain men they don't like and let robbers go." He added, "they are not the kind of men that should have power, as they are base tirants [*sic*]."[58]

Although General Burbridge had authorized retaliation against captured guerrillas, many state-guard officers had already taken matters into their own hands, resulting in summary executions. Unionist Captain J. J. Burrell, commanding the Thirty-Seventh Kentucky Mounted Infantry in Bloomfield, wrote D. W. Lindsey in mid-November documenting the shooting of three guerrillas earlier that month.[59] An affidavit from Nelson County sheriff James Wood and former provost marshal John A. Fennell attested to the fact that these three men were part of Sue Mundy's gang. Wood and Fennell provided detailed information about the executed, including their physical appearance. Homes Tinsdale and Harvey Standford were from Anderson County and Nelson County, respectively, but the officers identified John Parkhurst as a resident of Louisville, married with two children and "formerly of John Morgan Command." Burrell was obviously concerned about justifying his decision to execute the three men the morning after their capture, but Wood and Fennell further described the captain's operations against Mundy and Henry Magruder, including the mortal wounding of another member of the gang a week later.[60] The fighting had become quite personal, with Unionists hunting men they knew who had now turned to violence in order to exact revenge upon those who had supported the Union.

Unconditional Unionists urged greater support for state troops and more severe measures against the guerrillas and those who aided them. A state-guard officer in Louisville noted that it was becoming exceedingly difficult to mount troops to hunt guerrillas, for loyal men living in "rebel neighborhoods" feared that aiding them would expose themselves to guerrilla reprisals. The writer informed Lindsey that the only solution was "to press horses from rebels and Union men too, who would not furnish them." Even when mounted, Unionists found that rebel citizens had a network of runners who would go from farm to farm to give guerrillas ample notice to leave. The writer concluded that "some of them will have to be treated as guerrillas, before the county will be relieved of the guerrillas themselves." He added that Lieutenant Colonel George Jessee had supposedly told several individuals that "if his wife was made to leave the state, he would fill all the sink holes in the county with Union women."[61] Irregulars continued to rob and murder well into January 1865, including making continued attacks on discharged Union soldiers. George B. Cochran wrote to James Speed describing these problems and noting that returning volunteers should be mustered into state service to fight off guerrillas. Cochran was incensed that Burbridge would not allow the regiment to be formed and declared that the general "has no sense—is not fit for the part he fills and ought to be removed." Cochran added that he did not want Burbridge to learn of this comment, "for he would arrest me."[62]

By February 1865, Cochran would have no reason to fear Burbridge's wrath because Lincoln had replaced the embattled commander with Major General John M. Palmer. But Palmer's command also faced continued irregular violence. In December 1864, guerrillas killed fifteen black soldiers they took off a train outside of Frankfort, while the following month fifteen guerrillas attacked a group of black soldiers escorting a herd of cattle to Louisville, mercilessly killing thirty-five of the men. Despite the continued violence, Palmer did benefit from Bramlette's cooperation and the additional resources needed to significantly decrease partisan violence in the state.[63] But by this point the damage had already been done. Supporters of emancipation and rights for freedpeople knew better than to voice their opinions loudly. Many supporters of Union policies were now dead and long in the ground. Others had left the state to pursue peaceful lives among their neighbors north of the Ohio River. The last full year of the war was more crucial to Unionists in Kentucky than any other, and it signaled a significant defeat for their cause. With returning Confederates bolstering the conservative impulse to return to the status quo, the state would pay the price for Union victory but enjoy none of its benefits. No one individual can be held responsible, although Lincoln, Bramlette, and Burbridge all greatly influenced the course of events. But the principal actors were the home rebels, who continue to occupy the borders of historical sources. It was their desperate actions, and their willingness to take advantage of every opportunity to heap retribution on those who supported the Union government and the demise of slavery, that shaped postwar Kentucky society more than any single battle or military campaign.

NOTES

The author would like to thank Brandon Slone of the Kentucky Military History Museum for providing guidance through the state military records and James Prichard for his assistance with the manuscript collections at the Filson Historical Society and for sharing his knowledge of Kentucky guerrillas.

1. Elizabeth D. Leonard, *Lincoln's Forgotten Ally: Judge Advocate General Joseph Holt of Kentucky* (Chapel Hill: University of North Carolina Press, 2011), 157–60, 184–85; Joseph Holt to Edward M. Stanton, July 31, 1864, U.S. War Department, *War of the Rebellion,* ser. 1, 39(2):213 (hereafter cited as *O.R.*).

2. Phillips, *Civil War in the Border South,* Kindle ed., chap. 6, para. 29–33.

3. J. Michael Rhyne, "'A Blood Stained Sin': Slavery, Freedom, and Guerrilla Warfare in the Bluegrass Region of Kentucky, 1863–65," *Register of the Kentucky Historical Society* 112, no. 4 (Autumn 2014): 555.

4. Astor, *Rebels on the Border,* 152.

5. Stephen Rockenbach, "'The Weeds and the Flowers Are Closely Mixed': Allegiance, Law, and White Supremacy in Kentucky's Bluegrass Region, 1861–1865," *Register of Kentucky Historical Society* 111, no. 4 (Autumn 2013): 563–65.

6. The term "partisan violence" is used to differentiate the local and regional political motives common to smaller guerrilla bands from organized partisan rangers or other irregular operations related in some way to military campaigns or objectives. While home rebels are still subsumed under the definition of "guerrillas," their techniques and motives are distinct from irregular forces who harassed Union forces and supply lines. Home rebels targeted those with political authority or strong Unionist connections, which made this brand of guerrilla more difficult for Federal authorities to track and apprehend. Anonymous to Gen. Burbridge, June 21, 1864, RG 393, Records of the U.S. Army Continental Commands, 1821–1920, Department of Kentucky 1862–69, Pt. 1, Letters Received, Box 4, National Archives and Records Administration, Washington, D.C. (hereafter NARA).

7. Abraham Lincoln, "Proclamation 108—Amnesty and Reconstruction," Dec. 8, 1863, Gerhard Peters and John T. Woolley, The American Presidency Project, http://www.presidency.ucsb.edu/ws/?pid=69987.

8. Dennison to Lincoln, Dec. 10, 1863, Abraham Lincoln Papers at the Library of Congress, Manuscript Division American Memory Project, 2000–2002, http://memory.loc.gov/ammem/alhtml/malhome.html, accessed Jan. 15, 2015 (hereafter Abraham Lincoln Papers).

9. Russel A. Algers to John G. Nicolay, Feb. 1864, ibid.; R. T. Fulton to Abraham Lincoln, Jan. 21, 1864, ibid.

10. Proclamation about Amnesty, Mar. 26, 1864, ibid.

11. Harris, *Lincoln and the Border States,* 338–39.

12. Bland Ballard to Abraham Lincoln, Jun 11, 1864, Abraham Lincoln Papers.

13. Henderson to Blakely, June 18, 1864, ibid.

14. W. T. Sherman to Gen. Burbridge, June 21, 1864, *O.R.,* ser. 1, 39(2):135–36.

15. Leonard, *Lincoln's Forgotten Ally,* 184–87; Joseph Holt to Edward M. Stanton, *O.R.,* ser.1, 39(2):213–14.

16. Joseph Holt to Edward M. Stanton, *O.R.,* ser.1, 39(2):213–14.

17. Harris, *Lincoln and the Border States,* 235, 241; Phillips, *Civil War in the Border South,* Kindle ed., chap. 6, para. 13–16; Rhyne, "Blood Stained Sin," 553–62. Phillips points out that Federal impressment of black laborers, many of them "contrabands" or free men under the Emancipation Proclamation, had laid the precedent for black military participation and signaled the death of slavery in the state. Rhyne uses a postwar speech in 1867 to illustrate Bramlette's commitment to white supremacy in the state.

18. James M. Prichard, *Embattled Capital: Frankfort, Kentucky, in the Civil War,* (Frankfort: Heritage, 2014), 124–29, 130.

19. McKnight, *Contested Borderland,* 200–201.

20. Pritchard, *Embattled Capital,* 154–55; Capt. George Hamilton to Capt. J. E. Merritt, July 27, 1864, *O.R.,* ser. 1, 39(2):207; General Orders No. 59, July 16, 1864, ibid., 174; J. Bates Dickson to Brig. Gen. N. C. McLean, Nov. 2, 1864, ibid., 612. That same month, Union troops executed four guerrillas in response to the killing of two black men near Bardstown, and another four were put to death in Midway for the death of a white Unionist there.

21. Joseph Holt to Edward M. Stanton, *O.R.* ser.1, 39(2):213–14; RG 393, Pt. 1, Department of Kentucky, 1862–69, Provost Marshal, Oaths of Allegiance 1864–65, NARA.

22. "Reports from Kentucky," *Boston Herald,* Apr. 11, 1864, 4; "News from Below—A Special Dispatch from Cairo to the *St. Louis Republican,*" *New Albany Daily Ledger,* Aug. 19, 1864, 2.

23. H. H. Parker to Gov. Bramlette, Guerrilla Letters, Military History Museum, Kentucky Department of Military Affairs, Frankfort (hereafter MHM). This letter was answered by John Boyle, adjutant general of Kentucky, who responded that no new companies were being organized but added that Parker could apply to an existing company in order to enter service. Letter Book No. 2, 1864, MHM, 198. Parker was most likely serving as a private in the 2nd Kentucky Cavalry (C.S.) when he obtained his experience with raiding parties.

24. H. Faris to Gov. Bramlette, Apr. 24, 1864, Guerrilla Letters, MHM.

25. Ibid.

26. James B. Martin, "Black Flag over the Bluegrass: Guerrilla Warfare in Kentucky, 1862–65," *Register of the Kentucky Historical Society* 86, no. 4 (Autumn 1988): 359–61; Mackey, *Uncivil War,* 7–8.

27. Aloma Williams Dew, "'Between the Hawk and the Buzzard': Owensboro during the Civil War," *Register of the Kentucky Historical Society* 77, no. 1 (Winter 1979): 7–9.

28. Richard Massey to Gov. Bramlette, June 22, 1864, Guerrilla Letters, MHM.

29. John Reynolds to Gov. Bramlette, Aug. 17, 1864, ibid.

30. S. N. Starling to John Mason Brown, June 1, 1864, ibid.

31. McKnight, *Confederate Outlaw,* 123–27.

32. Richard Jenkins to James Speed, Apr. 1864, Speed Family Papers, A/S742/7, Filson Historical Society, Louisville, Ky. (hereafter FHS).

33. Lizzie Schreiber Diary, Stith-Moreman Papers, ibid.

34. Mackey, *Uncivil War,* 5–7. Mackey indicates that irregular cavalry operations were meant to bolster conventional campaigns, not incite insurrection behind lines. But Brig. Gen. John Hunt Morgan's cavalry served as a sort of incubator for guerrilla activity, adopting violent and destructive tactics when needed and training a cadre of cavalrymen to act as small-scale raiders. For interpretations that identify the connections between Morgan's cavalry and guerrilla warfare, see Astor, *Rebels on the Border,* 113–14; and Sutherland, *Savage Conflict,* 76–78.

35. John Hunt Morgan handbill, 1863, Kentucky Historical Society Library, Frankfort.

36. During both raids, Morgan's men took personal property, robbed banks and private citizens, and destroyed private property, much in keeping with the activities of many smaller guerrilla bands. Sutherland, *Savage Conflict,* 220–21; Stephen Rockenbach, "'This Just Hope of Ultimate Payment': The Indiana Morgan's Raid Claims Commission and Harrison County, Indiana, 1863–1887," *Indiana Magazine of History* 109, no. 1 (Mar. 2013): 45–60.

37. McKnight, *Confederate Outlaw,* 81, 87, 118, 123, 144–45.

38. *New Albany Daily Ledger,* July 20, 1863, 2.

39. "Guerrillas in Kentucky," *Daily Picayune,* Aug. 10, 1864, 4.

40. Schreiber Diary, Stith-Moreman Papers, FHS, 17.

41. "Guerrillas at Brandenburg," *New Albany Daily Ledger,* Oct. 18, 1864, 2.

42. "Refugees and Deserters," ibid., Aug. 19, 1864, 2; "Emigration from Kentucky," ibid., Sept. 28, 1864, 2.

43. Affidavits relating to the cases of James J. Mitchell and John A. McMahon, Feb. 11, 1865, RG 393, Pt. 1, Department of Kentucky, 1862–69, Provost Marshal, Correspondence, Affidavits, and Oaths Relating to Civilians Charged with Illegal or Disloyal Acts, Box 2, NARA.

44. Earl Saulman, "Blacks in Harrison County, Indiana: A History," unpublished manuscript, Corydon Genealogy and Local History Library, Corydon, Ind., 83, 92–93; Marion Lucas, *A History of Blacks in Kentucky* (Frankfort: Kentucky Historical Society, 1992), 183, 195.

45. Sutherland, *Savage Conflict,* 226–27.

46. "Guerrillas in Meade County," *New Albany Daily Ledger,* Aug. 9, 1864, 2.

47. Ibid., Aug. 19, 1864, 2; "Guerrillas Visit the Taracon," ibid., July 11, 1864, 2.

48. Schreiber Diary, Stith-Moreman Papers, FHS, 18.

49. "Guerrillas on the Ohio River," *New Albany Daily Ledger,* Dec. 21, 1864, 2.

50. Affidavits in the case of John Allen, Jan.3, 1865, Record Group 393, pt. 1 Department of Kentucky, 1862–69 Provost Marshal Correspondence, Affidavits, and Oaths Relating to Civilians Charged with Illegal or Disloyal Acts, Box 2; "From Kentucky," *Boston Herald,* Jan. 13, 1865, 4. Davidson's band was also responsible for burning the courthouse in Owensboro in January 1865. Union soldiers, including members of the U.S. Colored Troops, had garrisoned the building in 1864, which explains the guerrilla's actions. Dew, "Between the Hawk and the Buzzard," 10.

51. James Robinson to Thomas Bramlette, Aug. 8, 1864, Guerrilla Letters, MHM.

52. Report of Edgar Keenon, Mar. 14, 1865, 36th Regiment Kentucky Enrolled Militia records, MHM; and "List of Men Who Pursued Guerrillas," July 1864, ibid.

53. Lt. Valentine Grebenstein to Headquarters, July 24, 1864, RG 393, Sec. 1, Pt. 1, Department

of Kentucky, 1862–69, Provost Marshal, Box 4, NARA; Col. E. Ball to Major General Burbridge, July 28, 1864, *O.R.* ser. 1, 39(2):209; J. Bates Dickson to Brig. Gen. N. C. McLean, Nov. 2, 1864, ibid., 612.

54. Richard Brown to Gov. Bramlette, Nov. 29, 1864, Guerrilla Letters, MHM.

55. Nat Gaither et al. to Daniel Lindsey, Dec. 7, 1864, ibid.

56. "LSS" to E. Van Winkle, Nov. 1864, ibid.

57. James C. Culton, formerly of the 7th Kentucky, offered to organize the "Mountain Scouts" from discharged members of the regiment to protect Unionists targeted by guerrillas. James C. Culton to D. W. Lindsey, Nov. 22, 1864, ibid. James Wilson requested permission to recruit a company from discharged soldiers, who would furnish their own equipment, including Henry rifles. James Wilson to Gov. Bramlette, Nov. 8, 1864, ibid.

58. Jos. Buford to Bramlette, Nov. 4, 1864, ibid.

59. J. J. Burrell to D. W. Lindsey, Nov. 17, 1864, ibid.

60. James Wood and John A. Fennell to J. J. Burrell, Nov. 17, 1864, ibid.

61. Dupuy to D. W. Lindsey, Dec. 2, 1864, ibid.

62. G. B. Cochran to James Speed, Jan. 23, 1865, Speed Family Papers, A/S742f, 7, FHS.

63. Phillips, *Civil War in the Border South,* Kindle ed., chap. 6, para. 33; Harris, *Lincoln and the Border States,* 266.

"WHO IS 'TINKER DAVE' BEATY?"

Hunting Guerrilla Social Networks

AARON ASTOR

In a desperate March 1863 missive to Brigadier General James Garfield, Brigadier General George Crook complained of his command's inability to fight the numerous bands of Confederate cavalry attacking his supply lines along the upper Cumberland River. "I cannot entrap them in any possible way, for they have their spies and scouts all over this country, and I can make no movement without their being apprised of it before I can get to them with my infantry, and then, if it is not to their advantage to fight me, they get out of the way."[1] Rebel forces along the Kentucky-Tennessee state line continually attacked and seized boats stocked with corn and wheat, leading Crook to wonder how long he could remain secure at his post near Carthage, Tennessee. Finally, in exasperation and almost as a non sequitur, Crook asked Garfield, "Who is 'Tinker Dave' Beaty?"

Indeed, who was Tinker Dave Beaty? In the Upper Cumberland Plateau area of Tennessee, Beaty had already established a reputation by the spring of 1863 as one of the most ruthless and wily guerrillas for the Union side. His year-long battle with Confederate guerrilla leaders such as Champ Ferguson, Oliver Hamilton, Scott Bledsoe, and George Carter as well as his continued armed resistance against Southern military control around Fentress County made him a legendary figure. But what exactly did Crook mean in asking this question, especially one tucked in an otherwise hopeless communiqué? Did the general, appointed only recently to the region, not know who Beaty was? Or did he just not know how he could take advantage of Beaty's formidable network of guerrillas?

To conventional Civil War commanders tasked with the mundane responsibility of guarding civilians and military supplies in occupied areas, irregular fighters seemed to appear out of nowhere. After wreaking destruction on property and on people deemed "collaborators," they seemed to disappear into the landscape. Within a population of hostile civilians, guerrillas found sustenance, shelter, and moral support. But to hunt these men, commanders were forced to differentiate not only between loyal and disloyal persons but also between active guerrillas (and thus unlawful combatants, to use the modern term) and civilians sympathetic to, though not actively supporting, these irregulars.

In recent years, historians have come to appreciate the decisive role guerrillas played in the American Civil War.[2] Charismatic, desperate, and iconic figures like Ferguson, William Clarke Quantrill, Bloody Bill Anderson, Jesse James, and John S. Mosby have come in for significant reevaluation by scholars. Whether in full biographical portrayal or merely as symbols of unconquerable and ruthless resistance, guerrillas have captured the attention of military and cultural historians alike. We have developed more sophisticated understandings of the motivations of such men as well as irregular warfare itself, its strategic deployment, its link with politics, and its moral and legal implications.

Yet most studies of guerrillas have focused on the exploits and values of their leaders or on the experiences of specific kinds of violence. The charismatic and iconic guerrilla leaders captivated the public imagination and earned obsessive and hyperpersonalized attention from frustrated counterirregular commanders. Atrocities committed against helpless civilians also garnered significant attention from contemporaries and from recent historians. Less well known are the thousands of men who followed these guerrilla leaders. Who were the people who ran with Quantrill, Ferguson, and Beaty? What were their motivations? How did they come to join a guerrilla band, and what happened when their leader was captured or killed? Military commanders at the time certainly understood the threat posed by these largely faceless irregular fighters. The persistence of guerrilla violence vexed commanders accustomed to fighting more hierarchical conventional forces. Guerrilla units, by contrast, were typically cellular in structure, meaning that decapitation of a unit's leadership was not likely to staunch the problem of insurgency generally. Only a strategy targeting the rank and file among irregulars would be effective. And that would take many frustrating years of failure, gruesome violence, and the patient cataloging of names and relationships of suspected bushwhackers and their sympathizers.

It has proved just as vexing for modern historians as for counterirregular militias to identify and understand the extent of guerrilla participation. For several reasons, locating and identifying the membership in the network of men and women who supported guerrilla leaders is a difficult task. These commanders maintained inconsistent records of membership, especially as the legal status of, and bureaucratic requirements placed upon, irregulars changed throughout the war. With official records only partially sufficient, the task of identifying guerrilla warriors has fallen to local historians and genealogists, who record and collect stories passed down through generations in specific communities. Invaluable as these sources are, they are rarely deployed systematically so as to "connect the dots" among guerrillas.

The problem of locating and identifying the guerrilla rank and file poses a critical challenge for historians in the interpretation of irregular warfare as a phenomenon. Guerrillas, as we know, were not isolated bandits and almost never acted alone. Rather, they operated relationally, developing bonds of trust, lists of enemies, reliable lines of supply, routes of escape, houses of refuge, and structures of command based on informal but meaningful ties among members and between themselves and the wider community. These relationships typically built on existing prewar social networks that established certain persons as respected community leaders and drew certain members of the community more tightly together than others. To uncover these guerrilla networks, historians need to dig deeply into the nature of social relationships in areas where irregular warfare took place. By doing so, they can identify the priorities governing social relations of the community in peacetime and often the motivations of community members in wartime.

The term "social network" has a distinctly twenty-first-century ring to it, with a popular movie depicting the development of the social-media platform Facebook even titled *The Social Network*.[3] But the concept is deeply rooted in sociology and applies just as well to relations among rural nineteenth-century Southerners as it does to electronic connections between modern social-media users. The social-network model originated as a way to describe "an intertwined mesh of connections through which individuals were bound together."[4] Modern sociologists define this as a "structure of relationships linking social actors" wherein the individuals and the relationships between them are equally important.[5] Social-network analysts "reason from whole to part; from structure to relation to individual; from behavior to attitude."[6]

Classical German sociologists deployed the metaphor of interlocking textile threads to illustrate complex webs of social relations. Later scholars grounded the term in the fields of social psychology and anthropology, demonstrating the importance of "structures of friendship choices" and "informal interaction." Many constructed elaborate "sociograms" that mapped social relations in a particular community and graphically revealed the influence of certain influential leaders within the network. Sociologists and anthropologists found the social network to be particularly useful in the study of kinship relations and their connections with patterns of living and working.[7] Such analysis emerged by the 1970s as a useful way to depict not only the extent of social relations but also the quality, quantity, complexity, and intensity of them. It became apparent in the literature that common experiences and values, the structures of economy, kinship and governance, and qualities of individual leaders all influenced the shape and effectiveness of social networks.[8]

The modern U.S. military already applies social-network analysis to the study of guerrilla warfare. The 2006 U.S. Army Counterinsurgency Field Manual (formally FM 3-24), based in large part on the experience of the Iraq War, relies heavily on such analysis to develop a comprehensive response to insurgents of various stripes. An appendix to the field manual specifically addresses the elements of social networks, including natural topography, civilian infrastructure, civilian organizations, ideological and religious makeup, ethnic and kinship relations, and shared responses to external events.[9] Network analysis reveals the "form, efficiency and cohesion" of specific guerrilla organizations and, just as importantly, the connections between and among guerrilla outfits. It also assesses the density of guerrilla networks, especially as they coalesce and fragment depending on various circumstances of war and the social influence of certain leaders. The purpose of the field manual is to inform counterinsurgency policy and practice in today's U.S. military.[10] But its use of social-network analysis, "focusing on the preexisting relationships and ties that bind together such groups," can be just as helpful for historians studying guerrilla activity during the Civil War.[11]

As historians have come to understand, the Civil War included rampant guerrilla conflict on both sides, which could be found anywhere that conventional military activity took place. But irregular activity was strongest in places characterized by divided loyalties, lengthy military occupation, and terrain conducive to hit-and-run tactics. A social-network analysis uncovers the interconnected webs of partisan political allegiance, gendered kinship patterns, neighborhood and settlement, class and trade relations, and interactions between slaves, slaveholders, and nonslaveholding whites. The analysis can then be mapped onto the physical landscape in order to present a picture of the mental geography of civilians and guerrillas alike as they warily eyed one another.

Difficult as it can be to capture the dynamics of nineteenth-century social networks, new digital research tools make such an analysis much more fruitful. What follows is a guide for historians exploring guerrilla social networks, including some useful digital genealogical and historical programs. It must be stressed that while new digital tools are developed and made accessible every year, what matters most are the historical questions animating the researcher. Some technologically sophisticated programs might prove only marginally useful, while other, more clunky databases and map programs may nevertheless be especially helpful. Following the discussion of the research tools is an application of them to the study of one particular guerrilla band: Beaty's Independent Scouts.

The first place for historians of irregular warfare to explore is the physical and social geography of guerrilla-heavy areas. The Civil War was fought over highly variegated terrain, including rugged mountains, open prairies, rolling hills, swamps, sandy beaches, and dense forests. Guerrillas exploited local terrain better than other fighters. They typically grew up in the environment in which they fought and invariably understood local geomorphic peculiarities better than conventional commanders tasked with suppressing irregular activity. It behooves historians to get as strong a grasp of local geography as possible.[12]

In addition to the physical geography, historians should also engage as fully as possible with the social geography of people who lived in relatively circumscribed communities and who maintained an intimate understanding of the local landscape, often with very little knowledge of what lay beyond their neighborhood.[13] To be sure, people who remained close to home most of their lives were never exactly isolated. How they gathered and circulated information about the outside world is instructive. They obtained their outside news from important mediators like merchants, itinerant ministers, clerks and professionals, politicians, rural newspapers, commercial-oriented farmers and stock raisers, traveling laborers, and in many cases slaves.[14] To assess the mental geography of nineteenth-century Southerners, one must do more than simply examine maps.[15] One must also look at the trade connections, migration patterns, political boundaries, and other sinews of rural American life. Guerrillas operated on physical geography imperfectly replicable on maps.[16] Nevertheless, they knew of hideouts, safe and hostile zones, prominent citizens of different loyalties, navigable water routes, supply sources from friendly farmers, supply lines through forested trails, and likely counterirregular tactics thanks to their mental geography of their areas of operation.[17]

Still, maps are essential to the historian, and the more data layers that can be assessed the richer the analysis will be of the physical and mental geography of guerrilla war. Fortunately, most nineteenth-century maps have been digitized in some form and are easily available through public library, historical society, or genealogical society websites. These colorful charts typically include small population settlements, turnpikes, and other important physical features. Beyond these are available neighborhood, farm, or plat maps that illustrate the locations of specific farms and homes. Unfortunately, many states did not produce plat maps until the late nineteenth century, thus requiring the scholar to work backward from data in the 1880s and cross-reference family names with the census to ensure that the families did not arrive after the Civil War.

Military-campaign maps are also essential, especially as guerrilla operations often supported conventional activity. The invaluable *Atlas Accompanying the Original Records of the War of the Rebellion* includes several maps drawn by commanders with intimate, though often imperfect, knowledge of local terrain. A map of the gaps of Cumberland Mountain, for example, includes brief descriptions of the thoroughfares over the mountain. The atlas also contains larger operational maps that can be of great use for studying guerrillas operating over larger swaths of territory. For example, a map of the Southwest showing where Quantrill's Missouri guerrillas wintered in Texas says much about the thoroughfares through western Arkansas and Indian Territory, where rival guerrillas operated.[18] At the very least, these larger maps underscore the importance of food supply to sustain mounted irregular operations.

Historic U.S. Geologic Survey maps dating from the late nineteenth century are accessible as well and can be paired with satellite imagery and terrain maps readily available on any search engine.[19] The historic USGS maps are especially helpful because they include place names that have long disappeared as well as landscape features (such as rivers before construction of the Tennessee Valley Authority dams) more representative of mid-nineteenth-century America. In addition to these are Geographic Information Systems (GIS) programs that allow users to add data layers, superimpose historic maps on modern base maps, and plot socioeconomic data geographically. Some states, including Tennessee, have developed their own Civil War GIS programs that link to a wide range of historic and contemporary sources.[20] Though many guerrilla actions were too small-scale to show up on the Tennessee GIS program, there are enough other data to make a spatial analysis of guerrilla networks possible.

After uncovering the geography of warfare, the next challenge is to identify the participants. Shadowy as guerrilla bands were, they typically left some evidence of their membership in military and court records. Many groups received some kind of official recognition by either the Union or Confederate army at some point during the war. Whether as part of a Confederate partisan ranger unit, a guerrilla-oriented cavalry regiment, a state-militia organization, or a locally formed home guard, many outfits and their members were listed in muster rolls, adjutant general reports, or provost marshal records. The challenge in locating names of irregulars is the ever-changing "roster" of men throughout the course of the war. Many units filled out muster rolls early in the war but never bothered to update the lists, especially as members came to realize how capture of such information could lead to the deaths of dozens of close comrades in arms. Thus, initial muster rolls must be supplemented with other data gathered later in the war or even after the war ended.

Genealogists have done much of the hard work in uncovering lists of names. But digitized military search tools like Fold3.com, civilwardata.com, and Ancestry.com have made it possible to search entire guerrilla companies.[21] Among the many states that have generated their own roster lists is Tennessee. One compilation created during the Civil War centennial, *Tennesseans in the Civil War: A Military History of Confederate and Union Units with Available Rosters of Personnel,* is particularly thorough, especially as it has been mostly digitized.[22] Many guerrilla units began the war as official cavalry units, and so traditional Civil War service records accessible at Fold3.com and civilwardata.com can be a great resource, even in cases where guerrilla bands subsequently broke off from the official units. It is often essential to search these units at the company level since prewar social relations typically influenced the formation of the hundred-men companies; regiments, by contrast, were often cobbled together at recruitment camps and reveal less about social networks.

Beyond the easy pickings of national record sets are the local record databases. In many cases these must be obtained in manuscript form from county courthouses and state archives. But many of these local documents have been collected by state and regional archives and digitized for general use. One of the best examples of a local genealogical database, and the source for much of the research into Tinker Dave Beaty's command, is Bruce York's Fentress

County, Tennessee, database, which includes names, relationships, collected family stories, and census data for more than 360,000 people who lived in Fentress, Pickett, and Overton Counties as well as surrounding counties in Kentucky from the eighteenth century to the present. Housed on the Ancestry .com platform, York's database allows historians to generate family trees and follow kinship lines throughout the entire region. It is an extraordinary resource based on decades of genealogical research by York and many other current and former residents of the Upper Cumberland. But it is far from the only comprehensive genealogical database available, especially as Ancestry. com has made the collection of such data a much easier task than in the past.

Specific military records also shine a light on guerrilla activity and are invaluable in any research. Perhaps the most useful database for historians of Missouri's guerrilla war is the Provost Marshal General (PMG) file set. PMG files have long been microfilmed, including those contained in the collections "Relating to Two or More Civilians" and "Individual Civilians."[23] Since the early twenty-first century, many state records have been digitized and indexed in searchable form by the State Historical Society of Missouri. Since Michael Fellman first used these records for his book *Inside War,* historians have flocked to the PMG records for detailed descriptions of guerrilla activities, attitudes, and membership.[24]

For an example of how the PMG database can help map loyalties and guerrilla activity, a search in the Missouri index on the front page for Cooper County and the term "bushwhacker" reveals, among other results, a "list of disloyal citizens assessed for damages incurred" generated by two local Unionist women, Johanah Diehl and Mary Krohn.[25] The search result includes a summary of the file and a listing of the date, reel, frame, and file number of the actual document. A link on the main page to "Provost Marshal/USCT PDF images" takes the researcher to digitized microfilm rolls that can be accessed in full. Following the reel, frame, and file number of the example above, one finds the aforementioned list of names from Cooper County along with financial assessments for each man. What could the historian do with this information, especially one operating remotely and depending on other digitally available sources? Correlating these names with census figures, military rolls, other PMG files, and local genealogical data as well as digitally accessible plat maps could give the researcher a picture of the social network of Confederate loyalty in part of Cooper County, Missouri. Even more enterprising historians like Mark Geiger have found that the financial transactions of some of these "leading disloyal" citizens reveal a major financial fraud that would ultimately collapse and destroy the fortunes of many of these Confederate sympathizers—more effectively than did Unionist assessments.[26]

Postwar court testimony and personal recollections also help scholars map out guerrilla social networks. One must use caution here, for survivors may have incorrectly identified certain people as guerrillas in order to avoid disfranchisement or criminal proceedings. Still, testimony such as at the trial of Champ Ferguson offers the historian a rich source of names and, just as important, reflections on the workings of guerrilla social networks.[27] One sees in Ferguson's testimony and that of his Unionist enemies the mentality, motives, and social relations among the people of the Upper Cumberland throughout the war. It also becomes apparent in this testimony how much Ferguson's ruthless pursuit of anyone he deemed a potential threat would help catalyze and intensify what he called a "miscellaneous war" of revenge and brutality.[28]

With names and places in hand, the researcher can then turn to the social-history trove that is the U.S. manuscript census. In fact, the digitization of the 1860 Census has done more to make a social history of the Civil War possible than any other technological archival project. Fortunately, many genealogists have done the additional legwork of transcribing in table format the manuscript records, though the transcriptions vary in quality and depth. Census data include vital information about class, kinship, occupation, and location and are thus critical to uncovering guerrilla social networks. Census takers typically traveled through each district and recorded the names of residents in order. It is not uncommon to see multiple households with the same surname appearing consecutively since siblings often inherited portions of their parents' farms. Quite often people listed in households as "common laborers" are actually kin of some sort, having found employment on an uncle's farm. In urban districts similar patterns appear, with successive households often including a common surname, though occupations were more diversified.

An important variable in assessing guerrilla social identification is class. Generally speaking, historians have identified wealthy sons of slaveholders in Federally occupied territory as most likely to join Confederate guerrilla bands. At the same time, nonslaveholders in isolated mountain redoubts were most likely to form or join Unionist guerrilla outfits. But the presence of large numbers of wealthy, slaveholding Unionist guerrillas like Robert Byrd of Roane

County, Tennessee, and nonslaveholding Confederate leaders like George Carter, a blacksmith in Van Buren County, Tennessee, complicates any simple class-based analysis.[29]

The manuscript census lists "real wealth" and "personal wealth" for each household. With the additional use of the separate slave census and agricultural census, historians can determine whether the disparate wealth levels are a product of slave ownership or some other factor. Irregular bands certainly did not draw entirely from single economic classes, though certain groups were more likely to draw from sons of slaveholders or from town professionals than others. Also, in some counties small numbers of households owned a disproportionate share of the county's wealth, while in others the wealth was relatively evenly distributed. In Morgan County, Tennessee, home to a sizable German immigrant community at Wartburg, only 4 percent of households owned slaves; those heads of household possessed 21 percent of the county's real-estate wealth and 36 percent of its personal wealth. By contrast, in White County, 17 percent of households owned slaves, with slaveholders possessing 53 percent of the real-estate wealth and 71 percent of the personal wealth.[30] It stands to reason that ownership of slaves, both for their productive capacity and for their chattel property value, affected the social networks of influence. Put simply, slaveholders had comparatively more power in White County than they did in Morgan County. When it came time to weigh the threats to slavery against threats to the Union, relative distribution of wealth mattered a great deal. It is no coincidence that White County became a Confederate hotbed and Morgan County a Unionist redoubt, even though the two counties are close to each other and are topographically similar.

Beyond the census are records housed in archives and courthouses detailing social, kin, and political relationships. Deeds and land grants record transactions that reflect and often solidify antebellum social networks; legal and criminal transcripts may reveal preexisting disputes that tear asunder these social networks (such as with Champ Ferguson). Letters and diaries capture the richness and intensity of social relationships, though they are typically found only among elite members of society. Local newspapers shed light on political connections and partisan traditions while highlighting growing market relations outside the immediate area. As with national census and military records, these local records are increasingly digitized, allowing historians to make deeper forays into the sources and connect the nodes of social networks more efficiently. The essential Chronicling America project from the Library of Congress has digitized more than 100,000 pages from nineteenth-century newspapers of all sizes.[31] This tool is more useful in the study of some communities than others, but it is a very helpful resource in identifying commercial ties and political discourses.

With names, chronology, geography, and testimonies in hand, the historian can now perform the most important task: connecting the dots and interpreting the social world of the Civil War guerrilla. It is helpful, however, to think of guerrillas as operating in multiple social networks at once, many of them long predating the conflict. The Civil War effectively destroyed existing mechanisms for preserving order, causing civilians in many areas to activate new social networks that served the immediate purpose of maintaining security and defending ideological values under attack. Irregular bands thus built off previously existing networks just as they tore the more fragile old bonds apart. As war dragged on and counterirregular operations forced guerrilla bands to scatter in the face of enemy strength, the men often turned on one another, forming newer bonds based on trust and mutual self-protection.

What follows, then, is an example of a social-network analysis of a particular guerrilla band operating in the Upper Cumberland region of Tennessee. An examination of Fentress County, Tennessee, on the Upper Cumberland Plateau and along the Kentucky border, tells us how guerrilla social networks functioned. Following the methodology laid out above, this short study explores the makeup of the Upper Cumberland's guerrilla social networks, with an emphasis on one particular unit, Unionist guerrilla Tinker Dave Beaty's Independent Scouts.

An act of Congress in July 1870 generated a special postwar muster roll for what it called Beaty's Company, Independent Scouts, Tennessee. Though Beaty's men were never officially enrolled in the U.S. Army and were never officially paid until years after the war's completion, the congressional act "recognized" the organization as "engaged in suppressing the recent rebellion" so that "members thereof, on making proof of actual service, are declared to be entitled to same pay, pensions, as though they had been regularly mustered into the service of the United States as cavalry."[32] The muster roll was filed with the Fentress County Court in compliance with this act, though portions of the list were apparently destroyed in a later courthouse fire. David Crockett "Tinker Dave" Beaty verified the list's accuracy himself in 1870.[33] The centennial *Ten-*

nesseans in the Civil War recompiled the remainder of the company's muster list based on Civil War service records housed in the National Archives. Recent local histories include fairly standard and thorough lists of Beaty's scouts, with between ninety and one hundred men verified as members.[34]

According to Beaty's testimony at the trial of Champ Ferguson, his unit was formed shortly after the Battle of Mill Springs in January 1862. It fought off repeated attacks from Confederate cavalrymen operating under the leadership of Scott Bledsoe, John Hughs, Ferguson, and others. When told by Bledsoe's men that he must choose sides in early 1862, Beaty threw in his full lot with the Union and began organizing his company. In his testimony he admitted to killing "25 or more" men throughout the war, with that number likely a gross understatement.[35] Though Beaty's command was not the only Unionist guerrilla company drawn from Fentress County—Rufus Dowdy and Mitchell Millsaps each raised official, though often guerrilla-oriented, Union companies—Beaty's Independent Scouts would be best known in the Upper Cumberland for its fierce resistance to Ferguson.

A close examination of the ninety-four members of Tinker Dave's guerrilla band listed below shows an interconnected web of kinship that straddled the boundary between Fentress and Overton Counties but was concentrated in a few communities. Nearly every member was related to somebody else in the company or to the Beaty family. It is hardly surprising in such a close-knit, rural, and relatively isolated community like western Fentress County that a guerrilla unit would include such kin-based cohesiveness. But the extensiveness of this family network and its intensity around certain nodes are remarkable. In many cases, desire for retribution against Ferguson's band led men to join Tinker Dave, while in other cases simple geographic proximity and close kinship with the Beaty clan were incentive enough. A closer analysis of the social network that supported Beaty's Independent Scouts reveals varying levels of intensity and individual mini-networks that operated collectively.

A social-network analysis must examine characteristics of each node in the network—individual actors who make decisions based on values and circumstances—and on the links between nodes. In the Upper Cumberland Plateau, some elements of the social structure are more important than others to instigate military activity within the social network. The first consideration is geographic. Fentress County lies primarily atop the Cumberland Plateau, an elevated tableland of sandstone caprock dissected by numerous creeks and

Beaty's Independent Scouts—David C. "Tinker Dave" Beaty, Captain

Allred, Thomas	Hogue, Solomon	Smith, William C.
Beaty, Claiborne	Hoover, Madison	Sproul, John
Beaty, Fleming	Huff, John	Stephens, Burton
Beaty, George	Huff, Mac	Stephens, David
Beaty, Harvey	Johnson, Bill	Stephens, George
Beaty, James	Johnson, F. M.	Stephens, Isaiah
Boles, John, Sr.	King, John	Stephens, Jackson
Boles, John, Jr.	Livingston, Henry	Stephens, John, Sr.
Conatser, John	Livingston, John	Stephens, John, Jr.
Choate, Austin, Sr.	Livingston, P. T.	Stephens, Russell
Choate, Christopher, Sr.	Moody, John	Taylor, John
Choate, John	Moody, Jonathan	Taylor, Kiah
Choate, Sabe	Moody, Peter	Threet, Cullom
Choate, Thomas	Mullinix, Eli	Threet, Dean
Crabtree, William	Mullinix, John	Threet, George
Cravens, Peter	Padgett, John	Threet, James
Culver, Dow	Pile, Sherwood	Tipton, William
Culver, Tom	Piles, James	Turner, Jack
Delk, Sherwood	Ramsey, Sampson	Upchurch, Drury
Erwin, Wade H.	Reagen, Willliam	Upchurch, Henderson
Farrell, James	Reeder, Joseph	Whitehead, John
Francis, John	Riddle, Joseph	Williams, Elijah
Franklin, Tom	Roberts, George	Williams, Hardy
Frogg, Jack	Scroggins, John	Williams, Jack
Guffey, Harrison	Shilling, Harvey	Wilson, Berry
Gwinn, Martin	Shilling, James	Winningham, John, Sr.
Hatfield, Bob	Skinner, Reuben	Winningham, Seth
Hatfield, Eli	Smith, Asa	Woods, Isaac
Hatfield, Emanuel	Smith, Hijah	Wright, Silas
Hix, John	Smith, John, Sr.	York, George
Hogue, Milburn	Smith, Wash	York, Mitchell

rivers.[36] Where those creeks carved out wider hollows and coves, they left for settlers a relatively fertile zone amenable to agricultural settlement; otherwise, the terrain is extremely rugged. A few pockets in Fentress County lured farm families migrating from North Carolina, Virginia, Kentucky, and Pennsylvania to establish themselves. The Wolf River valley was perhaps the most inviting destination as its soil was richest and the river provided navigable access to markets in the Cumberland River watershed.[37]

Just as important as the pockets of fertile soil are the river-based economic links that connected these settlements with wider regional and national markets. While no Fentress County farmer was entirely self-sufficient, there are different levels of commercial engagement in evidence. Like elsewhere in antebellum America, communities along navigable transportation routes embraced commercial farming and stock raising more vigorously than did those living in relatively isolated environments. The Wolf River valley, which incorporated the neighborhood of Pall Mall, was a center of livestock raising and trading for the entire Cumberland River region of Kentucky and Tennessee; it was a major supplier of foodstuffs for Nashville downriver.

The Wolf River valley was also the area where slavery was most prevalent in the county, with the Andrew McGinnis farm at its heart. Compared to the rest of Tennessee or the South generally, slavery had a very light footprint in Fentress County, including in this fertile valley. Pleasant Miller and Andrew McGinnis owned fifteen and thirteen slaves apiece in 1860, making them the largest slaveholders in a tightly knit community of slaveholding commercial farmers and stock raisers. Pearson Miller, one of the earliest settlers in the valley, was one of the area's wealthiest men by 1860; his sons, Pleasant and James Miller, had also become prosperous farmers. McGinnis was likewise an early settler of the region and a successful farmer. His sons, Hamilton, Jarrett, and Fleming, became early officers in W. Scott Bledsoe's Confederate cavalry company, which would enroll Champ Ferguson in late 1861. Arch and Noble McGinnis, who were nephews, neighbors, and tenants of Andrew McGinnis, joined Ferguson's company during the war. Other neighbors of McGinnis, including Andrew J. Frogge, Rouse Rich, Harrison McFarland, William Frank Cummings, and Ephraim Crabtree, joined Bledsoe's Cavalry, with some riding with Ferguson throughout the war as well. McGinnis was wealthy and influential enough to host a major Confederate recruitment camp on his property, known officially as Camp McGinnis.[38]

Not everybody in Pall Mall supported Bledsoe, Ferguson, and the Confederate cause, however. In fact, some close neighbors like Mack and John Huff, William Crabtree, Emanuel Hatfield, Harrison Guffey, Sherwood Delk, Elijah and Hardy Williams, Drewry and Henderson Upchurch, and James and Sherwood Pile ended up fighting for Ferguson's archrival, Tinker Dave Beaty. How can we explain such divisions within a tightly knit geographic space? Surely all of these men knew each other quite well before the war. The Unionists of Pall Mall were not the wealthiest families in the neighborhood, but they were not exactly poor either; the Huffs and Upchurches even owned slaves. The answer is twofold: kinship and the circumstances of war.

As the guerrilla war wrought destruction and violence on the community, men vowed revenge on those who wronged their closest kin. The Manichean mind and ruthless intensity of Ferguson forced men of the region to pick sides. Neutrality was deemed suspect. If a Pall Mall boy did not support Ferguson for whatever reason, then he was an avowed enemy. And if he expected to live, he would need the protection of those capable of providing it. That would mean joining Tinker Dave Beaty. Some of the Pall Mall Beaty men were among the most militant, with Harrison Guffey naming his son born during the war General Manson Guffey (after Indiana Union general Mahlon Manson, who commanded forces in Tennessee) and another boy born after the war Tinker Guffey.[39]

A key moment in Pall Mall's Civil War was clearly Ferguson's murder of Conrad J. Pile in 1863.[40] Though Pile's brothers were divided in sentiment, his sons and sons-in-law vowed revenge. His sons James and Sherwood Pile joined Beaty and became notorious murderers in their own right during and after the war. Known locally as the Wolf River Gang, at one point they brutally killed James Rains, who lived on the McGinnis farm before the war, by slitting his throat and mutilating his body. Emanuel Hatfield, married to Conrad's daughter Elizabeth Pile, also joined Tinker Dave. Two nephews of Conrad (through his sister Susannah Pile Williams), Hardy and Elijah Williams, joined Beaty's men also. Sherwood Delk, nephew to Conrad's wife, Susannah Delk Pile, also fought with Tinker Dave's scouts. Though Beaty was not from the Wolf River valley, his force was the best organization through which these men could protect themselves and avenge Pile's death.

But what, then, should one make of the two wealthier sets of brothers, the Huffs and the Upchurches? Revenge plays an important role in both of these cases as well. Alexander Huff, father of John and Mack Huff, was murdered by Ferguson in 1862. The sons then joined Beaty's gang. A third son, Preston "Press" Huff, initially joined a different Unionist guerrilla band led by Eli Hatfield but joined Beaty later on.[41] Barely escaping Champ during the war, Press Huff was known as a terror to Confederate sympathizers in the latter months of the war, convincing many of them to leave for good; he was eventually killed a year after the war by a wartime rival. Drury and Elias Henderson Upchurch were the sons of merchant Joseph Upchurch, who had significant business and kin ties to Albany, Kentucky. Most of the Upchurch men joined Kentucky Union units at some point, making them targets for Ferguson. The direct connection between the Kentucky Upchurches and Drury and Henderson is unclear. But there were other members of their family who sided with the Confederacy, thus making the case even more complicated. The best that can be said is that the Upchurch family belonged to two overlapping social networks, each oriented toward different sides in the conflict.

Outside the mostly pro-Confederate Wolf River valley, Fentress County contained some relatively isolated pockets of tightly connected families, most of whom supported the Union cause with vigor. Settlement began in the 1810s in many of these areas, with settlers giving their names to the landscape: Skinner Mountain, Frogge Mountain, Moody Mountain, Gwinn Cove, the Obey River (named for Obediah Terrell), and communities like Winningham, Travisville, and Moodyville. These smaller settlement pockets invited migrants from North Carolina, Virginia, and Pennsylvania committed to a smaller-scale yeomanry. Between Jamestown and Livingston, county seats of Fentress and Overton Counties respectively, were communities surrounding creek bottoms along the East Fork of the Obey River, Piney Creek, Rockcastle Creek, and just over in Overton County, the West Fork of the Obey River. Poplar Cove, Buffalo Cove, Little Crab, Glenobey, Boatland, and West Fork were the most populous of these communities by 1860. It was in these pockets that members of Beaty's Independent Scouts were most likely to be found.

William "Billy" Beaty is likely the first of the family to settle in Pennsylvania from Ulster, though little is known about him. Seven of his children—James, Phoebe, Andrew, Alexander, John, David, and George—moved to the area around Overton County (from which Fentress County was carved), Tennessee, and Clinton County, Kentucky, in the late eighteenth century. The sons of George and David moved to the Boatland community along the East Fork of the Obey River in the 1810s and became patriarchs in the area. George's son was named David, after his uncle, and would become the famous Tinker Dave. George's brother named his son David Jr., thus putting a pair of first cousins named David Beaty at the heart of this kin-based guerrilla social network.

It was Tinker Dave's immediate family, however, who commanded the unit throughout the war. His two sons, James and Claiborne Beaty, were first and second lieutenants, titles that had no legal meaning for this unofficial band but clearly signified the leadership of Tinker Dave himself. A younger son named Harvey also fought in the unit. Three other Beaty men of Tinker Dave's generation—his brothers Fleming and George, and cousin David Jr.—were men of influence, convincing many others to join.

Radiating out from the Beaty core through marital and blood ties, Beaty's Independent Scouts included dozens of extended relations living in Boatland, Glenobey, Pine Springs, West Fork (Overton County), Travisville, and in Kentucky. Tinker Dave's sister, Matilda, married John Boles Sr., who joined the scouts at the ripe age of sixty. Interestingly, John Boles's son, John Jr., married his first cousin, Matilda, the daughter of Fleming Beaty. Meanwhile, Mary Ann, a daughter of John Boles Sr., married Thomas Allred, who joined his brother-in-law and father-in-law in Beaty's company.

Another sister of Tinker Dave named Mary Elizabeth, or Betsy, married Burton Stephens of nearby Poplar Cove. Not only did he join the company but so did members of his extended family, many of them connecting back to Tinker Dave in subsequent marriages. The roots of the Stephens clan go back to Thomas Grainger Stephens, who moved with his wife and children from South Carolina to what became Fentress County in the 1810s. One of his sons, Zorababel, was the father of Burton and Andrew Jackson Stephens, both of whom would join Beaty's Independent Scouts. Andrew Jackson Stephens even married one of Tinker Dave's other sisters, Charlotte—thus, a pair of Stephens brothers married a pair of Beaty sisters. A third son, Zoral Babel, sent his son, David Stephens, to fight with Tinker Dave as well. Another son of Thomas Grainger Stephens, David Stephens (for whom Babel's son was likely named), had even more ties to Tinker Dave. His son, Monroe Stephens, actually lived on Beaty's farm in 1860. Three other sons of David—Russell, Isaiah, and John Marion Stephens Sr.—all fought with Beaty's Independent Scouts.

Another family closely connected to Tinker Dave's scouts was the Choate clan, with five of its members joining the company. Like the Stephens family, the Choates were spread out among the Boatland, Pine Springs, and Travisville communities. Austin Choate Sr., sixty-five years old at the start of the war, lived next door to Beaty and ended up joining the unit as one of its oldest members. Two sons still living with Austin in 1860—John and Christopher Columbus Choate—joined the company, as did cousins Thomas and Sabe Choate.

Four members of the Moody family were connected via marriage to Beaty's inner core. Charlotte, Tinker Dave's oldest daughter, married Jonathan Moody, who was killed in October 1863. Jonathan's brother Peter and Peter's son, John, were also members of the scouts, though they survived the war. John Moody was also married to Thursa Jane Huff, daughter of Alexander Huff, murdered by Champ Ferguson; he thus had two reasons to join Beaty's command—kinship and revenge. Finally, Harvey Beaty, one of Tinker Dave's sons in the guerrilla band, married Margaret Moody, a sister of John. The Moodys were clustered around the Pine Springs section in what is now Pickett County and lent their name to the community known as Moodyville.

In many cases, men with little kinship link to the Beaty clan joined the scouts simply out of a desire for revenge against or protection from Ferguson. Lorenzo Dow Culver and his brother Tom joined the scouts after Champ murdered their father, John; Tom would be killed by Ferguson as well. Like the sons of Alexander Huff and Conrad Pile, the Culver boys lived in a place less easily protected by nature (Jamestown) and so depended on a wider guerrilla network for support.

But where kinship and revenge joined forces, Beaty's Independent Scouts provided an especially welcome home. James Beaty, son of Tinker Dave and "first lieutenant" of the company, married Elendor Jane Smith, whose father, David, and two brothers, Asa and Hijah, were all killed by Confederate guerrillas in 1863; her brothers had joined Tinker Dave's company, possibly in response to the death of their father. Brothers John and Hezekiah Taylor joined with Beaty shortly before their brother-in-law, James Reeder, was killed. Though it is uncertain who killed Reeder or why exactly the Taylor brothers joined the scouts, they all seem to have suffered the same grisly fate—John and Hezekiah Taylor were both killed while held as prisoners of war.

Kinship networks did not always yield common loyalty, especially in divided counties like Fentress. Most famously, Champ Ferguson and his brother Jim found themselves on opposite sides of the Civil War, with Jim participating in the very first military engagement in Tennessee at Travisville. More common than brothers lining up on different sides were cousins who lived in and among different networks of people and often found themselves on opposite sides. Such was the case with the Stephens family. Though most members supported the Union and many fought under Tinker Dave's command, some became victims of the scouts. Beaty's men killed Nicholas Stephens, the son of Josiah Stephens—a brother of Zorababel and David Stephens—along with two of Nicholas's sons.

Beaty's Independent Scouts also provided a refuge for deserters from the Confederate army. Knowing that Confederate provost marshals and cavalrymen hunted them, deserters often made for the most desperate irregular fighters of all. Entire companies and even regiments emerged along the Cumberland Plateau composed of deserters from the Confederacy. The most infamous was the 1st Alabama and Tennessee Independent Cavalry Vidette, organized west of Chattanooga during the Tullahoma Campaign and designed to harass General Braxton Bragg's men as they retreated toward Chickamauga Creek in Georgia. Cal Brixey, captain of Company D, was responsible for dozens of grisly murders of Confederate sympathizers in the Lower Cumberland Plateau before being captured and killed by Confederate cavalry. Though none of Beaty's men could match Brixey's exploits, the Threets followed a similar jagged path to the Union side. After Jesse D. Threet was killed at the Battle of Mill Springs while fighting as part of the Twenty-Fifth Tennessee (C.S.), his two sons, Dean and George, joined Beaty's command. The Confederate army dismissed another brother, James Threet, for being too young to serve. Age was not a consideration for service in Beaty's Independent Scouts, which took in young James. Another brother, Cullom Threet, joined Tinker Dave's organization and was later charged with the murder of a Lieutenant Matthew Baker of the Twenty-Eighth Tennessee (C.S.).[42]

What do these connections reveal about Beaty's Independent Scouts and about irregulars in the Civil War generally? For one thing, guerrillas historically fight in defense of what they perceive to be their homes and neighborhoods, so it stands to reason that most members of a guerrilla band would come from a common community. Yet irregulars defined "home" in different ways, some entirely localized to the household and others to the region or state. Moreover, guerrillas often operated in places where neighbors and kin fought on opposing sides. Thus, a simple top-level mapping of guerrilla households might not reveal the webs of loyalty so essential to guerrilla cohesion. Other layers, therefore, must be considered beyond geography, including and especially kinship. With the help of digitized genealogical data, it is now possible to connect the nodes among hundreds of people in a community and discover both blood and marital lines that defined a community's cohesive character. Since relationships among irregulars depended heavily on prewar connections, it is possible to map guerrillas' social networks by beginning with their leaders and searching antebellum kinship ties.

A social-network analysis also reveals the catalysts that intensified participation by some members. In the case of Beaty's Independent Scouts, the prime activator for membership beyond Tinker Dave's inner circle was Champ Ferguson. Relatives of those killed by Ferguson were likely to turn to Beaty's command for protection and to seek revenge, whether or not they were related to the core group of the Beaty, Stephens, or Choate families.

To be sure, a social-network analysis has its limits. It cannot speak to motives of individual members, although it can hint at them by revealing multiple close connections with other guerrillas. And it does little to explain why so many military-age siblings within guerrilla-heavy kinship networks chose not to fight at all. That said, by mapping the network of irregulars, it becomes apparent just how much a particular band was embedded in a particular community, and subsequently, why a community may have rallied to the defense of that unit. A social-network analysis will answer more than the question, Who is Tinker Dave Beaty? It also will answer, Who had the most to gain by fighting with Tinker Dave Beaty?

NOTES

Note: Some official Civil War sources spell Beatty with two "t"s; however, the single "t" spelling, "Beaty," has always been considered the most accurate.

1. George Crook to James Garfield, U.S. War Department, *War of the Rebellion,* ser. 1, 2:159–60.

2. Sutherland, *Savage Conflict.*

3. David Fincher, *The Social Network* (Columbia Pictures, 2010).

4. John Scott, "Trend Report: Social Network Analysis," *Sociology* 22, no. 1 (Feb. 1988): 110.

5. Bernice A. Pescosolido, "The Sociology of Social Networks," in *21st Century Sociology,* ed. Clifton D. Bryant and Dennis L. Peck (SAGE Publications, 2007), 1, published online Mar. 2012, SAGE Knowledge, http://dx.doi.org/10.4135/9781412939645.

6. Barry Wellman, "Social Network Analysis," in *Blackwell Encyclopedia of Sociology,* ed. George Ritzer (Malden, Mass.: Blackwell, 2007), 4490–91.

7. Scott, "Trend Report," 110.

8. David Knoke and Song Yang, *Social Network Analysis* (Los Angeles: SAGE, 2007), 1–3.

9. "Counterinsurgency," in Sarah Sewall et al., *The U.S. Army/Marine Corps Counterinsurgency Field Manual* (Chicago: University of Chicago Press, 2007), app. B.

10. A recent revision based on the experience in Afghanistan was published in 2014, though it adds little to the social-network analysis of the 2006 version. See K. J. Glueck, *Insurgencies and Countering Insurgencies* (Washington, D.C.: Department of the Army, 2014).

11. "Counterinsurgency," app. B, 17.

12. For a deeper analysis of the cultural constructions of space, see Richard White, *Railroaded: The Transcontinentals and the Making of Modern America* (New York: W. W. Norton, 2011), xxix; and Spatial History Project, Stanford University, accessed July 29, 2015, http://web.stanford.edu/group/spatialhistory/cgi-bin/site/index.php.

13. For an annotated bibliography of spatial history, social geography, and digital mapping, see "A Spatial History Annotated Bibliography," Spatial History Project, Stanford University, accessed July 29, 2015, http://web.stanford.edu/group/spatialhistory/cgi-bin/site/pub.php?id=89&project_id=.

14. For examples of excellent local guerrilla-war studies that assess relations with the outside world, see Crawford, *Ashe County's Civil War;* and Sarris, *Separate Civil War.*

15. Phillip Wright, "Challenging Assumptions: What Is a 'Human-Centred Geography'? Stretching the Geographical Imagination in Pursuit of Holism," *Geography* 96, no. 3 (Oct. 2011): 156–60.

16. On the geographic imagination in nineteenth-century America and the rise of mapmaking, see Susan Schulten, *Mapping the Nation: History and Cartography in Nineteenth-Century America* (Chicago: University of Chicago Press, 2013). On Civil War mapmaking in particular, see Earl B. McElfresh, *Maps and Mapmakers of the Civil War* (New York: Harry N. Abrams, 1999).

17. For an example of social geography and the study of Civil War guerrillas, see the excellent essay by Andrew Fialka, "Controlled Chaos: Spatiotemporal Patterns in Missouri's Irregular Civil War," in Beilein and Hulbert, *Civil War Guerrilla,* 43–69.

18. George B. Davis et al., *Atlas to Accompany the Official Records of the War of the Rebellion* (Washington, D.C.: Government Printing Office, 1891), https://archive.org/stream/atlastoaccompany00unit#page/n0/mode/1up , plates 95, 119.

19. ESRI, "United States Geological Survey Historical Topographic Map Explorer," *United States Geological Survey Historical Topographic Map Explorer,* 2014, http://historicalmaps.arcgis.com/usgs/.

20. Tennessee State Library and Archives, "Tennessee Civil War GIS Project," Tennessee Civil War GIS Project, 2013, http://tnmap.tn.gov/civilwar/.

21. Ancestry.com, 2015, http://home.ancestry.com/; Fold3, Ancestry.com, 2014, http://www.fold3.com/; Historical Data Systems, American Civil War Research Database, 2014, http://www.civilwardata.com/.

22. Tennessee Historical Commission, *Tennesseans in the Civil War: Part 2: A Military History of Confederate and Union Units with Available Rosters of Personnel* (Nashville: Civil War Centennial Commission of Tennessee, 1965). For the digitized version, see http://www.tngenweb.org/civilwar/.

23. Missouri Secretary of State, "Provost Marshal General Database for Missouri," Missouri's Union Provost Marshal Papers, 1861–1866, http://s1.sos.mo.gov/records/archives/archivesdb

/provost/default.aspx. Ancestry.com has also digitized the Provost Marshal General files, but it does not include a descriptive index.

24. Fellman, *Inside War.*

25. Search term "bushwhacker" on the index page, with location as Cooper County. Missouri Secretary of State, "Provost Marshal General Database for Missouri."

26. Geiger, *Financial Fraud and Guerrilla Violence.*

27. See especially McKnight, *Confederate Outlaw.*

28. *Nashville Union,* Oct. 21, 1865.

29. For the class origins of East Tennessee Confederate and Union guerrillas, see Fisher, *War at Every Door.*

30. "Eighth Population Census Manuscripts—1860," Ancestry.com, accessed Dec. 23, 2014, http://home.ancestry.com/; "Eighth Slave Census Manuscripts—1860," Ancestry.com, accessed Dec. 23, 2014, ibid.

31. Library of Congress, "Chronicling America," Chronicling America: Historic American Newspapers, 2013, http://chroniclingamerica.loc.gov/.

32. Each enlistment card includes the text of the congressional act. Ancestry.com, "Fold3."

33. Albert Hogue, *Mark Twain's Obedstown and Knobs of Tennessee: A History of Jamestown and Fentress County, Tennessee* (Jamestown, Tenn.: Cumberland, 1950), 59–60.

34. Caster D. Patton, *Conflict in the Cumberlands* (Jamestown, Tenn.: Fentress County Historical Society, 2010), 128–30.

35. Beaty's testimony in Hogue, *Mark Twain's Obedstown and Knobs of Tennessee,* 60.

36. Astor, *Civil War along Tennessee's Cumberland Plateau,* 15–38.

37. Albert Ross Hogue, *History of Fentress County, Tennessee: The Old Home of Mark Twain's Ancestors* (Baltimore: RPC, 2002).

38. Bruce York, "Fentress County Database," RootsWeb.com, 2014, http://wc.rootsweb.ancestry.com/cgi-bin/igm.cgi?db=bruceyork.

39. Ibid.

40. Sam K. Cowan, *Sergeant York and His People* (New York: Grosset and Dunlap, 1922), 127–28.

41. McKnight, *Confederate Outlaw,* 97–98.

42. *Knoxville Chronicle,* Jan. 19, 1879.

THE IRREGULAR WAR IN LOUDOUN COUNTY, VIRGINIA

SCOTT THOMPSON

On April 5, 1865, Confederate guerrilla leader John W. Mobberly approached a barn in which Sergeant Charles Stewart, Joseph Waters, and Mahlon H. Best of the Unionist Loudoun Rangers concealed themselves. As the three Federals prepared to rise and shoot, Stewart was about to conclude a personal campaign of retribution. Eleven months earlier, outside the village of Waterford in Loudoun County, Virginia, a combined group of Lieutenant Colonel John S. Mosby's partisan rangers and Mobberly's guerrillas attacked the Loudoun Rangers' pickets, one of whom was Stewart. As he and three others chased a decoy soldier, the rebels ambushed them. Stewart surrendered, but the ambushers fired at him anyway, knocking him off his horse and wounding him in four different places. Mobberly then rode his horse over Stewart's body, shot the ranger in the face, "and left him for dead."[1]

Afterward, a local Quaker named Rachel Steer and physician Thomas Bond nursed Stewart, helping him recover. Dr. Bond declared that Stewart's "only ambition in life was to live long enough to make another hell" for Mobberly as Stewart sought revenge for this vicious encounter. In early April 1865, the guerrilla leader planned to meet with a man named Luther M. Potterfield at Potterfield's barn in the Blue Ridge Mountains near the town of Lovettsville. Learning of this, Union forces at Harpers Ferry organized a party of five men to kill or capture Mobberly. Stewart seized the opportunity and requested to join the squad. After entering the barnyard, the guerrilla saw the Loudoun Rangers and yelled, "Oh, Lord I am gone!" They fired their revolvers at Mobberly; Stewart's "bullet pierced his brain, and he fell from his horse a corpse."[2]

These encounters constitute episodes of a local civil war within the American Civil War. This conflict occurred in Loudoun County, Virginia, an area situated along the Old Dominion's borders with Maryland and newly formed West Virginia, jointly occupied by both the Union and Confederate armies throughout the war and split between Unionist and secessionist populations. In and around the county, irregular units representing each rival republic and local faction frequently engaged each other and regular forces of the opposing side. As unconventional warriors, they operated behind enemy lines, served in units smaller than conventional commands, and made quick, stealthy attacks. This essay examines the loyalties and military service of three irregular cavalry units raised in the northern Virginia county: the Federal Independent Loudoun Rangers (sometimes referred to as the Loyal Virginia Cavalry), Lieutenant Colonel Elijah V. White's Confederate Thirty-Fifth Battalion Virginia Cavalry (nicknamed "the Comanches" for the wild manner in which they rode and the "ear-piercing yells" they made during combat), and John Mobberly's band of Confederate guerrillas.[3]

This examination of Loudoun's irregular war builds on the growing body of scholarship on soldier motivations and sociopolitical divisions in the Civil War South. While most historians identify *either* local concerns *or* political ideologies as the primary nature of Civil War loyalty and soldier motivations, Loudoun's unconventional troops were among those Americans who fought for their respective sides because of *both* an ideological allegiance to their republic *and* a sense of duty to protect their homes, neighbors, and families from enemy occupation. The county's irregular warriors thus understood political allegiance in the abstract, possessing ideas about which national government had constitutional legitimacy and which one undermined the American republican system. They also thought of loyalty practically, responding to concerns over the material effects of armed conflict on a local community.[4]

Loudoun County's irregular war enriches the scholarship on unconventional warfare in Civil War America. Joining the assortment of works on similar conflicts in Appalachia, Missouri, Texas, North Carolina, and Mississippi, this examination of an understudied local civil war helps paint a fuller picture of how unconventional warfare and local conflicts almost solely characterized the Civil War experience of many Americans. It also contributes to the subfield of counterirregular warfare by discussing Union and Confederate forces whose primary mission was to hunt down and kill or capture enemy irregulars infesting a particular geographic area.[5]

The irregular war in Loudoun County illustrates the importance of terminology when studying unconventional warfare. Some historians, following the Civil War generation's writings, have applied the blanket term "guerrilla" to all irregulars or use "guerrilla," "bushwhacker," "partisan," and "irregular" interchangeably. Such terminology obscures the complexity of irregular warfare. The conflict saw the emergence of various types of irregular units that, while having identical fighting styles, differed from each other in terms of composition, organization, and level of independence from the regular army. The unconventional warriors who served in Loudoun were variously "guerrillas," "partisans," and "regular raiders," corresponding to the three types scholar Robert Mackey identifies in the Middle South. The first term refers to disorganized, self-constituted armed groups of civilians or soldiers with little or no connection to or control by the regular army of the side for which they fought. The second term encompasses organized companies or battalions not attached to a regiment or brigade but subject to special orders from their government and regular army. Partisans, like regular troops, were formally mustered into their units, wore uniforms, received military pay, and officially represented a government. The third term refers to conventional soldiers who occasionally left their regiment or brigade for raids in which they fought irregularly. Loudoun stands out by being a single county in which all three types of irregulars waged war.[6]

Loudoun County's experience complicates our understanding of local unconventional conflicts seen throughout the Civil War South. As in other areas divided between Unionist and pro-Confederate populations and occupied by both armies, Loudouners responded to the war by arming themselves against neighbors and invaders who supported the enemy republic. Yet Loudoun lacked the civilian guerrillas and bands of deserters seen elsewhere. Rather, every participant in the county's war was a uniformed combatant who enlisted in a unit officially sponsored by one of the two competing republics, both of which conducted a widespread policy of utilizing irregular forces to win the war. Though Loudoun constituted a portion of "Mosby's Confederacy," the three local commands demonstrate that irregulars beside the Forty-Third Virginia shaped the county's experience with unconventional warfare. They reveal that Confederate partisan ranger units independent of the national and state partisan ranger systems existed. They also show that northern Virginia joined other regions in producing local Union forces and being home to a Confederate guerrilla band with a reputation among Federals for committing atrocities. As the political allegiances of Loudoun's irregulars highlight, the Civil War's irregular warriors were complex people who both tried to protect a local community's safety and subscribed to ideas of what the two competing national governments represented. Their motivations prompted them to resist attempts by their respective authorities to transfer them to the conventional service. As in other areas plagued by unconventional warfare, Loudoun's civilians found themselves either the victims of irregular depredations or the providers of material and emotional support for unconventional soldiers. The conflict in the county also resembles those elsewhere in that it provoked a parallel counter-irregular war aiming to eliminate the irregulars as a threat to each side's operations and authority in the region. The three Loudoun units, by participating in the counterirregular war in addition to being the targets of it, blurred the distinction between what was an irregular band and a counterirregular group. Civil War Loudoun presents an opportunity to examine how the two American militaries dealt with unconventional warfare in comparison and fought irregulars not in a peripheral region, but in a major theater of the war.

Loudoun County's irregular war began when a group of local secessionists sought to help secure Confederate independence and deliver their county from Union military forces by forming a single partisan unit under the official direction of Richmond and the Confederate army: Elijah V. White's independent cavalry company, the nucleus of the Thirty-Fifth Virginia. After the firing on Fort Sumter and Lincoln's call for volunteers to crush the rebellion in April 1861, a majority of Loudouners accompanied Virginia and the rest of the Middle South in joining the Confederacy and building its army. Due to its border with Maryland and proximity to both national capitals, the county faced a situation in which it would be among the first areas to be invaded by the Union army, which stationed itself along the Potomac River. The closeness of the enemy prompted Confederate commanders to send regular soldiers to Loudoun to guard the river and construct fortifications. To strengthen northern Virginia's defenses, they also formed a local force tasked with waging irregular warfare.[7]

A Marylander who had fought abolitionists in "Bleeding Kansas," acquired a Loudoun County farm in 1857, and helped defeat John Brown's Harpers Ferry raid, Elijah White enlisted in the Confederate army immediately after hostilities broke out. For distinguished service in the fall of 1861, Brigadier General Nathan "Shanks" Evans's officers recommended that White be awarded an army commission. White received authorization from Secretary of War Judah P. Benjamin to form an independent company that would conduct "ranging service" along the Union-Confederate border, report to the nearest Confederate general, and protect Loudoun's secessionist population from the Union army. Captain White began recruiting in secessionist-dominated Leesburg. In the winter of 1861–62, the partisans reported to Brigadier General A. P. Hill, who, as the closest high-ranking officer, assumed command over them while he was in the area. The formation of White's unit preceded both the creation of Virginia's State Rangers in March 1862 and the Confederate Congress's passage of the Partisan Ranger Act in April 1862. Yet the command resembled the units that emerged under those ranger systems in terms of recruitment, organization, tactics, and strategy. Overall, the company was an early example of the Confederacy's attempt to provide for local defense and hold its irregulars on a tight leash under a regulated structure.[8]

In his postbellum history of the battalion, Comanche officer and Waterford resident Frank M. Myers sheds light on the Confederate ideology of the secessionist Loudouners who joined the unit. Though written after the war and thus steeped in Lost Cause language, Myers's history also articulates the political views seen in conventional rebel soldiers' wartime writings and in the correspondence of Loudoun's pro-Confederate civilians. Just as other rebels demonized the Yankee enemy, Myers and his comrades interpreted the North, the Union army, and President Abraham Lincoln as anti-republican, satanic, and reminiscent of the old monarchical, aristocratic order of Europe. White's cavalrymen believed that the eleven states comprising the Confederacy possessed the right to separate themselves from the Union's compact. Since they possessed abstract ideas about the young Southern republic's constitutional authority and the nefarious, autocratic character of the Union, they shed light on the ideological nature of some Civil War irregulars.[9]

The views of White's cavalrymen toward pro-Union Loudouners illustrate the combined ideological-localist nature of their military motivations. As Myers reveals, a component of Comanche secessionism accused Loudoun's Unionists of treason against their state for being loyal to a country whose government threatened the Old Dominion's border and for incorrectly holding that the U.S. Constitution gave the national government supremacy over the states. The Thirty-Fifth's soldiers thus loathed tory neighbors because they challenged the Confederacy's right to exist and supported Northern invaders who posed a danger to the Virginia community.[10]

As a Confederate unit, White's cavalry defended the peculiar institution and recognized the threat Yankees posed to slavery. Myers derisively refers to the Union's invasion of the Confederacy as "the abolition crusade upon the South."

In February 1862, while Loudoun County's slaves fled across the Potomac to freedom in Maryland, White's company briefly acted as a slave patrol.[11]

White's Loudoun irregulars, of whom 170 are identifiable in the 1860 Census, tended to own little or no property, mostly consisted of farmers and laborers, and included a small number of slave owners—a profile resembling that of most Confederate units. The average value of real-estate property held by a member of White's original company was $401, and the average value of his personal property amounted to $378. In the sample, fifty-one soldiers were farmers before they enlisted and thirty-six worked as laborers in 1860. The average age of the Comanches at the time of enlistment was 24.2 years old. In their ranks, nine men owned 1–4 slaves, while two owned 5–9 slaves. Collectively, eleven Comanches owned a total of thirty people.[12]

Scouting operations, small engagements with Union forces, and the use of discretion when occasionally following the orders of superior Confederate officers in northern Virginia and along the Potomac characterized White's Cavalry's early military service, as with most partisan warfare. The company's first operations consisted of scouting and guarding the Potomac while encamped in the heavily Unionist Quaker town of Waterford. In late February 1862, Comanche squads began searching for Union forces to engage, including one partially comprised of Neersville farmer Thomas S. Grubb, Neersville carpenter John Tribbey, R. Ferro, and Waterford miller Charles Cooper.[13]

After General Hill withdrew to assist the Confederate army fighting on the Peninsula, Union forces launched their first counterirregular operation in Loudoun, which saw White's partisans unite with Confederate regular raiders. Colonel John Geary, with his Twenty-Eighth Pennsylvania Infantry and the First Michigan Cavalry, started hunting for any Confederate forces in Loudoun that threatened to attack the Baltimore and Ohio Railroad. Geary sent his men on a march to Leesburg, where he took possession of the town's buildings. Cut off from supplies, White's men could not effectively resist the Union cavalry and withdraw to a position outside the town. But four companies from the Second Virginia Cavalry came to White's aid. The combined force kept the Federals "in constant fear and trembling." The Confederates followed Geary's advance, attacked his pickets nightly, and later defeated his men in an engagement. Loudoun's rebel partisans thus found success against counterirregular troops by fighting alongside regular raiders.[14]

After spending the summer of 1862 delivering dispatches, fighting regular engagements, and being provost guards and couriers for Major General Richard S. Ewell's division in the Shenandoah Valley, White's company began to undergo changes in its structure and experienced a reinforcement of its identity as a partisan unit committed to local defense. In September and October, a Confederate Maryland partisan cavalry company under Captain George W. Chiswell, known as Chiswell's Exiles, and four newly recruited companies from other northern Virginia counties joined with the original Loudoun company to form the Thirty-Fifth Battalion, Virginia Cavalry. White's Loudouners became Company A; Chiswell's Marylanders transformed into Company B. The battalion unanimously elected White as its commander. After the original company first learned of the Marylanders' planned arrival in June, news arrived of the passage of the Partisan Ranger Act, through which the Richmond government approved, regulated, and aided the creation of other partisan units. Regarding the act, Myers, now captain of Company A, described how "this idea struck the minds of White's men very forcibly as containing the very principle upon which their company had been formed." The Loudouners hoped that, with the arrival of the additional companies, they could potentially become partisan rangers under the legislation, cease serving under the direct orders of generals, and resume "the more congenial and pleasant" duty "of once more scouting on the frontier."[15]

Following several months of service by White's cavalry, the Union army formed its own partisan company in Loudoun, the Loudoun Rangers, consisting of residents who both supported the preservation of the abstract Union and desired to rid their neighborhoods of Confederate occupiers. When Virginia seceded, the county's minority pro-Union community looked on in horror and shock at the prospect of disunion and civil war. For the crime of disloyalty, Confederate military forces occupying Loudoun subjected the county's Unionist civilians to surveillance, arrest, and imprisonment. These conditions, coupled with the Union army's need to establish a foothold in northern Virginia to conquer the Confederacy and travel to the major front lines, warranted a local-defense force representing a Federal counterpart to White's partisans.[16]

With each side of the divided county creating a rival partisan unit, Loudoun's unconventional war became a *civil* war, one that contrasts with other Southern inner wars in the level of its Union army involvement. The conflicts in the Appalachian Mountains, East Texas, the North Carolina Piedmont and coast, and Jones County, Mississippi, resulted from Unionist civilians or Confederate deserters, each of whom lacked any direct connection to the Federal army, banding together to violently resist Southern authorities. Though the self-constituted pro-Union guerrillas of East Tennessee, the Knight Company of Jones County, and Bill Owens's North Carolina band imitated official U.S. military organizations in their operations, Loudoun's civil war showcased a unit of Southern Unionists directly organized by the Federal government. The Loudoun Rangers ultimately represented a component of the Union army's policy of recruiting loyal white Southerners to help crush the rebellion.[17]

The rangers' commander for most of the war was Captain Samuel C. Means. A Waterford flour-mill owner, mercantile business owner in Point of Rocks, Maryland, and station agent for the Baltimore and Ohio Railroad, Means endured intimidation, confiscation, and coercion from the Confederate army for his Unionism. In response, he fled to safety in Point of Rocks, on the other side of the Potomac River from Loudoun, in July 1861. Here, Means served as a guide for Colonel Geary when his regiment entered Virginia. Viewing him as a traitor responsible for these raids, the Richmond government put a $5,000 bounty on Means's head that December. He shifted from an exiled Southern Unionist civilian to a Federal partisan commander in January 1862, when Secretary of War Edwin Stanton called him to Washington, D.C., and offered him a commission to raise a company. In May, Colonel Dixon Miles mustered the Loudoun Rangers into service at Harpers Ferry, and Captain Means established his headquarters in Waterford, where he initiated recruitment.[18]

Ranger sergeant John W. Forsythe, a shoemaker before the war, also decided to become a Federal partisan after suffering persecution and ostracism for his pro-Union sentiments. As a resident of Leesburg who "remained loyal to the government of the United States," he occupied a hazardous position. It pained Forsythe to witness his friends and acquaintances don the gray uniform during the initial wave of Confederate enlistments. He in good conscience could not, as he claimed in his memoir, "fight in defense of a cause so repugnant to my principles." When he took an oath of allegiance to the Union and pinned a small U.S. flag to his coat upon the entry of the Twenty-Eighth Pennsylvania into Leesburg, a group of secessionists assaulted him. Realizing that he could not remain a civilian at home in peace, he decided to join the Loudoun Rangers in early 1862. Forsythe resembles other Southern Unionists who also determined irregular warfare to be their best remedy for Confederate oppression.[19]

The Loudoun Rangers embodied a fusion of the irregular warrior and the counterirregular fighter. Like White's company, Means's partisan unit engaged in border service along the Potomac River, cherished and struggled to preserve its status as an independent command, occasionally took orders from a general, and executed quick ambushes behind enemy lines. Highlighting their concrete local concerns, the men considered their company to be one of counterirregular scouts who, as Forsythe declared, "were . . . mounted for service against bands of guerrillas who infested that part of the state, and who were engaged in committing depredations upon loyal citizens." Just as the Union army directed Blazer's Scouts to combat Mosby's rangers in northern Virginia and sent the Thirty-Sixth Ohio to look for and fight Confederate guerrillas in southern West Virginia, it also recruited the Loudoun Rangers to engage all rebel irregulars who could be found trespassing in Loudoun County. Despite being defenders of the Unionist population, the rangers also spent the war indiscriminately plundering and foraging from civilians of both sides.[20]

Private Briscoe Goodhart's postbellum unit history of the Loudoun Rangers discusses the ideological convictions of his comrades. Goodhart's work accompanied writings by other Southern white Union veterans. A number of these men never developed an explicitly pro–U.S. allegiance, opposing the Confederacy during the war because its impressment and conscription policies threatened their families' material subsistence. Yet to convince Northerners of their wartime loyalty and to counter the Lost Cause, their histories and memoirs portrayed themselves as patriotic, ideological Unionists. In contrast, the ideological language permeating throughout the wartime writings of Loudoun's Unionist civilians suggest that those who joined the rangers did indeed subscribe to at least some form of the abstract loyalty Goodhart said they did.[21]

The Loudoun Rangers upheld the prevalent view in nineteenth-century America that the Union was an absolute, idealized construct that could not be dissolved. Loudoun's Federal partisans viewed the Union as a compact of states over which the national government held supreme power. The loyal Virginians saw the Union war effort as the parent government disciplining its "adventurous and misguided" children, the seceded states, which had established an undemocratic government with "monarchical tendencies." They viewed the Union as "the best government that ever existed" and the Confederates' war against it as a "cruel and unjustifiable" attempt to "slay the goose that laid the golden egg." John Forsythe attributed his Unionism to an adherence to the U.S. Constitution and once denied the legitimacy of the Confederate States to a Libby Prison guard. The Loudoun Rangers' belief in an abstract Union places them among Northern soldiers and the Southerners who helped establish the state of West Virginia and made East Tennessee a militant pro-Union stronghold. They thus contrast with those Southern dissidents who entered the war as secessionists but became disillusioned with the Confederate cause after suffering battlefield defeats, conscription, and impressment in 1862 and 1863. Loudoun's loyal cavalrymen were irregular warriors who fought not only to protect their locality from hostile military forces but also to defend a constitutional system in which their home community participated.[22]

A function of eighteenth-century migration patterns, the religious and ethnic composition of the Loyal Virginia Cavalry reflected the predominantly Quaker, German, and Scots-Irish makeup of Loudoun County's minority Unionist faction. The Quakers' devotion to the Union motivated them to violate the pacifist tenet of their religion by joining a U.S. military unit. Of the ninety-nine Loudoun Rangers who can be identified in the 1860 census, eighteen members of the Society of Friends (including Captain Means), forty-three Germans, and seventeen Scots-Irish citizens, one of whom was Sergeant Forsythe, enlisted in the command.[23]

As a result of their ties to the county's Quaker community, whose members advocated for the abolition of slavery and for African American welfare in the antebellum period, the Loudoun Rangers subscribed to an antislavery form of Southern Unionism mirroring the North's free-labor ideology and hostility toward the slaveholding aristocracy that had founded the Confederacy. According to Goodhart, he and his comrades thought slavery degraded American labor. As Forsythe stated, "I was born in Virginia, and educated under the influences of slavery," but thought the peculiar institution unconstitutional. He referred to the slaveholder aristocracy as "the nobility" and chastised Confederate Loudouners for sacrificing "their lives upon the altar of slavery."[24]

The socioeconomic profile of the Loudoun Rangers reveals that its troops possessed less wealth than those of White's original company but held the same prewar occupations as their Confederate rivals. Though the overwhelming majority of rangers owned no property or were small property holders, the unit had one wealthy serviceman (Captain Means). The average value of real-estate property a ranger held was $298, and the rangers owned personal property averaging $181 in value. Forty-one pro-Union Virginia irregulars worked as laborers; thirty-three were farmers. When he enlisted, a Loudoun Ranger was on average 25.9 years of age. Although a tiny group of small slaveholders lived in the heavily Unionist sections of Loudoun County, the census and service records reveal that none enlisted in Means's command.[25]

The early operations of the Loudoun Rangers consisted of targeting Confederate resources and searching for rebel enemies. The Federal irregulars first disrupted a Confederate supply line extending from Baltimore to Leesburg. By midsummer 1862, the command had acquired fifty soldiers and relocated its camp first to a German Reformed church in Lovettsville, then to the Baptist church in Waterford. Here, the company became "engaged in active scouting" and acquired horses.[26]

In the early morning hours of August 27, 1862, the two Loudoun-based partisan companies fought their first engagement of the local civil war—a fight that pitted neighbors, friends, schoolmates, and family members against each other and demonstrated the involvement of civilians in irregular warfare. The skirmish resulted from the Comanches playing the role of both partisan and counterirregular while collaborating with regular raiders. It also represented the intersection of the twin Union and Confederate projects utilizing locally recruited, uniformed, and regulated unconventional soldiers to rid the Potomac border of enemy forces.

Lieutenant Colonel White left Ewell's Division and marched to Loudoun for the purpose of "chastising a band of renegades and Yankees . . . under Sam. Means." Members of Waterford's secessionist minority informed White's company of the Loudoun Rangers' encampment in the town. Shortly before 3:00 A.M., White, with twenty Comanches, twenty troops from the Fourth Virginia Cavalry, and six civilian pilots, galloped through farms and cornfields to Waterford. A slave arrived at the rangers' camp and warned the commander of the approaching Confederate force, but that officer gave no weight to the information. Several hours later, the Fourth Virginia evaded the ranger pickets, surrounded the camp, and caught the attention of the Unionists, of whom twenty-three were present. In response, with Captain Means at his home across town, Lieutenant Luther W. Slater formed a battle line. Hidden behind buildings and vegetation, the Confederates were hardly visible to the rangers. When Slater demanded that they identify themselves, the rebels fired their carbines, wounding some in the Union line, including Slater, who was shot in the temple, shoulder, arm, breast, and hand. The Confederates' volley awoke Sergeant Forsythe, who lay sleeping in front of the church. The rangers answered with carbine fire of their own before they fell back to the interior of the Baptist church. The Comanches then arrived on the scene, dismounted, and fired through the church's walls and windows. Goodhart recalled how "the Rangers returned the fire as vigorously as circumstances would permit," despite many lying "around in the church pews weltering in their blood, making the place look more like a slaughter pen than a house of worship." Amid this gruesome ordeal, the wounded cried for water. During the fight, members of the Unionist Walker family could hear soldiers ride horses, fire muskets and pistols, and give orders to charge.[27]

The end and immediate aftermath of the Waterford Baptist Church fight highlighted the extent to which civilians participated in and neighbors and kin fought each other in Loudoun's irregular war. Secessionist Lydia A. Virts permitted the Confederates to use her house, located across the street from the church, as a cover from which they fired on the rangers. The depletion of their ammunition convinced the Unionists to accept a truce offer, the conditions of which included immediate parole. Those partisans who bled in the church included Philomont farmer James A. Cox, James W. Gregg, and Thadeus W. Franklin of Waterford. Goresville cousins Charles and Henry Dixson, the former a farmer, the latter a laborer, were killed. One of Slater's wounds—from a bullet that crippled his right arm—forced him to resign as first lieutenant. In the service of the Confederacy, John Dove was wounded, Brook Hays died, and Peter J. Kabrick, a Waterford carpenter, received a mortal wound from which he perished on September 6. Both Goodhart and Myers reveal in their accounts that an unspecified number of those who fired on and struck each other during the fight had been friends and schoolmates prior to the outbreak of hostilities. When they met after the parole, Comanche William Snoots expressed a desire to murder his ranger brother Charles, but White's officers rebuked him. Following the engagement, the Loudoun Rangers guarded Potomac River fords, and White's command rejoined General Ewell. Waterford resident Susan Walker, who stalked the departing rebels, reported that the Comanches "seemed in high spirits" after the fight but regretted failing to take Means prisoner. Eliza Walker reported that children hidden in the cornfields listened to "many remarks—not very complementary" about the Unionist rangers.[28]

Noncombatants in the Loudoun County civil war looked to like-minded irregular and counterirregular warriors for local defense. In exchange for this service, civilians expressed gratitude. Once the Baptist church fight ended, Unionist Quakers of Waterford including Dr. Thomas Bond proceeded to the church to hastily gather the wounded rangers. P. S. Chalmers, a tailor, treated Private Henry Dixon until his death. The prominent Dutton family cared for Private Edward Jacobs, who would later be discharged for his injuries. Along the route to Ewell's camp, White's cavalry chased an unidentified Union force out of Leesburg. Frank Myers discussed how "the Southern people of that extremely Southern town . . . lionized to their heart's content the little band of boys in gray" for liberating them from "the galling rule of Yankeedom" and "their hated tyrants."[29]

In a demonstration of how irregulars could participate in a central theater of the war, the Loudoun Rangers and White's original company each aided their respective sides during the Antietam Campaign of September 1862. This operation witnessed the rangers encounter a group of counterirregular Confederates determined to rid the county of Unionist partisans. On September 2, joined by 125 members of Major Henry Cole's First Potomac Home Brigade, a Federal Maryland partisan unit, the rangers launched an expedition to Leesburg. After the Union force established pickets on the roads leading to town, Major General J. E. B. Stuart ordered 123 soldiers from Colonel Thomas Munford's Second Virginia to capture the party of marauders under Means, which "had so long infested that country." After a heavy back-and-forth fight, the Second Virginia drove the partisans to Waterford, where Munford ended his pursuit. Means's and Cole's men relocated to Harpers Ferry, where the rangers served as scouts, guides, pickets, flank guards, and dispatch riders for the Army of the Potomac. The engagement between Means's and Munford's forces highlights that whenever Confederate leaders learned of armed groups of Unionist irregulars roaming through an area, they sent in counterirregular forces to expel them.[30]

The contribution of White's partisans to the Antietam Campaign was to carry out ambushes. On September 12, Chiswell's Marylanders and White's Loudouners watched the movements of Major General George McClellan's army and defeated a Union infantry force on White's farm in Goresville. The command afterward rode to Leesburg, occupied by the Sixth Virginia Cavalry and forty Mississippi infantrymen. The county seat also fell along the path of four hundred Union cavalrymen led by Lieutenant Colonel Judson Kilpatrick on a raid in search for Confederate forces in Loudoun. The various rebel units took positions on the Leesburg Turnpike and in town and fired on the approaching Yankee raiders, forcing Kilpatrick to withdraw.[31]

White's cavalry ended 1862 and began 1863 with a challenge to its status as a partisan unit that best highlights the localist motivations of Loudouners serving in unconventional commands. While the Thirty-Fifth Virginia had served under the orders of Confederate generals and at times had performed conventional operations, it had never become officially absorbed into the larger army structure. But this changed after the Comanches reported to the camp of Brigadier General William E. Jones, commander of the Laurel Brigade, on Christmas. According to Myers's recollections, when Jones ordered Major White to command the Valley District, "here the battalion learned for the first time that its independence was gone and it was a portion of Gen. Jones' brigade permanently, and that," he added, "the men were regular troops." The transformation of the Comanches from partisans to regulars thus represents a precursor to the Confederacy's 1864 decision to dismantle most of its partisan ranger system and move its irregulars into conventional units.[32]

In response, Company A mutinied. The men declared that, as the original company, they amounted to an independent unit that served along the Union-Confederate border. They enlisted under the knowledge that, while they would report to the nearest commanding general, they would never be attached to any regiment or brigade without their consent. Also, as Myers described, the Loudouners' homes "were in the enemy's lines, and in the mountains, and as wild as they were they would have remained untamed for the remainder of the war."[33]

Major White eventually persuaded the mutineers to accept the changes and join the other companies in becoming a regular cavalry battalion, though not before detaching a group of incorrigible soldiers who refused to comply and permitting them to form a new guerrilla band under Private John Mobberly, a nineteen-year-old laborer from Harpers Ferry. White granted them their aspiration to continue operating in Loudoun and defending the secessionist population against the Federals. In essence, Mobberly's band possessed a level of independence greater than the Thirty-Fifth Virginia ever attained because it fought completely at its own discretion. Since this band was self-constituted and served the Confederacy with neither pay nor army regulation, when it broke off from the battalion, it became a group of guerrillas rather than partisans. But it contrasts with civilian and deserter guerrilla bands seen elsewhere in that it had official authorization from a regular Confederate officer. The creation of Mobberly's guerrilla band attests to the acute commitment of Loudouners to serve their republic only through fighting irregularly in their local area.[34]

Though the operations of the Thirty-Fifth Virginia frustrated the Union army throughout the war, the Federals despised Mobberly's band. Only Mosby's partisan rangers produced more worry among and condemnation by the Federals in northern Virginia. In official reports, Brigadier General John D. Stevenson defined the guerrilla leader as a "villain" leading "a gang of murderers." In an indication of the terror Mobberly brought to civilians, Charles Janney, a Unionist miller from the western Loudoun town of Hillsboro, compared the rebel's operations to Satan "going up and down the earth seeking whom" he may "devour."[35]

Mobberly's area of operations mainly consisted of the area between the Blue Ridge Mountains and Catoctin Mountain, in which he proved his band to be Loudoun's most vicious unconventional command. His guerrillas charged down mountain slopes, fired on Union troops, and quickly withdrew to thick trees. The band rarely took prisoners, often committed brutal acts against the prisoners it did take, and targeted both soldiers and civilians. Forsythe revealed that Mobberly sometimes took captured soldiers to hills, put them on their backs, placed large boulders on their limbs, and left them there to die of malnourishment and exposure. Late in the war, the guerrilla harassed Lovettsville Unionist John Everhart for voting against Virginia's secession ordinance. Mobberly's men arrested Everhart, struck him on the head with a stick, and tied him to a tree in the Blue Ridge. Arthur Newcomer, a member of Major Cole's cavalry, wrote after the war that the most common fate of those captured by Mobberly's band was to be instantly shot. During the Civil War, areas plagued by irregular warfare tended to produce notorious Confederate guerrilla leaders who gained a reputation for brutality: William Quantrill and "Bloody Bill" Anderson in Kansas and Missouri, John Gatewood in northern Georgia, and John Mobberly in Loudoun County.[36]

Very few sources regarding the members of Mobberly's band exist. As a gang of soldiers independent from the Confederate army, it never issued muster rolls. Official reports reveal that the unit had, at its largest size, twenty-six members including its leader. Out of this group only four, other than Mobberly, can be identified by name in the *Official Records* and the Thirty-Fifth Virginia's service records: Neersville resident James H. Riley, S. Mocks, William H. Tribette, and a Union defector named French Bill.[37]

Though the remaining men of White's command agreed to serve with the Thirty-Fifth Virginia for the rest of the war, they nevertheless always longed for a return to irregular service to launch surprise attacks on an unsuspecting enemy. Early 1863 provided the Comanches with such an opportunity to act as regular raiders. The presence of the Loudoun Rangers at Point of Rocks that summer prompted White to obtain permission from Ewell to detach from the brigade and "make a raid" there "in the hope of striking again his old enemy, Means." The Comanches used the same tactics as those of their partisan phase, but the battalion remained a component of a conventional brigade. White's force crossed the Potomac at Grubb's Ford, near Catoctin Creek, and landed three miles from Point of Rocks. Before assaulting Means's partisans, the raiders damaged a Union wagon train, railroad track, and telegraph wire. Company B struck the rangers from the north while the five other companies attacked from the south. The Comanches succeeded in routing their tory rivals; when the battalion arrived, many of the Federals were either cooking dinner or sleeping. Following the engagement, General Stuart allowed the Thirty-Fifth Virginia to raid Loudoun while still apart from Jones's Brigade in the summer and fall of 1863, during which it orchestrated ambushes against elements of the Army of the Potomac. Though White's cavalry experienced turbulence in its conversion to a regular battalion, it managed at times to become an unconventional unit again.[38]

But according to Frank Myers, serving in the Overland and Petersburg Campaigns of 1864 alongside the rest of the Laurel Brigade caused White's cavalrymen to begin to accept their status as regular soldiers who engaged a prepared enemy. Though they continued to dream of "roaming along the Potomac" again one day, they did not want to return to Loudoun until they defeated the Yankee invaders in central and eastern Virginia. Since they now realized that the importance of winning the national conflict exceeded that of fighting near their homes, the secessionist Loudouners' ideological commitment to Confederate independence now trumped the aspect of their loyalty based on local defense.[39]

Myers reveals that by 1865, unconventional warfare, once their "delight and pride," had become futile in the Comanches' minds. Three years of combat had produced great fatigue, reduced morale, and convinced them that their small, isolated raids and skirmishes were not sufficiently aiding the effort to defeat the invading Yankee hordes. They "all felt that to attain the liberty for which so much blood had already been spilled, there must be great . . . battles fought" by the regular Confederate army. The Thirty-Fifth Virginia thus spent the final months of the war willingly fighting for Southern independence wherever and in whatever style their republic needed them. The Comanches served conventionally for the remainder of the Petersburg and Appomattox Campaigns.[40]

The summer of 1863 highlighted the complex relationship between the Loudoun Rangers and Unionist civilians. The rangers' status as protectors of the county's pro-Union community caused this relationship to be mostly one of mutual aid and affection. During a brief stay in Waterford while the Gettysburg Campaign raged, the Loyal Virginia Cavalry received a joyous welcome from the inhabitants. As Goodhart claimed, "our command was a great favorite with the intensely loyal citizens of the Quaker village." With Unionist men exiled due to the threat of Confederate arrest, the mostly female population demonstrated their appreciation for the rangers' service by cheering them "with many a hurrah for the Union" and waving handkerchiefs and the U.S. flag.[41]

But interactions between the Loudoun Rangers and pro-Union civilians could also become antagonistic over the issue of foraging. After the unit relocated to Point of Rocks, Means's men captured a horse belonging to John Dutton, a Waterford merchant and prominent Quaker who had moved to the Maryland town to support his family when the war closed his store. Means refused to return the horse until Brigadier General John R. Kenly ordered him to do so. Despite his Unionist convictions, Dutton stated in a letter that since he moved to Point of Rocks, for reasons unclear, the ranger commander had "made frequent threats against my person and property" and "has urged some of his men to insult and abuse me."[42]

In March and April 1864, a challenge to the status of the Loudoun Rangers as partisan cavalry occurred, one which resembled that of the Thirty-Fifth Virginia in the winter of 1862–63, further highlighting the localist aspect of Loudoun County loyalty. At the end of March, the Department of West Virginia ordered Captain Means to send his command, then stationed at Point of Rocks, to Charleston, West Virginia, to be consolidated with the Third West Virginia Cavalry Regiment, which would transform the rangers into regular cavalrymen. Means and his men protested, refusing to comply with the order. They argued that the order violated the service Secretary Stanton had authorized for them when they first formed as a unit. As Means stated, "My command was raised in Loudoun . . . by special order of the War Department as an independent organization, mustered into service by myself with prescribed geographical limits." Therefore, the rangers, he maintained, have "no connection" with any conventional Union cavalry unit. The persistent refusal of Means to comply convinced Lincoln and Stanton to dismiss him from military service for disobeying orders. Yet Stanton also revoked the consolidation order, allowing the rest of the mutineers to remain partisans tasked with driving Confederate irregulars out of Loudoun for the duration of the war. Daniel M. Keyes replaced Means as captain. Loudouners fighting in irregular units conceived to scout, ambush, and raid in and around their county sought to put their lives on the line for their government only on the condition that they do so near their homes and with limited regulations. Through their resistance, the Loudoun Rangers were an irregular version of the regular Federal units consisting of Southerners who declined to perform missions far from their homes.[43]

As his band increased its activity in Loudoun County and along the Potomac River in 1864, John Mobberly became an ever-growing annoyance for the Union army, prompting the Yankees to conduct a series of counterirregular operations against his guerrillas. On November 11, Mobberly and twenty-five of his men ambushed eleven men of the Second Massachusetts Cavalry riding toward Harpers Ferry. At some point that year, he and his second in command, French Bill, murdered a Union surgeon after he surrendered. To put an end to these activities, General Stevenson, commander of Union forces in Harpers Ferry, selected the Loudoun Rangers for a mission to capture Bill in late November. With the aid of horse tracks on the snow-covered ground, four partisans tracked him down near Lovettsville. Bill fired his revolver at the rangers, but Waterford farmer Samuel Tritapoe and Joseph Ritchie of Gordonsville knocked the weapon out of his hand, captured him, and brought him into the custody of Union officials, who hanged Bill for his crime.[44]

The Loudouners' rivalries with Confederate irregulars concluded in early April 1865. On April 5, the Federal partisans attempted to capture or kill Mobberly. After he placed a bounty on Mobberly's head for "badly" scourging Loudoun County and becoming "such a terror" to its civilians, General Stevenson ordered a squad of three rangers "to wipe out the notorious guerrilla." After killing Mobberly and mortally wounding band member James Riley in an ambush in the Blue Ridge, the rangers returned to Harpers Ferry with the guerrilla leader's body. On April 6, 1865, fifty of Mosby's rangers executed a surprise assault on the Loyal Virginia Cavalry's camp near Halltown, capturing a large proportion of the command. The decisive victory in the counterirregular campaign against Mobberly and the crushing defeat at the hands of Mosby were the last engagements of the war for the Loudoun Rangers.[45]

After General Lee's army surrendered at Appomattox, the Comanches rode back to Loudoun, where they disbanded, received paroles, and felt anguish over the failure of the Confederate experiment. Upon hearing the news of the Army of Northern Virginia's defeat, Myers was devastated, commenting in a diary, "I am sure I was never in so much trouble in all my life." During the journey home, he felt "sick" and "worn out." Myers reflected on his military service of the last three years and several days: "I know I had rather been killed in my first battle . . . than pass thro the experience of the last three days." He could not "face that we are subjected," asserting, "If the people will do their duty, the Army will whip the Yankees yet." When he returned to his residence, the bitter Confederate Loudouner dreaded submitting to the Union army, but he regretfully received a parole on April 25. These sentiments attest to Myers's political allegiance to the national Confederacy rather than his localism.[46]

Meanwhile, the region's Union forces succeeded in eliminating what remained of Mobberly's band, thereby ending Loudoun County's irregular war. Upon the death of their leader, the remaining guerrillas surrendered to the Union army and acquired paroles on April 19, to the relief and satisfaction of the Federals in northern Virginia. Once the remaining elements of the Confederate army surrendered, the Loudoun Rangers mustered out at Bolivar, West Virginia, on May 31. Briscoe Goodhart concluded his narrative by stating that the rangers responded to Union victory and emancipation with jubilation.[47]

From 1862 to 1865, the Unionist and pro-Confederate populations of Loudoun County, Virginia, participated in a local irregular war with direct aid from their national governments. While the Loudoun Rangers played a key role in destroying an infamous Confederate guerrilla band and conducted the bulk of the Union army's counterirregular war in their county, the loyal cavalrymen ultimately failed in their mission to completely rid Loudoun of rebel irregulars and performed poorly in combat, barely avoiding their own elimination. In their on-and-off irregular campaign against Means's "renegades" and regular Yankee occupiers, the Comanches also could only claim a draw despite numerous victories. The only clear result in Loudoun County's irregular conflict is that Mobberly's guerrillas suffered defeat. Like the other inner civil wars, it was the end of the national conflict that convinced irregulars to put down their weapons. The three Loudoun-based unconventional commands ultimately demonstrate that the war's irregular fighters can shed light on Civil War–era political allegiances; on how each military combated the irregular threat; on different types of irregular warfare; on the often hazy boundaries between irregular, counterirregular, and conventional warfare; and on how irregular soldiers could play a role in a principal theater of the war. Further work is needed on how such combatants could be ideologically motivated as well as on additional variants of unconventional warfare. The Civil War's irregular is an elusive individual, but conflicts like Loudoun County's inner war help historians come closer to understanding the unconventional warrior and the world in which he lived.

NOTES

I extend my gratitude to local historians John and Bronwen Souders for giving me access to their collection of Civil War–era letters and diaries. I thank Barton Myers, Brian McKnight, Barbara Hahn, Gretchen Adams, James Sandy, Amanda Lancaster, and Tiffany González for critiquing earlier versions of this essay.

1. Forsythe, *Guerrilla Warfare and Life in Libby Prison,* 9; Goodhart, *Independent Loudoun Virginia Rangers,* 127.

2. Goodhart, *Independent Loudoun Virginia Rangers,* 127, 197–98; Forsythe, *Guerrilla Warfare and Life in Libby Prison,* 8–11.

3. John E. Divine, *35th Battalion Virginia Cavalry* (Lynchburg, Va.: H. E. Howard, 1985), 42.

4. The preeminent monograph espousing the ideological interpretation is James McPherson, *For Cause and Comrades: Why Men Fought in the Civil War* (New York: Oxford University Press, 1997). For works arguing that localism determined loyalties to a greater extent than other factors such as ideology, see Sarris, *Separate Civil War;* and Bynum, *Long Shadow of the Civil War.*

5. Mackey, *Uncivil War;* Sutherland, *Savage Conflict;* Fellman, *Inside War;* Sarris, *Separate Civil War;* Bynum, *Long Shadow of the Civil War;* Myers, *Rebels against the Confederacy,* chap. 4; Noe, "Exterminating Savages," 104–31.

6. Sutherland, *Savage Conflict,* vi–ix; Myers, *Executing Daniel Bright,* 45, 50–51; Mackey, *Uncivil War,* 5–11. Robert Mackey covers the guerrilla war in Arkansas, the partisan war in Virginia, and the regular cavalry raiding in Tennessee and Kentucky.

7. Charles Poland Jr., *From Frontier to Suburbia: Loudoun County, Virginia* (Westminster, Md.: Heritage Books, 2005), 179, 184–87; Samuel N. Grubb (no. 12667), Southern Claims Commission Approved Claims, 1871–80: Virginia, microfilm M2094, roll 28, Records of the Accounting Officers

of the Department of the Treasury, RG 217, National Archives and Records Administration, Washington, D.C. (hereafter NARA); James Fields (no. 11342), Barred and Disallowed Case Files of the Southern Claims Commission, 1871–80: Virginia, microfilm M1407, roll 27, Records of the U.S. House of Representatives, RG 233, NARA.

8. Frank M. Myers, *The Comanches: A History of White's Battalion, Virginia Cavalry, Laurel Brig., Hampton Div., A.N.V., C.S.A.* (Baltimore: Kelly, Piet, 1871), 8, 16, 18, 363; Sutherland, *Savage Conflict,* 91–94.

9. Franklin M. Myers Service Record, NARA, accessed via www.fold3.com; Myers, *Comanches,* 5, 19, 21, 219, 226, 336, 393. For the writings of a secessionist family in southern Loudoun that sent men to the Confederate army, see Margaret Ann Vogstberger, *The Dulanys of Welbourne: A Family in Mosby's Confederacy* (Berryville, Va.: Rockbridge, 1995). For a thorough examination of Confederate soldiers' cultural demonization of the Union army, see Jason Phillips, *Diehard Rebels: The Confederate Culture of Invincibility* (Athens: University of Georgia Press, 2007), 40–75.

10. Myers, *Comanches,* 278, 356.

11. Ibid., 21–22, 359.

12. U.S. Bureau of the Census, Population Schedule of the Eighth Census of the United States, 1860, Loudoun County, Va., NARA; 35th Battalion Service Records, NARA, accessed via www.fold3.com; U.S. Bureau of the Census, Slave Schedule of the Eighth Census of the United States, 1860, Loudoun County, Va., NARA.

13. Myers, *Comanches,* 19, 28–29, 36; U.S. Bureau of the Census, Population Schedule of the Eighth Census of the United States, 1860, Loudoun County, Va., NARA, microfilm 486, reel 166, microfilm 476, reel 156, microfilm 425, reel 105.

14. Myers, *Comanches,* 34–36; Report of John W. Geary, May 14, 1862, U.S. War Department, *War of the Rebellion,* ser. 1, 5:512–15 (hereafter cited as *O.R.*).

15. Myers, *Comanches,* 40, 71–72, 115, 121–22; Confederate Congress, *Partisan Ranger Act,* Apr. 21, 1862; Divine, *35th Battalion Virginia Cavalry,* 11, 13.

16. Rebecca Williams Diary, Apr. 25, May 20, Aug. 12, 18, 1861, William Williams Memoir, 1888, and Mollie Dutton to Franklin Steer, Mar. 1862, in John E. Divine, Bronwen C. Souders, and John M. Souders, *To Talk Is Treason: Quakers of Waterford, Virginia, on Life, Love, Death, and War in the Southern Confederacy* (Waterford, Va.: Waterford Foundation, 1996), 24, 28, 33, 35–37, 57–75; Alfred Fox (no. 11786), Southern Claims Commission Approved Claims.

17. Bynum, *Long Shadow of the Civil War;* Sarris, *Separate Civil War;* Fisher, *War at Every Door.* For works on Union soldiers recruited from the South, see Freehling, *South vs. The South;* and Richard N. Current, *Lincoln's Loyalists: Union Soldiers from the Confederacy* (Lebanon, N.H.: Northeastern University Press, 1992).

18. Goodhart, *Independent Loudoun Virginia Rangers,* 23–24, 26–27.

19. Forsythe, *Guerrilla Warfare and Life in Libby Prison,* 1–3.

20. Ibid., 4; Myers, *Comanches,* 360.

21. For a discussion on how Southern dissidents whose wartime allegiances primarily took the form of concrete local concerns crafted an ideological version of themselves in postwar memory, see Sarris, *Separate Civil War,* 144–80. Two sources articulating the ideology of Loudoun's pro-Union civilians are Charles P. Janney to Elisha H. Walker, May 13, 1861, Apr. 2, 1864, Walker Family Papers, Waterford Foundation Archives, Waterford, Va.

22. Goodhart, *Independent Loudoun Virginia Rangers,* 8, 11, 14, 199, 203; Forsythe, *Guerrilla Warfare and Life in Libby Prison,* 1, 28–47. For accounts on the "Absolute Union" in late-eighteenth and nineteenth-century American thought, see Paul C. Nigel, *One Nation Indivisible: The Union in American Thought, 1776–1861* (New York: Oxford University Press, 1964); and Myers, *Rebels against the Confederacy,* chap. 1.

23. A. Glenn Crothers, *Quakers Living in the Lion's Mouth: The Society of Friends in Northern Virginia, 1730–1865* (Gainesville: University Press of Florida, 2012), xi, 4; Goodhart, *Independent Loudoun Virginia Rangers,* 8–9; Forsythe, *Guerrilla Warfare and Life in Libby Prison,* 1.

24. Goodhart, *Independent Loudoun Virginia Rangers,* 199; Forsythe, *Guerrilla Warfare and Life in Libby Prison,* 1–2. For accounts that discuss Loudoun County Quaker abolitionism, see Fairfax Quarterly Meeting Minutes, Aug. 1861, Aug. 1865, Friends Historical Library, Fairfax, Va.; Fairfax Women's Quarterly Meeting Minutes, Aug. 1860, ibid.; and Samuel M. Janney, *Memoirs of Samuel M. Janney, Late of Lincoln, Loudoun County, Va., a Minister in the Religious Society of Friends* (Philadelphia: Friend's Book Association, 1890).

25. U.S. Bureau of the Census, Population Schedule of the Eighth Census of the United States, 1860, Loudoun County, Va., NARA; U.S. Bureau of the Census, Slave Schedule of the Eighth Census of the United States, 1860, Loudoun County, Va., NARA; Loudoun County Rangers Service Records, NARA, accessed via www.fold3.com.

26. Goodhart, *Independent Loudoun Virginia Rangers,* 29–30.

27. Myers, *Comanches,* 95, 97, 99; Forsythe, *Guerrilla Warfare and Life in Libby Prison,* 11, 25, 33–34; Robert R. Walker to James M. Walker, Aug. 27, 1862, Walker Family Papers, WFA; Eliza H. Walker to James M. Walker, Aug. 27, 1862, ibid.; William Williams to James W. Walker, Aug. 27, 1862, ibid.

28. Goodhart, *Independent Loudoun Virginia Rangers,* 33, 38–40; William Williams to James W. Walker, Aug. 27, 1862, Walker Family Papers, WFA; D. S. Miles to Halleck, Aug. 27, 1862, *O.R.,* ser. 1, 12(3):705; James A. Cox Service Record, James W. Gregg Service Record, Thadeus W. Franklin Service Record, Charles Dixson Service Record, and Henry Dixson Service Record, NARA, accessed via www.fold3.com; Myers, *Comanches,* 101–103, 395, 397; U.S. Bureau of the Census, Population Schedule of the Eighth Census of the United States, 1860, Loudoun County, Va., NARA, microfilm 463, reel 143, microfilm 623, reel 95, microfilm 422, reel 102, microfilm 413, reel 93, microfilm 412, reel 92; Luther W. Slater to William H. Chesenough, Feb. 16, 1863, Luther W. Slater Service Record, 9, NARA, accessed via www.fold3.com; Susan Walker to James M. Walker, Aug. 27, 1862, Walker Family Papers, WFA; Eliza H. Walker to James M. Walker, Aug. 27, 1862, ibid.

29. Goodhart, *Independent Loudoun Virginia Rangers,* 35–36; Eliza H. Walker to James M. Walker, Aug. 27, 1862, Walker Family Papers, WFA; Myers, *Comanches,* 102–104.

30. J. E. B. Stuart to R. H. Chilton, Feb. 13, 1864, *O.R.,* ser. 1, 12(2):745; Report of Thomas T. Munford, ibid., 749; Report of Dixon Miles, ibid., 805; Goodhart, *Independent Loudoun Virginia Rangers,* 41–44, 55–58.

31. Myers, *Comanches,* 109–11.

32. Ibid., 148; Sutherland, *Savage Conflict,* 476–78.

33. Myers, *Comanches,* 148–50.

34. U.S. Bureau of the Census, Population Schedule of the Eighth Census of the United States, 1860, Loudoun County, Va., NARA, microfilm 477, reel 157; Sutherland, *Savage Conflict,* 480.

35. J. D. Stevenson to E. M. Stanton, Mar. 28, 1865, *O.R.*, ser. 1, 46(3):240–41; John D. Stevenson to Morgan, Apr. 1, 1865, ibid., 444–45; Charles P. Janney to Elisha H. Walker, Apr. 2, 1864, Walker Family Papers, WFA; U.S. Bureau of the Census, Population Schedule of the Eighth Census of the United States, 1860, Loudoun County, Va., NARA, microfilm 635, reel 107.

36. Richard E. Crouch, *Rough-Riding Scout: The Story of John W. Mobberly, Loudoun's Own Civil War Guerrilla Hero* (Arlington, Va.: Elden Editions, 1994), 2; Forsythe, *Guerrilla Warfare and Life in Libby Prison,* 8; Joshua Everhart (no. 11653), Southern Claims Commission Approved Claims; C. Arthur Newcomer, *Cole's Cavalry; or, Three Years in the Saddle in the Shenandoah Valley* (Baltimore: Cushing, 1895), 93; Leslie, *Devil Knows How to Ride;* Castel and Goodrich, *Bloody Bill Anderson;* Sarris, *Separate Civil War,* 135–38.

37. C. Crowninshield to A. E. Dana, Nov. 11, 1864, *O.R.*, ser. 1, 43(2):604; John D. Stevenson to Morgan, Apr. 1, 1865, ibid., 46(3):444–45; James H. Riley Service Record and William H. Tribette Service Record, NARA, accessed via www.fold3.com; U.S. Bureau of the Census, Population Schedule of the Eighth Census of the United States, 1860, Loudoun County, Virginia, NARA, microfilm 475, reel 155, microfilm 327, reel 007.

38. E. V. White Service Record, 57, NARA, accessed via www.fold3.com; E. V. White to J. E. B. Stuart, June 18, 1863, *O.R.*, ser. 1, 27(2):770; J. W. Garrett to E. M. Stanton, June 18, 1863, ibid., 27(3):200–201; George D. Summers to R. Bruce, July 12, 1863, ibid., 27(2):203–204; Myers, *Comanches,* 188, 190; Goodhart, *Independent Loudoun Virginia Rangers,* 90; E. V. White to W. E. Jones, June 20, 1863, *O.R.*, ser. 1, 27(2):770–71. For the 35th Virginia's additional raids, see E. V. White to J. E. B. Stuart, Aug. 29, 1863, ibid., 29(1):92–93; E. V. White to J. E. B. Stuart, Sept. 2, 1863, ibid., 93; and E. V. White to J. E. B. Stuart, Oct. 2, 1863, ibid., 203–204.

39. Myers, *Comanches,* 255–312.

40. Ibid., 364–92.

41. Goodhart, *Independent Loudoun Virginia Rangers,* 101–102.

42. John Dutton to Anna Dutton, Apr. 28, 1863, in Divine, Souders, and Souders, *To Talk Is Treason,* 48–49.

43. Goodhart, *Independent Loudoun Virginia Rangers,* 123–24; Taylor M. Chamberlin and John M. Souders, *Between Reb and Yank: A Civil War History of Northern Loudoun County, Virginia* (Jefferson, N.C.: McFarland, 2011), 236; E. D. Townsend, Special Orders, Apr. 13, 1864, Samuel C. Means Service Record, 22, NARA, accessed via www.fold3.com; F. Sigel to Max Weber, Apr. 19, 1864, *O.R.*, ser. 1, 33:912; H. M. Burleigh to Provost Marshal, Apr. 24, 1864, ibid., 965; Max Weber to Averell, Apr. 13, 1864, ibid., 859–80; T. Melvin to Crook, Apr. 26, 1864, ibid., 989; Sarris, *Separate Civil War,* 128–29, 140.

44. Goodhart, *Independent Loudoun Virginia Rangers,* 173–74; C. Crowninshield to A. E. Dana, Nov. 11, 1864, *O.R.*, ser. 1, 43(2):604; D. Henry Bartnete to Stevenson, Dec. 1, 1864, ibid., 721; John D. Stevenson to Sheridan, Dec. 2, 1864, ibid., 727; U.S. Bureau of the Census, Population Schedule of the Eighth Census of the United States, 1860, Loudoun County, Va., NARA, microfilm 425, reel 105, microfilm 414, reel 94.

45. Goodhart, *Independent Loudoun Virginia Rangers,* 194–95, 197–98; Brig. J. D. Stevenson to E. M. Stanton, Mar. 28, 1865, *O.R.*, ser. 1, 46(3):240–41; Forsythe, *Guerrilla Warfare and Life in Libby Prison,* 10–11; J. D. Stevenson to E. M. Stanton, Apr. 5, 1865, *O.R.*, ser. 1, 46(3):590; Williamson, *Mosby's Rangers,* 364.

46. Frank M. Myers Diary, Apr. 9–25, May 12, 1865, Waterford Foundation Archives, Waterford, Va.; Myers, *Comanches,* 392.

47. John D. Stevenson to Mitchell, Apr. 19, 1865, *O.R.,* ser. 1, 46(3):840; W. G. Mitchell to Stevenson, Apr. 19, 1865, ibid., 841; Goodhart, *Independent Loudoun Virginia Rangers,* 199, 201.

AMERICAN WARLORD

Reconsidering "Guerrilla" Leader John Gatewood

ADAM H. DOMBY

Blackstone Hendricks died quickly. Around 11:00 P.M. on February 8, 1865, a party of some seventy-five to eighty horsemen surrounded Hendricks's home in Walker County, Georgia. When the armed men ordered him to come outside, he had no choice but to comply. He was then led fifty yards or so from the residence, at which point the red-bearded leader of the band, John Gatewood, shot him twice in rapid succession, once in the temple and once in the chest. The armed band then began shooting his corpse, leaving eighteen bullets in his body. With the deed done, the fun began for Gatewood and his men. The band ransacked Hendricks's house before riding to the home of Thomas Evatt and murdering him in the same manner. Gatewood and his men then headed south, away from Union lines.[1]

At first glance it would seem logical to explain Hendricks's death as an act of war. A thirty-eight-year-old farmer who had previously worked as a scout for the Union army, Hendricks surely had his share of enemies in northern Georgia due to his political allegiance.[2] But Gatewood was not a commissioned officer leading a cavalry unit, nor was he a champion of the Confederacy. Rather, he was something altogether different: a violent Confederate deserter whose loyalty belonged to the Confederacy only when it suited his purpose.

Originally from Fentress County, Tennessee, Gatewood initially enlisted in the Fourth Tennessee Cavalry but deserted in the winter of 1862–63 and joined Champ Ferguson's gang. Fairly quickly, Gatewood began exhibiting behavior that could be described as sociopathic, at one point braining three Union soldiers with a rock in order to save ammunition. In 1863 he left Ferguson's gang and formed his own militant band of deserters, recusant conscripts, and armed men who embarked on a reign of terror across northern Georgia and eastern Tennessee.[3] Numbering from fifty to one hundred members at any given time, his own gang killed, robbed, and intimidated civilians who did not flee the region during the last year of the war.[4] Gatewood was, by all accounts, extremely unstable and unpredictable, once sparing a man because "he had already killed a lot of men that day." By contrast, he once murdered twenty-five individuals, "including deserters, refugees, and innocent bystanders," in a two-day span. The total number of his victims will never be known, but the fear his actions instilled in citizens ensured that he became known as the "red-bearded beast from Georgia."[5]

These killings sometimes aligned with Confederate interests, but this was mostly a side effect of behavior benefiting Gatewood. Tellingly, few of his attacks were against Union soldiers. Even when he attacked them, it was usually a self-serving move to discourage pursuit or to profit materially.[6] Moreover, he routinely robbed individuals who were loyal to the Confederacy, including more than one "zealous supporter of the Southern cause."[7] In all likelihood, Gatewood targeted his victims not for their political beliefs, but for opposing his band of armed militants. Challenging his control of a region and his ability to do and steal as he pleased could lead to a shortened life expectancy.

For example, in November 1864 Gatewood and his men captured eight fleeing Unionists in Polk County, Tennessee. The captives were from Georgia and had been on their way to enlist in the Federal army, which would have provided an opportunity to return law and order to the region, protect the men's families, and allow them to seek revenge on those who had harmed them. Six of them would never get the opportunity. Instead, Gatewood lined the unarmed prisoners up and began shooting them in the head one at a time. Realizing their turn was soon to come, two of the captives made a run for it and escaped. The dead from the Madden Branch Massacre, as the event became known, were just the best known of Gatewood's many victims.[8] But they were not the only ones who died when attempting to impede Gatewood's free rein over the region.

While some might see the killing of Hendricks as an attack upon a Union sympathizer and an act of war on behalf of the Confederacy, the murder was also a personal deed. As a local citizen serving as an informant to Union forces, Hendricks represented a threat to Gatewood and his men. The occasional Union patrols that passed through the region hunted for such armed bands, and Hendricks's continued existence endangered their domination of the war-torn region. Indeed, the details of the murder are known to historians because a Union scout had left Hendricks's house just moments before the irregulars' arrival and witnessed the events from his hiding place in the woods.[9] Similarly, the Madden Branch victims were on their way to join a unit tasked with hunting Gatewood down.

And yet Gatewood has usually been remembered as a Confederate guerrilla. The only book-length biography of him is subtitled *Confederate Bushwhacker.*[10] But characterizing Gatewood as a devoted Confederate nationalist is profoundly unsatisfying and not supported by primary sources. A deep reading of these materials reveals that he was not much of a Confederate and that the term "guerrilla" is at best an inexact categorization.

The problem with the traditional characterization of Gatewood becomes evident when comparing him to a partisan ranger like John Singleton Mosby. While Mosby attacked Union supply lines, disrupted communications, and tied down a large number of Federal troops in northern Virginia, Gatewood was far less effective in hampering Union army operations. He ranged across a region that stretched from the southeastern tip of Tennessee across northeastern Georgia but attacked Northern supply lines only occasionally. Instead, Gatewood usually targeted civilians with Unionist sympathies for his own profit. Indeed, after November 1864 the region in which he operated had few if any Union troops in it, and yet he remained in the area stealing, killing, and intimidating inhabitants until after the war ended.[11]

Some historians have recognized the problems with characterizing Gatewood as a Confederate. Jonathan Dean Sarris's work has emphasized that identifying "sides" in northern Georgia's civil war was difficult, if not impossible, due to the importance of local issues and alliances. Though individuals might claim they were Unionists or Confederates to justify their actions, ideology and national politics were often not the driving forces behind their actions. Even Southern newspapers at the time recognized that the complexities of loyalty meant that most of the armed bands in North Georgia were "generally made up and headed by deserters from our [Confederate] army," though they often included recusant conscripts (essentially draft dodgers) and Union deserters as well. Sarris may have put it best when he observed that Gatewood's loyalty was "vague and malleable."[12]

This essay reassesses Gatewood's role in the Civil War. A reinterpretation of his movements during the fall of 1864 and the following winter provides an alternative potential narrative of his wartime career.[13] This new perspective presents Gatewood as a murderous criminal and deserter uninterested in the larger national conflict rather than a diehard Confederate who simply chafed under others' authority. A reexamination of much of the same evidence used by previous historians suggests that Gatewood was a man driven not by a desperate devotion to a dying nation but by his own desire to control the situation. Although previously understood as a highly effective Confederate guerrilla, Gatewood actually posed little threat to the Union war effort and rarely, if ever, worked with conventional Southern forces. An examination of northern Georgia's resemblances to a failed state and a consideration of the similarities (and differences) between twentieth-century warlords and Gatewood present the militant in a different light. Considering him not as Confederate but as an autonomous armed militant provides insights into Gatewood's larger influence on the war. Indeed, it becomes clear that he harmed the Confederate war effort by motivating Southern troops to desert and return home to protect their families. Finally, a comparison between Gatewood and other armed groups in the region shows that there were multiple types of militants in northern Georgia, and future scholars must work to distinguish between different types of armed groups fighting in the irregular conflicts across the South.[14]

* * *

One of the reasons historians have perceived Gatewood as a Confederate is that Union authorities did not distinguish between him and other Confederate guerrillas. Though Southern authorities viewed Gatewood as a deserter, Union troops saw him as a rebel robbing their supply lines. Fearing Gatewood intended to wreak havoc on his supply lines, Major General William T. Sherman himself ordered a brigade out to chase the militant leader on October 24, 1864, ordering the troops to "let the people also understand that . . . if they want to save what little corn and potatoes [they have], they must manage to get Gatewood disposed of, for he will bring ruin on them all." But it is not clear that his interpretation of Gatewood's intentions was correct. Indeed, an examination of Gatewood's movements suggests Sherman overestimated the danger he represented. Far from attacking Union forces, the militant was actually avoiding conflict with the army; when Federal troops arrived in his vicinity, he moved into a new area.[15]

On September 15, as Sherman's forces rested around the recently captured Atlanta, Gatewood was busy "indiscriminately" robbing individuals (of various espoused loyalties) west of Rome, Georgia, near the Alabama-Georgia border, far from Union lines.[16] In early October, General John Bell Hood's army moved north of Atlanta in an attempt to cut Union supply lines. Sherman chased the

Confederates north in a large loop through Snake Creek Gap and Villanow (in Walker County) before cutting southeast and ending in Cherokee County, Alabama, due west of Rome. On October 11, 1864, just five days before the Federals passed through the region in pursuit of Hood, a Union patrol reported a skirmish the previous day with Gatewood's force in the northernmost section of Floyd County, twenty miles south of Villanow. In late October, Sherman worried that the militant gang was aiming to attack his supply lines, which now stretched through Rome into Cherokee County.[17] To protect them, he ordered patrols out toward Dirt Town and Coosaville to meet the expected attack from Gatewood. The patrols, however, found no sign of him.[18]

The conventional interpretation by historians has been that Gatewood called off his planned attack on Union supply lines due to these patrols and instead went north into Walker County, arriving there by the end of October. In this version of events, he "sensed that his luck would run out if he lingered" in the area where Sherman's army was based.[19] This interpretation is largely based on documents created by Union troops. It assumes that the general and other Union officers understood Gatewood's actions and motivations correctly.

An alternate interpretation seems equally likely: Gatewood never had any intention of attacking the army and had already left Floyd County by the time Sherman's order was given.[20] Perhaps he had not moved south toward Sherman's supply lines but instead had moved north into Walker or Chattooga County to avoid Union forces.[21] If indeed it was his gang that the scouts encountered on October 10, it may indicate that instead of threatening Sherman, Gatewood was actually moving in front of and away from Hood, then advancing on the rail line at Resaca. After all, Gatewood was a deserter known to rob Confederate families, and he risked execution if captured by Southern forces.[22] In this version of events, Gatewood likely escaped northward before Sherman ever issued his order.

Sherman's October 24 order to hunt Gatewood was likely based on faulty intelligence. Scouts' reports were notoriously inaccurate, full of rumors and false information. In some of the surviving reports, Gatewood is incorrectly reported to be a Union deserter, dead, and to have gained a Confederate commission in exchange for stopping "the plundering and guerilla warfare" and returning to the army.[23] The first was incorrect, the latter two wishful thinking by civilian informants. While some Union scouts believed that Gatewood cooperated with Major General Joseph Wheeler's cavalry and other units, no wartime reports from a Confederate officer note working with the deserter in any official capacity.[24] Indeed, Wheeler's own men later actively disavowed Gatewood's activities, saying "not one of [Gatewood's men] belongs to [Wheeler's] command, unless he is a deserter."[25]

Even if one trusts the reports of Union scouts on Gatewood's movements, it seems likely that he was busy avoiding contact with the Federals during October 1864, and his movements over the remainder of the year also display a desire to avoid Union forces. On November 15, Sherman set off for Savannah, abandoning North Georgia. A week later, scouts brought back reports that Gatewood was in either Broomtown, Georgia, or Lebanon, Alabama—both far from any supply line or Union force. He would not stay along Georgia's western border for long. With the region between Atlanta and Chattanooga no longer heavily patrolled by troops protecting the railroad, Gatewood crossed northwestern Georgia and, by the end of November, was reportedly in Polk County, Tennessee, where he personally killed as many as twenty-two civilians.[26] On December 1, a patrol of locally raised Union troops, hunting gangs like Gatewood's, were said to have made contact with his band in northern Fannin County, causing him to flee again.[27] Gatewood's path during late 1864 constantly took him away from both the Union and Confederate armies into regions that were on the periphery of the war, purposefully avoiding those areas where the presence of troops kept them from devolving into anarchy.

Gatewood's avoidance of Union forces means that he represented no strategic threat to the army. Instead, he thrived in disordered regions that lacked any legal authority and only had occasional patrols passing through them. By November 22, the assistant adjutant general for the Union's District of the Etowah (encompassing North Georgia) had determined that "except for the damage inflicted upon loyal citizens, [Gatewood's men] do not appear to be worthy of much consideration."[28]

* * *

In examining northern Georgia from November 1864 to April 1865, one sees that the region bears more resemblance to Somalia in the 1990s than Richmond, Virginia, in 1865. With the withdrawal of Union forces, a war zone became an ignored backwater with no authorities controlling the region. All state apparatus that ensured domestic tranquility had disappeared with the retreat of the

Confederate army, and the withdrawal of Union troops left a power vacuum in North Georgia when the Confederacy simply failed to return. Huge segments of the population had fled as refugees from this liminal zone, either south before May 1864 or north with the Federal withdrawal in November. Armed bands roamed at will, and occasional Union patrols did little to protect civilians from the rampages of armed groups. After the Union withdrawal, one devout Southerner wrote to a friend, "we almost wish for the Yankees again since we can't have a Confederate force to protect us, the Yankees never came into our house to trouble us" as the armed men roaming the countryside did.[29] Although these bands often called themselves "Confederate scouts" or "Union home guards," rarely did they actually have any attachment to the state or either national cause.

The region looked more like a failed state than part of a nascent nation. Account after account notes how "the people generally were infinitely better off when the Yankees occupied the country." A letter to the *Atlanta Intelligencer* published in February 1865 from a man who had visited northern Georgia the month previous noted, "all of the northwestern counties are subjugated by those calling themselves Confederate scouts," most of whom were actually deserters. Conditions were so bad that without help, northern Georgia's "women and children must starve." Getting them food, however, would require the military. As the chronicler of woes wrote: "There is no civil law. Law and Order are put at defiance."[30]

Political scientists have defined failed states in a variety of ways, but key among them is a loss of control of a government's territory. Many scholars use Max Weber's definition of statehood, which requires a state to maintain "monopoly on the legitimate use of physical force." Among other features, failed states are characterized by an inability to maintain control and order within their borders, increased levels of political and criminal violence, the use of terror against civilian populations, a loss of infrastructure and government services, and food shortages—a description that fits North Georgia in the winter of 1864–65.[31]

During this last winter of the war, food shortages were severe, many North Georgia residents fled the region, and acts of violence by armed bands were a daily occurrence. In Ellijay, one report indicated that "scarcely a night passes away without some unoffending citizen being killed by these murderers." The use of torture to extort information and money, combined with the murder of any who resisted the bands of deserters, instilled fear in those civilians who remained.[32] In October 1864 the men of two Franklin County militia companies requested to be sent home to protect their farms from raids from Union forces and the "depredations of deserters from our own army." The petitioners also feared their families would not have enough to eat without someone to work the fields. Three months later, a letter to the governor of Georgia from twenty-eight citizens of Cartersville complained, "there are hundreds of lawless men traversing the county eating up the substance of the people with impunity, and if the authorities of our state do not come to our assistance the fertile fields in our valleys will not be cultivated and scores of helpless persons must starve for bread." The residents lamented the absence of any authority in the county: "[W]e now have no protection from any quarter. There is no legal organization of any kind in our county."[33]

The Confederate state ceased to exist in northern Georgia for all intents and purposes in May 1864, and it never really returned. Even mail service in Rome, which had stopped when Hood's army withdrew, would not restart until March 12, 1865, four months after Union forces withdrew from the town.[34] Slow mail was the least of the citizens' worries. In the power vacuum that remained, bands of deserters, recusant conscripts, and criminals banded together and took advantage of the prevailing anarchy.

Even Confederate officers recognized the failure of their nation to maintain their sovereignty and control over the region. In December 1864, Confederate brigadier general William T. Wofford reported to Congressman Warren Akin of Bartow County: "[B]ands of robbers are going through the country and taking any thing they want and killing who they please. . . . There is no law of any kind in that section." Similar situations existed across northern Georgia. After a swing through the region to round up deserters from his regiment, one Confederate officer wrote to the governor of Georgia and informed him that the peaceful and loyal civilians there were "greatly oppressed by predatory bands calling themselves confederate soldiers" but in truth had no legal sanction.[35]

Though northern Georgia fit many of the requirements of a failed state, some scholars might point out that it is only a region of the larger Confederacy or even the state of Georgia. Though this is perhaps a fair criticism, political scientists have fortunately provided us with the term "fragmented states" for governments that "have lost their authority over definable pieces of their territory." Northern Georgia, then, can be seen as a "fragmented area" of a failing state. It lacked public services, saw increased violence of all sorts, and experienced terror as a tool of control, food shortages, and an end to the state's monopoly on the use of force. After the Confederate retreat in May 1864 and the Union withdrawal that November, no state actors were paying much attention to the region, let alone controlling it. While bodies of armed men, including Gatewood's, remained, they were largely "non-state actors," or what Anthony Vinci has deemed "armed groups" with little connection to the state.[36] It was in this environment that Gatewood operated.

In studying armed groups in the twentieth and twenty-first centuries, political scientists have struggled with the fact that "one of the most daunting aspects [of studying conflict] is that armed groups differ not only from states but also radically from each other."[37] Vinci's scholarship has shined light on the distinctions among warlords, insurgencies, terrorist groups, militias, and other armed groups. Similarly, armed groups in northern Georgia were often quite distinct. These bands of armed men were not just part of the American Civil War but each also part of private civil wars. "Armed groups" in the region fell into multiple categories. Some were ad-hoc militias formed to protect a community, some were criminal bands, and some leaders, like Gatewood, bore a striking though imperfect resemblance to what scholars of the twentieth century called warlords.

* * *

Examining northern Georgia as a fragmented or failing state raises the question of whether Gatewood represents the equivalent of a Somali warlords. By examining Gatewood's similarities to warlords and contrasting his motivations and actions with other groups of armed northern Georgians, it becomes clear that our current vocabulary is in need of enlargement. While warlord is not an accurate description for Gatewood, neither is Confederate guerrilla.

Though Gatewood was not a warlord in the modern sense, the similarities reveal how poorly the label "Confederate guerrilla" fits him and his ilk. While the term is ahistorical to the period and an imperfect fit, Gatewood looks more like a warlord than a diehard Confederate. Warlords—or as Kimberly Marten sarcastically calls them, "local power brokers"—can be defined in a multitude of ways. Indeed, most scholarly works start with a clarification of what the term means. Marten's definition that warlords are *"individuals who control small pieces of territory using a combination of force and patronage*" provides an excellent starting point. No matter the description, most scholars recognize that warlords use violence to retain personal control of their dominion, or as Vinci terms it, they "purposefully commit atrocities and use rampages of barbaric violence to create disorder" in which they are able to thrive and profit. Warlords are by their nature parasitic and exist where state control is weak. John MacKinlay defines them as acting "without interference from the state" and "in a strictly predatory manner." Warlords worry less about maintaining popular support (as, for example, an insurgency might) and more about enriching themselves.[38] They are driven not by ideology, religion, or nationalism, but by a desire to maintain their personal power.

Thus, while the terminology was developed for modern conflicts and is anachronistic to the Civil War, Gatewood fits many of the characteristics that scholars attribute to warlords. He controlled various parts of northern Georgia, at times through violence, and thrived in the disorder created by his atrocities. He also provided patronage to a select group of allies. Like a warlord, Gatewood took care of the men who followed him on his raids and ensured that they were frequently rewarded. In February 1865, his gang stole $14,000 dollars in Confederate bills from Ellijay, of which "there was not one dollar of it captured from a Yankee."[39] Gatewood apparently kept his band together through their spoils, and while he may have preferred killing Unionists, a Confederate's money was still worth taking.

Gatewood offered most Confederate sympathizers no special protection. Newspapers reported that his men "have done the Yankees and tories much harm; but they are also a terror to our own people, and on the whole do us much more [harm] than good." Some Confederate sympathizers, however, managed to gain from their affiliation with Gatewood. Sean O'Brien has suggested that some members of his gang joined to avoid becoming victims of his wrath. Additionally, some civilians benefited by providing information, protection, or supplies. Gatewood sold stolen cattle to Southern civilians (thus making a profit), and his acts of violence against rival bands and Unionist scouts may have provided incidental protection to some noncombatants. Still, for every Confederate loyalist who loved Gatewood, at least two more wished him dead.[40]

Far from being a Confederate who only stole from rebel civilians when they were "greedy misers" who "horded their wealth, prolonging the misery of their less fortunate brethren," as one later author justified Gatewood's failure to distinguish between his victims, it seems more likely that he simply did not care.[41] While Gatewood may have felt some allegiance to the Confederacy, he did not let ideology get in the way of a good robbery or killing, especially one that provided him with wealth and ensured his reputation would continue to intimidate northern Georgians into subservience. He may have avoided attacking less well-off Confederate loyalists for fear of alienating the entire population of the region, only risking creating enemies of secessionists when the payoff was large enough to warrant the risk.

Gatewood's was not the only supposed band of "Confederate scouts" robbing civilians of all stripes while undermining the functions of the Southern state. For example, in February 1865 a group led by Jack Colquitt reportedly stole around four thousand dollars that Georgia had just distributed to support the indigent families of Confederate soldiers in Whitfield County. Feuds between groups that should have been natural allies demonstrate how tenuous a link to the Confederacy each band had. In fact, though both were deserters from the army, Colquitt and Gatewood were as much at odds with each other and with other bands of deserters as they were with the Union army. The two gangs' territories overlapped: while Colquitt operated in the Floyd County region, Gatewood ranged from Polk County, Georgia (south of Floyd), and Cherokee County, Alabama (west of Floyd), all the way into southeastern Tennessee. At least one report—of uncertain veracity—even indicates that Colquitt may have been Gatewood's "most deadly foe."[42] Gatewood, for his part, was rumored to have killed multiple other guerrilla leaders, both Union and Confederate. According to one historian, Gatewood's "policy" was "to exterminate the other leaders and bands wherever he could." Whether this is true or not, he clearly felt no need to form alliances to fight the Northern army. While being marched through northern Georgia as a captured Union soldier, the great satirist Ambrose Bierce heard that "Gatewood was a 'guerrilla' chief of local notoriety." His decision to put "guerrilla" in quotations is telling, for Bierce's Confederate captors viewed this band of raiders not as allies. Indeed, he reported, Gatewood was "a greater terror to his friends than to his other foes."[43]

The militant leader even drew the ire of Confederate authorities. For example, in December 1864, Brigadier General Wofford was named commander to the newly created Department of North Georgia and given orders to pacify the region using any men he could find. While some deserters joined Wofford's new command after he promised them a pardon and an opportunity to help restore order, most ignored him but stayed home peacefully. Yet Wofford acknowledged that some five hundred or so "guerrillas of the Gatewood class" resisted his efforts to concentrate troops and regain control of northern Georgia for the Confederacy. Instead, these men wished to continue their rampage and robbing. Wofford even warned Union major general George H. Thomas of a planned raid by Gatewood on Union cattle pens; he was negotiating a surrender for Georgia troops and feared that Gatewood's actions would be viewed as official and undermine the talks.[44]

Gatewood rarely risked an attack on a substantial Federal unit. Instead, he attacked civilians and other soft targets that would enhance his wealth and fearsome reputation. The vast majority of his killings were isolated Union recruits, sympathizers, or individuals with wealth. While Gatewood repeatedly attacked Unionist recruits heading north to enlist in the army, he avoided seeking out troops to attack except when he saw an immediate advantage to himself. Indeed, reports indicate that when bands "start out on a stealing expedition, and every man is at his post, but meet the enemy," nine out of ten would disappear.[45]

Gatewood contributed to historians later viewing him as a Confederate, claiming the label himself when it suited him. Although he and his men claimed legitimacy by pretending to be affiliated with the state, such groups were rarely actually sanctioned. Gatewood likely declared having legal authority for his actions to discourage resistance, but that does not mean he actually possessed it. Just as his reputation for violence discouraged standing against him, stating that he was a Confederate provided him with another tool to keep civilians and other armed groups subdued. Claims of official status combined with a fearsome reputation ensured few resisted when Gatewood and his men robbed them. It is possible that some of his killings were measured actions to provide him with a reputation that discouraged resistance.

These actions showed a lack of interest in the Confederate war effort. Gatewood's greatest achievement attacking Federal forces was the stealing of cattle from a lightly guarded corral in Rossville, Georgia, in January 1865. He and his men then took these beeves south to Gaylesville, Alabama, to distribute them. While some writers have used this raid to portray Gatewood as a "Confederate 'Robin Hood'" feeding starving civilians, others interpret this as an attempt to supply the rebel army with food. Overlooked by most scholars is evidence that reveals a capitalistic profit-making venture instead: a Union scout following

Gatewood after the raid reported that the gang had sold cattle to civilians as they traveled.[46] There is no evidence that the stolen livestock ever made it to the Confederate army. Perhaps instead of a warlord, Gatewood is best viewed as a violent capitalist.

Though similarities exist, Gatewood does not fit the definition of a modern warlord perfectly. The most obvious distinction between them is that he never controlled his range as thoroughly as a warlord might do. In fact, it is hard to even determine where Gatewood centered his operations. Some scholars have placed his home in Gaylesville, Alabama, while others have suggested McClemore's Cove in Walker County, Georgia. Another placed it in Chattooga County. In a manner, each was correct. It seems that Gatewood moved his base of operations as circumstances warranted throughout the war, always avoiding more powerful enemies and preying upon the weak. His actions were part of a separate conflict, or indeed separate conflicts, being fought across the South away from the armies slugging it out in Virginia and the Carolinas.[47]

While the comparison may be at times imperfect, considering Gatewood's similarities to a warlord suggests a new framework to consider the conflict in northern Georgia and displays the need for a robust discussion on how historians define the belligerents in the Civil War. Although Gatewood's actions are more characteristic of a warlord or a highwayman, he has historically been grouped with the guerrillas and other irregulars fighting *for* the Confederate state. Gatewood's effect on the Southern war effort is clearly different than that of Mosby or William Quantrill. Looking at the other armed groups that he is lumped with, it becomes clear that the variety of combatants in Georgia requires further study. To call all the armed bands fighting in northern Georgia the same thing, whether it be guerrilla, insurgent, or irregular, obscures how different these groups were from each other. Recognizing that they all had different purposes and goals reveals a more accurate depiction of the "inner war."[48]

Numerous other armed groups in North Georgia were not affiliated with the state in the last year of the war. In addition to bands of deserters and brigands, gangs of armed men protecting their families and communities (but not part of the Georgia militia system) sprang up in multiple communities. After the withdrawal of a Union garrison, the forty-odd men remaining in the town of

Rome formed an ad-hoc patrol in an attempt to defend themselves from raiders. Members of the patrol included both secessionists and Unionists who committed to protect their neighbors. The attempt proved ineffective, however, and resulted in the death of at least one man—a secessionist—at the hands of Colquitt's band. Later in Polk County, a posse with diverse loyalties and backgrounds formed to hunt down and exterminate Colquitt's gang. They killed Colquitt himself and numerous other members of his band, starting a feud that continued into Reconstruction. Escaped prisoner of war John Kellogg, while making his way to Union lines, was fortunate enough to find a "Union Home Guard" in Pickens County that consisted of "about a hundred men banded together for mutual protection." Some members had been recusant conscripts and avoided service, while others were Confederate deserters. Federal forces apparently did not trust this homegrown protection unit, which had no official sanction, but the men frequently fought against "a guerrilla company . . . used by the Confederates as scouts" led by Benjamin Jordan.[49]

As with Gatewood, the legitimacy of Jordan's band was questionable. After the war, numerous members, including its leader, were charged in county courts with crimes such as murder and robbery for their wartime actions.[50] Yet a February 11, 1865, newspaper article claimed that Jordan's men were one of just two bands that the author knew of in northern Georgia with official authorization. The same article noted by name three other bands, including Gatewood's, that were not authorized. Regardless of Jordan's sanction, most armed groups in the region clearly had no official connection to either the Union or the Confederacy. Their reasons for forming varied. One of the other groups mentioned in the article reportedly included both Union and Confederate deserters who "do not fight and don't intend to fight," having "joined these bogus organizations to keep from fighting."[51]

Though they had an influence on the larger war, the irregular groups fighting in North Georgia often cared little about the national conflict except for how it affected their own private war. The band that Kellogg visited even attempted to negotiate a truce with their local opponents, under the command of Jordan, in an attempt to protect their property and lives. While the effort failed, it is a testament to the role localism and local issues played in determining the loyalty of these bands.[52] These locally raised groups focused on protecting their own interests and persecuting their area opponents.[53]

Even official units tasked as counterguerrillas were frequently motivated by personal vendettas. The Union army's Fifth Tennessee Mounted Infantry, First Alabama Cavalry (Loyal), and First Georgia State Troops Volunteers were all notorious for their cruelty toward their opponents and for their disobedience of orders that conflicted with their personal missions in protecting their homes. They were also the most effective units for hunting down Gatewood and similar militants.[54]

* * *

So what did Gatewood accomplish for the Confederacy during the last six months of the war? Besides stealing eight hundred head of cattle, which did not appear to have caused the Union army to suffer noticeably, the answer appears to be not much.[55] While Gatewood's crimes ensured that the Federals sent out occasional patrols—primarily of Tennessee troops raised for that purpose—to hunt him, he failed to draw large numbers of regular troops away from the front. At a time when the Confederacy needed every man it could get at the front, Gatewood and his gang were robbing civilians, demoralizing the population, and spurring desertion from the army. Put in the context of migration studies, his harassment of soldiers' families and the general lawlessness to which he contributed represented major pull factors in leading Southern soldiers to desert during the last year of the war. Even when he was not fighting for the Confederacy, his effect on the war is undeniable.

The lawlessness created by Gatewood and other militants and the presence of armed bands within Southern communities harmed the Confederate war effort. While the extent of the damage caused by desertion is a hotly debated topic, there is no denying it had an effect. As Joseph Glatthaar has pointed out, "the Confederacy had a narrow margin of error in its efforts to win the war." The loss of any soldier narrowed that margin further. Though the exact numbers cannot be determined, the lawlessness back home drew many troops to desert to protect their families—a fact well known to officers. For example, Sherman's experiences in Georgia led him to incorporate soldiers' fears for their families into his grand strategy. On March 15, 1865, he declared to a subordinate that "all good soldiers must now be marching," that the destruction of the countryside need not be complete because "the simple fact that a man's home has been visited by an enemy makes a soldier in [Robert E.] Lee's and [Joseph E.] Johnston's army very anxious to get home to look after his family and property." A week earlier, Lee had also made clear to subordinates the ramifications of a fragmented state on his troops. He ordered that no prisoners should be taken "among those deserters who resist with arms the civil or military authorities" in North Carolina because "the immunity which these lawless organizations afford is a great cause of desertion." But for the Confederacy, it was too little too late; the monopoly on violence had already been lost, and soldiers recognized that an armed band at home might do a better job protecting their families than an army in the field. While entire militia units asked permission to return home, individual men simply went without asking.[56]

Even before Union forces marched south for Savannah, northern Georgia had been devolving into a lawless region. On July 1, 1864, while Sherman's and Johnston's armies faced each other at Kennesaw Mountain, eighteen miles (as the crow flies) northwest of the armies the commander of the Cartersville garrison wrote to his commanding officer complaining, "the neighborhood is infested with guerrillas." A few weeks later on July 20, a Union soldier in nearby Rome, writing about an influx of refugees from Polk County in his diary, noted that civilians reported, "the guerrillas are plundering everybody."[57] With the withdrawal of Union forces, the situation got worse.

The fall of northern Georgia demoralized Confederate troops, and the harassment of irregulars added to their worries. A mid-August Union intelligence report noted that Brigadier General Marcellus Stovall's brigade "has Georgia troops, and his men are very much demoralized, won't fight, and are constantly deserting."[58] While one might expect the Georgians to be the most dedicated in defending their home state, this ignores the complexities of Confederate soldiers' identities. Stovall's troops identified with their state, but more than that, they thought of themselves as from the counties and towns they resided in before the war. Most of these men were from the Upper Piedmont, areas that were occupied by Union troops or had been bypassed in their progression southward. Thus, the vast majority of Stovall's troops had already seen their home communities either occupied or abandoned during the Confederate retreat. Even those areas of northern Georgia that the Federals bypassed were not spared by the conflict. Occupation might have been more enjoyable for the residents since the withdrawal of Confederate forces was enough to send the area into anarchy. Years later, one resident complained about how Gatewood and other "guerrilla" groups had not actually protected Southerners from the Union army in the northeastern portion of the state. In a letter to an editor, this person wrote: "Scouts and guerillas! What use did we have for scouts and guerillas in Gilmer, Fannin, Pickens, Lumpkin, Union, and Hall counties, when any man of common sense knows there never was a genuine federal soldier in the counties, only those who were on the same mission [to rob and steal]."[59] Apparently, the locally raised Unionist troops that occasionally patrolled the region had alienated many of their neighbors as well.

The men of Stovall's Brigade had entered Confederate service to defend their homes from invasion, and their homes were now occupied by the enemy. With their families behind Federal lines, fighting for the rest of Georgia was little motivation for the individual soldier's war aims. Though not actively occupied by Union troops, northeastern Georgia was not in Confederate control anymore. It did not help that Governor Joseph E. Brown had called up the militia in July, exempting not only those behind enemy lines but also "the people of the counties of Rabun, Habersham, White, Lumpkin, Gilmer, Pickens, and Dawson on account of the great scarcity of provisions . . . [and] to preserve the lives of the inhabitants of those counties." The message was clear to the troops from these regions: their families did not have enough to eat.[60] Thus, Gatewood's gang and other armed bands of unclear loyalties destabilized the region and undermined confidence in the Confederacy.

* * *

Others have challenged the characterization of Gatewood as a Confederate. In 1932 Walker County historian James Alfred Sartain noted that none of the normal terms like "Raiders, Guerrillas, Tories, and Bushwackers . . . exactly suits" Gatewood and bands like his; Sartain settled on the term "terrorist." Michael O'Brien agreed with this, writing that the "wartime vacuum of northwest Georgia" provided the perfect environment for "a sadistic sociopath who seemed to enjoy killing for the sheer thrill of it." And long before Jonathan Sarris remarked on Gatewood's "vague and malleable" loyalty to the Confederacy, some of Gatewood's contemporaries pointed out the red-bearded militant's actual nature. In 1888 the *Atlanta Constitution* published an account of Gatewood protecting some civilians being preyed on by a band of "Tories" around Ellijay. At the time, publishing reminiscences of the war was a common practice in

Southern papers, which occasionally led to controversy. This was one such account, and the article "stir[red] up a hornet's nest" of debate. Letters poured in to the paper complaining about the positive characterization of Gatewood and Tom Edmondson, another leader of an armed group. One letter from Fannin County noted sarcastically that if Gatewood did indeed have a scout commission from the Confederacy, "he was the only one in the band who was anything but a deserter from either the federal or confederate armies."[61] The writer then pointed out that there was no reason for Confederate troops to be in Ellijay in the first place, as Union troops largely avoided the region at the time. Numerous rebuttals defended Edmondson as an authorized Confederate scout tasked with restoring order to the region. No one, however, wrote in specifically to defend Gatewood as a commissioned scout.

Even Gatewood's few defenders at the time had trouble claiming that his band was a legitimate Confederate force. An account published in June mentioned him positively, defending his status as a self-proclaimed commander by noting that although "at times exceeding the usages of civilized warfare," his gang was "recognized to the extent of being left unmolested by the authorities, and, therefore, they were practically an independent command."[62] As a general rule, "no one stopped him, so it must have been authorized" seems a dubious legal principle for historians to rely upon.

Twenty-three years after the war ended, even those defending Edmondson's band acknowledged how unauthorized roving bands of armed men had devastated communities. Writing to the *Atlanta Constitution,* one claimed only a bit hyperbolically that Edmondson had been charged with securing order because North Georgians were "so terrorized" by the lawless situation "that brave and true men, who had never flinched in battle, were leaving the confederate army by scores, influenced by the first law of nature—the protection of wives, mothers, and sisters."[63] Many of the victims of these loosely affiliated armed bands remembered Gatewood for what he was: a self-serving criminal, distinct from authorized guerrilla units, who harmed the Confederate war effort.

NOTES

The author would like to thank Lauren Simpson, Keith Bohannon, Jennifer Kosmin, Joseph Glatthaar, Fitzhugh Brundage, and the College of Charleston Graduate Historical Society Colloquium. Additionally, this essay benefited from the excellent editing and encouragement provided by Barton A. Myers and Brian D. McKnight.

1. Statement of Miron Ketchum, Feb. 11, 1865, Folder mislabeled Miram Ketchum, E 36, Correspondence, Reports, Appointments, and Other Records Relating to Individual Scouts, Guides, Spies, and Detectives, 1862–66, RG 110, Records of the Provost Marshal General's Bureau (Civil War), 1861–1907, National Archives and Records Administration, Washington, D.C. (hereafter NARA). See also Robert S. Gordon, Feb. 12, 1865, ibid.; Claim for James Evatt (19672), E 732, Settled Case Files for Claims Approved by the Southern Claims Commission, 1871–80, RG 217, Records of the Accounting Officers of the Department of the Treasury, 1775–1978, ibid. (accessed via Fold3 .com). For a physical description of Gatewood, see Jonathan Dean Sarris, "'Hellish Deeds . . . in a Christian Land': Southern Mountain Communities at War, 1861–1865" (Ph.D. diss., University of Georgia, 1998), 178. I am indebted to Keith Bohannon to alerting me the scout reports in RG 110 and for sharing with me his notes and thoughts about Gatewood.

2. Statement of Miron Ketchum, Feb. 11, 1865, E 36, RG 110, NARA; 1860 Census Population Schedule, M653, Eighth Census of the United States, 1860, RG 29, Records of the Bureau of the Census, 1790–2007, ibid. (accessed via Fold3.com).

3. Robert S. Davis, "Civil War Guerilla Fighter John P. Gatewood," *North Georgia Journal* 17 (Autumn 2000): 56; Stephens, *John P. Gatewood,* 49–50, 69. For the best descriptions of Gatewood's loyalty, see Sarris, "Hellish Deeds," 178–82; Jonathan D. Sarris, "Anatomy of an Atrocity: The Madden Branch Massacre and Guerrilla Warfare in North Georgia, 1861–1865," *Georgia Historical Quarterly* 77, no. 4 (Winter 1993): 679–710; and Keith Bohannon, "The Northeast Georgia Mountains during the Secession Crisis and Civil War" (Ph.D. diss., Pennsylvania State University, 2001), 222. Many other authors are often too trusting of their source material's accuracy.

4. Jonathan Sarris puts it at around fifty. Sarris, "Hellish Deeds," 178. Much has been written on Gatewood, and the secondary literature was extremely useful in determining his movements and actions. See, for example, Sarris, "Anatomy of an Atrocity"; Sarris, "Hellish Deeds," 178–87, 195, 203–204; Sarris, *Separate Civil War,* 135–39, 141, 155, 171; Stephens, *John P. Gatewood;* Davis, "Civil War Guerilla Fighter John P. Gatewood"; and Zack C. Waters, "The Last Blood Shed in the Civil War," *Alabama Heritage* 106 (Fall 2012): 6–15.

5. Sarris, *Separate Civil War,* 136; Gerald J. Smith, *"One of the Most Daring of Men": The Life of Confederate General William Tatum Wofford* (Murfreesboro, Tenn.: Southern Heritage, 1997), 100.

6. Most of the reports of him firing on Union forces refer to soldiers pursuing him or scouts hunting for him. For examples, see "An Incident," *Chattanooga Daily Gazette,* Nov. 29, 1864; and Stephens, *John P. Gatewood,* 130.

7. Sarris, *Separate Civil War,* 138.

8. Sarris, "Hellish Deeds," 180–81. See also Sarris, "Anatomy of an Atrocity." For other examples of reported murders by Gatewood, see *Connecticut Courant,* Aug. 6, 1864; "Twenty-Seven Guerilla Murders," *American Traveler,* Jan. 14, 1865; and *Daily National Intelligencer,* Feb. 24, 1865.

9. Statement of Miron Ketchum, Feb. 11, 1865, E 36, RG 110, NARA. The act was clearly illegal as the Confederacy did not condone summary executions of civilians without trials.

10. The footnotes in Stephens, *John P. Gatewood* (the only monograph on Gatewood), will prove useful for future scholars looking at him. Though I may disagree with some of his conclusions, Ste-

phens has done far more research on Gatewood than any other scholar. In retracing the irregular's movements, I found both the excellent work of Stephens and O'Brien, *Mountain Partisans,* 155–63, critical to my research.

11. For an example of report of robberies after April 1865, see "East Tennessee," *Macon Telegraph,* May 26, 1865.

12. Sarris, "Anatomy of an Atrocity," 680; Sarris, "Hellish Deeds," 178–79, 181; Murray, "Terrible State of Affairs in North Georgia," *Daily Constitutionalist,* Feb. 11, 1865; Sarris, *Separate Civil War,* 135.

13. My interpretation is based on a critical reading of the sources, valuing those with firsthand knowledge of events over those based on rumor or secondhand and thirdhand accounts of Gatewood. For example, reports of what a scout observed himself are deemed more trustworthy than what he heard from informants. A newspaper article based on statements made to a Mobile reporter "by trustworthy citizens of the region" is deemed less reliable than an account from someone "just returned from upper Georgia" who had passed "through the counties of Milton, Cherokee, Bartow, Gordon, Murray, Pickens, and the lower end of Whitfield." "Gatewood, The Regulator," *Augusta (Ga.) Chronicle,* Nov. 12, 1864; Murray, "Terrible State of Affairs in North Georgia," *Daily Constitutionalist,* Feb. 11, 1865.

14. Many scholars have recognized there were differences between these bands, but few have actively engaged in analyzing what that means for how we understand the war at home. For example, Daniel Sutherland acknowledges that Gatewood was a unique type of guerrilla, distinct from those protecting their homes. See Sutherland, *Savage Conflict,* 186–87.

15. U.S. War Department, *War of the Rebellion,* ser. 1, 39(3):415 (hereafter *O.R.*). Jonathan Sarris recognizes how rarely Gatewood attacked Union troops. Sarris, "Anatomy of an Atrocity," 698.

16. William T. Sherman, *Memoirs of General William T. Sherman,* vol. 2 (New York: D. Appleton, 1876), 138; David T. Dixon, "Enemy on the Home Front: A Georgia Plantation Owner Works against the Confederacy," *Georgia Backroads* 10, no. 2 (Summer 2011): 42; Stephens, *John P. Gatewood,* 98; O'Brien, *Mountain Partisans,* 158; *O.R.,* ser. 1, 52(1):639.

17. Sherman, *Memoirs,* 147–63; *O.R.,* ser. 1, 39(2):208. In Rome, supplies had to be transferred off the railroad and into wagons and taken overland, making this region less secure and easier to attack.

18. *O.R.,* ser. 1, 39(1):617, 619, 39(3):415.

19. Stephens, *John P. Gatewood,* 103.

20. Scholars have traditionally assumed that Sherman was correct about the threat Gatewood posed to his lines of communication. While a danger to small patrols that stumbled into his band (and to civilians), he presented little danger to any moderate-sized force of Union troops. Other groups of scouts—perhaps actually authorized by the Confederacy—likely posed a greater danger than Gatewood's band.

21. Statement of Wm. H. Burris, Nov. 21, 1864, E 36, RG 110, NARA. Burris met with a farmer six miles north of La Fayette who said that none of Gatewood's men "had come up as far as his place since nov. 1st," implying that perhaps they visited on or shortly before that date.

22. Historians have used a postwar account of Gatewood working with Confederate forces in October 1864 in La Fayette as evidence that he moved into Walker County in response to Sherman's order of October 24. If Gatewood did in fact join with Southern troops, however, it would have

occurred in early October (around October 12–15). If this account (much of which appears to be given secondhand or thirdhand) is to be believed, Gatewood was likely already on his way north toward Walker County when he stumbled into the Union patrol on the tenth. Additionally, if he did work with a Confederate cavalry unit at the time, he may have done so to avoid being suspected of desertion and soon separated from them. James Sartain, *History of Walker County, Georgia* (Dalton, Ga.: A. J. Showalter, 1932), 232–34; Stephens, *John P. Gatewood,* 103–105.

23. Statement of James W. Crandel, Nov. 12, 1864, E 36, RG 110, NARA; Statement of O. G. Frazier, Jan. 13, 1865, ibid.; Statement of Wm. H. Burris, Nov. 21, 1864, ibid. Similar reports ended up in newspapers. See "Dead," *Chattanooga Daily Gazette,* Jan. 4, 1865.

24. For one report of rumors of Gatewood working with Wheeler, see Statement of George M. Rose, Nov. 14, 1864, E 36, RG 110, NARA. For another example of an untrustworthy source indicating Gatewood working with Confederates in 1865, see "Fight at Ringgold," *Nashville Daily Union,* Feb. 25, 1865. This article recounts how he was in charge of an attack by 250 men on the Ringgold garrison. The *Daily Union* failed to disclose how Gatewood's identity was obtained, even though no prisoners were taken by the Federals since the Confederate wounded "were all carried off."

25. W. C. Dodson, *Campaigns of Wheeler and His Cavalry, 1862–1865: From Material Furnished by Gen. Joseph Wheeler* (Atlanta: Hudgins, 1899), 399.

26. *O.R.,* ser. 1, 45(1):990–91; Sarris, *Separate Civil War,* 136. For a primary-source account of this raid that gives a higher death count, see "Twenty-Seven Guerilla Murders," *American Traveler,* Jan. 14, 1865. Others provide a lower death tally. See, for example, "More Guerrilla Operations," *Chattanooga Daily Gazette,* Dec. 7, 1864.

27. "More Guerrilla Operations," *Chattanooga Daily Gazette,* Dec. 7, 1864; O'Brien, *Mountain Partisans,* 162–63; Stephens, *John P. Gatewood,* 121–22. The troops were under the command of James A. Davison, though the newspaper mistakenly reports his name as "Davidson." Compiled Service Record of James A. Davison, 5th Tennessee Mounted Infantry, Compiled Military Service Records of Volunteer Union Soldiers Belonging to Units Organized for Service from the State of Tennessee, RG 94, Records of the Adjutant General's Office, 1762–1984, M395, NARA (accessed via Fold3.com); *History of Tennessee from the Earliest Time to the Present: Together with an Historical and a Biographical Sketch of from Twenty-Five to Thirty Counties of East Tennessee,* vol. 4 [Nashville: Goodspeed, 1887], 948. By December 12, Gatewood was reported to be back in northeastern Georgia. Statement of W. H. Burris, Dec. 16, 1864, E 36, RG 110, NARA.

28. *O.R.,* ser. 1, 45(1):990.

29. Mary Noble to Lelia Montan, Nov. 20, 1864, Mary Noble Papers, Southern Historical Collection, Wilson Library, University of North Carolina, Chapel Hill.

30. Murray, "Terrible State of Affairs in North Georgia," *Daily Constitutionalist,* Feb. 11, 1865.

31. Anthony Vinci, "Anarchy, Failed States, and Armed Groups: Reconsidering Conventional Analysis," *International Studies Quarterly* 52, no. 2 (June 2008): 208; Robert I. Rotberg, "Failed States in a World of Terror," *Foreign Affairs* 81, no. 4 (Aug. 2008): 127–40.

32. *Columbus Daily Enquirer,* Feb. 10, 1864. For an example of torture, see Mary Noble to Lelia Montan, Nov. 20, 1864, Mary Noble Papers.

33. Companies A and F, 5th Regiment, 2nd Brigade, Georgia Militia to Joseph E. Brown, n.d., Petitions—Franklin County, Governor's Incoming Correspondence, Georgia State Archives, Morrow (accessed via Ancestry.com); E. G. Nelson et al. to Joseph E. Brown, Jan. 30, 1865, ibid.

By the summer of 1865, more than three thousand Bartow County residents would be "entirely destitute" and in need of government assistance for subsistence. *O.R.*, ser. 1, 49(2):1062. For more on the devastation, see Smith, *"One of the Most Daring of Men,"* 141–49.

34. R. S. Norton, "Diary," 87 (Mar. 12, 1865), transcription in Norton-Towers Family Papers, Atlanta History Center.

35. Warren Akin, *Letters of Warren Akin, Confederate Congressman*, ed. Bell Irvin Wiley, paperback ed. (Athens: University of Georgia Press, 2010), 65; John R. Hart to Joseph E. Brown, Feb. 2, 1865, Governor's Incoming Correspondence, Georgia State Archives, Morrow (accessed via Ancestry.com). See also Bohannon, "Northeast Georgia Mountains during the Secession Crisis and Civil War," 223. For the best overview of northeastern Georgia's Civil War, see ibid. Numerous county studies also provide excellent overviews, including Keith Scott Hebert, "Civil War and Reconstruction Era Cass/Bartow County, Georgia" (Ph.D. diss., Auburn University, 2007).

36. Vinci, "Anarchy, Failed States, and Armed Groups," 298; Anthony Vinci, *Armed Groups and the Balance of Power: The International Relations of Terrorists, Warlords and Insurgents* (New York: Routledge, 2009), 4.

37. Vinci, *Armed Groups and the Balance of Power* 3.

38. Kimberly Zisk Marten, *Warlords: Strong-Arm Brokers in Weak States* (Ithaca, N.Y.: Cornell University Press, 2012), 2, 3 (emphasis in original); Vinci, *Armed Groups and the Balance of Power*, 4; John MacKinlay, "Defining Warlords," *International Peacekeeping* 7, no. 1 (Apr. 2000): 49, 52.

39. Murray, "Terrible State of Affairs in North Georgia," *Daily Constitutionalist*, Feb. 11, 1865.

40. Ibid.; O'Brien, *Mountain Partisans*, 157. Historians often cite a newspaper report that Gatewood offered to trade Union prisoners for Confederate civilians being held hostage to demonstrate that Gatewood protected Confederate citizens. See "A Proposition from Gatewood" *Chattanooga Daily Gazette*, Jan. 19, 1865. As of yet, no official records have revealed that this offer was made. Additionally, two months earlier the same paper noted that the civilian hostages in question had been selected because they "have friends and relatives with Gatewood," implying a personal motivation for protecting those specific hostages as well as an ideological one. "If You Dare, Mr. Gatewood!," ibid., Nov. 16, 1864.

41. Stephens, *John P. Gatewood*, 127.

42. Murray, "Terrible State of Affairs in North Georgia," *Daily Constitutionalist*, Feb. 11, 1865; George Magruder Battey, *A History of Rome and Floyd County, State of Georgia, United States of America: Including Numerous Incidents of More Than Local Interest, 1540–1922* (Atlanta: Webb and Vary, 1922), 205–206; Stephens, *John P. Gatewood*, 124. The only primary source I have found for this rumor is a newspaper article of questionable accuracy, "Gatewood, the Regulator," *Columbus Daily Enquirer*, Nov. 4, 1864. The article refers to Colquitt as a Texas deserter named "Colbert," which is a clear mistake.

43. Battey, *History of Rome and Floyd County*, 206; Ambrose Bierce, *The Collected Works of Ambrose Bierce*, vol. 1 (New York: Neale, 1909), 310.

44. *O.R.*, ser. 1, 49(2):569, 605; Bohannon, "Northeast Georgia Mountains during the Secession Crisis and Civil War," 233; Smith, *"One of the Most Daring of Men,"* 141–42.

45. Murray, "Terrible State of Affairs in North Georgia," *Daily Constitutionalist*, Feb. 11, 1865. Killing local recruits made sense as the units they were joining were created to hunt down bands like Gatewood's.

46. Stephens, *John P. Gatewood,* 127–33; Davis, "Civil War Guerilla Fighter John P. Gatewood," 57; Waters, "Last Blood Shed," 13; Statement of Robert S. Gordon, Jan. 16, 1865, E 36, RG 110, NARA.

47. Waters, "Last Blood Shed"; Davis, "Civil War Guerilla Fighter John P. Gatewood," 57; Stephens, *John P. Gatewood,* 85; Sarris, "Hellish Deeds," 178; O'Brien, *Mountain Partisans,* 156. For more on the separate wars, see Sarris, *Separate Civil War,* esp. 3–4; William T. Auman, "Neighbor against Neighbor: The Inner Civil War in the Central Counties of Confederate North Carolina" (Ph.D. diss., University of North Carolina, 1988); and Adam H. Domby, "War within the States: Loyalty, Dissent, and Conflict in Southern Piedmont Communities, 1860–1876" (Ph.D. diss., University of North Carolina, 2015).

48. Auman, "Neighbor against Neighbor."

49. Court of Claims Case File 4997 for Peter Sheibley, E 22, Congressional Jurisdiction Case Files, RG 123, Records of the U.S. Court of Claims, 1835–1984, NARA; Domby, "War within the States," chap. 4; Gordon D. Sargent, "Bloody Legacy in Polk: A Frontier Family and Some Prior Commitments," *North Georgia Journal* (Summer 1995): 36–43; David T. Dixon, "'Til Secession Do Us Part," *Georgia Backroads* 11, no. 2 (Summer 2012): 14–18; Margaret Nola Burkley, "Floyd County, Georgia, during the Civil War Era" (Ph.D. diss., Florida State University, 1998), 313–14; Battey, *History of Rome and Floyd County,* 207; John Azor Kellogg, *Capture and Escape: A Narrative of Army and Prison Life* (Wisconsin History Commission, 1908), 166, 167–69.

50. Lucius Tate, *History of Pickens County* (Spartanburg, S.C.: Reprint Co., 1935), 213; Bohannon, "Northeast Georgia Mountains during the Secession Crisis and Civil War," 240. For more on similar trials, see Domby, "War within the States," chap. 6.

51. Murray, "Terrible State of Affairs in North Georgia," *Daily Constitutionalist,* Feb. 11, 1865.

52. Kellogg, *Capture and Escape,* 167, 179–80. They may have belonged to a series of auxiliaries raised by Brown during the occupation period. As no muster lists survived, the membership of the Union home guard is hard to establish. The unofficial nature of these units, much like that of the bands of deserters, means primary sources are scarce. The best work on it is Robert Scott Davis Jr., "The Curious Civil War Career of James George Brown, Spy," *Prologue* 26, no. 1 (Spring 1994): 17–31.

53. For more on the goals of these, see Bohannon, "Northeast Georgia Mountains During the Secession Crisis and Civil War," 202.

54. Domby, "War within the States," 155–59; Sarris, *Separate Civil War,* 138–41; Davis, "Curious Civil War Career of James George Brown"; Hebert, "Civil War and Reconstruction Era Cass/Bartow County," 257; McKnight, *Confederate Outlaw,* 124; Sarris, "Anatomy of an Atrocity," 695–96, 700–701, 703–704.

55. "Capture of Beeves," *Daily Constitutionalist,* Feb. 3, 1865.

56. Joseph T. Glatthaar, *General Lee's Army: From Victory to Collapse* (New York: Free Press, 2008), 441; *O.R.,* ser. 1, 49(2):857, 1354; Companies A and F, 5th Regiment, 2nd Brigade, Ga. Militia to Joseph E. Brown, Petitions—Franklin County, Governor's Incoming Correspondence, Georgia State Archives, Morrow (accessed via Ancestry.com). According to Joseph Glatthaar, deserters were more likely to have children than nondeserters, implying that fear for their offspring encouraged desertion. See Glatthaar, *General Lee's Army,* 410. Glatthaar's chapter on desertion is one of the best statistical studies of what motivated this action.

57. Col. William P. Innes to General Stedman, July 1, 1864, E 2657, Letters Received, District of the Etowah, RG 393, Records of U.S. Army Continental Commands, 1817–1947, Pt. 2, NARA; Lewis

Roe, *From Western Deserts to Carolina Swamps: A Civil War Soldier's Journals and Letters Home,* ed. John P. Wilson (Albuquerque: University of New Mexico Press, 2012), 110.

58. *O.R.,* ser. 1, 38(5):494. The compiled service records of the 43rd Georgia confirm numerous desertions around this period. James W. Bell, *The 43rd Georgia Infantry Regiment, Army of Tennessee. C.S.A.* (Hodges, S.C.: Lindy Publications, 1990), 49–177.

59. "The Georgia Brigade," General Barton and Stovall History & Heritage Association, accessed Mar. 26, 2015, http://www.generalbartonandstovall.com/brigade.html; Bell, *43rd Georgia Infantry,* 20, 31; Larry Blair et al., eds., *Organizational Summary of Military Organizations from Georgia in the Confederate States of America* (Louisville: Byrons Printing, 1999), 182–87, 196; "Tom Polk Edmondson: A Devoted Sister Comes to His Defense," *Atlanta Constitution,* May 1, 1888.

60. "Governor Brown's Proclamation to the People of Georgia," *Charleston Mercury,* July 14, 1864. For more on the effect of Sherman's advance on desertion, see Hebert, "Civil War and Reconstruction Era Cass/Bartow County," 175, 192, 204–206, 235.

61. Sartain, *History of Walker County, Georgia,* 120; O'Brien, *Mountain Partisans,* 153; Sarris, *Separate Civil War,* 135; Pea Jay, "John Gatewood: The Terrible Desperado of Gilmer County," *Atlanta Constitution,* Apr. 4, 1888; "Tom Polk Edmondson: A Devoted Sister Comes to His Defense," ibid., May 1, 1888.

62. "Unwritten History," *Atlanta Constitution,* June 24, 1888.

63. "Talk of the State: Gathered from the Mails and Exchanges," ibid., May 22, 1888.

THE UNION WAR ON WOMEN

LISA TENDRICH FRANK

In 1864 Union soldiers looted Caroline Davis's home in Virginia. They came in waves, successive assaults that turned her homestead into a battle scene. The invasion outraged her, for it seemed to betray her unstated sense of the limits of war. In her diary Davis bemoaned, "Our dear old home-stead has been ransacked from 'head to foot' seven times." Even though the numerous intruders scoured the house quickly, each small group ensured that her personal losses would tally greater than she could have imagined. "We have been deprived of nearly all our provisions & three valuable servants & two horses." The raiders treated the household's women with disdain and disrespect, "ordering one about as if they were dogs [and] prying into ladies wardrobes & portifolios [*sic*]." Their disregard for the private nature of her person and most intimate property magnified Davis's sense that the invasion was irregular. "It is hard *hard* to bear having these despicable men searching into every place, & stealing whatever valuables they can finds [*sic*]." When the soldiers finally left her home, Davis deemed herself a double victim. The extensive loss of personal property seemed an unnecessary cruelty as "their taunts & insults are hard enough to endure."[1]

Almost a year later, Union soldiers behaved in a surprisingly similar way when they invaded Loula Rogers's home in Georgia. Once again, troops ransacked a civilian homestead and in the process betrayed the commonly held image of war. "Well sure enough we have had a Yankee raid! Highway robbers and demons of torment to visit our quiet beautiful home, and commit all kinds of depredations." Indeed, the men seemed to behave remarkably irregularly. In her diary Rogers described the looting of her home. "Seven or eight times it was searched from top to bottom," she explained, as soldiers "stalked in without ceremony, opened all the bureau drawers, trunks, closets, and work boxes in the house, and stole whatever they wanted." The men revealed little sense of the tactical importance of the invasion. Instead, they acted as individuals, taking whatever valuables they could find and haul away before moving on to the next house. "I never saw such a sight in my life as all the rooms were, every thing out of place & scattered all over the floor." Rogers shared Davis's sense that the raiders behaved in ways that demanded condemnation. She understood that the pillaging of her home was not collateral damage but instead was a direct assault on her personal property that she saw as proof of the Union's utter disregard for women: "it was dreadful to see such great rough men prying into every secret drawer in our house, and we helpless women alone with no means of defiance among those who had no more respect for woman than a cow."[2]

The experiences of these two women and their reactions to them reflect a shared understanding of Union war tactics across the Confederate home front. When U.S. soldiers and rebel women came face to face, the distinction between home front and warfront frequently broke down. At the hands of regular soldiers, these white women experienced tactics that were widely viewed and understood as irregular. The use of such irregular tactics was especially true during the 1864–65 home-front campaigns in the Shenandoah Valley and in Georgia and the Carolinas. During these invasions, Union soldiers worked outside of the borders of formal military rules, and Confederate women felt as if lawless men had turned their world upside down. The Union invasions of the Southern home front had military objectives that did not necessarily require the rampant looting of residences, but these campaigns allowed many soldiers to pursue personal ambitions under the auspices of military action.[3] Their behavior led many Confederate women to conclude that they faced an enemy that betrayed the conventional understanding of war and otherwise acted in ways that typified guerrillas, partisans, and raiders. As one slaveholding woman from Georgia succinctly decried, "Was there ever any civilized land given up for such a length of time to lawless pillage and brutal inhumainities [*sic*]?"[4]

* * *

Union soldiers, officers, and politicians routinely denied that they waged irregular war on the Southern home front. At the same time, Federal commanders repeatedly expressed their frustration at facing Confederate guerrillas and dealing with their irregular tactics. As much as their political opponents in the North made feigned calls for war crimes, Union soldiers rarely committed more serious offenses like murder or rape, typically facing a court-martial when they did.[5] The gender, race, and class of their wealthy white female enemy on the Southern home front typically restrained and shaped the type of violence these soldiers committed. Nevertheless, the army routinely sanctioned irregular behavior that in many ways mirrored the actions they condemned by Confederate guerrillas. During the home-front campaigns through slaveholding areas, Union troops engaged in the theft and destruction of personal property as they promoted public disorder and the disrespect of white women. These military men turned homes into battlefields, arrested female civilians and confined them to their houses, pillaged parlors and bedrooms, used tactics designed to terrorize civilians, and relied on domestic spaces to shield themselves from harm. Furthermore, Union soldiers rejoiced in the successes of home-front campaigns such as Major General Philip Sheridan's in Virginia's Shenandoah Valley and Major General William T. Sherman's in Georgia and the Carolinas, which destroyed domestic spaces but otherwise lacked the "fronts or pitched battles" that typically define regular warfare.[6] Even as these actions stretched the conventional rules of war, Union officers successfully demonstrated how irregular behavior could be used acceptably in home-front campaigns; their actions showed these methods as neither part of a guerrilla campaign nor illegal in any way. Confederate women, not surprisingly, disagreed with this conclusion and condemned every aspect of these behaviors as irregular and uncivilized. Despite their differences, soldiers and civilians agreed about what actually took place during these campaigns: invading "regular" Union soldiers routinely broke what were recently understood as the stated and unstated rules of war. Southern women's descriptions of their interactions with enemy soldiers were not just "hostile and hysterical accounts," rhetorical flourishes, or functions of wishful Lost Cause memories as some scholars have dismissed them as being, nor were they merely a reflection of privileged elite women bemoaning the inherent difficulties of war.[7]

The shared contemporary understanding of what happened during Sherman's and Sheridan's campaigns blurs the scholarly distinction that frequently emphasizes the restraint of so-called regular soldiers in contrast with the cruelty of irregulars and guerrillas. Scholars too often point to a "consistent moral economy" that controlled the behavior of uniformed Federal soldiers, and they emphasize the code of conduct and rules of war to which the Union officially adhered. These rules—embodied in General Orders No. 100, or "Lieber's Code," and begun in Lieber's earlier pamphlet on "guerrilla parties"—proclaimed that guerrilla warfare was, among many things, "universally understood" as an "irregular band of armed men, carrying on an irregular war, not being able, according to their character as a guerilla party, to carry on what the law requires as *regular* law."[8] Yet this dichotomy broke down when Union soldiers confronted female civilians and violated gender norms that governed peacetime interactions. In their engagements with slaveholding Southern women, these men acted in ways that mirrored many of the characteristics of irregular war as Union officials had defined it; soldiers' actions paralleled the very behavior that they denounced as guerrilla warfare when their Southern enemy behaved in that fashion.[9] Although restrained by gender and class conventions that prohibited them from killing females, Union soldiers on several home-front campaigns routinely treated civilians as military objectives by assaulting their persons and private property; used "irregular" methods as they "attacked, harassed, and worried their foes"; pursued personal rather than generic objectives by focusing their efforts on specific families and households; acted on a desire to exact extralegal justice for perceived wrongs against the nation; and worked on the borders of Lieber's Code and the general understanding of the rules of war. They were more raiders than soldiers, more ransackers of homes and private property than they were destroyers of railroads and the machinery of war. As a result, many Confederate women believed themselves victims of unjust and irregular campaigns that violated nineteenth-century rules of war.[10]

Scholars have long recognized the hard-war tactics used by Union soldiers. Most notably, Mark Grimsley contends that Union warfare displayed a "combination of severity and restraint," with tactics chosen to instill "intimidation and fear" among the civilian population. Since the publication of Grimsley's influential work a generation ago, most scholarly accounts of the war have emphasized the restraint of Federal soldiers and the ways that they refrained from the twentieth-century concept of total war. In this process, women's experiences have been largely overlooked. Many historians integrate Southern "civilians" in the histories of military campaigns comprised of "organized armies and stand-up battles." But in most cases women are included in order to provide colorful anecdotes; they are not shown as central actors in the story. In essence, their gender has segregated women's wartime experiences. This unwillingness to listen to their voices combined with scholars' gendered understanding of destruction and loss has prevented hard-war tactics from being treated as irregular warfare. This exclusion of female civilians as actors unto themselves, for example, has led Mark Neely to sanitize Sherman's and Sheridan's campaigns. In Neely's assessment, Sheridan took great pains to reserve the worst treatment for those families who deserved it. "Sheridan and his men fought guerrillas in a different way and by different rules . . . than they fought the regularly constituted army," he writes. "The Union soldiers might destroy the subsistence and dwellings of the guerrillas and their families and abettors. They did not destroy the subsistence and dwellings of the other residents of the [Shenandoah] valley." Moreover, many historians have privileged physical damage over psychological damage and have thereby reduced the assessment of destruction to things that can be counted, such as houses, barns, factories, and other large items that could be inventoried. In addition, they have discounted the intangible personal property of women as inconsequential. This formal and masculine understanding of destruction allows scholars to emphasize how "the more unrestrained form of warfare never supplanted the restrained."[11]

Throughout the home-front campaigns, Union commanders recognized that the military was operating outside of the conventional way of war. The army's willingness to embrace "irregular" tactics became especially clear in the summer of 1864. Federal commanders—especially Lieutenant General Ulysses S. Grant, Major General Henry Halleck, Sheridan, and Sherman—explicitly proclaimed that the war required controversial tactics on the Southern home front. As scholars have noted, the Union armies thus employed a "strategy of raids."[12] Rather than shy away from the desire to fight an unconventional war with irregular tactics, Grant directed his forces in Virginia to "eat out Virginia clear and clean as far as they go, so that crows flying over it for the balance of this season will have to carry their provender with them."[13] Hyperbolic in ambition, these orders offered a vision of warfare that fit understandings forged in Sheridan's and Sherman's earlier campaigns against Native Americans and Confederate guerrillas. Both commanders adhered to the general premise of Grant's mandate, with Sherman's bummers becoming the most visible evidence of the policy. Indeed, Sheridan and Sherman fed their armies with the bounty of the Southern home front and typically took great pains to ensure that the food they left behind could not be consumed by enemy civilians. For example, troops repeatedly poured honey or molasses over grains or other items that they could not carry with them.[14]

Scholars frequently quote Grant's directive, but they typically do so when assessing its literal manifestation. Similarly, they have emphasized the limited damage caused by Sherman's and Sheridan's campaigns. Against the hyperbolic claims that their armies were to destroy everything, every standing house provides ammunition against the equally hyperbolic Lost Cause vilification of these Union leaders. By turning Grant's rhetorical ambitions into a literal measuring stick, scholars have minimized Sherman's and Sheridan's innovative and otherwise irregular tactics, and their power has been overlooked.[15] Yet scholars also accurately repeat proclamations by these generals that the destruction they caused helped end the war and therefore justified their irregular actions. Using these standards, other Union commanders determined that their unconventional warfare had succeeded. Sheridan responded to Grant's orders with language similar to his commander's—"I will go on and clean out the Valley"—and later proudly reported that "the Valley, from Winchester up to Staunton, ninety-two miles, will have but little in it for man or beast."[16] He proclaimed that he had accomplished his mission and in doing so acknowledged that cleaning out the Valley necessarily meant creating new hardships for civilians.

Throughout the home-front campaigns, Union soldiers explicitly treated female civilians as the enemy and as military objectives unto themselves. In verbal confrontations, they made it clear that their assault on Confederate women and their homes was not the unintended consequence of war. Women, for their part, did not accept these actions as regular military activity. One white woman in Virginia, for example, bristled at being a target of Major General David Hunter's invading soldiers. During the chaotic raid, "her house had been sacked, & *every thing* carried off—every particle of grain, meat, or food in every possible shape inanimate or living, 15 horses, furniture, clothing, bedding, silver." She bemoaned that she had lost "in fact all she owned in the world, save her wedding ring, & an indifferent change of clothing." The enemy did not stop at pillage, but instead "the house was not only completely stripped but the walls ripped open, & even the ashes barrels & *privies* searched for hidden articles." She explained to South Carolinian Emma Holmes that invading soldiers took special pleasure in the suffering they brought upon civilians. Rather than offering her protection from the raiders, a Union commander made "her wait an hour" before scolding her for complaining. "He told her, he was glad of it, for that the *women & children were* the *very fiends* of *this war,* sending their husbands, fathers & brothers into the army. He meant to humble the pride of the haughty Virginians to the very dust, & that if he did not do it that time he would sweep the earth so clean that it would be incapable of affording nourishment." Another Virginia woman's report similarly highlighted the soldiers' desire to punish Southerners. She wrote that "when remonstrated with in regard to their depredations their invariable reply was, 'This is nothing to the way the Rebs did in Maryland.'" Union soldiers' conversations with Georgian Mary Sharpe Jones highlighted the men's desire to punish women for their roles in the Confederacy. She was told "that I had no right even to wood or water" by the invading soldiers and "that I should be 'humbled in the very dust I walked upon,' a pistol and carbine presented to my breast, cursed & reviled as a Rebel, a hypocrite, a devil." In South Carolina, Pauline DeCaradeuc reported that Union soldiers claimed her home "was the root of the rebellion & burn it they would." Henry Hitchcock, a commander on Sherman's March to the Sea, similarly berated a woman: "You have done all you could to help the war, and have not done what you could to prevent it." Even Sherman revealed his disdain for Southern women, who were "the cause of the trouble in the country."[17]

In their own writings, Union soldiers reflected on their intention to inflict suffering on, but not kill, women and children. In the process, they subtly acknowledged that they were pushing, if not breaking, the widely held nineteenth-century assumption that regular soldiers should refrain from molesting civilians. A clergyman traveling with Sherman's army, for example, asserted that the traditional protections afforded to women did not apply to this situation. "So far as the *women* are concerned, we might as well spare our pity, for they are the worst secessionists, and why should *they* not suffer?" Women's roles in the war were vital, soldiers frequently asserted, and thus justified the irregular tactics used against them. "They have urged on the brutal treatment of Yankee prisoners. They have personally insulted these poor men, and would you now spare them a proper amount of suffering? We say no." Another Union chaplain similarly concluded that the gender of the enemy should not shield them from punishment. After all, he explained, "A pretty traitor is no better than an ugly one—male or female." Furthermore, although some of the "officers are boiling over with sympathy for those pretty female rebels, . . . I have none." One of Sherman's men boasted that the rough treatment female Confederates received at the hands of invading Union soldiers "serves them right for most of the *women* of the south are generally stronger secess[ionists] than the men." Confederate civilians, women included, deserved to feel the hard hand of war because it was "a horrible state of affairs [that] they had brought upon themselves." Just as importantly, soldiers rationalized their irregular tactics by placing the power to bring the war to an end on the civilians themselves. After evicting women from Atlanta, Sherman justified his order by asserting, "The only way the people of Atlanta can hope once more to live in peace and quiet at home, is to stop the war, which can only be done by admitting that it began in error and is perpetuated in pride."[18]

Although Union soldiers seemed to indiscriminantly inflict damage across their paths through Virginia and the Lower South, Sherman and Sheridan directed their soldiers to make sure specific families did not escape harm. Reminiscent of the directed personal attacks pursued by guerrillas, throughout their home-front campaigns both Sheridan and Sherman specifically targeted wealthy slaveholding areas and the homes and families of leading secessionists. To these ends, Sherman commanded that his soldiers should "discriminate between the rich, who are usually hostile, and the poor and industrious, usually neutral or friendly," especially because "the United States would be benefited by dispossessing a rich, prejudiced, hard-headed, and disloyal planter." Even Union troops noted that "the poor people are respected by the soldiers and their property protected" but "the rich are persecuted when caught and their barns, gins & houses fall victims to the invaders match." One soldier observed the specific punishment meted out to elite Southerners: "The Army are renting their spite on everything destructible & our line is marked each day by dense columns of black smoke curling up from the former residences of the 'chivalry.'" In Georgia, soldiers devastated Confederate politician and major general Howell Cobb's plantation and did not "feel much troubled about the destruction" because he was "one of the *head devils.*"[19] Similarly, in Charleston, Sherman's soldiers targeted secessionists and large planters by name, "asking 'Is this the home of Mr. Rhett?' and 'Is that the dwelling of Mr. Middleton?'" In addition, prominent "Charlestonians Arthur P. Hayne and Alfred Huger, were pulled about and struck" by the Northerners. Union soldiers also deliberately destroyed the homes of hundreds of well-known planters, including John Cheves, Maxcy Gregg, and Columbia mayor Thomas Jefferson Goodwyn.[20] Southern women too noted the direct attacks on the "chivalry." In South Carolina, Pauline DeCaradeuc complained about the soldiers' irregular behavior and described how the men raged against her class and her family. "They said that they had to arrest and shoot every influential citizen in S.C., every mover of secession, & from the accumulation of wealth, the quantities of food, books & clothes in this house . . . they knew Father was wealthy, literary, & influential." Furthermore, because the soldiers "had heard enough of him," they wanted "to make an example of him."[21]

In the home-front campaigns, Union soldiers routinely acted in ways that betrayed the officially stated justification for their raids. Rather than coordinated efforts to find, capture, or destroy wartime materiel, men marched in small groups to scour homesteads. In the process, they confiscated countless personal items that seemed unconnected to the war. One Virginia woman observed that in her home, "The wretches . . . did not so much as look into any place where there was any possibility of concealing arms and rebels but drawers and trunks and desks were ransacked." When a soldier "opened my top drawer and took out a small pin box," Virginian E. W. Harrison "could not resist the temptation of saying, Which do you expect to find in that, arms or rebels?" Another complained that the "stragglers intruded themselves and ran all over the house, ransacking bureau drawers, trunks and wardrobes," though not necessarily for valuables. Instead, the raiders insisted on "taking out the ladies' underclothes and dresses . . . [and] dressing themselves up in them" to humiliate the women. Many other Confederate women had similar experiences. Soldiers involved in home-front campaigns frequently searched bedrooms, parlors, and other feminine areas on the pretext of looking for guns and other military supplies. Yet the items they seized from these rooms—wedding gowns, sheet music, diaries, lingerie, personal letters, and other family keepsakes—were taken as souvenirs or as presents for loved ones, or sometimes simply to humiliate their owners. In addition, the directives to feed off the land allowed the men license to ransack kitchens, where they not only took foodstuffs for their own sustenance but also frequently dumped supplies that they could not carry, spilled honey and sorghum syrup on floors, and smashed china. Virginian Lucy Buck complained that after stealing one of her live ducks as well as other foodstuffs, "two miserable wretches . . . were running their fists down into my nice preserved blackberries and raspberries and Aunt C's pickles." Their constant harassment of civilians led one woman to note, "Yankee raiding parties are going everywhere & no one feels safe." In short, Union soldiers specifically sought out personal items instead of military materiel, and like irregulars they "attacked, harassed, and worried their foes."[22]

The lawlessness of the invading soldiers seemed clear to the white Southerners who witnessed it. Countless Confederates described the campaign with the language of theft and robbery. Susan Lining, in South Carolina, watched as soldiers looted what they could and "set fires all around us." "Every house in the Town was entered & each family robbed of every thing in the form of provisions, Silver jewelry, clothing, & what [the soldiers] could not carry off, they destroyed by fire or the axe." From Virginia, Caroline Davis observed that "hardly a house... has not been up turned & robbed." Mary Leverett condemned Sherman's men as "a regularly educated set of thieves, burglars robbers & house burners—& . . . accomplished villains." Another sympathized with a friend and bemoaned "the disgusting manner in which you were robbed, your house rifled & furniture mutilated." Similarly, Dolly Lunt Burge's day was filled with soldiers who "made a road through my back yard & lot field, driving their Stock & riding through, tearing down my fences & desolating my home." She saw their destruction of her home as intentional, emphasizing that the men were "wantonly doing it when there was no necessity for it."[23]

Women's complaints about the irregular behavior of Union soldiers were not confined to diaries or personal letters. In a vitriolic letter to Major General Hunter, Sheridan's predecessor, Virginian Henrietta Lee condemned the injustice she had faced. In it she demanded to know "What was my offence?" that warranted the irregular tactics of his "incendiary band" who "steal unaware upon helpless women and children, to insult and destroy." These soldiers, she complained, brought an illegal war upon the innocent when they "executed your infamous order and burned my house." Hunter's men indiscriminantly spread their destruction across the region, making them seem "Hyena-like . . . and demonlike" rather than like disciplined soldiers. As a result, their unwarranted actions against civilians would define them. "Your name will stand on history's pages as the Hunter of weak women, and innocent children; the Hunter to destroy defenceless villages and beautiful homes—to torture afresh the agonized hearts of widows; . . . the Hunter with the relentless heart of a wild beast, the face of a fiend, and the form of a man." An article in the *Richmond Enquirer* described how a house in Virginia was "despoiled in every conceivable manner. . . . [N]ice feather beds besmeared with filth." The physical destruction of homes, food, and personal items, however, were not the worst offenses. Soldiers, who civilians expected to be bound by the commonly understood rules of war, often committed depredations that betrayed those principles as well as those set out in the Articles of War and Lieber's Code. These "bands of scoundrels" had committed so many irregular acts that "[r]obbery, murder, & plunder is so common that it almost ceases to excite remark."[24]

Even Unionist women in the South noted the irregular behavior of uniformed Federal troops. From Georgia, Louisa Fletcher decried that "stragglers from the [Union] army rove about & commit many depredations upon peacable unoffending citizens." Although she longed for Union success and the destruction of the Confederacy, the tactical choice to unleash the chaos of a home-front war betrayed her expectations. She termed these constant raids the result of "aggressions of lawless soldiers." Months later, she again noted the guerrilla-like behavior of her countrymen. Their actions made for "gloomy days in the history of my country" because she saw no excuse for the "lawless Federal soldiers committing depredations on unprotected families depriving them of provision clothing cooking utensils & every thing necessary for house keeping & every one living in constant fear that their turn will come next."[25]

Loyal Northerners similarly questioned the legality of the home-front operations. A newspaper editor for Connecticut's *Republican Farmer* declared that the irregular campaign in the Shenandoah Valley was an outrage to American virtue and a violation of American law. He posited that "for real devilish malignity and cold-blooded brutality, the execution of [Grant's] order surpasses all the cruelty of Butler, and, in all save one particular, equals even the atrocity of Turchin." The editor urged his readers to consider the moral implications of "the wanton burning of twenty-seven hundred barns, filled with wheat, and corn," which, to the editor's disgust, was "done by soldiers of 'The Union,' with the Union flag waving over them." These uniformed soldiers were expected not to behave like guerrillas, especially not under the U.S. flag. As a result of their irregular behavior, "houses and barns alike . . . with all their contents, were reduced to a mass of smouldering ruins." Even so, "the worst remains to be told," the editor cautioned. He described one town where more than three hundred homes were burned on Sheridan's orders "with deliberation and without any other than the briefest warning to the inmates." As a result, "Tottering age and feeble infancy, delicate ladies, and women in that state which would find pity even in the eyes of a savage, were compelled to rush out of their houses, and then to witness their homes consumed before their eyes by devouring flames." He cringed at the thought of it. "What pen can describe the horrors of these scenes?" The editor thought the soldiers' irregular acts were done "[w]ith a refinement of malignity worthy of the evil one himself." Furthermore, he concluded, nothing could justify this "act that is not worthy of a general."[26]

For many Confederate women, the irregularity of the campaigns simply came down to the reality that soldiers purposefully inflicted punishment on civilians as part of the official ambitions for the operations. Virginian Ann

Jones commented that Union soldiers were "tearing down unhabited [*sic*] houses whenever it suits them. . . . [T]he whole neighborhood nearly seems turned out of doors." Furthermore, "houses are searched, things stolen, food taken. . . . They are fearfully desolating every place." From North Carolina, Catherine Edmondston, who would face Sherman's troops a few months later, noted that in Virginia, "The amount of misery endured by private citizens—noncombatants, who in all civilized warfare are exposed only to the unavoidable hardships incident to an upturned and unsettled country, exceeds beleif [*sic*]." In her mind, the trespasses made by the Union army were unforgivable and crossed the lines of what she considered civilized warfare. As a result, "The Yankee nation can never wipe out the stigma which this war has left upon them. It is indelible." After the invading soldiers "left us nothing but our wheat which is very little and the only living things in the place is the folks, a few *Chickens,* our dog and about a half dozen cats," a Georgia woman bemoaned the suffering that awaited her family. They had little to eat, and their personal belongings were similarly reduced to just "our wearing clothes." The constant raids and the personal nature of those invasions led her to determine, "I do not think the Demons from the bottomless pit could act much worse than the Yankees." The trauma inflicted by the invading soldiers reflected the guerrilla-like methods they employed. Georgian Dolly Lunt Burge offered a startling image of the regular troops that showed them as anything but regular. "Like Demons they rush in. . . . [L]ike famished wolves they come, breaking locks & whatever is in their way." The soldiers made quick work of all of her food, but there was nothing for her to do. She was "Utterly powerless" as she frantically worked to "save my house from plunder & fire."[27]

The sustained attacks on households, all part of a home-front campaign that one Union soldier referred to "as the biggest raid of the war," often occurred over several days and took their toll on Southern civilians. A Virginia woman complained, "they broke open the house [and] ransacked it from top to bottom at least fifty times." In Georgia, Loula Kendall Rogers found herself plagued by the terror caused by disordered raiders. "For two whole days they were coming in every few minutes in that way, and told so much about what the Infantry would do who were coming along behind, that we were heartsick with dread & fear." Another Georgian declared that what she had experienced would stay with her forever: "The day the Yankees left Atlanta will never be forgotten by those who lived on the road; it was a night of horrors to us all." Mary

Jones questioned the irregular tactics and those who committed them. "Do the annals of civilized, & I may add, Savage warfare, afford any record of brutality equaled in extent & duration to that which we have suffered? And which has been inflicted on us by the Yankees?" She continued with more details: "For one month our homes & all we possess on earth have been given up to lawless pillage. Officers & men have alike engaged in this work of degradation."[28] To these women, the soldiers' behavior on the Confederate home front seemed far outside the bounds of civilized warfare.

South Carolinian Emma Holmes agreed that Union troops behaved like guerrillas who seemed to relish the suffering of civilians. As a result, "all the barbarities of savage warfare followed in Sherman's wake—Fire, desolation, destruction of all property unremovable—all provisions, cattle & negroes carried away." That evidence of physical destruction was not even the worst of it. She particularly despised the "rape and consequent death or insanity of many ladies of the best families" by the uncivilized soldiers, insisting that no "pen can portray the sufferings inflicted by that army of demons." The constant raids, much like those led by Confederate guerrillas in western border states, led many to agree that it was "as if the lower regions had been turned inside out, such awful countenances as some had, really they looked too fiendish to live."[29]

Their insulting behavior toward civilians made Union troops seem undisciplined and therefore less than soldierly. As Louisianan Kate Stone noted, "The Yankee raids are no joke, though we laugh at each other for being frightened." She recorded the burning of Floyd and Pin Hook, where the soldiers did not allow "the people to remove any of their possessions from their houses." Even worse, the soldiers "were very rough and insulting in their language to the ladies, tore the pockets from their dresses and the rings from their fingers, cursing and swearing, and frightening the helpless folks nearly into fits." Stone was relieved that she and her family had left home and were not in the enemy's path because "[t]o lose everything is bad, but constant terror and insult are worse."[30] Safety was certainly not guaranteed in the presence of these irregularly acting Union soldiers.

Such destruction, encouraged by Union commanders even as they condemned similar acts by their enemies, fit within the limits of General Orders No. 100 and other directives. In a March 1865 letter to Sherman, Grant expressed his delight in Sheridan's home-front campaign. "Sheridan has made his raid and with splendid success so far as heard." In the formalized rules of war that he laid out in General Orders No. 100, Francis Lieber left room for interpretation by individual commanders. Although he stated that there was a "distinction between the private individual belonging to a hostile country and the hostile country itself, with its men in arms," and "that the unarmed citizen is to be spared in person, property, and honor as much as the exigencies of war will admit," these were merely suggestions. It was left to commanders in the field to define the "exigencies of war" as they marched across the Confederacy. Furthermore, Lieber's Code allowed that the vague notion of "[m]ilitary necessity . . . allows of all destruction of property, and obstruction of the ways and channels of traffic, travel, or communication, and of all withholding of sustenance or means of life from the enemy; of the appropriation of whatever an enemy's country affords necessary for the subsistence and safety of the army." Perhaps that justification allowed Sherman's men to proudly report that after leaving Columbia, South Carolina, "the Town was all burned except the out buildings Such destructians [*sic*] I Never did see."[31] Even within this set of rules that defined how the "regular" army should behave, "irregular" behavior was allowed, if not encouraged.

Lieber's Code also offered definitions of fighting groups that both connected the Union's home-front campaigns with and distinguished them from irregular warfare elsewhere. For starters, it defined "partisans [as] soldiers armed and wearing the uniform of their army, but belonging to a corps which acts detached from the main body for the purpose of making inroads into the territory occupied by the enemy." This definition encompasses both Confederate partisans and the soldiers in the home-front campaigns of Sheridan, Sherman, and other Union commanders. Yet Union officials rejected this connection for good reason: if the army considered Union raiders to be partisans, they would have been subject to severe punishments under Lieber's Code. "All wanton violence committed against persons in the invaded country, all destruction of property not commanded by the authorized officer, all robbery, all pillage or sacking, even after [the] taking [of] a place by main force, all rape, wounding, maiming, or killing of such inhabitants are prohibited under the penalty of death, or such other severe punishment as may seem adequate for the gravity of the offense." The soldiers in the home-front campaigns also escaped categorization as pillagers on account of some peculiarities in Lieber's definitions. Regular armies, he explained, would not act in ways that lived up to the popular definition of the crime: "the idea of intentional destruction for the sake of destruction" and the "general and heinous criminality, of robbery and lust." Instead, the crime of pillage could only be committed by "the guerrilla band, because, not being connected with the regular army, the men cannot provide for themselves, except by pillage." Not only did Lieber exclude Union soldiers from the probability of engaging in this illegal act, but his code also provided justification for it: "War is not carried on by arms alone. It is lawful to starve the hostile belligerent, armed or unarmed, so that it leads to the speedier subjection of the enemy."[32] In essence, Union soldiers may have behaved in ways that were comparable to Confederate pillagers, but Lieber explicitly excluded them from being tarnished by such charges.

After their renowned campaigns in the Shenandoah Valley, Georgia, and the Carolinas, Sheridan and Sherman both acknowledged that they crossed the line with the controversial approaches that they took. Sherman, who claimed to "know the vindictive nature of our enemy," cared little for Southerners' complaints about his disregard for the rules of war. He acknowledged that "a big howl is raised against my Barbarity—Butler is the Beast—Sherman the Brute & Grant the Butcher." These characterizations did not bother him. He dismissed the name calling as "somewhat on the order of the school bully who if he cant whip you, can call you hard names or make mouths as you listen." Sherman took particular pride in his irregular tactics on the home front. When pressed about it, he retorted, "War is cruelty, and you cannot refine it." He further felt justified in his actions because he believed that "those who brought war on the country deserve all the curses and maledictions a people can pour out."[33]

Sheridan also felt vindicated in his irregular actions in the Shenandoah Valley. His directive from Grant had been: "Do all the damage to railroads and crops you can. Carry off stock of all descriptions and negroes, so as to prevent further planting." Furthermore, the general in chief stressed, "If the war is to last another year we want the Shenandoah Valley to remain a barren waste." Sheridan did just that and reported, "The people here are getting sick of the war; hitherto they have had no reason to complain because they have been living in great abundance." After the conflict, Sheridan continued to justify his irregular tactics, asserting that he "[did] not believe war to be simply that lines should engage each other in battle." He further believed, like Sherman and Lieber, that "as war is a punishment . . . , if we can, by reducing its advocates to poverty, end it quicker, we are on the side of humanity." Sheridan also continued to take pride in his military performance, even if some judged it irregular. In an 1870 discussion with Sherman about current attacks on Indians, Sheridan unabashedly acknowledged and justified the irregular tactics he had employed during the Civil War and affirmed his commitment to continue using them: "In taking the offensive . . . , if a village is attacked and women and children killed, the responsibility is not with the soldiers but with the people whose crimes necessitated the attack. During the war did any one hesitate to attack a village or town occupied by the enemy because women or children were within its limits? Did we cease to throw shells into Vicksburg or Atlanta because women and children were there?" The general cared little for the sex or age of his enemy. These attitudes reflected the section of Lieber's Code that held, "The law of war, like the criminal law regarding other offenses, makes no difference on account of the difference of sexes, concerning the spy, the war-traitor, or the war-rebel."[34] Other Union soldiers felt the same.

* * *

In recent years, scholars have expanded the military history of the American Civil War to include a myriad of behaviors that betray the stereotypes of disciplined, if not scared, soldiers fighting one another in formal battles with discrete dates, orderly military formations, and hard rules. Although combat was not confined to men with clear ranks, uniforms, and objectives, most of the recorded memory of the war focuses on, and most historical accounts prioritize, "organized armies and stand-up battles."[35] Yet the distinction between the restraint of so-called regular soldiers and the cruelty of guerrillas is not as clear cut as historians portray it. Although scholars, like contemporary Union officers, have tried to define irregular war as a Southern problem, the participants in Sherman's and Sheridan's home-front campaigns employed methods used by the guerrillas they disdained. Soldiers acknowledged that they needed to follow a code of conduct, one that the Union laid out formally in Lieber's Code and that was informally understood and expressed in often unstated rules of war, but they frequently operated on the borders of these rules. As they demonstrated their willingness to make war personal for their enemies, Union soldiers worked with a shared sense of acceptable behavior and tactics.

By Lieber's definitions, Sherman's March to the Sea and Sheridan's Shenandoah Valley Campaign routinely embodied irregular tactics even as the code itself excused them. Indeed, these regular armies acted in ways that could be categorized as irregular, especially as they violated feminine space in their conduct toward and contact with Southern civilians. The Union victory allowed history to judge Northern army raiders as regular soldiers despite their use of what they defined for the enemy as irregular behavior. In addition, the tactics used during these campaigns have often been ignored because the violations committed were often gendered instead of merely physical; the destruction of women's private letters, dresses, and personal items has been minimized as inconsequential. But the rampant physical destruction of women's items proved a key to these campaigns. This reality was routinely acknowledged by the designers of the operations and by the soldiers who carried out the orders, even though they simultaneously denied the characterization that the war they waged was irregular and therefore punishable, illegal, and unethical. White Confederate women, the targets of these "irregular" attacks by "regular" Union troops, also acknowledged the soldiers' refusal to follow what they believed to be the laws of war. But the gender and politics of these witnesses have led scholars to largely dismiss Southern women's interpretations and observations and to minimize the relevance of their wartime experiences. When civilian accounts of the home-front campaigns are taken seriously, however, it becomes evident that irregular warfare during the Civil War was not, in fact, very irregular at all.

NOTES

1. Caroline Kean (Hill) Davis Diary, June 12, 1864, Virginia Historical Society, Richmond.

2. Loula Kendall Rogers, Apr. 30, 1865, Loula Kendall Rogers Papers, Special Collections Department, Robert W. Woodruff Library, Emory University, Atlanta, Ga.

3. Elsewhere I argue that these acts were tactical attempts to demoralize women, but for purposes of this essay, the intent is not necessary. See Frank, *Civilian War.*

4. Mary Sharpe Jones and Mary Jones Mallard, *Yankees a'Coming: One Month's Experience during the Invasion of Liberty County, Georgia, 1864–1865*, ed. Haskell Monroe (Tuscaloosa: Confederate Publishing, 1959), 62 (Dec. 28. 1864).

5. Contemporary references to the punishment of soldiers for rape include Charles Brown Tompkins to Mollie Tomkins, Apr. 2, 1865, Tomkins Papers, Rare Book and Manuscript Library, Duke University, Durham, N.C.; John "General Jack" Casement to Francis Marion Jennings Casement, Apr. 2, 1865, Casement Collection, Henry E. Huntington Library, San Marino, Calif.; Esther Hill Hawks, *Woman Doctor's Civil War: Esther Hill Hawks' Diary,* ed. Gerald Schartz (Columbia: University of South Carolina Press, 1989), 61 (Feb. 1864); and John J. Hight, *History of the Fifty-*

Eighth Regiment of Indiana Volunteer Infantry, Its Organization, Campaigns and Battles from 1861 to 1865. From the Manuscript Prepared by the Late Chaplain John J. Hight during His Service with the Regiment in the Field, ed. Gilbert R. Stormont (Princeton, N.J.: Press of the Clarion, 1895), 416 (Nov. 17, 1864). For a discussion of rape during Civil War campaigns, see E. Susan Barber and Charles Ritter, "'Physical Abuse . . . and Rough Handling': Race, Gender, and Sexual Justice in the Occupied South," in Whites and Long, *Occupied Women,* 49–64; Crystal Feimster, "General Benjamin Butler and the Threat of Sexual Violence during the American Civil War," *Daedalus* (Spring 2009): 126–34; Feimster, "'How Are the Daughters of Eve Punished?': Rape during the Civil War," in *Writing Women's History: A Tribute to Anne Firor Scott,* ed. Elizabeth Anne Payne (Jackson: University Press of Mississippi, 2011), 64–81; Susan Brownmiller, *Against Our Will: Men, Women, and Rape* (New York: Simon & Schuster, 1975), 88; and Thomas P. Lowry, *The Stories the Soldiers Wouldn't Tell: Sex in the Civil War* (Mechanicsburg, Pa.: Stackpole Books, 1994), 123–31.

6. Fellman, *Inside War,* 81.

7. Quotation in Neely, *Civil War and the Limits of Destruction,* 112.

8. Hulbert, "Constructing Guerrilla Memory," 60; Lieber, *Guerrilla Parties,* 7; Lieber, *Instructions.* For recent scholarship on General Orders No. 100, see Witt, *Lincoln's Code;* Matthew J. Mancini, "Francis Lieber, Slavery, and the 'Genesis' of the Laws of War," *Journal of Southern History* 77, no. 2 (May 2011): 325–48; and D. H. Dilbeck, "'The Genesis of this Little Tablet with My Name': Francis Lieber and the Wartime Origins of General Orders No. 100," *Journal of the Civil War Era* 5, no. 2 (June 2015): 231–53.

9. In his introduction, Lieber notes: "[T]he term Guerrilla is often inaccurately used, and its application has been particularly confused at the present time. . . . [I]t is besides exposed to the mischievous process, so often employed in our day, of throwing the mantle of a novel term around an old and well-known offence, in the expectation that a legalizing effect will result from the adoption of a new word having a technical sound." Lieber, *Guerrilla Parties,* 5.

10. Sutherland, *Savage Conflict,* xii (quote). Sheridan acknowledged personal motives behind some of his actions against civilians in the Shenandoah Valley. For example, after his engineer officer, John Meigs, was killed, he declared, "For this atrocious act all the houses within an area of five miles were burned." Sheridan to Grant, Oct. 7, 1864, U.S. War Department, *War of the Rebellion,* ser. 1, 43(2):308 (hereafter cited as *O.R.*). This essay joins the work of an emerging group of scholars who use gender to interpret the interactions between fighting men and female civilians. Following the work of LeeAnn Whites, who adeptly points to the centrality of gender and women in the guerrilla campaigns in Missouri and Kansas, the essay contends that the confrontations between Confederate women and Union soldiers frequently mirrored those with guerrillas. Whites, "Forty Shirts and a Wagonload of Wheat." See also Whites and Long, *Occupied Women;* and Frank, *Civilian War.*

11. Grimsley, *Hard Hand of War,* 2–3; Steve Newton, "Irregular Warfare, 1861–1865," *North & South: The Official Magazine of the Civil War Society* 11, no. 3 (2009): 19; Neely, *Civil War and the Limits of Destruction,* 131.

12. See Herman Hattaway and Archer Jones, *How the North Won: A Military History of the Civil War* (Urbana: University of Illinois Press, 1991), esp. 487–96; and Grimsley, *Hard Hand of War,* esp. 162–70.

13. Ulysses S. Grant to Henry Halleck, July 14, 1864, *O.R.,* ser. 1, 37(2):301. Grant also directed

Halleck that Maj. Gen. David Hunter "should make all of the Valley south of the B & O road a desert." Grant to Halleck, July 15, 1864, ibid., 329.

14. On Sheridan's and Sherman's campaigns as deliberate attacks on the home front and civilians, see Frank, *Civilian War;* Frank "Bedrooms as Battlefields"; and Frank, "War Comes Home."

15. For examples of works that minimize the damage done by these campaigns, see Neely, *Civil War and the Limits of Destruction;* Lee Kennett, *Marching through Georgia: The Story of Soldiers and Civilians during Sherman's Campaign* (New York: Harper Perennial, 2001), esp. 322; and Wesley Moody, *Demon of the Lost Cause: Sherman and Civil War History* (Columbia: University of Missouri Press, 2011).

16. Sheridan to Grant, Sept. 29, 1864, *O.R.,* ser. 1, 43(2):210; Sheridan to Grant, Oct. 7, 1864, ibid., 43(1):31.

17. Emma E. Holmes Diary, Aug. 2, [1864], South Caroliniana Library, University of South Carolina, Columbia; Lucy Rebecca Buck, *Shadows on My Heart: The Civil War Diary of Lucy Rebecca Buck of Virginia,* ed. Elizabeth R. Baer (Athens: University of Georgia Press, 1997), 301 (Aug. 18, 1864); Jones and Mallard, *Yankees a'Coming,* 73 (Jan. 7, 1865); Pauline DeCaradeuc Heyward, *A Confederate Lady Comes of Age: The Journal of Pauline DeCaradeuc Heyward, 1863–1888,* ed. Mary D. Robertson (Columbia: University of South Carolina Press, 1992), 65–68 (Feb. 18, 1865); Henry Hitchcock, *Marching with Sherman,* ed. M. A. DeWolfe Howe (Lincoln: University of Nebraska Press, 1995), 92 (Nov. 25, 1864); Ellen Devereux Hinsdale to Child, Mar. 23, 1865, Hinsdale Family Papers, Duke University, Durham, N.C. Also see Sue Sample, Nov. 29, 1864 diary entry, in *When Sherman Came: Southern Women and the "Great March,"* ed. Katherine M. Jones (New York: Bobbs-Merrill, 1964), 48.

18. Rev. G. S. Bradley, *The Star Corps: or Notes of an Army Chaplain During Sherman's Famous "March to the Sea"* (Milwaukee: Jermain & Brightman, 1865), 225 (Dec. 28, 1864); Hight, *History of the Fifty-Eighth Regiment of Indiana Volunteer Infantry,* 416 (Jan. 19, 1865); J. Dexter Cotton to Wife, Sept. 17, 1864, Cotton Papers, Library of Congress, Washington, D.C.; James Leath Journal, Dec. 23, 1864, Henry E. Huntington Library, San Marino, Calif.; William T. Sherman to James M. Calhoun, Mayor; E. E. Rawson; and S. C. Wells, representing the City Council of Atlanta, Sept. 12, 1864, William T. Sherman, *Sherman's Civil War: Selected Correspondence of William T. Sherman, 1860–1865,* ed. Brooks D. Simpson and Jean V. Berlin (Chapel Hill: University of North Carolina Press, 1999), 708.

19. Special Field Orders No. 120, Nov. 9, 1864, *O.R.,* ser. 1, 39(3):713; William T. Sherman to R. M. Sawyer, Jan. 31, 1864, ibid., 32(2):279; Charles Cox to Katie, Feb. 1, 1865, in "'Gone for a Soldier': The Civil War Letters of Charles Harding Cox," ed. Lorna Lutes Sylvester, *Indiana Magazine of History* 68 (Sept. 1972): 229; Divine to J. H. Everett, Jan. 25, 1865, Everett Papers, Georgia Historical Society, Savannah; Hitchcock, *Marching with Sherman,* 84–85 (Nov. 22, 1864). As described by Hitchcock, Cobb's plantation was "about 6000 acres, and worked 100 hands. . . . No thrift or neatness about the place."

20. See Royster, *Destructive War,* 21. See also E. P. Burton, *Diary of E. P. Burton, Surgeon 7th Reg. Ill., 3rd Big. 2nd Div. 16 A. C.* (Des Moines: Historical Records Survey, 1939), 37 (Oct. 27, 1864); Charles S. Brown to Mother and Etta, Dec. 16, 1864, Brown Papers, Duke University, Durham, N.C.; Taylor Diary, Nov. 23, 1864, Taylor Collection, Emory University, Atlanta, Ga.; and James C. Bonner, "Sherman at Milledgeville in 1864," *Journal of Southern History* 22 (Jan. 1931): 281.

21. Heyward, *Confederate Lady Comes of Age,* 67 (Feb. 18, 1865). Some scholars propose that Sherman designed his campaign with the intention of striking hardest at the Southern elite. For example, see Michael Fellman, *Citizen Sherman: A Life of William Tecumseh Sherman* (New York: Random House, 1995), 214–15; and Frank, *Civilian War.*

22. Buck, *Shadows on My Heart,* 298 (Aug. 18, 1864), 300 (Aug. 18, 1864); E. W. Harrison to Mrs. James L. Henderson, Mar. 11, 1865, in "Sheridan's Raiders," *William and Mary College Quarterly Historical Magazine* 17 (Apr. 1909): 289–90; Susan Leigh Blackford to Charles Minor Blackford, Mar. 6, 1865, in *Letters from Lee's Army,* ed. Charles Minor Blackford III (Lincoln: University of Nebraska Press, 1998), 283; Emma E. Holmes Diary, Feb. 18, 1865, South Caroliniana Library, University of South Carolina, Columbia; Sutherland, *Savage Conflict,* xii. Sutherland asserts that "at least two things defined nearly all 'guerrillas.' . . . First, there was the 'irregular' way they attacked, harassed, and worried their foes. . . . Second, their principal responsibility, their very reason for being in most cases, was local defense. . . . Guerrillas often stretched and tested the second of these conditions."

23. Susan Bowen Lining to Sister, Mar. 16, 1865, South Carolina Historical Society, Charleston; Caroline Keen (Hill) Davis Diary, June 12, 1864, Virginia Historical Society, Richmond; Mary Bull Maxcy Leverett to Caroline Pinckney Seabrook, Mar. 18, 1865, South Caroliniana Library, University of South Carolina, Columbia; E. V. Ravenel to Allan Macfarlan, Mar. 21, 1865, Allan Macfarlan Papers, ibid.; Dolly Lunt Burge, *The Diary of Dolly Lunt Burge, 1848–1879,* ed. Christine Jacobson Carter (Athens: University of Georgia Press, 1997), 161–62 (Nov. 19, 1864).

24. Henrietta B. Lee to General [David] Hunter, July 20, 1864, Civil War Collection—Confederate Items, Swem Library, College of William and Mary, Williamsburg, Va.; "Vandalism," *Richmond Enquirer,* May 21, 1864, 1; Catherine Edmondston, *"Journal of a Secesh Lady": The Diary of Catherine Ann Devereux Edmondston, 1860–1866,* ed. Beth G. Crabtree and James W. Patton (Raleigh: Division of Archives and History, Department of Cultural Resources, 1979), 589–90 (July 14, 1864).

25. Louisa Warren Patch Fletcher Journal, July 25, Oct. 12, 1864, Georgia Department of Archives and History, Atlanta, Ga.

26. "The Way in Which Grant's Order Was Carried Out," *Republican Farmer,* Oct. 21, 1864, 2.

27. Ann C. R. Jones to Lucy R. Parkhill, Nov. 30, 1864, in *Defend the Valley: A Shenandoah Family in the Civil War,* ed. Margaretta Barton Colt (New York: Oxford University Press, 1994), 350–51; Edmondston, *"Journal of a Secesh Lady,"* 588 (July 11, 1864); A. E. D. to Brother, Dec. 6, 1864, Confederate Miscellany I, Special Collections Department, Robert W. Woodruff Library, Emory University, Atlanta, Ga.; Burge, *Diary,* 159–60 (Nov. 19, 1864).

28. Bradley, *Star Corps,* 183 (Nov. 17, 1864); Letter, Maria Linsey Dobyns Roane Garnett, June 17, 1864, Virginia Historical Society, Richmond; Loula Kendall Rogers Journal, Apr. 30, 1865, Loula Kendall Rogers Papers, Special Collections Department, Robert W. Woodruff Library, Emory University, Atlanta, Ga.; A. E. D. to Brother, Dec. 6, 1864, Confederate Miscellany I, ibid.; Jones and Mallard, *Yankees a'Coming,* 72–73 (Jan. 7, 1865).

29. Emma E. Homes Diary, Nov. 12, 1864, South Caroliniana Library, University of South Carolina, Columbia; Sarah Jane Sams to Randolph Sams [husband], Feb. 13, 1865, Sarah Jane Sams Letter, ibid.

30. Kate Stone, *Brokenburn: The Journal of Kate Stone, 1861–1868,* ed. John Q. Anderson (Baton Rouge: Louisiana State University Press, 1972), 297–98 (Sept. 5, 1864).

31. Ulysses S. Grant to William T. Sherman, Mar. 16, 1865, *O.R.*, ser. 1, 47(2):860; Lieber, *Instructions,* Articles 15, 22; Jesse S. Bean Diary, Feb. 18, 1865, Southern Historical Collection, University of North Carolina, Chapel Hill.

32. Lieber, *Instructions,* Articles 17, 44, 81; Lieber, *Guerrilla Parties,* 8.

33. William T. Sherman to James M. Calhoun, Mayor; E. E. Rawson; and S. C. Wells, representing the City Council of Atlanta, Sept. 12, 1864, Sherman, *Sherman's Civil War,* 707; William T. Sherman to Eugene Casserly, Sept. 17, 1864, ibid., 713.

34. Ulysses S. Grant to Philip Sheridan, Aug. 26, 1864, *O.R.,* ser. 1, 43(1):916–17; Philip Sheridan to Ulysses S. Grant, Oct. 7, 1864, ibid., 43(2):30; Philip Sheridan to A. A. Humphreys, May 13, 1866, ibid., 36(1):801; Philip Sheridan to William T. Sherman, Mar. 18, 1870, *Executive Documents Printed by the Order of the House of Representatives during the Second Session of the Forty-first Congress, 1869–70* (Washington, D.C.: Government Printing Office, 1870), 70 (exec. doc. 269); Lieber, *Instructions,* Article 102.

35. Newton, "Irregular Warfare," 19.

GUERRILLA WARFARE AND THE ENVIRONMENT IN THE TRANS-MISSISSIPPI THEATER

MATTHEW M. STITH

As the guerrilla war in the Trans-Mississippi theater reached its peak intensity in early 1864, regular Union forces struggled for ways to effectively combat the "bushwhacker" menace. Commanders increasingly based their counterguerrilla strategy on the environment. More specifically, they explored ways to beat guerrillas at their own game. To this end, Federal officers, according to one order, should "acquire a perfect knowledge of the country, its resources in forage, its covers, forests, [and] hiding places for marauding parties." A similar order called for guerrilla hunters to carefully search the "brush and low grounds that would be likely to afford cover for guerrillas." These counterguerrilla soldiers came to identify themselves as hunters, and they developed strategies that might allow them to successfully manipulate what had become the guerrillas' greatest ally: the environment. "While on the hunt," one Federal commander implored, "no talking or other loud noises will be made, except signals, which should be the imitation of some forest bird or animals." In the cover of darkness, guerrilla hunters should abstain from smoking while skulking about the brush for the enemy in their own habitat. These precautions, the frustrated Federals hoped, would make it impossible for guerrillas to hide from these patrols. While using birdcalls and sneaking thin the dark forest might have brought some success, Union forces generally failed in their attempts to match the guerrillas in the brush. By August 1864, influential Unionist B. W. Lewis wrote with urgency to Brigadier General Clinton Fisk about the situation in Glasgow, Missouri. "I am firmly of the opinion that the knights of the brush have it in their power to crush us," Lewis warned, "whenever they think it policy to do so." The guerrillas had pinned Lewis and his local militia in, and they had quite literally used the brush—and the environment in general—as leverage to even the odds against their better-supplied and more numerous foe.[1]

Just as Union troops found it difficult to catch guerrillas in the field, historians still struggle to fully define guerrilla, or "irregular," warfare and those who perpetuated it. Much of the problem in definition rests with the levels of violence and lawfulness that irregulars practiced in the field. For the purposes of this essay, irregulars represent both Confederate guerrillas and Union "jayhawkers" who operated in the vast area between the Mississippi River and the eastern sections of Texas, Indian Territory, and Kansas. Both Union and Confederate forces generally defined irregulars during the war as those who fought outside the bounds of conventional warfare—without proper uniforms, leadership, or structure. Irregulars fought what had widely become known as a skulking kind of war. They perfected hit-and-run tactics against both enemy supply and communication lines, and they struck hard and often against enemy morale. For historian Daniel E. Sutherland, almost all guerrillas—Confederate and Union—used irregular tactics and engaged in a local war to "protect" their homes and communities. While the former is indisputable, the latter is far more complicated and often proved to be half-hearted justifications for sheer violence. Isaac Gause, a member of the Second Ohio Cavalry, provided a thorough contemporary description. The irregulars who "infested" much of the Trans-Mississippi, he said, "were not confined to the army alone; some were secessionists, and others Union, while others were, strictly speaking, seeking revenge for actual or supposed wrongs perpetrated on themselves or families, and still others were depredating for the spoils." Not only did Gause have a sophisticated understanding of what motivated irregulars, but he also knew well their style of warfare. "They were constantly making raids, driving off stock, and carrying off provisions of every kind, [and] robbing and burning houses," he wrote. As the Ohio Yankee made clear, irregular warfare was complicated, unpredictable, and destructive.[2]

While Sutherland's and Gause's definitions hold true, one universal essential factor has heretofore remained out of focus: irregulars from both sides relied almost entirely on the environment to ply their trade. Guerrilla warfare's gravitational center rested squarely on the natural and manmade environment. Mountains, rivers, forests, and swamps proved to be key sanctuaries for irregular warfare, just as stolen cattle, pigs, corn, and wheat fueled the guerrillas and those who chased them. The environment was also central to cultural perceptions of this contest. Both Union and Confederate irregulars hid in the "brush" and were hunted like wild game. The same rhetoric used by nineteenth-century bear hunters to describe their expeditions flavored the speech of Union and Confederate soldiers who stalked humans in the bush.

More than just representing the foundational element in irregular warfare, the environment defined how soldiers, guerrillas, and civilians *perceived* their conflict. The guerrilla war happened in the brush. It occurred in the shadows, thickets, swamps, and hills that spanned the Trans-Mississippi and other parts of the South. The guerrillas themselves—variously called bushwhackers, rebels, secesh, butternuts, and a variety of other terms—had come to represent for most nonguerrillas a kind of dangerous and skulking wild animal. As such, Union troops "hunted" guerrillas much as they would wild hogs or black bears. They used extra caution, sure, but they brought with them a sense of the manly hunt in a wilderness of war that harbored what they considered the lowest order but most dangerous of combatants, who used the forests, hills, and swamps as their ally. In sum, it is impossible to fully appreciate the guerrilla war's significance without also understanding the environment's robust and decisive role in shaping its course. To this end, the Trans-Mississippi—a region including Kansas, Missouri, Indian Territory, Arkansas, Texas, and Louisiana—serves as an ideal arena for evaluating the intricate relationship between guerrillas and the environment. The region not only was home to the most intense and protracted guerrilla fighting in the American Civil War but also featured one of the most diverse environments in the South. Indeed, the natural environment allowed for and helped perpetuate the especially brutal guerrilla war that occurred there.[3]

War and environment are inseparable in any context, and this is even more pronounced in an irregular war. Guerrilla monikers like "bushwhacker" or "knights of the brush" reflect their greatest asset. For the Federals who chased them, such environmental allies such as topography, foliage, weather, and other natural factors exacerbated their ever-growing frustration. Avowed Confederate guerrilla Samuel S. Hildebrand put the guerrilla perspective frankly: "I was fully satisfied that the 'Bushwhacking department' was the place for me, with the continent for a battlefield and everlasting woods for my headquarters."[4] By 1864, the Union army had taken the war to the Southern home front in an effort to silence or at least control guerrilla activity. But Hildebrand's "everlasting woods" was only a part of the irregular battleground. Guerrillas, those they hunted, and those who hunted them, were all inextricably connected to the built environment as well. Livestock and crops, although increasingly rare in much of the Trans-Mississippi by midwar, had become the fulcrum for conflict among combatants and noncombatants alike. War in the region pitted civilians against soldiers and guerrillas in a series of battles that raged in or over homes, yards, pigpens, and corncribs. And although women and children (depending on their age) rarely were in direct mortal danger, their lives and livelihoods were threatened when they lost their only food and shelter. At best, they became refugees in crowded, disease-ridden camps. At worst, they succumbed to the hardships wrought by a war in which they were directly involved.[5]

The natural and built environment directly shaped the course and consequences of the guerrilla war west of the Mississippi River. It was a key ally of guerrillas and helped them perpetuate a particularly brutal conflict that led to an enlarged Union presence and an increasingly harsh Federal policy toward Confederate civilians. In sum, the irregular war changed the nature of warfare on the Southern home front, eroded the Confederate war effort by prompting a Union hard-war policy, and ultimately played a decisive role in shaping the outcome of the Civil War. Yet scholars of the guerrilla war have largely missed the very medium in which irregulars wrought such significant damage even as Federal guerrilla hunters knew well that they were fighting the forests, hills, and food supplies as much as they were the fighters who relied on these environmental factors for survival and success.

Civil War scholars have only recently started to give the environment the attention it deserves. Indeed, the unrelenting and often deadly environment shaped the irregular, civilian-centered war as much as it did larger campaigns. It was an integral and altogether inseparable part of the Civil War everywhere, but especially in the Trans-Mississippi. Historians have long included the environment in their analyses of the conflict, yet few have used it as a central vehicle with which to more fully understand the war. Lisa M. Brady argues that the environment became an increasingly important factor in Union military strategy against the Confederacy. By destroying the built Southern landscape, the Union army effectively eroded civilian morale and eventually their willingness and ability to continue the war. "By targeting the South's agricultural sector," she contends, "this new Union strategy undermined the region's most basic relationship to the natural world. It destroyed the Confederacy's agroecological foundations and contributed significantly to ultimate Federal victory." For Megan Kate Nelson, the war's inherent destruction, or "ruination," spread to every section of society. Neither natural nor manmade environments were immune. Southern homes were torched for a variety of reasons, not the least of which was a new Union strategy aimed at the heart of civilian support for the Confederate war effort. The subsequent destruction, Nelson contends, manifested itself as "the ultimate invasion of privacy and a gendered attack on a space previously sanctified but rendered profane." At the least, domestic destruction represented "a morally disastrous turn in the conduct of the war" in which Victorian sensibilities were obliterated with houses and forests. What's more, such devastation—though quickly cleaned and rebuilt—became an important weapon to be wielded against the Union in the war for memory long after the physical fighting had ended.[6]

As the new cohort of Civil War environmental scholars have shown, terrain, animals, weather, and other natural factors played significant roles in shaping warfare, and this was certainly the case in the Trans-Mississippi. The region featured some of the most intense, demanding, and dangerous terrain in the eastern half of the United States. For civilians living along the Trans-Mississippi border, the environment represented an integral part of their existence. As evidenced by thousands of letters, diary entries, and memoirs, the environment's influence on society was second to none. These written records mention weather, disease, animals, and food as much as they do any societal phenomenon. The environment, in its many facets, indelibly shaped society and warfare on the border. It deserves as much emphasis as the Union and Confederate forces in any fully developed study of this region, perhaps more. While trench networks, roving armies, and redirected rivers certainly scarred the landscape, in the end, the environment did much more to scar people. In short, combined with a cross-cultural border where political boundaries meant little, the environment, frontier society, and war congealed to foster economic, social, and physical destruction to an extent not previously witnessed in American history.[7]

At times, Confederate commanders endorsed what they called "partisan" warfare. Major General Thomas Hindman leveraged the national Partisan Ranger Act in Arkansas and called for small companies of irregulars to harass Federals and hinder their ability to make war. In eastern Arkansas, the actions he recommended these guerrillas take included "blockading roads, burning bridges, destroying all supplies, growing crops included, and polluting the water by killing cattle, ripping the carcasses, and throwing them in." Hindman recognized the role landscape and agriculture played in shaping the conflict, and he urged guerrillas—and civilians in general—to manipulate the environment in order to stymie the enemy. As Union major general Samuel Curtis threatened

Arkansas's White River valley in the summer of 1862, Hindman pleaded with all Arkansans who would listen to "lay in ambush and surprise his detachments, shoot his mounted officers, destroy every pound of meat and flour, every ear of corn and stack of fodder, oats and wheat that can fall into his hands." Hindman, in short, urged Confederate civilians and irregulars to wage an environmentally focused guerrilla war against the Union army.[8]

In turn, thousands of Union troops dedicated much of their fighting career to hunting guerrillas in the Trans-Mississippi. According to one Federal officer in 1863, "hunting and in some cases exterminating bushwhackers" was an "everyday business." Another boasted that his troops could "track the bushmen like a dog will a deer," while other reports reflect a general strategy of hunting guerrillas in the timber and underbrush. "I keep my men scouring the country in all directions," wrote a frustrated officer in southern Missouri, "hunting those thieves and meting summary justice to them." Reflecting on a march in western Arkansas, one of Charles Jennison's infamous jayhawkers reported that they "scouted the country . . . for miles, and not without occasionally flushing a cover of the 'night hawks.'" The guerrillas, the frustrated and no less brutal Union trooper complained, "hang, like cossacks upon our rear, and better were a man with a millstone about his neck in the middle of Missouri than alone anywhere in the *brush* after the command has passed." They were frustratingly elusive. A small Union cavalry patrol in Missouri "discovered 16 Bushwhackers who were beating a lively retreat, our boys started in pursuit but lost their game." The same cavalrymen later "commenced a hunt" for a guerrilla band and quickly had them "fleeing wildly in the woods."[9] Another Federal cavalry patrol in southwestern Missouri engaged a band of guerrillas who had set up an ambush near their winter supplies of corn and wheat. After a brief but intense exchange of gunfire, the "bushwhackers . . . fled to their holes in the nearby rugged hills." Union soldiers tracked, flushed, and hunted guerrillas throughout the region, but they rarely harvested all of their game.

For the Union pursuers, such a deadly game of chase proved at once thrilling and maddening. A Kansas newspaper editor put it most succinctly: "A squad of troops may march and counter-march all over the country, and not find a single bushwhacker, and yet hundreds of them lied concealed within twenty rods of the columns." An intricate system of civilian support in tandem with the rugged terrain and brush made it nearly impossible for patrols to hunt them down. Much like a wily game animal wary of the hunter, guerrillas used the environment to survive and ply their trade. Historian Michael Fellman has likened the pursuit to something close to "blood sport." For Union troops, Fellman contends, these irregulars represented "beasts to be hunted down like other animals." Guerrilla hunting was akin to "vermin eradication." Union brigadier general John Schofield clarified Federal intentions toward their quarry in General Orders No. 18. "The utmost vigilance and energy are enjoined upon all the troops of [Missouri]," he ordered, "in hunting down and destroying these robbers and assassins." Schofield continued: "When caught in arms, engaged in this unlawful warfare, they will be shot down upon the spot."[10]

Union soldiers followed Schofield's directive and the many other "black flag" orders passed down by commanders in the Trans-Mississippi. In the rugged northern Arkansas Ozarks, Union lieutenant Charles W. Porter and his Wisconsin cavalry gave chase to a dozen bushwhackers who had fired into their column. They managed to kill two of the assailants and capture three—a high percentage for the typical fight in this difficult terrain. The rest, Porter lamented, "escaped in the brush." Knowing well the ramifications for accused guerrillas, the three captives claimed to be regular Confederate soldiers and, as such, privileged to the rights thereof. Porter and his men spared them for the first evening and scheduled a speedy trial for the morning. At that time they found the men guilty and sentenced them to immediate execution. Porter took "charge of the execution of these Knights of the brush" and ordered two cavalry troopers from each company to march the condemned men off the road to be shot. Just after the lieutenant read the prisoners their sentence, "the doomed men made no reply, but started to run when the boys fired on them with their carbine[s], killing them instantly."[11] The Federals had caught some of their elusive and deadly quarry, but they still had a nearly inexhaustible supply of guerrillas to track down. Porter and his troopers hunted on.

It was difficult to catch and kill guerrillas, but some Union officers had grown quite adept at controlling them. Union major general John McNeil excelled at the task. For him, the best way to effectively hunt guerrillas was to adapt to their style of warfare. Writing to Colonel M. LaRue Harrison, who commanded the First Arkansas Cavalry (U.S.), a remarkably effective counterguerrilla unit, McNeil made clear that little good would come from hunting irregulars on the regular roadways in Arkansas. Instead, he wrote, "the byways and mountain paths your men know so well are the real tracks to glory and honor." The general added that "night marches, sudden attacks, ambuscades, and untiring pursuit are the only cure for bushwhackers and guerrillaism." In other words, to effectively counter guerrillas, it was imperative to fight on their terms. By midwar if not before, Union troops like those from the First Arkansas Cavalry took to the woods, hills, and swamps to pursue their prey. The overwhelming frustration and constant hunt led many guerrilla chasers to treat their quarry little better than pests in need of eradication. In September 1864, troopers in the Third Wisconsin Cavalry surprised a small group of nine guerrillas in a thicket, promptly killing two; the others got away. The Wisconsin troopers took some horses and supplies, and they "left the two men for the wolves and buzzards to hold a grand feast over." In 1864 Union brigadier general Clinton B. Fisk reported from eastern Missouri that "guerrilla hunters are doing good service. Small squads of the rascals are raked out of the brush and mustered out on the spot."[12]

The rhetoric and reality of the "hunt" went both ways. Union irregulars, or jayhawkers as many Confederates called them, came to be identified as vermin to be hunted much like their rebel counterparts. In August 1863 a band of nearly fifty jayhawkers attacked some Texas cavalrymen near Opelousas, Louisiana. The bloody little fight, like so many other irregular skirmishes, was brief but intense. The angry Confederates launched a search-and-destroy mission against the Unionists the next day. The rebel troops lined up side by side for the hunt, searching through the thick terrain. According to one Texan, "we scoured the woods and country for miles . . . across bodies of timber and swamps—driving for them as if for deer." The effort yielded four jayhawker prisoners, who were summarily shot the following day.[13]

Farther north, Confederate guerrillas chased Unionists, who used the very same environment so well adapted by the rebel guerrillas to elude their pursuers. In a desperate 1864 letter to Major General William Rosecrans, a Unionist named Richard Hudson from southeastern Missouri complained about the treacherous nature of his part of the state. "The Union men are hunted, and if found are shot or killed in some other way," the Ironton man wrote; "our families are shamefully and grossly insulted by these desperate bloody-handed bushwhackers." But being hunted by rebel irregulars was not all. The guerrilla war's intensity and persistence by midwar had precluded the opportunity of most citizens to provide for themselves. Not only could they not plant and grow a crop, but most of the food and supplies they already had were subject to theft or destruction. "We not having the liberty to make a crop last year, and our property and provisions being taken away from us by those bands," Hudson continued, "there are families [who] without relief shortly will be reduced to starvation." In northwestern Arkansas, Unionists had been forced to take refuge in the same rugged Ozarks that the guerrillas used to their advantage. "Guerrilla bands are numerous," Union major general James Blunt reported in the summer of 1863, and they have been "hunting Union men who have fled to the mountains." He continued: "Many of them have been compelled by starvation to come in, when they have been shot or hung." For Unionists in southeastern Missouri and northwestern Arkansas alike, the war had deteriorated into one of survival, and it had become a struggle entirely centered on the environment.[14]

Unionists in East Texas suffered a similar fate. Without mountains to hide in, some took refuge in the Big Thicket. This dense forest in the east-central part of the state served as an ideal hideout until late 1864. In November a "reserve corps" of local Confederate Texans went hunting for these jayhawkers, much like they would any wild game. The similarities are striking. They brought along the "redoubtable old bear hunter" Richard Williams and his hunting dogs to lead the chase. The dogs caught scent of their quarry in a thick canebrake that stretched over a mile, where the Unionists had built an elaborate camp resplendent with gardens and shanties. But their security was shattered when the old bear hunter, "with marvelous sagacity . . . tracked their foot-prints through cane brake and thicket, and the fierce cries of his dogs warn[ed] him that the wolves . . . [were] 'at bay.'" This quest yielded over twenty captives. The hunting analogy was no accident. The jayhawkers had become akin to game beasts or even vermin so far as those who hunted them were concerned. They were pests who hid out in the same woods as the wild pigs, black bears, and wolves, and they needed to be eradicated.[15]

Terrain played as important a role in shaping irregular warfare as it did in regular campaigns, especially in the Trans-Mississippi. Indeed, one of the most widely used names for Confederate guerrillas was based on terrain: bushwhacker. Union forces used the term with disgust. From an environmental standpoint, whether in the Trans-Mississippi border or the Appalachian backcountry, the moniker represents an adroit example of environment's influence on irregular warfare. Save for a handful of large set-piece battles in the Trans-Mississippi, irregular warfare occurred quite literally in the brush. Guerrilla bands used thickets, hills, hollows, and swamps to surprise and evade Union patrols. Nasty descriptor or not, Federal forces themselves soon adopted the "bushwhacker" style of fighting. Patrols often attempted to "beat bushwhackers . . . at their own game." In one instance a small cavalry command received orders to "lie in the brush for three or four days" and ambush roving guerrilla bands. These cavalrymen, and thousands more, adapted to the irregular style of warfare dealt them in the border area by immersing in the natural terrain in an attempt to silence local guerrillas.[16]

Pursuing guerrillas in the brush was an exasperating affair. Irregulars captured along the border region were often swiftly and brutally punished. After coming under sudden fire while patrolling a wooded area, one young Union officer ordered an immediate counterattack that resulted in the capture of the three assailants. The men were quickly tried and convicted for engaging in guerrilla warfare. Standing before a hastily gathered firing squad, the condemned attempted to escape, but the "Knights of the brush," as the young officer quipped, were immediately shot down. Frustration among Union soldiers patrolling the border Trans-Mississippi continued to build throughout the war. Perpetually pursuing irregular warriors along heavily wooded rivers and creeks or through the vast and rocky Ozarks was maddening, the victories rare and largely ungratifying. Their foe used the environment to its greatest potential, not just feasting on stolen pork and corn but also melting into the landscape after inflicting casualties. Blending back into society or more commonly hiding in forests and caves, these irregulars seemed untouchable by Union troops. When caught, though, their punishment was often death.[17]

Guerrillas were no easy quarry, and this had a lot to do with the mountainous landscape throughout much of the Trans-Mississippi that afforded them ample room to run and hide. In the Ozarks of northern Arkansas and southern Missouri, Federal perceptions of the region quickly evolved from a sense of awe to sheer loathing. The rocks, trees, and brambles became as much the enemy as the guerrillas they harbored. Wisconsin soldier Jacob Haas lamented in his diary, "the deep ravines and very high rocky banks of the [White] river . . . are excellent hiding places for criminals, rebels and bushwhackers." Another Federal complained that he could not "see anything that would entice me to leave a civilized and white man's country to dwell in this wilderness among the rocks and hills where even the sun fails to shine more than eight hours in twenty-four." Major William Thompson wrote to his wife about a march through the rocky hills and steep ravines of southern Missouri, complaining that a "more God forsaken Country than that over which we have marched I have never seen." The deadly landscape had become, as another Union soldier put it, "a dreary and uninviting wilderness."[18]

A different kind of terrain challenged guerrilla hunters in Louisiana, where swamps and thickets proved ideal hiding places for "swamp guerrillas" bent on harassing Union patrols. In the La Fourche region southwest of New Orleans, swamps and lowlands proved a critical ally for irregulars. One New York Yankee vented his fear and frustration in a poem that exclaimed, in part, "Hark, A shot comes sharply ringing on the air; From the foe in hiding there. In the deep dark wood and firs." The same guerrillas who lurked in the shadowy wetlands and dark woods compared themselves to Revolutionary War guerrilla Francis Marion, the "Swamp Fox." Much as Marion had used the swamps of the Carolinas to offset his imbalance in manpower and supplies against the British, the outnumbered and outsupplied swamp guerrillas of southern Louisiana leveraged the landscape to even the odds against the Federals.[19]

The guerrillas' use of forests and terrain to enhance their effectiveness against the Union army had increasingly harsh consequences. Not only had a "black flag" policy been widely adopted by Federals, but severe and immediate retribution at the community level often followed guerrilla attacks—especially by midwar. In the spring of 1863, guerrillas struck one of Colonel William Weer's foraging parties in northern Arkansas. For the Yankees in the rugged terrain, the guerrillas seemed to lurk behind every bush, tree, and rock—"the woods about here are alive with bushwhackers," wrote one of Weer's Ohio soldiers. As for the attack on the Yankee foragers, the colonel had been "so annoyed at this that he ordered a party to go out . . . where the citizens are outspoken secesh and very saucy to boot, and burn all their dwellings." His order was clear: "destroy every house and farm, etc., owned by secessionists, together with their property; . . . kill every bushwhacker you find; bring away the women and children to this place."[20] Even if Weer and his fellow officers in the Trans-Mississippi could not catch all of the elusive guerrillas who leveraged the environment to increase their effectiveness, the frustrated Federals *could* torch homes and entire communities. With their failure to control the irregulars themselves, Union forces made war on the Confederate home front more generally—a move that ultimately helped erode the ability and desire for the Confederacy to continue the fight both in the Trans-Mississippi and across the South.

The Trans-Mississippi landscape was not all that stymied Union guerrilla hunters. One Illinois soldier complained to his parents about the hordes of insects and animals that plagued him and his comrades near Shreveport, Louisiana. "It is anything but pleasant here," he wrote. "The flies, fleas, spiders, crickets, slugs, beetles, giggers, lice and all kinds of vermin bother so one has no peace or quiet." This was not all. After dark, the swamps came alive with unrelenting noise: "The frogs, owls, aligators, musquitoes, and all creeping things keep up such an ever lasting hissing. . . . The musquitoes present their bills for liquidation, the fleas play backgammon on my anatomy all night and I wake up in the morning more tired than when I laid down." An Ohio soldier in Baton Rouge focused his lamentations squarely on mosquitoes. At a loss for words to adequately describe the swarms around him, he wrote simply: "The 'skeeters' here are—well, there is no use talking. You never can imagine the like—I never seen the like before." Reflecting sarcastically on the swampy environment that surrounded them, an Iowa infantryman told his brother, "musketoes, gallinippers, crab fish, gars and alligators are some of the luxuries of the country."[21]

Louisiana did not hold a monopoly on irksome fauna, however. Near Fort Scott, Kansas, the Third Wisconsin Cavalry—a noted counterguerrilla force on the Trans-Mississippi border—found themselves in a bloody fight with stinging insects. According to one lieutenant, they spent a great deal of time "desperately fighting flies and mosquitos which continually bit and sting us day and night, and remind us that the Devils dominions are located at this place, or his imps in miniature form are on a tour of inspection." The hordes of biting flies and mosquitoes had occupied the guerrilla hunters such that any protracted assault against bushwhackers in the area simply had not been practical. For the young lieutenant, the insect infestation was not far removed from the guerrilla infestation. He confided in his diary the next day, "we are of the opinion that every foot of hell is here exhibited and we have free tickets."[22]

From early in the conflict, Union counterguerrilla efforts increasingly focused on the large rivers coursing through the Trans-Mississippi. Infantry and cavalry struggled to cross dangerous, guerrilla-infested forests, hills, and swamps, but the major tributaries of the Mississippi River—namely the Missouri, White, Arkansas, and Red Rivers—formed large, navigable highways on which to transport supplies and soldiers far more safely and efficiently. Confederate irregulars did everything they could to complicate these supply routes. By late 1862, constant guerrilla harassment on the rivers led the Union army to develop the Mississippi Marine Brigade. This unit's primary mission was to protect Federal vessels by fighting and deterring guerrilla attacks. In sum, they had been tasked to control irregulars who had become quite effective at ambushing Union steamboats from the thick brush along the riverbanks. The special brigade had been designed as a counterguerrilla strike force. Horses, men, and supplies maintained a state of readiness to respond to enemy harassment as quickly as their steamer could get them to the scene. Such an amphibious assault force worked well on paper, but leadership issues and the troops' inability to effectively thwart the guerrillas they were chasing proved the brigade's undoing. One officer writing from near Lake Village, Arkansas, got straight to the problem in a letter home. Added to the discomforts of "the malarial water we are compelled to drink, and the excessive hot weather" that "make us sigh for Peace," the Federal wrote, was the "trying guerrilla war-fare, phoenix-like in its character, subdued, yet day after day rising up out of the ashes of its defeat again to menace us." If nothing more, the Marine Brigade's very development reflects the Union army's continued attempts to control the guerrilla problem—one wholly exacerbated by the thick mud and brush that lined the brown rivers of the Trans-Mississippi.[23]

In June 1863, a small group of Confederate guerrillas opened fire on the gunboat USS *Marmora* as it steamed down the Mississippi River near Eunice, Arkansas. Union lieutenant Robert Getty later reported that not only had the rebels fired at his ship, but they shouted at him "with curses to come to and land." Instead of surrendering to the small band, Getty turned the boat and "threw some shell at them" before anchoring near town. The next day the guerrillas had moved closer to Eunice and poured harassing fire at more Union ships. Instead of hopelessly chasing the elusive irregulars through the thick brush and mud lining the river, Getty and the other vessels "commenced shelling the town and woods." The enraged Federals attempted to destroy their unseen foes by bombarding Eunice and two miles of shoreline on the river's western bank. Not content with the bombardment, the Federals landed and torched the town, including a depot, locomotive, warehouse, and "every house and shed within a mile of the landing." In the end, Getty made clear, "not a vestige of the town of Eunice can be seen."[24]

This intense and exacting Union response to guerrilla harassment in southeastern Arkansas reflects the literal and figurative nature of irregular warfare in the Trans-Mississippi theater. Although there had been no Union casualties in the initial attacks, the Federals responded with overwhelming force. In the end, the officers found no guerrilla casualties in the burned-out town, though they likely never expected to. Instead, they destroyed Eunice—and other towns up and down the Mississippi, White, and Arkansas Rivers—in a show of force to intimidate and dissuade the guerrillas and their supporters. Being sniped at for over two years, and being continually frustrated in any attempts to thwart it, led to a number of counterguerrilla measures, not the least of which included outright destruction of property. Major General William T. Sherman echoed such growing Union fear and paranoia in an 1863 letter to Admiral David D. Porter in which he yearned for the day when their men would no longer fear "the howling shell at each bend in the river or the more fatal bullet of the guerrilla at each thicket." Eunice's destruction reflects the natural environment's direct and ubiquitous role in shaping the conflict. Indeed, the riverbanks of mud, brambles, and altogether inhospitable terrain served as the guerrillas' top ally. The guerrilla-infested thickets that Sherman feared forced the Union army and navy to allocate countless resources to the Trans-Mississippi river systems to little avail. Rather than engaging in a usually futile attempt to chase the assailants down, the Federals instead opted to shell the woods and any nearby town that harbored them. For them, the guerrillas and the natural environment had become one and the same.[25]

As late as 1865, guerrillas in western Arkansas ambushed a small flotilla of five boats on the Arkansas River. They first disabled the lead steamer with several well-placed artillery rounds while simultaneously firing several volleys into the boat. Union troops aboard the other steamboats fired back, and three of the vessels were able to run the gauntlet. The other two fell to the guerrillas, who summarily burned one and took over the other. Most of the victims on the burned boat were civilian refugees, "who jumped overboard and were drowned." The families on the captured steamboat were "left on the shore to starve." The attackers also killed dozens of recently mustered-out Kansas soldiers on their way home. Even in the last months of the war, guerrillas had used the rivers and brush to orchestrate a successful attack. While their broader activity led to an increased, and increasingly harsh, Union presence, their smaller fights often ended with some success.[26]

Civilians represent the core of any guerrilla war, and the civilian-centered conflict in the Trans-Mississippi had been shaped entirely and irrevocably by the natural and built environment. In the first years of the war, civilians—mostly women, children, and the elderly—struggled to maintain some level of livelihood, but most in Kansas, Missouri, Indian Territory, and Arkansas instead quickly found that they were intricately immersed in what can only be defined as localized total war. By midwar, every function of society had broken down or completely collapsed. Law and order ceased to exist beyond whomever might have yielded the most military power at a specific time and place—guerrillas, Federals, or Confederates. Possession of a modicum of judicial power not only constantly fluctuated among a variety of disparate forces, but those who enjoyed the temporary upper hand—irregulars and regulars alike—had been unpredictable, destructive, and often deadly. The economic system in the Trans-Mississippi had also eroded. What once was a thriving agricultural economy had turned into an almost purely subsistence society in which everyone feared for their livestock, crops, and lives.[27]

It is little surprise, then, that by the last two years of war, thousands of civilians gave up. Their houses had been torched, farms laid waste, or hogs stolen. Livelihoods and life itself had moved to an increasingly sharp edge. A visit from a Union patrol or guerrilla band was often all it took to push women and children over the edge and render them homeless and destitute. With the breakdown of any sense or level of government and amid a guerrilla war that had directly involved noncombatants as much as it had combatants, it was clear to most who remained to the end of the war that the region had fallen into "a state of perfect anarchy." While the constant and maddening game of chase between regular and irregular fighters reflected a significant part of the guerrilla war, the civilian conflict encapsulated the most brutal and all-encompassing aspect of the war in the Trans-Mississippi specifically and the South as a whole.[28]

Such anarchy manifested itself with disturbing regularity. Infamous Confederate guerrilla William Anderson, better known as "Bloody Bill," helped as much as anyone to shape Union perceptions of their elusive enemy. In the summer of 1864, Anderson wrote a threatening letter to Union brigadier general Egbert B. Brown. "I do not like the idea of warring with women and children," Anderson said, "but if you do not release all the women you have arrested . . . I will hold the Union ladies in the community as hostages." Using rhetoric that would define him, Anderson warned Brown that he would "tie them by the neck in the brush and starve them" until or unless the Confederate women were released.[29]

While Anderson's tactics were extreme by any measure, they accurately reflect the central role women played in shaping the guerrilla war in the Trans-

Mississippi. Like their male counterparts, whether Union or Confederate, women relied on the environment for survival. For them and their children, survival meant protecting their farms and livestock from Confederate or Union theft and destruction. Keeping a hog alive for the winter made the difference between staying home and becoming refugees, as did properly hiding corn or other food items from marauding guerrillas and Union troops. Women were active in ways beyond survival as well. In March 1864 in Arkadelphia, Arkansas, Confederate women took the war into their own hands. A Union detachment had recently arrived in the town, and "several fine ladies . . . had planted poisonous molasses before their homes," knowing well that the Union troops would readily take it. Those soldiers who did partake became "dangerously sick," and the Southern ladies were promptly arrested. But most women and children eventually lost everything regardless of their activity, becoming refugees in a war-torn region that had, in a way, returned to wilderness.[30]

The guerrilla war in the Trans-Mississippi led to one of the most brutal and widespread refugee problems in the South during the Civil War. Those who made it to designated refugee camps found unsanitary conditions amplified by disease and malnourishment. As the war dragged on, tensions between civilians and their military protectors increased. Yet even under such conditions, the "destitute mortals," as one Federal soldier put it, preferred the relative safety of the crowded camps to their rural homesteads.[31] While a significant part of the fighting had been focused between irregular and regular fighters, residents quickly became a key ingredient in the conflict. To be sure, any guerrilla war in any time period incorporates civilians as key actors, and the Civil War was no exception. Furthermore, much like guerrillas and their pursuers, noncombatants caught in the internecine conflict both relied upon and suffered from the natural and built environments. For civilians as much as for combatants, disease, weather, and food issues shaped their very survival. By midwar, thousands of civilian refugees—Union and Confederate—flocked to relative safe havens in the Trans-Mississippi. Many Confederate sympathizers fled to Texas or Louisiana, while others mingled with Union refugees in Federal strongholds in Indian Territory, Arkansas, Kansas, and Missouri. Any town or fort with a strong Union presence had its share of white and black refugees, and by 1864 the flood of homeless, sick, and generally destitute women, children, and elderly caused a severe logistical problem for Federal authorities.

As early as 1862, hundreds of refugees from Arkansas and Missouri fled to

Union lines. Most had lost everything in the war and sought food, shelter, and security within Federally controlled areas like Fort Scott, Kansas, and eventually Fort Smith, Arkansas. Riding north through the rugged Boston Mountains to the Ozark Plateau, a Union cavalryman noted in his diary, "a large number of refugees and Negroes came with us . . . and they presented a terrible state of poverty and wretchedness." A soldier from the Nineteenth Iowa was shocked to see a steady line of refugees "pass through almost every day on their way north; they look pitiable indeed, with their skeleton teams, ragged clothes and pallid, restless children." Civilians, white and black, had been fighting their own war of survival in the guerrilla conflict. With their homes destroyed and livelihoods lost, women and children struggled to survive in the bitter cold. That same December, as the mud froze hard enough for horses and wagons to pass over, a Kansas newspaper reported that "the number of inhabitants in [Fort Scott] has been considerably increased within the last two months by a number of refugee Union families." Overcrowding and a lack of supplies exacerbated their already impoverished condition. Hundreds of women, children, and elderly men had trudged through difficult terrain and dangerous conditions to Fort Scott only to find poor conditions and few supplies awaiting them. "They are in a very destitute condition," an editor observed, "some of them actually suffering for the necessities of life." With very little shelter, the homeless civilians built their own accommodations out of scrap wood and extra wagon covers—rarely enough to stop the cold winter winds. Conditions had worsened by the next summer. The number of destitute civilians had grown, and "nine-tenths of them are in great suffering for food and clothing." Without adequate supplies, starvation and disease would soon hit the camp. Union major T. J. Insley wrote an urgent letter to a U.S. sanitary agent urging him to send relief to Fort Scott in order to offset the suffering. The refugees, he wrote, "are numerous, and in great need of all kinds of clothing, particularly for women and children." Bedding and medicine were also in very short supply.[32]

In 1863, Union posts in the Trans-Mississippi became increasingly inundated with civilians who had lost everything. An editor for the *Fort Smith New Era* complained in November that "the town is full of refugees from the country." The problem for him was not the refugees stressing the available supplies, but the consequent lack of production from the farms they left behind. The situation was "deplorable . . . from the injury the community at large is receiving by the almost total suspension of farming operations. The cause of all this is bush-whacking." In sum, the guerrilla war in western Arkansas forced farmers into refugee status and precluded any future crop yield. The impending food shortage in tandem with increased refugee numbers meant potential starvation for the coming year. If the refugees could not get back into the fields, the editor lamented, "there will be ten times more applications for rations than now, and the suffering among the people must necessarily be great." His article concluded, "the only remedy is to clean out the bush-whackers, and give them no mercy wherever and whenever found." By the summer of 1864, Fayetteville resident Robert W. Mecklin noted hundreds of homeless women and children trudging through northwestern Arkansas en route to refugee camps in Kansas. In his view, the noncombatants he witnessed were "in a state of starvation."[33]

Warfare in the Trans-Mississippi undermined perceived notions of environmental control as much as it obliterated the "moral structure" and societal norms that had existed prior to the conflict. War destroyed antebellum limits and ideals in the region, with no true amelioration occurring until one or two years after the war. It also ruined the built environment and dramatically altered the natural one. Nineteenth-century Americans had worked tirelessly to control the wilderness around them, and the war on the border fundamentally and dramatically reshaped the human-environment relationship. Nature became both an ally and enemy to soldiers and civilians. But mostly, the conflict inaugurated a return to antebellum concepts of wilderness. By the spring of 1865, one could travel miles without seeing a standing structure or encountering a human being not labeled a Union soldier or Confederate guerrilla. Such social and environmental reconfiguration was manifested by the destruction of homes, farms, and in some cases entire towns. Ruined communities, wild animals, destitute civilians, and war-hardened combatants came to define the region. As one Union soldier observed as early as 1862, "nothing remains but one barren waste. The country is deserted and given up to the destroyer—WAR."[34]

NOTES

The author would like to thank Brian D. McKnight and Barton A. Myers for their helpful comments and suggestions. Thanks also to David Schieffler and Alan Thompson for their good-humored advice and valuable ongoing conversation about the Civil War west of the Mississippi River.

1. Col. James H. Ford to Maj. J. N. Smith, Feb. 23, 1864, U.S. War Department, *War of the Rebellion,* ser. 1, 41(2):656 (hereafter cited as *O.R.*); B. W. Lewis to Brig. Gen. Clinton B. Fisk, Aug. 11, 1864, ibid., 34(2):459, 478–79.

2. Sutherland, *Savage Conflict,* xi–xii; Isaac Gause, *Four Years with Five Armies* (New York: Neale, 1908), 48–49.

3. Stith, "'Deplorable Condition of the Country.'"

4. Samuel S. Hildebrand, *Autobiography of Samuel S. Hildebrand,* ed. Kirby Ross (Fayetteville: University of Arkansas Press, 2005), 14, 17, 20.

5. See especially Lisa M. Brady, *War upon the Land: Military Strategy and the Transformation of Southern Landscapes during the American Civil War* (Athens: University of Georgia Press, 2012).

6. Lisa M. Brady, "From Battlefield to Fertile Ground," *Civil War History* 58 (Sept. 2012): 305–21; Brady, *War upon the Land,* 23, 48; Nelson, *Ruin Nation,* 101.

7. For the burgeoning scholarship on Civil War environmental history, see especially Brian Allen Drake, ed., *The Blue, the Gray, and the Green: Toward an Environmental History of the Civil War* (Athens: University of Georgia Press, 2015); Kathryn Shively Meier, *Nature's Civil War: Common Soldiers and the Environment in 1862 Virginia* (Chapel Hill: University of North Carolina Press, 2013); Jim Downs, *Sick from Freedom: African-American Illness and Suffering during the Civil War and Reconstruction* (New York: Oxford University Press, 2012); Brady, "From Battlefield to Fertile Ground"; Megan Kate Nelson, "Looking at Landscapes of War," *Journal of the Civil War Era* 3 (Sept. 2013): 439–49; Nelson, *Ruin Nation;* Stith, "'Deplorable Condition of the Country'"; Mark Fiege, "Gettysburg and the Organic Nature of the American Civil War," in *Natural Enemy, Natural Ally: Toward an Environmental History of Warfare,* ed. Richard Tucker and Edmund Russell (Corvallis: Oregon State University Press, 2004); Ted Steinberg, "The Great Food Fight," in *Down to Earth;* and Jack Temple Kirby, "The Civil War: An Environmental View," *Nature Transformed* (Washington D.C.: National Humanities Center, 2001).

8. Maj. Gen. Thomas Hindman, General Orders No. 1, May 31, 1862, *O.R.* ser. 1, 13(1):37; *Arkansas State Gazette,* June 28, 1862; George David Schieffler, "Too Little, Too Late to Save Vicksburg: The Battle of Helena, Arkansas, July 4, 1863" (M.A. thesis, University of Arkansas, 2005), 14, 17. Schieffler's outstanding study places the Battle of Helena in the context of the irregular operations in eastern Arkansas at midwar.

9. Col. Chester Harding to Col. H. V. Colburn, June 6, 1863, Letters Sent File 567, RG 393, National Archives and Records Administration, Washington, D.C.; *O.R.,* ser. 1, 48(1):293. Also see Fellman, *Inside War,* 176–79; Charles W. Porter, *In the Devil's Dominions: A Union Soldier's Adventures in "Bushwhacker Country,"* ed. Patrick Brophy (Nevada, Mo.: Vernon County Historical Society, 1998), 72, 89; and Samuel J. Crawford, *Kansas in the Sixties* (A. C. McClurg, 1911), 64.

10. Fellman, *Inside War,* 178–79; Brig. Gen. John Schofield, General Orders No. 18, *O.R.,* ser. 1, 22(1):866; *Leavenworth (Kans.) Daily Times,* Aug. 15, 1863; Maj. Waldemar Fischer to Brig. Gen. Thomas A. Davies, May 3, 1863, *O.R.* ser. 1, 22(2):267–68.

11. Porter, *In the Devil's Dominions,* 55–56.

12. Col. M. LaRue Harrison to Brig. Gen. John McNeil, Sept. 8, 1863, *O.R.,* ser. 1, 22(2):518; Porter, *In the Devil's Dominions,* 164; *O.R.,* ser. 1, 41(2):422.

13. *Houston Tri-Weekly Telegraph,* Aug. 29, 1863. Also see Donald S. Frazier, "'Out of Stinking Distance': The Guerrilla War in Louisiana," in Sutherland, *Guerrillas, Unionists, and Violence,* 165.

14. Richard Hudson to Maj. Gen. William Rosecrans, Mar. 2, 1864, *O.R.,* ser. 1, 34(2):485; Maj. Gen. James Blunt to Maj. Gen. John M. Schofield, July 30, 1863, ibid., 22(2):411.

15. *Houston Tri-Weekly Telegraph,* Dec. 21, 1864.

16. Lt. Col. Joseph A. Eppstein to Col. Albert Sigel, July 9, 1862, *O.R.,* ser. 1, 13(1):140. For a discussion of terrain and irregular warfare, see Sutherland, "Guerrillas," 138.

17. Porter, *In the Devil's Dominions,* 56–57.

18. Henry A. Strong, *"A Rough Introduction to this Sunny Land": The Civil War Diary of Private Henry A. Strong, Co. K, Twelfth Kansas Infantry,* ed. Tom Wing (Little Rock: Butler Center for Arkansas Studies, 2006), 33; Jacob Haas, *"This Day We Marched Again": A Union Soldier's Account of War in Arkansas and the Trans-Mississippi,* ed. Mark Christ (Little Rock: Butler Center for Arkansas Studies, 2014), 54. Edwin C. Bearrs, ed., "Civil War Letters of Major William Thompson," *Annals of Iowa* 38 (1966), 437; Shea, "Semi-Savage State," 312–13 (quote).

19. Quoted in Stephen S. Minchot, "'War Is Still Raging in this Part of the Country': Oath-Taking, Conscription, and Guerrilla War in Louisiana's Lafourche Region," *Louisiana History* 38 (Spring 1997): 162. See especially Samuel C. Hyde Jr., "A Threshold of Unobtainable Commitment: Irregular Operations in Louisiana's Florida Parishes, 1862–1865," in *A Fierce and Fractious Frontier: The Curious Development of Louisiana's Florida Parishes, 1699–2000* (Baton Rouge: Louisiana State University Press, 2004), 109, 113.

20. Robert T. McMahan, *Reluctant Cannoneer: The Diary of Robert T. McMahan of the Twenty-fifth Independent Ohio Light Artillery,* ed. Michael E. Banasik (Iowa City: Camp Pope Bookshop, 2000), 138; *O.R.,* ser. 1, 22(2):197–98.

21. Kelby Ouchley, *Flora and Fauna of the Civil War: An Environmental Reference Guide* (Baton Rouge: Louisiana State University Press, 2010), 151, 152–53.

22. Porter, *In the Devil's Dominions,* 152–53.

23. Anne J. Bailey, "The Mississippi Marine Brigade: Fighting Rebel Guerrillas on Western Waters," *Military History of the Southwest* 22 (Spring 1992), 34; Chester G. Hearn, *Ellet's Brigade: The Strangest Outfit of All* (Baton Rouge: Louisiana State University Press, 2000), 231.

24. Lt. Robert Getty to Lt. Cmdr. James M. Prichett, June 14, 1863, U.S. Navy Department, *Official Records of the Union and Confederate Navies in the War of the Rebellion* (Washington, D.C.: GPO, 1884–1922), ser. 1, 25:173.

25. Maj. Gen. William T. Sherman to Adm. David D. Porter, July 19, 1863, ibid., 314.

26. *Leavenworth (Kans.) Daily Times,* Feb. 5, 1865; Strong, *"Rough Introduction,"* 74.

27. For perspective on the destruction wrought by the guerrilla war, see especially Shea, "War We Have Lost," 105–106, and Stith, "'Deplorable Condition of the Country,'" 345–47.

28. Carl H. Moneyhon, "1865: A State of Perfect Anarchy," in *Rugged and Sublime: The Civil War in Arkansas,* ed. Mark Christ (Fayetteville: University of Arkansas Press, 1994), 158. Several scholars have addressed the civilian problem in the Trans-Mississippi. See especially Fellman, *Inside War,* 23–80, 193–230; and Carl H. Moneyhon, *Impact of the Civil War and Reconstruction on Arkansas: Persistence in the Midst of Ruin* (Baton Rouge: Louisiana State University Press, 1994), 124–39.

29. William Anderson to Brig. Gen. E. B. Brown, *O.R.* ser. 1, 41(2):76. For important analyses of guerrillas—including "Bloody Bill" Anderson—and women, see Joseph M. Beilein Jr., "The Guerrilla Shirt: A Labor of Love and the Style of Rebellion in Civil War Missouri," in *Bleeding Kansas,*

Bleeding Missouri: The Long Civil War on the Border (Lawrence: University Press of Kansas, 2013); Whites, "Forty Shirts and a Wagonload of Wheat"; and Elle Harvell, "Cope, Cooperate, Combat: Civilian Responses to Union Occupation in Saline County, Missouri, during the Civil War" (M.A. thesis, University of Texas at Tyler, 2012). Harvell contends that rather than being passive victims of a particularly nasty guerrilla war, women played a direct and active role in the conflict and their own survival.

30. Haas, *"This Day We Marched Again,"* 96.

31. Bradbury, "'Buckwheat Cake Philanthropy,'" 240, 244. See also Robert R. Mackey, "Bushwhackers, Provosts, and Tories: The Guerrilla War in Arkansas," in Sutherland, *Guerrillas, Unionists, and Violence,* 182–83.

32. Porter, *In the Devil's Dominions,* 46; J. Irvine Dungan, *History of the Nineteenth Regiment Iowa Volunteer Infantry* (Davenport, Iowa: Luse & Griggs, 1865), 72; *Leavenworth (Kans.) Daily Times,* Dec. 18, 1862, Aug. 14, 1863.

33. *Fort Smith New Era,* Nov. 14, 1863; and W. J. Lemke, ed., "The Mecklin Letters," *Washington County Historical Society Bulletin* 10 (1955): 7.

34. "Creek" [Col. A. C. Ellithorpe], "From the Army on the Western Frontier," *Chicago Evening Journal,* Dec. 1, 1862.

IRREGULAR NAVAL WARFARE ALONG THE LOWER MISSISSIPPI

LAURA JUNE DAVIS

Within weeks of the first volley at Fort Sumter, South Carolina, New Orleans bore witness to an altogether different salvo. On the evening of May 6, 1861, the docks at Algiers, Louisiana, burst into flames when a fire broke out on the steamboat *General Pike.* The fire soon crumbled its moorings—and those of two neighboring boats—resulting in a blazing procession of vessels floating downstream. In less than one hour the whipping wind spread the flames "with terrific rapidity" to six more vessels. In the ensuing comedy of errors, the alarm bells did not sound; the arriving firemen "ran about at random," not knowing how to proceed. With a cloudy sky above and the dark Mississippi River rushing below, the light from the flames "reflected luridly down upon the city," washing it in an eerie glow. Ultimately, nine commercial steamboats—*General Pike, Editor, Grenada, Telegram, Baltic, Republic, Madison, Dollie Webb,* and *Conqueror*—mysteriously caught fire. In a matter of moments, over 4,500 tons of timber splintered into kindling, thousands of pounds of cotton were immolated, and a combined investment of $28,500 disintegrated into ash.[1]

Yet the event drew little local interest or concern. Despite the magnitude of such a multivessel conflagration, the inferno was unremarkable. After all, steamboat fires—usually attributed to boiler explosions—were fairly common in the nineteenth century. On average, 21 percent of all antebellum riverboats burned or exploded. Between 1847 and 1857 alone, 232 steamers caught fire and another 56 exploded. Between 1816 and 1848, 1,433 people lost their lives to steamboat explosions along the western waters. As citizens of a prominent port town, New Orleanians would have been cognizant of the innate danger and combustibility of steamboats. As such, local officials quickly dismissed the incident as an accident, signifying that the notion of intentional boat burning had not yet entered into the public consciousness.[2]

Interestingly, at least one party thought the 1861 New Orleans fire *was* intentional. *The Cincinnati Daily Press* reported that the inferno was the work of a "negro incendiary." Whether the newspaper meant that the culprit was an African American, an abolitionist Republican, or simply a degenerate was unclear. What was apparent was the paper's declaration that the steamboat burnings were an act of deliberate sabotage. The veracity of such an allegation remains unknown, but it stood as a portent of things to come.[3]

With the fall of Vicksburg in July 1863, the Union seemingly gained unfettered access to the mighty Mississippi—an essential transportation, trade, and communication route. Soon thereafter, President Abraham Lincoln penned his bold declaration, "the Father of Waters again goes unvexed to the sea." Gripped by the dual victories at Gettysburg and Vicksburg, Lincoln misinterpreted the situation: conventional siege operations and naval battles along the river may have been drawing to a close, but brown-water irregular warfare was just beginning. The rebels had failed to defend or maintain control of the Mississippi River, but that very failure also revealed the extent to which they might employ naval guerrilla warfare to thwart Federal jurisdiction; after Vicksburg, the Confederate naval war took on a more sinister posture. For the final two years of the conflict, rebels quite literally blazed a path of resistance up and down the lower Mississippi River: the 1,190-mile stretch from St. Louis to New Orleans was the boat burners' primary target.[4]

One of the earliest, and perhaps the most costly, boat-burning disasters was the destruction of the *Ruth* on August 4, 1863. According to reports, this "terrible calamity" arose when the steamer caught fire midstream between Cairo, Illinois, and Vicksburg. Haplessly, the *Ruth*'s cargo contained the perfect ingredients for a conflagration: bituminous coal, dry wood, and "an immense quantity of bacon"—all resting directly below four U.S. Treasury boxes with $2,600,000 in Federal funds destined for Major General Ulysses S. Grant's army. The *Ruth*'s incineration resulted in thousands of dollars in damages plus the loss of all the government greenbacks. More tragic was the resulting deaths of twenty-six people, including a Union paymaster, three clerks, one African American woman, and three freedmen. Most of the casualties were drowning victims who fell into the water when the fire collapsed the ship's plank; only the *Ruth*'s crew managed to survive the inferno. While early reports claimed, "there is no satisfactory theory as to how the fire originated," locals believed it to be the work of naval guerrillas working on behalf of the Confederacy. Ultimately, the Federal government agreed as an official investigation into the conflagration ruled: "the steamer Ruth was fired by an incendiary—not for the particular purpose, although that may have been an additional object, of destroying the public funds on board, but in conformity with, what appears to be a plan of the Rebels, for the destruction of the water transportation in the valley of the Mississippi, and thus crippling the movements of our Armies." At one time or another, the provost marshal attributed the conflagration to four different suspects—William Murphy, John McKennon, Robert Louden, and Isaac Aleshire—all members of an organized band of boat burners operating out of St. Louis.[5]

The August 19, 1863, explosion of the steamer *City of Madison* also foretold the imminent dangers on the Mississippi River. While docked at Vicksburg, the *City of Madison* was loaded with ammunition destined for Union troops. Halfway through the packing process, a "negro carrying a percussion shell on board let it fall." Almost instantaneously, the steamer caught fire. The flames quickly spread to the stockpile of ammunition, causing an explosion. William G. Christie saw "a great cloud of smoke flame and steam, and [heard] a loud prolonged roar as if a great gun had Burst." The $40,000 boat "shivered into thousands of atoms, and pieces of the machinery, wood work, and human beings, were thrown high into the air." By the time help arrived, the boat was destroyed; its upper deck and stern were beside the wheelhouse, and mangled bodies lay over a hundred yards away. Of the 160 travelers aboard at the time, only four managed to survive, making the *City of Madison*'s explosion one of the most lethal incidents on western waters. Christie stated that he could not "write about it with any other feelings than those of horror." Perhaps his dismay was heightened by the one hundred African Americans secured in the steamer's hold who accounted for most of the fatalities. While contemporaries declared the explosion an accident due to negligence, the *City of Madison* would later be included in Provost Marshal J. H. Baker's list of losses attributed to the St. Louis boat burners—likely because Aleshire purportedly confided that he was the culprit behind the conflagration. The *City of Madison* therefore represents a key turning point in the Federals' understanding of asymmetric naval warfare: what had been accepted universally as an accident in 1863 would become embroiled in a greater conspiracy of sabotage by 1865. Right or wrong, evidence or not, the Union was beginning to associate all steamboat fires along the river with sabotage.[6]

The destruction of the *Ruth* and the *City of Madison* also marked a dramatic shift in the Confederate war effort along the Mississippi River. Initially, the river was defended by the fourteen vessels of the River Defense Fleet, but after the loss of New Orleans and the destruction of all but one warship at the Battle of Memphis, the fleet disbanded on June 21, 1862. The Confederate States Navy fared little better. But while the navy and the short-lived River Defense Fleet had failed to hold the Mississippi in the face of a stronger and more powerful Union fleet, the rebels did not consider the river lost. They refused to go quietly or to relinquish control of the waterway. Accepting their limited numbers and capabilities, the Southerners turned toward unconventional warfare. Employing individuals and small groups, Confederate boat burners targeted civilian steamers—especially those aiding the Union cause by transporting troops or government goods—as they traveled up and down the Mississippi between St. Louis and New Orleans.[7]

Boat burners operated along the watery margins between shoreline and waterway. They took their cause to the water, making steamships and river ports their battlefields of choice. Referred to as "incendiaries" or "naval guerrillas" by contemporaries, boat burners differed markedly from bushwhackers or partisan rangers. While irregular fighters such as William Quantrill and "Bloody Bill" Anderson flaunted their exploits, bushwhackers wore flamboyant shirts, and partisan rangers operated under the authority of the Confederate government, naval guerrillas intentionally operated in the shadows; they skulked along the docks, secreted themselves aboard vessels, or insinuated themselves into a steamboat crew. Shock and awe may have been their aims, but secrecy and terror were their watchwords of choice.[8]

The Civil War boat burners complicate our existing taxonomy of guerrilla warfare. A self-constituted group of saboteurs, they focused their attentions exclusively on the waterways and actually boarded their targets rather than shooting at them from the shoreline. These naval guerrillas engaged in a "hidden war," operating within the sinister intersections of irregular warfare, sabotage, and espionage. Planting incendiary devices and setting fire to civilian riverboats and government transports, they embraced hard-war measures and consciously sought to destroy human lives and Federal property. Terrorists *avant la lettre,* they were a unique brand of incendiary who limited their arson to commercial vessels and steamboats. And while the boat burners may not have been guerrillas in the customary context, they did embody a unique form of irregular fighter: one focused on riverine warfare, a classification echoed by contemporaries who dubbed them "naval guerrillas." Thus, "boat burners," "incendiaries," and "naval guerrillas" are interchangeable terms that can (and will here) be ascribed to these nineteenth-century "terrorists."[9]

The actual scope of the boat burners' accomplishments is difficult to quantify, especially because of the inherently secretive and subversive nature of their actions. Newspapers of the time estimated that two hundred vessels fell victim to naval guerrillas. This was an overestimation induced by fear; the actual number was likely much smaller. By cross-referencing all of the Mississippi steamers listed as burned or exploded in *"The Lytle-Holdcamper List"* of merchant steam vessels, *Way's Packet Directory,* and W. Craig Gaines's *Encyclopedia of Civil War Shipwrecks* with contemporary accounts, diaries, newspapers, provost marshal records, and the *Official Records,* I have identified at least forty steamboats—totaling over 13,300 tons—traveling along the lower Mississippi that likely fell victim to boat burners over the course of the war.[10]

Trying to paint the collective portrait of naval guerrillas is also a daunting task. Just as there are no official muster rolls for guerrillas, an official roster of Southern boat burners does not exist. Provost Marshal J. H. Baker did, in fact, provide Union officials with a list of nineteen men operating out of St. Louis, and the judge advocate general identified thirty-five people, including Jefferson Davis, as part of a boat-burning conspiracy, but such registers emphasized organized gangs of naval guerrillas; they completely ignored or dismissed individual agents or small groups of saboteurs operating along the river. Ultimately, historians must paint a collective portrait from old newspaper reports, provost marshal investigations, and official records—sources that so vilified the incendiaries, it can be difficult to take their human measure. For example, newspapers cast the culprit of a July 15, 1864, inferno as "some Devil, in the shape o' a human Being." Despite the imagery of fire and brimstone that blazing steamboats certainly evoked, this incendiary was a man, not a demon.[11]

If we take a broader look at naval guerrillas, several recurring themes and attributes do emerge. Many had previous work experience aboard steamboats. For example, Robert Louden (Lowden) was a steamboat painter and pilot; Isaac Aleshire (Eleshire) had been a mate, deckhand, and watchman prior to the war; and Edward Frazer (Frasier or Frazier) served as both a second engineer and an assistant striker on various steamers. Boat burners like Aleshire, Frazer, and Louden with previous steamboat experience could have easily disguised themselves as members of a crew. In fact, Frazer later testified that the agent who set fire to the *Robert Campbell, Jr.* (in September 1863) was, in fact, aboard ship during its incineration, though he refused to identify the saboteur by name. Such intelligence justified U.S. Army chief quartermaster Robert Allen's allegations that "the incendiary, when it serves his purpose, becomes one of the crew, and thus secures himself from detection. I apprehend that there are disloyal men in disguise in the employ of every steamer." While the likelihood of such universal deception is dubious, the terror created by even a handful of confirmed naval-guerrilla attacks was immeasurable. Other boat burners were local men of influence who could utilize their power and authority to advantage. As Franklin Archibald Dick explained, "there is a large number of active, intelligent, wealthy, disloyal men in St. Louis who keep up a constant intercourse with the rebels in arms"—among them, J. W. Frick, a newspaper editor, and Joseph W. Tucker, a former Missouri politician and newspaperman. Such local celebrities could have easily found friends and supporters to aid them in their cause or in the evasion of Federal authorities. Thus, Union officials and river-town populations endured a pervasive threat because they never knew when or where the boat burners would strike, let alone who the saboteurs might really be. The corresponding fear was palpable as the perpetrators hid in plain sight.[12]

By being members of the local community, if not prominent citizens of a river town, several naval guerrillas established networks of support. For example, provost marshal reports indicated that Cornwell Keefer and George Foster, both of St. Louis, were known accomplices of boat burners; they often harbored incendiaries in their homes. Confederate sympathizers, especially those living along the riverbanks or near the wharves like Mary J. Callahan of St. Louis, could have easily hidden naval guerrillas while giving them easy access to their intended targets: commercial steamships. Ties between the boat burners and other rebel agents were common. Mollie Lewis, the wife of suspected boat burner Tip Fox, often boarded the wife of Frazer, the suspected boat-burner leader, at her house on Fifth Street. Frazer himself admitted to spending time with both Lewis and Fox. Allegedly, John R. Barrett was a member of the Order of American Knights, a secret society purportedly trying to overthrow the U.S. government and establish a Northwest Confederacy. With thousands of members in Missouri, Barrett would have an extended network of allies to help him in his boat-burning cause. Robert Louden was a mail runner along with his wife, Mary, and his good friend, Absalom Grimes. For Louden, boat burning was a family affair, his brother-in-law Arthur McCoy also being an incendiary. This strong correlation between the St. Louis mail runners and boat burners likely provided the naval guerrillas with vital intelligence. The fact that several boat burners had ties to area saloons and whorehouses was no accident either; places like Frazer's bar and Kate Clarke's brothel loosened tongues with their spirits and wares. The intelligence thus gathered must have proven invaluable to the incendiaries. While evidence suggests that wives, female friends, and prostitutes aided and abetted naval guerrillas, no female boat burners have come to light, though the possibility certainly exists, especially since the fires that destroyed at least three vessels—the *Hope* (September 11, 1863), *Chancellor* (October 1, 1863), and *Black Hawk* (May 28, 1864)—started in ladies' cabins.[13]

Taken together, these images and portrayals provide a composite portrait of the naval guerrilla. He was a Confederate sympathizer from a river city: St. Louis, New Orleans, Memphis, or Mobile. He was a working or well-connected man who did not directly benefit from slavery or the slave economy, although plantation owners and slave traders may have frequented his saloon, traveled aboard his steamship, or stayed in his lodgings. Certainly, steamboat workers carried slave-produced cotton if not slaves themselves aboard their ships. He was most likely white, although at least one alleged boat burner was dark skinned. Most importantly, he had strong ties to his community, by virtue of either his position or his gregarious nature, which offered him a support network to aid in his nefarious activities and to hide him away from Union authorities whenever necessary.

While many naval guerrillas may have acted alone, some appear to have worked in small groups. In October 1863 the Sixth Iowa Cavalry captured three boat burners in Memphis. That December, a Secret Service agent arrested a pair of boat burners at the mouth of the White River in Arkansas. In July of the following year, two men faced trial for the contingent burnings of the *Cherokee, E. F. Dix, Glasgow, Northerner, Sunshine,* and *Welcome.* Such duos and trios were not unusual. One naval guerrilla likely stood watch while his partner(s) boarded the vessel to either set a fire or stow away an incendiary device; their small numbers helped them evade detection or public notice.[14]

Further evidence suggests that a gang of boat burners did, in fact, exist. William Murphy, a member of the organized incendiaries, gave a full confession to Provost Marshal J. H. Baker. According to Murphy, Frazer led a band of nineteen secret agents whose mission was to destroy Federal property and steamboats. By war's end, Frazer himself gave a full confession—likely in hopes of reprieving his imprisonment. According to him, Miner Majors was the true mastermind of the boat-burning conspiracy. Ultimately, Provost Martial Baker determined that Judge Tucker was the ringleader, operating directly under Confederate secretary of war James Seddon; Majors was his second in command, and Barrett supervised the land operations.[15]

Whether the incendiaries acted alone, in small groups, or as part of an organized gang, they all seemed to have the (sometime) sanction of the Confederate government. Two boat burners captured in December 1863 by S. B. Morehouse of the Secret Service's Department of Vicksburg carried papers resembling letters of marque; these documents authorized them to "seize and destroy all Government transports and other property on the Mississippi and its tributaries." Murphy confessed that the St. Louis boat burners "were employed by the rebel authorities" and that the Confederate government endorsed their actions. As part of a February 1864 act, the Confederate Congress authorized the organization of "bodies for the capture and destruction of the enemy's property by land or sea, and to authorize compensation for the same." As part of this bill, Congress authorized Secretary of War Seddon to "organize secret expeditions against the enemy for the purpose of destroying their property on the high seas, on the rivers, lakes and harbors in the United States." In exchange for their efforts, the secretary of war was authorized to pay the perpetrators up to 50 percent of the damaged property's value. The actions of the St. Louis boat burners fell under this act, explaining why several traveled to Richmond in the summer of 1864 to be paid; Frazer, Murphy, and others received $35,000 for their efforts to date. While there, the six boat burners met with both Seddon and President Davis to discuss the logistics of their activities. Such verbal endorsements seemingly legitimized the naval guerrillas' explosive actions.[16]

By September 1863, the boat-burning plot was in effect. Minor Majors had arrived in St. Louis to recruit agents for his incendiary scheme. Authorized by the Confederate government for the express purpose of engaging naval guerrillas, Majors repeatedly met with Frazer to discuss "the subject of burning boats on the Mississippi River." No doubt, Judge Tucker was also recruiting saboteurs from various river towns. Eventually, Murphy, Louden, McCoy, Aleshire, and thirteen others would join the plot. And while the majority of incidents described below have been attributed to this organized gang of naval guerrillas out of St. Louis, an unknown number of mysterious perpetrators also engaged in irregular warfare along the inland waters.[17]

Also by September, the boat burners were adding torpedoes and other devices to their arsenal. Union officers learned that "amongst other devilish inventions [of the Confederacy] is a torpedo resembling a lump of coal, to be placed in coal piles and amongst the coal put on board vessels." For example, the "new and elegant" steamer *Hope* fell victim to rebel incendiaries. Docked at the Market Street landing in St. Louis, the vessel was preparing passengers and cargo for a trip downriver to Memphis. On Friday, September 11, just before midnight, a fire was "discovered issuing from the transom of one of the staterooms near the Ladies' cabin." Around the same time, a "rascal" was spotted leaving the steamer; he disappeared into the night, never to be seen again. Meanwhile, steamboat bells rang in frantic alarm. The dock became frenzied as numerous watchmen raced to the scene. Guards from neighboring vessels worked together to create an impromptu bucket brigade. The rescue team managed to subdue the flames before they spread to any other part of the ship; the fire damaged only one stateroom and a neighboring cabin's ceiling. Purportedly, the incendiary utilized a homemade explosive device to cause the fire; he threw a bottle of ignited turpentine through the transom into the stateroom. Luckily, the damages were minimal—less than a hundred dollars—so the *Hope* soon continued on her way. Tragically, it was never destined to reach Memphis. A few days later the steamer snagged above Cairo, and a fire was discovered in her hold. After the narrow escape from the enemy's clutches the weekend before, the crew did not want the *Hope* to fall into rebel hands now. They sunk the ship to extinguish the fire and kept a guard nearby to protect it from capture.[18]

Within twenty-four hours of the *Hope*'s initial blaze, another massive steamboat fire broke out in St. Louis. Around six o'clock on the evening of September 13, a dense cloud of smoke descended upon the port. Alarm bells clamored; the telegraph alarm sounded. An impenetrable wall of smoke ascended from the steamer *Imperial,* where a fire had broken out in its nursery. Dozens flocked to the riverbank to witness "an extensive conflagration." Within minutes, the *Imperial* was reduced to "a mass of flame and burning coal from stem to stern." The fire fed on the nursery's shuck mattresses, sheets, and comforters, growing in size and communicating to the nearby *Hiawatha.* That vessel's wheelhouse soon ignited, and within twelve minutes the steamer was "hopelessly aflame." The *Hiawatha*'s twenty-odd passengers endeavored to save what possessions they could before being driven from the ship in the wake of a "demon of fire in the shape of a mass of flame and illuminated smoke." The *Post Boy*'s wheelhouse and sides also caught fire, threatening the nearby *Jesse K. Bell.* The crew tried to save their ship, cutting it loose from its moorings and sending it swirling into the water. Yet the *Jesse K. Bell* did not escape the inferno's wrath, and those who had tried to save the steamer ended up jumping overboard into the river or nearby skiffs.[19]

Despite such efforts, the fire soon spread across the docks, making "such headway that it was impossible to stop" it. Confusion abounded. The inferno traveled with such rapidity "that only those who witnessed the fire can realize the sudden and complete devastation of the hungry flames." The combustible nature of the steamships only exacerbated matters. Attempts by the ferryboat *John Trendley* to spray water from its fire engine did little to abate the flames. The erratic explosions of combustibles "intermingled with the roaring and crackling of the flames," heightening the drama of the scene. Smoke ascended, darkening the sky. The smell of scorched wood filled the air, the roar of the fire overwhelming the once-serene landscape. The ever-growing crowd of onlookers soon found themselves in danger. A panicked cry of "powder aboard" rang out as someone suspected that the gunboat *Ozark* would soon catch fire. With an explosion imminent, the curious throngs ran for their lives, not stopping until they were several blocks away. Fortunately, the *Ozark* remained out of harm's way as did the *J. C. Swon,* which was cut loose from the docks and floated down to the safety of Plum Street landing. Ultimately, the contiguous burning resulted in the demise of four steamers: *Imperial, Hiawatha, Post Boy,* and *Jesse K. Bell.*[20]

One newspaper claimed that "the sluggish river seemed a party in the plot to engender misfortune to the doomed" crafts, moving so slowly that the endangered vessels could not escape their fiery demise. For hours, locals could see "cinders and smoke . . . dancing and whirling fantastically in the air." The real culprit, however, was a rebel boat burner—or as the *Daily Missouri Republican* declared, a "devilish spirit which actuated some scoundrel to set fire" to the boats. As the *Imperial* and *Hiawatha* had been lying idle for weeks, there was no logical explanation—save sabotage—for why a fire would break out. While no lives were lost, damages totaled $200,000. Meanwhile, the floating wrecks of the four steamers became tourist attractions. What had once been floating palaces now were "shapeless and burning masses of floating rubbish." According to Charles F. Vogel, large crowds flocked to the river's edge to view the smoldering remains. It was becoming evident to the citizens of St. Louis that a great conspiracy to destroy all steamers along the lower Mississippi River was wreaking havoc on their lives, livelihoods, shipping, and commerce. In addition to the physical threat that this conflagration posed, it also represented a symbolic challenge to the Federal government. The *Imperial* had been the first steamer to traverse the Mississippi once it officially "opened" after Vicksburg's fall. Likewise, the *Jesse K. Bell* had transported the first contrabands to St. Louis in March 1863. Whether or not the naval guerrillas intentionally targeted these vessels because of their roles in heralding Union control of the river and ending slavery, their destruction suggests the possibility that some of the boat burners' targets were specifically chosen and not just the victims of chance or happenstance.[21]

In just over two months since the fall of Vicksburg, seven commercial steamers had fallen victim to pro-Confederate boat burners. In less than a week, St. Louis steamboats alone suffered $300,000 worth of damages. And while steamer explosions had been common in the antebellum and early war periods, those living in the Mississippi River valley could not simply dismiss such wholesale destruction as accidents. Something nefarious seemed to be afoot. Rumors of a conspiracy began to emerge. As no one knew if a single individual or a group perpetrated the crimes, locals became apprehensive. Officials urged steamboatmen to be vigilant. The *Daily Missouri Republican* circulated a rumor of an "existing conspiracy to burn all the transports which have been or may be employed by the Government." Already, those living along the river were drawing connections between the attack on the *Hope* and the St. Louis fire. They were not alone; the news of the "Great Fire in St. Louis" reached Ohio, Nashville, New York City, the Carolinas, and West Virginia.[22]

While the unanticipated loss of commercial steamboat property elevated fears for those living in St. Louis, New Orleans, and Memphis, Unionists across the continent bemoaned the new vexations rising up along the lower Mississippi. So much was at stake—militarily, economically, strategically, and psychologically—that any threat to the safe passage of troops, supplies, or civilians along the river had be dealt with immediately. In the wake of such threats, Major General William Tecumseh Sherman bluntly exclaimed: "It is not war. Any boat captain who caught incendiaries should drop them overboard and let them find the bottom in their own way." Sherman, who shared the populace's frustrations over irregular warfare, remained steadfast in his assertion that the Mississippi was essential to the success of the Union war effort. Earlier he had written to General Grant stating that he intended to "fight till the death for the Mississippi River. This is my hobby, . . . [and] I am daily more and more convinced that we should hold the river absolutely." With the Union's control of the Mississippi tenuous at best, Sherman and many others would propose radical action to keep the river under Federal jurisdiction.[23]

As September 1863 rolled on, so did the firestorms. On September 22, the *Champion* caught fire. A commercial steamboat chartered by the U.S. government, the *Champion* carried 600 bales of hay and 130 head of cattle, explaining why rebel incendiaries likely targeted the ship: they wanted to destroy war materiel destined for Federal troops. According to its captain, John Molloy, while the *Champion* backed out of a Memphis wharf, a watchman reported a fire in the kitchen. Molloy ordered the soldiers aboard to get ashore and then headed to the engine room. At that point everything turned to excitement as the *Champion*'s crew tried to tame the flames, which had broken through the main deck. The intense heat and dense smoke made this difficult; the large stockpile of hay fed the blaze. The steamer was soon "perfectly wrapped in a sheet of flame." Molloy realized that the boat could not be salvaged and gave orders for the crew to abandon ship and save themselves. By some miracle, one of the clerks managed to get into the office, unlock the safe, and secure the steamer's books and papers by throwing them into a pillowcase. The burning boat began to drift downstream, "with her living freight"—the cattle—crying out in "almost human groans of agony." All told, the destroyed cargo and steamer were valued at $120,000. Two guards, a doctor, and an unnamed African American presumably died in the fire. As the steamer was in service to the Union government and had all its after hatches locked, Captain Molloy was "fully convinced that the fire was the work of an incendiary."[24]

Three more incidents that September signaled the devastating threat that boat burners posed to traffic on the lower Mississippi River. On September 26, the *Choteau* caught fire below Columbus, Kentucky. Little was known about the incident, but as it was "on a Government trip," many supposed the inferno "to be the work of an incendiary." The crew managed to scuttle the vessel, saving all of the government freight. Two days later a naval guerrilla snuck aboard the *Platte Valley,* setting it on fire. At around one o'clock in the morning, the guard "discovered a fire kindled in the watchman's locker," where he had been just moments before. With little effort the man extinguished the flames, preventing their spread. In the interim "the villain had effectually made his escape." Almost simultaneously, another mishap occurred near Milliken's Bend, Louisiana, as a Caucasian incendiary with a painted black face reportedly destroyed the *Robert Campbell, Jr.* by setting fire to its hold. Around six o'clock in the morning, cries of fire sounded aboard ship. Flames progressed rapidly. The passengers had mere moments to rise from their beds and flee overboard before the fire reached their quarters. Dozens of travelers escaped the inferno only to drown in the river's strong currents. The officers on board tried to rescue the passengers in distress; one second mate even swam back from shore to save a Mrs. Cooley. Of the forty-odd victims, four were Federal soldiers, two were Mrs. Cooley's children, and one was an invalid woman. The *Robert Campbell, Jr.* itself was valued at $60,000 and insured for $25,000. Because the steamer was in service to the Federal government at the time of its incineration, John H. Shaw, its owner, sued the U.S. government for $70,000. Shaw claimed that Assistant Quartermaster Charles Parsons impressed his steamer into military service for "especial duty between Memphis and Vicksburg, loaded [it] with army stores and troops," and traveled downstream. While Shaw received some money courtesy of insurance payments, the court ruled in favor of the United States as *Robert Campbell, Jr.*'s service was voluntary and contractual, not impressed.[25]

What Shaw, the newspapers, and the locals did not know at the time was that the *Robert Campbell, Jr.*—and its Federal freight—had been a specific target of the St. Louis boat burners. Miner Majors had explicitly urged Frazer to destroy the ship while it was docked at the levee. When Frazer refused, claiming it would "create too much excitement," Majors then ordered him to plant an incendiary device on board. This would ensure that the *Robert Campbell, Jr.* would explode between St. Louis and Cairo, preventing the identification of the perpetrator. Accordingly, Frazer went down to the docks before the steamer's scheduled departure, but two detectives inspecting the boiler deck scared him away. Tragically for the *Robert Campbell, Jr.*, the boat-burner network was quite extensive. Frazer was not the only incendiary tasked with destroying the vessel. As it turned out, Judge Tucker had also solicited an agent, Isaac Aleshire, who succeeded where Frazer had not, receiving $5,000 for his fire starting.[26]

Not surprisingly, those living along the lower Mississippi River quickly linked all of these conflagrations together. With a dozen or so vessels burned in a matter of weeks, it was logical to make such a connection—one river paper stated, the "coincidence in time of the burning of boats hundreds of miles apart, shows there is a band of men employed in this hellish business" and operating all along the lower Mississippi. Conspicuously, St. Louis seemed to bear the brunt of the damage. The *Daily Missouri Republican* fretted on behalf of the town's commercial and social interests, urging the immediate termination of such fiery exploits. Otherwise, "there is no predicting how far it may involve the very safety of our city and its millions of property." What still eluded understanding was the full scope of the plot or the number of saboteurs involved.[27]

As the number of steamers falling victim to pro-Confederate boat burners rose, so did the ire of St. Louis residents. It was becoming evident that any steamer moored at the river city—especially if impressed or commissioned by the Federal government—was at grave risk. While torpedoes, incendiary devices, and Greek fire were used on occasion, the naval guerrillas preferred to set fire to steamers when they were docked near other vessels, offering the opportunity to destroy multiple Union ships with a single fire. The *Gallipolis Journal* in Ohio put into print what everyone was thinking: "there is a conspiracy to destroy all the boats on the Western rivers, in this way, so as to embarrass the Government in moving troops and supplies; and this having been accomplished the rebels think they might again get possession of the Mississippi." The boat burners' industrious scheme to terminate shipping and transportation along the river was multifaceted; it had economic, strategic, military, and political components. The incineration of twelve valuable Union vessels was proof positive that a design to "suppress the commerce of the lower Mississippi by the villainous work of the incendiary" was quite effective. As the list of victims increased with frightful speed, some Unionists feared that replacements could not be built fast enough; one report lamented that "one steamer is not built for every five that are destroyed." Without an immediate end to such destruction, some feared the "irreparable depletion of our river marine," which was already falling substantially behind the economic, military, and transportation needs of the Union.[28]

Psychological warfare also figured into the tactical assaults of naval guerrillas along the river as they sought to scare Unionists into submission. And they were quite successful at invoking fear; the *Memphis Daily Appeal* revealed that "steamboat disasters succeed each other in such rapid succession that the excitement naturally occasioned by one is scarcely allayed before it is again aroused to as high a pitch by another." Local governments up and down the river called for vigilance and military protection. Even communities in the interior—Ohio, West Virginia, and Washington, D.C.—understood that "the emissaries of Jeff. Davis are at work in our midst, and it behooves loyal citizens to be on the alert." Fear and terror proved the boat burners' greatest tools, and they were cognizant of this fact. A February 1865 letter to President Davis sheds light on the naval guerrillas' terroristic motivations. W. S. Oldham advised that the rebels should "burn every transport and gunboat on the Mississippi river, as well as devastate the country of the enemy, and fill his people with terror and consternation."[29]

The primary reason for constant vigilance along the river was "the new style of rebel warfare" that the boat burners invoked. As the *Daily Intelligencer* explained, reports "that the rebels have organized a gang of incendiaries to burn the steamers on the Mississippi river, would have excited little attention and less belief, did not the facts indicate the truth of it. It is evident that the rebels intend to do by treachery what they are unable to do by a fair contest, keep the Mississippi clear of federal steamers." Noticeably, the boat burners were not operating by any conventional rules of naval warfare—and that was what was so frightening and frustrating. The *Daily Missouri Republican* complained, "if this be 'civilized warfare,' of which the Southern chivalry so much love to prate, we wonder what are their ideas of barbarity!" Especially troubling was the grim reality that boats were ignited midstream while carrying women and children asleep "in fancied security," subjecting innocent civilians to the dangers of fire and drowning. That the Confederacy seemed to condone such tactics as legitimate warfare was more disconcerting. Unionists exclaimed that "to apply the torch to river craft lying peaceably at wharves that have never been inside the adversary's lines, or plying their legitimate trade upon a stream wholly in Federal possession, is a kind of diabolism without precedent in any way." Neither the Union military nor its people living in river towns understood this new game of arson, destruction, and murder. All they understood was that naval guerrillas wished to destroy "the spirit of liberty," overthrow the Federal government, "and erect upon its ruins a miserable anarchy." As the *Daily Missouri Republican* bemoaned, "steamboats seem to hold their existence by a very slight tenure of late, and where the wholesale destruction will stop, it is impossible" to know.[30]

Yet the flames raged on. On October 1, 1863, a steamboat docked at the Carondolet in St. Louis fell victim to rebel incendiaries. Three deckhands aboard the *Chancellor* smelled smoke while eating their supper below deck before noticing a hole burning into the dining cabin. According to an officer, "some scoundrel slipped on board unperceived and setting fire to a spread, placed it in a state room in the ladies' cabin then locked the doors and dodged ashore undetected." The crew managed to extinguish the flames before any material injury or loss of life ensued. As the *Chancellor* was docked near the *St. Louis, Sioux City,* and two new steamboat hulls, Federal authorities believed that the incendiary intended to inflict substantial damage. The *Daily Missouri Republican* reported that such "conduct is of a piece with the monstrous and murderous villainy which has lately consigned so many boats to destruction."[31]

But the *Chancellor*'s good fortune was short lived. Three days later the commercial steamer again fell victim to naval guerrillas. At half past one o'clock in the afternoon, young Charles Woodworth discovered a fire in the *Chancellor*'s carpenter shop. Watchmen stationed nearby sounded the alarm. Ferryboats and firemen rushed to the scene. The conflagration quickly advanced beyond containment, reducing the *Chancellor* to ember and ash. Also victim to the flames were the *Catahoula,* which lay just below the *Chancellor* in a seemingly protective cove, and the *Forest Queen.* Dozens of passengers aboard the latter vessel jumped into the river to escape the inferno. Nearby skiffs and ferryboats came to the assistance of all but two—a pair of freedmen who drowned in the chaos. The *Daily Missouri Republican* reported that "the fire was doubtless the work of an incendiary, but no clue can be obtained relative to the guilty parties." More inflammatory was the subsequent remark: "it is somewhat singular that, not withstanding the double watch lately placed on all steamboats, none of the boat burners have been caught." Stranger still was the failure to link this inferno with the previous fire aboard the *Chancellor.* It seems little coincidence that naval guerrillas struck the same steamship twice in four days; evidently, the rebel agents considered the *Chancellor* a significant target. Even more apparent was their preference to inflict the greatest damage possible by selecting commercial steamers docked close to one another.[32]

For many in St. Louis and other river towns, the *Chancellor*'s demise was the last straw. Such wholesale destruction in such a short amount of time frightened and infuriated them. Chief Quartermaster Allen reported, "there is evidently a band of incendiaries organized for the destruction of our own transports." In October 1863 he further declared: "[T]he continued destruction of steamboats, by fire, on these waters is assuming a very alarming feature. Unquestionably, there is an organized band of incendiaries, members, of which are stationed at every landing . . . Already some fourteen first-class boats have been burned, and this is equivalent to 10 per cent of the whole river transportation." But the mayhem only continued. As Allen explained, the "increase of watchmen and extra vigilance do not seem to arrest this insidious enemy." Despite two years of warfare and professed Union control of the Mississippi, Federal officials realized that river towns like St. Louis and New Orleans were home to thousands of Confederate sympathizers and boat burners.[33]

In the fall of 1863, the Union military finally took concerted action to stop the plague of boat burning. The *Memphis Daily Appeal* reported in late September that "Vicksburg, Natchez, Port Hudson, Lake Providence and Greenville are to be permanently occupied, to be fortified so as to enable them to be held by comparatively few men, and to be used as points of rendezvous for the troopers who will . . . keep the banks of the river clear of boat burners." Ultimately, the Union pursued a two-pronged defense of the river: gunboats patrolled the Mississippi while local police were pressed into protection duty for commercial steamboats. In October 1863, Federal authorities began placing undercover agents in port towns and on steamers. Rear Admiral David Dixon Porter ordered several precautions "to prevent fire to public vessels by incendiaries." These included stationing sentries at major ports, refusing nighttime access to public property, and stopping of all small boats traversing the river after dark. Porter reiterated, "it behooves every officer and man to be watchful at this time and see that no attempt to burn the property under their charge shall succeed." Lastly, trade was restricted to "any one of approved loyalty, and for the present, will be carried on by means of large store-boats, protected by gunboats." Many predicted that such arrangements would be permanent, likely enduring until war's end. By December 1863, Sherman was frustrated by the unchecked "boldness of our enemy in attacking boats on the Mississippi." He directed Admiral Porter to take more aggressive action. The general himself said that "to secure the safety of the navigation of the Mississippi River I would slay millions."[34]

The local populace was not happy with such measures. On the one hand, they were "seriously distressed and annoyed by this strolling police. There is no escape for them except in abandoning their homes until [the Union is] once more in possession of our river." On the other hand, many citizens of river towns did not trust the U.S. government to "ensure a greater degree of safety to life and property on the river than has been enjoyed for some time past." They often criticized troops for their inability to protect Union steamships, safeguard civilian passengers, or hold the saboteurs accountable for their nefarious actions. The frequency of boat burnings along the lower Mississippi further supported claims that the government failed in its duty to protect commercial vessels.[35]

Vulnerable, the local populace took matters into their own hands. Many felt that it was the duty of all river people to help detect and punish the perpetrators. Unionists declared that "if any of the villains engaged in this work can be caught, a long rope and a short shrift should be awarded them." Meanwhile, local police increased their vigilance. Detectives set out to discover the boat burners. Steamboat owners and officers took additional measures to protect their charges. On October 10, 1863, St. Louis steamboat owners gathered together to discuss "the danger which now surrounds steamboat property from fire, and to endeavor by concerted action to remove [said] evil." As they ultimately desired to make the riverways and steamers safer for commercial and leisure travel, they too increased the number of watchmen on the docks. Despite such efforts, neither the Federal government nor the steamboat captains succeeded in their aim. For the duration of the war, the incendiaries evaded authorities and continued to target steamers along the lower Mississippi River.[36]

In the end, naval guerrillas destroyed some forty-odd steamers throughout the course of the war, the majority during the fall of 1863. These conflagrations resulted in dozens of civilian casualties, substantial economic losses, and the arrest of six incendiaries, including William Murphy and Robert Louden. The explosive integration of irregular and naval warfare also resulted in a dramatic shift in public perception. While Union officials quickly dismissed the 1861 New Orleans steamboat fires as an accident, by mid-1863 they made the opposite assumption—that every steamboat calamity was the act of deliberate sabotage and arson. The fact that the boat burners had effectively diverted Union commanders from their primary military objectives required them to alter strategies, and the forced reallocation of soldiers to the port towns indicated the success of the naval guerrillas' exploits. Their victimization of women, children, and commercial steamers signaled a new *modus operandi* in naval warfare. And the Federals' belief that rebel secret agents intent on sabotage were aboard virtually every vessel traveling the Mississippi River became accepted fact. While the likelihood of such universal deception is unlikely, the terror created by a handful of confirmed boat burnings was immeasurable. Fear, it proved, was the naval guerrillas' greatest weapon.[37]

The effectiveness of the boat burners' intimidation campaign revealed itself at war's end. Newspapers claimed that "during the war over two hundred steamers of all kinds valued at from $15,060 to $150,000 each, were destroyed by this chivalrous band, involving not only an immense pecuniary to the Government but the sacrifice of hundreds of valuable lives." The elevated number of participants and sabotaged vessels (from forty to two hundred) revealed the efficacy of irregular warfare. As terrorists, the boat burners' greatest accomplishment was convincing Federal officials and local populations that their reach was much farther than it actually was. Whether or not the naval guerrillas actually sabotaged two hundred vessels was not important; the fact that the Union believed them to be the agents of such wholesale destruction was. The Father of the Waters may have been under Federal jurisdiction, but there was no way for the Yankees to retain complete control. The pro-Confederate boat burners revealed how murky the waters of the West really were as they vexed the Union war effort long after Vicksburg fell.[38]

NOTES

The author thanks Stephen Berry, James Hill Welborn III, Daniel E. Sutherland, Joseph M. Beilein, and Nicholas Benson for their feedback on earlier versions and presentations of this essay. She also thanks David J. Gerleman for his invaluable assistance in locating pertinent records of the boat burners in the National Archives. Generous grants from the Willson Center for Humanities & Arts, the University of Georgia Graduate School, the Greg and Amanda Gregory Graduate Studies Enhancement Fund, the Vincent J. Dooley Graduate Research Award in History, and the University of Georgia History Department aided in the research of this project.

1. "Big Fire over the River," *New Orleans Daily Crescent,* May 6, 1861; U.S. War Department, *The Annual Report of the Secretary of War* (Washington, D.C.: U.S. Government Printing Office, 1866), 195.

2. Paskoff, *Troubled Waters,* 20; Hunter, *Steamboats on the Western Rivers,* 287; Gudmestead, *Steamboats and the Rise of the Cotton Kingdom,* 108.

3. "Varieties," *Cincinnati Daily Press,* May 17, 1861.

4. Abraham Lincoln, *Collected Works of Abraham Lincoln,* vol. 6, ed. Roy P. Basler (New Brunswick: Rutgers University Press, 1953), 409.

5. "Terrible Calamity," *Daily Missouri Republican,* Aug. 6, 1863; Proceedings of a Court of Inquiry Commenced the Special Orders No. 408, War Department, Adjutant General's Office, Washington, Sept. 11, 1863; Destruction of Steamer *Ruth* by Fire, Nathan S. Brinton Papers, 1863–1864, Filson Historical Society, Louisville, Ky.; "Burning of the *Ruth*—Additional Particulars," *Daily Missouri Republican,* Aug. 7, 1863; "Affairs Down River," *Daily Missouri Republican,* Aug. 11, 1863;

John McKennon, roll 1200, U.S. War Department, Union Provost Marshal Files of Individual Civilians, 1861–1866 (hereafter Provost Marshal Files of Individual Civilians); William Murphy, roll 1249, ibid.; Isaac Elshire [*sic*], roll 1311, ibid.; Robert Lowden [*sic*], roll 1363, ibid.

6. "Another Disaster on the Mississippi," *New York Times,* Aug. 26, 1863; William G. Christie to Alexander S. Christie, Aug. 20, 1863, Minnesota Historical Society, Civil War Letters of the Christie Family, accessed Mar. 23, 3015, http://www.mnhs.org/library/christie/letters/0820631.php; "Appalling Accident to a Cincinnati Steamer," *Dollar Weekly Bulletin* (Maysville, Ky.), Aug. 27, 1863; J. H. Baker to C. A. Dana, Apr. 25, 1865, U.S. War Department, *War of the Rebellion,* ser. 1, 48(2):195 (hereafter cited as *O.R.*); "Edward Frazer," in *The Lincoln Assassination: The Evidence,* ed. William C. Edwards and Edwards Steers Jr. (Urbana: University of Illinois Press, 2009), 568. The large number of African Americans traveling on the *City of Madison* is not surprising given the plethora of plantations in the Mississippi River valley and the prominent role that the river played in the Union's efforts to recruit black troops. According to Gary Gallagher, "most black men in Federal service from Confederate states came from those bordering the Mississippi River. Louisiana sent 24,052, which constituted 31 percent of that state's black men between the ages of 18 and 45; Tennessee sent 20,133 (39 percent); and Mississippi 17,869 (21 percent). Arkansas, another state bordering the Mississippi, contributed 5,526 black men, 24 percent of its overall number." Gallagher, *The Union War* (Cambridge: Harvard University Press, 2011), 146.

7. The River Defense Fleet was a set of fourteen Confederate vessels under the command of Capts. Joseph E. Montgomery and James H. Townsend. Its purpose was to defend the Mississippi River from Federal attack, but after the loss of New Orleans and the destruction of all but one vessel at the Battle of Memphis, the fleet disbanded on June 21, 1862. See Edward B. McCaul, *To Retain Command of the Mississippi: The Civil War Naval Campaign for Memphis* (Knoxville: University of Tennessee Press, 2014). It is not surprising that pro-Confederate boat burners focused their efforts on the Mississippi River. By 1861, the Mississippi was the nation's premier economic, transportation, and communications highway. Cotton, grain, hogs, chickens, sugar, and people traveled from St. Louis to New Orleans (or vice versa) in as little as four days. With the advent of steamboats, 160,000 tons of shipping carried $200 million worth of goods aboard 700 vessels. For the economic importance of the Mississippi, see Johnson, *River of Dark Dreams,* introduction; Hunter, *Steamboats on the Western Rivers;* and Louis Hunter, "The Commercial Growth and Greatness of the West," *Hunt's Merchants' Magazine* 17 (1847): 495–503.

8. For information on the role of the guerrilla shirt, see Joseph M. Beilein Jr., "The Guerrilla Shirt: A Labor of Love and the Style of Rebellion in Civil War Missouri," *Civil War History* 58, no. 2 (June 2012): 151–79. For information on Confederate mail running, especially the role of women, see LeeAnn Whites, "Corresponding with the Enemy: Mobilizing the Relational Field of Battle in St. Louis," in Whites and Long, *Occupied Women,* 103–16.

9. Abraham Lincoln to James C. Conkling, Aug. 26, 1863, in Lincoln, *Collected Works,* 409. In his introduction to *American Civil War Guerrillas,* Daniel Sutherland declares: "[T]here was terrorism during the Civil War. . . . One finds their roots during the American Civil War in the guerrilla conflict that raged between 1861 and 1865, a conflict that caused either directly or indirectly most of the terrorism and counterterrorism that we associate with that war." Sutherland, *American Civil War Guerrillas,* xiii. While historians such as Richard Brownlee, Michael Fellman, Mark Grimsley, Robert Mackey, and Sutherland have demonstrated the pivotal role of guerrillas in the

Civil War, none considered naval guerrillas or boat burners. Fellman, Grimsley, and Mackey failed to even mention this type of irregular fighter, while Sutherland classified them as either privateers or sailors aboard torpedo gunboats. Such universal disregard of boat burners illuminates a hole in the historiography of irregular warfare that this essay addresses.

10. "The Rebel Boat-Burners," *American Citizen,* Sept. 27, 1865. For statistical information on steamboat disasters, see William M. Lytle and Forrest R. Holdcamper, *Merchant Steam Vessels of the United States, 1790–1868: "The Lytle-Holdcamper List,"* ed. C. Bradford Mitchell (State Island: Steamship Historical Society of American, 1975); Frederick Way Jr., *Way's Packet Directory, 1848–1994: Passenger Steamboats of the Mississippi River System since the Advent of Photography in Mid-Continent America,* rev. ed. (Athens: Ohio University Press, 1994); and W. Craig Gaines, *Encyclopedia of Civil War Shipwrecks* (Baton Rouge: Louisiana State University Press, 2008).

11. J. H. Baker to C. A. Dana, Apr. 25, 1865, *O.R.,* ser. 1, 48(2):194–95; "River News," *Daily Missouri Republican,* July 16, 1864.

12. Edward Frazer and Isaac Elshire, roll F1311, Provost Marshal Files of Individual Civilians; Benn Pitman, ed., *The Assassination of President Lincoln and the Trial of the Conspirators* (Clark, NJ: The Lawbook Exchange, Ltd., 2006), 49; Robt. Allen to H. W. Hallack, Oct. 5, 1863, *O.R.,* ser. 1, 22:607; F. A. Dick to Col. W. Hoffman, Mar. 5, 1863, in Archibald Kirk, *Troubled State: Civil War Journals of Franklin Archibald Dick,* ed. Gari Carter (Kirksville, Mo.: Truman State University Press, 2008), 118; *O.R.,* ser. 1, 48(2):194–95.

13. Court-Martial NN-1074, RG 153, Records of the Office of the Judge Advocate General, 1792–2010, NARA (hereafter RG 153); Cornwell Keefer and George Foster, roll F1637, U.S. War Department, Union Provost Marshal Files, Two or More Civilians, 1861–67, NARA; Mollie Levis, Tip Fox, and Edward Frazer, roll F1632, ibid.; "Edward Frazer," in Edwards and Steers, *Lincoln Assassination,* 567. For more information on guerrilla communities, see Whites, "Forty Shirts and a Wagonload of Wheat," and "Corresponding with the Enemy." The Organization of American Knights was an offshoot of the Knights of the Golden Circle, organized in 1863. See Joseph Holt, *Report of the Judge Advocate General on "The Order of American Knights," Alias "The Sons of Liberty": A Western Conspiracy in Aid of the Southern Rebellion* (Washington, D.C.: Government Printing Office, 1864); and David C. Keehn, *Knights of the Golden Circle: Secret Empire, Southern Secession, Civil War* (Baton Rouge: Louisiana State University Press, 2013).

14. "By Telegraph," *Nashville Daily Union,* Oct. 18, 1863; "Important Arrest of Rebels," *Chicago Tribune,* Dec. 19, 1863.

15. Court-Martial MM-1967, RG 153; J. H. Baker to C. A. Dana, Apr. 25, 1865, *O.R.,* ser. 1, 48(2):194–98; J. H. Baker to E. R. S. Canby, Apr. 26, 1865, ibid., ser. 2, 8:516; "Edward Frazer," in Edwards and Steers, *Lincoln Assassination,* 566.

16. "Important Arrest of Rebels," *Chicago Tribune,* Dec. 19, 1863; J. H. Baker to C. A. Dana, Apr. 25, 1865, *O.R.,* ser. 1, 48(2):196; "Confederate S.A. Documents No. 2 s. 194," in Edwards and Steers, *Lincoln Assassination,* 376–77. See also "Every Steamboat Navigating the Lower Mississippi and Ohio Rivers to be Destroyed by Rebel Emissaries," *Daily Missouri Republican,* Oct. 8, 1864; and "The Trial at St. Louis Complicity of Jeff. Davis, Seddon and Benjamin," *New York Times,* Oct. 1, 1863.

17. "Edward Frazer," Edwards and Steers, *Lincoln Assassination,* 566; J. H. Baker to C. A. Dana, Apr. 25, 1865, *O.R,* ser. 1, 48(2):195.

18. "Report of Rear Admiral Porter, U.S. Navy, Transmitting Captured Letters Referring to Institution of Torpedo Service," May 20, 1864, *Official Records of the Union and Confederate Navies* (Washington, 1894–1922), ser. 1, 26:186 (hereafter *O.R.N.*); Robt. Allen to H. W. Hallack, Oct.5, 1863, *O.R.*, ser. 1, 22:607; "River News," *Daily Missouri Republican*, Sept. 11, 1863; "Late Steamboat Disasters," *Memphis Daily Appeal*, Sept. 28, 1863; "From the Lower Mississippi," *Daily Intelligencer*, Sept. 16, 1863.

19. "Extensive Conflagration," *Daily Missouri Republican*, Sept. 14, 1863; "River News," *Daily Missouri Republican*, Sept. 14, 1863.

20. "Extensive Conflagration." *Daily Missouri Republican*, Sept. 14, 1863; "The Fire Yesterday," ibid.

21. "Extensive Conflagration," ibid.; Charles F. Vogel Diary, Sept. 13, 1863, Z/0656.000: Vogel (Charles F.) Diary, Mississippi Department of Archives and History, Jackson; "Opening of the Mississippi," *Harper's Weekly*, Aug. 8, 1863; Louis S. Gerteis, *Civil War St. Louis* (Lawrence: University Press of Kansas, 2001), 273. Surprisingly, some of the owners of the burned steamers bought a replacement boat a day after the fire. See "River News," *Daily Missouri Republican*, Sept. 15, 1863.

22. "Late Steamboat Disasters," *Memphis Daily Appeal*, Sept. 28, 1863; "Extensive Conflagration," *Daily Missouri Republican*, Sept. 14, 1863. For nonlocal coverage of the St. Louis fire, see "By Telegraph," *Nashville Daily Union*, Sept. 15, 1863; "Destructive Fire in St. Louis—Four Steamboats Burned," *Daily Intelligencer*, Sept. 15, 1863; "Last Night's Dispatches," *Daily Ohio Statesman* (Columbus), Sept. 15, 1863; "Great Fire in St. Louis," *New-York Daily Tribune*, Sept. 18, 1863, "From the West," *Western Democrat* (Charlotte, N.C.), Sept. 29, 1863, and "Editorial Items," *Yorkville (S.C.) Enquirer*, Sept. 30, 1863.

23. W. T. Sherman to W. S. Rosecrans, Apr. 23, 1864, *O.R.*, ser. 1, 32(3):464; W. T. Sherman to U. S. Grant, Oct. 4, 1862, ibid., 17(2)260.

24. "The Champion Conflagration," *Daily Missouri Republican*, Sept. 29, 1863; "Destruction of the Steamboat *Champion*," *Gallipolis (Ohio) Journal*, Oct. 1, 1863; "Steamboat Disaster at the Memphis Landing," *Memphis Daily Appeal*, Oct. 5, 1863; "From the *Cincinnati Gazette*, 26th: News of the Day," *Gallipolis (Ohio) Journal*, Oct. 1, 1863.

25. "Latest by Telegraph," *Daily Missouri Republican*, Sept. 28, 1863; "Attempt to Burn the Steamer *Platte Valley*," ibid., Sept. 29, 1863; "Mississippi River News," *Cleveland Morning Leader*, Oct. 2, 1863; "From Memphis," *Daily Missouri Republican*, Oct. 6, 1863; "By Telegraph," ibid., Oct. 4, 1863; "Three Steamers Burned at St. Louis," *Washington (D.C.) Evening Star*, Oct. 6, 1863; *Shaw v. United States*, 93 U.S. 235, 23 L.Ed. 880 (1876), PublicResource.org, accessed Mar. 25, 2015, https://law.resource.org/pub/us/case/reporter/US/93/93.US.235.html. This was not the first time rebels tried to destroy the *Platte Valley*. On June 18, 1863, guerrillas at Bradford's Landing fired into the steamer, killing three passengers and wounding several others. Their primary objective, the cotton aboard ship, eluded them. See "Rebel Attack on the Steamer *Platte Valley*," *Daily Intelligencer*, June 19, 1863.

26. "Edward Frazer," Edwards and Steers, *Lincoln Assassination*, 567–68.

27. "Incendiarism," *Daily Missouri Republican*, Oct. 6, 1863. See also "The New Style of Rebel Warfare, *Daily Intelligencer*, Oct. 10, 1863; and "Rebel Incendiarism," *Lancaster (Ohio) Gazette*, Oct. 15, 1863.

28. "From the Cincinnati Gazette, 26th: News of the Day," *Gallipolis (Ohio) Journal*, Oct. 1, 1863; and "More steamboat property sacrificed," *Memphis Daily Appeal*, Oct. 22, 1863.

29. "Steamboat Disaster at the Memphis Landing," *Memphis Daily Appeal,* Oct. 5, 1863; "Rebel Incendiarism," *Lancaster (Ohio) Gazette,* Oct. 15, 1863; Sutherland, *Savage Conflict,* 70, 165; W. S. Oldham to Jefferson Davis, Feb. 11, 1865, Entry 12, General Records of the Adjutant General's Office, Correspondence, 1800–1947, RG 94, Letters Received by the Office of the Adjutant General (Main Series), 1861–70, NARA.

30. "The New Style of Rebel Warfare, *Daily Intelligencer,* Oct. 10, 1863; "Incendiarism," *Daily Missouri Republican,* Oct. 6, 1863; "Rebel Incendiarism," *Lancaster (Ohio) Gazette,* Oct. 15, 1863; "Another Extensive Steamboat Fire," *Daily Missouri Republican,* Oct. 5, 1863.

31. "More Steamboat Incendiarism—Attempt to Burn Boats at Carondolet," *Daily Missouri Republican,* Oct. 5, 1863.

32. "Another Extensive Steamboat Fire," ibid.

33. Robert Allen to Hurlbut, Sept. 15, 1863, *O.R.,* ser. 1, 30(3):641; Robt. Allen to H. W. Hallack, Oct. 5, 1863, ibid., 22:607.

34. "Letters from Canton, Miss.," *Memphis Daily Appeal,* Sept. 29, 1863; W. T. Sherman to John A. Logan, Dec. 21, 1863, *O.R.,* ser. 1, 31(3):459. As any efforts to allay the boat burners' havoc failed, the Department of the Missouri issued General Orders No. 119 (July 1864), outlining new protections against incendiaries: the stationing of three towboats along the harbor to serve as a firefighting force, the removal of any vessels not loading or discharging freight from the docks, and the prevention of small vessels from plying the harbor. General Orders No. 119, July 15, 1864, ibid., 41(2):199–200. R. Adm. S. P. Lee passed a similar order for the Mississippi Squadron in December. See General Order, No. 23, Dec. 29, 1864, *O.R.N.,* ser. 1, 26:766–67.

35. "Letters from Canton, Miss.," *Memphis Daily Appeal,* Sept. 29, 1863; "Meeting of Steamboat Owners," *Daily Missouri Republican,* Oct. 6, 1863.

36. "The New Style of Rebel Warfare, *Daily Intelligencer,* Oct. 10, 1863; "Meeting of Steamboat Owners," *Daily Missouri Republican,* Oct. 6, 1863.

37. Robt. Allen to Hurlbut, Sept. 15, 1863, *O.R.,* ser. 1, 30(3):641; Robt. Allen to H. W. Halleck, Oct. 5, 1863, ibid., 22:607; "Destructive Fire at the Wharf," *Daily Missouri Republican,* July 16, 1864. See also Court-Martials MM-1967, NN 1074, RG 153; and *In Re: Murphy,* 17 F.Cas. 1030 (1867), PublicResource.org, accessed Jan. 21, 2015, https://law.resource.org/pub/us/case/reporter/F.Cas/0017.f.cas/0017.f.cas.1030.2.html. Ultimately, Robert Louden was found guilty of transgressing the laws and customs of war, espionage, and boat burning but managed to escape imprisonment—and the hangman's noose. In 1865 William Murphy was sentenced to ten years of hard labor for boat burning and transgressing the laws and customs of war; his sentence was commuted two years later.

38. J. H. Baker to C. A. Dana, Apr. 25, 1865, *O.R.,* ser. 1, 48(2):195–96; "The Rebel Boat-Burners," *American Citizen* (New York City), Sept. 27, 1865.

WHISKEY, WILD MEN, AND MISSOURI'S GUERRILLA WAR

JOSEPH M. BEILEIN JR.

When R. M. Burgess awoke on September 27, 1864, in Centralia, Missouri, he could hardly have imagined what madness would ensue. Burgess, who was in town to sell livestock, remembered it was "one of those cool, bracing, lovely autumn mornings." This otherwise beautiful day was disrupted when Bill Anderson and his company of guerrillas rode into town, a group that Burgess called "the finest looking body of horsemen" he had ever seen. The guerrillas were on the hunt for contraband and easy prey; in Centralia they found both. Although he was terrified, Burgess remembered the horsemen being polite and jovial, especially Dave Pool. Upon his arrival in town, Pool recognized Burgess's companion, a man who had ridden with the band earlier in the war before retiring from fighting, and came over to say hello to the two civilians. Moments after their meeting, Pool uncovered a barrel of whiskey. Looking around for glassware or a ladle to drink the booze, the guerrilla instead found a case of brand-new shoes. For these fast-drinking men, the boots would serve as well as tumblers for getting the firewater from the barrel into their bellies. Burgess remembered that Pool approached him "with a boot full of whisky and boisterously insisted that I should drink with him." Burgess hastily tipped the boot, drinking some and spilling much more. This was how the rest of the morning proceeded: drinking, toasting, and treating each other until they heard the low-chugging sound of a distant but approaching train.[1]

It was a riotous scene to roll into: perhaps seventy-five guerrillas, with their wild beards and long hair, wearing cavalry boots, slouch hats, and the uniform jackets of Union troopers, most of them drunk on whiskey gulped from boots, staggering here and riding there. It was this absurd revelry that a train carrying an untold number of noncombatants and twenty-three Union soldiers on leave from Major General William T. Sherman's army in Georgia pulled into. The drunken guerrillas quickly swarmed the cars and boarded them, their guns waving this way and that. With the burn of whiskey lingering on their tongues, they shouted at the passengers to surrender their valuables and ordered the unarmed Union soldiers off. These men were lined up next to the train and executed, with the exception of Thomas Goodman, a sergeant who was taken captive in the hope of exchanging him for a guerrilla who had been captured by Union forces. Whether or not Burgess's drinking partner, the fun-loving Pool, was among the executioners is unclear. Indeed, by that time, things in Centralia had become blurry for all involved. Years later, looking back on the massacre through the fog of that day's inebriation, Burgess conceded that the rapacious drinking "may in some degree have been responsible for the dreadful tragedy."[2]

As Burgess suggested, the Centralia massacre was influenced by alcohol. Other witnesses to the slaughter put a greater emphasis on the correlation. W. F. Bassett, who left a somewhat flawed account of the event, nevertheless pointed to whiskey as an important contributor to the bloodshed. He remembered that before the train arrived, the guerrillas were "working themselves up by frequent potations." Goodman, the lone survivor among the Union soldiers, remarked on their inebriated state after the massacre. He remembered that while he was their prisoner, "Twice, my guard had all they could do to prevent a drunken squad of them from taking me from them." At Centralia and throughout the war, bushwhackers were prone to both violence and drinking; exactly how the two were related was less obvious to their victims and witnesses. Examining the connection between violence and drinking among the guerrillas, one can see that it was necessary for many of the men to imbibe in order to participate in the conflict and that the men who drank were the best equipped to deal with the escalation of violence. By the end, the guerrilla war was an all-out binge of whiskey and blood in which the wild men and heavy drinkers (often one and the same) came to the forefront and did the most to shape the war's final years.[3]

It is well accepted among scholars that guerrillas operating in Missouri imbibed. Beginning with their antebellum forebearers—the border ruffian and the aptly named puke—and ending with the postwar, saloon-dwelling outlaws who sprang forth from the irregular ranks, most scholars work from the assumption that the guerrillas and their ilk were drinkers. In what is representative of the historical understanding of the guerrillas' drinking habits, one scholar of the irregular war sees the effects of alcohol in the context of the psychological framework of "character doubling" and a loose Freudian interpretation of the war that makes these fighters out to be infantile boys warring against the authority of their father in the form of the Federal government. Some men, when captured, "claimed that they had been drunk while committing guerrilla acts and were therefore not responsible for whatever they had said or done." In other words, there was the drunk self and the sober (real) self; one was not responsible for the other. The implication of this analysis is that getting tight was merely an excuse for inexcusable behavior. This observation, however, is as far as any analysis of the drinking patterns among the guerrillas has gone.[4]

Like so many aspects of the guerrilla war, alcohol and its use grew out of antebellum life in Missouri. Tracking the locations of alcohol production can be difficult, given the tumultuous history of the relationship between the distiller and the taxman. Many distillers and brewers did their work "underground" rather than disclose their production to government auditors who would apply a tax to their annual yields. Although it may be impossible to know exactly how much alcohol was produced in the state, according to the manufacturing census of 1860, there were ninety-one businesses in Missouri producing liquor. Twenty-two of these businesses produced distilled spirits, sixty-four produced malted liquor, and five produced rectified liquor (high-proof grain alcohol without any flavoring). For a frame of reference, the state of Kentucky—traditionally known for its bourbon whiskey—had 243 establishments listed, whereas the state of Mississippi does not list a single alcohol-producing business. Additionally, in Missouri 27,827 gallons of wine were produced on an annual basis, and 2,263 pounds of hops were grown, presumably for brewing beer.[5]

In Little Dixie—the mostly rural region of the state comprising around fifteen counties on either side of the Missouri River and where most of the guerrilla fighting took place—alcohol was an accepted part of everyday life. In some parts of the country, particularly the urban areas of the North, drinking had become a contentious issue and a source of conflict between reformers and the working classes and ethnic groups. Since the late 1820s, temperance societies had tried to reduce the large amounts of alcohol consumed by Americans. They tended to target densely populated cities, where alcohol contributed to a myriad of social problems—vagrancy, prostitution, gambling, brawling, domestic abuse, and the spread of venereal disease—and by at least one measure they were successful, reducing the average American's overall consumption of alcohol by several gallons a year. Yet they were largely ineffective in rural areas, especially in the South, where all reform efforts were lumped together with abolitionism. In these areas, alcohol consumption remained much as it had and varied from household to household. Like nearly every other part of life, alcohol and its production and consumption fell under the sway of the head of household. Certainly, if grain harvested from a farm was used as an ingredient in whiskey or land was used as the site for a still house, it would have to be approved by the man in charge, if the distilling was not done under his direct supervision already. The purchase of alcohol from a local store or neighborhood distillery would also need to be cleared with the head of household. Of course, the actual imbibing could only be done with the acquiescence of the father or boss, even if such permission was implied. Thus, the amount, frequency, and reasons for drinking ran the gamut and depended on the culture of the family in question. There were families of teetotalers and families of drunkards, but the majority fell in between those two extremes.[6]

Drinking became a part of guerrilla culture. That is not to say that all such men were drunks or binge drinkers or even that every single one of them drank. Rather, alcohol in its various forms was present during this time and many guerrillas partook. At times they drank before battle, other times it was after battle, and there were even times when they drank during battle. They were aware of alcohol's effects on the body and on behavior, at least in the context of their nineteenth-century worldview. Some of these effects were negative: men losing control of their senses and making themselves vulnerable to their enemies, belligerence between friends, illness, and dependency. They nevertheless imbued cultural meanings into alcohol and the act of drinking. Whiskey helped increase bravery (or lessen fear, depending on the perspective), made killing another man easier, and helped fighters endure the physical and emotional pain of warfare in a manly way. Drinking together could promote amicable relations among strangers, who were potential enemies in the context of the guerrilla war. It could also instill among a cohort of fighting men a sense of brotherhood: celebrating a victory with a toast, honoring each other with a treat, testing each other with the offer of a nip, proving themselves by tipping the bottle, increasing their prowess with a long pull from the demijohn. For many men in the nineteenth century and for fighters especially, strong drink was a central element of what made them men.[7]

From the very start of the war, the guerrillas drank. On the first page of his memoir, Andrew Walker lets the reader know, "I was wild." Initially, it is unclear whether or not being wild meant that he was a heavy drinker, but there is evidence throughout his memoir suggesting that a wild man was a man who drank. Throughout his recollection of the war, he mentions quite a few occasions when he and fellow guerrillas got into their cups. One time early in the war, Walker remembers that they "robbed a mail hack . . . and relieved the driver of a jug of whiskey bound for a bibulous farmer." He notes, "The liquor was found to be of good quality and the jug was passed around at short intervals." At Lawrence, after the killing was done and it was nearly time to ride out of the burning town, Walker "dismounted, went into a saloon, swallowed a couple of drams, ate a can of sardines, and took enough canned stuff to fill my saddle pockets." Having sated his thirst for liquor, Walker joined the rest of the men assembled to leave.[8]

Walker and his cohorts in Jackson County were not the only guerrillas who made whiskey a part of their war. Whiskey distillation and consumption was a focal point of the war for fighters across the state. In February 1862, Southern irregulars in southwestern Missouri used still houses (or distillation houses, or simply stills) as meeting places. This became very troubling for at least one Union commander. John Richardson, a captain in the militia around Springfield, Missouri, reported that he "marched to Mallard's still-house from the northwest. The rebels had fled before us." Elaborating on the raid, he said: "There were two reasons for destroying the still-houses: First, they were places of rendezvous for the forming secession bands for plunder; secondly, bad men would get drunk there, and go to Union men's [homes and] expose their naked persons to Union women." Richardson pleaded, "I hope you will, and I know every good woman in the state will, indorse the destruction—the burning of those still-houses." To Richardson, secessionists were bad men and bad men were drunks, whereas the women of Union men were inherently good, and good men and women were sober. Although his views were not universal among Unionists in Missouri, it was clear that this captain believed he was not only waging a war against the South but also fighting against immorality and depravity.[9]

Many commanders in blue and gray would have commended Richardson's actions. Although many officers in the conventional armies drank, the general view of alcohol consumption among the upper echelons of the Union and Confederate armies was a negative one. In the only study of alcohol in the Civil War, historian Thomas Lowry examines drunkenness in the Union army. Using mostly court-martial records, he seeks to answer whether drinking-related stereotypes were grounded in truth. Looking at three groups—Irish immigrants, German immigrants, and American-born troops—he confirms long-held stereotypes (or confirms that these stereotypes prejudiced the officers who leveled charges against the men). Within the total number of charges brought against the three groups, the Irish had the largest percentage that were alcohol related, then the Germans, then native-born Americans. Additionally, he offers a conclusion that would make men like George McClellan quite happy: drinking was detrimental to the army.[10]

The formal armies of the Union and the Confederacy required discipline built upon sobriety. The firm organizational structure of strict hierarchy required men to follow a protocol that governed nearly all aspects of their lives while they were in the military. Within that soldierly experience, alcohol was not entirely prohibited; it could not be. But its place was made small by restriction, pushed to the fringe away from the battlefield and outside of the regulation of the army. Distance, privilege, and furtiveness provided opportunities for imbibing: common soldiers would find whiskey away from the front lines, often while foraging or on leave; officers used their status to discreetly ply themselves with drink while in camp and during battle; and the man reliant upon alcohol to function—soldier or officer—kept his drinking secret, hiding away bottles or concealing a flask. Any of these men could find himself sanctioned for a number of violations, though mostly for drunkenness in some degree.[11]

Unlike the guerrilla ranks, in which the consumption of alcohol was an accepted practice, the formal army hierarchy did not mix well with alcohol. The problematic factor in this immiscible relationship depended on one's perspective. For the most part, general officers—whether they were veritable teetotalers like McClellan or Robert E. Lee, or men like Ulysses S. Grant and Joseph Hooker, who were known for imbibing—believed alcohol to be a deterrent to the proper order of their armies. In contrast, the common men who walked to war from farms and from working-class neighborhoods in burgeoning cities saw discipline at odds with a key component of their lifestyle. Both perspectives can be understood. Generals thrived on power and absolute authority, which required complete deference by the men under them as well as their clear-minded competency to carry out orders. Booze could obstruct the necessary conditions for effective generalship. Yet for men in the rank and file who had drank all of their adult lives, alcohol had never been a problem. It was the army and the discipline imposed on them from external sources that created an issue where one had not existed, one that had little bearing upon their will to fight or their fighting ability—or so these tipplers thought.[12]

Externally imposed discipline did not occur among the guerrillas. More organic forces determined whether or not men could drink, when they could drink, and how much they could drink. Although the exact antebellum circumstances in which men partook in alcohol consumption had been disrupted—the rhythm of farm work and the oversight of the household patriarch—the principles on which they were based remained: task-oriented labor and familial bonds. Order was built on kinship and friendship bonds. Older brothers and cousins were the leaders of these bands, whose members often came from the same families. No matter their "rank," men were driven by the twin tasks of killing and staying alive. These were the sources of power that determined the drinking habits of the guerrillas. If their leaders gave approval or if the war opened an opportunity, then men could drink. It was not prohibited merely for the sake of prohibition, but men did not drink to excess all of the time simply because there was no one there to flog them or subject them to bucking-and-gagging.[13]

The consumption of alcohol influenced the guerrillas' performance. Irregular war knew no front lines, no home front, and no such thing as leave. It was an inclusive experience; combat could occur anywhere at any time. Whenever the guerrillas imbibed, they did so within this context. Walker remembered that after he and his comrades drank the jug of fine whiskey liberated from the postman, they "got to the stage of feeling good." Unfortunately, the buzzed guerrillas failed to put out a picket, preoccupied as they were with the whiskey and the fun that inevitably ensued. Riding upon an ascending wave of emotion brought on by the initial digestion of the spirits, "one of the boys looked out and saw, two miles away, a scout of Yankees." Buoyed by the whiskey, all of the guerrillas wanted to fight. Walker thought back on the moment and noted: "Now if sober, we would have remained in the barn. As it was, every man was eager for the fun." The guerrillas poured out of the barn, "leaped" into their saddles, and charged off looking for a fight. The tipsy bushwhackers ambushed and defeated the Union troopers.[14]

The inclination to partake in strong drink could also lead men astray and expose their personal vulnerabilities. For all the stories of the positive effects of so-called liquid courage, there were an equal number of instances of men succumbing to the weakening influence of alcohol. Whether they made poor decisions, had their marksmanship or horsemanship affected by inebriation, or were literally caught napping, drinking could make killing the irregulars quite a bit easier. Walker recalled one time when alcohol was the primary factor in two guerrillas' demise. During the first winter of the war, his band was hiding out in the brush and running low on food, so Jim Reed and Sam Montgomery went out for supplies. After picking up some food and visiting Reed's wife, the two made their way back toward camp. They stopped at John Hampton's house on the way, where they discovered that Hampton "had brought a jug from Kansas City, and they all got drunk." Once the bushwhackers were inebriated, "Hampton betrayed them to a scout of Federals, who killed them on the spot." Here, whiskey was a weapon used against the guerrillas.[15]

Leadership was an important factor in moderating drinking and hopefully mitigating the potential dangers of imbibing in a war zone. In a relationship that was not dissimilar to that between a head of household and his dependents, the chief of a guerrilla band held sway over his men, who deferred to him. Unlike the regular army, guerrillas did not drink *in spite of* the leadership or hierarchy of their band. Instead, if the men in a particular group partook in drink, they did so *because of* their leader. Service in the ranks and deference to a particular leader was voluntary, which meant that guerrilla bands were more or less self-selecting. Although it seemed that all guerrilla leaders allowed some measure of imbibing, men who enjoyed drinking and associated activities would join together or fight for someone who allowed (and even facilitated) the desired amount and frequency of their drinking. That is not to diminish the political, social, or economic motivations for fighting but instead to assert that alcohol could influence who individuals fought alongside. No matter how permissive a guerrilla captain was, he was also entrusted with the safety of the band. Whether it was putting out pickets and vedettes or simply making sure that some members remained sober, it was up to the leader to take the appropriate precautions to protect his men.

During the first half of the war, permissive sobriety was the stance taken by many guerrilla leaders. The primary example of a sober irregular captain was William Clarke Quantrill. The famous (or infamous) guerrilla leader let his men partake in hard drink while he personally tended to stay away from it. Walker, who was perhaps the closest man to Quantrill early in the war, only saw the chieftain imbibe once. Upon their departure from Lawrence, the guerrilla army stopped after a few miles and partook in a celebratory drink from an enormous demijohn of whiskey. It was only then, after the exhilarating raid, that Quantrill took a drink with his men. Even though the captain mostly abstained from strong drink, he indulged his men's appetite for whiskey—up to a point. His men had to be able to fight when the time came, and they had to respect the Southern-sympathizing populace of Missouri. Sober, drunk, or somewhere in between, if they could do these two things, they would remain in good standing with their leader. Quantrill knew that his authority depended on his followers' voluntary allegiance. If he tried to stymie their thirst, his status would be reduced, and he might even be pushed out of the band altogether. As a result, Quantrill was lenient regarding the drinking habits of his men, fostering a loose atmosphere within the band and creating a culture of tolerance that unified the command under his leadership.[16]

Other guerrilla captains were drinkers. Bill Anderson offers an alternative to Quantrill's sober leadership. "Bloody Bill" embraced drinking as a mechanism for maintaining authority over his men. His captainship was an outgrowth of his prowess as a man, and that prowess was confirmed and reinforced by drinking with his followers. For these men, to gather and tip the bottle, including the leaders of the group, was to band together over strong drink. Once unity was affirmed, the group setting would quickly become a venue for masculine contestation. As the bottle made its way around the circle, men would challenge each other by taking longer and longer pulls of whiskey—the deeper the drink, the bigger the man. The real test, though, was in winning the long game. Each man then had to demonstrate how well he could hold his liquor by drinking without vomiting and by staying disproportionately sober for the amount of whiskey he had ingested. In this context, Anderson was probably able to hold his own when the bottle went around.[17]

Although drinking had always been essential to guerrilla culture, it remained a moderate part of guerrilla identity for the first two years of the war. The great guerrilla binge began during the winter of 1863–64, and it would change the shape of the irregular war until its end. Following the raid on Lawrence, General Orders No. 11, and the Battle of Baxter Springs, the army of several hundred guerrillas under the command of Quantrill migrated south to Texas, where they settled around the town of Sherman. Many of the men fell into a pattern of drunken debauchery that helped create tension within the band. Walker recalled one such example of a destructive binge. Anderson's command entered Sherman one night and got deep into the whiskey, but the men passed out without much trouble. Waking up in town, almost certainly hung over, they procured an old remedy for their pain, taking down the hair of the dog that bit them—in other words, they started drinking again. Building on the foundation of whiskey already in their blood, the guerrillas got wildly drunk. Walker remembered it as "a riotous breakfast" that culminated with the men riding through the streets, shooting the doorknobs off doors. After this loud, dangerous, and drunken parade made its circuit around Sherman, the men rode their horses into the lobby of their hotel, jumped them over the furniture, and redecorated the walls with bullet holes. Despite several close calls, no one was hurt, at least not with the bullets. But there were probably quite a few aching heads once the bender finally ended.[18]

Such indulgent drinking persisted during this particular winter because it was the longest time during the war when the guerrillas found themselves away from combat. The physical distance from the fighting of the Missouri brush became problematic, at least for the citizens of Sherman. Without the discipline of warfare, the guerrillas could drink without having to worry about keeping their guard up. Yet the mindset of these men was such that they never put down the mantle of the gun-toting bushwhacker. This was a dangerous mix: men drank to excess and then, once they were blind drunk, looked to their revolvers and their horses for sport and mischief. As far as the historical record is concerned, there were no instances of alcohol poisoning or accidental deaths among the irregulars. Although we do not know for sure, the guerrillas' heavy drinking may have led to the robbery and murder of a few citizens of Texas. It certainly did not help. Regardless, with the absence of the whetstone of combat, the usually sharp edge of this band of killers began to soften and become dull. While their desire to cut loose was similar to that of many Civil War soldiers who found themselves away from home and also on leave from the front lines, the presence of firearms, the unending desire to prove their manhood, and the incredible power and autonomy retained by each individual made for a messy bit of merriment.[19]

During their time in Texas, the guerrillas became personae-non-grata among the Confederate commanders in the area. Their drunken shooting matches and riding contests in Sherman probably agitated the local citizenry, civilian leadership, and military commanders. Indeed, reckless behavior has been cited through the years as a big reason for the problems between the guerrillas and the formal Confederate armies as well as a source of dissolution within the guerrilla bands. Regarding the former, the guerrillas' alcohol-related behavior did not appear in the Confederate reports compiled in the *Official*

Records as a reason for the discord. Rather, there was much concern that the guerrillas were looting locals under the guise of Confederate deserters and that the blue Federal uniforms they wore indicated that they were turncoats who would fight for the Union; there is no mention of intoxicated bushwhackers discharging their weapons in town. Yet stories like the one described by Walker trickle down through the years as linked to a general character flaw among the guerrilla population: they were wild, without discipline, and operating at cross-purposes with the conventional and orderly war effort of the Confederacy. Perhaps worse than that, they were nothing but drunken riffraff with guns.[20]

Whatever the original reasons for the discord with Confederate officials, alcohol cost Quantrill his status as the overall leader of the guerrillas. He remained in camp during the guerrillas' many alcohol-fueled sprees. In a postwar letter to Quantrill's childhood friend W. W. Scott, a guerrilla named Fletch Taylor recalled the chieftain's absence from the wild binges in Texas and that he seemed to discourage the drinking and carousing. Taylor mentioned that Quantrill "staid in camp most all the time while the rest of his officers were having a good time in riding in Gen Blunts buggy and ambulance," the conveyances being trophies of the guerrillas' victory over Major General James Blunt at Baxter Springs in October 1863. Additionally, Quantrill was openly critical of a popular saloon owner, Jim Crow Chiles, who was himself a Missourian and a friend to many of the men. Chiles's establishment in Sherman was at the center of the raucous behavior that winter. Although Quantrill did not seem to disrupt the party all that much through his conspicuous absence and his open denigration of Chiles, he pitted himself against the merrymaking and imbibing guerrillas who made up the majority of his band. It was likely that his men felt these acts were an attempt by their leader to enforce something akin to regular-army discipline, just the type of censorship and authority they had actively sought to avoid by joining the guerrilla ranks.[21]

The hard-drinking Anderson usurped Quantrill's authority around this time. More and more of Quantrill's men began to ally themselves with the reckless Anderson, a man who would never force them to bend into the constricting mold of the regular-army stooge because he was incapable of such restriction. Indeed, Anderson saw the merit in leading a force of men as wild and thirsty as himself, so he concocted a way to commandeer Quantrill's band. The source of the final break between the guerrillas was said to have been a murder. Quantrill suspected and arrested one of Anderson's men for killing a local farmer, then had the man executed before his rival could intervene. In response, Anderson framed Quantrill for the crime, telling Brigadier General Henry McCulloch that the guerrilla chief was responsible for the murder and all of the other mayhem in the region. McCulloch sent for Quantrill and placed him under arrest. While in the general's quarters, Quantrill was able to grab his guns, get the drop on his guards, and escape back to camp. By then, though, many of his men had left for the excitement promised by Anderson's leadership.[22]

By the time the men returned to Missouri in the spring of 1864, the character of the guerrilla forces had changed, and along with it the shape of the war. In fact, the paradigm of leadership for the remainder of the conflict shifted from the permissive sobriety of Quantrill to the participatory binging of Anderson, who had taken command of a force that would range in size from forty to around one hundred wild and bloodthirsty men. To make matters worse for Quantrill, following their departure, George Todd took control of what remained of his own band. Less wild than Anderson but just as deadly, Todd humiliated Quantrill during a card game and sent him with his tail between his legs into the wilderness. While a few men went with their old leader, most of those who remained would fight under Todd until his death. Although Todd was somewhat like his predecessor, both groups of guerrillas—Anderson's and Todd's—became wilder and bloodier than any had been before that winter in Texas.[23]

There were a couple of reasons for the guerrillas' full embrace of rowdiness. First, Sherman was a venue where battlefield skill and leadership was less important than a man's talent in the barroom. As long as the guerrillas remained in Texas, the disproportionate value placed on imbibing and hell-raising continued to increase, and Anderson's advantage over the sober Quantrill grew. Apparently, the Missourians stayed there just long enough for Anderson to take power from his prudish rival. Second, the war was taking a toll on the veterans of the band. The individual acts of killing and the losses of family members, friends, and comrades left their psychic imprints on the minds of these men. Moreover, omnipresent battle, the likes of which were unique to the guerrilla experience, required constant lubrication of the fighting mechanism. To be forever vigilant and constantly prepared to kill could sap the mind and the spirit. These stresses, though, could be reduced and vitality restored with a swallow of whiskey.[24]

After the return from Texas, a new brand of guerrilla came to the forefront: the wild man. These men embraced drinking as much as they embraced fighting.

While they had always been there—men like Andrew Walker—they began to thrive in the new conditions the guerrillas created for themselves. Even as the war became bloodier and deadlier, these fighters imbibed in the face of death, destruction, and tragedy. One of these wild men was Dave Pool, who came into his own as a bushwhacker in 1864. His wartime record was impressive. Despite his consumption of alcohol, or perhaps because of it, he fought well for the duration of the conflict, rose in rank, and lived to see the other side of war. Among his fellow guerrillas, Pool was spoken of in glowing terms. Other sources confirm that he was an active and effective guerrilla fighter. At different times he fought under the command of Todd or Anderson, and by 1863 he was considered a leader in the movement. Eventually, when Todd was killed in the fall of 1864, just a few weeks after the events at Centralia, Pool took over his command, thus becoming one of the central figures in the guerrilla war. His promotion was certainly due to his skills as a bushwhacker, but just as much to the fact that he had outlived all of the men above him while keeping his head in the process—not an easy task in war, especially an irregular contest as bloody as that in Missouri. By the spring of 1865, Pool led forty men. That May, he rode into Lexington at the head of his column of bushwhackers and surrendered.[25]

As much as he was known for his bushwhacking, Pool was better known for his personality. John N. Edwards, who tried his best to make the guerrillas out to be the great heroes of the Civil War in his book *Noted Guerrillas,* offered descriptions of each "noted" bushwhacker's persona. Although much of Edwards's work can be discarded as propaganda, it is important to remember that he knew most of the guerrillas personally, granting him insight into their character as individuals. He called Pool "an unschooled Aristophanes of the civil war, [who] laughed at calamity and mocked when any man's fear came. . . . [H]is speech would have been comedy personified. He laughed loudest when he was deadliest, and treated fortune with no more dignity in one extreme or another." Sifting through this highfaluting language makes clear that Pool was the comedian among the guerrillas. William H. Gregg, Quantrill's right-hand man, recalled "a laughable incident" when Pool's sense of humor was put to the test amid battle. Acting as a picket and standing in a farmer's field, Pool was simultaneously attacked by Union troopers and charged by a kicking, braying mule. His fellow guerrillas watched with great amusement as their comrade was chased this way and that, ducking Union bullets and dodging the spooked jack. He survived the wild skirmish with angry men and an even angrier animal, and he did so with a smile on his face.[26]

Drinking and fighting went hand in hand for Pool. In addition to the "boot bash" in Centralia, an event that was supremely representative of his character, he was linked to booze on a number of other occasions. The most telling piece of evidence for the important place of alcohol in Pool's life is one photograph. At some point during the war, he and two other men had their likenesses made together. Since then, the image has made its way around the histories of the war and also the internet, not so much because of Pool but because it features his friend and drinking partner Archie Clements, one of the most infamous guerrillas. With a cigar clamped between his teeth, a revolver in his right hand, his thumb on the hammer and his finger on the trigger, Clements looks every bit the wild and fearsome killer that he was. Pool's pose, however, is much more unique and fascinating. Standing between his two seated friends, Pool sports long, curly hair, and his beard is downright radical. With his hat tilted to the side, he stares blankly into the lens—a presence equal parts boastful and menacing. In his right hand he holds a pistol, not as he might use it but rather as an object for display. In his left hand, with a cigar butt between his fingers, he grips a bottle of whiskey as if he had just taken it from his lips. In their portraits most guerrillas posed like Clements; they were happy to brandish a revolver. Pool brought whiskey into the picture, looking much more apt to use the bottle than the gun. Nonetheless, the message was clear, the two items—the two tools for making war—provided balance for the guerrilla; one required the other.[27]

The best example of the intersection of Pool's drinking prowess and fighting skill came at Centralia. After the drunken massacre in the streets of the town, the guerrillas knew that another fight was coming. With their prisoner—Sergeant Goodman—in tow, Anderson and his men rode out of town to a camp in the brush some two and a half miles away. Goodman remembered that "the men threw themselves upon the ground, and in a little while the majority were soundly sleeping away the effects of their inebriation." Not everyone succumbed to the deflating effects of the whiskey, however. While their comrades rested, several men spread across the countryside, covering all of the major roads going to and from Centralia, scouting for any Union patrols that might respond to the day's bloody events. It is likely that Pool was among these scouts. Whether it was his genetic makeup that gave him a higher tolerance for alcohol or a greater frequency of drinking experiences, Pool remained vigilant and active despite the amount of whiskey he drank. After a couple of hours ranging about the local environs, one of the scouts—perhaps Pool himself—spotted a Union column and sprinted back to camp with the news.[28]

Pool then offered a perfect demonstration of the bloody art of bushwhacking. After a brief meeting, the guerrilla captains in the camp—probably Anderson, George Todd, Thomas Todd, John Thrailkill, Clifton Holtzclaw, and Jim Jackson—decided on a course of action: using a small band of men as bait, they would lure the Union force of over one hundred into the field next to their wooded camp, where several hundred guerrillas would then spring out from the tree line on three sides and engulf their prey. Pool was picked to head ten men to confront the Union force, feign retreat, and pull the unsuspecting troopers into the trap. He performed his task exquisitely. The guerrillas trotted their horses to within a few hundred yards of the lead element of the Union force, acted surprised, fired off a few shots from their pistols and a few curses from their mouths, and then wheeled around and set off toward the killing zone. Occasionally, when they thought their prey was slipping off the line, they would rein up, let the Federals catch up, exchange some lead, and then scamper away again. The guerrillas were able to successfully trick the larger Union force back to the ambush site. This type of action took great savvy. If the guerrillas ran away too quickly, they would outrun the troopers and would never get them into the trap. If they waited too long or stopped too many times, then the troopers would suspect the ambush. Using his feel for combat, Pool played his enemies to perfection, showing a remarkable knack for combat in the brush.[29]

Rousted from their alcohol-induced slumber, the guerrillas were ready for a brawl. Pool and his men came flying into the killing field down toward the camp at the base of the U-shaped tree line. They dismounted for a second to cinch up their saddles, preparing for a charge. As they readied their mounts, the Union troops—115 sober fighting men led by Major A. V. E. Johnston—rode over a crest at the center of the field, dismounted, and got in line. Pool's small band was joined by the rest of Anderson's company, together charging straight at the blue troops in front of them. Simultaneously, groups of a hundred or so men emerged from the woods on either side of Johnston's command. From Goodman's perspective in the woods, he remembered, "I saw the defeat of my friends was inevitable." Then as soon as the Federals broke and ran or tried to surrender, the guerrillas unleashed violence on their prey. As the sergeant described it, "Hell was suddenly transferred to earth, and all the fiends of darkness summoned to join the carnival of blood." He offered the rhetorical question to his audience: "were it possible for human souls to grow drunk on blood?" Goodman certainly seemed to think so: "[T]he idea may offer some palliation for the scenes enacted there. . . . Men's heads were severed from their lifeless bodies, exchanged as to bodies, labelled with rough and obscene epitaphs and inscriptions, stuck upon their carbine points, tied to their saddle bows, or sat grinning at each other from the tops of fence stakes and stumps around the scene."[30]

For Goodman, the debauchery was just beginning. Following this latest slaughter, the guerrillas removed to another predetermined camp several miles away in the brush. The rendezvous site had been prepped by a detachment of men under Todd, who had been drinking since their arrival. Goodman remarked, "Todd was drunk as a lord, and evidently in a bad humor." At that spot in the woods, the guerrillas "seemed to possess some sort of a depository or commissary . . . and both 'grub and whisky' were dispensed with a liberal hand." As darkness fell, nearly all the irregulars "were drunk even to madness. . . . They whooped, ran, jumped and yelled like so many savages." Goodman, who "trembled for [his] own safety," watched as "Anderson, leaping on a horse, rode wildly through the crowd; firing his revolvers indiscriminately, and yelling like one possessed." After so much frenzied celebration, the guerrillas drifted off to sleep, one at a time until nearly the whole company was passed out. The chaotic scene might have given the sergeant an opportunity to escape, except that his guards were teetotalers—surely not the coincidence Goodman thought it to be.[31]

Goodman conflated violence and intoxication, especially the heavy drinking done by the bushwhackers and the brutality used in irregular warfare. While the guerrillas were destroying Johnston's command and then mutilating the corpses, he wondered if men could "grow drunk on blood." During the nocturnal revelry of Anderson's and Todd's bands, alcohol caused men to be in "bad humor" and generally led them to a state of "madness" and "savagery." In other words, just as gory violence could be intoxicating, binge drinking made men act brutally. As a soldier, Goodman knew that violence was necessary, but it was a well-ordered violence administered by sober men with their wits about them that was the appropriate, even righteous, way. Although he was probably not a drinker, the sergeant seemed to have accepted imbibing by other men in certain situations, though miles away from the front and detached from combat. In Goodman's mind, violence and alcohol should reside in different worlds, and never the twain shall meet. Such a mixture would be too much for any man, making him witless and primitive, even animalistic in his actions and urges.[32]

Modern analysis of the relationship between alcohol and violence help explain Goodman's anxiety. Ingesting alcohol can make violence a more acceptable response for men under the influence. Even those who have not been drinking can be put on edge by the presence of alcohol. In fact, without having had a drop of liquor, a man can become more likely to react in a violent way if he is surrounded by bottles of booze and a crowd of drunkards—not to mention gun-toting, murderous tipplers who have openly proclaimed their desire to kill you. Goodman was not only immersed in a company of men who were more likely to shoot him than they would be if they were sober but also was likely to have his back up and resist them by force. But he was never abused by his captors, let alone killed. Nor did the captive become so jumpy that he acted out against his intoxicated abductors.[33]

Exactly how alcohol affected the Centralia massacre was a different matter. For men like Burgess, who were not bushwhackers but joined them in drinking, the whiskey may have saved their lives. Although they were not initially targeted by the guerrillas, sharing a cordial with the raiders helped ease any tension between the strangers and even bond them together. With good feelings established between the guerrillas and the townspeople participating in the toasting and treating, a basic but fundamental level of trust was established, and some of the fear or skepticism that must have existed in both groups dissipated. To think about this in a different way, to refuse a drink from a guerrilla would be equivalent to rejecting a gift or denying a host his privilege of hospitality. Such an insult was interpreted as a declaration of war in the intensely personal guerrilla conflict. By raising the boot with Pool or any of his comrades, a man caught in the middle of the fighting greatly increased his chances of surviving their encounter with the wild men of the brush.[34]

While drinking saved some men, booze was in some degree responsible for the execution of Goodman's twenty-two comrades. Yet alcohol did not cause the massacre. By that point in the war, guerrillas were not taking prisoners. This was especially true of Anderson's men, who employed no quarter and mutilation as twin components of a strategy of fear against Union occupation forces. Typically, this type of guerrilla violence was experienced by armed combatants, men who had just surrendered, or notorious Union militiamen caught off guard at their homes or otherwise away from their garrison. To have a trainload of unarmed soldiers fall into their lap was an anomaly; their execution was not. While it may be going too far to suggest that the army was responsible for the deaths of Goodman's comrades, Union officers knew the form of violence that characterized guerrilla warfare in 1864, which made their decision to send uniformed men through the state unarmed a shocking act of negligence. That the guerrillas were drunk when the train arrived merely made them more pliable and accepting of the killing: it prevented any of them from stepping in to stop the massacre or suggest an alternative action, assuming that there was an alternative action.[35]

Of course, there was no alternative. It did not matter if men were blind drunk or were sober and clear minded—the bloodletting would go on. Drinking did matter in regard to the strength of the killers' psyches. They had to kill, but they did not have to do it sober and did not have to remember every waking moment of their bloody deeds, even if they were proud of them. If only a temporary departure, whiskey could separate men from their pasts. Moreover, whiskey brought these men together. Faced with weighty stress, they found relief in the emotional elevation brought about by communal drinking. These men sharing the sacred rite of the bottle together could endure any weight, take on larger and more powerful forces, and convince themselves that they could accomplish any feat. Whiskey could set them free from their nasty world and simultaneously join them together with their brothers and cousins in the brush. In their minds, alcohol was a necessary element of their war, but it did not cause it, nor did it make it bloodier.[36]

The guerrillas' binge eventually came to an end as they all do. Drunk on blood and alcohol, Anderson's gory bender came to an abrupt halt on October 26, 1864. His command was surprised by a Union patrol led by Indian tracker Samuel Cox, and rather than turn and run, Anderson charged headlong into the line of enemy soldiers, only to be shot down and killed. His decision to charge has been attributed to megalomania. Whether it was his contemporaries or historians, the belief is that Anderson's mind had slipped into a delusional space where he began to imagine that he truly could not be killed. Yet it seems highly unlikely that a man with the moniker "Bloody" could conceive of a world in which a man, no matter how special or unique, could not be shot, beaten, cut, burned, crushed, or hanged to death. That said, he must have seen the value in other men—both his followers and his enemies—thinking of him as somehow harder to kill than a normal person. It made convincing his followers to fight in the face of pain and almost certain death a little easier. The major drawback of making men believe that you could not be killed, however, was that the guerrilla leader had to perform the acts of an immortal—completely fearless, unaffected by the looming presence of death—and whiskey made such actions easier. As Anderson broke loose from his band on that fateful day, liquid courage coursed through his veins, enough to make a man feel as if he could live forever.

* * *

For Anderson, there would be no hangover. The men who survived the guerrilla war in western Missouri, however, would not be so lucky. Although most of the conventional armies of the Confederacy surrendered in the spring of 1865, hostilities continued in Missouri. Many of the irregulars stayed in the brush or returned to the brush intermittently during the postwar years. Using the same tactics that had been so successful during the formal conflict, they harassed and killed Unionists and blacks, destroyed Unionist-owned banks and companies, and used the threat of violence to influence local politics. During the fall of 1866, the town of Lexington became a focal point of the struggle between the guerrillas and the Republican-led state authorities. Here, the guerrillas were able to successfully prevent the election of local Republicans despite their own inability to vote.[37]

Alcohol was as much a part of this phase of the war as it had been before the spring of 1865. On December 13, 1866, liquor would break the stalemate between the guerrillas and the state authority. J. M. Turley, lieutenant colonel of the state militia, was sent to Lexington by Governor Thomas Fletcher with three companies of locally raised troops—two companies of black infantrymen and one company of white cavalrymen. Under instruction from the governor, Turley employed a new strategy: he would try to avoid a direct confrontation while ending the state's passive, defensive posture in its attempts to mollify the guerrillas. Turley rode out to a nearby field and met with Dave Pool—now the overall commander of the guerrillas around Lexington—and two other leaders, Jesse and Frank James. The bushwhackers were probably surprised by Turley's proposition: he wanted them to join the militia. The three guerrillas agreed to his terms. To the surprise of the townspeople, a column of 115 irregulars rode into Lexington later that day and made their way to the courthouse, where they were sworn in and signed their names to the militia roll. Immediately following their enrollment, Turley led his new company of galvanized militia to a store, where he "ordered a case of whiskey," lined the men up, and treated them all to a drink. Whiskey was a sure way to warm the heart of a bushwhacker.[38]

One man refused to toast with a Unionist. As Turley was passing the whiskey around, he "heard some one ask, 'where is Arch Clements?' One of the James boys said he was at Cather's Hotel drunk; and Dave Pool remarked that he would get killed before he got out of town." Turley then heard that Clements had not enrolled in the militia. Since he had a warrant for him, the officer was forced to go and try to arrest the infamous bushwhacker. With another man, Turley went to Cather's Hotel and found that "Clements was drunk," standing at the bar talking to James Cather, a Southerner who had fought with Brigadier General Jo Shelby during the war. Reluctantly, Turley approached Little Arch from behind, put his hand on the guerrilla's shoulder, and told him he was under arrest. In a flash Clements spun around, drew his revolvers, and fired both of them point blank into either side of his would-be captor. "Flesh wounds just above the hips" was how Turley remembered the effect of Clements's pistols. Arch then made his way for the door, "firing as he went." The guerrilla was shot in the shoulder by Turley's companion, George Moses, forcing him to drop the gun in his right hand. Although he was still blasting away with the gun in his left hand, Clements "was so drunk his aim was not true."[39]

Drunk and bleeding, Clements stumbled into the street. With Turley in pursuit, he made his way down the street and around a corner to where his horse was tied up. Clements mounted his horse, placed the reins in his teeth, and continued to fire with his good hand. Turley leapt onto his own horse, and the two commenced a wild, running firefight through Lexington. At one point Clements's horse took a spill on a slippery sidewalk but was able to get up and keep galloping. Now, however, Turley was right on his tail. The officer fired six balls into the back of Clements. Eventually, after a half-mile more, the guerrilla fell from his horse. Turley dismounted and pounced on Clements, who was trying to cock his pistol with his teeth. Feeling no pain, the intoxicated man refused to give up the fight despite wounds that would prove mortal.[40]

Clements was belligerent to the very end. After Turley took away his pistol, he noticed that his quarry's "eyes were glassy and said to him, 'Arch, you are dying. What do you want me to do with you?'" According to the officer, Clements uttered, "I've done what I always said I'd do,—die before I'd surrender." That was not all, though. "Take me back to Cather's Hotel" was the dying man's last request—almost certainly for one more drink. Several men helped load Clements into an ambulance; Turley placed the guerrilla's head in his lap. As Clements lay in the back of the wagon, being rocked and jostled about, numbed by alcohol and chilled by the loss of blood, his muscles seized for the last time before going limp. No longer in need of one more potation to ease him into the unknown, he was taken to the courthouse. When inspecting the corpse, Turley noted that the man was wearing the overcoat of a Federal cavalryman and was carrying a Bowie knife fourteen inches in length, objects that would seem to confirm his dying sentiments: he was a guerrilla until the bitter end. Turley then had the mud and blood washed off the body, and just as they had done with his mentor, Bloody Bill Anderson, and would do fifteen years later with his protégé Jesse James, they propped him up "in a big chair on the porch" and took a picture of the notorious bushwhacker. Turley and his men probably raised a glass knowing that Clements would drink no more.[41]

Eventually, after a long and painful hangover, Missouri's guerrilla war ended. Whether we mark the end of the conflict with the death of Clements and the absorption of Pool's rebels into the militia or with the assassination of Jesse James, the lingering agony eventually subsided. The damage was done, though. With a bottle in one hand and a Colt Navy revolver in the other, the guerrillas made their particular brand of warfare the deadliest, bloodiest, and longest lasting of the Civil War. It would be a mistake to think that whiskey was the cause of the violence, however. It would be equally misguided to think that being drunk was simply an excuse or an alibi. Rather, alcohol made these men capable of waging the type of nasty, destructive warfare that was required of them. While some men were more damaged by the whiskey than others—alcohol caused its fair share of problems—in and of itself, the liquor was neither good nor bad. Instead, in the hands of an experienced drinker, whiskey was a tool that could be used to either sharpen a man or to take the edge off. In the right hands, alcohol could be used by a guerrilla to maintain and even perfect the most deadly weapon of the war—man.

NOTES

I would especially like to thank Bruce Bartholow, a good friend and professor of psychology at the University of Missouri, for teaching me a great deal about alcohol and violence from the perspective of a psychologist. He provided invaluable guidance in developing this essay and did much to improve it. Also, I would be remiss if I did not thank the innumerable bartenders who provided inspiration for this piece.

1. Account of R. M. Burgess in "An Oft Told Story," *Paris Mercury,* reprinted in *Shelbyville (Mo.) Herald,* Oct. 27, 1897.

2. Ibid.; Goodrich, *Black Flag,* 139–42. His name also appears as "Poole."

3. W. F. Bassett, "The Famous Centralia Fight: The Old Story Related with Variations, Graphic Account of Bill Anderson's Famous Raid," *St. Joseph (Mo.) Argus,* n.d., in Jim Cummins, *Jim Cummins's Book Written by Himself* (Denver: Reed, 1903), 62–67; Thomas Goodman, *A Thrilling Record: Founded on Facts and Observations Obtained during Ten Days' Experience with Colonel William T. Anderson* (Des Moines: Mills, 1868), 27. For histories examining alcohol during the antebellum period, see W. J. Rorabaugh, *The Alcoholic Republic: An American Tradition* (New York: Oxford University Press, 1979); Mark Edward Lender and James Kirby Martin, *Drinking in America: A History* (New York: Free Press, 1987); and Eric Burns, *The Spirits of America: A Social History of Alcohol* (Philadelphia: Temple University Press, 2004).

4. Fellman, *Inside War,* 144. For other studies of the guerrilla conflict that comment on the guerrillas' drinking but offer little explicit analysis, see Brownlee, *Gray Ghosts of the Confederacy,* 124, 216; Castel, *William Clarke Quantrill,* 10, 46, 56, 134, 153; and Sutherland, *Savage Conflict,* 142, 159.

5. *Manufactures of the United States in 1860, Compiled from the Original Returns of the Eight Census* (Washington: Government Printing Office, 1863), 317–18; *Agriculture of the United States in 1860; Compiled from the Original Returns of the Eighth Census* (Washington: Government Printing Office, 1864), 94.

6. Rorabaugh, *Alcoholic Republic,* 95–122. In his study of alcohol in Appalachia, Bruce Stewart contends that there were some inroads made by the temperance movement in the antebellum South. But those who joined the movement seemed to be confined to the burgeoning middle class, which was sprouting up mostly in urban areas. See Stewart, *Moonshiners and Prohibitionists: The Battle over Alcohol in Southern Appalachia* (Lexington: University Press of Kentucky, 2011), 31–60.

7. For a study of the various ways in which people believe that alcohol creates changes in the drinker, both positive and negative, see Barbara Critchlow, "The Powers of John Barleycorn: Beliefs about the Effects of Alcohol on Social Behavior," *American Psychologist* 41, no. 7 (July 1986): 751–64. References to drinking appear in all of the major historical sources of the guerrilla war. Guerrillas spoke of imbibing in their memoirs. Using "whiskey" as the search term, a keyword search of the provost marshal records of Missouri reveals 268 hits. Even the *Official Records,* the very bedrock of military history for the Civil War, makes mention of booze. With hardly any digging at all, one can discover that alcohol was a fact of life for the guerrillas, their supporters, and the Union army. For a survey of guerrilla writings, see Babe Watts, *Babe of the Company: An Unfolded Leaf from the Forest of Never To-Be-Forgotten Years* (Fayette, Mo.: Democrat-Leader Press, 1913); Samuel S. Hildebrand, *Autobiography of Samuel S. Hildebrand: The Renowned Missouri Bushwhacker* (Fayetteville: University of Arkansas Press, 2005); John McCorkle, *Three Years with Quantrill: A True Story Told by His Scout,* written by O. S. Barton (1914; reprint, Norman: University of Oklahoma Press, 1992); William H. Gregg, "A Little Dab of History without Embellishment," Western Historical Manuscript Collection, Columbia, Mo.; Cole Younger, *The Autobiography of Cole Younger* (1903; reprint, New

York: Fireship, 2007); James Cummings, *Jim Cummins, The Guerrilla* (Excelsior Springs, Mo.: Daily Journal, 1908); Joanne Chiles Eakin, *Recollections of Quantrill's Guerrillas: As Told by A. J. Walker of Weatherford, Texas to Victor E. Martin in 1910* (Independence, Mo.: Two Trails, 1996) (hereafter, Walker, *Recollections of Quantrill's Guerrillas*); Harrison Trow, *Charles W. Quantrell: A True History of his Guerrilla Warfare on the Missouri and Kansas Border during the Civil War of 1861 to 1865,* ed. and written by J. P. Burch (Vega: J. P. Burch, 1923); Sidney Drake Jackman, *Behind Enemy Lines: The Memoirs and Writings of Brigadier General Sidney Drake Jackman* (Springfield, Mo.: Oak Hills, 1997); Bailey, *Confederate Guerrilla;* U.S. War Department, *War of the Rebellion,* http://ehistory.osu.edu/books/official-records (hereafter cited as *O.R.*); Missouri's Union Provost Marshal Papers: 1862–1866, Missouri Digital Heritage, http://www.sos.mo.gov/Records/Archives/ArchivesDb/provost; and Rorabaugh, *Alcoholic Tradition.*

8. Walker, *Recollections of Quantrill's Guerrillas,* 2, 35, 62.

9. *O.R.,* ser. 1, 28:72.

10. Thomas P. Lowry, *Irish & German, Whiskey & Beer: Drinking Patterns in the Civil War* (CreateSpace, 2011).

11. Lowry lists fifty-three terms for drinking-related charges brought against men. Ibid., 89–92.

12. Ibid., 5–12.

13. For a description of order, organization, and discipline within the guerrilla ranks, see Beilein, *Bushwhackers,* 50–110.

14. Walker, *Recollections of Quantrill's Guerrillas,* 36.

15. Ibid., 24.

16. Ibid., 64; Beilein, *Bushwhackers,* 78–110.

17. Beilein, *Bushwhackers,* 78–110. For the definitive study of Anderson, see Castel and Goodrich, *Bloody Bill Anderson.*

18. Walker, *Recollections of Quantrill's Guerrillas,* 80–81.

19. For a summary of the events over the winter of 1863–64, see Castel, *William Clarke Quantrill,* 155–72.

20. *O.R.,* ser. 1, 38:430.

21. Letters, Fletch Taylor to W. W. Scott, File 3, Box 1, Ser. 1, William Elsay Connelley Collection, Denver Public Library.

22. Castel, *William Clarke Quantrill,* 164–67.

23. Ibid., 155–72.

24. In recent years, quite a bit of important scholarship has been undertaken to understand exactly how alcohol shapes human behavior. Psychologists confirm the long-held belief that alcohol consumption "frees" people from their memories or the stresses of their day-to-day existence. See especially Catharine E. Fairbairn and Michael A. Sayette, "The Effect of Alcohol on Emotional Inertia: A Test of Alcohol Myopia," *Journal of Abnormal Psychology* 122, no. 3 (2013): 770–81.

25. *O.R.,* ser. 1, 60:528.

26. Edwards, *Noted Guerrillas,* 54; Gregg, "Little Dab of History," 18–19.

27. Unlabeled photograph, Prints and Photographs Collection, Library of Congress, Washington, D.C.

28. Goodman, *Thrilling Record,* 28–29. Unfortunately, the record is silent on the precise amount of whiskey imbibed by Pool or his comrades, so any analysis of their digestion and processing of

alcohol would lack this critical data. Furthermore, the reasons for variations in tolerance for alcohol consumption and digestion are still unclear. Yet studies suggest that the two major factors in the "level of response" to alcohol (or "alcohol sensitivity") are genetics and degree of drinking experience. At this time, it is generally accepted that genetics is responsible for 40–60 percent of the variability between people in their response to alcohol. See Meghan E. Morean and William R. Corbin, "Subjective Response to Alcohol: A Critical Review of the Literature," *Alcoholism: Clinical and Experimental Research* 34, no. 3 (Mar. 2010): 385–95; and Patrick D. Quinn and Kim Fromme, "Subjective Response to Alcohol Challenge: A Quantitative Review," *Alcoholism: Clinical and Experimental Research* 35, no. 10 (Oct. 2011): 1759–70.

29. For a summary of the events that unfolded at Centralia, see Castel and Goodrich, *Bloody Bill Anderson,* 79–98; and Stiles, *Jesse James,* 119–27.

30. Castel and Goodrich, *Bloody Bill Anderson,* 79–98; Stiles, *Jesse James,* 119–27; Goodman, *Thrilling Record,* 34–35.

31. Goodman, *Thrilling Record,* 47–48. Whether or not the guerrilla chief would risk being discovered by firing his guns for no reason is up for debate. It is possible they knew their place to be safe from discovery, even with such a ruckus.

32. Ibid., 34–35, 47–48.

33. The relationship between violence and alcohol consumption is an important topic for social psychologists, and their conclusions inform the analysis here. For some of the cutting-edge work in this area, see Bruce Bartholow and Adrienne Heinz, "Alcohol and Aggression without Consumption: Alcohol Cues, Aggressive Thoughts, and Hostile Perception Bias," *Psychological Science* 17 (2006): 30–37; Ronald Friedman, Denis McCarthy, Bruce Bartholow, and Joshua Hicks, "Interactive Effects of Alcohol Outcome Expectancies and Alcohol Cues on Nonconsumptive Behavior," *Experimental and Clinical Psychology* 15, no. 1 (2007): 102–14; and William C. Pederson, Eduardo A. Vasquez, Bartholow, Marianne Grosvenor, and Ana Truong, "Are You Insulting Me?: Exposure to Alcohol Primes Increases Aggression Following Ambiguous Provocation," *Personality and Social Psychology Bulletin* 40, no. 8 (2014): 1037–49.

34. Michael A. Sayette, Kasey G. Creswell, John D. Dimoff, Catherine E. Fairbairn, Jeffrey F. Cohn, Bryan W. Heckman, Thomas R. Kircher, John M. Levine, and Richard L. Moreland, "Alcohol and Group Formation: A Multimodal Investigation of the Effects of Alcohol on Emotion and Social Bonding," *Psychological Science* 20 (2012): 1–10.

35. Bartholow and Heinz, "Alcohol and Aggression without Consumption"; Friedman et al., "Interactive Effects of Alcohol Outcome Expectancies and Alcohol Cues on Nonconsumptive Behavior"; Pederson et al., "Are You Insulting Me?"

36. For a summary of the escalation of violence and brutality, see Beilein, *Bushwhackers,* 215–41

37. Statement of J. M. Turley, William Elsay Connelley Collection, Denver Public Library, Denver, Colo.; Stiles, *Jesse James,* 149–87.

38. Statement of J. M. Turley; Stiles, *Jesse James,* 184–85.

39. Statement of J. M. Turley. Turley actually had warrants for several of the men, but their enrollment in the militia placed them back in the good graces of the government. Stiles, *Jesse James,* 185–87.

40. Statement of J. M. Turley.

41. Ibid.

LARKIN M. SKAGGS AND THE MASSACRE(S) AT LAWRENCE

MATTHEW C. HULBERT

In the predawn heat of August 21, 1863, a lone rider in possession of vital intelligence set out from his home on the outskirts of Eudora, Kansas. Soon after and without warning, the horse faltered at full gallop; man and beast tumbled to the ground as one. The weight of his crippled mount crushed the body of Mr. J. Reed beyond the restorative powers of medicine in mid-nineteenth-century America; he died early the next day. Reed's precious information—that the dreaded guerrilla leader William Clarke Quantrill and several hundred Missouri bushwhackers had last been seen riding in the direction of Lawrence, Kansas—never made it to the unsuspecting town. Later that morning, for want of a horse's footing, the townspeople of Lawrence would pay dearly in human life and property.[1] How to remember what transpired there has been studied and contested for more than 150 years.

* * *

When Quantrill and his men reached Lawrence around sunrise on the morning of August 21, their total force measured roughly three hundred. (Some estimates range as high as five hundred, but such claims are unsubstantiated.) Most of the town's residents were still in their beds—soon awakened to the jarring discord of hooves pounding, men whooping and shouting, and revolvers reporting. The guerrillas immediately bore down on camps occupied by new recruits of the Fourteenth Kansas Regiment and the Second Kansas Colored Volunteers. Hopelessly outnumbered, lacking in arms, and caught entirely off guard, these troops in training could offer no effective resistance and were slaughtered. With their would-be protectors routed, civilians in Lawrence had to fend for themselves.[2]

To more efficiently traverse the town, guerrillas next split into smaller detachments. They moved from street to street, building to building, looting businesses, pillaging and torching houses, and gunning down men (and boys) of all ages. For his part, after a visit to the Eldridge Hotel, Quantrill watched most of the assault unfold from atop Mount Oread, a steep hill that overlooks Lawrence, now as then. He observed victory—militarily, psychologically, materially—in virtually every sense of the word: sobbing women and children ran for the shelter of cornfields; smoke enveloped the town as Massachusetts Street and surrounding blocks went up in flames; guerrillas dragged men outside and executed them, while still more victims were simply shot within their homes and left to burn.[3]

According to official reports, guerrillas burned more than 182 buildings—80 of them brick and 65 on Massachusetts Street alone. Estimates of the material damage typically hover around $2 million in 1863 currency (approximately $38 million in 2013 currency). That said, the tolls exacted in human life and emotional trauma far exceeded any ledgers of material or economic ruin. Quantrill's raid ultimately claimed around two hundred male inhabitants of Lawrence. Victims were both white and black—though in some cases, race was useless when attempting to identify the dead because the remains were literally charred beyond recognition. From merchants to farmers, doctors, and even mere schoolboys, the slain had hailed from all tiers of society. Even Reverend Snyder of the United Brethren Church was found "riddled with bullets." Newly made widows numbered approximately eighty, newly made orphans, 250. By any metric, the raid on Lawrence truly was a massacre.[4]

While the fighting, however one-sided, lasted only a few hours, the battle to control how it could and should be remembered began almost immediately—and has continued to rage ever since. On one side, defenders of Quantrill and his pro-Confederate guerrillas frequently contended (and still contend) that the collapse of a makeshift Union prison for women in Kansas City triggered the brutal assault. The building in question, owned by the artist George Caleb Bingham, literally imploded, killing or crippling the female kin of several bushwhackers, including the sisters of William "Bloody Bill" Anderson. Moreover, the pro-Quantrill camp asserted that Lawrence, as a hotbed of abolitionism, had functioned as a headquarters for slave-kidnappers and Unionist guerrillas called "jayhawkers" who had been harassing law-abiding Missourians since the 1850s.[5]

On the other side, critics of Quantrill and the Lawrence Massacre, including survivors, have argued that the guerrillas had begun plotting to destroy the town well before the collapse of the Kansas City prison—which, they maintained, had been an unfortunate accident. Furthermore, Unionists opined that Quantrill and his men had represented little more than border trash: banditti, deserters, and sociopaths who utilized the chaos of war to slake their ghoulish desires. Finally, and perhaps most important of all, detractors of the August 21 assault firmly believed that Lawrence had never constituted a legitimate military target. According to one survivor, the Reverend Richard Cordley: "The killing was indiscriminate and mostly in cold blood. . . . [T]here was no provocation and no resistance." As such, the pinnacle achievement of Quantrill's career as a would-be Confederate commander had, in reality, been an unprecedented act of mass murder, not a stunningly lopsided martial operation waged in the context of a Confederate war effort.[6]

The immediate aftermath of the raid proved no less controversial. Newspaper headlines from Kansas to New York announced "The Burning of Lawrence!" One article, printed by the *Daily Times* of Leavenworth, Kansas, the day after the massacre, lamented that "Kansas has been invaded and many of her best citizens murdered by rebel outlaws from Missouri." "Justice," the paper declared, "cries aloud for vengeance and expiation. The destruction of Lawrence must be avenged . . . and woe betide their [Quantrill's guerrillas] sympathizers all along the border." The article concluded by avowing that "the sword of vengeance is unsheathed; let it not rest or be stayed from its fearful mission, until it has purchased at the cost of much blood, *perfect* immunity from such terrible calamities as have befallen our State in the burning of Lawrence."[7]

Just a few days later, the Union army did draw its "sword of vengeance." In direct reaction to the assault on Lawrence and as part of a wider effort to stamp out pro-Confederate guerrilla activity emanating from western Missouri once and for all, Brigadier General Thomas Ewing issued General Orders No. 11 on August 25, 1863. The edict was specifically designed to strike at the families of guerrillas in the field: it required rural residents of Jackson, Cass, and Bates Counties, along with portions of Vernon County, who could not explicitly prove their loyalty to the Union to remove themselves from the district within fifteen days. In short, if Ewing's troops could not catch up with Quantrill's raiders and their ilk, the immobile kin of the guerrillas would pay the price for their irregular activities. Virtually none could meet the loyalty requirements; left unguarded, the homes and farms of exiled Missourians were frequently pillaged and burned by jayhawkers. The targeting and expulsion of civilians drew heavy criticism in Missouri and abroad, but many Kansans lauded the measure as just retribution for the Lawrence Massacre.[8]

Interpreting Ewing's General Orders No. 11 as "official" proof that Quantrill's raid was an illegal atrocity that had prompted unprecedented action against the families of his men, Unionist Kansans—many based in Lawrence—gradually crafted a narrative in which they had been completely innocent of any provocation prior to the massacre and helpless to defend themselves militarily as it unfolded. They constructed a moral dualism that juxtaposed their own pure, righteous, honorable behavior with the hellish intentions and dastardly conduct of the invading bushwhackers. Pro-Unionist partisans felt that such an immediate and absolute seizure of the moral high ground would afford them the best opportunity to control the massacre's long-term legacy and, by extension, the legacy of their most-reviled foe: William Clarke Quantrill.

By way of speeches, pamphlets, newspaper articles, books, reunion ceremonies, and other commemorative activities, Kansans made a concerted effort to tout Lawrence as a refuge for innocent and peace-loving people—as a place literally "founded in the spirit of human liberty." At the same time, they depicted the Missouri guerrillas as "ruffians" and "perpetrators of inhuman butchery" whose behavior in Lawrence "was characterized by the most cowardly barbarism." The most damning imagery was reserved for Quantrill: "He made his name a Cain's mark and a curse to those condemned to bear it. . . . [B]ecause of him widows wailed, orphans cried, maidens wept, as they lifted the lifeless forms of loved ones from bloody fields and bore them reeking to untimely graves." In short, the architect of the Lawrence Massacre should forever be remembered as a "gory monster" with a "thirst for blood" that "towered above the men of his time."[9]

With all of this in mind, the story of one particular guerrilla's demise, a man named Larkin Milton Skaggs, posed a serious threat to this commemorative agenda—not despite his death, as one might expect, but because of it. Speaking plainly, the people of Lawrence had butchered Skaggs and defiled his corpse. And now in the interest of preserving a commemorative strategy founded upon wholesomeness and victimhood, they needed to explain the *other* massacre that took place in their town on August 21, 1863.

* * *

The vast majority of the guerrillas who followed Quantrill to Lawrence were native-born Missourians. Military historian Don R. Bowen notes that the average age of a guerrilla in western Missouri (Quantrill's prime recruitment pipeline) was just twenty, and the majority of them had another blood relation—most often a brother or cousin—active in the guerrilla war. Oftentimes, young bushwhackers, despite the lowly connotation of their title, were the scions of relatively well-to-do slaveholding families with clear Confederate sympathies.[10]

Based on these criteria, Larkin Skaggs was an enigma from the moment he joined Quantrill's command. Skaggs hailed from Kentucky. There he had served as a Baptist preacher, of all things, before swapping Bible for revolver; emigrating from Green County, Kentucky, to Cass County, Missouri; and wading headlong into the border conflict of the 1850s that became known as "Bleeding Kansas." Born in 1831, Skaggs was thirty-two years old at the time of the Lawrence Massacre. Thus, while still a relatively young man by modern standards, he was significantly older than nearly all of his comrades, including even Quantrill, who was twenty-seven in 1863 and himself an elder among his men.[11]

By the summer of the "Great Raid," Quantrill's regulars were well versed in what historian Joseph M. Beilein Jr. has dubbed "household warfare."[12] Within this system of waging irregular war at the community and neighborhood levels, guerrillas lacked formal linkages to the Confederate government and intentionally ranged close to home. Therein men fought from the bush while the women of their kinship networks—wives, sisters, mothers, cousins, and grandmothers—worked as quartermasters and spies, providing both accouterments and intelligence. Instead of pitched, Napoleonic battles, they targeted houses, barns, stores, and even churches; domestic environs in which arson, torture, rape, murder, and massacre all fell within the normal bounds of irregular combat. Guerrillas used disguises, sprang roadside ambuscades, and carried out moonlit raids. And they fully understood the correlation of speed and mobility to survival, favoring revolver over rifled musket and superior horseflesh over fortification.[13]

Yet even among the grizzled veterans of household war—men renowned for generating terror up and down the Missouri-Kansas border—Skaggs's résumé was again unique. He had not only been to Lawrence before, he had actually helped sack it. In May 1856, as part of a mob of proslavery zealots, Skaggs had viewed the town as the epicenter of abolitionism in the Border West and as a haven for slave-kidnapping jayhawkers; as recompense, he and his cohorts torched the Free State Hotel, plundered homes, and razed newspaper offices before finally disappearing back into Missouri.[14] So in August 1863, as Quantrill dreamed of notching a major victory for the Confederacy and establishing himself as a bona fide field commander, Skaggs planned to finish what he had started seven years before: the utter ruination of Lawrence. Fulfilling this quest would cost the holy-man-turned-marauder his life.

Details of the objective variety are scant concerning Skaggs's execution and what became of his remains. Foremost among them: he was the only man from Quantrill's command killed *during* the Lawrence Massacre. (Others were hunted down and killed after the fact, but only Skaggs fell while actually raiding the town.)[15] Skaggs was captured in the surrounding countryside but later executed within the town proper. It is clear that he became separated from the rest of Quantrill's command, unsuccessfully fled from Lawrence upon realizing this, and was brought back under arms to meet his death. Finally, Skaggs's body was grotesquely mutilated and then never formally interred.[16] As fellow guerrilla William H. Gregg said of this handling years later in 1912, no Kansan killed at Lawrence had been "treated with the cruelty Jim Skaggs was subjected to who was captured by the 'red legs.'"[17]

From these basic facts, many more questions emerge. Who actually pulled the trigger that killed Larkin Skaggs? Who authorized the desecration of his corpse? Most critically, what might the responses to those queries—or perhaps the inability of historians to provide them—explain about how memories of the Lawrence Massacre and guerrilla warfare on the Missouri-Kansas borderlands have been constructed and interpreted for decades?

For this, we will examine the four most extensive accounts of Skaggs's debauchery and downfall in Lawrence on August 21, 1863. All recorded in the early 1900s, they are the pieced-together narrative of a pseudohistorian, the testimonial of a freedman who witnessed Skaggs's death, the newspaper editorial of a white man who survived the massacre, and the speech of yet another surviving witness delivered in commemoration of the raid's fiftieth anniversary. By "reading between the lines" of these sources, new light can be shone on the morbid saga of Larkin Skaggs, and the process dissected through which individual recollections were gradually amalgamated to form a collective narrative.

Additionally, this also works to reconcile Quantrill's raid with the cutting-edge understandings of household warfare, domestic trauma, and guerrilla memory. Historians of guerrilla warfare habitually point to the Lawrence

Massacre as both the best-known irregular incident of the Civil War and the one least representative of how Civil War guerrillas generally operated. By reapplying the commemorative principles gleaned from the story behind the Skaggs story, we can reinterpret the Lawrence Massacre as a series of massacres and take new stock of how and where it fits within the broader corpus of guerrilla studies.

* * *

With *Quantrill and the Border Wars,* published in 1909, William E. Connelley offered the first widely disseminated account of Larkin Skaggs's behavior and death in Lawrence. As Connelley told the story, Quantrill and his men abandoned the town after a few hours, but Skaggs, with two other guerrillas, "rode back to the City Hotel, called out the landlord Mr. Stone, and shot him dead." Having murdered Stone, Skaggs and his pair of companions rode to catch up with the rest of the command but again detoured. They stopped at the home of John Speer, a prominent citizen in Lawrence well known as the publisher of a local newspaper. Skaggs and company "brutally treated his [Speer's] wife, holding her by the wrists while they fired the house." When enough smoke had accumulated to make breathing inside the structure impossible, the guerrillas dragged Mrs. Speer outside and refused to let her extinguish the flames." Next, Connelley added, Skaggs and his followers "robbed her of a pair of little gold armlets belonging to her dead babe." (Unknown to Mrs. Speer, Skaggs had already robbed and then gunned down another one of her sons earlier in the day.)[18]

Exiting the Speer house, Skaggs and company again looked to link up with Quantrill and the rest of the retreating guerrilla band. This time, however, the trio ran into a group of farmers riding in the nearby countryside. During the course of this encounter, William Speer (the third son of John Speer and his wife) "appeared upon the scene with a loaded rifle he had found." William had informed his mother that his two younger brothers, John Jr. and Robert, had been murdered, and hearing this she replied: "There is one of them—go and shoot him." On his mother's orders, William fired at Skaggs, who then fled from the group of farmers that had cut off his escape route. Connelley contended, based on personal interviews and the testimony of witnesses to the scene, that Speer's shot found its mark, and "the dust flew out from where the ball struck

Skaggs in the shoulder-blade." That said, Connelley credited Skaggs's actual death to another man, a Delaware Indian named White Turkey. As Connelley's rendition of the story ends, immediately after Speer fired his rifle, White Turkey exclaimed, "Oh! He kill everybody! Me kill him!" and then shot Skaggs through the heart with a bow and arrow, killing the cornered guerrilla in his tracks.[19]

Connelley's narrative of events is problematic to say the least. For one, the guerrilla's two companions vanish without a trace, calling into question whether or not Skaggs had actually been by himself all along. This possibility—which is actually quite likely correct—recasts his capture and execution significantly; instead of a violent standoff between dangerous parties, it takes the shape of an individual lynched by a much larger group, or as its own separate massacre. Moreover, description of the fatal shot by the usually detail-oriented, adjective-loving Connelley was uncharacteristically concise and does not even chronicle the spot where Skaggs's body fell lifeless to the ground. Most interesting of all, however, is that as part of this inexplicable ambiguity on the matter, Connelley also allowed—perhaps just a little too conveniently—a Native American (White Turkey), instead of the white William Speer, to take ultimate responsibility for killing Skaggs and *not* turning him over to Union military authorities as a captured Confederate bushwhacker.

It warrants mention that Connelley was a vehement critic of Quantrill and of rebel guerrillas in general. So it is not altogether surprising that he would relegate to a footnote what the people of Lawrence did to Skaggs's body postmortem. In that citation, well before he began to reveal the ceremonial mutilation of Skaggs's corpse, Connelley first paused to remind readers that the guerrilla had been a man of ill repute, a ne'er-do-well even among his own friends and family. "The author," he stated, "knew many of the relatives of Skaggs in Kentucky" and "knows that the family was a good one." Thus, while the details to follow would be gruesome for some readers, Skaggs's character in life and treatment after death somehow went hand in hand. Even then, Connelley avoided trying to justify outright the "indignities to which his body was subjected." He called the mutilation of Skaggs's corpse "barbarous and inexcusable" before immediately proffering an excuse that such behavior "never would have been permitted in Lawrence at any other time" than right after the massacre. "Resentment," Connelley concluded, "should have stopped at death and would have done so but for the excitement under which the people labored after that bloody and terrible day."[20]

Granted, Connelley provided all of this text in a citation *before* actually exposing to readers what was done to the corpse—at which point he enlisted the published testimony of a third party and refused to verify the account with his own authorial voice. Thus, by way of C. M. Chase, who claimed to have witnessed everything, he reported that African American residents of Lawrence had outfitted the corpse with a noose, tied the rope to a saddle hitch, and then dragged the body up and down the streets while an excited crowd chased after the body and assaulted it with stones. "There was an attempt," Chase's account asserted, "by the negroes [*sic*] to burn the body, which was not successful." As a result, "the bones lay naked all winter in a ravine in the town," where "negroes and boys sawed finger rings from some of them." "No part of the body," he concluded, "was ever given burial." For his part, Connelley added nothing to Chase's description, nor did he take anything away.[21]

The next version of the story was penned in the early 1900s by Andrew Williams, a semiliterate former slave who had taken up residence in Lawrence by the time of the massacre and who, as a result, claimed to have witnessed the execution of Skaggs firsthand. It is worth noting that Williams's story is one of the few surviving accounts—if not the *only*—of an African American witness to the events at Lawrence. Also worthy of mention is the fact that he worked as Connelley's gardener in Topeka for three years, from 1908 to 1910.[22] Subsequently, it is virtually impossible to presume that Connelley, then working full-time on *Quantrill and the Border Wars,* would not have been aware of Williams's tale (or perhaps even influenced it). In fact, odds are quite good that his connection to Connelley is the only reason Williams wrote down his experiences in the first place. The closeness of their relationship, however, did not translate into their accounts emphasizing the same details—not by a long shot, actually.

According to Williams's handwritten log, he had been living in Lawrence for approximately five months when "Quantrell done his murdering." When the raid began, "a bout 400 men he [Quantrill] came right by our house it was a little after day light [they] had on all sorts of uniforms some in their Reed Shirt Sleeves." Like some of his neighbors, he thought Quantrill's men were actually Union soldiers until "one in the crowd broke ranks then they scattered in all directions." As the guerrillas swarmed the town, Williams reported, "we seen one Bushwacker call out one man and talking a minut to him they shot him downe."[23]

Then Williams turned his attention to Larkin Skaggs. "Thir was one of them that got so drunk he could not get away," he wrote. The guerrilla "was shoot in the Back of the head and the Ball come out through his mouth knocking all of his teeth out." And, Williams stated definitively, "it was William Sphear that shoot him" and delivered the death blow. With Skaggs dead, "they takn him and hitched a Rope around his beck and atached a horse and drug him all over town." Next, Skaggs's corpse was taken "down to a Revene" where the unnamed men in question "burned him up." Williams also disclosed another violent incident that played out in the wake of the raid. "The faew men that was lucky a nugh to scape and save their lives," he asserted, "found a man that was living in Lawrence at the time of the Rade" who had been seen helping bushwhackers locate the hiding places of men in town. In retribution, this man was apprehended, taken to a barn, and hanged. His captors "made him [step] up on a dry box and taken it out from under him and be four he was dead shot him half dozen times while hanging."[24]

Juxtaposed with Connelley's story, Williams's account presents striking differences. Chief among them, rather than claiming that a Delaware Indian dispatched Skaggs, the former slave stated that William Speer had shot and killed the guerrilla while the latter had been severely incapacitated by alcohol; White Turkey failed to even appear in his narrative. Additionally, while Connelley provided a footnote that related another man's account of the mutilation of Skaggs's body—one that claimed those responsible for the depredations were African American—Williams made no secret of the treatment unleashed upon the corpse nor did his testimony conclusively state, on way or the other, that the men responsible were black. These points concerning race are intriguing on their own; they become especially more so when combined with the fact that Connelley neglected to inform his readers that white men in Lawrence had apparently lynched *another* man, this time *not* one of Quantrill's guerrillas, in the aftermath of the raid. Such an allegation not only damaged the peace-loving image of Lawrence that Connelley had constructed, but it also undercut the "one time only" excuse he had provided for the abuse of Skaggs. With all of this in mind, the explanation as to why Connelley chose to cite the account of C. M. Chase rather than his own gardener seems quite clear.

As part of a twenty-five-page speech delivered at a reunion of Lawrence Massacre survivors in August 1913, S. A. Riggs detailed his personal encounter with Larkin Skaggs some fifty years earlier. The guerrilla, he recalled, "rode up to me where I was standing and as they all did, demanded my arms and money." After handing over what little paper currency he had left, Riggs struck up a "profitless discussion" with Skaggs, during which the raider actually attempted—unsuccessfully by Riggs's reckoning—to justify the attack. As the two men spoke, Skaggs remained atop his horse with a revolver strewn across his lap; at this point Riggs suggested that "he [Skaggs] was full of liquor which was showing its effect in his blinking eyes and occasional short periods of absent-mindedness."[25]

Intoxicated or not, as the conversation ended, Skaggs took hold of the revolver in his lap and raised it "within a foot of my [Riggs's] breast and pulled the trigger." The hammer snapped down, and much to the surprise of both men, the weapon failed to discharge. With Skaggs momentarily distracted by his malfunctioned firearm, Riggs made the most of his good luck and began wrestling with the guerrilla for control of the gun. According to Riggs, after a brief tussle, he decided to make a run for the shelter of a nearby side street.[26]

In this version of the story, as Skaggs wheeled his mount to give chase—a race that Riggs likely would have lost to the mounted guerrilla—Riggs's wife appeared from behind, "at once seized the bridle reins," and began yanking the horse around in circles. This act of bravery bought ample time for a successful getaway, and after Skaggs had spent a few minutes roaming the area in search of Riggs, the disoriented raider decided to take "a southeasterly course to find and join the command." Shortly thereafter, he was "intercepted by William Hughes and others coming from the east, and was run down and killed," with nearly $1,500 of stolen money in his possession.[27]

"Later that day," Riggs stated, "as I was going home to the west part of town I saw the iron grey horse on which Skaggs had been riding in the possession of a colored man who [was] riding it bareback and singing at the top of his voice 'John Brown's body lies mouldering in the grave.'" The unnamed African American "was dragging north through the dust of Massachusetts Street the naked body of a dead man—without doubt the body of a man [*sic*] Skaggs." "It was a terribly repulsive sight," Riggs concluded, "but seemingly a just retributive ending to his [Skaggs's] brutally savage work of the morning."[28]

Despite his very clear recollection of details related to a firsthand encounter with Skaggs, Riggs—unlike Connelley or Williams—suddenly became succinct when narrating the final moments of the guerrilla's life. He suggested that a party of mostly unnamed men intercepted the lost (and very inebriated) bushwhacker, chased him down, and killed him. From this telling, it is impossible to derive whether or not Skaggs was brought back to Lawrence (and we know that he was) or how his execution eventually took place. "Run down and killed," as Riggs put it, could have meant any number of possibilities.

Furthermore, Riggs's story did not place blame on White Turkey, the Delaware Indian who delivered Skaggs a final blow in Connelley's rendition, or on William Speer, the local boy who gunned down the fleeing guerrilla in Williams's account. Rather than dwelling on these potentially damning details, Riggs pivoted to the mutilation of the corpse, at which point he resumed the provision of minute details: the mistreatment of Skaggs's dead body had been spearheaded by jubilant African Americans in Lawrence. He even remembered the route of the triumphant procession as it dragged the corpse northward through the smoking ruins of Massachusetts Street, an end that, in Riggs's estimation, was "terribly repulsive" but ultimately fit for a brutal savage like Skaggs.

In September 1913 another survivor of the Lawrence Massacre named J. M. Henry provided his own version of Skaggs's execution to a local newspaper because, according to him, so many others contained incorrect information. He opened by stating that the guerrilla had become separated from the "main body" of Quantrill's command when they evacuated Lawrence and lingered for nearly half an hour on his own. The raiders rode due south out of town, he continued, but when it finally dawned on the "bewildered" Skaggs to beat his own retreat, he chose his direction poorly and "started east on the Eudora road."[29]

Along that road, Skaggs "discovered his mistake" after stumbling into a large group of men gathered near the farm of H. L. Enos. Recognizing that the guerrilla was lost and alone, "the farmers gave chase on their horses" and managed to wound Skaggs's mount. Unable to escape on a lame animal, he fell into the custody of the men, whose party, according to Henry, included Miles Walters, Thomas McFarland, Robert Peebles, and several others. It was Walters, Henry contended, who "had personal charge of Skaggs, having disarmed him." In any event, the farmers now led the captured guerrilla back to the smoking ruins of Lawrence.[30]

In town the group holding the prisoner merged with another crowd of enraged townspeople on horseback. Then a man described as "a volunteer soldier" allegedly rode up to Skaggs, struck him violently in the face, ordered him off his mount, and commanded him to make a run for it. "Skaggs immediately sprang from the horse and ran east toward the brush half a mile away," but the escape attempt had been doomed from the start. The soldier chased closely behind Skaggs and attempted to shoot him in the back of the head but missed. The powder from the shot, Henry noted, set fire to Skaggs's shirt, "which was still burning when we fell." At this, the rest of the group opened fire on the scrambling guerrilla; several shots found their mark, but Skaggs remained afoot and continued to flee for his life. Henry suggested that Skaggs, slowed by his wounds, made an easy target for White Turkey, the Delaware Indian, who proceeded to shoot an arrow through the bushwhacker's midsection. With the shaft protruding from his ribs, Skaggs *again* regained his footing, but another Indian, this one named Little Beaver, also a Delaware, "then shot with his big buffalo rifle," and at the crack of the gun Skaggs fell forward on his face. The last guerrilla left in Lawrence was apparently dead before he hit the ground.[31]

Little Beaver then approached the body of the fallen bushwhacker and removed his boots; they had supposedly been stolen during the raid hours earlier. The Indian also "turned Skaggs's pockets inside out but found nothing." Before leaving the scene, Little Beaver "caught Skaggs by the hair of the head" and before the assembled crowd "made a motion pretending to scalp him." As for himself, Henry claimed that he had had no desire to shoot at Skaggs personally because so many others did and would not have allowed the guerrilla to escape. He also confessed that, at the time of his capture and execution, Skaggs had been drunk. And in addition to his inebriation, the guerrilla "had no cartridges or ammunition to load his revolver and was completely without means of defense." Perhaps this is why the man in charge of Skaggs (Miles Walters), as Henry revealed toward the end of his story, "made a desperate effort to protect him, intending to turn him over to the sheriff of Douglas County." Either way, Henry was certain that Little Beaver had fired the fatal shot.[32]

While factually out of line with Connelley, Williams, and Riggs, Henry's story is equally illuminating; in more ways than one, it seems to reveal damning details about the Kansans despite itself. First, Henry asserted that he had been a firsthand witness to the whole event, but his testimony completely ignored the mutilation of the corpse. Next, he openly admitted that Skaggs had been both drunk and unarmed when captured and then forced to run for his life. Perhaps ashamed of the spectacular manner in which the townspeople gunned down the guerrilla, Henry rather weakly pinned the blame on a stranger, the unknown "volunteer soldier" who ordered Skaggs to run and began the entire process of execution.[33]

Moreover, this rendition not only places the responsibility for killing Skaggs on a nonwhite character, it actually introduces a second, Little Beaver, who is completely absent in *Quantrill and the Border Wars,* Williams's account, and Riggs's speech. In very suspicious fashion, Henry replaced the upstanding William Speer, the rifleman reported by Williams to have shot Skaggs to death, with a Native American while simultaneously offering that Walters, another respectable white man, had desperately wanted to do the morally correct thing and turn Skaggs over to the law for punishment. Therein J. M. Henry inadvertently let slip that, raid or no raid, massacring the raider in the street had been extralegal—a lynch mob, essentially—and that guilt needed to reside with an Indian, not a member of the white Speer family or any other white residents of Lawrence possibly involved in the shooting.[34]

After probing each account in turn and then as a collective, what truths concerning the death of Larkin M. Skaggs surface? Only one: that Skaggs, at one point the massacre's most eager predator, by raid's end had become prey himself—a victim of the very style of violence he had let loose upon the people of Lawrence. Aside from this, it is extremely likely that William Speer fired the fatal shot. William's own father, John Speer, penned a newspaper article just days after the massacre—before the whitewashing could begin—confirming that his son had killed Skaggs. Moreover, if actually present, White Turkey and Little Beaver probably played no seminal role in the killing. And a mob of white *and* black residents of Lawrence almost certainly participated in the mutilation of the bushwhacker's corpse.[35]

Modern authors, perhaps the most successful of which is Edward Leslie, have settled on a version of the story that borrows elements from all four accounts. In *The Devil Knows How to Ride: The True Story of William Clarke Quantrill,* published in 1996, he offered a rendition in which:

> A party of men who were in pursuit of Quantrill spotted him [Skaggs] and gave chase, turning him so that he raced northeast toward Eudora. His horse was very strong and fast and, cutting across fields and brakes and jumping fences, gradually pulled away from the pursuers. Skaggs might have gotten away except he ran into a small party of men in a lane in front of him. He was disarmed, knocked from his horse, and herded back toward town.... Speer stepped out into the street and started toward the crowd just as Skaggs managed to break free and run toward him. Billy drew a bead on

> the drunken preacher, who was only ten feet away and closing, and hit him in the shoulder, dropping him. White Turkey, one of a party of Delaware Indians who were passing through town in pursuit of the raiders, put an arrow into Skaggs's chest and then scalped him. Other men then cut loose with their firearms. . . . His body was hung from a tree, and vengeful survivors pelted it with stones and riddled it with lead. The next day some blacks cut it down and dragged it behind a horse—just as he had dragged the U.S. flag behind his horse—while a mob ran behind, throwing rocks at it. When all the clothes and skin had been worn off, the blacks threw what was left of the corpse into a ravine and set it on fire. The bones were left for scavengers. Sometimes during the following winter small boys visited the ravine and broke off the finger bones to retrieve Skaggs's rings.[36]

The consolidation of plot elements and racial symbolism in Leslie's writing is unmistakable. After a party of men captured Skaggs and dragged him back to town, he made a run for his life. As the guerrilla ran, William Speer wounded him in the shoulder with a rifle, which allowed White Turkey to move in for the kill and to claim Skaggs's scalp. Following the bushwhacker's execution, a mob of African Americans took control of the remains, mutilated them beyond recognition, and then left the body to rot without burial. Translation: as evidenced by popular narratives more than 130 years later, Kansans had managed to censor their behavior that most resembled the depravity of Quantrill's men. Essentially, they whitewashed one massacre to retain control of how another would be remembered, and this collective memory allowed the moral dualism of good (the people of Lawrence) against evil (guerrilla hordes personified by Larkin Skaggs) to survive. But as we have just been reminded, collective memories are inherently distorted; based upon elision and the smoothing over of rough edges, such narratives do not exist naturally in the "wilds" of history.

Therefore, the value of a memory study of Larkin Skaggs and the *other* massacre at Lawrence is not—and was never—that it provides a more definitive account of what happened to Skaggs. Personal recollections are not a substitute for raw facts; rather, they are mechanisms for understanding how those details have been interpreted and manipulated for consumption. Nor is the modus operandi here to further "complicate" the past by conceding our inability to retell the story from start to finish in its entirety. The past is infinitely complex and needs no help from us to remain so. Historians of social memory often point to the processes through which collective-memory narratives are pieced together, how they are designed and regulated for specific partisan purposes, how they evolve to remain relevant amid shifting political environments, and even how they fade into obscurity when a new narrative ascends to dominance. This saga's true contribution, with all of its conflicting testimony, is that it actually allows us to work backward through that process of collectivization.

Very rarely are observers granted the opportunity to view each phase of a collective memory narrative as it takes shape over time: as seedy details are sanitized, as new characters emerge to assume responsibility for what cannot be explained away, as new plot twists make sense of new characters, and as the rough edges are polished clean until multiple individual accounts—those of Connelley, Williams, Riggs, and Henry—are melded into a single version, loaded with social, cultural, and political symbolism. In other words, a dissection of the Skaggs narrative's formation serves to temporarily pause the work of collectivization and makes it possible to assess the quality of each individual fragment prior to fusion. It also provides an important reminder that collective memories of traumatic events are not born "whole," and that to better understand how they were experienced in real time, historians must be willing to excavate beneath the façade of uniformity and admit when we simply do not—or cannot—totally explain an occurrence, even one as notorious as the Skaggs killing.

In the same way that an individual soldier might have recalled combat in the Slaughter Pens of Chickamauga as hopelessly chaotic—with artillery raining down and men shouting, fleeing, and groaning their last—and disconnected from the "big picture" of the battle going on around him, so too did individual memories exist within an array of overlapping but ultimately unique accounts. Only after a regimen of distilling and ordering could the disparate memories of thousands of soldiers be transformed into neatly arranged red and blue lines on a map. Likewise, a dominant rendition of Skaggs's murder could only emerge after completing a similar course of collectivization. Leslie's telling in *The Devil Knows How to Ride* is a case in point of this arrangement.

What, then, is the result of applying this tactic of commemorative dissection to the Lawrence Massacre itself? For years, historians have struggled with the task of properly situating Quantrill's raid within the context of the guerrilla war in Missouri and Kansas and of the Civil War's irregular conflict more broadly conceived. Taken as a whole, guerrillas inflicted more casualties at Lawrence than in any other raid. There were more men involved at Lawrence than in any other irregular assault, and the fact that they operated under a unified command structure (Quantrill and his lieutenants) made their presence all the more anomalous. In trekking from western Missouri through miles of enemy territory on the Kansas side of the border, Quantrill and his men ranged much farther from home than was standard and carried out the large-scale ambush in broad daylight.

Disclaimers related to these characteristics of the massacre are especially troublesome for historians of the guerrilla conflict for two reasons. First, primary documents chronicling the events at Lawrence constitute a substantial portion of guerrilla-history sources from the Missouri-Kansas borderlands. One need only reference the holdings of the State Historical Society of Missouri, the Kansas State Historical Society, or the Kenneth Spencer Research Library at the University of Kansas to verify this claim. Second, the Lawrence Massacre is often cited in popular histories of the Civil War, prominent Civil War reference works, and in university-level textbooks as a prime example of irregular warfare.[37] Readers are thus introduced to the Lawrence Massacre not only as a fantastic atrocity (which is quite a label within a broader conflict that managed to wipe out some 750,000 men) but also, by implication, as a representation of how other guerrilla raids worked. Our examination of the Skaggs narrative provides a path around these issues.

In the same way that witnesses to Skaggs's execution and the desecration of his corpse each experienced the events individually and recorded their version to match, so too did the victims of the massacre that preceded his death experience the raid on personal terms. Mayor George W. Collamore attempted to hide from the guerrillas in a well and suffocated to death when flaming pieces of his home fell down on top of him; Judge Louis Carpenter was shot in the head at point-blank range even as his wife tried to shield him from harm; Ellis, the blacksmith, was cut down while clutching his only child; Anthony Oldham, an African American preacher, answered his door and was immediately shot dead in front of his daughter; Edward Fitch was shot eight times by guerrillas who then forced his distraught wife to watch his body be burned; and bushwhackers wounded Daniel Palmer, bound his hands and legs, and threw him into a burning building. Dozens of similar scenes played out all over town.[38]

Collectively, these tales combine to form the Lawrence Massacre as so many know it today. But none of these victims experienced the massacre in this fashion; very few would have understood what was happening to random individuals across town or hidden in wells and burning to death in basements. In his oft-consulted history of the raid, Reverend Cordley, himself a survivor, went so far as to say that "every man was so isolated by the presence of the raiders in every part of the town, that each knew only what he saw. . . . [T]he magnitude of the disaster was beyond the wildest thought of even those who were in the midst of it."[39] These were privately experienced moments of agony, suffering, and death. The same principle applied to the guerrillas themselves: after arriving in Lawrence they split into small squadrons and dispersed throughout the town, none witnessing the attack in anything near its entirety. Only after the process of collectivization had done its work did anyone understand the raid as a linear sequence of interconnected events.

Consequently, if the Lawrence Massacre is reimagined as a series of massacres, it can be reconciled with the ways guerrilla warfare operated as a system of household war. As previously noted, within this paradigm, men waged war from the forests and countryside; women served as the quartermasters and intelligence gatherers for their husbands, brothers, sons, and cousins; and as a result, because individual households functioned as centers of the system that made irregular warfare possible on the Missouri-Kansas borderlands, those same households became the chief targets of enemy guerrillas. Accordingly, when the massacre is broken down into a momentous wave of home invasions perpetrated by pro-Confederate bushwhackers against the households they believed were allowing jayhawkers to function efficiently as pro-Union guerrillas, it much more closely resembles how irregulars themselves understood the waging of war in the Missouri-Kansas guerrilla theater.

* * *

At a reunion of the Quantrill Men Survivor Association in 1913, William H. Gregg explained the Lawrence Massacre to a reporter. "There's been so much written about the Lawrence raid from the standpoint of the Kansans that I would just like to tell our side once." "Quantrell didn't want to make that raid," Gregg asserted. "He held off for months, but the old men clamored for revenge on the 'red legs' of Kansans." Those Red Legs, Gregg claimed, "had come over here and stolen our teams, loaded up our household goods in our wagons, insulted our mothers and sisters and set fire to our homes."[40] While he certainly had much to gain by regulating details of the assault in the press, particularly what had motivated it, Gregg probably did genuinely remember it as a very condensed series of "normal" guerrilla raids against Kansans in response to another series of "normal" attacks against Missourians. And this is how historians of irregular warfare should begin to approach the massacres at Lawrence, just so long as they also remember that historically recontextualizing a bloodbath—be it one drunken bushwhacker or two hundred unsuspecting Kansans—is not the same as morally justifying it.

NOTES

In addition to my colleagues at the Southern Roundtable, I would especially like to thank Kylie A. Hulbert, Andrew W. Fialka, and Joseph M. Beilein Jr. for their insightful critiques.

1. U.S. War Department, *War of the Rebellion,* ser. 1, 24(2):583 (hereafter cited as *O.R.*).

2. Ibid., 578, 579–81, 24(3):467, 470; Richard Cordley, *A History of Lawrence, Kansas: From the First Settlement to the Close of the Close of the Rebellion* (Lawrence, Kans.: E. F. Caldwell, 1895): 202–206. In 1863, immediately following the raid, the Rev. Richard Cordley penned an account for the newspaper the *Congressional Record.* It is believed to be the most complete narrative written by a firsthand survivor of the attack and is often cited as near definitive by modern historians. Cordley's coverage of the Lawrence Massacre in *A History of Lawrence* is based almost entirely on the 1863 article. For an edited version of Cordley's narrative, see Richard Cordley, *William Clarke Quantrill and the Civil War Raid on Lawrence, Kansas, August 21, 1863: An Eyewitness Account,* ed. Richard B. Sheridan (Lawrence, Kans.: R. B. Sheridan, 1999).

3. Sophia Bissell to Cousins, Sept. 8, 1863, Chicago History Museum Research Center, 2–3, 6–7; Mary Savage to Mother and Sister, Oct. 10, 1863, Mary Savage Correspondence, 3–4, Kansas Memory, http://www.kansasmemory.org/item/225701; Thomas Gleed, "Formal Memorial Address for the Fiftieth Anniversary of Lawrence Massacre," Kansas State Historical Society, Topeka, 14–16; Alan Conway, "The Sacking of Lawrence," *Kansas Historical Quarterly* 24, no. 2 (Summer 1958): 147–49; Isadora Allison, "A Night of Terror," RH MS P241, Kenneth Spencer Research Library, University of Kansas, Lawrence, 1–3. Also see L. D. Bailey, *Quantrell's Raid on Lawrence* (Lyndon, Kans.: C. R. Green, 1899).

4. *O.R.,* ser. 1, 24(3):487–88; "The Lawrence Massacre—An Appeal," *New York Times,* Aug. 27, 1863; Charles S. Gleed, "Kansas City Journal, Memorial Address," MC159, Recollections of Quantrill Raid: For Fiftieth Anniversary of Lawrence Massacre, 1913, Kansas Historical Society, Topeka, 14; Cordley, *History of Lawrence,* 240–44, 246; and Richard B. Sheridan, "A Most Unusual Gathering: The 1913 Semi-Centennial Memorial Reunion of the Survivors of Quantrill's Raid on Lawrence," *Kansas History* 20, no. 3 (Autumn 1997): 177–78. According to most relative value calculators, $2 million in 1863 is equivalent to $38 million in 2013 currency, or roughly $200,000

per building burned or destroyed during the raid. For a reliable currency converter, see http://www.measuringworth.com.

5. For the published foundations of the pro-Quantrill position, see Edwards, *Noted Guerrillas.* For more-recent attempts to justify the Lawrence Massacre, see Paul R. Petersen, *Quantrill at Lawrence: The Untold Story* (Gretna, La.: Pelican, 2011).

6. Cordley, *History of Lawrence,* 195. By far the best-known example of this ideological faction is William Elsey Connelley, *Quantrill and the Border Wars* (New York: Smithmark, 1909). For an analysis of Connelley's partisanship, see Joseph M. Beilein Jr., "'Nothing but Truth Is History': William E. Connelley, William H. Gregg, and the Pillaging of Guerrilla History," in Beilein and Hulbert, *Civil War Guerrilla,* 207–29.

7. "The Burning of Lawrence," *Leavenworth Daily Times,* Aug. 22, 1863.

8. *O.R.,* ser. 1, 24(2):578, 579–81, 24(3):471–73.

9. Connelley, *Quantrill and the Border Wars,* 41.

10. Bowen, "Quantrill, James, Younger, et al.," 43–45; Bowen, "Guerrilla War in Western Missouri," 39–40, 43, 44, 46.

11. Ancestry.com. *1850 United States Federal Census* [database online]. Provo, UT, USA: Ancestry.com Operations, Inc., 2009. Images reproduced by FamilySearch; Ancestry.com. *1860 United States Federal Census* [database online]. Provo, UT, USA: Ancestry.com Operations, Inc., 2009. Images reproduced by FamilySearch. On fact vs. fiction in the case of Larkin Skaggs, also see Matthew C. Hulbert, "Casualties of War: Larkin Milton Skaggs," *Civil War Monitor* 4, no. 2 (Summer 2014): 27, 74.

12. For a book-length treatment on the specifics of "household warfare," see Beilein, *Bushwhackers.* On female quartermasters, see Whites, "Forty Shirts and a Wagonload of Wheat," 56–78; and Joseph M. Beilein Jr., "The Guerrilla Shirt: A Labor of Love and the Style of Rebellion in Civil War Missouri," *Civil War History* 58, no. 2 (June 2012): 151–79.

13. On the fundamentals of guerrilla warfare in the Missouri-Kansas borderlands, see Brownlee, *Gray Ghosts of the Confederacy;* Castel, *William Clarke Quantrill;* Fellman, *Inside War;* Hulbert, "How to Remember 'This Damnable Guerrilla Warfare'"; Hulbert, "Regularly Irregular War"; and Andrew W. Fialka, "Controlled Chaos: Spatiotemporal Patterns within Missouri's Irregular Civil War," in Beilein and Hulbert, *Civil War Guerrilla,* 43–69.

14. Connelley, *Quantrill and the Border Wars,* 356, 381–82n1.

15. The official reports of Lt. Col. Charles S. Clark, Ninth Kansas Cavalry, and Lt. Col. Bazel F. Lazaear, First Missouri State Militia Cavalry, detail some of the efforts made to hunt down Quantrill and his men after the raid. See *O.R.,* ser. 1, 24(3):586–88.

16. An article published by the *Lawrence Daily Journal-World* in 1912 alleged that a skeleton discovered by men digging sewers in the city was the remains of Larkin Skaggs: "Workmen digging sewer ditches in Central Park this morning unearthed the human bones of a man believed by some of the old settlers to be those of one of Quantrell's guerrilla band who was killed here in Lawrence at the time of that horrible event in Kansas history—Quantrell's raid on Lawrence. After almost fifty years of quiet in this secluded spot these bones were brought to the surface this morning." The article verified that Skaggs was executed and then mutilated but offered no explanation as to who was responsible for either incident.

17. "*Proud of* Their Campaigns," *Kansas City Post,* Oct. 4, 1913, in *The William Clarke Quantrill Men Reunions, 1898–1929,* ed. Donald R. Hale (Independence, Mo.: Blue & Grey Book Shoppe, 2001). The term "red legs" referred to a specific group of Kansas guerrillas known to wear red leggings.

18. Connelley, *Quantrill and the Border Wars,* 391.

19. Ibid., 392.

20. Ibid., 382.

21. Ibid.

22. Andrew Williams died in 1913.

23. "Narrative of a Former Slave," Andrew Williams Collection, Kenneth Spencer Research Library, University of Kansas, Lawrence, 8–9.

24. Ibid., 9–10.

25. "Paper Prepared by S. A. Riggs and Read at the Meeting," MC159, Recollections of Quantrill Raid: For Fiftieth Anniversary of Lawrence Massacre, 1913, Kansas Historical Society, Topeka, 20–21.

26. Ibid., 21–22.

27. Ibid., 23.

28. Ibid.

29. "Account of Eye Witness J. M. Henry," Mrs. A. W. Phillips Collection, Kenneth Spencer Research Library, University of Kansas, Lawrence, 1.

30. Ibid.

31. Ibid., 2.

32. Ibid., 2–3.

33. In a brief description of the Lawrence Massacre, local resident George White claimed that two men, Austin White and George Black, took Skaggs from the possession of a man named "Dr. Hennell" (who intended to turn the guerrilla over to authorities) before each shot the guerrilla in the chest with revolvers. When he fled from them—though how he did this with multiple bullets in his breast is unexplained—White Turkey shot him through the cheek with an arrow. William Speer does not feature in White's version of events in any way. George White, "Statement on the Killing of Skaggs," Douglas County Historical Society, Lawrence, Kans., 2.

34. At first glance, it would seem most logical for Unionists to have written this episode out of the Lawrence Massacre narrative completely. But because many pro-Confederate narratives reference the killing of Skaggs—including Edwards, *Noted Guerrillas*—the story was likely well known enough that it could not simply be ignored.

35. Long held as definitive, Richard Cordley's account of the entire Lawrence Massacre offers strikingly little on the matter of Skaggs's killing but seems to corroborate Speer's newspaper story. Cordley wrote that "a son of John Speer, two of whose brothers were dead, had just picked up a loaded rifle which one of the raiders had dropped. Seeing the fellow [Skaggs] hurrying off he leveled the gun and fired and brought him to the ground. This was said to be 'Elder Scraggs,' the hard-shell preacher, who was the hardest of all that company." *History of Lawrence,* 231. In his own undated account of the killing, William Speer claimed to have fired at Skaggs but that several others (including "an Indian") fired at the fleeing guerrilla, who did not die immediately following the gunfire. William Speer, "My Story of the Quantrell Massacre," Kansas Historical Society, Topeka, 5.

36. Leslie, *Devil Knows How to Ride,* 233–34. For a similar account published in a popular title, see Schultz, *Quantrill's War,* 213.

37. As examples of prominent Civil War textbooks, see McPherson, *Battle Cry of Freedom,* 784–87; and Michael Fellman, Lesley J. Gordon, and Daniel E. Sutherland, eds., *This Terrible War: The Civil War and Its Aftermath* (New York: Pearson, 2008), 203–204. As an example of a prominent Civil War reference book, see Margaret E. Wagner, Gary W. Gallagher, and Paul Finkelman, eds., *The Library of Congress Civil War Desk Reference* (New York: Simon & Schuster, 2002), 449–50. And for popular narratives of the war that offer such treatments of Lawrence, see Harry Hansen, *The Civil War: A History* (New York: New American Library, 1991), 492–93; and Louis P. Masur, *The Civil War: A Concise History* (Oxford: Oxford University Press, 2011), 59.

38. Cordley, *History of Lawrence,* 211–12, 213–15, 216, 219.

39. Ibid., 240.

40. "Lawrence Raid for Revenge," *Kansas City Post,* Oct. 4, 1913.

A SPATIAL APPROACH TO CIVIL WAR MISSOURI'S DOMESTIC SUPPLY LINE

ANDREW FIALKA

Scenes of desolation all too familiar throughout the occupied South reached an apex in Civil War Missouri. Irregular warfare shattered the state's political, social, and economic institutions; made blackened chimneys a regular landmark throughout the environment; left parts of Osceola, Rocheport, and Centralia in smoldering ruins; and displaced thousands of panic-stricken refugees from their ravaged homesteads. After the war, grieving Missourians (and later on, curious historians) struggled to answer *who* caused the devastation, *how* soldiers and guerrillas could act so savagely, and *why* irregular fighting so plagued the state. Painter-turned-politician-turned-officer George Caleb Bingham demonized in historical memory the man he felt most responsible for the rampant death and destruction: his superior and commander of the District of the (Kansas-Missouri) Border, Union brigadier general Thomas Ewing Jr. Bingham's massive 56-by-78-inch painting *Civil War: As Realized in the Desolation of Border Counties of Missouri during the Operation of "General Order No. 11," Issued by Brigadier General Ewing, from His Head Quarters, Kansas City, August 25, 1863* (1865–70) portrays Ewing and his troops wielding an "anti-republican and despotic" power in the act of robbing and murdering innocent civilians and destroying their property (figure 1).[1] Bingham's depiction was far from historical fabrication; Union troops under Ewing's command committed plenty of similar acts against civilians throughout his assigned district (figure 2). But the general felt that the unique context of irregular warfare justified his policies. He did not consider these civilians to be nonmilitarized innocents, nor did he view their houses solely as familial homes or centers of personal economic production. Male civilians (including boys) in guerrilla war zones "morphed" into soldiers, while the women (and some children and elderly men) became distributors, "messengers, and spies" in a robust domestic supply line. Their households operated as "command centers, communication hubs, and supply depots" for the guerrilla resistance, and their home front—the environment that included all of these domestic places and spaces—became

Fig. 1. George Caleb Bingham, *Civil War: As Realized in the Desolation of Border Counties of Missouri during the Operation of "General Order No. 11 . . ."* (1865–70). (State Historical Society of Missouri, Ellis Library, University of Missouri, Columbia)

one continuous irregular battlefield, encompassing everyone and everything in them.[2]

Ewing's actions support this conclusion. His war-making policies directly targeting civilians (most infamously General Orders No. 10 and No. 11 in August 1863) reflected his reclassification of the home front as an irregular war zone and his recategorization of affected civilians as legitimate combatants, whether they wanted to participate in the guerrilla war or not. The general made war on the guerrillas' terms, on their battlefields, and against their logistical war-making machine: the household. In point of fact, he personally cataloged his army's irregular (and female) enemies and used hand-drawn maps of guerrilla activity to *integrate* irregular warfare's entangled home and battle spaces and to more effectively operate within them (figure 3).[3] With General Orders No. 11, he established a systematic antiguerrilla strategy that targeted the household and consequently meshed the conventional and unconventional conflicts into a "household war."[4] Ewing believed this synthesis of regular and irregular strat-

Fig. 2. General Ewing's District of the Border, June 9, 1863. (Map by author)

egy would prove successful because he understood that Missouri's Confederate guerrillas operated within the context of their hierarchical slave communities, which depended on the household to rightfully organize its members and to produce its economic wealth. Guerrillas rarely fought on open and distinguished battlefields, they were not supplied by a governmental entity, and they did not utilize a bureaucratic power for information. Instead, irregulars made war

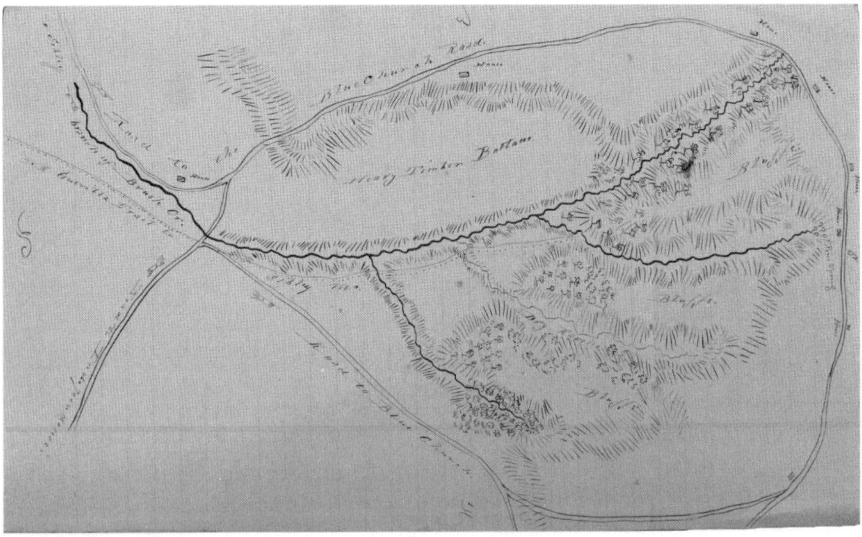

Fig. 3. Hand-drawn map of guerrilla activity in Ewing's district, noting a "Guerrilla Trail" (notation on far left) and nearby households. (Unknown author, Order No. 11, 1863, Box 212, Thomas Ewing Family Papers, 1757–1941, Library of Congress)

with the resources and within the shared space of their society's people and households. Despite the official definitions on the books at any given point in time, any person—commander, soldier, guerrilla, or citizen—living within the irregular theater recognized that they were in a unique household war zone and acted accordingly.[5]

Numerous historians side with Ewing and cite Union officers' uneven application of "hard war" strategy toward Southern civilians throughout the Confederacy to argue that the irregular conflict blurred the line between battlefield and home front.[6] Furthermore, scholarship on the increasingly political actions of rebel women and guerrillas' communal nature demonstrates that male combatants relied on a domestic supply line for their war-making capabilities.[7] Joseph Beilein argues that the household anchored guerrillas' political, economic, and gendered senses of identity. Indeed, guerrillas "were so attached to their households that they saw no distinction between themselves and that institution" and were willing to die for its preservation. Irregular warfare practiced by Southerners was indeed an extension of slave society, which exemplified the "communal nature of resistance" against professedly unjust Federal aggression. Moreover, Union occupiers quickly identified and targeted the communal nature of irregular warfare by subjecting civilians who served as the guerrillas' domestic supply line to fines, jail time, banishment, and even violence. In Missouri especially, several factors exacerbated conditions for irregular warfare. Among these were the state's close proximity to the American frontier, the bitter and violent legacy of the 1850s border war with Kansas settlers, and a predominantly Southern-sympathizing population under the yoke of Federal control from sporadic Union occupation with no in-state Confederate army to join.[8] These qualitative arguments present the uncomfortable assimilation of unconventional practices to conventional policies in a state already conducive to irregular war.[9]

In addition to previous scholarship, this essay shifts historical investigation away from immediately asking *who, how,* and *why* and instead privileges a detailed examination of *when* and *where* to gain additional perspectives—one spatial and one temporal—on the nature of irregular warfare.[10] Not surprisingly, these perspectives reinforce General Ewing's and historians' conceptualization of guerrillas as extensions of their communities, households, and the women who lived there. But more importantly, spatial and temporal methods add quantitative support to these arguments and erase ambiguities present in our understanding of irregular war by *making sense* of guerrillas' and Union occupiers' savage actions. By discovering when and where instances of guerrilla violence occurred in relation to the civilians and soldiers present in the built and natural environment, we can literally see that irregulars, their households, and the Union army operated in distinct spaces at predictable time intervals. It was in this symbiotic space that participants continuously reinvented their war-making policies, procedures, and the justifications for both. As a result, my argument is twofold: first, digital maps of Southern-sympathizing and guerrilla-aiding households (referred to collectively as rebel households), guerrilla violence, and Union army activity illustrate a vast theater where the home front and conventional battlefield were *not* separate entities but a single irregular war zone. Second, visualizing the effects of Ewing's antiguerrilla policies on irregular activity—most specifically those of Orders No. 11—demonstrates that the general was right: the only way to end "household war" was to end the households. Only two parameters eradicated Missouri's irregular violence: a regular and conventional ending to the war, and the complete evacuation or destruction of the guerrillas' domestic supply line—the civilian population.[11]

A digital and spatiotemporal method is necessary to properly conduct this type of research; that is, only animated maps that display guerrilla warfare's participants as they appeared in time and space can sufficiently illustrate the complexities of the irregular contest. My digital model of Missouri's irregular theater, "Of Methods and Madness," currently utilizes three distinct sources to map irregular warfare and guerrillas' domestic supply line.[12] First, beginning on July 18, 1861, the Union army defined the "authority of the provost marshal" to "preserv[e] order" in Union-occupied territories. Among their many tasks, provost marshals investigated "charges or acts of treason and arrest[ed] deserters, spies . . . persons deemed disloyal," and guerrillas. Items in the Missouri Union Provost Marshals Papers identify spatiotemporal information concerning irregulars' domestic supply line by including citizen complaints of guerrillas' actions, petitions for Union occupation, lists of Southern sympathizers, and investigations of guerrillas' aiders and abettors.[13] Second, these papers, along with selected memoirs, autobiographies, and secondary literature on the state's most active guerrilla leaders, depict instances of guerrilla violence.[14] Lastly, the Union army's location assists in illustrating the shared battlefield of regular and irregular participants during war. Frederick H. Dyer's *Compendium of the War of the Rebellion* is the most comprehensive description of the entire army's spatial location throughout the war.[15] Historians engaged in digital scholarship projects at Tufts University and the University of Richmond digitized the *Compendium* in order to spatially manipulate its data.[16] Collectively, evidence from the provost marshals' papers, primary and secondary documents on the state's most notorious guerrillas, and the digitized version of Dyer's *Compendium* allowed me to confidently map where guerrillas attacked, what they destroyed, where they received support from rebel households, and where Federal forces conducted short- and long-term occupations. While traditional military histories and static maps tend to separate guerrillas from their homes and the Union army from guerrillas' battlefields—their backyards, the roads connecting their homes, and their communal spaces—"Of Methods and Madness" welds together these spaces, consolidating disconnected definitions of guerrilla warfare's actors and identifying patterns within these participants' shared battlefields.[17]

Two demonstrations of a spatiotemporal methodology help support the claims herein and consequently entrench the domestic supply line's foundational role in Missouri's Civil War. In the first case, envisioning the concentration of guerrilla activity before and after General Orders No. 11 shows that Ewing's near-total war on guerrillas' households virtually ended the irregular conflict in parts of the District of the Border. Secondly, it is useful to compare and combine historians' research techniques concerning an anecdote of irregular warfare. Different approaches reveal diverse characteristics about Missouri's guerrilla war; qualitative analysis depicts the chaotic ways in which Missourians and Union troops experienced warfare, while the addition of a spatiotemporal method uncovers patterns of violence within the irregular theater.

General Ewing issued General Orders No. 11 on August 25, 1863, in retaliation to guerrillas' raid on and near-complete destruction of Lawrence, Kansas. The document stated: "*All persons* living in Jackson, Cass, and Bates Counties, Missouri, and in that part of Vernon included in this district . . . are hereby ordered to remove from their present places of residence within fifteen days from the date hereof." Unfortunately, Ewing entrusted the order's execution to Kansas troops, some of whom had participated in pro-Union guerrilla-style raids into Missouri territory during the 1850s border war. As a result, "[a]pproximately 20,000 people were forced to evacuate their homes, almost all of which then were burned." Guerrillas also vacated the state after the sacking of Lawrence by fleeing to Texas during the winter of 1863–64.[18]

Mapping the spatial density of guerrilla violence before and after General Orders No. 11 indicates that the nexus of irregular warfare shifted away from western Missouri after the army's enforcement evacuated guerrillas' families from their homes (figures 4 and 5). After August 25, guerrillas had to shift their operations to other parts of the state in order to maintain communal support. Most refugees headed east (in Bingham's painting, note that Union troops are heading west, back to Kansas, while the stream of now-homeless civilians are marching one county east, the signpost directing them to Lexington, Missouri) and continued to sustain the guerrilla war throughout central Missouri in 1864. While some instances of violence still occurred in western Missouri after the order, the vast majority took place where rebel households had not been systematically destroyed by Union troops. Ewing's war on Missourians' households effectively quelled guerrilla violence in the irregular theater subject to General Orders No. 11. Other than the gradual cessation of hostilities following the Confederacy's conventional surrender, nothing more successfully ended irregular violence in Civil War Missouri than Ewing's assault on the guerrillas' domestic supply line.

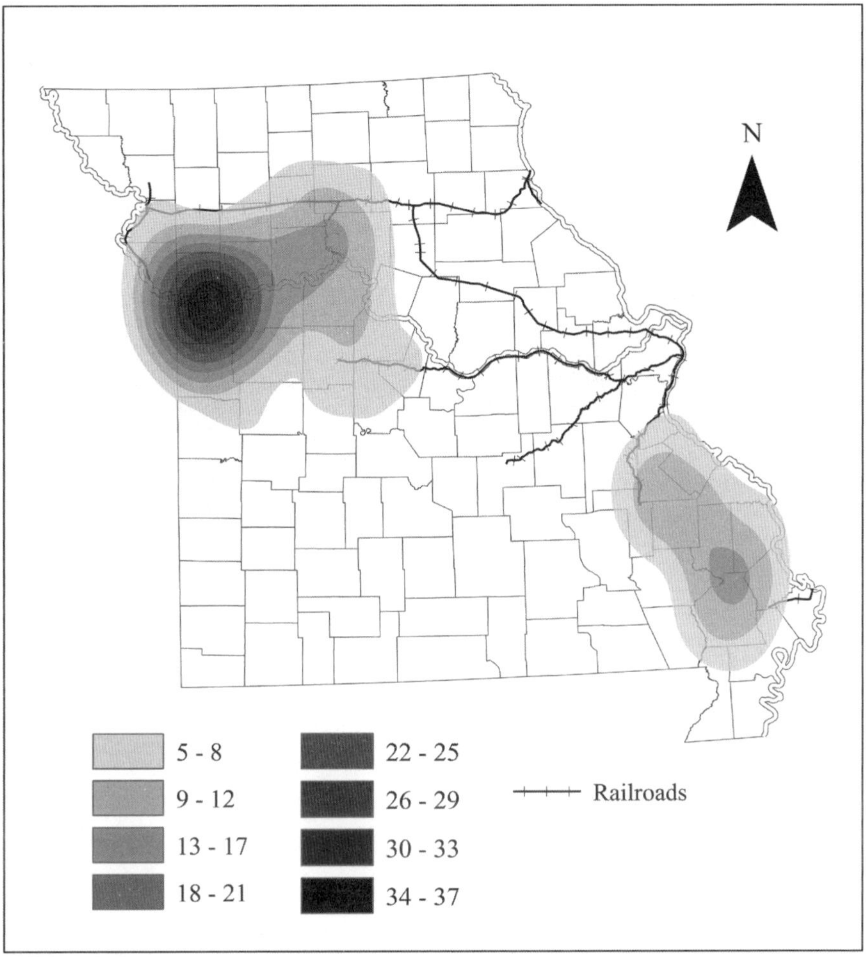

Fig. 4. Instances of Guerrilla Violence before Order No. 11. (Map by author)

Additionally, situating qualitative evidence in a spatiotemporal framework elucidates the chaotic nature of the guerrilla war at statewide, county, and city levels. At the macro level, instances of guerrilla violence, Union occupational forces, and rebel households concentrated among one another and also corresponded with the state's wealthiest counties along the Missouri and Mississippi Rivers and those that contained railroad lines and depots (figures 6, 7, and 8).[19] The close proximity of guerrilla violence and Union occupation to rebel

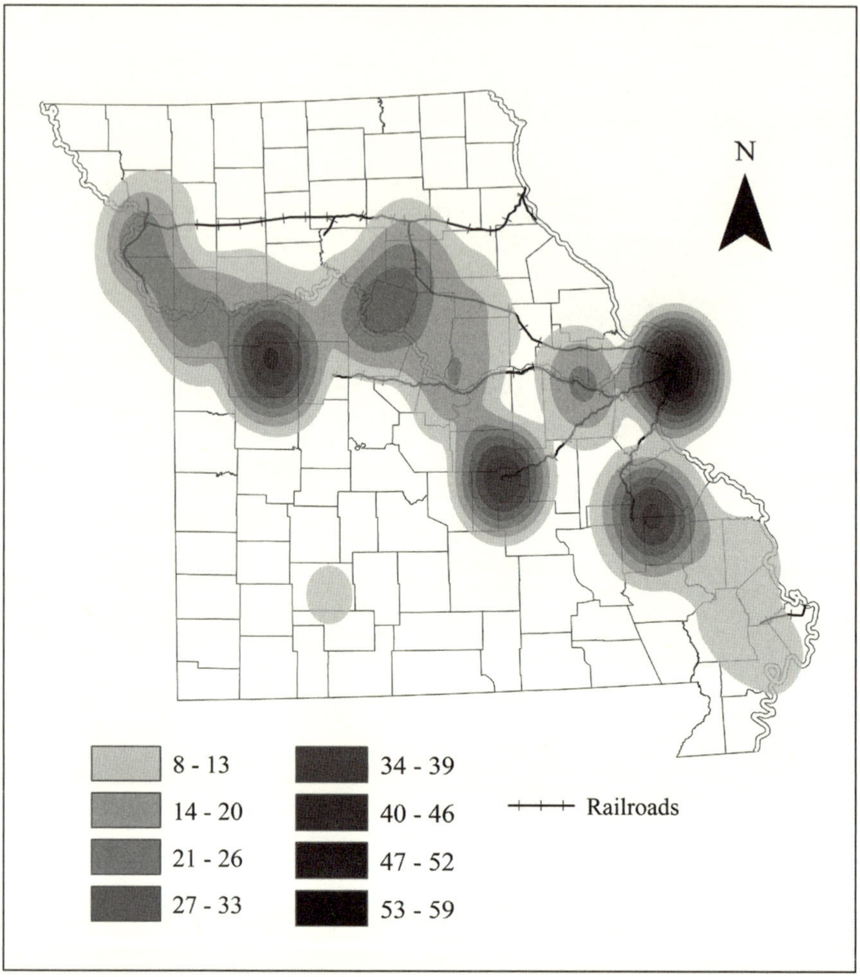

Fig. 5. Instances of Guerrilla Violence after Order No. 11. (Map by author)

households and national transportation networks in Missouri demonstrates two important points. First, the spatial association between irregular participants and transportation networks supports claims that most guerrillas emanated from wealthy slaveholding and landowning families.[20] Second, guerrillas throughout the state mainly operated in counties that offered support from sympathetic households—better illustrating the irregular as an extension of his community—while the Union army consciously included rebel households and

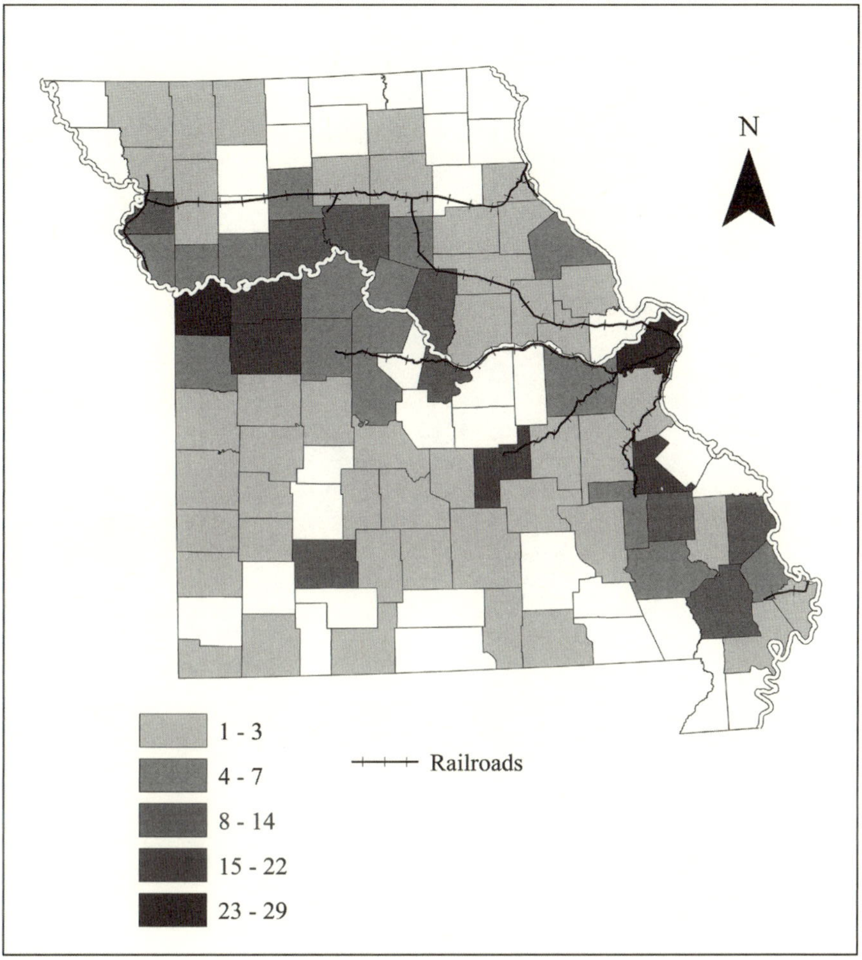

Fig. 6. Instances of Guerrilla Violence by County, 1861–1865. (Map by author)

civilians connected to the domestic supply line in its antiguerrilla strategies. The state's irregular war was actually a phenomenon of several groups of actors in a shared space who simultaneously sustained the unconventional war effort, greatly influenced Union war policies, and shaped the wartime experience for a majority of Missourians.

At the micro level, spatiotemporal information adds crucial context to anecdotal evidence. For example, provost marshal documents indicate that the

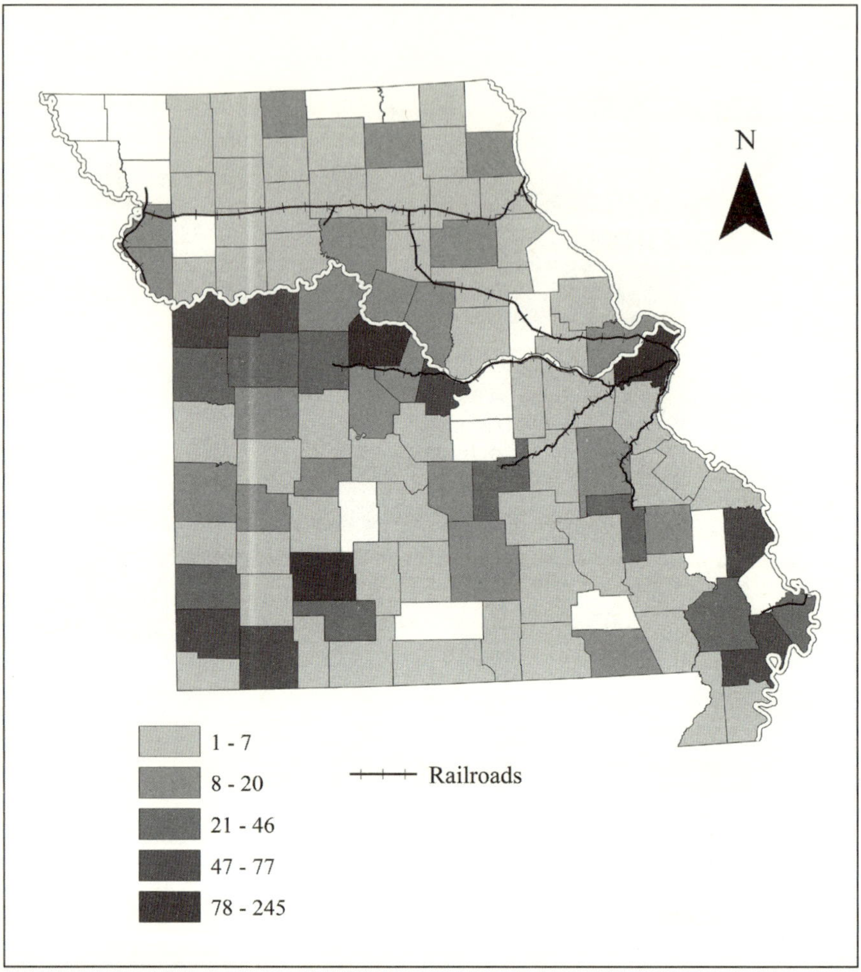

Fig. 7. Instances of Union Occupation by County, 1861–1865. (Map by author)

Fox household of Chariton County, Missouri, participated in aiding guerrillas and consequently suffered retribution at the hands of Federal officials such as Captain Harry Truman, a Union "detective." Peter Fox was a typical antebellum Missourian. Originally from North Carolina, Fox followed his Southern kin westward and settled within ten miles of the Missouri River. As of 1860, he farmed seventy-five acres of improved land with the help of his wife, two sons, three daughters, a woman who did not share their surname, and no slaves.

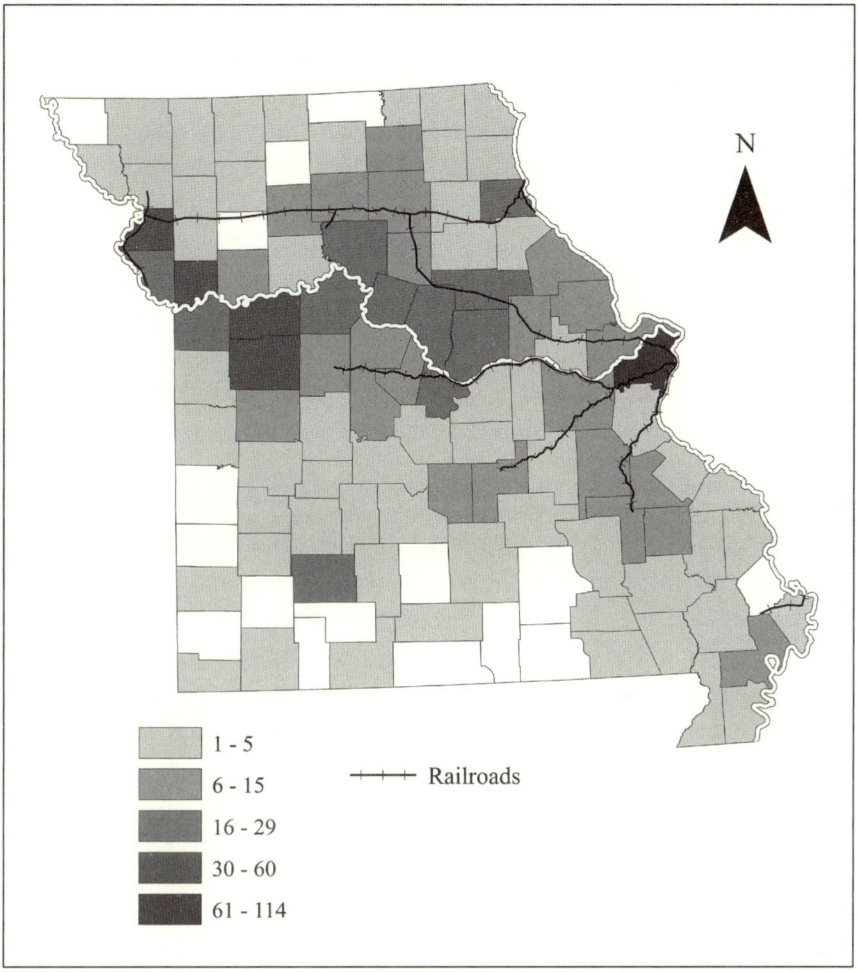

Fig. 8. Instances of Rebel Households by County, 1861–1865. (Map by author)

Although Fox, age fifty, and his two sons, ages five and ten, never served in the Confederate military or took up arms as bushwhackers, the family sympathized with guerrillas who targeted Federal troops in middle Missouri.[21]

In testimonies taken by provost marshals in 1865, civilians of Keytesville, Missouri, professed that the Fox family was particularly disloyal. D. B. Kellogg accused them of maintaining "a reputation for harboring bushwhackers, feeding them and making them clothing," while Marilla Carmon witnessed "Isabella

[Fox, Peter's wife,] read *Art of War* with bushwhackers" and claimed she "[fed] and harbor[ed] them often."[22] Other civilians leveled more serious accusations against the women of the household by asserting that Isabella kept "a house of ill-fame," meaning that her daughters slept with men (and more shockingly, guerrillas) out of wedlock. More specifically, John Dewey alleged that Mellisa, Isabella's second-oldest daughter, rode "with bushwhackers and entertain[ed] them with a dance." It is imperative to note that these charges purposefully incriminated the men *and* women of the Fox household, acknowledging that both sexes possessed the agency to "keep" a house and support guerrilla warfare. During the war, Missouri's male civilians relied on women's ability to sustain a household and simultaneously support roving bands of irregulars by utilizing their domestic resources. In June 1864 the ill-reputed Fox household attracted the ire of Union officials.[23]

Between June 1 and June 12, J. W. Terman, a Union detective under the guise of Captain Harry Truman, led a twenty-man detachment through Chariton County with soldiers from the Ninth Cavalry, Missouri State Militia. Truman and his men disguised themselves as guerrillas to entrap Southern sympathizers into admitting their relation to the irregulars' domestic supply line.[24] While in and around the town of Keytesville, Truman and his men robbed ten homes, murdered seven men, and burned down another man's home before fleeing the county on June 12.[25] Among their many victims were Peter Fox and Fox's son-in-law, Henry C. Jennings.

During his raid, Captain Truman temporarily employed "Ephraim Clark, Polk Young, [and] one Mott"—members of the Keytesville Unionist League—to serve as his "guides." He urged Clark, Young, Mott, and a member of the Ninth Cavalry "to go to Fox and [his son-in-law and ex-Confederate soldier] Jennings and kill them." Clark led the four-man detachment to the homestead, where they found Peter Fox in a field tending to his crops and Henry Jennings in a second-floor bedroom stricken with illness. The detachment escorted both Fox and Jennings "about 200 yards from Fox's house into a woodland pasture" and stated their orders from Captain Truman. The two men begged for a final visit with their families, but the detachment rejected their pleas and instead permitted them only the opportunity to pray. Seconds later, "all four [men of Truman's outfit] discharged their pistols," shooting the father of five and his son-in-law "while Jennings was still on his knees in prayer." Jennings fell limp instantly, while the detachment left for dead the fatally wounded Fox as he attempted to crawl back to his home. The men then stopped at the household and explained to Isabella that they had killed her husband and son-in-law because they "were charged with general disloyalty and dishonesty."[26] A downward spiral of local violence ensued: two days after Truman's exit, local Southern sympathizers (*or* guerrillas) murdered between four and nine Unionist civilians who had offered Truman assistance during his "scouting expedition."[27] In response to these actions, the Thirty-Fifth Missouri Infantry scouted Chariton County July 27–30, while Unionists (whether acting alone *or* in cooperation with local Union troops) "burned down . . . the dwellings of nearly every citizen against Truman" between June and December.[28]

Seven months later, Isabella and Mellisa Fox issued statements from their holding cells at the Gratiot Street Prison in St. Louis after being arrested by the Union army for aiding and abetting guerrillas. Both Isabella and her seventeen-year-old daughter confessed to making shirts for bushwhackers and feeding guerrillas under Clifton Holtzclaw and Jim Jackson on three occasions in 1864. Yet perhaps in an effort to return to their crippled homestead, Isabella stated that she fed and harbored guerrillas against her will and that she "*ha[d] been* a Southern Sympathizer but for the past year 'since [she] ha[d] got light,' [was] loyal, and desire[d] the South put down and the authority of the U. States Govt. restored over them." The provost marshal record does not indicate whether or not the army permitted the two women to return to their home. On the other hand, Captain Truman served a year-long hard-labor sentence in Alton Prison before the army reinstated him.[29]

This extraordinary example from the provost marshal papers reveals the opaque nature of historical sources concerning irregular warfare. Read at an individual scale and without spatial knowledge of Chariton County's previous Union occupation, guerrilla activity, and rebel households, this example can lead historians to conclude that a spontaneous and endless cycle of retaliation among guerrillas, civilians, and ill-disciplined Union troops characterized Missouri's Civil War. Yet information from sources like these records cannot confidently determine if secessionist civilians and Unionist civilians murdered each other in cold blood, if guerrillas and local Unionist militias squared off at every opportunity, or even draw a clear line between civilians and irregular combatants. But placing the Fox household, Unionist "detectives," and guerrilla violence in a larger spatiotemporal framework reveals an entire community mobilizing against Union occupation in systematic ways. Such a framework illustrates a spacious, irregular battlefield with combatants, rules, and identities unique from their conventional counterparts.

To start, we can situate the Foxes' home county, Chariton, in the larger context of Missouri's guerrilla theater. Chariton County stretches along twenty miles of the Missouri River's northern bank in the central region of the state. Keytesville and Brunswick, its county seat and main trading center, respectively, rest near the river and served as a central location for farmer's crops and westward travelers. Like many other counties close to the Missouri, Chariton's lush farmland lured a large population of Southern migrants—along with their slave property—while its strategic location on the waterway attracted intermittent but substantial attention from the Federal army and navy during the war. Much like other large trade-oriented cities located along the state's major rivers and railroads, Brunswick and Keytesville entertained the vast majority of its county's guerrilla war. Simply put, Southern farmers and merchants migrated to these types of cities for their financial opportunities, the Union army reclaimed these locations for their strategic and logistical value, the sons of the wealthiest resident farmers and merchants targeted the army in order to protect their future investments (including in slaves), and the women of those men's households enabled them to operate.[30]

Chariton County, containing thirty-seven identified rebel households, endured ten instances of guerrilla violence and eleven visitations from Union troops, all figures well above the state's averages. Illustrating this data in space and time provides a better sense of how the irregular war unfolded around the Fox family. Reports concerning guerrillas' aiders and abettors in the county started as early as October 1862. On October 11, Philip Hoover told Union authorities of a "secessionist meeting to aid guerrillas in crossing [the] Missouri River and to assassinate Col. William Moberly, Maj. A. Griffin, and Capt. Hancock." In this all-too-typical case, guerrillas and members of their community cooperated to target Union forces. Four more provost marshal cases from 1863 illustrate how Southern sympathizers in Chariton County deliberately wielded different identities to aid irregular fighters, operate *as* guerrillas, and avoid punitive treatment from Federal agents. For example, the case records of Andrew C. Watson state that Watson was a "notorious bushwhacker" who forfeited his bond and "ran off" in the summer of 1862 to "avoid arrest." John Watson, most likely Andrew's relative, used his "considerable wealth" to "harbor" the bushwhacker and conceal him from Union eyes. In another case, Collins Coy aided guerrillas by hiring out his slave, Abram, to a group of Chariton bushwhackers. Several more cases from 1864 and 1865 depict county residents feeding irregulars, providing them with information and clothing, and acting as guerrillas during certain times of the year. In these ways, the Chariton County community interchangeably played the roles of guerrilla, aider and abettor, and innocent bystander to protect themselves from and actively resist the army. Visualizing cases of guerrilla violence and Union occupation in the same space and time as these rebel households allows us to see that the community did not operate in a vacuum; instead, residents mobilized in organized and expected ways.[31]

Between August 17, 1861, and April 5, 1862, four separate Union cavalry companies paid visits to Brunswick and Keytesville, home to most of the county's Southern-sympathizing civilians. Dyer's *Compendium* lists each company in the towns for only one day and does not include a description of their actions while on duty. Furthermore, the Second California Infantry Regiment conducted a ten-day "expedition" throughout the county in April 1863. The army sent troops into Chariton six more times after the Second California's expedition, never for more than three days at once. Moreover, Dyer notes that most of the men visiting the county were organized in "detachments" or "companies"—not regiments—and he uses the words "affair" and "scout" to describe the small Union forces' actions. I categorize these short-term and small-scale Federal raids, expeditions, and scouting missions in Missouri as *temporary* Union occupations that dealt specifically with the irregular conflict. Soldiers in small groups that engaged in temporary practices were more likely to ignore their official codes of conduct and target any and all persons involved in the guerrilla war. Not surprisingly, 70 percent of the guerrilla violence in Chariton County took place *after* these instances of temporary occupation, and half of them occurred in either Brunswick or Keytesville.[32]

It is vital to understand the *nature* of Union occupation in Chariton—small groups of troops conducting quick scouts and expeditions—and the *nature* of irregular violence—residents' communal effort to provide the men and women required for guerrilla warfare against a distinct enemy in the Union army (only one case depicts guerrillas savagely attacking civilians). These participants operated in the same spaces, and all of them acted *irregularly;* civilians intermittently operated as combatants, while Union troops often targeted noncombatant men and women. Yet because of the communal nature of guerrilla violence, all of these participants understood themselves to be within the irregular theater and subject to its unique set of rules and combat.

These examples, illustrating the density of guerrilla violence before and after General Orders No. 11 and placing Chariton County in the larger context of Missouri's irregular theater, are just two demonstrations of how spatio-temporal methods can help us better understand the communal and domestic nature of irregular warfare. In an overwhelming majority of cities and counties throughout Missouri, high levels of guerrilla attacks, Union occupation, and rebel households existed in (dis)harmony. This evidence reveals the fused relationship between irregular warfare's participants and further exhibits the need for historians to frame discussion of the Civil War's guerrilla experience within and through the household.

Patterns discovered at the state, county, and city levels complement each other and mutually reinforce the necessary role of domestic spaces in guerrilla warfare. Heretofore scholars have often studied irregular warfare in pursuit of professional legitimacy—they have illustrated that it was decisive, or have proved something about gender, or have viewed it as some microcosm of war itself, anarchic and devastating. This scholarship is essential to our understanding of *all* warfare—regular and irregular—and responsible for a more comprehensive perspective of military history. Moving forward, historians need to further discipline the study of guerrilla warfare, paying very careful attention to local context; this essay posits that if scholars ask precisely *where* and *when* a guerrilla incident occurred, they can get closer to the answer of *why* it occurred, which gets closer to understanding its essential nature.

NOTES

The author would like to thank the following individuals for reading drafts of this essay, their academic guidance, and technical assistance: LeeAnn Whites, Joseph M. Beilein Jr., Matthew C. Hulbert, Aaron Sheehan-Dean, Stephen Berry, Brian Luskey, Katherine Brackett Fialka, Lorien Foote, Tim Mashburn, David Holcomb, and Mike Perkins.

1. For a thorough exploration of the painting's diverse reception and interpretations in the postwar period, see Joan Stack, "Toward an Emancipationist Interpretation of George Caleb Bingham's General Order No. 11: The Reception History of the Painting and the Remembered Civil War in Missouri," *Missouri Historical Review* 107, no. 4 (July 2013): 203–21. Concerning Ewing's district, Maj. Gen. John Schofield ordered on June 9, 1863: "The State of Kansas north

of the 38th parallel, and the two western tiers of counties of Missouri north of the same parallel and south of the Missouri River will constitute the District of the Border, and will be commanded by Brig. Gen. Thomas Ewing, Jr.; headquarters at Kansas City." The Missouri counties in Ewing's district encompassed approximately 5,000 square miles and more than 15,000 citizens. See U.S. War Department, *War of the Rebellion,* ser. 1, 22(2):315 (hereafter cited as *O.R.*).

2. Michael Edward Shapiro, Barbara Groseclose, Elizabeth Johns, Paul C. Nagel, and John Wilmerding, *George Caleb Bingham* (New York: St. Louis Art Museum, in association with Harry N. Abrams, 1990), 43; Hulbert, "Regularly Irregular War," accessed Jan. 31, 2015.

3. For a thorough description of Ewing's list of female guerrilla supporters and further analysis on guerrillas' domestic supply line, see LeeAnn Whites, "Forty Shirts and a Wagonload of Wheat: Women, the Domestic Supply Line, and the Civil War on the Western Border," *Journal of the Civil War Era* 1, no. 1 (March 2011): 56–78. The conclusions drawn throughout this essay lend quantitative support to arguments made in Whites's article. Special thanks to Megan Biram for acquiring an image of the hand-drawn map featured in this essay.

4. Ewing issued General Orders No. 10 on August 18, 1863, which forcefully exiled *only* bushwhacker families and their supporters from his district. General Orders No. 11 was issued on August 25 and expelled from their homes *all* Missourians, whether they be loyal or disloyal, from over three border counties. General Orders No. 10 and No. 11, *O.R.,* ser. 1, 22(2):460–61, 473. Some clarification is required on the execution of these directives: before Union troops could mobilize to execute G.O. No. 10, roughly 300 guerrillas under William Clarke Quantrill sacked Lawrence, Kansas, prompting Ewing to take the more drastic measures in G.O. No. 11, albeit in a smaller area of his district. But G.O. No. 11 allowed for "the provisions of General Orders, No. 10 . . . [to be] at once vigorously executed by officers commanding in the parts of the district . . . and especially in the towns of Independence, Westport, and Kansas City." The Missouri portion of the District of the Border included six full counties and parts of two others, meaning that G.O. No. 11 legalized the systematic removal of *all* families in over three counties and families deemed disloyal in over three more counties.

5. The following conclusions concerning definitions of "guerrilla," "citizen," and "combatant" and applications of the laws of war were influenced by conversations with Joseph M. Beilein Jr., Matthew C. Hulbert, and Lorien L. Foote and the consultation of these scholars' unfinished manuscripts. For the most thorough presentation of the irregular conflict as "household war," see Joseph M. Beilein, "Household War: Guerrilla Men, Rebel Women, and Guerrilla Warfare in Civil War Missouri" (PhD diss., University of Missouri–Columbia, 2012). Historians debate whether it is proper or useful to define women and members of guerrillas' domestic supply line as legitimate combatants. During the Civil War, Union policymakers relied on the writings of the military theorist Francis Lieber to define legitimate and illegitimate war parties and to provide official instructions for how soldiers in the field should conduct themselves in relation to these parties and civilians. To view Lieber's definitions of "guerrilla," "war rebel," and "bushwhacker," and to see his "extermination policy" regarding all three, see Francis Lieber, "Guerrilla Parties Considered with Reference to the Laws and Usages of War," April 1863, *O.R.,* ser. 3, 2(1):301–309. There are two main opposing interpretations of Lieber's guerrilla policy. First, *by his definition,* only "men, or squads of men" can be defined as combatants. Scholars who take the definition of "combatant" literally often portray a chaotic rendition of guerrilla war in which innocent civilians (men and

women) could suffer random depredations at any given point in time because, technically, they were not combatants even if they enabled guerrillas. This portrayal downplays the orderly patterns in which the irregular war's chaotic events took place. On the other hand, John Fabian Witt has noted that "Lieber's analysis of the irregular warfare problem . . . was hardly definitive. It left wide discretion in the hands of officers in the field. One of the most striking features of Union treatment of guerrilla fighters . . . was its variability from region to region and command to command." I assert that historians should not apply Lieber's definitions concerning guerrillas and combatants too literally because of their questionable degree of application. It is problematic for historians to categorize the irregular war by Leiber's standards if guerrillas, civilians, and soldiers in the field did not routinely apply his policies. See Witt, *Lincoln's Code,* 195.

6. For the best work pertaining to official Union policies against Southern civilians, see Grimsley, *Hard Hand of War.* For the leading arguments that "women were an integral part of the war of occupation" and that "guerrillas were . . . created by their domestic line of supply," see Whites and Long, *Occupied Women,* 7; Ash, *When the Yankees Came,* 49; Beilein, "Household War"; and Fellman, *Inside War,* 205.

7. Prime examples from the rich literature detailing women's increasingly political actions in the Civil War include McCurry, *Confederate Reckoning;* and Kristen L. Streater, "She-Rebels on the Border: Gender and Politics in Civil War Kentucky" (Ph.D. diss., University of Kentucky, 2001).

8. The 1854 Kansas-Nebraska Act repealed the 1820 Missouri Compromise by allowing popular sovereignty to decide if Kansas would be admitted into the Union as a slave or free state. Proslavery Missourians flooded into Kansas Territory to fraudulently vote in favor of slavery. Political contestation boiled over into violence on both sides of the Missouri-Kansas border throughout the late 1850s as Missourians violently suppressed antislavery Kansans from voting and Kansas "jayhawkers," led by men such as Jim Lane and Charles Jennison, attacked Missouri civilians.

9. Beilein, "Household War," 24; Ash, *Middle Tennessee Society Transformed,* 147–48, 155–58. Other works depicting the relationship between the household and soldiers' motivations on the battlefield include Whites and Long, *Occupied Women;* Fellman, *Inside War;* Ash, *When the Yankees Came;* and Aaron Sheehan-Dean, *Why Confederates Fought: Family and Nation in Civil War Virginia* (Chapel Hill: University of North Carolina Press, 2007). Several works from the field of community studies emphasize the role of localism in soldiers' and guerrillas' motivations. Two prime examples related to guerrillas are Paul Horton, "Submitting to the 'Shadow of Slavery': The Secession Crisis and Civil War in Alabama's Lawrence County," *Civil War History* 44 (June 1998): 112, 122; and Sarris, *Separate Civil War,* 3, 72–75, 102. The household holds greater importance in areas of Union occupation due to the shortened distance between homes, families, and Federal authorities. In areas of direct occupation, guerrillas stuck closer to their homes to better protect them.

10. Stephen Ash's *When the Yankees Came* utilizes a spatial methodology and contains our best static model (or "schematic representation") for Union-occupied territory and guerrillas' area of operations. Ash's national study of Union occupation depicts "three spheres" of control throughout Confederate territory. The first two spheres, Union-controlled garrisoned towns and the Confederate frontier, offered protection by their respective national-government, local-government, and home-guard companies. The areas outside these two spheres resembled a "no-man's-land" that seethed "with hostility and guerrilla violence" due in large part to waves of "Yankee rapine[,] violence . . . '[t]heft, plunder, arson, murder and every other crime of the black catalogue.'" The

citizens living in no-man's-land experienced their own battle zone characterized by constant fear, anxiety, and terror as local governments collapsed and Federal foraging squads provided more death than protection. Ash acknowledges the fluidity of his model by stating that because of "the ebb and flow of military campaigns . . . , what was a garrisoned town or no-man's-land one day might be Confederate frontier the next." Moreover, he states that his description of garrisoned towns lacks continuity because "[s]ome of the smaller ones were simply swallowed up by Union occupation." These ambiguities in Ash's schematic cloud historians' understanding of guerrilla warfare's nature but can be partly remedied with digital methods. See Ash, *When the Yankees Came,* 76–77, 88, 91–93, 105.

11. This essay is not concerned with claiming that the Civil War was or was not a "total war." The master narrative of my generation claims that the Civil War was total; see McPherson, *Battle Cry of Freedom.* Michael Fellman claimed that the guerrilla conflict in Missouri was the closest thing to a total war but cannot be defined as such because rebel guerrillas and Union troops restrained from attacking white women; see Fellman, *Inside War,* 201. For the argument that the war was "hard" but not total, see Grimsley, *Hard Hand of War;* and Wayne Wei-Siang, "Total War and the American Civil War Reconsidered: The End of an Outdated 'Master Narrative,'" *Journal of the Civil War Era* 1, no. 3 (Sept. 2011): 394–408. For the leading arguments that the Civil War was not a total war but a limited and restrained one, see Neely, "Was the Civil War a Total War?" and *Civil War and the Limits of Destruction.*

12. For more information on ArcGIS, the mapping software used in this essay, see ESRI Software Products, "ArcGIS," ESRI, accessed Aug. 9, 2015, http://www.esri.com/software/arcgis. This essay is part of an ongoing project to map guerrilla warfare in the Civil War entitled "Of Methods and Madness: A Spatial History Approach to the Civil War's Guerrilla Violence." A majority of the quantitative evidence in this essay comes from Andrew William Fialka, "Reassessing Guerrillas: A Spatial and Temporal Analysis of Missouri's Civil War" (M.A. thesis, West Virginia University, 2013). But the University of Georgia's Center for Virtual History currently hosts an expanding version of the data sets and maps used in this essay. For more information and to view the animated maps discussed in this essay, please visit "Of Methods and Madness," eHistory, http://www.ehistory.org/projects/of-methods-and-madness.html.

13. For a thorough description of Missouri's Union Provost Marshal Papers and to view the online database, see State Historical Society of Missouri, "Missouri's Union Provost Marshal Papers: 1861–1865," Missouri State Library, accessed Aug. 9, 2015, www.sos.mo.gov/Records/Archives/ArchivesDb/Provost/. These papers are still an imperfect source because they are incomplete and disorganized. Many items omit locations and dates. Moreover, provost marshals existed in a limited number of cities. Some citizens had to travel to a central location to make a report, calling into question the validity of the recorded dates and locations. For example, numerous cases ended up being filed in the Union's most permanent garrison, St. Louis, toward the end of the war even though the subject of a case's material took place earlier in the conflict and in a different city. While these challenges seem to jeopardize the legitimacy of the project, Missouri's Union Provost Marshal Papers remains one of the best sources for the civilian experience of guerrilla warfare. I argue that I get closer to avoiding Union subjectivity because a great deal of these records contain civilians' own words from sworn statements, testimonies, and trials.

14. Some of the state's most notorious guerrillas—William Clarke Quantrill, "Bloody Bill" An-

derson, and Samuel S. Hildebrand—do not show up in the Provost Marshal Papers because reports of their attacks bypassed local provost marshals in favor of actual combat officers. To acquire some of these instances of violence, I used O. S. Barton, *Three Years with Quantrell: A True Story Told by his Scout John McCorkle* (New York: Buffalo-Head, 1966); Samuel S. Hildebrand, *Autobiography of Samuel S. Hildebrand, the Renowned Missouri "Bushwhacker" . . . Being His Complete Confession, Recently Made to the Writers, and Carefully compiled by James W. Evans and A. Wendell Keith . . . Together with All the Facts Connected with His Early History* (Jefferson City: State Times Printing House, 1870); and Castel and Goodrich, *Bloody Bill Anderson.*

15. Frederick H. Dyer, *A Compendium of the War of the Rebellion* (New York: Sagamore, 1908). Many known and unknown errors exist in the *Compendium:* Dyer worked at the regimental level and did not include many company-level movements in his work. This poses a problem as the Union military sent many companies on search-and-destroy missions targeting guerrillas and their supporters in Missouri. Dyer drew much of his evidence from the *Official Records,* so any errors or omissions in that source transmitted to the *Compendium.* A large amount of guerrilla violence enacted against civilians targeted members of local Unionist militia. Dyer does not account for local home guards or civilian militias; this omission further leads historians to assume that guerrillas attacked civilians randomly. Lastly, Dyer was a Union veteran, and his subjectivity must be taken into account.

16. These digital scholarship projects include University of Richmond, "Digital Scholarship Lab," Boatwright Memorial Library, Mar. 28, 2015, http://dsl.richmond.edu/; and Gregory R. Crane, "Perseus Digital Library," Tufts University, accessed Mar. 28, 2015, http://www.perseus.tufts.edu/hopper/. While errors also exist in these two projects' digitizing processes, their collective work is among the best in the field. Scott Nesbit wrote the necessary code to organize a digitized XML file of Dyer's *Compendium* in a format compatible with ArcGIS for a project entitled "Visualizing Emancipation." To view and download this data set, visit "Visualizing Emancipation," University of Richmond, accessed Aug. 9, 2015, http://dsl.richmond.edu/emancipation/data-download/. I am especially grateful to Scott Nesbit for his expertise and insight concerning data manipulation and available resources for digital historians.

17. Although useful, quantitative analysis can be misleading without a qualitative supplement. In the "Of Methods and Madness" database, each numerical instance of violence, occupation, and rebel household does not reflect the *degree* of violence, the *nature* of occupation, or the *level* of guerrilla support. For example, regarding the Centralia Massacre, each of the more than one hundred Union soldiers who perished and a guerrilla robbing a Unionist of his/her horse both count equally as one instance of guerrilla violence. I did not attempt to quantify the effects of robbery, terror, anxiety, fear, or death because every human interprets and experiences these actions and emotions in different ways. Therefore, historians should utilize the statistical conclusions present in this essay in combination with more qualitative analysis, as I have attempted to do here.

18. *O.R.,* ser. 1, 22(2):473 (emphasis added); Fellman, *Inside War,* 95. Joseph Beilein argues that "General Order No. 11 . . . effectively destroyed the logistical side of the . . . entire rebel supply line" and rendered guerrilla warfare defunct in the border counties subject to General Orders No. 11. Beilein's argument stands in stark contrast to Castel's and Goodrich's claim that G.O. No. 11 "had no such effect . . . of making it impossible for the guerrillas to maintain themselves in th[e] region." Beilein, "Household War," 77–78; Castel and Goodrich, *Bloody Bill Anderson,* 31.

19. Figures 6, 7, and 8 contain approximate data for multiple reasons. In addition to the difficulties outlined in notes 13 and 15, it is problematic to define and quantify diverse psychological motives, controversial definitions, cryptic messages, and incomplete evidence. Yet the digital nature of "Of Methods and Madness" allows me to constantly update and improve its quantitative data. These figures are current as of February 3, 2015. During the Civil War, Missouri contained 113 counties. My sample includes 383 instances of guerrilla violence (including both when guerrillas targeted the Union army and when they targeted civilians), 855 potential rebel households (including the homes of accused Southern sympathizers and the homes of Missourians convicted of aiding guerrillas), and 1,712 instances of Union occupation. Each case in the Provost Marshal Papers counts as one instance. Averages per county are 3.39 cases of violence, 7.57 rebel households, and 15.15 Union occupiers (this last figure drops *dramatically,* to 4, when calculating median as opposed to average due to extreme numerical outliers from Union staging grounds in St. Louis, Cooper, and Green Counties). I use the median number (4) in my textual description of Chariton and Jackson Counties throughout this essay.

20. Counties along Missouri's river and railroad networks contained the highest percentage of slaves in the total population, the largest agricultural production in the state, and the most numerous instances of guerrilla warfare. Don Bowen's application of relative deprivation—the "experience of being deprived of something to which one believes oneself to be entitled to have"—to guerrillas in western Missouri helps explain the personal motivations of bushwhackers there. Bowen analyzed census record information from 194 known guerrillas in Jackson County to argue that most irregulars were the eldest sons of slaveholding and landowning families. Union military occupation posed a distinct threat to these men's future property, wealth, and status and compelled them to defend their entitled inheritances by acting as guerrillas. Furthermore, the threat of economic insecurity and loss triggered their aggressive acts of violence. See Bowen, "Guerrilla War in Western Missouri," 30–51. For the best overview of Missouri's antebellum history and demographics as they relate to the guerrilla war, see Fellman, *Inside War,* 3–22.

21. 1860 U.S. Manuscript Census, Chariton County, Mo.; 1860 U.S. Agricultural Census, Chariton County, Mo.; 1860 U.S. Census Slave Schedule, Chariton County, Mo. For a detailed description of the Fox household's complete agricultural and livestock output and categorization as a disorderly household in support of guerrillas, see Joseph M. Beilein Jr., "'The Presence of These Families Is the Cause of the Presence There of the Guerrillas': The Influence of Little Dixie Households on the Civil War in Missouri" (M.A. thesis, University of Missouri–Columbia, 2006), 48–73.

22. Marilla Carmon did not specify the author of the *Art of War* in question, and several works share this title—most notably those penned by ancient Chinese general Sun Tzu (written before the Common Era but first published in English in 1910), Italian Renaissance philosopher Niccolò Machiavelli (English translation, 1636), and French military general and theorist Antoine-Henri Jomini (English translation, 1862). A case can be made for all three: Tzu's theories were widely borrowed and published in other military texts throughout the Common Era. These theories stressed deception, mobility, secrecy, and only attacking the enemy's weakest points—tactics associated with guerrilla warfare. Historians still debate Jomini's relevance in American Civil War strategy, but his work may have been the most accessible. Yet Jomini briefly acknowledges the effectiveness of guerrilla tactics but clearly emphasizes a regular standing army's discipline and professionalism. Machiavelli provides a synthesis of regular and irregular tactics but is more

concerned with exploring civil-military relations in a regular army. See Carol Reardon, *With a Sword in One Hand & Jomini in the Other: The Problem of Military Thought in the Civil War North* (Chapel Hill: University of North Carolina Press, 2012).

23. Case against Isabella Fox, 1865 Missouri Union Provost Marshal File of Papers Relating to Individual Citizens, Ellis Library Special Collections, University of Missouri–Columbia.

24. File 10159, 1864 Missouri Union Provost Marshal File for Two or More Individuals, ibid.

25. Case against J. W. Terman, Court-Martial Case Files, compiled 12/1800–10/1894, National Archives, Washington D.C. (hereafter Truman's Military Commission Case), 226–28. Truman's case indicates that he was found guilty on seven of nine murder charges, three of nine robbery charges, seven of twelve larceny charges, and one arson charge.

26. File 10159, 1864, Missouri Union Provost Marshal File for Two or More Individuals, Ellis Library Special Collections, Columbia, Mo., 14–16; Truman's Military Commission Case, 14–16, 40.

27. Truman's Military Commission Case, 221; *O.R.*, ser. 1, 34(4):372.

28. *O.R.*, ser. 1, 41(4):815.

29. Case against Isabella Fox, 1865 Missouri Union Provost Marshal File of Papers Relating to Individual Citizens, Ellis Library Special Collections, Columbia, Mo.; Case against Mellisa Fox, 1865 Missouri Union Provost Marshal File of Papers Relating to Individual Citizens, ibid.

30. Fellman, *Inside War,* xiv–22.

31. File 2591, 1862 Missouri Union Provost Marshal File for Two or More Individuals, Ellis Library Special Collections, Columbia, Mo.; Case against Andrew C. Watson, 1863 Missouri Union Provost Marshal File of Papers Relating to Individual Citizens, ibid.; Case against Collins Coy, ibid.

32. See "Of Methods and Madness."

CHALLENGING THE UNION CITIZEN-SOLDIER IDEAL

ANDREW F. LANG

During times of crisis, the nineteenth-century American citizen-soldier ideal obligated free white males to defend their nation, thereby upholding the Republic's unique value of civic virtue. Their service would be quick and temporary; military duty was assumed to be neither professional nor bureaucratic. Volunteers, clothed in their uniforms and armed with muskets, would battle one another in formal combat to determine the fate of nations. Amateur soldiers accepted the reality of death on the altar of their respective national cause. Upon resolution of the crisis, volunteers would remove their uniforms, discard their weapons, and shed their identities as soldiers, once again returning to private life and taking up the tools of civilian trade.[1]

Volunteerism flourished during the American Civil War, inspiring millions of men to enlist and reflecting the citizenry's profound attachment to the republican military tradition. Notions of an honorable and disinterested service guided volunteers through the maelstrom of war. U.S. soldiers remained in the ranks, even amid battle and the absence from home, bolstered by their faith in the exceptional promise of Union. Thus, the Civil War was in many ways a standard mid-nineteenth-century military conflict. The Union and Confederacy each conducted war as modern nation-states, relying on massive volunteer armies and looking to events on the formal field of battle to govern the course of war.[2]

Yet for the Union, launching grand forays into an enemy's territory and waging battle on distant fields proved immensely complicated. The war also contained an equally decisive, largely unexpected element: negotiating the aftermath of invasion, a relatively new component to the U.S. military tradition. Few national precedents had conditioned Americans, especially Northern volunteers, to the complex undertaking of regulating peoples and regions long after the principal armies had departed. Although employed in the brief conflict against Mexico (1846–48), wartime occupation had never before been a formal feature of American military practice. The invasion, acquisition, and management of territory symbolized a quasiwar that undermined notions of a quick, decisive, romantic struggle. Indeed, the critical importance of battlefield victories meant only so much if the acquired lands could not be governed by the army.[3]

Approximately one-third of all Union volunteers served as forces of occupation during the war. While many soldiers fought in formal battle to obtain Confederate territory, the unforeseen realities of wartime occupation—governing rebellious civilians, administering martial law, unfolding the process of emancipation, and ensuring the loyalty of wayward states—collided with the citizen-soldier ideal. Union volunteers equated armies of occupation with formal, permanent, bureaucratic military institutions and feared that their roles as occupiers accelerated a detachment from republican values. Acting as arbiters of martial governance, serving in what they defined as standing armies, and witnessing the social dislocation wrought by the military's presence, Northern volunteers became anxious about the changing nature of American military culture.[4]

Northern men discovered that the environment of occupation held an additional element that exposed the unrestrained, brutal underside of war. Relegated to garrisons or patrolling the Southern countryside, volunteers came face to face with an enemy who did not engage in formal combat, who refused a soldier's uniform, and who attacked with clandestine ferocity. The military occupation of the Confederacy spawned a widespread guerrilla resistance that thrust unsuspecting volunteers into a chaotic contest far removed from the nineteenth-century American martial imagination. Isolated in a sea of unrestricted warfare, Northern volunteers learned that honorable military practices did not exist in arenas of occupation.[5]

Guerrillas and combatants dressed as private citizens reflected a very different kind of war from what Union soldiers expected. This was not combat conducted on distant fields of battle in which organized ranks of uniformed soldiers engaged one another. On the contrary, the irregular war raged in the streets of towns and in the desolate countryside, where traditional rules of engagement and "civilized" combat rarely pertained. Unorganized violence flourished, forcing Union soldiers to adopt powerful modes of recourse, changing them in the process. Soon they no longer waited to be attacked; they no longer acted confused about the nature of their enemy. Instead, they craved revenge, sometimes meted out on their assailants in a grisly fashion.

The sporadic, furtive violence of guerrilla warfare forced U.S. volunteers to alter their conceptions of the citizen-soldier ideal. Identifying a faceless enemy and waging a counterguerrilla war required targeting elements of society traditionally removed from previous American conflicts: civilians, landscapes, towns, and private property. This irregular war unleashed waves of punishment against both occupier and occupied, often shattering the limits of civility and restraint and creating the sense of an endless battle. As historian Michael Fellman has written, "guerrillas broke all the conventions of honorable war and led the occupying forces into a deepening cycle of attack and counterattack, revenge and retaliation, in a war that blurred all distinctions between the civilian and the military, thus deepening war and brutalizing combatants."[6]

Although they became willing participants, Union soldiers were deeply troubled by the implications of their vicious conduct and actions. Waging a counterguerrilla war required adopting guerrilla tactics, thus revealing the fundamental tension underlying the entire irregular war. Perceiving that wars of occupation transformed volunteers into the very embodiment of violence that they resisted, Union soldiers believed that their virtue as individual men, provisional soldiers, and a collective army had been irrevocably altered. Northern volunteers thus struggled to define the consequences of irregular warfare upon the republican military tradition. They sensed that the moral nature of volunteer service had been discarded, rendering the American citizen-soldier little more than a guerrilla.

Union soldiers' efforts to catalog the repercussions of counterguerrilla actions reveal key historiographical implications. Departing from the traditional paradigm of "why they fought and endured," this essay instead emphasizes how soldiers participated in what is now termed the "dark side" of Civil War history. This emerging literature seeks to revise our understanding of the war as a noble, unifying event, instead emphasizing the fragmented traits that composed an incoherent conflict. The violent obscurity of guerrilla warfare resides within this realm of dark history and is revealed by participants who wrote with startling candor about their experiences. To fully appreciate this turn, however, necessitates a balanced understanding of the war as a whole. If some Union volunteers sensed that irregular warfare corrupted the citizen-soldier ideal, many others, especially those in the principal armies far removed from theaters of occupation, might well have thought otherwise. This examination, therefore, offers an alternative way of looking at the multifaceted dimensions of the soldiering experience, rather than seeking to make universal claims about Billy Yank's Civil War.[7]

* * *

Guerrilla warfare represented an organic response to both the tangible and the imagined nature of Union military occupation, offering an unorganized alternative to the more traditional battles fought on the fields of Shiloh, Antietam, and Gettysburg. Guerrillas unleashed murder and thievery; destruction of bridges, towns, railroads, and supply lines; intimidation of Unionists and African Americans; and even the capturing and kidnapping of civilians and enemy soldiers. Exposure to the insurgent, sinister dynamics of guerrilla conduct pushed Union occupiers to redefine their preconceived notions about the enemy in particular and the war in general.[8]

Soldiers encountered sparse guerrilla activity in the wake of the initial forays into the South. During the spring of 1862, although minor attacks annoyed Union rear guards, full-scale assaults rarely occurred. This tepid resistance convinced invading troops that occupation might be relatively peaceful. Yet as the Yankee presence grew and it became clear to white Southerners that their unwelcome guests would not soon depart, guerrilla resistance mounted and spiraled out of control. Much of the occupied Confederacy erupted into a muddled, disorderly war in which small bands of irregular forces rode the countryside and harassed the occupying soldiers in their midst. Flouting the conventional and "proper" rules of conventional warfare, guerrillas convinced Union soldiers of their precarious and dangerous position. "There is not a Garrison in Tennessee where a man can go beyond the sight of the flagstaff without being shot or captured," Major General William T. Sherman wrote during the late summer of 1862. Indeed, it became quite difficult to combat these irregular forces: they operated at night, disguised themselves in civilian clothes, and employed hit-and-run tactics expressly to inspire fear and terror.[9]

Union occupiers believed that the guerrilla war distorted traditional conceptions of "the enemy." Insurgents behind the lines hardly resembled and functioned as the gray-clad soldiers in the principal Confederate armies. Writing from Nashville, John M. King, whose unit occupied Middle Tennessee for much of 1863, characterized this problem. "The citizens were all rebel in sympathy and to guard those magazines and store houses was no easy task. Rebel spies and bushwhackers were going in and coming out [of the city] dressed as farmers, women, negroes, and the like, crawling through the guard line under the cover of darkness, getting ammunition and supplies to shoot our men from behind a tree or under a bush."[10]

King's description outlined the challenge of defining a civilian-combatant. Acting largely independent of any formal guidelines, Yankee soldiers often followed the definitions established by their commanding officers. Guerrilla warfare, Major General William S. Rosecrans declared, embodied "bands of armed men [who] are let loose upon the country with the instincts and the means for the exercise of lawless power and with few if any restraints of military rule." Major General John Pope, who commanded the Army of Virginia in July 1862, similarly indicted those "lawless bands of individuals not forming part of the organized forces of the enemy," who rejected "the garb of soldiers, who, seeking and obtaining safety on pretext of being peaceful citizens," harassed the Union army, murdered U.S. soldiers, devastated railroads and bridges, "and commit[ed] outrages disgraceful to civilized people and revolting to humanity."[11]

The blurry distinctions between civilian and guerrilla spread paranoia among the occupiers, who believed that both groups conspired as a single body to dislodge the Yankee presence. Charles Harding Cox, whose Seventieth Indiana Volunteers protected the rail lines in Tennessee, commented, "Our career as railroad guards was tended with a great deal more danger . . . as we were scattered in small squads in a strong secesh [country], where guerrilla bands were thick as hail, and the citizens would aid them against us any moment." In Rolla, Missouri, Henry J. Seaman related how one of his commanding officers in the Thirteenth Illinois led a small detachment that "captured every man woman and child that was capable of conveying intelligence to the [local guerrillas]." Union soldiers also sensed that they were constantly watched, believing that the shadowy guerrilla bands outnumbered them and threatened to kill anyone who dared to leave a garrison. "Last night there was considerable confusion in camp as the gurillas attacked our Pickets," wrote an Indiana soldier stationed in eastern Arkansas. "We do not know on going to Bed any night but what we may be aroused up during the night to fight the devils as they are hovering around us day and night watching an oportunity to surprise us."[12]

Guerrillas operated with a frightening combination of viciousness and unpredictability; Yankee soldiers continuously remained on edge, wondering when the next attack, murder, or theft might occur. "I have felt very uneasy about [our current location at Fort Donelson, Tennessee,] on account of the trouble along the river," wrote Jerome Spilman of the Fifth Iowa Cavalry. "At this place we know not what a day may bring forth. Gurilla bands are roving all over the country. . . . We sleep on our arms every night." Courtland G. Stanton of the Twenty-First Connecticut agreed, believing his position at Suffolk, Virginia, to be quite dangerous: "The people are all Secesh & the country is full of Guerilas." Although his unit had recently constructed a fort, Stanton believed that they were only minimally safe. "Picket duty here," he explained to his wife, "is such as you have heard of where the pickets have to keep themselves hid and are liable to get poped over it any time."[13]

Indeed, guerrillas indiscriminately hanged soldiers, burned their remains, and left their bodies behind as physical reminders of the occupiers' unwanted presence. Northern volunteers were often killed in a deliberate yet random style intended to intimidate the rank and file. Frank Twitchell, who served in Louisiana, revealed the varied ways his comrades died, describing their disfigured bodies. "The guerrilas captured a transport and burned it with 15 officers and a few soldiers," he reported, "what was done with them is more than wee know." A few days later he better understood. "An officer of the 128th NY went across the river to look for some cotton that was hiden in the woods, he was found the other day hung by the neck to a tree." Twitchell concluded that "those Officers on the boat may of [*sic*] shared the same fate," ultimately learning that several soldiers ventured a "little ways from the camp after some brush to make brooms [and] they found a human skeleton laying in the weeds very likely it was one of our own men shot [by] the guerrilas."[14]

Rather than falling honorably in formal combat, the occupiers' comrades had been slain indiscriminately by lawless bands of assassins. Iowan Charles O. Musser distinguished between various modes of wartime death, judging that guerrilla warfare near Helena, Arkansas, produced "not so much bloodshed as murder." Being "killed in battle and [dying] of sickness," Musser wrote in 1863, were far different from succumbing to the arbitrary will of guerrillas. Countless Union soldiers, such as Musser, had entered the army prepared to die on the field of battle—not to be murdered in the Southern backwoods. The lack of honor and dignity attached to this form of passing added to the volunteers' reluctance to be exposed to these random acts of violence.[15]

Stationed in remote areas, protected only by small garrisons, and enduring haphazard, arbitrary, and terrifying encounters with guerrillas, occupation soldiers questioned the honor and legitimacy of their clandestine foes. Irregular warfare epitomized anything but the grand battlefield encounters between troops clothed in the blue and gray that would decide the war. Instead, the guerrilla presence inspired an ambiguous outlook about the conflict. A Connecticut major wrote from Louisiana that his regiment had battled irregulars continuously. "Nearly every day we have [fought] them to a fair engagement distant from our support," he recollected. Yet "[o]n each occasion we obtained only dissolving views of them. . . . [T]hey are activated by no motive but plunder, they fight only from ambuscade and war indiscriminately, upon friend and foe."[16]

Thus, it seemed that guerrillas existed merely to perpetuate chaos and spread violence. Union soldiers learned that they could not fight a fair, open battle against irregular bands in which a decisive outcome might be achieved. This led many occupiers to conclude that guerrillas were, in the words of John Vreeland of the Nineteenth Illinois, "equalled only by the Cowardly Mexicans." Others similarly categorized irregulars as dishonorable cultural inferiors. "The expeditions sent out to break up guerrilla dens & seize & bring in there [*sic*] effects are always attended with a good deal of fatigue, & sometimes, but rarely, with skirmishing," explained an officer in the Department of the Gulf, "which is generally after the Indian fashion of skulking thro' the woods & bushes thus approaching their object or lying in wait. The general weapon of the Guerrillas is a double-barreled gun loaded with buckshot. His appearance & his qualities those of a white Indian." Even General Rosecrans argued that guerrillas "scalping their victims is all that is wanting to make their warfare like that which seventy or eighty years ago was waged by the Indians against the white race."[17]

In labeling guerrillas as inferior racial and cultural groups, Union soldiers classified as dishonorable the entire experience of irregular warfare. The essence of wartime military governance and its accompanying violent resistance from white Southerners resembled a destabilized environment in which chaos and disarray ruled supreme. Such attributes disturbed Northern men who attached themselves intimately to societal order and balance. By employing scornful tropes about races and cultures considered inferior, Union soldiers suggested that guerrilla defiance resembled dislocated Mexican regimes and loose-knit Indian nations, always on the verge of collapse and upheaval. Guerrillas, in the minds of the occupiers, represented the ignoble and fragmented components of these societies.[18]

Union soldiers' descriptions of fierce Indians creeping beyond the bushes through dense forests, established their definitions—or perhaps imaginations—of a clandestine enemy. Likewise, the "uncivilized" character of guerrilla conduct came to be associated with the remote, untamed fringes of the Southern landscape, as Northerners connected primitive warfare with the region's wild spaces. Irregular combatants used the natural environment to perpetuate grisly attacks upon unsuspecting soldiers, reorienting both the face and landscape of war. Union soldiers thus linked the South's unimproved terrains, thick gnarled woods, and twisted underbrush with the crude manner in which its people fought.[19]

The occupiers produced a discourse unique to the irregular war, employing environmental rhetoric merged with traditional military expression. This language fused guerrillas with the natural environment, which transformed the local geography into an active, violent setting. "[H]aving been shot at from the brush," an Illinois soldier wrote from Mississippi, the "infantry always thinks the enemy is just out of gunshot of them." The brush extended indefinitely, concealing the prowling guerrilla, offering impenetrable safety. Stephen F. Fleharty, an officer in northern Middle Tennessee, described riding in a supply train "thundering along through a wild uncivilized region, when as we approached a dense wood it suddenly stopped, and bang! bang! bang! went firearms in the woods near by." Equating the remote lands with the guerrillas who utilized the woods, Fleharty and his comrades later were "busy at work felling trees that might protect an attacking party."[20]

The unruly environment and the wild enemy it concealed became synonymous, each symbolizing the South's violent, archaic character. Union soldiers often did not distinguish between their adversaries and the landscape, instead seeing man and nature as a single object. Ironically, though, the dearth of improved land seemed to sprout and nourish guerrillas, providing sustenance for their violent conditions. "The country looks desolate about this place," Michigander David Millspaugh wrote from Nashville, "the thick scrubby cedar grows along the road offering a good place for rebs to hide and prowl about." William Whitney, a volunteer in the Thirty-Eighth Massachusetts, described how the guerrillas' "mode of action is to hide in the bushes when they hear of the approach of travelers and jumping out suddenly presenting a pistol. . . . Such is the state of the country."[21]

Linking the untamed backwoods with irregular combatants, finding their comrades' mutilated bodies, and enduring fear, stress, and worry about suddenly being murdered collectively transformed Union occupiers' understanding of a meaningful conflict. Guerrillas merged their identities as civilians and combatants through, according to Northern volunteers, peculiar incarnations of savage Indians and feral landscapes. Thus, the disarrayed milieu of irregular warfare strained the occupiers' own blurring line between private civilian and combatant. The citizen-soldier ideal necessitated that those who threatened the nation must be killed or defeated, determined by a code of ethical wartime conduct.

Yet guerrillas completely repudiated the basic requirements and assumptions of the citizen-soldier concept. Their identity as civilians-turned-combatants relied on murder and secrecy, evident in their disregard for moral law and military custom. Union occupiers had to adapt to this model themselves or be killed. But they struggled with the implications of this dilemma, primarily because they retained so much of their *own* civilian identities. In their minds, the guerrillas did not function as formal soldiers but rather as rebellious and dangerous civilians. In peacetime society, private citizens naturally would remove themselves from the presence of such uncouth individuals. And civilians certainly were not granted the legal or moral recourse to act in such a warlike manner.

The experience of occupation thrust these contradictory elements directly at Union soldiers, challenging them to decide how best to wage a counterguerrilla war. Killing functioned as a universally acknowledged component of warfare, blurring the lines between civilian and combatant, and arbitrary murder did not. Their immediate enemies thrived *exclusively* on this brand of lawlessness, yet methods of conventional warfare failed to work within the occupation environment. Ultimately, the Union's citizen-soldiers would have to adopt guerrilla tactics, which transformed the volunteer's relationship to the army and American society.[22]

* * *

As Charles Wright Wills and his comrades in the Seventh Illinois Cavalry rode through northern Alabama, confiscating cotton and displaying their martial authority, he outlined the citizen-soldier's emerging role as a counterguerrilla force. "It makes the chivalry howl," he rejoiced in August 1862, "which is glorious music in our ears." Yet Wills tempered his enthusiasm when he recalled "the murders of Bob McCook, a dozen of men in this command and hundreds in the army," who allegedly died at the hands of guerrillas. "[W]e are satisfied that citizens do ten-elevenths of such work," he estimated, "and nothing less than the removal of every citizen beyond our lines . . . will satisfy us."[23]

Several months later, while guarding the railroads near Holly Springs, Mississippi, Wills had a darker perspective, though not due to guerrilla violence. Instead, he was struggling to accept the counterguerrilla tactics employed by his fellow occupation soldiers. Although he hardly sympathized with rebellious Southerners, Wills admitted, "'tis shocking and enough to make one's blood boil to see the manner in which some of our folks have treated them." Disgusted at the sight of his comrades destroying private property in the name of vengeance, he declared: "The army is becoming awfully depraved. How the civilized home folks will ever be able to live with them after the war, is, I think something of a question. If we don't degenerate into a nation of thieves, 'twill not be for lack of example set by a fair portion of our army."[24]

Wills outlined one of the great challenges of military occupation in the citizen-soldier tradition. Expecting a war governed by restraint and civilized conduct, he instead saw firsthand how insurgencies flouted traditional assumptions of warfare. The enemy had changed tactics, arbitrarily killing Union soldiers beyond the bounds of mutually accepted combat. The common Union soldier, therefore, would have to change *his* approach to war too. But for Wills, the implications were stark: the long-term virtue of the common citizen-soldier was at stake. Could volunteers wage a counterguerrilla war while also safeguarding the exceptional nature of the American citizen-soldier ideal?[25]

Although Union troops strove to fulfill the obligations of the volunteer tradition, they believed that guerrillas could not be fully eradicated. Their enemies refused to fight in an honorable and open manner, straining available means of retaliation. But instead of skulking in fear and struggling to abide by more muted approaches to war, the occupiers embarked on a campaign of destructiveness and violence, hoping to punish the perpetrators of irregular warfare. Soldiers justified an overwhelming response against guerrillas, stretching the limits of restraint and widening the gulf between wartime civility and annihilation. Officers learned that their men could not be convinced to withhold their anger; thus, they sanctioned, sometimes unofficially, wide-ranging tactics to counter the guerrilla presence. The occupation war was now reshaped, defined by vengeance and measured by devastation, altered by a profound shift in the citizen-soldier's mentality.[26]

Writing from Memphis in the summer of 1862, General Sherman summarized the evolving convictions of countless Union troops. "The Government of the United States may now safely proceed on the proper Rule that all in the South are Enemies of all in the North," he declared, "and not only are they unfriendly, but all who can procure arms now bear them as organized Regiments or Guerrillas." While one can debate the accuracy of Sherman's claim, *he* believed it to be true, as did many soldiers, thus dictating how they would conduct a counterguerrilla war. Since all white Southerners were potentially complicit in inflicting harm on U.S. armies, and all were considered impediments to the restoration of the Union, nothing short of annihilation would settle the issue. Of course, widespread extermination never occurred, but that misses the point. The *mind* and *practice* of the citizen-soldier was irrevocably altered in the realization that new methods of reprisal were now justified.[27]

The occupiers channeled their retribution through two distinct modes of recourse. First, they attacked the Southern landscape, targeting local environs, towns, buildings, and private homes. Second, they trained their sights directly on irregular combatants, the physical embodiment of insurgent brutality. Union armies of occupation conducted this new war through patrols and scouting expeditions, deploying small squads to move swiftly and efficiently across the countryside. Using fortified garrisons as bases of operation, counterguerrilla forces often moved at night, ambushing guerrilla dens and surprising communities suspected of harboring irregular warriors. These approaches were not unique—they were the same ones employed by the guerrillas themselves.[28]

A key distinction needs to be drawn between the nature of reprisals and the ways in which Union occupiers understood their new roles in the irregular conflict. Desires for retaliation certainly inspired the evolution of counterguerrilla warfare. Yet it is crucial to recognize the constraints placed on the conduct of Union armies. Although most soldiers and commanders sought to extend "the hard hand of war" against guerrillas and sympathetic civilians, appropriate calculations were made on the acceptable limits of retribution. Rather than murdering or imprisoning whole communities, Union authorities instead countered the guerrilla presence by burning private dwellings thought to be the sources of irregular violence, even banishing and dislocating citizens from entire towns. The targets of such actions were particular residents suspected of harboring, funding, or operating as guerrillas. These pragmatic policies nonetheless conditioned the troops in the art of waging war against the countryside and ununiformed civilians.[29]

Edward F. Noyes, an Ohio soldier, summarized the emerging tension. "As I go through this traitor country," he wrote, "two impulses are struggling in my heart, one to lay waste as we go—like destroying angels, to kill & burn and make the way of the transgressors hard—the other is to wage a civilized warfare." Union policymakers and military authorities initially sought the latter path, but the troops chose differently. "[I]n view of the atrocities of the rebels," Noyes concluded, "our boys only wait for the word, to make the land desolate."[30]

Lieutenant Colonel John A. Keith of the Twenty-First Indiana Volunteers expanded on Noyes's wavering but ultimate acceptance of attacking the physical landscape in retribution for guerrilla warfare. Stationed in southeastern Louisiana, Keith received orders to take a detachment of troops into Terrebonne Parish to "arrest and punish" those guilty of killing wounded Union soldiers. The dead soldiers "were robbed of everything . . . [their] bodies after being brutally and disgustingly abused, being kicked and beaten, the face of [one soldier] scarcely retaining the semblance of a human being." Keith, along with 240 members of the Twenty-First Indiana, arrested several citizens of Houma, learning that the primary culprit was a prominent attorney and newspaper editor who plotted the murders of other local citizens. The officer demanded that other residents come forward who could provide information, then declared that "the foul and unnatural murder of two American soldiers, repugnant alike to the instincts of humanity and the practice of civilized warfare," had resulted in the perpetual occupation of the town. "The atrocious nature of the crime itself," he continued, "the indecent, shameless and un-Christianlike burial and robbery of the dead . . . have forever disgraced the town of Houma."[31]

Because the citizens of Houma opted to embrace an uncivilized mode of warfare, Keith implied, Union occupiers were justified to respond in kind. After the officer ordered residents to rebury the dead soldiers, he left a flag atop the courthouse as a reminder that "terrible consequences" would befall the town and its population if the graves were disturbed or future attacks attempted. Indeed, local residents were given forty-eight hours to identify and turn in the culprits. If they failed to comply, Keith warned, "not a vestige of the town of Houma shall be left to identify its former location, and the plantations in the parish of Terrebonne shall suffer in a like degree." Southern civilians and the physical landscape were no longer passive actors in the drama of wartime occupation. All were now brought into the purview of Union occupation, used as symbols of retribution and vengeance.[32]

Houma, Louisiana, escaped the destruction of the U.S. military; other Southern communities were not so fortunate. As the guerrilla threat continued unabated, Union armies unleashed the very tactics threatened by Lieutenant Colonel Keith. With meticulous commitment, occupiers exacted devastation on towns. Addison McPheeters Jr. of the Twenty-First Illinois Volunteers commented, "the boys are raising hell in Nashville every night, I would not care if they would burn it to ashes, it is no uncommon thing to see houses burning here." McPheeters explained that such occurrences are "the best way to put down the rebellion, burn them out, damn them." His fellow Illinoisan Wills agreed. "This little town had when the war commenced some 40 house," he wrote from Middleton, Tennessee, in June 1863. "[N]ow it boasts of not more than 12 or 15. . . . This country has literally been scraped, swept and scoured."[33]

Such tactics were crucial to reconstruct what McPheeters and Wills considered an archaic, rebellious society. Union soldiers believed that a reunited nation must be rid of the physical emblems of violent resistance. Guided by an acute sense of national cleansing, Major James A. Connolly of the 123rd Illinois declared in 1864, "We'll burn every house, barn, church, . . . and nothing but the most complete desolation will be found in our track." If civilians, Connolly continued, "play the guerrilla against us, neither youth nor age, nor sex will be respected. Everything must be destroyed." Indeed, irregular violence symbolized what Union soldiers considered to be outmoded relics of the Southern culture of honor. Everything in the Southern world, from its agricultural staples to its rural lands to its embrace of guerrillas, must be extinguished. The postwar Union needed a singular identity, they believed, one drawn in the Northern image.[34]

Citizen-soldiers realized that national rejuvenation could come only through great destruction and violence. Rather than expressing shock or confusion in the wake of clandestine attacks, the occupiers unleashed absolute devastation on properties suspected of harboring the assailants. As he traveled on a railroad transport to Huntsville, Alabama, John Beaty described how guerrillas attacked the train, wounding multiple Yankees and slashing telegraph lines. Informing the residents of nearby Paint Rock "that this bushwhacking must cease," Beaty "then set fire to the town, took three citizens with me, returned to the train, and proceeded to Huntsville." Irregular combatants, he explained, did not have a place in formal warfare: "If they wanted to fight they should enter the army, meet us like honorable men, and not, assassin-like, fire at us from the woods and run." He pledged thenceforth to hold all citizens responsible for similar conduct, "mak[ing] them more uncomfortable than they would be in hell."[35]

While Union soldiers made a deliberate decision to target both the Southern countryside and local towns, they also trained their vengeance on the bodies and physical presence of their guerrilla adversaries. The choice to integrate a corporeal element into the irregular war created an intimate, yet deeply violent bond between the rivals. Guerrillas had long disgraced the occupiers' bodies through mutilation, hanging, and disfigurement. Union soldiers now responded in kind, applying methods that they believed would smother the irregular threat, redefining a war that lacked structure and clarity.

The guerrilla war had always been an acutely personal affair. Thus, Union volunteers justified many modes of unconventional recourse against their enemies' bodies, refusing to acknowledge irregulars to be official soldiers deserving of honorable treatment. Capturing a leader from a guerrilla company roaming the countryside near Bayou Boeuf, Louisiana, "evidently for the purpose of shooting down our soldiers," one officer issued a directive outlining the rebel's destiny. The guerrilla would "be shot to death . . . as a warning to all men not soldiers to remain peaceably at their homes, if they desire the protection of the Government of the 'United States.'" The crime was simple, the verdict a warning to other potential civilian combatants: "And the fate of this man shall be the fate of every man found with arms in his hands not belonging to the so-called Army of the Confederate States of America." An honorable man, in the minds of Union occupiers, would enlist in the regular military and fight his nation's battles in uniform. If he chose an alternative course, he would meet a fate similar to the very type of war he perpetrated.[36]

The occupiers implemented a similar variety of violent procedures, which ranged from hangings, executions, beatings, chases through the woods, and even knocking on suspected guerrillas' doors and pulling the trigger. If Northern men were targeted, killed, and mutilated in a shameful fashion, then their aggressors would endure the same destiny. Union soldiers sought to demonstrate that they too could play the game of irregular warfare while reducing their enemy to nothing more than a skeleton. Simple killing and burial, practiced only by the uniformed, principal armies, was unsatisfactory. A new code governed the irregular war, with competitions of power directing its course.[37]

Oftentimes, soldiers were instructed to avoid capturing and imprisoning guerrillas. One officer ordered his troops, who picketed the lines outside of New Orleans, "if attacked by such infernal rascals to bring no prisoners in, only their dead carcasses, of those that they are successful in securing." A Michigan colonel stationed in Middle Tennessee replied to similar orders in July 1863: "I propose to bring some of the scoundrels to grief if I can. I have no doubt they intend the same thing by me." Over the next few months, his regiment captured numerous bushwhackers, most of whom were sent to Nashville for imprisonment. Yet the colonel kept "two or three to hang when we want a little fun."[38]

Union occupiers indeed used hanging as an effective means of retribution. Iowan Musser explained to his father that although reports of such executions rarely appeared in Northern newspapers, "that is no sign that it is not done." In fact, Musser acknowledged that when captured, guerrillas were often hanged. As early as August 1861, the commander at Cape Girardeau, Missouri, declared that if local guerrillas made war on the local population or army, "I will hang them, and take a bitter revenge on you in other respects." And the practice continued more than three years later, following the murders of three Union troops at Powder Springs, Georgia. The guerrilla perpetrators were caught and ordered to "be either shot or hung in retaliation."[39]

Although grisly, no-quarter retaliation provided soldiers with significant martial leverage. Mirroring guerrilla tactics allowed the Yankees to exert a degree of power and control that they believed had been undermined by irregular warfare. A Massachusetts soldier disagreed with imprisoning guerrillas, calling on his officers "to take everyone they catch and shoot them." And Taylor Peirce's comrades in Missouri did exactly that. "[W]e gather up [the guerrillas] as we go along and shoot them," he wrote in February 1863. "They are a set of murderers and are not fit to live to encumber society." One local resident, who allegedly fired at Peirce's officers, was eventually apprehended and shot near his house. "When we came along he was lying by the side of the road and his wife was crying over him," Peirce wrote. "It looks hard to me to see a man shot and his wife and children left alone but these men are the ones that keep up the cruelties that are continually being practiced in this part of Missouri."[40]

The male image emerged as the central target in this sphere of violence. Yet some modes of recourse, while grounded in masculine humiliation, represented basic forms of peace, innocence, and even a sense of playful restraint. Considering guerrilla tactics to be acts of purposeful emasculation, the occupiers fashioned ways to make their enemies endure the shame of their conduct. As the Ninety-Second New York Volunteers picketed the cold, dark shores of the Neuse River in coastal North Carolina, they experienced nightly battles with guerrillas, whom they "hated cordially, and were disposed to show them but little mercy." The irregular combatants often dressed in civilian clothes, professing to be "unionists, neutrals, or 'know nothings,'" often shooting "our men in cold blood." After a scouting mission departed to rout a guerrilla band, the rebel leader challenged one of the occupation officers to a fight. The two parties squared off in the woods, riding, yelling, and shooting in a violent rampage.[41]

When the fighting ceased, men on both sides lay killed or wounded, while some of the guerrillas were captured and taken to the Union garrison at New Bern. "One prisoner was marched through the city," an observer noted, "with a woman's skirt on, and on his back a placard with the words, 'guerrilla caught dressed in woman's clothes.'" The soldiers simply could have killed their prized catch, leaving his body to rot in the woods enveloped only by the peace of nature. Indeed, many Union occupiers had experienced their final moments alone and isolated. But the spectacle of subjecting guerrillas' masculinity to uncensored public humiliation in the broad daylight of Southern society seemed much too tempting to resist. Cloaking the male body in women's attire, in this instance, was far superior to wasting a bullet.[42]

The corpus of Union reprisals extended far beyond gendered humiliation. Perhaps the most peculiar tactic in the war against Confederate guerrillas was not a variation in military strategy or conduct. Rather, it was a change in language, an alteration of an imagined mentality. Union soldiers transformed expeditions and battles against guerrillas into a symbolic hunt, reminiscent of their prewar days in pursuit of deer, quail, or other wild game. Converting guerrillas into a faceless foe, devoid of personality or humanity, allowed the occupiers to pursue their adversaries without concern for moral bearing. Instead, the hunt for guerrillas evolved into a game, a competition to see who could acquire the best prize. The environment of occupation, which threatened the core of Northern masculinity, permitted the occupiers to exhibit the virtues of manly contest. There were no rules, no limitations, and no referees. Only raw instinct guided the soldier against his prey.[43]

The guerrilla body, indeed the "dead carcasses" of deceased opponents, became the trophy in this competition. Soldiers carefully gauged the score, always noting the number of dead opponents compared to survived comrades. "Captain Bishop with some 25 men of Companies A and G did a splendid thing last Thursday night," Charles Wills exclaimed. "He surprised Saulstreet [*sic,* S. G. Street] and 20 of his gang . . . , killed three wounded and captured five and six sound prisoners, without losing one of our men or getting scratched. Three of the wounded guerrillas have since died." The hunt had commenced.[44]

Cloaking the battle against guerrillas in familiar, prewar language allowed the occupiers to distance themselves from the horrors of irregular war. But their rhetoric also reveals the troubling extent to which they had become desensitized to shocking conduct. Characterizing their opponents merely as animals implicitly sanctioned a mode of warfare that stripped the humanity away from both the hunter and the hunted. "I have just returned from a grand guerrilla hunt of over a week," Connecticut officer Frank Peck reported from New Orleans. The pursuit, though, proved difficult because "they never fight openly" and often "skedaddled" when the hunters appeared.[45]

Yet such hunts offered a uniquely challenging element: the crafty and clever intellects of the human prey. Henry C. Gilbert, colonel of the Nineteenth Michigan Volunteers, described a recent guerrilla pursuit in Tennessee. "Our hunting still goes on," he wrote in March 1864, "'the hunting of men.' Over 40 of the guerrillas have been shot since Feb." The search parties, he reported, "go on foot & hunt men as they would deer. . . . It is awful but there is an excitement about it that places it far above anything recorded by Cumming and Gerard the Lion Hunter. Their game were mere brutes without intelligence. Here we hunt men with brains." Gilbert exhibited an acute sense of pride, celebrating the sport's great difficulty and praising his victims' shrewdness and quickness. Thus, the thrill of securing a human trophy appeared all the more satisfying.[46]

The hunting paradigm not only functioned as a metaphor or an imagined discourse but also morphed into official military policy. A circular distributed throughout central Missouri instructed Union forces on how to blend into the local landscape. "The brush and low grounds that would be likely to afford cover for guerrillas must be closely examined," the directive stated, "to move secretly, the men will be marched across the prairies at night." The environmental dimensions of guerrilla warfare had come full circle. Soldiers who had once been victims of the wild landscape now became part of the untamed bush. "[W]hile on the hunt no talking or other loud noises will be made," the order charged, "except signals, which should be the imitation of some forest bird or animal." If troops followed these instructions carefully, "it [would] not be possible for bands of guerrillas to remain concealed in any portion of this district." Thus, the guerrilla-turned-prey signified an object to be killed, not captured. In a war stripped of honor and control, the language of hunting—employed by either guerrillas or Union soldiers—assumed a hierarchical structure, with a superior assailant tracking a less powerful foe who always fled for his life.[47]

* * *

The hunt for men testified to Union authorities' increasing concern that the guerrilla war had spiraled dangerously out of control. Soldiers in service to the Republic, some reasoned, did not adopt irregular, brutal tactics, but rather adhered to the standards of civilized warfare. An inspector general from the U.S. Army, writing from St. Louis in March 1864, perhaps best summarized the implications of the occupiers' violent retributions. "It has been the custom in many parts of the department for officers and soldiers, when operating against guerrillas, to immediately put to death all who fall into their hands," he disclosed, "even after they have thrown down their arms and asked for mercy." The inspector reported that most officers prohibited taking prisoners, explaining that these unyielding tactics prolonged the nature of irregular warfare by inducing the enemy to "to fight to desperation." The guerrilla war would continue as long as occupation continued, he concluded, "where murder, highway robbery, pillage, and other kindred crimes are now of almost daily occurrence."[48]

The inspector further outlined his concerns about the tactics adopted by local counterguerrilla forces. Acknowledging that "bushwhackers undoubtedly deserve the most severe chastisement for the atrocities they have committed," he nonetheless wondered if imprisonment and military tribunals—traditional modes of recourse—would provide "the opportunity to prove their innocence before being executed." The inspector's disquietude emerged not out of sympathy for suspected guerrillas, but from a deep-seated anxiety that the Republic's citizen-soldiers had themselves morphed into bodies of unrestrained, chaotic violence. "The existing practice," he conceded, "enables evil-disposed soldiers to rob and murder loyal and inoffensive citizens under the plea that they were acting as bushwhackers, and it unquestionably tends to demoralize the troops."[49]

Ironically, the inspector general's report appeared one year *after* civil and military authorities sought to address the consequences of Union soldiers' participation in the irregular war. In the spring of 1863, General in Chief Henry W. Halleck enlisted Francis Lieber, a German-born political philosopher, historian, and expert on international military conduct, to codify the U.S. counterguerrilla doctrine. In a pamphlet entitled *Guerrilla Parties: Considered with Reference to the Laws and Usages of War,* Lieber defined nearly a dozen forms of irregular combatants, concluding that the nature of guerrilla warfare presented the greatest threat to an effective military governance. He considered all forms of guerrilla warfare, and the individuals who perpetrated it, to be illegitimate, and therefore not to be utilized or acknowledged by civilized nations. Though he argued that "guerrillamen" should be captured and tried as war criminals, and sometimes even subject to decisive modes of recourse, Lieber understood that theoretical applications of irregular warfare were "much diminished by the fact that the soldier generally decides these cases for himself."[50]

Lieber's pamphlet culminated in General Orders No. 100, a codified system of conduct for armies of occupation. Published in April 1863, the code incorporated the nebulous "laws of war" into systematized legal theory. Hoping to define the Union's war of occupation in positive, moral, and humanitarian terms, "Lieber's Code" gave instructions on the proper ways to conduct martial law, to protect civilians' rights and private property, and to accommodate prisoners of war. The code grew out of Lieber's concern about the implications of wartime destruction, targeting of civilians, and seemingly wanton rampage perpetrated by Union armies. Inspired to introduce a level of moral consideration to wartime occupation, he believed that "[m]en who take up arms against one another in public war do not cease on this account to be moral beings, responsible to one another and to God."[51]

The insistence on morality and restraint functioned at the heart of Lieber's quest. He authorized wide latitude for Union armies as they swept across the South, employing "those measures which are indispensable for securing the ends of the war." Lieber merely wanted to curb what he considered *unnecessary* or *unauthorized* pillaging, destruction, or killing. The definitions of such terms, though, were left to the discretion of soldiers and field commanders. In fact, General Orders No. 100 suggested that protection of enemy civilians and property were exceptions to the rule. Above all, Lieber's Code was hazy on particular guidelines. On the one hand, armies of occupation were instructed to practice civilized restraint, while on the other, they were given substantial leeway to measure their destruction of hostile environments and people.[52]

Although seemingly ambiguous and at times contradictory, General Orders No. 100 held deeper significance. Lieber's writings conveyed a sense of discomfort with the apparent cultural degradation of the Union's citizen-armies as they became mired in the long-term occupation of the rebel South. Military governance created unprecedented challenges, including waging an expansive counterguerrilla war against hostile civilians. Lieber's Code implied that the United States simply did not have a grounded experience in wars of occupation or a martial culture dedicated to regulating the behavior of white citizens. Indeed, large, static, invading armies, even in wartime, were believed to spawn depravity and violence and to fragment society. Occupation sought to restore peace and loyalty to rebellious regions, yet sometimes the exact opposite occurred. White Southerners resisted, and blue-clad troops pushed back until explosive chaos ensued.

General Orders No. 100, then, was the U.S. government's attempt to articulate a national position on the ethical integrity of the Republic's soldiers. The code suggested that the *troops* were to blame if they committed acts of destruction or violently engaged enemy combatants, while the *nation* would be exonerated. Those occupiers who defied the conditions of the orders would be interpreted as men who failed to abide by the official ethical standards of the army. Lieber therefore sought to return a degree of virtue and restraint to military institutions he considered had become devoid of moral direction. The United States must win this war, he concluded, or else all efforts to rededicate the nation to a system of moral wartime conduct would be irrelevant. Thus, Lieber's Code was less an inflexible legal decree and more a commentary on maintaining the honorable standards of a citizen army.[53]

Lieber's Code also gave voice to Union soldiers' broader anxieties that counterguerrilla warfare had fundamentally transformed the American citizen-soldier tradition. These men came to consider that their conduct, while necessary, also had damaging consequences. Guerrilla attacks outside of New Orleans, for example, pushed local occupation commanders to order the destruction of nearby Donaldsonville, Louisiana. F. A. Roe, a lieutenant on the USS *Katahdin,* implored his commanding officers to halt what he considered the needless leveling of the town. "I am desirous of encountering enemies and of injuring them in every manly manner," he protested, "but I cannot further prostitute the dignity of my profession." Roe believed, "It is disgraceful and humiliating to me to be ordered on guard duty of soldiers employed in pillaging ladies' dresses and petticoats, and I respectfully request that I may be relieved from such service."[54]

Likewise, James W. Denver, a brigadier general of volunteers stationed near Corinth, Mississippi, described the intellectual and practical transformations of soldiers as they embarked on expeditions. The troops, he wrote in late 1862, "seem to be possessed with the idea that in order to carry on war men must throw aside civilization and become savages." He related "some most heart-rending cases, and I do not see how men claiming to be enlightened and educated do such things." Denver revealed how his troops engaged civilians and destroyed private property, acknowledging that occupation soldiers had become devoid of restraint and virtue. Using language reminiscent of earlier depictions of guerrilla conduct, and even their allusions to Mexicans and Indians, Denver worried, "It will not be long before the soldier will be sunk in the cowardly plunderer—for men loaded with plunder are always cowards—and instead of an army we will have an undisciplined mob."[55]

Charles Henry Moulton, a private in the Sixth Michigan Volunteers, built on Denver's perspective, believing that occupation and guerrilla warfare fundamentally altered the character of Northern volunteers. In the wake of a recent expedition and guerrilla hunt through the swamps near New Orleans, Moulton wrote, "I am getting so I dont care for anything. let a man be in the army," he warned, "and he is more like a Savage than a man." As early as October 1862, he suggested that the irregular war had taken its toll on his fellow Michiganders occupying southern Louisiana. Their violent responses functioned as the great agents in their changed attitudes. "Our men is all sick and tired of the war," he moaned, "and are discouraged." The war seemed "as though it would never get done," primarily because guerrillas appeared to be self-perpetuating, never fully eradicated. Thus, Union soldiers, Moulton concluded with troubled expression, became hardened and distant, adopting a callous disregard for civilized conduct and human dignity.[56]

Conceptions of participating in an army both surrounded and inculcated by haphazard violence infected soldiers' perspectives of themselves. Like Moulton, Charles Musser of the Twenty-Ninth Iowa admitted in February 1863 that he served in "what would be called the dark side of soldiering." After waging war against guerrillas for several months, he recognized that "the boys are geting so that they do not care much for anything." Indeed, the constant firing upon Union pickets and the hit-and-run tactics employed by clandestine foes inspired deep-seated hatred for all white Southerners. "[W]e are in for fighting to the last rather than give way to traitors and rebels," he declared in April, and "we will kill, 'burn,' and destroy every thing before us to gain our end. I never want to come home untill the war is ended." Musser's brand of demoralization culminated with a desire not to leave the army, but rather to lay waste to the people and region he associated with irregular war. "I have no pity, no mercy," he acknowledged. "I would rather put a minne ball through the brain of one of them renegades than the . . . [regular-army] rebel down here."[57]

The transformation of soldiers into "savages" who sought unmitigated vengeance against communities and enemy combatants caused some Yankees to believe that they also had transformed Union armies into destabilizing institutions. Military occupation sought to restore peace and calm to rebellious regions, yet according to Sergeant Major Stephen F. Fleharty, invading armies only spawned guerrilla resistance. "A bitter feeling of hostility is naturally engendered," he wrote as a result of the incursions into Tennessee, "and we find the citizens ever willing to aid the armed rebels in all their designs against us." Anti-Union sentiment and guerrilla conduct accordingly pushed volunteers into extreme forms of retaliation, fueling a self-perpetuating cycle of violence.[58]

Northern men wrote that, while still citizen-soldiers, their perceptions of volunteer service, their understanding of the enemy, and the nature of their military art had been fundamentally changed by the irregular war. As the inspector general in St. Louis suggested, little distinguished guerrilla from occupier. The ethos of occupation brought them both together, merging their identities as collective agents of violence. Robert Gould Shaw, the white colonel of the famed all-black Fifty-Fourth Massachusetts Volunteers, perhaps best articulated the blurring line between citizen-soldier and guerrilla. Shaw pledged himself to civilized warfare, trusting that belligerents on both sides would remain wedded to controlled, moral conduct. Guerrilla warfare, he believed, unleashed Union soldiers to perform acts of peculiar violence against people, property, and the environment. "Besides my own distaste for this barbarous sort of warfare," he acknowledged, the guerrilla conflict was fraught with disrepute and disgrace, sinking the citizen-soldier "into a plunderer or robber."[59]

The abnormal culture of occupation, he observed, spawned an equally strange mode of warfare, which Shaw considered unprofessional and simplistic. He criticized his colleague in the Department of the South, Colonel James Montgomery, for adopting irregular tactics to combat the insurgent presence. "He is a guerrilla-man," Shaw scoffed. "He is an Indian in his mode of warfare. . . . I can't say I admire it. It isn't like a fair stand up such as our Potomac Army is accustomed to." Distinguishing between his former service in the Union's principal field army and the guerrilla war in South Carolina and Georgia, Shaw denounced Montgomery's tactics. He displayed a willingness to burn and destroy "wherever he goes with great gusto, & looks as if he had quite a taste for hanging people & throat-cutting whenever a suitable subject offers."[60]

While disgusted by Montgomery's tactics, Shaw also worried about the broader implications of his comrade's conduct. Denigrating him a "bushwhacker," he believed that Montgomery reflected the larger body of soldiers who relished wanton destruction and unnecessary violence. Montgomery evidently had been converted by the dictates of counterguerrilla operations, claiming that Union soldiers were no longer bound by traditional modes of warfare. "[T]hat makes it none the less revolting to wreak our vengeance on the innocent and defenseless," Shaw grumbled in June 1863, following the burning of Darien, Georgia, which he believed degraded the character of citizen armies. Referring to it as a "dirty piece of business," he noticed the stark differences between occupying territory in the Department of the South and serving in the field with the Army of the Potomac. "For myself, I have gone through the war so far without dishonour," he acknowledged, yet the very acts of committing war upon civilians, hanging guerrilla enemies, or skulking through the woods, he believed, were all devoid of "pluck or courage."[61]

If, though, the army had fought honorably for possession of territory, such as it did in Virginia, Shaw explained, "there might have been some reason for Montgomery's acting as he did; but as the case stands, I can't see any justification." Outlining the spirit of the citizen-soldier ideal, Shaw suggested that "[i]f it were the order of our government to overrun the South with fire and sword, I might look at it in a different light." But "[a]s the case stands, we are no better than 'Semmes,' who attacks and destroys defenceless vessels, and haven't even the poor excuse of gaining anything by it." He concluded, "After going through the hard campaigning and hard fighting in Virginia, this makes me very much ashamed of myself."[62]

Colonel Shaw witnessed both wars during his time in the service. He was exposed to the massive eastern armies that confronted one another on the formal field of battle, generally devoid of contact with civilians, and focused on deciding the fate of the nation. He considered himself a citizen-soldier in this conflict, performing his civic duty and accepting the possibility of an honorable death. Guided by a sense of moral integrity that accompanied his identity as a volunteer, Shaw subscribed to an awareness of control and discipline. As a participant in the irregular war, though, he witnessed what he perceived to be the devolution of the citizen-soldier's moral character. The ethos of war in the occupied Confederacy, he learned, was far different from that in the eastern theater. Although disgusted with Montgomery's contention, "we are outlawed, and therefore not bound by the rules of regular warfare," Shaw could not deny the sentiment's truth. The irregular war, populated by vicious guerrillas, vengeful soldiers, and suspicious civilians, enveloped all participants in its violent fold, changing everyone in the process.[63]

The American Civil War and even its aftermath were nowhere near as destructive as other nineteenth-century conflicts in, for example, Napoleonic Europe or dynastic China. The tolls of human death and environmental annihilation fell far short of these international episodes. But Shaw highlighted a curious feature when he attempted to interpret the problematic nature of the Civil War's irregular conflict. Underscoring the influence of both individual experience and collective national identity, Shaw implied that focusing on numbers of dead soldiers or civilians missed a startling reality about the changing character of American warfare. Indeed, he witnessed far more deaths on the fields at Antietam than he did in the destruction of Darien, Georgia. Yet as indicated by his adverse reaction to the latter, Shaw emphasized the fast-evolving integrity of the citizen-soldier ideal in occupied zones.[64]

Americans believed that they lived in an exceptional nation in which free citizens were obligated to protect and defend the Republic, which safeguarded their liberty. So when Shaw perceived that citizen-soldiers might discard the obligations of morality and honor and engage in modes of warfare reflective of guerrilla tactics, he considered the ethic of republican citizenship to be threatened. This idea revealed the fundamental tension underlying the entire irregular war. Although Union occupiers actually behaved with considerable restraint, especially when compared with other nineteenth-century civil conflicts, Shaw presumed that their *participation* in counterguerrilla warfare had pushed them into an inescapable arena of perceived immorality, far removed from the romanticized citizen-soldier tradition.

Part of the problem stemmed from the character of their enemy: white Southerners. Yankee troops hated their Confederate and irregular foes, believing that the South had to be remade into a Northern image. U.S. armies, though, did not set the entire region ablaze nor imprison and murder millions of civilians. Yet for each home that was burned, each community that was destroyed, and each guerrilla who was hunted, Union soldiers feared the symbolism of what they considered violent conduct against American environs and white American citizens.

And herein lay the ironic tragedy of military occupation and counterguerrilla and guerrilla combat during the American Civil War. Union citizen-soldiers who participated in irregular conflict underwent a striking alteration in their intellectual conceptions of war, their definitions of the enemy, and their understandings of traditional, civilized conduct. Occupiers learned that war was not a restricted event in which only formal armies battled for the fate of nations. Instead, occupation sometimes necessitated making war on civilians, destroying private homes, and wrecking the landscape. Union soldiers thus recognized that their particular war was directed against *white* civilians, *private* property, and *American* environs—ingredients central to the concept of national exceptionalism. Contemporaries could not escape the unsettling reality that white citizen-soldiers conducted war against white citizens, all of whom claimed a common national heritage and who might again inhabit the same nation. The long-term implications of this troubling fact were yet to be seen.[65]

NOTES

The author recognizes all who read and critiqued earlier versions of this piece; thanks Barton Myers and Brian McKnight for the invitation to contribute; and is grateful to Aaron Sheehan-Dean for sharing sources from his research in the Department of the Gulf Records at the National Archives.

1. Ricardo A. Herrera, "Self-Governance and the American Citizen as Soldier, 1775–1861," *Journal of Military History* 65 (Jan. 2001): 21–52.

2. Earl J. Hess, *The Union Soldier in Battle: Enduring the Ordeal of Combat* (Lawrence: University Press of Kansas, 1997), ix–xii; James M. McPherson, *For Cause and Comrades: Why Men Fought in the Civil War* (New York: Oxford University Press, 1997), 22–24, 94–105, 131, 110–14,

170–76; Gary W. Gallagher, *The Union War* (Cambridge, Mass.: Harvard University Press, 2011), 3, 26–27, 64, 120, 124.

3. The most comprehensive books on occupation during the Civil War are Ash, *When the Yankees Came;* and Grimsley, *Hard Hand of War.* See also Andrew F. Lang, "The Garrison War: Culture, Race, and the Problem of Military Occupation during the American Civil War Era" (Ph.D., diss., Rice University, 2013). On the Mexican-American War, see Robert W. Johannsen, *To the Halls of the Montezumas: The Mexican War in the American Imagination* (New York: Oxford University Press, 1985), 45–107; James M. McCaffrey, *Army of Manifest Destiny: The American Soldier in the Mexican War, 1846–1848* (New York: New York University Press, 1992); Richard Bruce Winders, *Mr. Polk's Army: The American Military Experience in the Mexican War* (College Station: Texas A&M University Press, 1997); and Foos, *Short, Offhand, Killing Affair.*

4. Birtle, *U.S. Army Counterinsurgency and Contingency Operations Doctrine,* 23; Lang, "Republicanism, Race, and Reconstruction," esp. 560–65.

5. Reid Mitchell, *Civil War Soldiers* (New York: Viking, 1988), 134. For the most recent comprehensive treatment of guerrilla war during the Civil War, see Sutherland, *Savage Conflict.*

6. Michael Fellman, *Citizen Sherman: A Life of William Tecumseh Sherman* (New York: Random House, 1995), 140.

7. For literature on the "dark turn" in Civil War history, see Fellman, *Views from the Dark Side of American History;* Berry, *Weirding the War;* Michael C. C. Adams, *Living Hell: The Dark Side of the Civil War* (Baltimore: Johns Hopkins University Press, 2014); and Sternhell, "Revisionism Reinvented?" On seeking a balance between the dark turn and traditional literatures, see Gallagher and Meier, "Coming to Terms with Civil War Military History," 487–508, 492. For a recent historiographical treatment of the Civil War soldiering experience, see Lorien Foote, "Soldiers," in *A Companion to the U.S. Civil War,* ed. Aaron Sheehan-Dean, 2 vols. (Hoboken, N.J.: Wiley-Blackwell, 2014), 1:114–31.

8. Scholars have given excellent attention to the creation and evolution of the guerrilla war, its purpose, and its leading figures. See, for example, Fellman, *Inside War,* 149–66; Mitchell, *Civil War Soldiers,* 132–38; Ash, *When the Yankees Came,* 21–22, 47–50, 64–65, 63–67; Sutherland, *Guerrillas, Unionists, and Violence;* Mackey, *Uncivil War;* McKnight, *Contested Borderland;* George S. Burkhardt, *Confederate Rage, Yankee Wrath: No Quarter in the Civil War* (Carbondale: Southern Illinois University Press, 2007); Mountcastle, *Punitive War;* Myers, *Executing Daniel Bright;* Sutherland, *Savage Conflict;* Geiger, *Financial Fraud and Guerrilla Violence;* and McKnight, *Confederate Outlaw.*

9. William T. Sherman to Salmon P. Chase, Aug. 11, 1862, William T. Sherman, *Sherman's Civil War: Selected Correspondence of William T. Sherman, 1860–1865,* ed. Brooks D. Simpson and Jean V. Berlin (Chapel Hill: University of North Carolina Press, 1999), 269; Ash, *When the Yankees Came,* 34, 46–50; Sutherland, *Savage Conflict.*

10. John M. King, *Three Years with the 92d Illinois: The Civil War Diary of John M. King,* ed. Claire E. Swedburg (Mechanicsburg, Pa.: Stackpole Books, 1999), 52 (Feb. 10, 1863).

11. W. S. Rosecrans to Sterling Price, Oct. 16, 1862, U.S. War Department, *War of the Rebellion,* ser. 1, 4:627 (hereafter cited as *O.R.*); John Pope, General Orders No. 7, ibid., 12(2):51; Birtle, *U.S. Army Counterinsurgency and Contingency Operations Doctrine,* chap. 2.

12. Charles Harding Cox to My dear Sister, Feb. 13, 1863, in Lorna Lutes Sylvester, ed., "Civil War Letters of Charles Harding Cox," *Indiana Magazine of History* 68 (Mar. 1972): 48; Diary entry, Feb. 26, 1862, Henry J. Seaman Diary, Civil War Times Illustrated Collection, U.S. Army History Education Center, Carlisle Barracks, Carlisle, Pa. (hereafter cited as USAHEC); Samuel Kerr to Dear Malvina, Dec. 26, 1862, DL0522.57, Kerr Letters, John L. Nau III Civil War Collection, Houston, Tex. (hereafter cited as JLNC). See also Frank Marcotte to Dear Mother, July 25, 1862, in Frank B. Marcotte, ed., *Private Osborne, Massachusetts 23rd Volunteers: Burnside Expedition, Roanoke Island, Second Front against Richmond* (Gretna, La.: Pelican, 1999), 92–93; and Dexter Ladd Diary, July 22, 1862, Civil War Miscellaneous Collection, USAHEC.

13. Jerome Spilman to Dear Wife, July 23 [1862], Jerome Spilman Letters, Civil War Times Illustrated Collection, USAHEC; Courtland G. Stanton to wife, [Mar. or Apr.] 5, 1863, DL0011.032, Courtland G. Stanton Letters, JLNC; See also Browning, "'I Am Not So Patriotic as I Was Once,'" 230.

14. Frank Twitchell to [unknown], Apr. 3, 1864, Mss. 3367, Louisiana and Lower Mississippi Valley Collections, Hill Memorial Library, Louisiana State University, Baton Rouge.

15. Charles O. Musser to Dear Father, Feb. 12, 1863, Charles O. Musser, *Soldier Boy: The Civil War Letters of Charles O. Musser, 29th Iowa*, ed. Barry Popchock (Iowa City: University of Iowa Press, 1995), 27. See also D. Leib Ambrose Diary, Sept. 15, 1863, in Daniel E. Sutherland, ed., *From Shiloh to Savannah: The Seventh Illinois Infantry in the Civil War* (DeKalb: Northern Illinois University Press, 2003), 134; and Drew Gilpin Faust, *This Republic of Suffering: Death and the American Civil War* (New York: Alfred A. Knopf, 2008), 6–17, 28–31.

16. Frank H. Peck to mother, Aug. 3, 1862, Montgomery Family Papers, 1771–1974, Peck Correspondence, Library of Congress, Washington, D. C. (hereafter cited as LC).

17. Justus F. Gale to Dear Father, Nov. 7, 1862, in Nina Silber and Mary Beth Sievens, eds., *Yankee Correspondence: Civil War Letters between New Englanders and the Home Front* (Charlottesville: University Press of Virginia, 1996), 140; John Vreeland to Dear Parents, Mar. 17, 1862, John Vreeland Letters, Vreeland-Warden Collection, USAHEC; Report of Brig. Gen. Thomas Williams, June 10, 1862, No. 1756, Box 1, Letters Received 1862, RG 393, Part 1, Department of the Gulf, National Archives and Records Administration, Washington, D.C. (hereafter cited as NARA); William S. Rosecrans, "To the Loyal Citizens of Western Virginia," Aug. 20, 1861, *O.R.*, 5(1):576; Sutherland, *Savage Conflict*, 28.

18. Gregory P. Downs, "The Mexicanization of American Politics: The United States' Transnational Path from Civil War to Stabilization," *American Historical Review* 117 (Apr. 2012): 387–409.

19. Lisa M. Brady has recently called for historians to consider "how ideas about what is wild and what is civilized affected conduct during war," especially in the realm of guerrilla conflict. See "The Future of Civil War Studies: Environmental Histories," *Journal of the Civil War Era*, http://journalofthecivilwarera.org/forum-the-future-of-civil-war-era-studies/the-future-of-civil-war-era-studies-environmental-histories/.

20. Diary, June 9, 1862, Charles Wright Wills, *Army Life of an Illinois Soldier*, comp. Mary E. Kellog (Washington, D.C.: Globe, 1906), 100; Stephen F. Fleharty letters, May 3, June 19, 1863, S. F. Fleharty, *Jottings from Dixie: The Civil War Dispatches of Sergeant Major Stephen F. Fleharty, U.S.A.*, ed. Terry L. Wilson (Baton Rouge: Louisiana State University Press, 1999), 111, 121. See also Diary,

Apr. 4, 1863, Charles W. Porter, *In the Devil's Dominions: A Union Soldier's Adventures in "Bushwhacker Country,"* ed. Patrick Brophy (Nevada, Mo.: Vernon County Historical Society, 1998), 89.

21. David Millspaugh Diary, Apr. 21, 1863, Michigan in the Civil War Military Collections, Bentley Historical Library, University of Michigan, Ann Arbor; William H. Whitney to Dear Brother Frankie, Jan. 21, 1864, in Tara Zachary Laver, ed., "'Where Duty Shall Call': The Baton Rouge Civil War Letters of William H. Whitney," *Louisiana History* 46 (Summer 2005): 360–61.

22. Fellman, *Inside War,* 149–66.

23. Diary, Aug. 14, 1862, Wills, *Army Life of an Illinois Soldier,* 125.

24. Diary, Dec. 12, 1862, ibid., 136.

25. Lang, "Republicanism, Race, and Reconstruction," 564–65.

26. Mitchell, *Civil War Soldiers,* 135.

27. William T. Sherman to Salmon P. Chase, Aug. 11, 1862, Sherman, *Sherman's Civil War,* 269.

28. On the specific components of counterguerrilla/counterinsurgency policy and practice, see Birtle, *U.S. Army Counterinsurgency and Contingency Operations Doctrine,* 23–47; Noe, "Exterminating Savages."

29. Birtle, *U.S. Army Counterinsurgency and Contingency Operations Doctrine,* 23–47; Noe, "Exterminating Savages"; Grimsley, *Hard Hand of War,* 111–19, 184–85.

30. Edward F. Noyes to R. H. Stephenson, Sept. 21, 1861, quoted in Sutherland, *Savage Conflict,* 59; Mountcastle, *Punitive War,* 66–67; Fellman, *Citizen Sherman,* 140. For an interpretation of the Union's initial policy of conciliation, see Grimsley, *Hard Hand of War,* 7–66.

31. John A. Keith to Benjamin Butler, May 22, 1862, No. 1756, Box 1, Letters Received, RG 393, Part 1, Department of the Gulf, NARA.

32. Ibid.

33. Addison McPheeters Jr. to R. P. McPheeters, Nov. 25, 1862, McPheeters Family Papers, USAHEC; Diary, June 4, 1863, Wills, *Army Life of an Illinois Soldier,* 178. Historians have devoted great attention to the nature of the destruction wrought by the Union army, especially the shifts in national policy from conciliation to "hard war." Attempting not to repeat what scholars have already successfully established, this essay focuses more on the shifting mindsets, and their implications, of Union soldiers who adopted such tactics. For studies on the former, see Ash, *When the Yankees Came,* 13–75; Grimsley, *Hard Hand of War,* 67–170; Mountcastle, *Punitive War,* 1, 6–7, 24–25, 59, 71–72, 106–108, 126–28; and Danielson, *War's Desolating Scourge,* 45–91.

34. Diary, Nov. 26, 1864, James A. Connolly, *Three Years in the Army of Cumberland: The Letters and Diary of Major James A. Connolly,* ed. Paul M. Angle (Bloomington: Indiana University Press, 1969), 324; Joseph Allen Frank, *With Ballot and Bayonet: The Political Socialization of American Civil War Soldiers* (Athens: University of Georgia Press, 1998), 79–80; Mitchell, *Civil War Soldiers,* 138. For a broader discussion of Union soldiers' motivation to reshape Confederate society in the image of the Union, see Gallagher, *Union War,* 54–71.

35. Diary, May 2, 1862, John Beaty, *The Citizen-Soldier: Or, Memoirs of a Volunteer* (Cincinnati: Wilstatch, Baldwin, 1879), 138–39. The destruction of private property was one of the most common forms of counterguerrilla doctrine. For additional examples of similar episodes, see Sutherland, *Savage Conflict,* 124–25, 153, 178, 234–35; Mountcastle, *Punitive War,* 56–84; Grimsley, *Hard Hand of War,* 78–119; and Birtle, *U.S. Army Counterinsurgency and Contingency Operations Doctrine,* 36–40.

36. Special Orders No. 211, May 6, 1863, No. 1756, Box 3, Letters Received 1863, RG 393, Part 1, Department of the Gulf, NARA. See also Department of Arkansas, Circular No. 1, Mar. 23, 1864, *O.R.*, ser. 1, 34(2):705; and J. Holt to Edward M. Stanton, Aug. 5, 1864, ibid., ser. 3, 4(1):577.

37. For a specific interpretation of targeting of the male body, by both sides, during the guerrilla war, see Fellman, *Inside War*, 186–89.

38. Dudley to Davis, Sept. 6, 1862, No. 1756, Box 1, Letters Received 1863, RG 393, Part 1, Department of the Gulf, NARA; Henry C. Gilbert to My Dear Wife, July 18, Nov. 4, 1863, Henry C. Gilbert Papers, 1826–64, James S. Schoff Civil War Collection, William J. Clements Library, University of Michigan, Ann Arbor (hereafter cited as SCWC).

39. Charles O. Musser to Dear Father, Nov. 9, 1864, Musser, *Soldier Boy*, 161; Thomas C. Reynolds to C. C. Marsh, Aug. 10, 1861, *O.R.*, ser. 1, 3(1):449; William D. Whipple to John Bell Hood, Feb. 1, 1865, ibid., ser. 2, 8(1):164. Other counterguerrilla methods included Union soldiers disguising themselves in guerrilla dress and infiltrating enemy camps. See Sutherland, *Savage Conflict*, 113.

40. Taylor Peirce to Dear Catherine, Feb. 16, 1863, in Richard L. Kiper, ed., *Dear Catherine, Dear Taylor: The Civil War Letters of a Union Soldier and His Wife* (Lawrence: University Press of Kansas, 2002), 80.

41. Albert W. Mann, *History of the Forty-Fifth Regiment Massachusetts Volunteer Militia, "the Cadet Regiment"* (Jamaica Plain, Mass.: Brookside Print, 1908), 219.

42. Ibid. Northerners commonly practiced the feminization of their wartime political and military opponents. See, for example, Nina Silber, "Intemperate Men, Spiteful Women, and Jefferson Davis: Northern Views of the Defeated South," *American Quarterly* 41 (Dec. 1989): 614–35.

43. Michael Fellman introduced the concept of the guerrilla war as analogous to a wild-game hunt in *Inside War*, 176–84.

44. Dudley to Davis, Sept. 6, 1862, No. 1756, Box 1, Letters Received 1863, RG 393, Part 1, Department of the Gulf, NARA; Diary, May 29, 1863, Wills, *Army Life of an Illinois Soldier*, 177. See also Diary, Apr. 4, 1863, Porter, *In the Devil's Dominions*, 54–55.

45. Frank Peck to Dear David, Aug. 10, 1862, Montgomery Family Papers, Peck Correspondence, LC.

46. Henry C. Gilbert to Dear Wife, Mar. 23, 1864, Gilbert Papers, SCWC. Roualeyn George Gordon-Cumming was a Scottish traveler, sportsman, and author who spent much of the mid-nineteenth century hunting big game in Africa. He wrote of his exploits in *Five Years of a Hunter: Life in the Far Interior of South Africa* (1850). Jules Gérard, known popularly during the nineteenth century as "the lion hunter," was a French sportsman and author who wrote *Lion Hunting and Sporting Life in Algeria* (1856).

47. District of Central Missouri, Circular No. 2, Mar. 1, 1864, *O.R.*, ser. 1, 34(2):478–79; Fellman, *Inside War*, 178.

48. R. B. Marcy to Maj. O. D. Greene, Mar. 29, 1864, *O.R.*, ser. 1, 34(2):775–76.

49. Ibid., 776.

50. Francis Lieber, "Guerrilla Parties: Considered with Reference to the Laws Usages of War," ibid., ser. 3, 2:301–309; Henry W. Halleck to Francis Lieber, Aug. 6, 1862, ibid., 301; Frank Burt Freidel, *Francis Lieber: Nineteenth Century Liberal* (Baton Rouge: Louisiana State University Press, 1947); Peter W. Becker, "Lieber's Place in History," in *Francis Lieber and the Culture of the Mind*, ed. Charles R. Mack and Henry H. Lesesne (Columbia: University of South Carolina Press, 2005), 1–7; Sutherland, *Savage Conflict*, 126–28.

51. General Orders No. 100, "Instructions for the Government of Armies of the United States in the Field," Apr. 24, 1863, *O.R.*, ser. 3, 3:148–64; Grimsley, *Hard Hand of War,* 148–51; Frank Freidel, "General Orders 100 and Military Government," *Mississippi Valley Historical Review* 32 (Mar. 1946): 541–56; Ralph H. Gabriel, "American Experience with Military Government," *American Historical Review* 49 (July 1944): 637–39; Matthew J. Mancini, "Francis Lieber, Slavery, and the 'Genesis' of the Laws of War," *Journal of Southern History* 77 (May 2011): 325–48; Witt, *Lincoln's Code,* 170–96.

52. General Orders No. 100, *O.R.*, ser. 3, 3:150; Grimsley, *Hard Hand of War,* 150.

53. L. Lynn Hogue, "Lieber's Military Code and its Legacy," in Mack and Lesesne, eds., *Francis Lieber and the Culture of the Mind,* 51–61.

54. F. A. Roe to Henry W. Morris, Sept. 11, 1862, *O.R.*, ser. 1, 15(1):569; Mountcastle, *Punitive War,* 71.

55. James W. Denver to My Dear Wife, Nov. 29, 1862, James W. Denver Leter, Harrisburg Civil War Roundtable Collection, USAHEC.

56. Charles Henry Moulton to Dear Bro and Sister, Oct. 31, 1862, Charles Henry Moulton Papers, 1835–1916, Michigan in the Civil War Collection, Bentley Library, University of Michigan, Ann Arbor.

57. Charles O. Musser, undated letter fragment, [probably Feb. 3, 1863], and Musser to Dear Father and Mother, Apr. 29, 1863, Musser, *Soldier Boy,* 25, 49, 54.

58. Stephen F. Fleharty letter, Dec. 31, 1862, Fleharty, *Jottings from Dixie,* 88.

59. Robert Gould Shaw to My Dearest Annie, June 9, 1863, Robert Gould Shaw, *Blue-Eyed Child of Fortune: The Civil War Letters of Colonel Robert Gould Shaw,* ed. Russell Duncan (Athens: University of Georgia Press, 1992), 343.

60. Robert Gould Shaw to My Dearest Annie, June 6, 1863, ibid., 339.

61. Shaw to My Dearest Annie, June 9, 1863, ibid., 343.

62. Ibid., 343–44.

63. Ibid., 343.

64. For a comparative context of these events, see Hsieh, "Total War and the American Civil War Reconsidered."

65. Mitchell, *Civil War Soldiers,* 138; Grimsley, *Hard Hand of War,* 184–85, 224.

CIVIL WAR GUERRILLAS IN A GLOBAL, COMPARATIVE CONTEXT

EARL J. HESS

Captain Cyrus Clay Carpenter, a Federal commissary officer and future governor of Iowa, reflected on the progress of Union arms while stationed at Hamburg, Tennessee, on July 4, 1862. He was pleased with the accomplishments of Abraham Lincoln's large, regularly organized armies, believing they had mostly broken up regularly organized Confederate forces in the Mississippi Valley. But Carpenter predicted a different kind of conflict to emerge from that defeat. He was sure that "the war henceforth here will be of the Guerilla and Spanish kind and I think will not last long."[1] Carpenter certainly was right to predict a guerrilla uprising—in fact, it already was well underway by July 4. He also reflected a common awareness that the Spanish Uprising against Napoleon more than half a century earlier was the best international model for what might develop in the way of guerrilla warfare during the American Civil War.

This essay explores how far the guerrilla phenomenon of the 1860s in America mirrored the past and foretold the future of irregular warfare within a global context. The international perspective sheds light on the nature of guerrilla warfare in the Civil War and connects that phenomenon with trends in the larger world community. Several examples of guerrilla war have been selected for comparison, beginning with the Spanish Uprising initiated fifty-three years before the firing on Fort Sumter, and extending to American participation in the Vietnam War one hundred years after Appomattox. General characteristics of each example will be briefly compared with the guerrilla phenomenon of the 1860s and suggestions drawn as to how Civil War historians can meaningfully interpret that phenomenon.

The intrusion of French forces into the kingdom of Spain sparked a popular uprising in May 1808 that came to define guerrilla warfare in the Western world. It was a complicated phenomenon that combined a genuine insurrection of the people with a calculated effort to use what was left of the regularly organized Spanish army as irregular fighters. To a degree, regularly organized

British forces also participated in the bloody struggle that developed in Spain and lasted six years before dying out by April 1814.[2]

Spanish writers have long extolled the guerrilla as proof of the valor of the Spanish people, viewing the uprising through romantic and nationalistic lenses. While not all historians and commentators have agreed, most Spanish writers have assumed that the guerrillas were effective fighters and have argued that they played a large role in the ultimate defeat of Napoleon. The image of the "Spanish Ulcer," working with the unwise invasion of Russia in 1812, tends to dominate discussion of why the Napoleonic Empire weakened and eventually collapsed. The uprising has long been viewed as a major component of Spanish national identity in the modern world.[3]

Recent historians have questioned the overly positive image of "la guerrilla." Charles J. Esdaile's thorough study of the uprising portrays it as unique in the Napoleonic era. Nowhere else in the French empire was there such a large and sustained irregular effort against Napoleon's troops. The geography and culture of Spain proved to be fruitful ground for the growth of an insurrection against hated occupying forces. Genuine guerrilla bands ("self-constituted," as Francis Lieber of the Civil War era called them, created as grassroots organizations rather than by governmental authority) certainly cropped up by the summer of 1808. But many other elements became involved in fighting the French on irregular terms, including Spanish militia, units of the Spanish regular army, and outside forces provided by the British Army. Esdaile portrays all these components as achieving some degree of success in their efforts, though far less than necessary to support the generous historical view of the guerrillas' influence on the course of history.[4]

Esdaile argues that popular hatred of Napoleon and support for the guerrillas was far more limited than previously thought. He believes that "the bulk of the population had little interest in the war." Motives for joining guerrilla bands included hatred of the French, a love of adventure, a desire for material gain (plunder), and the crushing necessity of finding some way to feed oneself in a society that even in peacetime lived on the margin of subsistence. Some French deserters joined irregular bands as well, with motives one can only guess.[5]

Esdaile identified a sample of 1,166 guerrillas and discovered the occupation of 322 of them. All came from the better classes of Spanish society rather than the lower classes. He argues that even if the other 844 were all peasants, it still indicates that the guerrilla movement was not dominated by the poorest elements of society. At the least, "groups representing fewer than 10% of the population provided 17% of the guerrilla movement." Of 371 men Esdaile identified as heading a guerrilla band, 103 came from the middle or upper classes, 37 came from the lower classes, and 222 had undetermined origins. At least 27 percent of the leadership came from the better elements of society, while barely 10 percent came from the lower classes.[6]

Local governments tried to organize guerrilla bands, with at best uneven success. More effective were Spanish army personnel who participated in the irregular warfare. Esdaile argues that the more effective guerrilla bands also were those headed by leaders who realized that creating tighter control over their men, adapting to regular tactics, and cooperating more closely with regular units led to a higher degree of success. "In the case of the smaller and less militarized bands contact with the invader was infrequent. . . , the military capacities of such forces were very limited." Even the better groups were not consistently successful.[7]

Esdaile also fully documents the many examples of guerrilla bands that barely saw French soldiers, using their weapons instead against Spanish civilians. Band leaders often displayed rampant jealousy, greed, and callousness, plundering citizens freely without fighting the invader. Esdaile argues that the guerrilla movement contributed to the decline of the regular Spanish army as men of military age often chose to be an irregular, and contact with guerrilla bands often led to a breakdown of discipline among regular units operating with them.[8]

It is true that provinces such as Navarre and Aragon were largely self-liberated, but Napoleon helped the guerrillas dominate those areas by stripping them of French troops as he transferred 25,000 men from occupation duty in Spain to support his 1812 invasion of Russia.[9]

Although a quarter of a million French troops occupied Spain, they could not eliminate "la guerrilla." But it is equally true that the irregulars could not defeat the occupiers. Only when French commitments in other parts of the empire reduced troop numbers could the guerrilla have better chances of success. As the empire weakened and died due to factors beyond the borders of Spain, the guerrillas could claim a small role in its defeat.[10]

Esdaile argues persuasively that "the impact of the Spanish guerrillas was much less impressive than has generally been thought to be the case." Efforts by the Spanish government at all levels to control these bands normally ended in failure. In fact, Esdaile believes that the guerrillas ultimately were a negative factor in the war against Napoleon. "Consuming disproportionate quantities of food, revenue and other resources, they sapped the strength of the Spanish regulars whilst increasing the discontent and alienation of the populace."[11]

The end of the war did not spell the end of the guerrillas. They "ended, much as they had begun, in banditry and opportunism. Always primarily the product of the poverty and social disruption brought about by the impact of war, invasion and economic collapse on a society whose resources were at the best of times very sparse, the *partidas* were motivated by what contemporary observers called 'greed' as much as they were by a desire to fight the French." After the invader evacuated Spain, many guerrilla bands continued to plunder the populace and ignore efforts by the resurrected government to enforce law and order. That government had to make war on the guerrillas in order to bring peace to Spain.[12]

C. C. Carpenter could not have known how right he was when he predicted that the Southern guerrilla war would be of the "Spanish kind." There were many similarities between the guerrilla phenomenon of the Civil War and the Spanish Uprising. A variety of irregular forces participated in the Southern war against Federal occupiers, including many self-constituted bands, regularly organized units of cavalrymen detailed from their parent regiments behind enemy lines, and a formal partisan organization created by the Confederate government. Rebel authorities in Richmond never seem to have consciously used the Spanish Uprising as a model, but they encouraged self-constituted bands to rise, utilized their regular forces in irregular ways, and tried on their own to experiment with a formal organization that occupied middle ground between a self-constituted band and a volunteer regiment.

Confederate authorities received many petitions to authorize what B. W. Blakewood called "a regiment of mounted men, on the guerrilla order." Many of these petitions included extraordinary freedom of action for the members of such units. D. M. K. Campbell of Alabama wanted authority for his men to fight as they pleased and to keep any captured Union property and equipment for their own use. Campbell asked "that our Government will not interfere with our movements or hold us accountable in after time for the part taken in the premises. As regards the enemy, we will take care of ourselves." He asked if the Richmond authorities would "look upon us as unlawful bands that ought to be dispersed, capture us, and hold us amenable to the laws of the country?

Or would not the Government, as well as all good citizens, applaud rather than condemn such a movement?" The answer was clear: the Confederate government could not condone such tactics and urged Campbell and his colleagues to form a regularly organized unit for volunteer service in the army.[13]

Despite that initial policy, some Confederate officials later in the war condoned self-constituted guerrilla bands and encouraged their activities. Major General Sterling Price was among the most active, urging the notorious irregulars in Missouri to rise up and support his planned invasion of that border state in the late summer of 1864; "Bloody Bill" Anderson actually held a commission from the Confederate army. With some justification, many Union officers blamed Richmond for the rise of guerrilla bands and the destruction that attended their activities as well as Federal countermeasures to suppress them.[14]

But it is important to keep in mind that the Confederate government never officially condoned or supported self-constituted bands, and most officials felt that the guerrillas were a force set apart from formal channels. The Richmond authorities certainly did see the utility of irregular warfare against the North. Many local commanders detailed fragments of volunteer cavalry regiments to act in guerrilla fashion behind enemy lines by attacking railroad communications. This caused a good deal of confusion for Union officers; when members of regularly organized units hid in the brush and sniped at trains or Federal patrols, it naturally was impossible to know if they were true guerrillas or troops organized and supported by the Confederate government. Much of this kind of irregular warfare occurred during the Atlanta Campaign as rebel officers sought ways to hamper Major General William T. Sherman's relentless drive toward the city in the summer of 1864.[15]

Detaching units from volunteer regiments could only supply a handful of men to the irregular operations behind Union lines, and the self-constituted bands were by definition beyond any hope of control by Confederate authorities. Therefore, Richmond tried to create a new force designed for permanent duty behind enemy lines but authorized by central authority and thus under some degree of control by regular officers. Congress authorized the creation of a partisan force in April 1862, organized within Union-occupied territory and armed by the recruits themselves as far as possible. "Though raised and intended immediately for the defense of their own section of country," Secretary of War George W. Randolph wrote, "they . . . will be subject to the orders of the general commanding the military department in which they are included."

Anyone liable to the Conscription Act was not allowed to join the partisan force. Partisans would receive the same pay as regularly organized soldiers and were expected to obey the same laws. About one hundred companies had been raised or were in the process of being organized by September 1862.[16]

Because partisans held commissions and muster rolls from the Confederate government, the Federals officially counted them as soldiers, not as guerrillas. But the nature of partisan service created so many gray areas that any attempt to categorize the men as one or the other inevitably fell apart. They were to a surprising degree self-constituted bands that often did not wear Confederate uniforms or use regularly issued Confederate weapons. It was easy for true guerrillas to claim to be partisans when captured, even if they could not prove it, and many arguments arose between Union and Confederate officers charged with managing the complicated prisoner-exchange system as a result. In the field, it mattered little whether someone was a true partisan or a true guerrilla, for their attack had the same effect on Union soldiers charged with defending a railroad or a town.[17]

Confederate authorities found the partisan experiment to have largely failed by the war's midpoint. They recognized the need for stricter control, and Secretary of War James L. Seddon was compelled to admit by the fall of 1863 that the few benefits of the system had been more than counterbalanced by the problems. Offered prize money and with a great deal of freedom to do as they pleased, the partisans had committed "grave mischiefs" in the form of depredations on the civilian population. Many noncombatants considered Confederate irregulars "as more formidable and destructive to our own people than to the enemy." Men eager to command a partisan company siphoned off recruits from regularly organized units, and the depredating tendency of partisan units tended to rub off on volunteer units that came into contact with them. One of the few partisan leaders of the war who fulfilled the hopes of the government was Lieutenant Colonel John S. Mosby, a former member of a regularly organized volunteer unit who exerted an unusual amount of discipline and control over the Forty-Third Battalion, Virginia Cavalry, and mercilessly harassed Union troops in Virginia during the last months of the Civil War.[18]

Federal authorities relied heavily on Major General Henry W. Halleck, commander of the Department of the Missouri, to define the guerrilla in a military-legal sense. A keen student of history and military science, Halleck early in the war set his definition within the context of those two subjects. "It is a well-established principle," he wrote in a general order, "that insurgents, not militarily organized under the laws of the State, predatory partisans, and guerrilla bands are not entitled" to be treated as prisoners of war. "They are, in a legal sense, mere freebooters and banditti, and are liable to the same punishment which was imposed upon guerrilla bands by Napoleon in Spain and by Scott in Mexico." For Halleck, the key point was administrative, whether a legitimate state or putative state had organized, armed, clothed, and disciplined a military force or if the group was self-constituted.[19]

When Halleck asked Lieber for his opinion, the professor fully concurred with his view of the case. At the general's request, Lieber wrote a pamphlet defining what "guerrilla" and "partisan" meant to legal scholars and the Federal government alike. A guerrilla band was "either self-constituted or constituted by the call of a single individual, not according to the general law of levy, conscription, or volunteering." Lieber acknowledged that partisans such as those raised by the Confederate government were indeed soldiers who shared a tradition in the European military past with light infantry, operating outside the confines of the field army to interrupt enemy logistics and communications. This definition was officially adopted by the War Department in General Orders No. 100 in April 1863.[20]

Esdaile contributed his most important findings when focusing on the self-constituted guerrilla bands of the Spanish Uprising, and the same is true of Civil War historians. Unlike the situation before, where French forces evacuated Spain to give the guerrillas some opportunity to claim they played a role in Napoleon's defeat, the Confederate government not only decisively lost the Civil War but also was dismantled in the process. Despite the claims of recent historians that irregular warfare occupied center stage and even played a decisive role in shaping the Civil War, no one on the Federal side saw it that way. High-level Union commanders always considered the guerrilla threat to be marginal compared to the major purpose of Union field forces, which was to deal with the large, regularly organized Confederate army. The highest estimate of guerrilla strength is 50,000 men, a small force compared to the more than one million troops at Lincoln's disposal by war's end. It is also a comparatively small force when stacked up against the 400,000 or so Confederate troops at Jefferson Davis's disposal at any given time during the war. The guerrillas operated in bands that ranged in size from a few dozen to 1,000 men.[21]

It is true that for lower-level Federal officers assigned occupation duty in guerrilla-infested areas, combating the irregulars was a grueling, energy-sapping job. But occupation troops had other responsibilities as well, including combating regularly organized Confederate units, dealing with civilians, and protecting communications from a variety of threats. "The army of the Confederacy is the South," General Sherman stated in late 1863. "I am not going to bother myself about guerrillas and citizens. If they can't do our main arteries harm, is all I aim at." As long as the guerrilla threat remained marginal, Federal officials detached limited manpower to it and reserved the bulk of their troops for major campaigning against the principal armies of the Richmond government. "I pay but little attention to guerrillas," Sherman told Major General Nathaniel P. Banks. "They have never attacked any place of note, and are chiefly engaged in harassing their own people."[22]

While Southern irregulars could not claim strategic success in the Civil War, they could inflict tactical defeat on occupying Federal troops now and then. As Esdaile has pointed out for the Spanish guerrillas, the level of tactical effectiveness among Confederate guerrilla bands varied according to the extent of their organization, armament, planning, and quality of leadership. Those groups led by men with a military mind who imposed some degree of discipline became serious threats to local Union forces. While much of the Federal soldiers' exposure to guerrillas consisted of futile efforts to run them down, at times they got a regular battle out of them.[23]

When confronting partisan units, the level of tactical effectiveness often increased. Captain Francis T. Moore of the Second Illinois Cavalry recalled encountering one of the most effective partisan leaders, Colonel William C. Falkner, in western Tennessee during the fall of 1862; Falkner led an authorized partisan regiment of about three hundred men. Moore engaged in a tough fight with the partisans, even though heavily outnumbered, and barely was able to extricate his Illinois cavalrymen before they were overwhelmed. Falkner conducted the battle with skill, "handling his men more like soldiers than a mob," as Moore put it. The colonel was later captured, and Moore had an opportunity to converse with him. He dressed in Confederate gray but carried no insignia of rank. "Very proud and erect in his bearing, he was a man that from his very appearance would anywhere command respect. He is said to be a good commander, reckless and daring." But by 1863, many of Falkner's troops committed depredations on Southern civilians while he ran afoul of Confederate authorities for siphoning off men liable to the draft.[24]

Civil War observers fully documented the many examples of guerrilla failures on the tactical level. Many bands avoided Union soldiers altogether and instead hit defenseless civilians to acquire horses, money, and food. Plunder was a major motivation for many Southern irregulars, and it often is difficult to see that protecting civilians, driving out the invader, or sustaining the Confederate government played any role in their actions or view of the sectional crisis. Leaders often had difficulty controlling their men. Far more often than not, these fighters became more troublesome to Southern civilians than to Union occupiers. It must be pointed out that many Unionist guerrillas within the Confederacy caused a good deal of trouble for the rebel government, which had fewer resources to devote to antiguerrilla duty than did its Federal counterpart.

The degree to which Southern civilians tried to resist guerrilla depredations was limited at best. There is little wonder that faced with the greater task of subduing regularly organized Confederate forces, many Union commanders gave up trying to protect defenseless residents. As Sherman told Major General Stephen A. Hurlbut in November 1863: "It is none of our business to protect a people that has sent all its youth, and arms, and horses, and all that is of any account to war against us. . . . All you need to do is to protect the interests and property of the United States. The people have done all the harm they can, so let them reap the consequences." Sherman kept the core objective of Federal armies in sight. "Our duty is to strike and break up the large armies of the Confederacy," he told Hurlbut.[25]

Esdaile has concluded that Spanish guerrillas could not lay much if any claim to having won the war against French occupiers. In fact, he argues that they hampered the war against Napoleon rather than helped it. Much the same could be said of Southern irregulars. They destabilized Southern society, inflicted terrible suffering on friend and foe alike, and opened the door for many people to satisfy personal grudges with neighbors. Overall, the guerrillas increased the suffering attendant on sectional warfare by many times without a corresponding benefit that can be counted as worth the cost. Confederate efforts to control irregular warfare through the partisan law can only be counted a limited success that ultimately failed to achieve its purpose.[26]

The question of whether organized Confederate armies should have dispersed into the countryside and conducted massive guerrilla warfare rather than surrender in 1865 has fascinated historians for some time. It seems a fit option for the defeated government, and President Davis's message of April 4, 1865, to the South seems to many scholars a call for taking to the woods and converting the failed conventional war into a massive guerrilla effort. But as historian William B. Feis has pointed out, Davis was not really making a call for guerrilla warfare. Instead, he advocated using regularly organized units to operate in a highly mobile fashion inside the interior of what was left of the Confederacy, similar to the strategy employed by George Washington and the Continental Army during the Revolutionary War. The majority of Confederates, from General Robert E. Lee down to the lowest private, either rejected the guerrilla option or remained indifferent to the prospect of hiding out in the brush for years to come in a futile effort to redeem the lost fortunes of the Confederacy.[27]

In the waning days of the war, a number of local rebel commanders even offered to cooperate with their Federal counterparts in combating guerrillas and restoring peace and order to civilian society. Colonel Josiah Patterson of the Fifth Alabama Cavalry put it well when he informed Brigadier General Robert S. Granger that Lee's surrender ended all reasonable hope of Southern victory. "A further shedding of blood would be suicidal. Guerrilla or partisan warfare would be the only warfare that we could resort to, and that would prove disastrous alike to friend and foe. However much may have been said heretofore of guerrilla warfare as a last resort, yet no good man, however patriotic he might be, would encourage, much less participate in, such a struggle."[28]

Even before Lee's surrender, Lieutenant General Nathan Bedford Forrest expressed his disdain for Southern guerrillas. When Colonel John G. Parkhurst met Forrest under a flag of truce to arrange for an exchange of prisoners in late February 1865, the Confederate general "remarked that he was as anxious to rid the country of them as was any officer in the U.S. Army, and that he would esteem it a favor if General [George H.] Thomas would hang every one he caught."[29]

Anyone captivated by the prospect of a massive guerrilla war in the South following Lee's surrender should also keep in mind that the Federals devoted very limited numbers of troops to contend with guerrillas during the war. With major Confederate armies defeated and more than one million troops under arms, Union commanders would have been able to devote their entire military force to the task. As early as September 1862, Sherman warned Confederate major general Thomas C. Hindman what would happen if the Federals devoted massive manpower to the anti-irregular conflict: "At that game your guerrillas would meet their equals, and the world would be shocked by the acts of atrocity resulting from such warfare."[30]

There was a widespread assumption on both sides that if the Confederacy could not win its independence by using large conventional armies, it could not do so through irregular warfare even on a massive scale. The Southern guerrilla effort and its corresponding Union counterirregular effort always were sideshows of the big show from a military standpoint, even though they had an important and devastating effect on society that historians are beginning to measure. Any escalation or continuation of the guerrilla conflict would have failed to achieve the desired military goals while exponentially increasing the war's horrible consequences on the lives of millions of civilians throughout the ex-Confederacy.

Much the same can be said about the military versus societal effect of the Spanish Uprising. But the Civil War guerrilla phenomenon differs remarkably from its Spanish predecessor in the memory of the historical event in the minds of those who lived through the tragic era of 1861–65. While Spanish guerrillas achieved the status of heroes in the eyes of many writers following the collapse of the Napoleonic Empire, Southern irregulars found very few champions after Appomattox. A survey of articles published in the *Confederate Veteran* reveals that the overwhelming majority of them viewed wartime guerrillas in a negative light. In short, most veterans of organized Confederate units had no regard for bushwhackers, portraying them as ruthless killers who terrorized innocent civilians as much as they bothered Union occupiers. "I was always strongly opposed to guerrilla warfare," wrote W. J. Courtney, a veteran of the Fifth Missouri Cavalry (C.S.), "believing it wrong and a poor way to settle anything." These Confederate veterans wrote in the same way about Unionist guerrillas they encountered in strongly loyalist areas of the South or of Federal deserters who became plunderers in Southern territory.[31]

As time passed and the bitterness of the war morphed into Lost Cause mythology, Southern guerrillas who had survived the war found that they had no place in Confederate memory. That is why some of them wrote their memoirs and tried to join veterans' organizations—to find some degree of acceptance. But they never were accorded a significant role in the development of the South's memory of the Civil War.[32]

One can assume the primary reason for this is that, unlike the Spanish guerrillas, Southern guerrillas were on the losing side in the conflict. But that did not stop veterans of regularly organized Confederate units from claiming a remarkable degree of honor out of a disastrously lost bid for independence. Moreover, Federal veterans rarely if ever extolled the exploits of Unionist guerrillas operating in East Tennessee or other heavily loyalist areas of the Confederacy, even though they fought on the winning side. Guerrillas were personas non grata for the vast majority of Union and Confederate veterans, regardless of which side they appeared to be fighting on.

The history of guerrilla warfare after 1865 exhibits a remarkable development toward greater organization of irregular fighters by governments, either established or putative. One of the first major examples of this took place in the Philippines only thirty-four years after Appomattox. Emilio Aguinaldo's Filipino independence movement created a nascent, although small, government to push for autonomy, but the U.S. government refused to grant it. The bloody war that followed, lasting from 1899 to 1902, involved a native force that was highly organized and surprisingly modern in its conception of guerrilla conflict. Equally surprising, the U.S. Army managed not just to contain the guerrilla effort, as it had done during the Civil War, but also to defeat it more thoroughly than in 1861–65. American officers experimented successfully with a number of tactics and strategies to deal with Aguinaldo's forces and with the regional warlords who succeeded them after his capture. Success was based on a smart approach to the problem, understanding the differing cultures of the Filipino peoples and of the various regions, and using a large degree of nonmilitary pacification approaches as well as military action.[33]

The Filipino War was the first modern guerrilla conflict, and in many ways it was quite different from the Spanish Uprising and the Civil War irregular experience. The most salient difference lies in the high degree of control by guerrilla commanders over a relatively large force (amounting to about 10,000 men under Aguinaldo's leadership). An equally important feature was the large counterguerrilla force that approached the problem with tact, discernment, and intelligent planning. The Filipino War should serve as a brilliant case study for counterinsurgency and a corrective to any idea that guerrilla efforts are usually successful.

Additional guerrilla conflicts throughout the first half of the twentieth century resemble the Filipino example. After the failed Easter Rising of April 1916, nationalists organized a guerrilla force to destabilize British control of Ireland. It was well organized, with more than 112,000 men by mid-1921. Only a small part of them were well armed and trained, while the British Army deployed nearly 58,000 troops to combat the Irish Republican Army. The best that can be said is that the British fought the Republicans to a standstill; they could not develop an effective strategy to crush them. Political pressure built up in London, which led the government to make peace and grant independence to most of Ireland in 1921.[34]

Political pressure also played a key role in the British Army's inability to crush another insurgency in Palestine right after World War II. Jewish nationalists organized an effective political and military force in Haganah, which had 45,000 men by 1946. Although deploying more than twice that number of troops, the British could not crush the military wing of Haganah, relying too heavily on military force and not enough on political approaches to the problem of maintaining their mandate over Palestine. Army officers too often conducted massive sweeps, which rarely succeeded in rooting out the insurgents, rather than well-planned small-unit operations. The British failed to win the propaganda war, they failed to gather intelligence effectively, and they failed to learn and adapt. Changes in the London government also hampered the military effort as the army switched from a passive job of maintaining law and order to large offensives against the guerrillas, which satisfied politicians but failed to capture Haganah fighters. In the end, domestic economic and political factors were more important in Britain's decision to give up the Palestine Mandate than the military successes of Haganah.[35]

Most historians argue that the French army conducted a smart and effective counterinsurgency effort in Algeria from 1954 until 1962. The Algerian National Liberation Front (ANLF) organized a military force of 25,000 men by 1960, while the French deployed close to 400,000 troops in counterinsurgency operations. French strategy included sealing off Algeria from friendly populations in neighboring Tunisia and Morocco and then mounting an effective strategy to find and attack the scattered units of the ANLF, reducing their numbers by at least half. The open terrain of the area, French proximity to Algeria, and control of the coast and its ports all aided the counterinsurgency effort. But political factors combined with a general attitude that the huge expenditure of funds to maintain the military effort was not worth the gain finally brought victory to the ANLF in 1962. It was, however, a political victory rather than a military triumph for Algerian nationalists.[36]

The degree to which political influences played a role in the Spanish Uprising and irregular warfare in the Civil War is questionable in light of post-Appomattox examples. Grassroots guerrilla phenomena can happen based on a variety of motives that have little if anything to do with a single political goal. The extent to which a guerrilla movement was molded by a military or governmental leader presupposes a unitary motive and goal. With that we enter the era of insurgency, a more clearly defined effort to undermine an existing governmental power than is evident in grassroots guerrilla movements like those to be seen in Napoleonic Spain and Civil War America. If, for example, more than half the guerrilla bands targeted civilians to obtain horses and food, there seems to be little in the way of insurgency or political motives in operation.

Equally important is the nature of the counterguerrilla effort, which, as we have seen, was very successful in the Philippines, largely so in Algeria, but unsuccessful in Ireland and Palestine. The U.S Army experimented a bit with different strategies during the Civil War, but there could be little in the way of political action in that case. The U.S. government meant to restore its authority in the South and could not compromise on that issue. Military action largely had to suffice, barring the re-creation of effective state, county, and municipal governments in occupied Confederate territory. While Union authorities tried to resurrect state and local governments in areas their armies conquered, they had little success in doing so. Fighting the guerrillas to a standstill while using relatively limited numbers of troops, the Federals held them off until the organized rebel armies were soundly defeated. After that, the guerrilla movement collapsed too.

Anyone who believes the Confederates would have had a good chance to win their independence by conducting a massive guerrilla war with the veterans of Lee's army should take a lesson from history. There seems to be no example of a government winning its goals by guerrilla action *after* losing a conventional war. In the South African War of 1899–1902, exactly coinciding with the Filipino War, the British defeated the Boer republics of Transvaal and the Orange Free State in conventional warfare. The Boers organized a sizable irregular effort after that, in December 1900, against occupying British troops. Using a combination of fortified barriers to restrict guerrilla movement, punishment or internment of civilian collaborators, and massive military sweeps across the countryside, the British Army subdued the guerrilla effort in eighteen months.[37]

This international perspective reveals that the Civil War guerrilla conflict had no show on the global stage. Military forces in other nations did not study irregular warfare during the Civil War; they do not even seem to have been aware that such fighting broke out during the struggle between North and South. While the Spanish Uprising was known internationally, no one looked upon the Civil War for lessons in counterirregular warfare. To a degree, the Mexican War served as a model for Civil War commanders in this regard, but there is no evidence that American officers looked to Union counterirregular methods as a model for how to deal with Aguinaldo's Filipinos. When the U.S. Marine Corps crafted its small-wars doctrine in the 1920s and 1930s, officers created strategies similar to what their predecessors had successfully used in the Filipino War but did not look farther back in American history for instruction.[38]

The British effort in Malaya from 1948 to 1960 has emerged on the international scene as the ultimate example of success in counterinsurgency strategy. It has been studied by scholars and examined by military officers engaged in or preparing for their own counterinsurgency challenges. The effort in Malaya represents an impressive case study of learning on the job what works, thinking anew about old problems, and moving forward on multiple military, diplomatic, social, and cultural fronts. Moreover, it was a genuine triumph of combined effort by military, political, and diplomatic personnel. The global example of how not to conduct a counterinsurgency operation has always been the U.S. effort in Vietnam from 1965 to 1973. Faced with many historical case studies, and although experimenting with a number of promising strategies, the U.S. Army chose to concentrate on massive firepower supporting huge troop deployments against an enemy not necessarily vulnerable to such strengths.[39]

An international perspective also highlights Civil War guerrilla conflict as decidedly old-fashioned in its dispersed, uncoordinated character, far more similar to the Spanish Uprising than to Aguinaldo's guerrilla war. The trend for governmental organization of irregulars reached an apogee in the effort mounted by the Soviet government behind German lines along the eastern front of World War II. From virtually nothing, Moscow raised a guerrilla force in enemy-occupied territory, equipped it, directed its attacks on lines of communication and other targets, and maintained political discipline by dispatching commissars to each guerrilla band. By early 1944, more than 180,000 partisans were operating behind German lines in small bands of less than 1,000 men each. Some Red Army personnel were part of this effort, and to a degree the bands had to steal food from the civilian population to survive, but overwhelmingly, the Soviet partisan effort of World War II was far more successful than the Confederate partisan effort of the Civil War. One could hardly expect a polity like the Confederacy, with its loose bonds of cooperation, to achieve a degree of control across enemy lines so complete as to rival the efforts of the most highly centralized state in European history. The culture of the southern United States in the mid-nineteenth century severely limited an effective governmental control over irregular forces.[40]

The Civil War guerrilla conflict has admittedly been ignored even by Civil War military historians. It has emerged as the preserve of social and cultural historians, and for good reason. By their nature, guerrilla forces kept no records such as battle reports, service records, or letter and order books. The normal type of documentary evidence that reveals the history of regularly organized military forces is absent for the self-constituted bands. Growing more directly and obscurely from the populace, the true guerrilla's story has to be told largely by social and cultural historians, although there is yet room for a true military history of his experiences during the Civil War.[41]

NOTES

1. Mildred Throne, ed., "A Commissary in the Union Army: Letters of C. C. Carpenter," *Iowa Journal of History* 53, no. 1 (Jan. 1955): 64.

2. Charles J. Esdaile, *Fighting Napoleon: Guerrillas, Bandits and Adventurers in Spain, 1808–1814* (New Haven, Conn.: Yale University Press, 2004), 43–44, 51–53.

3. Ibid., 1–25.

4. Ibid., 27–28, 31–40. For a more positive analysis of the effect of Spanish guerrillas on the course of events, see Ronald Fraser, *Napoleon's Cursed War: Spanish Popular Resistance in the Peninsular War, 1808–1814* (London: Verso, 2008), 390–431.

5. Esdaile, *Fighting Napoleon,* 88–89, 112–23. On the role of deserters in the Spanish irregular forces, see also Fraser, *Napoleon's Cursed War,* 346.

6. Esdaile, *Fighting Napoleon,* 93. Ronald Fraser compiled a database of 751 guerrillas and came out with similar statistics concerning their social origins. He also estimates total guerrilla numbers at 55,000 men. Fraser, *Napoleon's Cursed War,* 394, 497–507.

7. Esdaile, *Fighting Napoleon,* 105–108, 159. In his study of *petite guerre* in early American history, John Grenier notes that scholars use many terms in reference to it, including "guerrilla."

But his definition of the concept indicates that, to be effective, this mode of warfare had to be pretty tightly controlled by a regular military force rather than relying on self-constituted bands. Grenier, *The First Way of War: American War Making on the Frontier, 1607–1814* (New York: Cambridge University Press, 2005), 1, 10–11, 225.

8. Esdaile, *Fighting Napoleon,* 138–49, 154.

9. Ibid., 136, 159.

10. John A. Nagl, *Counterinsurgency Lessons from Malaya and Vietnam: Learning to Eat Soup with a Knife* (Westport, Conn.: Praeger, 2002), 15.

11. Esdaile, *Fighting Napoleon,* 159–89.

12. Ibid., 191–92.

13. Blakewood to Walker, July 13, 1861, U.S. War Department, *War of the Rebellion,* ser. 4, 1:475 (hereafter cited as *O.R.*); Campbell to Walker, July 26, 1861, ibid., 505; Benjamin to Barkham, Mar. 19, 1862, ibid., 1008.

14. Fisk to Greene, Aug. 15, 1864, ibid., ser. 1, 41(2):719; Sherman to Rawlins, Nov. 19, 1862, ibid., 17(2):871; Forsyth to Merritt, Nov. 27, 1864, ibid., 43(2):679.

15. Hines to Breckinridge, Mar. 3, 1863, *Supplement to the Official Records of the Union and Confederate Armies,* 100 vols. (Wilmington, N.C.: Broadfoot, 1993–2000), pt. 1, 4:185–86; Bolick to unknown, [Nov. 1863], *O.R.,* ser. 1, 29(1):496–97; Garrard to Sherman, July 10, 1864, ibid., 38(5):111.

16. Adjutant and Inspector General's Office, General Orders No. 30, Apr. 28, 1862, *O.R.,* ser. 4, 1:1094–95; Adjutant and Inspector General's Office, General Orders No. 53, July 31, 1862, ibid., 2:26; Cooper to Randolph, Sept. 12, 1862, ibid., 82–83; Randolph to Seawell, Aug. 22, 1862, ibid., 303.

17. Adjutant General's Office, General Orders No. 100, Apr. 24, 1863, *O.R.,* ser. 2, 5:676; Holt to Stanton, June 11, 1863, ibid., 6:1–2.

18. Clark to Randolph, July 13, 1862, ibid., ser. 4, 2:4–5; Adjutant and Inspector General's Office, General Orders No. 82, June 12, 1863, ibid., 585; Seddon to Davis, Nov. 26, 1863, ibid., 1003; Longstreet to Cooper, Dec. 26, 1863, ibid., ser. 1, 31(3):871; Myers, *Rebels against the Confederacy,* 129–37; John S. Mosby, *Stuart's Cavalry in the Gettysburg Campaign* (New York: Moffat, Yard, 1908), 61; Lee to Seddon, Jan. 21, 1864, *O.R.,* ser. 1, 33:1113.

19. Headquarters, Department of the Missouri, General Orders No. 1, Jan. 1, 1862, *O.R.,* ser. 1, 8:477–78.

20. Halleck to Lieber, Aug. 6, 1862, ibid., ser. 3, 2:301; Lieber, *Guerrilla Parties,* 7–8, 11–12; Adjutant General's Office, General Orders No. 100, Apr. 24, 1863, *O.R.,* ser. 2, 5:677.

21. Sutherland, *Savage Conflict,* x; Sutherland, *American Civil War Guerrillas,* xii; Mountcastle, *Punitive War;* Dils to Wright, Oct. 25, 1862, *O.R.,* ser. 1, 16(2):644; Holloway to Greene, July 11, 1864, ibid., 41(2):133.

22. Sherman to John Sherman, Dec. 29, 1863, William T. Sherman, *Sherman's Civil War: Selected Correspondence of William T. Sherman, 1860–1865,* ed. Brooks D. Simpson and Jean V. Berlin (Chapel Hill: University of North Carolina Press, 1999), 578; Sherman to Porter, Nov. 8, 1863, *Official Records of the Union and Confederate Navies* (Washington, 1894–1922), 25:540; Sherman to Banks, Jan. 16, 1864, *O.R.,* ser. 1, 32(2):115.

23. Crowninshield to Forsyth, Oct. 1, 1864, *O.R.,* ser. 1, 43(2):250; Parke to Pleasanton, Aug. 30, 1864, ibid., 41(1):300.

24. Francis T. Moore, *The Story of My Campaign: The Civil War Memoir of Captain Francis T. Moore, Second Illinois Cavalry,* ed. Thomas H. Bahde (DeKalb: Northern Illinois University Press, 2011), 104–108; Sutherland, *Savage Conflict,* 110–11, 172.

25. Watson to Bryson, Feb. 28, 1865, *OR,* ser. 1, 49(1):788–89; Sherman to Hurlbut, Nov. 9, 18, 1863, ibid., 31(3):101, 187.

26. Eads to Totten, June 17, 1862, ibid., 13:437; Fisk to DuBois, Nov. 12, 1864, ibid., 41(4):548; Julie Holcomb, ed., *Southern Sons, Northern Soldiers: The Civil War Letters of the Remley Brothers, 22nd Iowa Infantry* (DeKalb: Northern Illinois University Press, 2004), 29; Edward J. Wood, *A Fierce, Wild Joy: The Civil War Letters of Colonel Edward J. Wood, 48th Indiana Volunteer Infantry Regiment,* ed. Stephen E. Towne (Knoxville: University of Tennessee Press, 2007), 208.

27. Feis, "Jefferson Davis and the 'Guerrilla Option,'" 105–106, 110, 115–17, 122.

28. Patterson to Granger, Apr. 26, 1865, *O.R.,* ser. 1, 49(2):505.

29. Parkhurst to Whipple, Mar. 1, 1865, ibid., ser. 2, 8:325.

30. Sherman to Hindman, Sept. 28, 1862, ibid., ser. 1, 13:683.

31. Courtney, "Guerrilla Warfare in Missouri," *Confederate Veteran* 29 (1921): 104. For other examples of a negative view of guerrillas, see Cunningham, "A Night with Guerrillas," *Confederate Veteran* 31 (1923): 465; Lewis, "Chasing Guerrillas in Arkansas," *Confederate Veteran,* 29, (1921): 220–22; and "Typical Guerrillas of the War Period," *Confederate Veteran* 27 (1919): 132–36. For a rare example of a positive portrayal of guerrillas, see Thompson, "Prince of Dare-Devils," *Confederate Veteran* 28 (1920): 288–89.

32. Sutherland, *American Civil War Guerrillas,* 101–110.

33. Brian McAllister Linn, *The U.S. Army and Counterinsurgency in the Philippine War, 1899–1902* (Chapel Hill: University of North Carolina Press, 1989), 12–13, 16–25, 61, 76–77, 84–85, 95, 98–100, 118, 120, 123, 136–60, 168–70.

34. Joseph McKenna, *Guerrilla Warfare in the Irish War of Independence, 1919–1921* (Jefferson, N.C.: McFarland, 2011), 38–65, 250, 252–54.

35. David A. Charters, *The British Army and Jewish Insurgency in Palestine, 1945–1947* (Houndmills, U.K.: MacMillan, 1989), 1–11, 42–82, 85, 88, 100–101, 111, 131, 133, 137, 172.

36. Charles R. Shrader, *The First Helicopter War: Logistics and Mobility in Algeria, 1954–1962* (Westport, Conn.: Praeger, 1999), xvi, 2–3, 41–42, 131–32, 145–46, 153, 155, 206, 227, 229–33.

37. Denis Judd and Keith Surridge, *The Boer War* (Houndmills, U.K.: Palgrave Macmillan, 2002), 3, 10, 56–57, 76, 87, 105–17, 125, 173–86, 191–96, 214–17.

38. Keith B. Bickel, *Mars Learning: The Marine Corps Development of Small Wars Doctrine, 1915–1940* (Boulder, Colo.: Westview, 2001), xi, 1, 91, 128–33, 178–79.

39. Nagl, *Counterinsurgency Lessons,* xiv, 9, 59–64, 66–75, 92–93, 95, 102–103, 115–33, 154–56; Donald W. Hamilton, *The Art of Insurgency: American Military Policy and the Failure of Strategy in Southeast Asia* (Westport, Conn.: Praeger, 1998), 14, 21–29, 33.

40. Kenneth Slepyan, *Stalin's Guerrillas: Soviet Partisans in World War II* (Lawrence: University Press of Kansas, 2006), 15–17, 28–33, 39–40, 51–52, 62, 79–84, 93, 161, 173–77, 270, 273.

41. Thus far, the only real military history of Civil War guerrilla conflict is Mackey, *Uncivil War,* although other studies, by default if for no other reason, deal to a limited degree with a military-history perspective on the subject. Mackey's work also is not a complete or fully convincing mili-

tary study but goes much further toward that goal than any other. Daniel E. Sutherland, in *Savage Conflict,* devotes quite a lot of attention to the military aspects of irregular warfare and its influence on the course of the larger conflict. But the literature still lacks a study of irregular conflict in the Civil War that employs a comprehensive use of the sources, methods, and insights available to the military historian.

AFTERWORD

DANIEL E. SUTHERLAND

I had not been long at the University of Arkansas when the editor of the *Arkansas Historical Quarterly* asked me to write an article about Civil War guerrillas. I was working on a book about the war in Virginia at the time and so tried to beg off by saying that I knew very little about guerrillas, in Arkansas or anywhere else. The editor, not one easily deterred, replied, "Oh, just read a few books!"

The problem, I discovered, was that there were not many books, certainly not good ones, about the guerrilla war, let alone about guerrillas in Arkansas. Like most people—scholars and nonscholars alike—I thought of Civil War guerrillas as being one of two types, although I was not at all sure how to explain the duality. Tradition had it that they were either desperadoes or chivalrous *beau sabres,* with William C. Quantrill being the poster boy for the former and John S. Mosby representing the latter. The division also seemed to mean that the guerrilla war—again, for the vaguest of reasons—had been restricted to Missouri and Virginia. The names Champ Ferguson and Sue Mundy rang a bell, but I could not say why.

I eventually came across an article about guerrillas in northern Arkansas by Leo E. Huff that had been published in the *AHQ* twenty-five years earlier. Dated as it was, Huff's article was the only scholarly work of its kind. More significantly, I discovered Michael Fellman's book about the guerrilla war in Missouri. Despite, for my purposes, its geographical limitations, Fellman's work suggested the wider analytical possibilities of the guerrilla story. The fact that I had "discovered" his book two years after it was published spoke volumes. I had some catching up to do.[1]

I slowly unearthed an entirely new historical world, and with roots sunk deeper into the past than I had imagined. Not only did I find pioneer writers about Civil War guerrillas, such as Virgil C. Jones, Richard S. Brownlee, Jay Monaghan, Thurman Sensing, Carl Breihan, Barnes S. Lathrop, Carl E. Grant, Richard O. Curry, F. Gerald Ham, and Albert Castel, but I also came to appreciate the much broader scope of guerrilla studies. Most of the authors writing in the 1950s and 1960s, such as Jac Weller, Joseph P. Kutger, Chalmers A. Johnson, Peter Paret, Charles W. Thayer, Otto Heilbrunn, Irwin R. Blacker, and Virgil Ney, provided historical context for the American experience, but they were principally interested in using the past to understand contemporary insurgencies in Malaysia, Indochina, and Cuba. I also found how useful it could be to trace "modern" guerrilla warfare to its source, which is to say, through the writings of its early participants and practitioners, from C. E. Callwell and T. E. Lawrence to Lenin, Mao Tse-tung, and Che Guevara.[2]

It was already a cliché by the 1960s that Civil War guerrillas (which almost universally meant Confederates) had been slighted as an unimportant sideshow of the war, but it was the interest in contemporary irregular operations after World War II that finally convinced Civil War historians to examine their guerrilla conflict. Virgil Jones, for instance, admitted that one of the reasons he had written his landmark book *Gray Ghosts and Rebel Raiders* (1956) was because of the subject's relevance in his own day. As he put it, "[O]ur modern fighting machine, from top to bottom, recognizes irregular warfare as highly effective, a weapon sometimes employed for results that not even an army can attain."[3]

Unlike Jones, I had no interest in modern irregular wars, but I learned soon enough, in a historical context, that he had been right about the effectiveness of guerrilla warfare. As I wrote my article, I even described the guerrilla conflict as the "real war" in Arkansas, the single most important factor in determining how most people—soldiers and civilians—experienced the struggle. I was emboldened by the fact that Fellman offered a similar interpretation of events in Missouri, and a splattering of Civil War scholars not previously known for acknowledging the importance of guerrillas, such as Robert L. Kerby, Don R. Bowen, William L. Barney, and Phillip Paludan, had also taken notice by the 1990s. Similarly, the findings of non–Civil War scholars, including Walter Laqueur, N. I. Klonis, Robert B. Asprey, Emanuel Halicz, John M. Gates, Brian M. Linn, and John Ellis, continued to emphasize the broader global and contemporary significance of what Asprey called "war in the shadows."[4]

Still, having done my bit for the *AHQ*, I readily returned to the conventional war, though not for long. Within a couple of years, I was back at it, fascinated by this dimension of the conflict. I became particularly impressed by the similarities one found in the guerrilla war as it had been waged in very different parts of the South. Nor did it take long for me to appreciate the geographical breadth of that fighting. Far from being restricted to Virginia and Missouri, or even to the Border and Middle South (cue Ferguson and Mundy), I found it to be pervasive throughout the Confederate states and a not-insignificant factor in the lower Midwest.

What was needed, I decided, was a survey of the guerrilla war, one that would draw on its similarities and turn the conflict into an understandable whole, rather than a collection of random, violent episodes. The closest thing I could find to this approach was a special issue of *Civil War Times Illustrated* written by Albert Castel in 1974. Like so much of Castel's work, his long essay suggested a new way of looking at the war. He still made the nexus of the guerrilla contest the Border South, but he at least brought portions of the Deep South into the conversation. What remained to be written, I believed, was a more penetrating and broader analysis based on existing local studies of the guerrilla conflict and a bit more original research.[5]

Unfortunately, it turned out that a significant amount of original research, about a decade's worth, was required. The local studies I had hoped to find did not exist. Again, there was lots about Missouri and Virginia, and a fair amount for Tennessee and Kentucky, but everything else was pretty much a wasteland, at least in terms of reliably documented work.

As I began serious research—and this would have been around 1995—I was helped by a spate of excellent new work that touched on the guerrilla war in that broader context. Mark Grimsley's *Hard Hand of War* and Stephen V. Ash's *When the Yankees Came* pointed to new possibilities in telling the guerrilla story. Kenneth W. Noe and Shannon H. Wilson had produced an edited volume, *The Civil War in Appalachia,* that added layers of sophistication to my knowledge of that region. Benjamin Franklin Cooling, in *Fort Donelson's Legacy,* demonstrated, like Noe and Wilson, the futility of trying to understand the guerrilla war solely within the boundaries of individual states. Sean Michael O'Brien's *Mountain Partisans,* though based entirely on published sources, made the same point. Then there was Robert R. Mackey's *The Uncivil War,* which underscored the need, as had Grimsley, to integrate guerrilla operations with counterguerrilla strategies and to understand how those strategies both differed and remained consistent across the South. Still, useful as all this and much more scholarship would prove to be, many more gaps had to be filled.[6]

Equally important, I was convinced that the guerrilla story must be told in chronological order, something that had rarely been done even at the local level. I was impressed by how much Cooling's work had benefited from following this rule, as had the salient parts of Grimsley's book. By the same token, it was the principal flaw in Fellman's explanation of the war in Missouri, which he had organized topically. The result, which suited Fellman's intensely iconoclastic nature, was a book full of passion and insight, but one that also failed to explain satisfactorily the evolution of the guerrilla war or how the conflict in Missouri reflected or influenced the contest elsewhere in the South. That proved to be the toughest part of my assignment, to tell the story not just in chronological order but also from a variety of different perspectives across the whole of the South and lower Midwest. History is linear, a messy continuum of cause and effect, which makes it impossible to understand events in July 1864 without appreciating what happened in May 1862. Conditions and circumstances were not the same in 1862 and 1864, and to conflate them by using documentary evidence in ways that ignore those differences obscures important nuances and meaningful distinctions. Then too there was the satisfaction of telling (and of reading) a story as it unfolded, even when one knew the outcome.

I was satisfied with the results of that project, published in 2009 as *A Savage Conflict,* but even as I wrote, I caught myself thinking, "Hmm, I wonder if more might be said about this issue," or "Gosh, that bit should be documented more thoroughly." Of course, every sensible author has those thoughts. No piece of historical writing is definitive. So what might be better understood, more convincingly argued, or reformulated when considering the guerrilla war of 1861–65? The essays in this volume both reinforce prevailing interpretations and pose intriguing new questions. As a reflection of their contributions, here are some additional—or sometimes complementary—thoughts on what might yet be done.[7]

Placing both the conventional war and guerrilla wars in a global context, as suggested by Earl Hess, has been needed for some time. The writers on strategy in the 1950s–70s took a stab at it, but often writing in such journals as *Orbis, World Conflict, Parameters, Journal of Contemporary History,* and *Journal of the Royal United Service Institution,* they generally used the American war to explain contemporary warfare, rather than to understand it in a nineteenth-century context. That trend has continued into the twenty-first century with such authors, besides those cited by Hess, as Caleb Carr, David Rooney, Anthony James Joes, and Ian F. W. Beckett. There are certainly many similarities between the organization, operation, and goals of America's guerrillas and the insurgents of earlier foreign conflicts, including the Napoleonic and Mexican

Wars. Some authors, such as Joes, have also traced the evolution of irregular warfare through the exclusively American experience, from the Revolution to the modern Middle East. Fellman tried his hand at that sort of analysis in a later book, although he defined it as American "terrorism." Yet none of these approaches, which still tend to define the American experience in terms of Missouri and Virginia, has integrated the Civil War in a satisfactory way.[8]

Sad to say, only scholars writing specifically about irregular warfare acknowledge its significance in either the Civil War or in the general military history of the United States. In their introduction, Brian D. McKnight and Barton A. Myers rightly challenge Civil War military historians to give irregular fighters more credit for shaping the nature of the war. I would point as well to a recent discussion of the "antiwar turn" in Civil War scholarship that surveys many of the defining elements of irregular warfare, including unchecked violence, Union and Confederate atrocities, and definitions of "heroism" and "villainy," without ever mentioning the guerrilla war. Its absence is also conspicuously noticed in recent historiographical reviews of both American and world military history.[9]

This is no small point, for it is the persistence of precisely this attitude of exclusion or segregation that inhibits more serious consideration of the guerrilla war. A paradox is at fault. Scholars who still consider it a sideshow, peripheral to the larger contest, mistakenly define the guerrilla war in exclusively military terms. The fact that it is equally grounded in social history—the story of families, communities, lawlessness, profiteering, cultural conflict, and much more—perplexes them, and rather than grapple with that complexity, they dismiss it entirely. I thought we had learned long ago, with the advent of the "new" military history, that the stuff of wars extends far beyond the conventional battlefield. And after all, guerrilla wars are "irregular" wars.

Other military historians justify pigeonholing guerrillas by saying they played no *decisive* role in the larger war. This is a more difficult obstacle to overcome, especially when even those scholars willing to consider the significance of the guerrilla contest give it short shrift. Grimsley, for instance, credits rebel guerrillas with helping alter Union military policy but fails to follow that insight to its logical conclusion or to appreciate the ramifications of the guerrilla war beyond mere policy. Kerby, George M. Fredrickson, and Richard Beringer's crew, in *Why the South Lost the Civil War,* see the potential consequences of guerrilla resistance for Confederate success, but for them it was largely the dog that did not bark in the night.[10]

Returning to the irregular war's cultural and societal roots, other issues require fuller explanations. Most importantly, who were these fighters? What motivated them? How might they be characterized in cultural terms? Were Civil War guerrillas, beyond similarities in organization and tactics, cultural or ideological cousins of the Spaniards who opposed Napoleon, the Filipinos who defied Arthur MacArthur, or the Russians who fought the Nazi Wehrmacht? That certainly would not be true—to take an extreme example—of Native Americans who operated as guerrillas. Should irregular fighters be compared to Eric Hobsbawm's "primitive rebels" or "bandits?" Francis Lieber, drawing incidentally on models from European history, would have endorsed the Marxist historian, having famously categorized most Confederate guerrillas as freebooters, marauders, robbers, and brigands. In any event, as Ellis insists in his *Short History of Guerrilla Warfare,* published in 1976, "it is quite impossible to discuss guerrilla warfare without paying attention to the social, economic and political configurations of a particular society," a characterization that must always be borne in mind.[11]

A few notable biographies of individual rebel guerrillas have been written. Naturally, Quantrill and Mosby lead the pack, but admirable work has also been published on William Anderson, Champ Ferguson, and some other lesser-knowns; one might even add John Hunt Morgan and Turner Ashby, depending on how one defines "partisan" warfare. Unfortunately, we are unlikely to gain much headway with this approach. We simply do not know enough about the lives of individual guerrillas to produce useful biographies of particular people. For instance, a recent biography of Jack Hinson, a celebrated rebel bushwhacker on the Tennessee-Kentucky border, is based largely on oral tradition and contains a good bit of speculation. In that sense, a more fruitful approach to individual biographies might be to publish closely edited editions of postwar memoirs or reminiscences written by guerrillas. A fine example of this alternative is T. Lindsay Baker's treatment of an Arkansas rebel.[12]

A more plausible approach to identifying these people and understanding their motivations is offered in this volume by Myers, McKnight, Aaron Astor, Adam H. Domby, and Joseph M. Beilein Jr., who examine groups of guerrillas. Astor's essay, which focuses on Unionist rather than the more usual Confederate guerrillas, is particularly intriguing in that it explores the composition of an entire band of men from a single region. This methodology mirrors Noe's classic 2003 treatment of rebel guerrillas in western Virginia; while difficult to achieve, it is a model worth emulating. Given that the guerrilla war was, at its heart, a series of intense local struggles for control of communities across the South, it is also a quite sensible approach. Mark W. Geiger's explanation of the political divisions in Missouri offers an equally innovative model, though perhaps uniquely so, given the difficulty of finding in other states the comprehensive court and banking records on which he depended. But Geiger's work brings to mind a similar topic badly in need of investigation, the role of guerrillas in the wartime South's black-market economy. A fuller appreciation of rebel motivations will also very likely undermine, as McKnight and Myers suggest in their introduction, the historiographical case for Confederate nationalism.[13]

Having mentioned Unionist guerrillas, I will also advocate more work on their side of the story. It still surprises people, including some scholars, when they discover *two* guerrilla wars in the South. The most recognized one was fought by the Confederates, but the Federals had their guerrilla bands too. To miss or obscure this dimension of the war is to mistake the core of the irregular contest, which always had more to do with neighbors fighting neighbors than with rebel guerrillas taking on the Union army. Too few scholars have pursued this path, but it alone can reveal the totality of the guerrilla struggle. Probing only one side is akin to explaining conventional military operations exclusively from a Union or Confederate perspective.[14]

Closely related to Unionist opposition are the Union army's counterguerrilla measures, which are dealt with quite handily in this volume by Stephen Rockenbach, Scott Thompson, Andrew F. Lang, and Lisa Tendrich Frank. Frank's essay is especially revealing in that it highlights the retaliatory nature of the Union policy against noncombatants, who were, in fact, the most frequent targets of those operations. This has become a standard way of explaining the Union reaction to the guerrilla war. It formed the heart of Robert Mackey's book, and insofar as Grimsley addresses the guerrilla problem, he too takes account of it. Clay Mountcastle has pursued the same theme even more forcefully, as have several unpublished theses and dissertations. The most common way of treating the subject is to combine the response of Unionist guerrillas and the Union army to recalcitrant communities, regions, or states. Yet if we are to use the microcosm as a way of testing large suppositions, more work on particular counterguerrilla units, as has been done by Darl L. Stephenson and Gordon L. Olson, might provide sharper insights. Equally welcome would be similar studies of units of Southern Unionist "guerrilla hunters."[15]

Union counterguerrilla policy also raises the issue of slavery, which perhaps more than any other topic has been slighted in guerrilla studies. Slaves played several roles in the guerrilla war and were central to it. First of all, they served as reliable informants on guerrilla movements to the Union army. Second, they were often targeted by pro-Southern irregulars responsible for controlling the black population, catching fugitives, and harassing refugee camps. This policing role, in particular, complicates the suggestion made by some scholars that the chaos inherent in a guerrilla war necessarily increased the likelihood of slave insurrection. Finally, some fugitive slaves joined with Union deserters and Confederate draft dodgers to form dangerous gangs that threatened Southern communities. An ideal study of the relationship between slavery and the guerrilla war would explain the interaction of each of these parts from both a Union and Confederate perspective.[16]

Another area in need of more research is the geographical scope of the guerrilla war. It is gratifying to see six of the current essays—by Myers, Domby, Frank, Brian Steel Wills, Laura June Davis, and Matthew M. Stith—venture beyond the Border South, and in ways too that offer suggestive comparisons between that region and the Deep South. Indeed, the expanse of the guerrilla war is one of the underlying themes of this book. But while Davis plies the waters, so to speak, of the lower Mississippi River valley, Domby explores the nature of guerrillas in Georgia, and Frank follows William T. Sherman's march through Georgia and the Carolinas, more scholars need to jump four-square into such states as Louisiana, Mississippi, Alabama, South Carolina, and even Florida—and again, we cannot forget the lower Midwest. The border war between Kansas and Missouri has received much attention, but we have barely touched on events and circumstances in Iowa, Illinois, Indiana, and Ohio. Frank's reminder that the drama of the irregular war could be found as often on Southern rivers as in its hills and swamps is especially relevant in looking at those neglected regions.

Several of these same essays also underscore, as noted, the need for more comparative work on the strength, utility, and nature of the guerrilla war in different parts of the South. Superficially, at least, there seem to have been few differences between, say, Missouri and Georgia, or Kentucky and Louisiana.

But was that so? We tend to forget that Missouri and Kentucky were Union states. Did that affect contemporary impressions of rebel aggression, let alone Union military policy? Did guerrilla operations seem more outrageous and more dangerous in those states than in the Confederacy? Stith's essay takes this issue in an even more provocative direction by showing that differences in the natural environment in widely divergent places could define the guerrilla war in unique ways. This is not to retreat from my position that state boundaries were often irrelevant in the guerrilla war (a point verified by several of the contributors), but we can only compare such peculiarities with carefully researched investigations of additional individual states.

And what about the legacy of the guerrilla war? Like all of the issues addressed in this volume, postwar impressions of the conflict are also beginning to receive the attention they deserve. Matthew C. Hulbert, who is emerging as an expert on this issue as it affected popular memory, offers a fine example of this methodology in his analysis of the Lawrence raid. It is a relatively new way of looking at history, and certainly one that would not have occurred to the first generation of guerrilla historians.[17]

And by legacy, I do not mean memory studies alone. I would also include under that heading an examination of the postwar lives of former guerrillas. Of particular interest would be the role of ex-guerrillas in the political upheaval of Reconstruction. We know all about the James and Younger brothers, but what about those irregulars who retired quietly to civilian life? Or the ones who, quite possibly, formed the core of such postwar terrorist groups as the Ku Klux Klan? Much attention has been directed in the past decade at the postwar lives of Union and Confederate soldiers, but nothing of the sort exists for ex-guerrillas. Several good books address the enduring legacy—as opposed, strictly speaking, to memories—of the guerrilla war, some of which follow the postwar careers of both rebel and Unionist fighters. Ideally, we will come to hear more of how these men responded to the rigors of peace and how they remembered the war and their roles in it.[18]

Finally, the ultimate goal of all of this should be a more complete integration of the guerrilla story with general histories of the Civil War. It is also the toughest assignment. I tried to place the guerrilla war in the context of the larger war in *A Savage Conflict,* but the next step should be to make it a seamless part of the national struggle, alongside the conventional battles, political elections, draft riots, and diplomatic intrigue. I doubt that it can be done at the moment.

More digging, along the lines of the splendid offerings in this volume, is needed before we can tell that grander story. There is, though, a more glittering prize to be won.

NOTES

1. Huff, "Guerrillas, Jayhawkers, and Bushwhackers in Northern Arkansas"; Fellman, *Inside War.*

2. I later tried to do this historiographical legacy justice in "Sideshow No Longer."

3. V. Jones, "Problem of Writing about the Guerrillas," 21.

4. Sutherland, "Guerrillas"; Asprey, *War in the Shadows.*

5. Castel, "Guerrilla War."

6. Grimsley, *Hard Hand of War;* Ash, *When the Yankees Came;* Noe and Wilson, *Civil War in Appalachia;* Cooling, *Fort Donelson's Legacy;* O'Brien, *Mountain Partisans;* Mackey, *Uncivil War.* For a brief review of some of the most important other works, especially those published since 2000, see Sutherland, *American Civil War Guerrillas,* 149–55.

7. Sutherland, *Savage Conflict.*

8. Carr, *Lessons of Terror;* Rooney, *Guerrilla;* Joes, *Guerrilla Conflict before the Cold War;* Joes, *America and Guerrilla Warfare;* Joes, *Resisting Rebellion;* Beckett, *Modern Insurgencies and Counter-Insurgencies;* Fellman, *In the Name of God and Country.*

9. Gallagher and Meier, "Coming to Terms with Military History," 492–93; Sternhell, "Revisionism Reinvented?"; Lee et al., "American Military History"; Citino, "Military Histories Old and New."

10. Berry, "Future of Civil War Studies"; Kerby, "Why the Confederacy Lost"; Fredrickson, *Why the Confederacy Did Not Fight a Guerrilla War;* Beringer et al., *Why the South Lost the Civil War,* 430–36.

11. Eric Hobsbawm, *Primitive Rebels: Studies in Archaic Forms of Social Movement in the 19th and 20th Centuries* (New York: Norton, 1959); Hobsbawm, *Bandits* (1969; reprint, London: Weidenfeld & Nicolson, 2000); J. Ellis, *Short History of Guerrilla Warfare,* 7.

12. The best Quantrill and Mosby biographies are Leslie, *Devil Knows How to Ride;* and Ramage, *Gray Ghost.* In addition, we have Castel and Goodrich, *Bloody Bill Anderson;* Myers, *Executing Daniel Bright;* McKnight, *Confederate Outlaw;* Ramage, *Rebel Raider;* Paul Anderson, *Blood Image;* Stephens, *John P. Gatewood;* McKenney, *Jack Hinson's One-Man War;* and J. Bailey, *Confederate Guerrilla* (T. Lindsay Baker, ed.).

13. Noe, "Who Were the Bushwhackers?"; Geiger, *Financial Fraud and Guerrilla Violence.*

14. Other examples of this approach are Barnes, "Williams Clan"; Stevens, *Rebels in Blue;* and Pickering and Falls, *Brush Men and Vigilantes.*

15. Mountcastle, *Punitive War;* Durrill, *War of Another Kind;* Fisher, *War at Every Door;* Storey, *Loyalty and Loss;* Ash, *Middle Tennessee Society Transformed;* Sarris, *Separate Civil War;* Browning, *Shifting Loyalties;* Myers, *Rebels against the Confederacy;* Stephenson, *Headquarters in the Brush;* Olson, *Isaac Earl and His Scouts.*

16. Gary W. Gallagher suggests that the Confederate government refused to endorse a widespread guerrilla war because of the upheaval it would have caused, but the context in which he makes the argument is ill conceived. Gallagher, *Confederate War,* 146–51.

17. For the latest work on the "memory" of the guerrilla war, see Beilein and Hulbert, *Civil War Guerrilla;* and Hulbert, *Irregular Recollections.*

18. Storey, *Loyalty and Loss;* Bynum, *Long Shadow of the Civil War;* Hutton, *Bloody Breathitt.* Two possible models, one each from the Union and Confederate perspective, are Evans, *To Die Game;* and Crouch and Brice, *Cullen Montgomery Baker.* I have attempted the last-mentioned assignment in "Memories of a Rooted Sorrow."

A READER'S BIBLIOGRAPHY OF CIVIL WAR GUERRILLA STUDIES

Anderson, Paul Christopher. *Blood Image: Turner Ashby in the Civil War and the Southern Mind.* Baton Rouge: Louisiana State University Press, 2002.

Arenson, Adam, and Andrew R. Graybill, eds. *Civil War Wests: Testing the Limits of the United States.* Berkeley: University of California Press, 2015.

Ash, Stephen V. *Middle Tennessee Society Transformed, 1860–1870.* 1988; Knoxville: University of Tennessee Press, 2006.

——. *When the Yankees Came: Conflict and Chaos in the Occupied South, 1861–1865.* Chapel Hill: University of North Carolina Press, 1995.

Ashdown, Paul, and Edward Caudill. *The Mosby Myth: A Confederate Hero in Life and Legend.* Wilmington, Del.: Scholarly Resources, 2002.

Asprey, Robert B. *War in the Shadows: The Guerrilla in History.* 2 vols. Garden City, N.Y.: Doubleday, 1975.

Astor, Aaron. *The Civil War along Tennessee's Cumberland Plateau.* Charleston, S.C.: History Press, 2015.

——. *Rebels on the Border: Civil War, Emancipation, and the Reconstruction of Kentucky and Missouri.* Baton Rouge: Louisiana State University Press, 2012.

Avirett, James Battle. *The Memoirs of General Turner Ashby and His Compeers.* Baltimore, Md.: Selby & Dulany, 1867.

Baggett, James Alex. *Homegrown Yankees: Tennessee's Union Cavalry during the Civil War.* Baton Rouge: Louisiana State University Press, 2009.

Bailey, Anne J. *Invisible Southerners: Ethnicity in the Civil War.* Athens: University of Georgia Press, 2006.

Bailey, Anne J., and Daniel E. Sutherland, eds. *Civil War Arkansas: Beyond Battles and Leaders.* Fayetteville: University of Arkansas Press, 2000.

Bailey, Joseph. *Confederate Guerrilla: The Civil War Memoir of Joseph Bailey.* Edited by T. Lindsay Baker. Fayetteville: University of Arkansas Press, 2007.

Barnes, Kenneth C. "The Williams Clan: Mountain Farmers and Union Fighters in North Central Arkansas." In Bailey and Sutherland, *Civil War Arkansas,* 155–76.

Beckett, Ian F. W. *Modern Insurgencies and Counter-Insurgencies: Guerrillas and Their Opponents since 1750.* London: Routledge, 2001.

Beilein, Joseph M., Jr. *Bushwhackers: Guerrilla Warfare, Manhood, and the Household in Civil War Missouri.* Kent, Ohio: Kent State University Press, 2016.

Beilein, Joseph M., Jr., and Matthew C. Hulbert, eds. *The Civil War Guerrilla: Unfolding the Black Flag in History, Memory, and Myth.* Lexington: University Press of Kentucky, 2015.

Benedict, Bryce. *Jayhawkers: The Civil War Brigade of James Henry Lane.* Norman: University of Oklahoma Press, 2009.

Beringer, Richard E., Herman Hattaway, Archer Jones, and William N. Still Jr. *Why the South Lost the Civil War.* Athens: University of Georgia Press, 1986.

Berry, Stephen W. "The Future of Civil War Studies: Predictions." *Journal of the Civil War Era* 2, no. 1 (March 2012): 3.

——, ed. *Weirding the War: Stories from the Civil War's Ragged Edges.* Athens: University of Georgia Press, 2011.

Birtle, Andrew J. *U.S. Army Counterinsurgency and Contingency Operations Doctrine, 1860–1941.* Washington, D.C.: U.S. Army Center of Military History, 2009.

Blackford, W. W. *War Years with Jeb Stuart.* New York: Scribner, 1945.

Boot, Max. *Invisible Armies: An Epic History of Guerrilla Warfare from Ancient Times to the Present.* New York: Liveright, 2013.

Borcke, Heros von. *Memoirs of the Confederate War for Independence.* New York: P. Smith, 1938.

Bohannon, Keith S. "They Had Determined to Root Us Out: Dual Memoirs by a Unionist Couple in Blue Ridge Georgia." In *Enemies of the Country: New Perspectives on Unionists in the Civil War South,* 97–120. Athens: University of Georgia Press, 2001.

Bowen, Don R. "Guerrilla War in Western Missouri, 1862–1865: Historical Extensions of the Relative Deprivation Hypothesis." *Comparative Studies in History and Society* 19 (1979): 30–51.

——. "Quantrill, James, Younger, et al.: Leadership in a Guerrilla Movement, Missouri, 1861–1865." *Military Affairs* 1 (1977): 42–48.

Bradbury, John F., Jr. "'Buckwheat Cake Philanthropy': Refugees and the Union Army in the Ozarks." *Arkansas Historical Quarterly* 57 (1998): 233–54.

Bradley, Michael. *Nathan Bedford Forrest's Escort and Staff.* Gretna, La.: Pelican, 2006.

Brant, Marley. *The Outlaw Youngers: A Confederate Brotherhood.* Lanham, Md.: Madison Books, 1995.

Brents, J. A. *The Patriots and Guerillas of East Tennessee and Kentucky.* New York: J. A. Brents, 1863.

Browning, Judkin. "'I Am Not So Patriotic as I Was Once': The Effects of Military Occupation on the Occupying Soldiers during the Civil War." *Civil War History* 55 (2009): 217–43.

——. *Shifting Loyalties: The Union Occupation of Eastern North Carolina.* Chapel Hill: University of North Carolina Press, 2011.

Brownlee, Richard S. *Gray Ghosts of the Confederacy: Guerrilla Warfare in the West, 1861–1865.* Baton Rouge: Louisiana State University Press, 1958.

Budiansky, Stephen. *The Bloody Shirt: Terror after Appomattox.* New York: Viking, 2008.

Bushong, Millard K. *General Turner Ashby and Stonewall's Valley Campaign.* Verona, Va.: McClure, 1980.

Bynum, Victoria E. *The Free State of Jones: Mississippi's Longest Civil War.* Chapel Hill: University of North Carolina Press, 2001.

———. *The Long Shadow of the Civil War: Southern Dissent and Its Legacies.* Chapel Hill: University of North Carolina Press, 2010.

———. *Unruly Women: The Politics of Social and Sexual Control in the Old South.* Chapel Hill: University of North Carolina Press, 1992.

Carr, Caleb. *The Lessons of Terror: A History of Warfare against Civilians: Why It Has Always Failed and Why It Will Fail Again.* New York: Random House, 2002.

Castel, Albert E. "The Guerrilla War, 1861–1865." *Civil War Times Illustrated* spec. issue (October 1974).

———. "Quantrill's Bushwhackers: A Case Study in Partisan Warfare." *Civil War History* 13 (1967): 40–50.

———. *William Clarke Quantrill: His Life and Times.* Norman: University of Oklahoma Press, 1999.

Castel, Albert E., and Thomas Goodrich. *Bloody Bill Anderson: The Short, Savage Life of a Civil War Guerrilla.* Mechanicsburg, Pa.: Stackpole Books, 1998.

Citino, Robert M. "Military Histories Old and New: A Reintroduction," *American Historical Review* 112 (October 2007): 1070–90.

Cooling, Benjamin Franklin. *Fort Donelson's Legacy: War and Society in Kentucky and Tennessee, 1862–1863.* Knoxville: University of Tennessee Press, 1997.

Crawford, Martin. *Ashe County's Civil War: Community and Society in the Appalachian South.* Charlottesville: University Press of Virginia, 2001.

Crouch, Barry A., and Donaly E. Brice. *Cullen Montgomery Baker, Reconstruction Desperado.* Baton Rouge: Louisiana State University Press, 1997.

Croy, Homer. *Last of the Great Outlaws: The Story of Cole Younger.* New York: Duell, Sloan, and Pearce, 1956.

Cunningham, Frank. *Knight of the Confederacy: Gen. Turner Ashby.* San Antonio, Tex.: Naylor, 1960.

Danielson, Joseph W. *War's Desolating Scourge: The Union's Occupation of North Alabama.* Lawrence: University Press of Kansas, 2012.

Davis, Burke. *Jeb Stuart: The Last Cavalier.* New York: Rinehart, 1957.

Davis, Michael. "The Legend of Bill Dark: Guerrilla Warfare, Oral History, and the Unmaking of an Arkansas Bushwhacker." *Arkansas Historical Quarterly* 58 (1999): 414–29.

Davis, William C., and Meredith L. Swentor, eds. *Bluegrass Confederate: The Headquarters Diary of Edward O. Guerrant.* Baton Rouge: Louisiana State University Press, 1999.

Davison, Eddy W., and Daniel Foxx. *Nathan Bedford Forrest: In Search of an Enigma.* Gretna, La.: Pelican, 2006.

Degler, Carl N. *The Other South: Southern Dissenters in the Nineteenth Century.* New York: Harper and Row, 1974.

Dollar, Kent T., Larry Whiteaker, and W. Calvin Dickinson, eds. *Sister States, Enemy States: The Civil War in Kentucky and Tennessee.* Lexington: University Press of Kentucky, 2009.

Duke, Basil W. *A History of Morgan's Cavalry.* Cincinnati, Ohio: Miami, 1867.

——. *The Civil War Reminiscences of General Basil W. Duke, C.S.A.* New York: Cooper Square, 2001.

Durrill, Wayne K. *War of Another Kind: A Southern Community in the Great Rebellion.* New York: Oxford University Press, 1990.

Earle, Jonathan, and Diane Mutti-Burke. *Bleeding Kansas, Bleeding Missouri: The Long Civil War on the Border.* Lawrence: University Press of Kansas, 2013.

Edwards, John Newman. *Noted Guerrillas; or, The Warfare of the Border.* St. Louis, Mo.: Bryan, Brand, 1877.

Ellis, Daniel. *Thrilling Adventures of Daniel Ellis.* New York: Harper and Brothers, 1867.

Ellis, John. *A Short History of Guerrilla Warfare.* New York: St. Martin's, 1976.

Erwin, James W. *Guerrilla Hunters in Civil War Missouri.* Charleston, S.C.: History Press, 2013.

——. *Guerrillas in Civil War Missouri.* Charleston, S.C.: History Press, 2012.

——. *The Homefront in Civil War Missouri.* Charleston, S.C.: History Press, 2014.

Escott, Paul D. *After Secession: Jefferson Davis and the Failure of Confederate Nationalism.* Baton Rouge: Louisiana State University Press, 1978.

——. *Many Excellent People: Power and Privilege in North Carolina, 1850–1900.* Chapel Hill: University of North Carolina Press, 1985.

——, ed. *North Carolinians in the Era of Civil War and Reconstruction.* Chapel Hill: University of North Carolina Press, 2007.

Etcheson, Nicole. *Bleeding Kansas: Contested Liberty in the Civil War Era.* Lawrence: University Press of Kansas, 2004.

Evans, William McKee. *To Die Game: The Story of the Lowry Band, Indian Guerillas of Reconstruction.* Syracuse, N.Y.: Syracuse University Press, 1995.

Feis, William B. "Jefferson Davis and the 'Guerrilla Option': A Reexamination." In *The Collapse of the Confederacy,* edited by Mark Grimsley and Brooks D. Simpson, 104–28. Lincoln: University of Nebraska Press, 2001.

Fellman, Michael. *Inside War: The Guerrilla Conflict in Missouri during the American Civil War.* New York: Oxford University Press, 1989.

——. *In the Name of God and Country: Reconsidering Terrorism in American History.* New Haven: Yale University Press, 2010.

——. *Views from the Dark Side of American History.* Baton Rouge: Louisiana State University Press, 2011.

——. "Women and Guerrilla Warfare." In *Divided Houses: Gender and the Civil War,* edited by Catherine Clinton and Nina Silber, 147–66. New York: Oxford University Press, 1992.

Fisher, Noel C. *The Civil War in the Smokies.* Gatlinburg, Tenn.: Great Smoky Mountains Association, 2005.

——. *War at Every Door: Partisan Politics and Guerrilla Violence in East Tennessee, 1860–1869.* Chapel Hill: University of North Carolina Press, 1997.

Foos, Paul. *A Short, Offhand, Killing Affair: Soldiers and Social Conflict during the Mexican-American War.* Chapel Hill: University of North Carolina Press, 2002.

Forsythe, John W. *Guerrilla Warfare and Life in Libby Prison.* Edited by Melvin L. Steadman. Annadale, Va.: Turnpike, 1967.

Frank, Lisa Tendrich. "Bedrooms as Battlefields: The Role of Gender Politics in Sherman's March." In Whites and Long, *Occupied Women,* 33–48.

——. *The Civilian War: Confederate Women and Union Soldiers during Sherman's March.* Baton Rouge: Louisiana State University Press, 2015.

——. "War Comes Home: Confederate Women and Union Soldiers." In *Virginia's Civil War,* edited by Peter Wallenstein and Bertram Wyatt-Brown, 123–36. Charlottesville: University of Virginia Press, 2005.

Fredrickson, George M. *Why the Confederacy Did Not Fight a Guerrilla War after the Fall of Richmond: A Comparative View.* Gettysburg: Gettysburg College, 1996.

Freehling, William W. *The South vs. the South: How Anti-Confederate Southerners Shaped the Course of the Civil War.* New York: Oxford University Press, 2001.

Gallagher, Gary W. *The Confederate War: How Popular Will, Nationalism, and Military Strategy Could Not Stave Off Defeat.* Cambridge, Mass.: Harvard University Press, 1997.

——, ed. *Fighting for the Confederacy: The Personal Recollections of General Edward Porter Alexander.* Chapel Hill: University of North Carolina Press, 1989.

Gallagher, Gary W., and Kathryn Shively Meier. "Coming to Terms with Civil War Military History." *Journal of the Civil War Era* 4 (2014): 487–508.

Geiger, Mark W. *Financial Fraud and Guerrilla Violence in Missouri's Civil War.* New Haven, Conn.: Yale University Press, 2010.

Gildrie, Richard P. "Guerrilla Warfare in the Lower Cumberland River Valley, 1862–1865." *Tennessee Historical Quarterly* 49 (1990): 161–76.

Goodhart, Briscoe. *History of the Independent Loudoun Virginia Rangers: U.S. Vol. Cav. (Scouts) 1862–65.* Washington, D.C.: McGill and Wallace, 1896.

Goodrich, Thomas. *Black Flag: Guerrilla Warfare on the Western Border, 1861–1865.* Bloomington: Indiana University Press, 1995.

——. *Bloody Dawn: The Story of the Lawrence Massacre.* Kent, Ohio: Kent State University Press, 1991.

Grimsley, Mark. *The Hard Hand of War: Union Military Policy toward Southern Civilians.* New York: Cambridge University Press, 1995.

——. "Wars for the American South: The First and Second Reconstructions Considered as Insurgencies." *Civil War History* 58, no. 1 (2012): 6–36.

Groce, W. Todd. *Mountain Rebels: East Tennessee Confederates and the Civil War.* Knoxville: University of Tennessee Press, 1999.

Gudmested, Robert H. *Steamboats and the Rise of the Cotton Kingdom.* Baton Rouge: Louisiana State University Press, 2011.

Harris, William C. *Lincoln and the Border States: Preserving the Union.* Lawrence: University Press of Kansas, 2011.

Hogue, James K. *Uncivil War: Five New Orleans Street Battles and the Rise and Fall of Radical Reconstruction.* Baton Rouge: Louisiana State University Press, 2006.

Horwitz, Lester V. *The Longest Raid of the Civil War: Little-Known & Untold Stories of Morgan's Raid into Kentucky, Indiana, & Ohio.* Loveland, Ohio: Farmcourt, 1999.

Hsieh, Wayne Wei-Siang. "Total War and the American Civil War Reconsidered: The End of an Outdated 'Master Narrative.'" *Journal of the Civil War Era* 1 (2011): 394–408.

Huff, Leo E. "Guerrillas, Jayhawkers, and Bushwhackers in Northern Arkansas during the Civil War." *Arkansas Historical Quarterly* 24 (1965): 127–48.

Hulbert, Matthew C. "Constructing Guerrilla Memory: John Newman Edwards and Missouri's Irregular Lost Cause." *Journal of the Civil War Era* 2 (2012): 58–81.

——. *The Ghosts of Guerrilla Memory: How Civil War Bushwhackers became Gunslingers in the American West.* Athens: University of Georgia Press, 2016.

——. "How to Remember 'This Damnable Guerrilla Warfare': Four Vignettes from Civil War Missouri." *Civil War History* 59 (2013): 142–67.

——. "The Regularly Irregular War: Domestic Violation, Women, and Remembrance in Missouri's Guerrilla Theater." *Common-Place* 14, no. 2 (Winter 2014). http://www.common-place-archives.org/vol-14/no-02/hulbert/#.VMzN7S75HLp.

——. "Texas Bound and Down: An Untold Narrative of Missouri's Guerrilla War on Film." *Journal of the West* 50 (2011): 27–33.

Humes, Thomas. *The Loyal Mountaineers of Tennessee.* Knoxville, Tenn.: Ogden Brothers, 1888.

Hunter, Louis C. *Steamboats on the Western Rivers: An Economic and Technological History.* Cambridge, Mass.: Harvard University Press, 1949.

Hutton, T. R. C. *Bloody Breathitt: Politics and Violence in the Appalachian South.* Lexington: University Press of Kentucky, 2013.

Inscoe, John C. "'Moving through Deserter Country': Fugitive Accounts of the Inner Civil War in Southern Appalachia." In Noe and Wilson, *Civil War in Appalachia,* 158–86.

——. *Race, War, and Remembrance in the Appalachian South.* Lexington: University Press of Kentucky, 2008.

Inscoe, John C., and Robert Kenzer, eds. *Enemies of the Country: New Perspectives on Unionists in the Civil War South.* Athens: University of Georgia Press, 2001.

Inscoe, John C., and Gordon B. McKinney. *The Heart of Confederate Appalachia: Western North Carolina in the Civil War.* Chapel Hill: University of North Carolina Press, 2000.

Joes, Anthony James. *America and Guerrilla Warfare.* Lexington: University Press of Kentucky, 2000.

——. *Guerrilla Conflict before the Cold War.* Westport, Conn.: Praeger, 1996.

——. *Resisting Rebellion: The History and Politics of Counterinsurgency.* Lexington: University Press of Kentucky, 2004.

Johnson, Adam Rankin. *The Partisan Rangers of the Confederate States Army.* Louisville, Ky.: George G. Fetter, 1904.

Johnson, Walter. *River of Dark Dreams: Slavery and Empire in the Cotton Kingdom.* Cambridge, Mass.: Harvard University Press, 2013.

Joiner, Gary D. *Mr. Lincoln's Brown Water Navy: The Mississippi Squadron.* Lanham, Md.: Rowman and Littlefield, 2007.

Jones, J. William, et al., eds. *Southern Historical Society Papers.* 52 vols. Richmond: Virginia Historical Society, 1876–1959.

Jones, Virgil Carrington. *Gray Ghosts and Rebel Raiders: The Daring Exploits of the Confederate Guerrillas.* New York: Holt, Rinehart, and Winston, 1956.

——. "The Problem of Writing about the Guerrillas." *Military Affairs* 21 (Summer 1958): 21–25.

——. *Ranger Mosby.* Chapel Hill: University of North Carolina Press, 1944.

Keen, Hugh C. *43rd Battalion, Virginia Cavalry, Mosby's Command.* Lynchburg, Va.: H. E. Howard, 1993.

Kerby, Robert L. "Why the Confederacy Lost." *Review of Politics* 35 (July 1973): 326–45.

Lang, Andrew F. "Republicanism, Race, and Reconstruction: The Ethos of Military Occupation in Civil War America." *Journal of the Civil War Era* 4 (2014): 559–89.

——. *Waging Peace in the Wake of War: Military Occupation and Civil War America.* Baton Rouge: Louisiana State University Press, forthcoming.

Laqueur, Walter. *Guerrilla Warfare: A Historical and Critical Study.* Boston: Little, Brown, 1976.

Lause, Mark A. *Race and Radicalism in the Union Army.* Urbana: University of Illinois Press, 2009.

Lee, Robert E. *The Wartime Papers of Robert E. Lee.* Edited by Clifford Dowdey and Louis H. Manarin. Boston: Da Capo, 1961.

Lee, Wayne E., et al. "American Military History: A Round Table." *Journal of American History* 93 (March 2007): 1116–62.

Lemman, Nicholas. *Redemption: The Last Battle of the Civil War.* New York: Farrar, Straus, and Giroux, 2006.

Leslie, Edward E. *The Devil Knows How to Ride: The True Story of William Clarke Quantrill and His Confederate Raiders.* New York: Random House, 1996.

Lieber, Francis H. *Guerrilla Parties: Considered with the Reference to the Laws and Usages of War.* New York: D. Van Nostrand, 1862.

——. *Instructions for the Government of Armies of the United States in the Field.* Originally issued as General Orders No. 100, Adjutant General's Office, 1863. Washington, D.C.: Government Printing Office, 1898.

Longacre, Edward G. *Mounted Raids of the Civil War.* South Brunswick, N.J.: A. S. Barnes, 1975.

Lucas, Scott J. "'Indignities, Wrongs, and Outrages': Military and Guerrilla Incursions on Kentucky's Civil War Home Front." *Filson Club History Quarterly* 73 (1999): 355–76.

Lytle, Andrew Nelson. *Bedford Forrest and His Critter Company.* New York: Minton, Balch, 1931.

Mackey, Robert R. *The Uncivil War: Irregular Warfare in the Upper South, 1861–1865.* Norman: University of Oklahoma Press, 2004.

Mann, Ralph. "Ezekiel Counts's Sand Lick Company: Civil War and Localism in the Mountain South." In Noe and Wilson, *Civil War in Appalachia,* 78–103.

———. "Family Group, Family Migration, and the Civil War in the Sandy Basin of Virginia." *Journal of the Appalachian Studies Association* 19 (1992): 374–93.

———. "Mountains, Land, and Kin Networks: Burke's Garden, Virginia, in the 1840s and 1850s." *Journal of Southern History* 58 (1992): 411–34.

Martin, James B. "Black Flag over the Bluegrass: Guerrilla Warfare in Kentucky, 1863–1865." *Register of the Kentucky Historical Society* 86, no 4 (Autumn 1988): 352–75.

Matthews, Gary Robert. *Basil Wilson Duke, C.S.A.: The Right Man in the Right Place.* Lexington: University Press of Kentucky, 2005.

McCaslin, Richard B. *Tainted Breeze: The Great Hanging at Gainesville, Texas, 1862.* Baton Rouge: Louisiana State University Press, 1994.

McClellan, H. B. *I Rode with Jeb Stuart: The Life and Campaigns of Major General J. E. B. Stuart.* Bloomington: Indiana University Press, 1958.

McCorkle, John. *Three Years with Quantrill: A True Story.* Armstrong, Mo.: Armstrong Herald Print, 1914.

McCurry, Stephanie. *Confederate Reckoning: Power and Politics in the Civil War South.* Cambridge, Mass.: Harvard University Press, 2010.

McKenney, Tom C. *Jack Hinson's One Man War: A Civil War Sniper.* Gretna, La.: Pelican, 2009.

McKenzie, Robert Tracy. *Lincolnites and Rebels: A Divided Town in the American Civil War.* New York: Oxford University Press, 2006.

McKnight, Brian D. *Confederate Outlaw: Champ Ferguson and the Civil War in Appalachia.* Baton Rouge: Louisiana State University Press, 2011.

———. *Contested Borderland: The Civil War in Appalachian Kentucky and Virginia.* Lexington: University Press of Kentucky, 2006.

McPherson, James M. *Battle Cry of Freedom: The Civil War Era.* New York: Oxford University Press, 1988.

Miller, Randall, and Paul Cimbala, eds. *The Great Task Remaining before Us: Reconstruction as America's Continuing Civil War.* New York: Fordham University Press, 2010.

Moore, Albert Burton. *Conscription and Conflict in the Confederacy.* New York: Macmillan, 1924.

Mountcastle, R. Clay. *The Punitive War: Confederate Guerrillas and Union Reprisals.* Lawrence: University Press of Kansas, 2009.

Munson, John W. *Reminiscences of a Mosby Guerrilla.* Washington, D.C.: Zenger, 1983.

Myers, Barton A. "Dissecting the Torture of Mrs. Owens: The Story of a Civil War Atrocity." In Berry, *Weirding the War,* 141–59.

——. *Executing Daniel Bright: Race, Loyalty, and Guerrilla Violence in a Coastal Carolina Community, 1861–1865.* Baton Rouge: Louisiana State University Press, 2009.

——. "The Future of Civil War Era Studies: Military History." *Journal of the Civil War Era* 2, no. 1 (March 2012): 6. Full entry at http://journalofthecivilwarera.org/forum-the-future-of-civil-war-era-studies.

——. "A More Rigorous Style of Warfare: Wild's Raid, Guerrilla Violence, and Negotiated Neutrality in Northeastern North Carolina." In Escott, *North Carolinians in the Era of the Civil War and Reconstruction,* 37–68.

——. *Rebels against the Confederacy: North Carolina's Unionists.* New York: Cambridge University Press, 2014.

Neely, Jeremy. *The Border between Them: Violence and Reconciliation on the Kansas-Missouri Line.* Columbia: University of Missouri Press, 2011.

Neely, Mark E. *The Civil War and the Limits of Destruction.* Cambridge, Mass.: Harvard University Press, 2007.

——. "Was the Civil War a Total War?" *Civil War History* 37 (1991): 5–28.

Nelson, Megan Kate. "Indians Make the Best Guerrillas: Native Americans and the War for the Desert Southwest, 1861–1862." In Beilein and Hulbert, *Civil War Guerrilla,* 99–122.

——. *Ruin Nation: Destruction and the American Civil War.* Athens: University of Georgia Press, 2012.

Nichols, Bruce. *Guerrilla Warfare in Civil War Missouri. Vol. 1, 1862.* Jefferson, N.C.: McFarland, 2004.

——. *Guerrilla Warfare in Civil War Missouri. Vol. 2, 1863.* Jefferson, N.C.: McFarland, 2007.

——. *Guerrilla Warfare in Civil War Missouri. Vol. 4, September 1864–June 1865.* Jefferson, N.C.: McFarland, 2014.

Noe, Kenneth W. "Exterminating Savages: The Union Army and Mountain Guerrillas in Southern West Virginia" In Noe and Wilson, *Civil War in Appalachia,* 104–30.

——. "Who Were the Bushwhackers? Age, Class, Kin, and Western Virginia's Confederate Guerrillas, 1861–1862." *Civil War History* 49 (2003): 5–31.

Noe, Kenneth W., and Shannon Wilson, eds. *Civil War in Appalachia: Collected Essays.* Knoxville: University of Tennessee Press, 1997.

O'Brien, Sean Michael. *Mountain Partisans: Guerrilla Warfare in the Southern Appalachians, 1861–1865.* Westport, Conn.: Praeger, 1999.

Olson, Gordon L. *The Notorious Isaac Earl and His Scouts.* Grand Rapids, Mich.: William B. Eerdmans, 2014.

Paludan, Phillip Shaw. *Victims: A True Story of the Civil War.* Knoxville: University of Tennessee Press, 1981.

Parrish, William. *Turbulent Partnership: Missouri and the Union, 1861–1865.* Columbia: University of Missouri Press, 1963.

Paskoff, Paul F. *Troubled Waters: Steamboat Disasters, River Improvements, and American Public Policy, 1821–1860.* Baton Rouge: Louisiana State University Press, 2007.

Perry, Robert. *Jack May's War: Colonel Andrew Jackson May and the Civil War in Eastern Kentucky, Eastern Tennessee, and Southwest Virginia.* Johnson City, Tenn.: Overmountain, 1998.

Phillips, Christopher. *The Civil War in the Border South.* Santa Barbara, Calif.: Praeger, 2013.

Pickering, David, and Judy Falls. *Brush Men and Vigilantes: Civil War Dissent in Texas.* College Station: Texas A&M University Press, 2000.

Ramage, James A. *Gray Ghost: The Life of Col. John Singleton Mosby.* Lexington: University Press of Kentucky, 1999.

——. *Rebel Raider: The Life of General John Hunt Morgan.* Lexington: University Press of Kentucky, 1986.

——. "Recent Historiography of Guerrilla Warfare in the Civil War—A Review Essay." *Register of the Kentucky Historical Society* 103 (2005): 517–41.

Rhyne, J. Michael. "'A Murderous Affair in Lincoln County': Politics, Murder, and Memory in a Civil War Era Kentucky Community." *American Nineteenth Century History* 7 (2006): 337–59.

Rockenbach, Stephen. *"War upon Our Border": Two Ohio Communities Navigate the Civil War.* Charlottesville: University of Virginia Press, 2016.

Rooney, David. *Guerrilla: Insurgents, Patriots, and Terrorists from Sun Tzu to Bin Laden.* London: Brassey's, 2004.

Ross, Kirby, ed. *Autobiography of Samuel Hildebrand: The Renowned Missouri Bushwhacker.* Fayetteville: University of Arkansas Press, 2005.

Royster, Charles. *The Destructive War: William Tecumseh Sherman, Stonewall Jackson, and the Americans.* New York: Vintage, 1993.

Russell, Charles Wells, ed. *The Memoirs of Colonel John S. Mosby.* Boston: Little, Brown, 1917.

Sandow, Robert M. *Deserter Country: Civil War Opposition in the Pennsylvania Appalachians.* New York: Fordham University Press, 2009.

Sarris, Jonathan Dean. *A Separate Civil War: Communities in Conflict in the Mountain South.* Charlottesville: University of Virginia Press, 2006.

Scharff, Virginia, ed. *Empire and Liberty: The Civil War and the West.* Berkeley: University of California Press, 2015.

Schultz, Duane. *Quantrill's War: The Life & Times of William Clarke Quantrill, 1837–1865.* New York: St. Martin's, 1996.

Scott, John. *Partisan Life with Col. John S. Mosby.* New York: Harper and Brothers, 1967.

Sensing, Thurman. *Champ Ferguson: Confederate Guerrilla.* Nashville: Vanderbilt University Press, 1942.

Shea, William L. "A Semi-Savage State: The Image of Arkansas in the Civil War." *Arkansas Historical Quarterly* 48 (1989): 309–28.

——. "The War We Have Lost." *Arkansas Historical Quarterly* 70 (2011): 100–108.

Siburt, James T. "Colonel John M. Hughs: Brigade Commander and Confederate Guerrilla." *Tennessee Historical Quarterly* 51 (1992): 87–95.

Siepel, Kevin H. *Rebel: The Life and Times of John Singleton Mosby.* New York: St. Martin's Press, 1983.

Smith, Ronald T. *Thomas Ewing, Jr.: Frontier Lawyer and Civil War General.* Columbia: University of Missouri Press, 2008.

Starr, Stephen Z. *Jennison's Jayhawkers: A Civil War Cavalry Regiment and Its Commander.* Baton Rouge: Louisiana State University Press, 1974.

———. *The Union Cavalry in the Civil War.* 3 vols. Baton Rouge: Louisiana State University Press, 1979–85.

Stephens, Larry D. *John P. Gatewood: Confederate Bushwhacker.* Gretna, La.: Pelican, 2012.

Stephenson, Darl L. *Headquarters in the Brush: Blazer's Independent Union Scouts.* Athens: Ohio University Press, 2001.

Sternhell, Yael A. "Revisionism Reinvented? The Antiwar Turn in Civil War Scholarship." *Journal of the Civil War Era* 3 (June 2013): 239–56.

Stevens, Peter F. *Rebels in Blue: The Story of Keith and Malinda Blalock.* Dallas: Taylor, 2000.

Stiles, T. J. *Jesse James: Last Rebel of the Civil War.* New York: Alfred A. Knopf, 2002.

Stith, Matthew M. "'The Deplorable Condition of the Country': Nature, Society, and War on the Trans-Mississippi Frontier." *Civil War History* 58 (2012): 322–47.

———. *Extreme Civil War: Guerrilla Warfare, Environment, and Race on the Trans-Mississippi Frontier.* Baton Rouge: Louisiana State University Press, 2016.

Storey, Margaret M. *Loyalty and Loss: Alabama's Unionists in the Civil War and Reconstruction.* Baton Rouge: Louisiana State University Press, 2004.

Sutherland, Daniel E. *American Civil War Guerrillas: Changing the Rules of Warfare.* Westport, Conn.: Praeger, 2013.

———. "Guerrillas: The Real War in Arkansas." *Arkansas Historical Quarterly* 52 (Autumn 1993): 257–85.

———, ed. *Guerrillas, Unionists, and Violence on the Confederate Home Front.* Fayetteville: University of Arkansas Press, 1999.

———. "Guerrilla Warfare, Democracy, and the Fate of the Confederacy." *Journal of Southern History* 68 (2002): 259–92.

———. "Memories of a Rooted Sorrow: The Legacy of the Guerrilla War." *Civil War History* 62 (March 2016): 8–35.

———. *A Savage Conflict: The Decisive Role of Guerrillas in the American Civil War.* Chapel Hill: University of North Carolina Press, 2009.

———. "Sideshow No Longer: A Historiographical Review of the Guerrilla War." *Civil War History* 46 (2000): 5–23.

Tarrant, Eastham. *The Wild Riders of the First Kentucky Cavalry.* Louisville, Ky.: R. H. Carothers, 1894.

Tatum, Georgia Lee. *Disloyalty in the Confederacy.* Chapel Hill: University of North Carolina Press, 1934.

Thomas, Edison H. *John Hunt Morgan and His Raiders.* Lexington: University Press of Kentucky, 1975.

Thomas, Emory M. *Bold Dragoon: The Life of J. E. B. Stuart.* New York: Harper and Row, 1986.

Trelease, Allen W. *White Terror: The Ku Klux Klan Conspiracy and Southern Reconstruction.* New York: Harper and Row, 1971.

Tucker, Spencer C. *Brigadier General John D. Imboden: Confederate Commanders in the Shenandoah.* Lexington: University Press of Kentucky, 2002.

Twain, Mark. "A Private History of a Campaign that Failed." *Century Magazine* 31, no. 2 (1885): 193–204.

U.S. War Department. *The War of the Rebellion: A Compilation of the Official Records of the Union and Confederate Armies.* 128 vols. Washington, D.C.: Government Printing Office, 1880–1901.

Valentine, L. L. "Sue Mundy of Kentucky." *Register of the Kentucky Historical Society* 66 (1968): 175–205.

——. "Sue Mundy of Kentucky, Part II." *Register of the Kentucky Historical Society* 66 (1968): 278–306.

Watson, Thomas S., and Perry A. Brantley. *Confederate Guerrilla Sue Mundy: A Biography of Kentucky Soldier Jerome Clarke.* Jeffersonville, N.C.: McFarland, 2007.

Weber, Jennifer L. *Copperheads: The Rise and Fall of Lincoln's Opponents in the North.* New York: Oxford University Press, 2006.

Wert, Jeffry D. *Cavalryman of the Lost Cause: A Biography of J. E. B. Stuart.* New York: Simon and Schuster, 2008.

——. *Mosby's Rangers.* New York: Simon and Schuster, 1990.

Wesley, Charles H. *The Collapse of the Confederacy.* Columbia: University of South Carolina Press, 2001.

Whites, LeeAnn. "Corresponding with the Enemy: Mobilizing the Relational Field of Battle in St. Louis." In Whites and Long, *Occupied Women,* 103–16.

——. "Forty Shirts and a Wagonload of Wheat: Women, the Domestic Supply Line, and the Civil War on the Western Border." *Journal of the Civil War Era* 1, no. 1 (Mar. 2011): 56–78.

——. "The Tale of Three Kates: Outlaw Women, Loyalty, and Missouri's Long Civil War." In Berry, *Weirding the War,* 73–94.

Whites, LeeAnn, and Alecia P. Long, eds. *Occupied Women: Gender, Military Occupation, and the American Civil War.* Baton Rouge: Louisiana State University Press, 2009.

Williams, David. *Bitterly Divided: The South's Inner Civil War.* New York: New Press, 2008.

——. *A People's History of the Civil War: Struggles for the Meaning of Freedom.* New York: New Press, 2005.

Williamson, James J. *Mosby's Rangers: A Record of the Operations of the Forty-Third Battalion of Virginia Cavalry from Its Organization to the Surrender.* New York: Ralph B. Kenyon, 1896.

Wills, Brian Steel. *A Battle from the Start: The Life of Nathan Bedford Forrest.* New York: HarperCollins, 1992.

Witt, John Fabian. *Lincoln's Code: The Laws of War in American History.* New York: Free Press, 2012.

Wyeth, John A. *That Devil Forrest: Life of General Nathan Bedford Forrest.* New York: Harper and Row, 1959.

Younger, Cole. *Story of Cole Younger: By Himself.* Chicago: Press of the Henneberry Company, 1903.

CONTRIBUTORS

AARON ASTOR, associate professor of history at Maryville College, is the author of *Rebels on the Border: Civil War, Emancipation, and the Reconstruction of Kentucky and Missouri* and *The Civil War along Tennessee's Cumberland Plateau.* An expert on the Upper and Border South, he holds a Ph.D. from Northwestern University.

JOSEPH M. BEILEIN JR. is a scholar of the Civil War with interests in guerrilla warfare and gender. He is the author of *Bushwhackers: Guerrilla Warfare, Manhood, and the Household in Civil War Missouri* and coeditor of *The Civil War Guerrilla: Unfolding the Black Flag in History, Memory, and Myth.* He is assistant professor of history at Penn State–Erie, the Behrend College.

LAURA JUNE DAVIS is assistant professor of history at Southern Utah University. Her current book project is entitled "Vexed Waters: Naval Guerrillas, Masculinity, and Mayhem along the Lower Mississippi River, 1861–1865." She also serves as a contributing editor for the *Civil War Monitor.*

ADAM H. DOMBY is assistant professor of history at the College of Charleston. He received his Ph.D. from the University of North Carolina at Chapel Hill.

ANDREW FIALKA, a Ph.D. student at the University of Georgia, works at the Center for Virtual History (eHistory.org) on projects such as "CSI: Dixie," "Civil War GIS," and "Of Methods and Madness: A Spatial History Approach to the Civil War's Guerrilla Violence."

LISA TENDRICH FRANK holds a Ph.D. from the University of Florida and is an independent scholar who has taught at several universities in the United States. She is author and editor of several books and articles in Civil War history, including *The Civilian War: Confederate Women and Union Soldiers during Sherman's March.*

EARL J. HESS, Stewart W. McClelland Chair in History at Lincoln Memorial University, has written twenty-two books and thirty-two articles, most of them on Civil War military history. His more recent publications include *Civil War Infantry Tactics: Training, Combat, and Small-Unit Effectiveness.*

MATTHEW C. HULBERT is a lecturer in the Department of History, Political Science & Philosophy at Texas A&M University–Kingsville. He is the author of *The Ghosts of Guerrilla Memory: How Civil War Bushwhackers Became Gunslingers in the American West* and coeditor of *The Civil War Guerrilla: Unfolding the Black Flag in History, Memory, and Myth.*

ANDREW F. LANG is assistant professor of history at Mississippi State University and the author of *Waging Peace in the Wake of War: Military Occupation and Civil War America,* which will be published by LSU Press in 2017.

KENNETH W. NOE is the Draughon Professor of Southern History at Auburn University. He is most recently the author of *Reluctant Rebels: The Confederates Who Joined the Army after 1861.* His current research involves the influence of climate and weather on the war.

STEPHEN ROCKENBACH is professor of history at Virginia State University. His book *"War upon Our Border": Two Ohio Valley Communities Navigate the Civil War* compares the wartime experience of the residents of Corydon, Indiana, and Frankfort, Kentucky.

MATTHEW M. STITH is assistant professor of history at the University of Texas at Tyler and the author of *Extreme Civil War: Guerrilla Warfare, Environment, and Race on the Trans-Mississippi Frontier.*

DANIEL E. SUTHERLAND is Distinguished Professor of History at the University of Arkansas, where he has taught since 1989. He is the author of *A Savage Conflict: The Decisive Role of Guerrillas in the American Civil War* and *American Civil War Guerrillas: Changing the Rules of Warfare.*

SCOTT THOMPSON is a Ph.D. student at West Virginia University. He wrote his master's thesis on Civil War–era Loudoun County while attending Texas

Tech University. A social historian of the American Civil War, he researches loyalty, dissent, emancipation, soldier motivations, the civilian experience, and irregular warfare.

BRIAN STEEL WILLS is director of the Center for the Study of the Civil War Era and professor of history at Kennesaw State University. He is the author of numerous books and is best known for his extensive work on Nathan Bedford Forrest, including the biography *A Battle from the Start: The Life of Nathan Bedford Forrest,* which remains the most influential on the subject.

INDEX